Historic Ship Models

Wolfram zu Mondfeld

Sterling Publishing Co., Inc. New York

Library of Congress Cataloging-in-Publication Data

Mondfeld, Wolfram zu.
[Historische Schiffsmodelle. English]
Historic ship models / Wolfram zu Mondfeld.
p. cm.
Includes index.
ISBN 0-8069-5733-6
1. Sailing ships—Models. I. Title.
VM298.M5913 1989 89-11380
623.8′203—dc20 CIP

9 10 8

Published in 1989 by Sterling Publishing Co., Inc.
387 Park Avenue South, New York, N.Y. 10016
First published in West Germany by Mosaik Verlag
GmbH, Munich 54,
Distributed in Canada by Sterling Publishing
% Canadian Manda Group, P.O. Box 920, Station U
Toronto, Ontario, Canada M8Z 5P9
Manufactured in the United States of America

Sterling ISBN 0-8069-5733-6 Paper

Contents

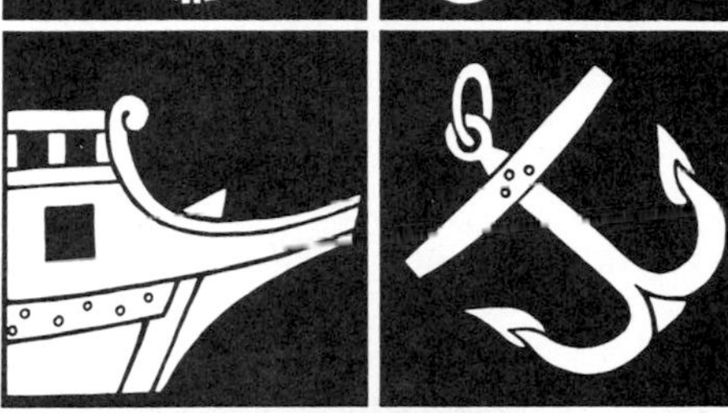

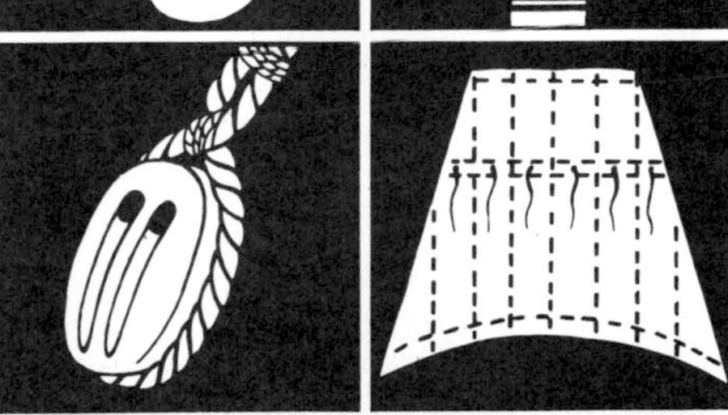

History and research

Introduction · Previous knowledge · Plan · Sources Types of model · Scale · Cost Expenses

Ship modelling is an ancient craft – as old as shipbuilding and sea travel themselves.

From the dawn of time, water and the ocean have nurtured and sustained life, though at the same time threatening and destroying life in equal measure. Once any person falls under their spell, he will never again be entirely free of it. It is not therefore surprising that man wove this fundamental element into his beliefs and his religion, and included with it the ship, which, despite its weakness and fragility, faced and exploited these gigantic and uncontrollable forces.

Traces of the ship's mystical and religious significance have lingered on into our own times, tied up with the individual personality which was assigned to all ships. Signs of this are to be found in the fact that ships have names, that they are "christened", that they are always called "she" – never "it" – that in the Mediterranean you still find an eye at the bow of the ship, that the ship had a figurehead which represented the spirit and personality of the ship, and which only disappeared 100 years ago. Not least in this is the vivid superstition of all seamen throughout the world, as alive today as ever.

All the things which are said of a ship, whether justified or not, apply in equal measure to its miniature counterpart, the model.

On 14th April 1912 the mighty passenger ship *Titanic* of the White Star Line collided with an iceberg while attempting to win the coveted "Blue Riband"; she was ripped open from bow to midships on one side, and sank within 2½ hours. About 60 years later a modeller was driving to an international competition with a model of the *Titanic*, which, according to many experts, had excellent prospects of winning this event. Another car cross his path, forcing him to brake sharply, and the model jumped out of its retainers and scraped along an ashtray – ripping the hull open from the bow to midships on one side . . . just a coincidence, of course.

Originally the model represented the full-size ship, and served religious or cult purposes; even today, if you look in churches along many coasts you will find votive ships displayed on stands, or hanging up. The date of the first model ships is lost in the mists of history; the oldest surviving examples date from the 5th and 4th millennia before Christ, and were made in Egypt and Chaldea. Later the Babylonians, the Cypriots, the Greeks and all the other ancient nations produced their own models.

These first model ships were often moulded in clay, but silver, gold and stone were also used. Wood was only used very rarely. In most cases these little models were of extreme simplicity, representing just the idea of a ship, rather than an accurate replica.

Models in our sense, i.e. exact small-scale reproductions of the original ship, began to be made in Egypt around the year 2000 B.C., and from these beginnings a tradition developed of making model ships by no means only for cult purposes, but also to satisfy the decorative needs and the whims of their owners. This tradition lasted for a thousand years; in the tomb of Tutankh-amun there were a good two dozen model ships ranging from the cult barks of the Gods to the King's state ship. From the late period of ancient history until the 15th century this tradition lapsed into oblivion. Since then ship modelling has seen an enormous, glorious upswing, and today it is more widespread than ever before, with the number of enthusiastic model ship builders exceeding the million mark worldwide.

Some of the oldest remaining ships in the world. The boat from Ur was made from bitumen, and the other models were made of clay.

Boat from Ur in Chaldea, around 3400 B.C.

Cretan boat from Mochlos, around 2600 B.C.

Boat from Cyprus around 800 B.C.

Merchant ship from Cyprus around 800 B.C.

Greek merchant ship from Tarent around 600 B.C.

Greek warship from Sparta around 600 B.C.

Requirements

Figure from the stern of the French galley La Réale *of 1669.*

"I could never do that!"
Is there a modeller who has not heard this lament, when he presented his latest model to relatives, friends and acquaintances for their perusal? And is there a modeller who does not feel the slightest twinge of sly satisfaction at such an expression of amazement and admiration? Hand on heart, could you reply like this: "It's not really so hard, you know, and if you were to just make the effort, you could probably do the same"? Just between you and me, model building is really not so frightfully difficult if you just know some of the wrinkles – or is it? The difficulties inherent in building period ship models are often greatly over-estimated, and many modellers are only too happy to reinforce this misconception. And so one more art takes its place among the unattainable skills and unfathomable knowledges.
What do you really need to know, and what abilities are really required, if you wish to join this apparently exclusive band of period ship modellers? You need absolutely no previous knowledge, as everything can be learned in time, although it must be admitted that there is a vast amount to learn – let's not pretend any different.
What you do need is a few personal qualities; if you don't possess these, you would do well to leave period ship building alone.
These qualities are: a certain degree of manual skill. Even though there are machine tools and ready-made components available in specialist shops which can save you a large amount of troublesome detail work, you still cannot manage without some degree of manual dexterity.
The second quality is a knowledge of your limitations. Many boat modellers come to grief right at the start, just because they over-estimate their abilities, and this dissolves their enthusiasm altogether. What a shame! And quite unnecessary, too; if only the modeller could admit in good time that the splendid 17th century three-decker is simply beyond his capabilities, while a small brig, a Viking ship or a Hansa Cog might be ideally suited to his talents, and could turn out to be a genuine masterpiece.
A consistent approach. I will mention this characteristic again later. But for now: once you have made a decision, do not subsequently change your mind, otherwise your house will soon be full of half-made models, with nothing ever finished.
Finally, the most important quality: patience, patience and even more patience! A period ship is not a thing which you can assemble in a few weekends. Models of high quality demand time, an enormous amount of time. The real expert model makers work on a model for one, two or three years. But it is not only the finished model which gives you pleasure, it is the building itself. A finely balanced anchor, a ship's wheel which looks just right, a well-laid rope lashing, a splendidly carved figurehead – which may well be the third or fourth attempt at it . . .
If you can apply these four qualities, manual skill, self-criticism, consistency and patience of a very high order, there is really no reason why you should not aspire to the highest levels in the building of period model ships.
Everything else can be learned, and this book is intended to help you a little on the way, to show you the "wrinkles", the best way of making this or that, and to point out some common errors. To some extent it can be considered as a guide through the maze, for you to follow steadily from the preparations and plans for your model right through to its completion, from keel to truck.

La Renommée, *French 5th rate ship of the line of 1790.*
Stern, quarter and head decoration from the most glorious era of shipbuilding.
The richly gilded carvings were placed against a cobalt blue background.

The Plan

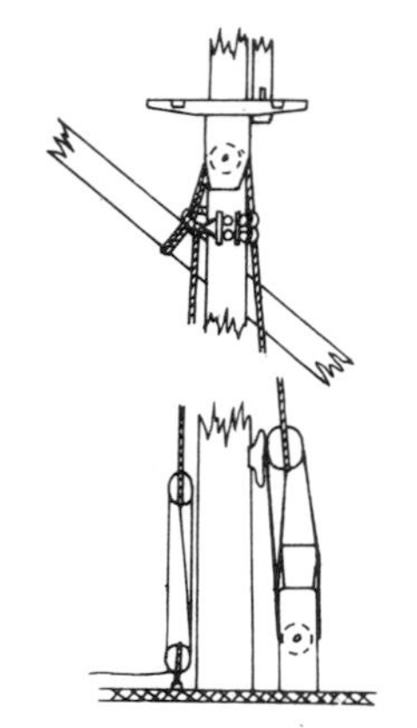

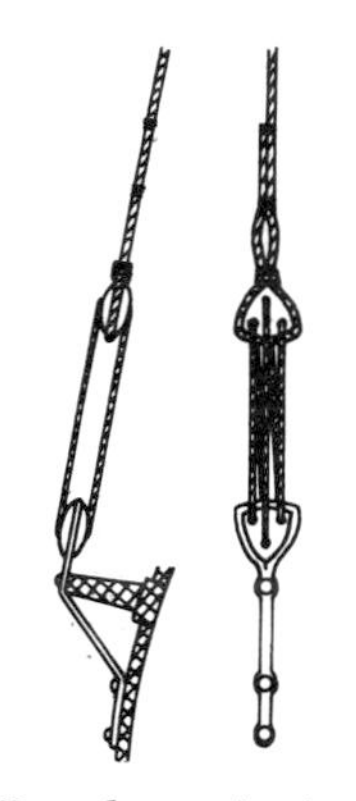

Mizen halyard and parral

Deadeye rigging

Kevel

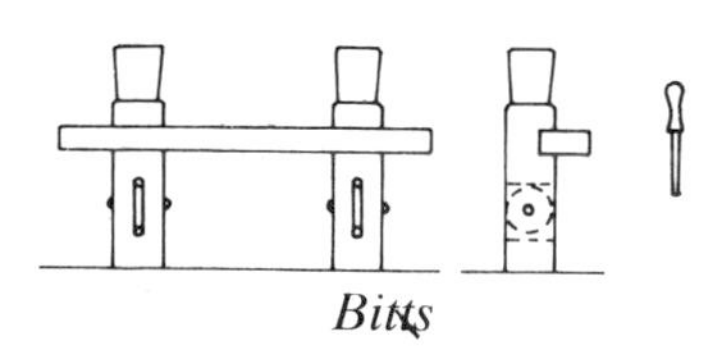

Bitts

Detail drawings to a larger scale.

The basic requirement for the construction of an historically accurate model ship is a plan of correspondingly high quality.
This really goes without saying. However, when you look at some of the construction plans available in model shops, you may feel an attack of the creeping horrors coming on. Good ship construction plans are almost so rare as to be collectors' items! This is sad, because many modellers simply do not know enough about the matter to be able to differentiate between a good and a bad plan, and this fact is often exploited.
On this and the next double page I have drawn up a list of the factors which show how an accurate and practical model construction plan should look, if your aim is to produce a historically accurate model.
Sheer plan: Shows the outline of the hull from the side, the position of the water lines and the frames.
Half-breadth plan: Shows the water lines and deck lines as seen from above, and also the position of the frames.
Body plan: Shows the outline of the frames and the position of the water lines. We will discuss these three plans in greater detail, and how they are used, in the section on building the hull.
External profile: Shows the hull from the side with the exact position of the wales, the gunports, etc. This drawing should also provide information on the ship's colour scheme.
Internal profile: Shows the hull in section along the plane of the keel. This plan shows the position of the decks, how they are divided, and the location of the fittings (capstans, pumps, bitts, masts, etc.).
Deck plan: Shows the plan view of the hull with the various deck fittings, such as gratings, hatches, cannon, channels, catheads, etc.
Bow elevation: Shows the ship from the front and the bow bulkhead, and is especially important for the construction of the head.
Stern elevation: Shows the ship from behind, and is indispensable for building and detailing the transom.
Cross-sections: Show parts of the deck equipment and especially the appearance of the various bulkheads (quarter deck bulkhead, beakhead bulkhead, etc.).
Rigging plan: Shows the masts, yards, sails and all the standing and running rigging. The flags and colouring should also be included. The rigging is often drawn on several individual plans, to make the information easier to understand.
Belaying plan: Shows where the individual lines of the standing and running rigging are attached (often included in the deck plan).
Detail drawings: Show difficult individual components of the ship, often to an enlarged scale.
Scale: An absolute necessity on any usable model ship plan, so that one knows the degree of reduction of the model as shown on the plans.
Signed plans are generally more reliable, as somebody has been prepared to acknowledge his own work.

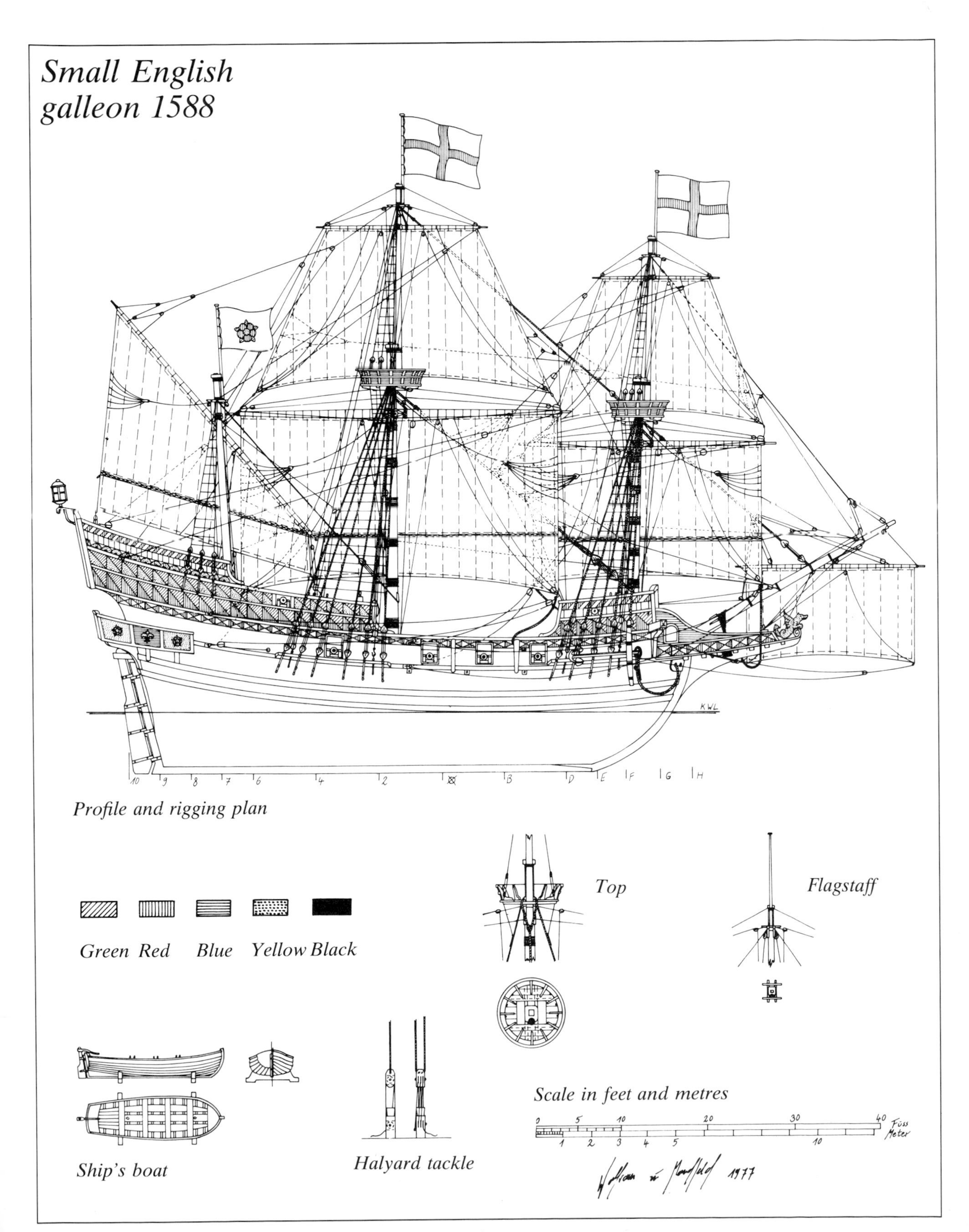
Small English galleon 1588
KWL
10
9
8
7
6
4
2
B
D
E
F
G
H
Profile and rigging plan
Top
Flagstaff
Green
Red
Blue
Yellow
Black
Ship's boat
Halyard tackle
Scale in feet and metres
0
5
10
20
30
40
Füss
Meter
1
2
3
4
5
10
1977

The Plan

Key to the Belaying Plan

Spritsail

1 Halyard
2 Braces
3 Preventer braces
4 Sheets
5 Clew lines
6 Anchor cat tackle

Fore Course

7 Halyard
8 Truss pendants
9 Lifts
10 Sheets
11 Tacks
12 Braces
13 Clew garnets
14 Leech lines
15 Bowlines
16 Stay tackle
17 Backstay

Fore topsail

18 Stay lanyard
19 Halyard
20 Lifts
21 Sheets
22 Braces
23 Clew lines
24 Bowlines

Main Course

25 Halyard
26 Truss pendants
27 Lifts
28 Sheets
29 Tacks
30 Braces
31 Clew garnets
32 Leech lines
33 Bowlines
34 Stay tackle
35 Backstay

Main topsail

36 Halyard
37 Lifts
38 Sheets
39 Braces
40 Clew lines
41 Bowlines

Mizen Course

42 Halyard
43 Truss pendant
44 Lifts
45 Clew garnet
46 Leech and bunt lines
47 Throat halyard
48 Tack tackle
49 Sheet

Same belaying point on starboard and port sides

Small English galleon 1588

Plans, sections and profiles

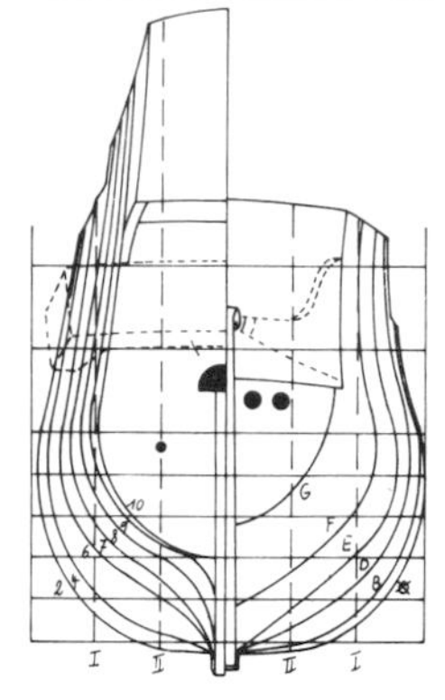
Body plan

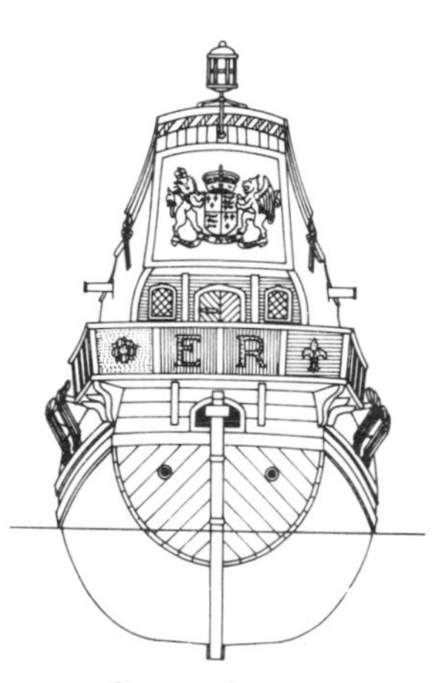

Stern elevation

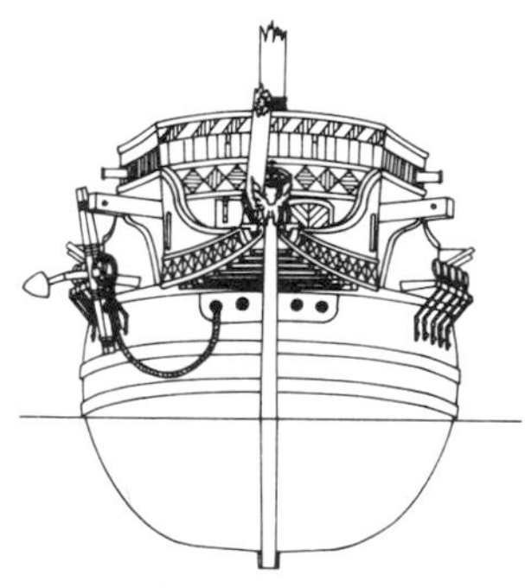
Bow elevation

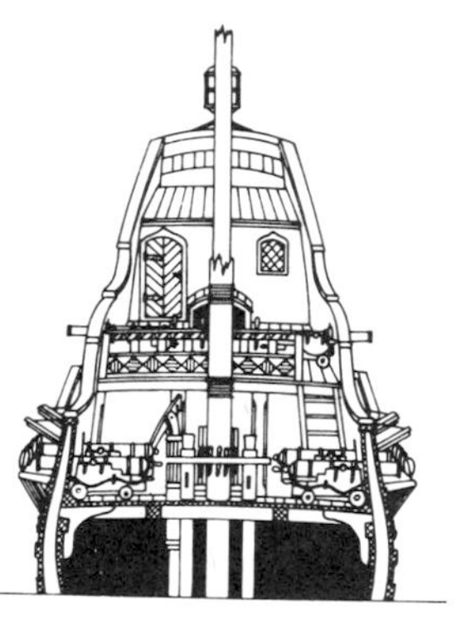
Cross section at midships frame looking aft

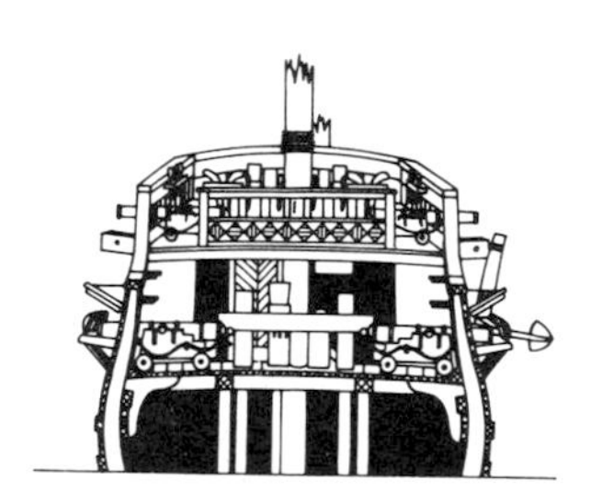
Cross section at midships frame looking forward

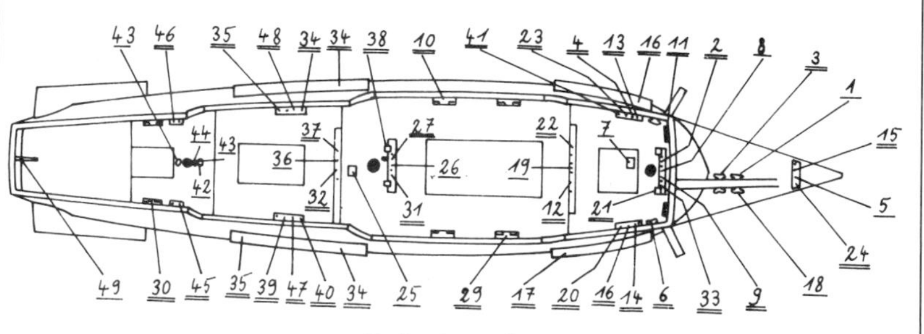

Belaying plan

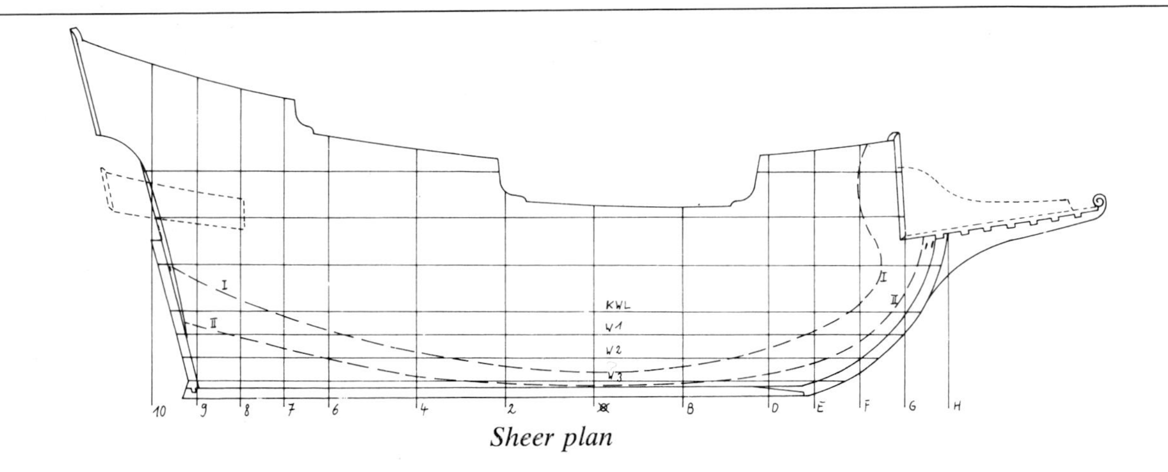

Sheer plan

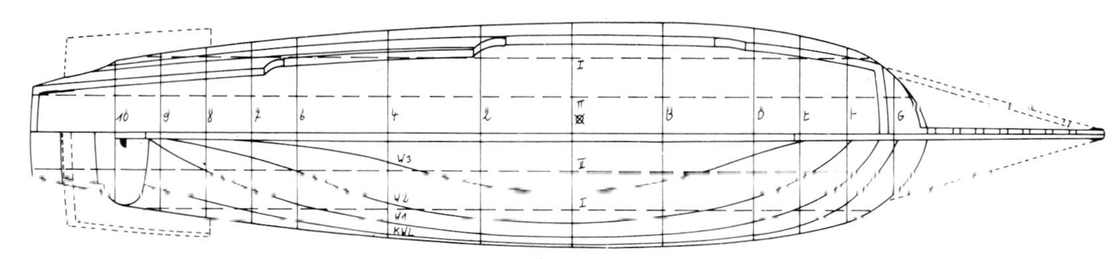
Bulwarks and maximum breadth (upper half): Half breadth (lower half)

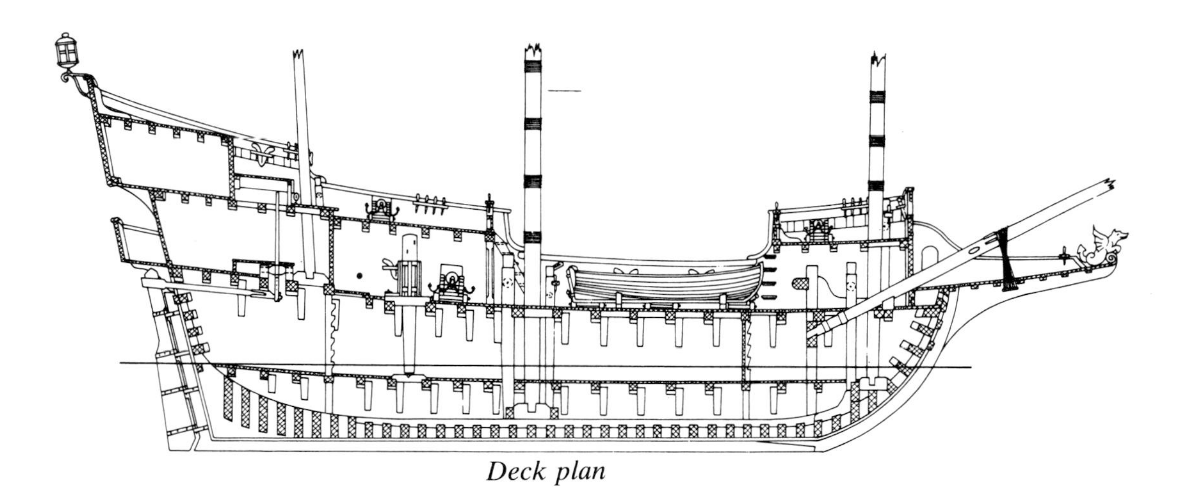
Deck plan

Profile

Sources

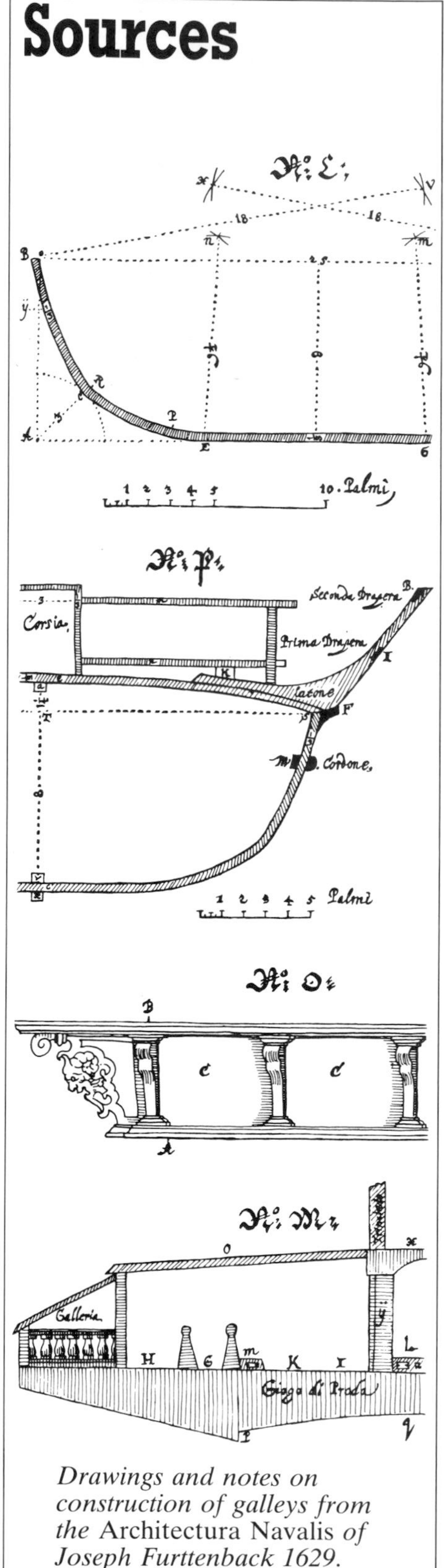

Drawings and notes on construction of galleys from the Architectura Navalis *of Joseph Furttenback 1629.*

Do not trust any plan!

Of course, this entreaty certainly applies to the poor quality (and worse) plans which are so often offered by commercial suppliers. They deserve only this comment: do yourself and the many thousands of enthusiastic model boat builders a great favour, and refuse outright to use poor quality plans. Resist all such offers! Force the manufacturers to supply better quality – it is in your power to do so. As long as rubbish continues to sell, the manufacturers do not need to invest money in producing goods of high quality. But if only a few hundred modellers would turn their backs on such companies, the situation would rapidly change for the better.

But don't even trust a good plan! Even on the best model construction plans there are a few small errors and inaccuracies that have crept in, even if only in respect of some parts which are simply not shown as clearly and unambiguously as the modeller would like.

If the basic drawings are correct – and on a high quality plan this will be the case – small areas which are less than clear are of no concern. In fact they make the whole business of period ship modelling really exciting! And the reason? Well, this is your opportunity to take an active interest: to check your plans, to improve them, to make discoveries, to clear up areas of doubt, to make corrections – in short, building a model which is better and more accurate than the plan, rather than just sticking rigidly to the drawings. For example, kit models can almost always be improved considerably by such methods, with the result that worthy and historically accurate pieces are produced. The aim and purpose of period ship modelling is not, after all, just a good-looking model; the ship should be as accurate a reproduction of the original as possible, the only difference being that it is 50, 75 or 100 times smaller than the original.

The study of source material is one of the obligatory tasks for any genuine model ship builder.

Certainly this study of source material takes up time, and it can also be laborious, but it can be a lot of fun, once you have acquired the taste for it. Occasionally you will need to develop the "fingertip" feel of a true detective in order to unearth this or that detail from your sources, but once you have started, you will find that this sort of modelling detective work becomes a real passion.

Oh yes, I know: when an interesting plan is spread out before you, it casts a spell, doesn't it? You just have to get on and build it. Nevertheless, don't do it! Take a little time and rummage through all the information you can find on this ship. I can promise you this: when the model is finished, you will look upon it with double the pleasure and double the pride!

Fortunately there are numerous sources of material available for checking and improving the plans – far more than you would believe, perhaps. In the appendix of this book I have listed a few museums and books which may be of use to you in this respect.

Let us look at the possibilities open to us: ideally, of course, the ship which you wish to model would still exist. If this is the case, you can swiftly clear up any problems and doubts.

The number of period ships which have survived until the present time is understandably small. The most famous is probably the *Victory*, Lord Nelson's flagship at Trafalgar in 1805, which is now in dry dock at Portsmouth. Other ships include the bark *Seute Deern*, at the German Maritime museum in Bremerhaven, the clipper *Cutty Sark* at Greenwich, the schooner *Amphion* at Stockholm, and the American frigate *Constitution* at Boston, Massachusetts.

If you are interested in the smaller coastal ships, or inland water boats, you will find a wide range of these preserved in the various naval and

Page from the handwritten Fragments of Ancient English Shipwrightry *from the end of the 16th century, attributed to the master shipwright Matthew Baker of 1586*

Sources

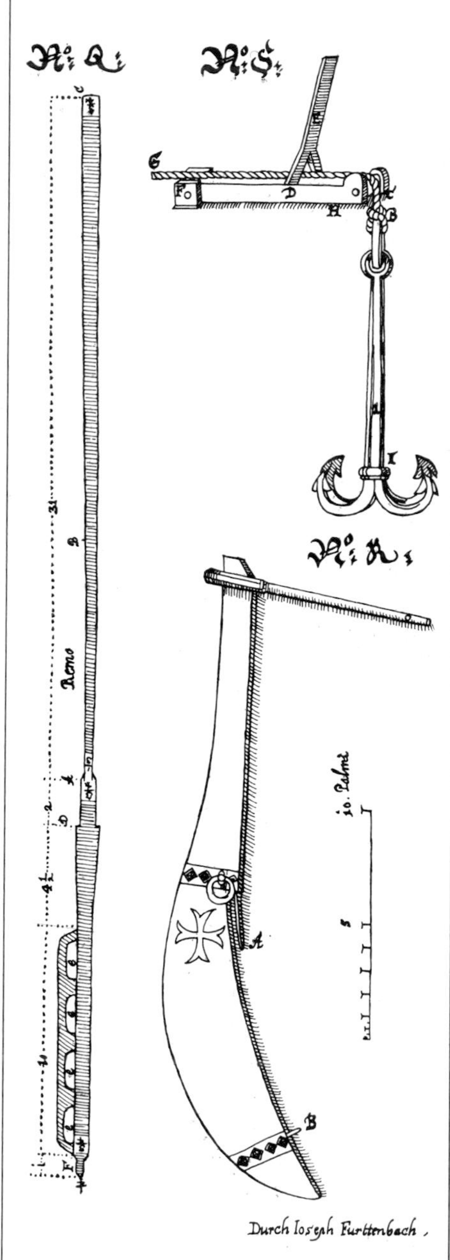

maritime museums.
Some ships have been dug up, or raised from the seabed, including the gigantic Roman state ship which lay in Lake Nemi in central Italy, the famous Viking ships of Gokstad and Oseberg in Norway and Roskilde in Denmark, a cog at Bremen, which is at present undergoing restoration in the German maritime museum, and the royal ship *Wasa* which sank in Stockholm harbour in 1628.
Another possible source is the stock of original and dockyard models which can be relied upon for absolute accuracy. The most famous collection of this type is probably the British "Admiralty models", which represent almost the entire British Royal Fleet in the form of splendidly worked models. They cover a period of a century starting around 1660-70, and no types are omitted. There are other models of the highest quality covering a very wide range of ships, although not including a compete series encompassing any particular period. These are to be found in Holland, Belgium, France, Spain, Sweden, the USA and Italy, and in quality they are by no means inferior to the British examples.
The votive ships and church models which also survive should be treated with some caution. They do indeed date from the period, but are usually simplified to an extreme degree, and are of less help to the modeller seeking information; on the other hand these models do include some exact replicas, which are suitable as source material.
Old dockyard drawings and original shipbuilding instructions often do not include a scale, and are rather unclear; they often contain more sketches than technical drawings in the present-day sense.
However, if you study them thoroughly enough, they will prove to contain much valuable information, made the more useful because there are nearly always tables accompanying the sketches, which give exact dimensions; these dimensions then have to be converted to our present-day units.
Three famous works must be mentioned here:
The oldest is the *Architectura Navalis* by Joseph Furttenbach, dating from the year 1629, the first work to publish the strictly guarded secrets and traditions of the various great shipbuilding families. This book still does not include plans in our sense, at best dimensioned drawings and sketches, but the text is very thorough, and is of the greatest interest, especially to the modeller whose principal interest is Mediterranean vessels.
The second is the *Architectura Navalis Mercatoria* by the famous Swedish master shipwright Fredrik Henrik af Chapman, written in 1768. This work contains hundreds of very accurate scaled plans of Swedish merchant ships, and also of pirate, postal and luxury ships.
The third is the collection *Souvenirs de Marine* by the French Vice-Admiral Edmond Paris, dating from about 1884. This work, in several volumes, also contains hundreds of scaled plans, not only of French ships, but of vessels from the widest range of periods and from all nations – from Japan and China, as well as from the American and European areas.
One excellent source of information is the wealth of oil paintings and engravings of individual ships, and also those depicting naval battles and fleet parades. In the 17th century certain painters were particularly famous for their accurate representations of ships: the Dutchmen Willem van de Velde the Elder and the Younger, Abraham Stork and Pieter Cornelis Soest. In other centuries look for Titian, Holbein, Scott, Serres, Chambers, Pocock, Dighton, Withcomb, van Beest, Canaletto and Roux.
Other useful sources of information are seals, coins, plaques, etc., which are virtually indispensable if you are studying the appearance of

Two original models of ancient Egyptian Nile boats dating from around 1500 B.C.

Sources

Ship illustrations of 13th Century seals. Top: seal of the Port of Winchelsea. Bottom: seal of the Port of Sandwich.

ships in the Middle Ages. Vase paintings have opened up whole epochs in the ancient arts of shipbuilding.

You should also consider mosaics, statues, fountains, tombstones, icons, small sculptures, book illustrations, church windows, wall hangings, votive pictures – there are vast numbers of pictures of ships, and many of them turn out to be excellent sources on close study.

In many cases, the acquisition of original source material on a particular ship may involve great trouble and often great expense. Often such research is simply beyond the resources of the ordinary modeller. The solution here is to find a sensible, practical middle path between the "too little" and the "too much" in source material. The best, surest path always leads to the museums, archives and libraries.

Here you will find that experts have spent decades assembling documents, and it is not uncommon to find that the results have been published in book form. I have quite deliberately omitted a comprehensive bibliography in this book – it would be quite beyond its scope. A vast avalanche of books has been written on the subject of ships, shipbuilding and even model shipbuilding; they include some splendid examples and a large number of moderate ones.

A few names should be borne in mind: there are a number of internationally recognized authors who really understand their subject, have written first-class books, and whose information can be depended upon in every way. They include Anderson, Boudriot, Chapelle, Hoeckel, Longridge, MacGregor, Petrejus, Underhill and Winter.

There is another way in which the museums provide almost indispensable aid to the modeller. They contain the largest collections of models. Probably every single type of ship, and every moderately famous individual ship in history, has been modelled at some time, and the model will be in some museum or other.

Of course, the majority of these are not original models, but recently constructed ones, made in the museum's workshops. However, these workshops are equipped to produce superb models, and employ skilled staff of the highest order, as well as having documents, books and plans available to them of which an ordinary modeller could only dream.

As a rule museum models are built to a superb standard, and are historically absolutely reliable. They are a safe, easy to use source. Together with a good plan and some specialized literature, there is hardly any excuse for errors in the building of your model.

It is not difficult to get hold of photographs of museum models: all naval, shipbuilding and maritime museums have a picture library which is usually very well organized. They will send the photos you want to your door, with an average waiting time of three to six weeks.

Naturally the chance to view the model "in the flesh" is better than any number of archive photos. Ask if you can photograph the model yourself, and take at least double the number of pictures that you think you need, especially of all the details. You can never have too many pictures, but you will often have too few. If photography is forbidden, make your own sketches and drawings – they do not need to be beautiful, the main thing is that they provide you with the information.

You might also consider for a moment whether you really need to spend the next Easter holiday on some beach at the Adriatic . . . would it not be much more interesting to go to Rotterdam or Paris to see "your" model, for example?

The splendid stern of the museum model of the Danish three-decker Sophia Amalia *of 1649*

Types of model

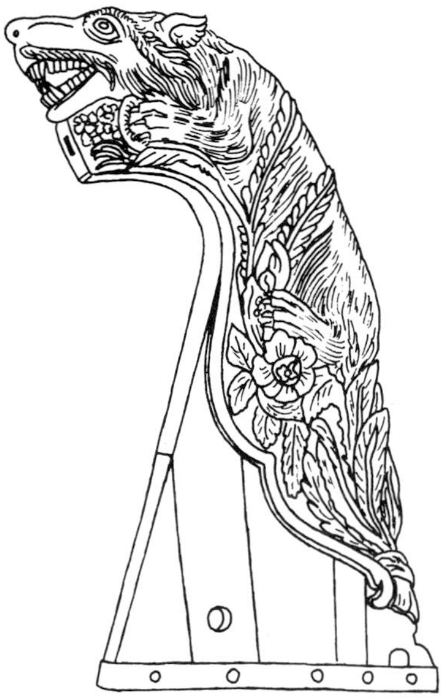

Dutch rudder head of the 18th Century

Once you have assembled your documentation, the next question to answer is this: what will the ship look like when it is finished?
This question may seem easy enough to answer, but it is really not so straightforward. There is a whole range of model types, all of which have their particular merits and function.

Frame models are design models, whose function is to show the exact appearance and precise location of the keel, the keelson, the stem and stern, the frames, the deck beams including all the important decorative elements and fittings. Frame models not only look complex, they *are* complex! Only experienced modellers should consider this type of model, and only then if they are familiar with the vast mass of theoretical knowledge behind period shipbuilding. To all other modellers the message is simple: steer clear of frame models!

Hull models show nothing but the finished, planked hull with its equipment and decoration (sometimes with, sometimes without guns), but do not include masts or rigging at all.
Well constructed hull models can be quite attractive, the more so to the modeller because they are the simplest to make of all period ship models, simply because of the absence of masts and rigging. Of course, hull models cannot show the appearance of a ship as it sailed the seas, but anyone who is fearful of tackling the rigging, which can be exceedingly complicated, will be attracted to this type of model, as it opens up rich scope for work.

Block models are also a type of hull model, but in this case they are not assembled from individual components, but are carved from a single block of wood, with the fittings completely omitted. Block models do not have all that much to offer the model builder, unless they are the type which are put in a bottle, but these have no place in this book.

Half-models represent a further type of hull model, and show half of the hull as far as the centreline. They were used in the 19th century in preference to dockyard models, when their purpose was to investigate the most favourable hull shapes; they have little attraction for the model builder.

Waterline models show the fully-rigged ship, but only down as far as the waterline, that is, as the vessel would be seen when afloat. An idea with obvious attractions, and many models of modern ships are built in this form. However, it is not so suitable for period ships. Indeed, except for what are classed as "miniatures" they are rarely seen at all, and for this reason we cannot recommend waterline models to the builder of period ships.

Admiralty models were an English invention of the 17th century, when the British Admiralty demanded a model as well as the plans of each new type of ship. The characteristic feature of Admiralty models was the underwater hull, which was built as a frame model. The part above the waterline was fully planked, and the decks again were unplanked, in order to show the design of the deck beams. Admiralty models, which are amongst the most magnificent achievements in model shipbuilding of all time, were built with or without guns, as hull models, or as fully rigged models.
The same applies here as for the frame type of model. A broad background of theoretical and practical experience are required before a modeller should dare to tackle this type of model. If in doubt, steer a wide berth, or you risk a fiasco!

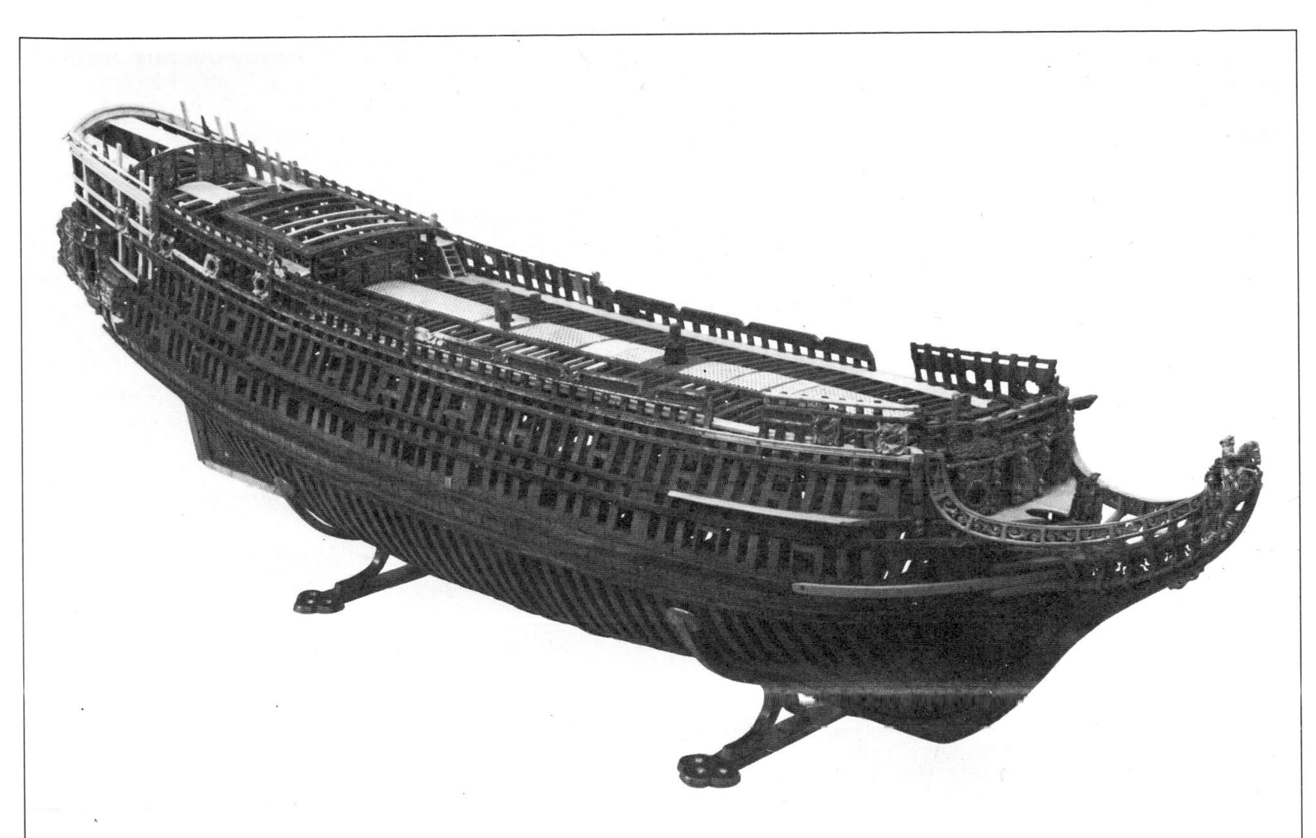

Frame model of a British three-decker of 1660

Hull model of an 18 gun brig of 1800

Types of model

Dutch rudder heads of the 18th Century

Fully rigged models are really what everyone imagines a proper model ship should be. Here the beauty of a period ship, with all its proportions so finely balanced, can be shown to best effect; it is also the first model type we have discussed which shows the overall scheme of how the ship operated. If you walk through the collections of the great naval and maritime museums, you will find that you go past many hull or frame models, no matter how skilfully constructed, almost without a second glance, only to be almost magically drawn to the splendour of the fully rigged models.
Without wishing to denigrate other types of model, I would strongly recommend the fully rigged model to any model maker who does not have an irreversible repulsion to the vast number of cords and threads involved in the rigging. The rigged model type can also be sub-divided into four versions:

Fully rigged models without sails: among the most popular type of rigged model. Many model makers are of the opinion that sails would conceal far too much of the masts and the rigging. However, this problem can be avoided, if a few tips are followed – more on this later. In any case, a model without sails quite certainly has its own great charm, with its filigree network of masts, topmasts, yards and all the ropework.

Fully-rigged models with furled sails: similar reasoning has led to the idea of showing the sails of the model rolled up, that is, furled at the yards. This method requires knowledge of a few "tricks of the trade", as we will see in the chapter on sails. Such models are comparatively rare.

Fully-rigged models with partially set sails: these are much more popular. Usually the top and topgallant sails are set, while the lower sails are furled at the yards, or at least brailed up, to permit a better view of the deck. On such models the staysails are absent, generally speaking.

Fully-rigged models with sails set: of course, the full function of the rigging in all its complexity can only be shown if all the sails available are set, complete with staysails and even the studding sails, if fitted. Nobody would doubt that a model ship with all sails set is a thoroughly glorious sight. However, in the final analysis it is up to the individual modeller which type of model comes closest to his wishes and conceptions.

Waterline model of an English galleon of 1580

Scale

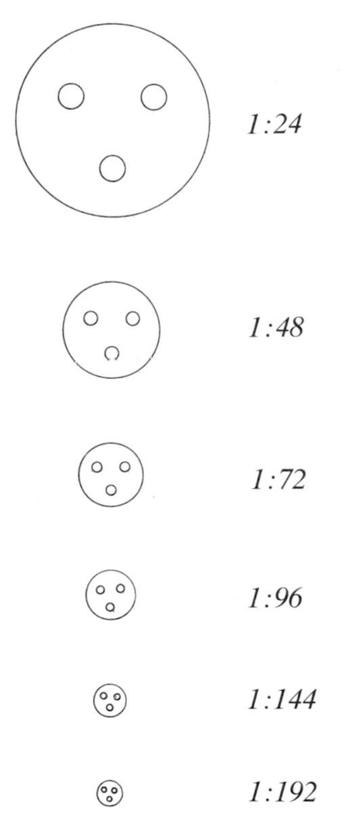

An example of scale: a deadeye in various scales.

The next stage is to establish the scale of the planned model ship, i.e. the degree of reduction to which the model is to be built. Hence a scale of, for example, 1:50 means that the model will be 50 times smaller than the original.

Commercial plans are available in all possible – and impossible – scales; hence it is up to the model maker to decide which scale is the ideal one for his model, and to which scale he can best bring his ideas to realization. I would not usually advise sticking rigidly to the scale of the plans, since they are usually drawn to a smaller scale than is desirable for model building, in order to prevent the paper sizes getting out of hand. One further point here is that it is advisable to keep to one of the standard scales.

On the continent of Europe these are 1:200, 1:150, 1:100, 1:75, 1:50, 1:25. In Britain and, usually, America (to make calculations easier in Imperial units): 1:192, 1:144, 1:96, 1:72, 1:48, 1:24. (1:192 is 1/16in to 1ft, 1:96 is 1/8in to 1ft, etc.)

Each of these scales has its advantages and disadvantages. Please consider for a moment where in your home the finished model is to stand, and whether there is really space for it there. You would not be the first to suffer a nasty surprise. A modelling friend of mine had to half de-rig his very fine, very large-scale model, because it would not pass through the door . . .

1:200 (1:192). Very great reduction. For: Modern ships, which are often more than 650ft long, can be reduced to a reasonable model size at this scale. Against: Details disappear almost completely, or cannot be made at all because of their miniscule size.

1:150 (1:144). Also a very great reduction, and the same applies as above.

1:100 (1:96). For: The large sailing ships (e.g. clippers) or steam/sail driven ships of the last century can be well represented at this scale. Against: Many details again have to be omitted, as they turn out too small.

1:75 (1:72). For: Good possibilities for representing period ships at a sensible size, without involving too much intricate work. Beginners, modellers with less patience, or constructors who shy away from too many details (although this fear is largely unfounded) are recommended to work at this scale. It is often selected for kits by model firms, and not without justification. Against: Model makers who place a high priority on the accurate reproduction of even the smallest details must be discouraged from using this scale, as the smallest parts still turn out very minute, and are correspondingly difficult to make. Very large ships, e.g. three-deckers of the seventeenth and eighteenth centuries, occasionally demand this scale, although you might in this case consider whether the construction of a smaller original to a larger scale would not be a better solution.

1:50 (1:48). This is widely regarded as the "ideal scale" for period ships; for example, all the English Admiralty models are constructed to 1/4in-1ft (1:48) scale. For: This scale is large enough for the exact scale rendition of almost all the details, and yet small enough that the model can be displayed in a normal home (for a ship of average size up to about 1750, the model would be no larger than 4ft 6in long). This scale of 1:50 (or 1:48 in British practice) can be recommended most warmly to model builders, and it has proved its value a thousand times over. Against: It forces you to undertake detail work. If you omit this work, the model will look poor. If you prefer to gloss over the detail work, choose a smaller scale (1:75).

1:25 (1:24). Very large scale. For: At this scale you can include even the tiniest details. Connoisseurs of model building have the chance to pull out all the stops. Against: the models rapidly assume gigantic

Admiralty model of the British First Rate Prince *of 1670*

Scale

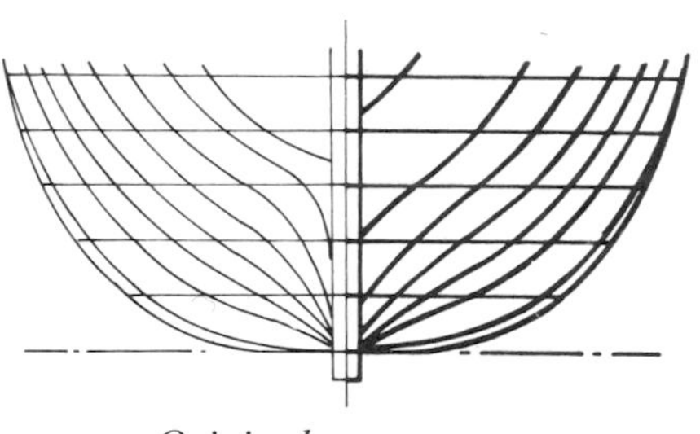

Original:
Left side – fine lines
Right side – thick lines

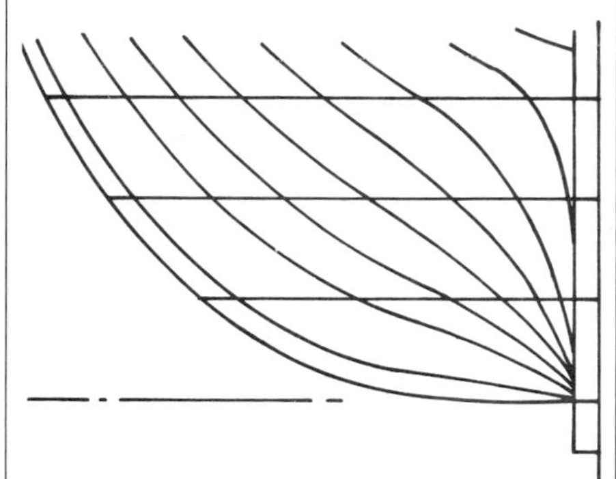

Enlargement of left side:
Lines remain sharp
Enlargement usable

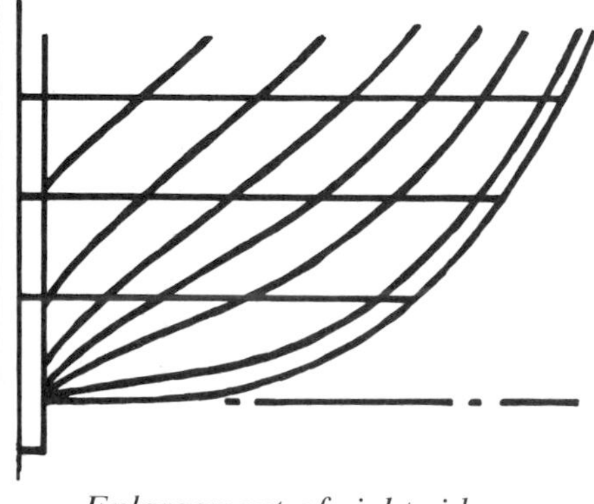

Enlargement of right side:
Lines become too thick
Enlargement useless

proportions (a two-decker from the mid-18th century will be over 9 feet long, and almost equally tall). Only small vessels can really be built to this scale.
Other scales: These are occasionally offered on plans, but they are not all that welcome – even at international competitions. There is a widely held view – and not without justification – that models should be built to a limited range of specific scales which shows the models in a clear dimensional relationship to each other; this also makes it easier for the onlooker to make direct comparisons.
Unfortunately the scale of the plans from which the modeller wishes to build is rarely the same as the scale at which he has decided to work. This raises a problem: the drawings shown on the plans are often not directly usable for the modeller's own model. They have to be redrawn – a task which few modellers enjoy, but which is often necessary, alas. You should under no circumstances allow yourself to be dictated to by the scale of the plans; never build a model to a smaller scale simply because you want to save yourself the trouble of redrawing!
There are two methods of re-scaling plans, one of which is tedious, and the other rather expensive.
The tedious method is to draw the most important outlines neatly on transparent squared paper, and then transfer the lines point by point onto a second sheet at the required degree of enlargement, using dividers, straight edge, and, if necessary, a calculator or slide-rule. The points on the original should be no farther apart than ⅛in, and 1/16in is much better, otherwise inaccuracies will creep in. This job is cased somewhat by the use of proportional dividers, on which the degree of enlargement can be set.
The expensive method is to have the plans enlarged photo-mechanically. By this method plans can be altered to any size you desire without any difficulty. The photo-copying service round the corner will not be accustomed to dealing with such large sizes, so it is best to look up "Reprographic services" in the Yellow Pages, which are usually willing to carry out such work. This costs money, of course, perhaps from £10 to £40 according to size, and for this reason it is sensible to select certain vital drawings for enlargement, rather than have all of them processed. After all, a lot can be achieved with the dividers method. The most important and most difficult parts include the frame outlines, the waterline plan, and the internal profile. One important point in photo-mechanical enlargement is that the lines on the original drawing must be very fine. If the lines on the original are already thick, they will become even thicker on enlargement, and the tolerance will then be far too great.
Finally, it makes sense to trace your own exact copy of the plan on transparent squared paper, from this enlargement. This does not take all that long, and it will make some later stages much easier, e.g. the exact drawing of the frames.

Fully rigged model without sails of an English frigate of 1785

Costs

Figure from the stern of the ship Die Admiralität von Hamburg *of 1691*

It is an amazing fact that authors of model shipbuilding books are unanimous on one point: period ship modelling is uncommonly cheap. The modeller can get by with the minimum of tools, and the few odd sheets and strips of wood, string and pins hardly cost anything at all. Alas, I cannot join my voice to this opinion without certain reservations, neither regarding the tools, nor the materials.

I will admit that period ship modelling can by no means be classified as an expensive hobby, and I can state this as a fact. Moreover if you calculate the costs on an investment per month basis, the overall figures will seem incredibly low.

Another factor is that a well built model ship will be worth many times more than the costs incurred in building it. But when we hear of the "minimal number of tools required", and the "cheapness of the materials", these statements may well apply to the beginner, and for him there is the enormous advantage that he needs only invest a small amount to find out whether he is likely to stick with his new hobby.

The beginner may well find he can manage with a fretsaw, a hand-drill, a file, a carving chisel, a few paintbrushes, a hammer, a pair of pliers and some clothes pegs for tools; for materials he can start with plywood and spruce and obechi stripwood. But this only applies to the beginner!

If you intend to take up period shipbuilding seriously, you will eventually need to build up a considerable assortment of tools (more details in the next chapter), and materials such as walnut, pearwood, boxwood are all quite costly. Wood stain, paint and dyes are by no means cheap, and gold leaf is incredibly expensive – the only compensation being that not very much is ever needed of any of them.

When we move on to detail fittings (blocks, deadeyes, guns, cleats, etc) costs really start to rocket upwards, particularly if you buy them ready made from a model shop. You will rapidly get through a considerable amount of money in this way. The plans are not exactly given away, either. A good plan could cost £5 to £10 or more, and this is one area in which you should not attempt to save money.

All in all, a well-constructed model ship of average size can be reckoned to cost £100 to £200 (less tools). A beginner with a simple model may well manage comfortably on a fifth of this amount.

On the other hand the construction of a good model takes a lot of time. If we reckon on 12 months' building time, and an outlay of £100, then that is around £8 per month. In model making terms this amount is about right for somebody who sits in his miniature dockyard just about every weekend. This amounts to less than £2 per weekend. You could spend more money much more quickly on another hobby, or on petrol, in order to creep along the motorway at snail's pace, breathing your neighbour's exhaust fumes, hoping to reach a favourite spot for a picnic before it is time to go home again.

Large Venetian carrack Santa Elena *of around 1500 under full sail. (Model by the author for Aeronaut Modellbau)*

Decision

English lion figurehead of the early 18th century

There is one method of ensuring that you build your model badly, that you leave it half-way through, or simply lose the pleasure at some stage, and that is to grab your saw, your file and your drill and get hacking at the wood – failure is then guaranteed!

If you are keen on nasty surprises, start by all means on the building, and make your decisions as and when they become necessary – you will surprise yourself!

The construction of a good model requires a considerable amount of initial thinking and planning; you have to find answers for a whole series of questions, and you have to make decisions before construction can start.

To put it quite plainly: before you take the first piece of wood in your hand, you must know exactly how your ship will look when it is finished. Give yourself time. Think it all through carefully. Flip through this book once more. Take another look at the particularly critical and difficult areas of your model, e.g. the stern, the head, the armaments, the poop lantern, the ship's boats, the carvings etc. You should also decide in what situation you wish to show the ship, e.g. in the harbour, under way or in battle. In harbour sails are secured to the yards or completely struck while open hatches, dangling anchors on the cat-heads and unlashed barrels on deck are completely justified – things that with the sails set, that is with the ship under way, would, of course, be absolute nonsense!

Bury yourself once more in your rigging plan, let your sails wind themselves through your head again, gaze anew at the photos of the museum models, and then make your decisions. Now, *before* you start. And then stick to what you have decided.

As well as a degree of manual skill and patience, consistency is an essential asset, if you are to be successful in building period ship models. Of course you will change your mind now and then, and go back on decisions you have made here and there in the course of the work. That is only human, and quite understandable. But bear this in mind: the less you alter in your original conception, the less trouble, frustration and difficulties you will encounter.

On the opposite page I have assembled a list of 41 questions. Before you start building a model ship, sit yourself down one quiet evening, and answer these questions – in writing. Please be quite honest, and be critical in respect of your ambitions – you are not doing yourself a favour by deceiving yourself.

Make your decisions without the least hint of a "maybe", "I'm not really sure", "possibly", "we'll see", "let's see what turns up" . . .

If you are unable to give a clear answer to any one question, immerse yourself again in your plans, photos, books and other documentation. Weigh up the various possibilities again in your mind.

Have patience, even with yourself. Allow yourself plenty of time, time and more time! As long as you need, until you know absolutely precisely what you want. Then – and only then – start work.

Questionnaire

Ship:
1 Is the model attractive enough to me to make me work on it, probably for many months?
2 Are there other models which might be even more attractive?
3 Am I really sure of this ship?
4 Really??

Basic questions:
5 Is my manual skill sufficient for this model?
6 Am I not overstretching myself with this ship?
7 Should I not perhaps select a simpler one?
8 Are my hand tools up to the demands of this model?
9 How are my finances for the ship (materials and perhaps some tools)?

Documentation:
10 Are my plans thorough enough?
11 Do they agree with each other?
12 Are there any other plans available for my ship?
13 Do I have all the museum photos which are available?
14 Do I have access to the specialized literature pertaining to my ship?
15 Are there any other documents which I could or should have?

Preparation:
16 What type of model should I select?
17 Which scale will I choose?
18 Will the finished model fit the space in which it is intended to stand?

Construction:
19 What type of construction shall I choose?
20 Can I cope with the stern?
21 Can I cope with the head?
22 Can I really do the carvings?
23 Am I sure, or should I carry out a few experiments beforehand?
24 Which timber do I choose?
25 Where can I get hold of the wood?
26 Can I guarantee that it is sufficiently well-seasoned?
27 How will the guns be shown?
28 Can I manage the anchors?
29 Can I make the poop lantern?
30 Where can I get hold of equipment and fittings which I cannot make myself?
31 Does my supplier have everything in stock which I will need?
32 Of appropriate quality?
33 Should I show my ship in rigged form?
34 Am I well acquainted with my rigging plans?
35 Do they agree with each other?
36 Do I have a belaying plan?
37 Where can I obtain rigging thread?
38 Do I want sails?
39 Who is going to sew up my sails?

Final questions:
40 Am I still sure that I want to build this ship and no other?
41 Am I still certain that I can finish the job?

If the answer is yes, then start work and I wish you all success!

Materials and tools

Material preferences
Material scale · Wood · Metal
Glass · Ropes · Sails · Tools
Machines · Chemicals
Working area · Working
wood and metal · Carving
Punching · Etching · Joining
materials · Glueing · Pins
Screws · Soldering · Dowels
Rivets · Synthetic resin casting
Metal casting · Electro-plating
Paints · Dyes · Bleaching
Gilding · Paint and lacquer
Blackening metal
Ageing wood

For the construction of a good model ship the choice of materials is of the greatest importance, as also is the question whether the modeller has the tools to work the materials properly.
A further point is that the materials and tools should be appropriate to the abilities of the model maker. Good materials and a comprehensive selection of machine tools are by no means a guarantee of high quality results!
On the other hand real experts are often able to produce the most unbelievable models even with the cheapest means, indeed almost without tools altogether. A famous example of this is the "Prisoner of War models" which were made by captured French sailors in the Napoleonic wars, often out of bones – yes, you read that right – bones!. These modellers had nothing more refined than a knife to work with, plus perhaps crude tools made from needles, nails, hoop-iron and the like.
Now, these are exceptions.
Today's ship modeller is offered almost too many materials and tools; his problem is that of deciding what he really needs, and what he can do without.
In the following section I will try to give you a little help, whether you are a beginner or an expert.
What tools must the modeller own, what should he have, and what can be regarded as a luxury? How is the tool used, which materials are suitable for which purpose, how are technical difficulties overcome, or circumnavigated? What other paths lead to the same goal? For example, to turn gun barrels from brass you need a watchmaker's lathe, and this machine is very expensive. However, gun barrels of equally high quality can be cast by the modeller himself in tin alloy, and if you treat them correctly afterwards, no person on earth will be able to tell the difference in the end.
There is one basic tenet which the historical ship modeller really should adopt right from the start: do not accept inferior quality!
When you buy something, buy the best available. As far as tools are concerned, this applies equally to beginner and expert. The beginner may not need a giant workshop full of machinery, but what he has in the way of tools must be of top quality.
With materials, of course, this only applies to the advanced and expert modeller. For the beginner a degree of moderation is advised. If the beginner tries to handle boxwood and gold leaf, he is throwing money away. But if an expert works with spruce and gold paint, he is devaluing his own skilled labour.
It goes without saying that the best quality is never cheap – it cannot be. But the amount of material – even the most expensive – which you need for a model ship is not great; as for the costly tools and machines you may need in the course of time – well, what are Christmas, birthdays and other feast days for?
And one more thing: if you build quickly, if you use poor quality tools and cut-price materials, you will usually produce a poor result.

French 74 gun ship Le Vengeur *from the end of the 18th Century. This model was built from bone by a French prisoner-of-war sailor around 1806*

Choice of materials

There are four basic materials in period ship modelling: wood, metal, sailcloth and rope.
Sailcloth and rope are covered in detail in the chapters BLOCKS AND ROPES and THE SAILS, hence we can devote this section to wood and metal and everything the modeller needs to know about working with these materials.
Every model maker has his strengths and weaknesses concerning these two basic materials. To put it another way: every modeller has a basic preference either for the one or the other material; he feels more at home with it, and he has a better understanding of how the material is worked.
As I have already said, the modeller must be self-critical with regard to his abilities and facilities. Herr Anton Happach is German Champion, European Champion, etc, etc, and models built by him are on display in the German Museum, Munich, and in the German Maritime Museum, Bremerhaven. He is one of the most brilliant modellers I have ever met, but he quite openly admits, for example, that carving is not really in his line. For this reason he has specialised in ships of the nineteenth century.
It matters not one jot if you cannot quite come to grips with one or other technique; you just need to get to know your preferences and leanings, your strengths and weaknesses in the working of wood or metal, and select your model with this in mind.
Here is one general rule: If you are not happy working with metal, you should stick to ships dating from 1820 or earlier. Of course, even these models cannot be made entirely without metal parts, but their number is quite small.
The modeller who enjoys working with metal should select ships from 1820 onwards, as they will give him the opportunity to indulge himself to his heart's content.

Material scale

We have already discussed scales in some detail in the section on planning your model. So what is this subject cropping up here again so soon? A very great deal, that's what. A common error, seen again and again, is the selection of the wrong material (especially the choice of the wrong wood), which is not appropriate to the scale of the model. An example might show this more clearly. The most important shipbuilding timber was oak, a hard, short-grained wood with a distinct grain pattern. Many model makers are of the opinion that the choice of oak for the model is bound to be right, as you could hardly get any closer to the original. Viewed in this light, the facts appear indisputable. But what these modellers overlook is the fact that the materials have to match the scale of the model. In practice, this is the result: At a scale of ¼in to a foot, all the parts of the model are 48 times smaller than the original, except that the wood, in our example oak, remains at a scale of 1:1, and is therefore 48 times larger and coarser than it should be. If we reduce everything 48 times, then the oak must also be reduced by 48 times. And since that is technically impossible, of course, we have to select a timber whose structure corresponds to oak – reduced 48 times – pear, walnut or box, for example.
Material scale means nothing less than selecting your materials to correspond in structural terms to the scale reduction of the original material.
Please bear this in mind, especially when selecting your timbers.

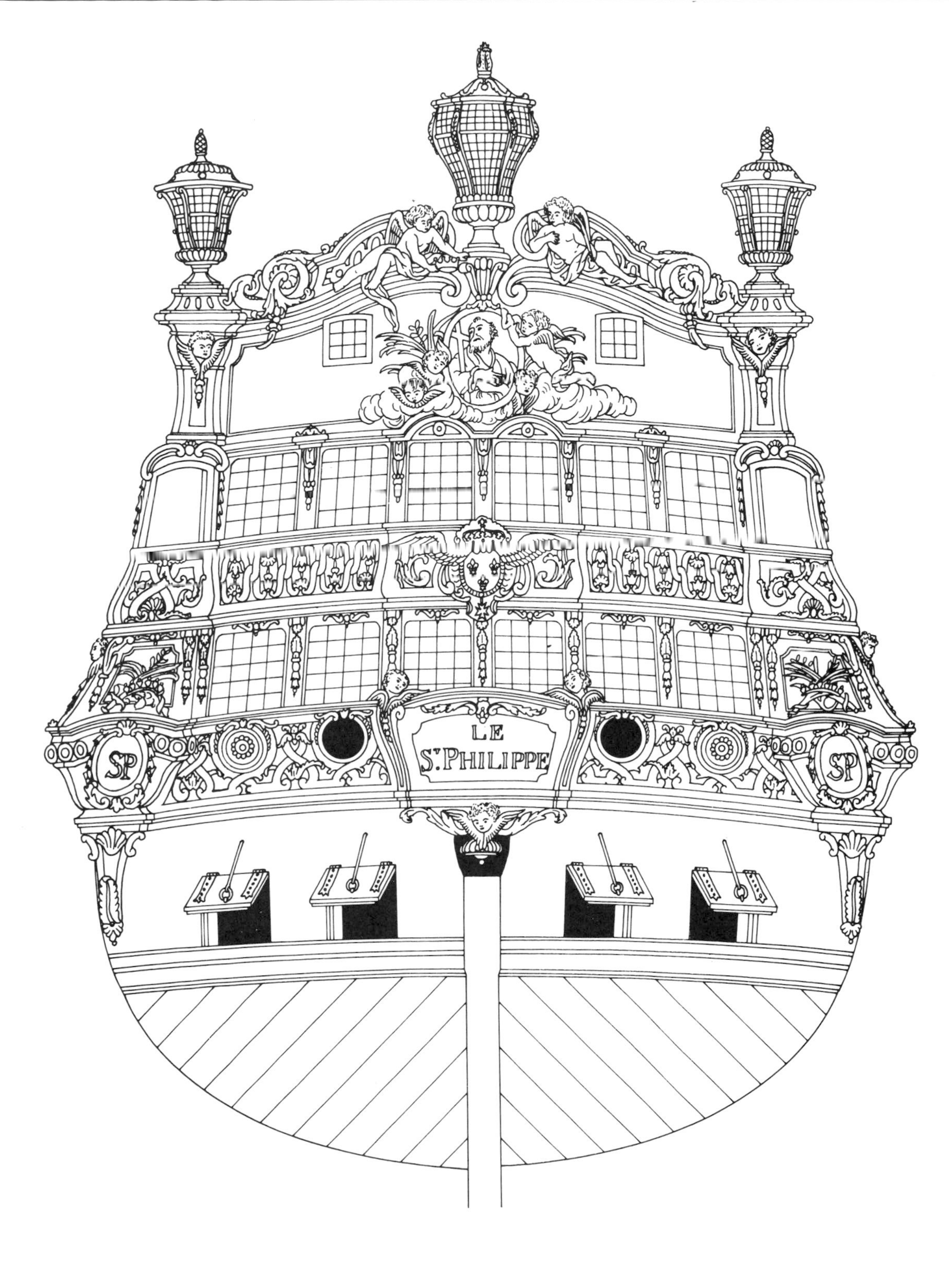

Stern of the French 2nd rate ship of the line Le St. Philippe, *1721*

Wood

1 x 1 1 x 2 1 x 3 1 x 5 1 x 8 1 x 10

2 x 2 2 x 3 2 x 4 2 x 5 2 x 7 2 x 8

2 x 10 2 x 15 2 x 20

3 x 3 3 x 5 3 x 8 3 x 10

4 x 4

5 x 5 5 x 8 5 x 10 5 x 15

6 x 6

8 x 8

10 x 10 10 x 15 10 x 20

2 3 4 5

6 8 10

12 14

The standard strip and dowelling sizes of imported ship modelling timbers, dimensions in mm

Undoubtedly the most important material in shipbuilding up to the second half of the last century – and hence in the whole era of period shipbuilding – was wood.
At one time shipbuilding stripped whole countries of their forests, e.g. England, Italy, Yugoslavia and Greece. Bitter wars have been fought over shipbuilding timber, for example between Holland, England, Denmark and Sweden, when the favour of the great European wood supplier, namely Russia, and hence free access to her timber, was at stake. In the area controlled by the city of Venice it was a punishable offence to fell a tree before a state commissioner had checked whether the tree was suitable for shipbuilding use.
These problems do not exist for the ship modeller, as he has access to woods from all parts of the world. For him, the important point is that he should have a sound knowledge of what is suitable and what is not. Please bear the following basic rule in mind: wood is an organic material, which reacts to warmth and cold, damp and dryness. The older and the better seasoned the wood is, the less it will "move", the less it will tend to split, to warp and to change colour.
Whatever your timber merchant may tell you about the adequate seasoning of his wood, do not believe him, as today a really well seasoned piece of wood is scarcely available at all. But don't let this put you off. It just means store your wood yourself for at least one to two years after purchasing it (the longer, the better), and ideally in a dry, airy room. I don't know any serious model ship builder who does not have a small wood store of this type.
The only exception to this rule is veneer. This is in the form of thin sheets of hardwood, which have a maximum thickness of ·040 inches, and are used for various purposes in ship modelling. Here is a list of the most important types of wood, which you can obtain from hobby shops, timber merchants or cabinet makers; it includes notes on their usefulness for modelling and an indication of *comparative* cost.

Obechi
Soft, yellowish, open-grained, tough. Obechi is extremely easy to work, holds nails well (in contrast to balsa), is less fragile, and is preferable in all respects to balsa wood. Does not warp! Hence it is ideal for the keelson and the in-fill pieces of fully planked hulls. Available as stripwood in virtually all imaginable sizes, it is suitable for the base planking of double-planked hulls, as it is tough and flexible, and does not splinter readily. Cheap.

Balsa
Very soft, white, porous, fragile. Easy to work but does not look good and can only be used for in-fill pieces at the bow and stern. Does not hold nails. Of very little use for ship modelling. Cheap.

Pear
Medium-hard, light to medium brown in colour, slightly reddish, short fibres, plain grain pattern. Pear is excellent to work and to carve, as it hardly splinters at all. Represents one of the ideal timbers for period shipbuilding. Use for virtually everything: visible frames, planking, deck strakes, all kinds of deck erections and fittings, also carvings. Expensive.

Beech
Medium-hard, red-brown to brown, long-fibred, very tough, plain grain pattern. Suitable for masts and yards, also for frames. Cheap.

British Stuart royal yacht around 1675

Wood

Flexible beech stripwood
Very flexible, red-brown to brown, long-fibred, very tough, plain grain pattern. Flexible wood has been subjected to special processing, and is available in strip form through commercial outlets. Flexible wood strip is very difficult to break, and can be bent and twisted into any shape imaginable. On the other hand, it is almost impossible to nail it and very difficult to glue it or dowel it, and these qualities make it much less suitable for period ship modelling than you might have thought at first. Medium price.

Boxwood
Hard, yellow, close-grained, plain grain pattern, very strong. Although hard, it is good to work and to carve, but tends to splinter when nailed (pilot drill all holes). It is ideal for all small parts, especially for carvings and blocks, deadeyes, thimbles and similar, also for visible frames, planking and similar parts. Represents one of the ideal timbers for period model shipbuilding. Very expensive and difficult to obtain.

Oak
Hard, light to medium grey-brown, tough, short-fibred, distinctive grain structure. In full-size shipbuilding oak was probably the most commonly used timber, but its coarse structure makes it less suitable for model building. It is also difficult to work. Medium price.

Spruce
Medium-hard, yellowish to whitish-pink, tough, long-grained, medium to strong grain pattern. Spruce is often supplied in kits as planking material, and is available commercially in strip form in all imaginable sizes. Only moderately suited to period ship modelling except perhaps for underplanking. Cheap (and a model in which spruce is largely used also looks cheap).

Lime
Soft, white, tough, long-fibred, plain grain pattern. Lime is easy to work and does not splinter. Highly suitable for planking, deck strakes, wales, decorative strips, etc. Somewhat overrated for carving, as lime does not work very cleanly across the grain, and breaks easily along the grain when used for very small parts. Quite unsuitable for parts which have to withstand any strain, such as blocks and deadeyes. Lime is available commercially as sheet, block and strip in all possible dimensions. Cheap.

Mahogany
Hard, red to brown, short-fibred, distinct grain pattern. Used widely for full-size shipbuilding in the late 19th century, but, like oak, is only moderately suitable for modelling because of its coarse structure; mahogany also splinters very easily. Unfortunately its colouring is very difficult to represent with other woods or dyes. Medium price.

Walnut
Hard, in a wide variety of colours from light brown to dark brown, short-fibred, tough, plain grain pattern. Often looks very like oak in colour, and is relatively easy to work and bend, despite its hardness, as it hardly splinters at all. Also carves well. One of the ideal woods for period ship modelling. American walnut has approximately the same qualities as the European, while African walnut is cheaper, although more difficult to work. Walnut can be used for virtually everything, such as visible frames, keel, planking, deck strakes, small parts (even blocks and deadeyes), and carving. Expensive.

Olive wood
Initially soft, then hard, yellowish to white, short-fibred, plain grain pattern, very strong. Used principally in Southern Europe, olive has similar properties to boxwood. Young wood is soft and easy to work. After seasoning olive becomes very hard, and is then almost impossible to work. Hence the modeller must use young wood, make the required parts, but then leave them to season for at least one year before fitting them on the model. Fairly cheap.

Pitch pine
Medium hard, whitish to yellowish, long-fibred, tough, plain grain pattern, rather resinous. Suitable for masts and yards, as it does not break easily and is not prone to splintering. Care required at points where resin exudes, as these often reject paint, stain or varnish. Cheap.

Plywood
Consists of several laminations of wood glued together with the grain running at right-angles in adjacent layers. Available commercially in numerous thicknesses from 1/64in (·4mm). Plywood is easy to saw, drill and nail, and it has the advantage that the grain direction, which needs to be watched with all other types of wood, is of no importance. Plywood has little tendency to warp.
The available types are as follows: birch ply (best quality), beech ply (medium quality) and poplar ply (worst quality). Other types, such as oak or mahogany ply, are of no interest to model makers.
Plywood looks poor, and for this reason it should only be used in period ship modelling where it will not be exposed (frames and keelsons of fully planked hulls, deck beams, etc). In invisible locations plywood should be used wherever possible because of its otherwise good properties. Cheap.

Cembra pine
Soft, yellowish to pink, close-grained, short-fibred, plain grain pattern, but with many dark eyes, and resinous. Easy to work and to carve. Is widely used in ship modelling – especially in Southern Europe. The numerous knots are easy to work, but sometimes insist on showing as dark spots or points. The resinous nature can lead to problems in painting, varnishing, staining and gilding. Fairly cheap. Also known as Swiss Pine and Siberian Yellow Pine.

Other types of wood
Cedar, maple, teak, yellow and white pine, fir, elm, yew, lemon and other woods are seldom used in period ship modelling, although this does not mean that they are not useful in some areas. It may well be worthwhile for the experienced modeller to experiment with these neglected timbers. However, it is not within the scope of this book to cover them all.

Examples of how variously shaped components for timber shipbuilding could be cut from trees. The model maker does not need "grown knees", but he should nevertheless consider carefully the best grain direction for each part.

Metal

The second important material is metal, and not only for ships after the middle of the 19th century, although metal played a far more dominant role on these ships than previously.
The two metals with which the historic ship modeller will work are brass and copper. What you need are sheets of various thickness down to ·004in (e.g. for copper sheathing of hulls), round rod for turning (e.g. for gun barrels), and tubes of various diameter (e.g. for funnels or galley chimneys, etc).
In contrast to wood, there is no point in setting up a small store of all possible sizes of rod, tube and sheet metal, which you will perhaps need at some time or other – that would be far too expensive. In this case it makes much more sense to measure up your immediate needs in terms of shapes, lengths and diameters from the plan, and then buy in a stock to suit your project.
Sources of supply: The larger thicknesses and diameters should be available in well-stocked model shops, and the very thin metal foils and similar materials from special non-ferrous metal suppliers (almost all larger towns have such a store); check up in the Yellow Pages, or enquire at a good model shop.
Small flat brass strip, and L, T and U section strip in brass, as occasionally required when building models after the middle of the 19th century, are available in good model shops – in the railway department.
Very small diameter wires in brass, nickel silver and similar materials can be purchased from good model shops or model engineering mail order suppliers.

Glass

The representation of glass has been a problem for a very long time, as real glass cannot really be used.
The traditional solution is to use the so-called "glass colours", i.e. the windows and poop lantern, etc are fabricated from wood, and then painted with a colour which meant "glass". These colours were green (emerald to chromium oxide green), a mid to dark blue and black, sometimes with white spots. This does not really look very true to life, but many ultra-conservative model makers declare that this is the only possible method, simply because it has been done in this way for centuries.
If you wish to have windows or skylights which look natural, you can use celluloid or photographic film, from which the emulsion has been removed in warm water. Smoked perspex is also very suitable. This is obtainable from plastics merchants. The material is worked like wood (sawing, etc). But do take care to avoid scratching the surface.
For complex glass components, e.g. poop lanterns, clear casting resin has proved ideal (see CASTING RESIN). Using this method, splendid imitations of even the lattice-like leaded windows used on windows of ships up to the beginning of the 18th century are possible.

Ropes & Sails

The materials used for ropes and sails are discussed in detail in the appropriate chapters, so we will not repeat the information here.

Two French warships shortly after the middle of the 19th century.
Top: the 1st rate scout cruiser Le Bouvet, *1866.*
Bottom: the armoured ship Le Solferino, *1861.*

Hand & power tools

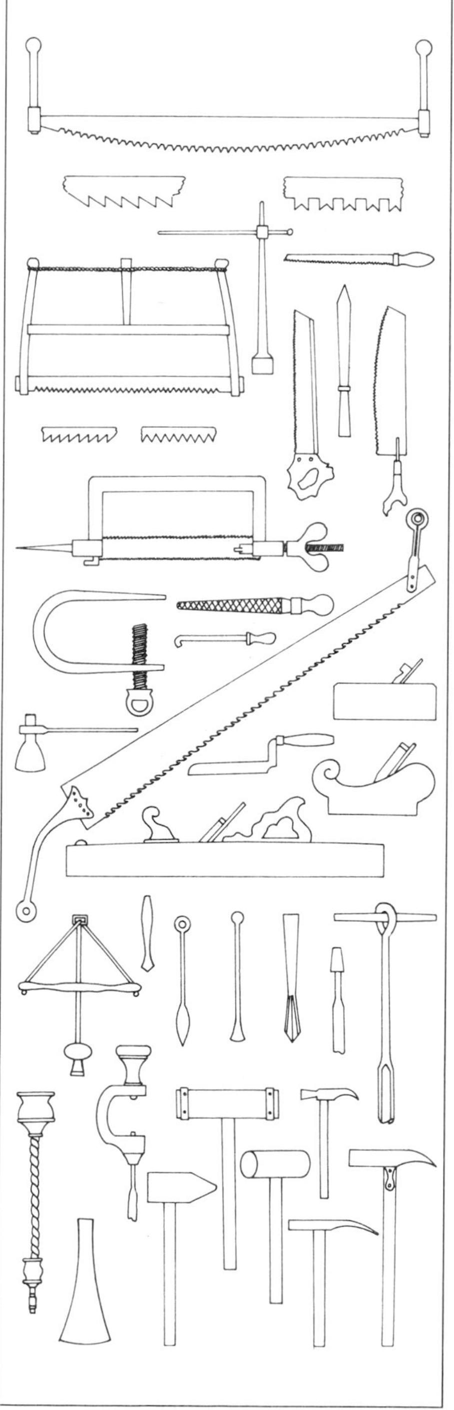

As I have already stated, good tools are a basic requirement for good work!

In the following section I have assembled a list of tools which you will need for period ship modelling. Please do not be frightened off by the length of the list – many of the items may not be needed at all, especially when you are a beginner, and you will only need to acquire them over the years. Sources of supply: where not otherwise stated, all these tools are obtainable in good model shops and well-stocked metal suppliers. Once again, accept nothing less than the best quality – you will not get far using the ordinary home hobbyist's tools. Each group is made up as follows: the first items in each group are those tools which you will certainly need. Then – after the dash – you will find those tools which, although very useful, are not absolutely essential.

Measuring: Rule, compasses, dividers, set-square, protractor, steel straight-edge – slide rule or calculator (all these items available in stationers and drawing office suppliers).

Drawing: Hard pencils, tracing paper, squared tracing paper, carbon paper (typewriter variety, which does not smudge so readily). (Stationers or drawing office suppliers).

Sawing: Fretsaw with table and clamp, fretsaw blades for wood and metal from 0 to 4 – small handsaw with mitre guide for cutting angles.

Cutting wood: An assortment of carving chisels, whetstone for sharpening the blades (the softer the wood, the more rapidly the blades become blunt) – scalpel with replaceable blades (very sharp! Available from good model shops) side cutters as used in electronics (good tool shops).

Cutting metal: Small tin snips – die stock, and dies.

Drilling: Hand-drill with twist drills for wood and metal from 1/32in to 1/4in diameter, countersink bit, tap wrench and taps (only for metal).

Smoothing: Wood rasp, small plane, balsa planes (razor planes) with interchangeable blades are very good, files of all sizes and shapes including needle files (files wear out more quickly on wood than on metal), glasspaper and emery cloth down to the finest grade available.

Hammering: Hammer of about 6 ounces weight, punches of various lengths with small heads.

Soldering: Soldering iron with various tip inserts and accessories, also a suitable stand.

Work holding: Screw clamps of various sizes, a large vice, a small vice (watchmaker's vice) for small components, clothes pegs.

Gripping: Small pliers with a tip diameter of 1/32in to 1/16in with round, flat and flat pointed tips, tweezers with round, flat, pointed, long and short angled shanks (a very good assortment is available at model shops).

Cleaning: The finest grade of steel wool, glass fibre brush from model railway shops – wire brushes, steel and brass.

Painting: Paint brushes of the widest variety of sizes you can obtain, but of the very best quality only, as lesser types leave bristles behind; old toothbrushes, ruling pen.

Aids to vision: Magnifying glass – suspended magnifier, which can be placed in a frame, leaving both hands free for work.

Other items: Screwdrivers, scissors, pins, needles, thin crochet hook (which I have used for years in rigging work), dental tools (these do not need to be new – ask your dentist for his worn-out tools).

Power tools

If the above-mentioned tools generally speaking are available for a few pounds, things get a little expensive when you start to collect machine tools. For this reason you should consider carefully which machines you really need, and then buy them only in first class model shops, or from specialist traders. I strongly advise you to steer clear of Do-It-Yourself shops.

Small electric drill: This is a small machine, hardly as big as your hand, and not very expensive to buy. Not very powerful, but is almost indispensable for drilling holes in difficult positions, where there is no room for a standard hand-drill, e.g. on the inside of the bulwark.

Circular saw: An accurate circular saw with the appropriate stops, mitre guides and saw blades is almost essential for the average model builder. It is needed for cutting strips, making gratings, blocks and other items. The circular saw blades are available commercially in a variety of thicknesses. The best blade to use for cutting stripwood is what is known as a side-cutter, which has cutting edges on its sides also. It is expensive, but does cut much more accurately than a normal circular saw blade.

Lathe: The more advanced modeller should have a lathe and its accessories to hand, with which he can make gun barrels, railing stanchions and many other turned parts. For the ordinary modeller the Unimat is possibly the best and comparatively cheap to buy. With the appropriate accessory fittings the lathe can usually be converted into a circular saw, so that one only needs to buy one basic machine – bear this in mind when buying.

Power fretsaw: Opinions among top modellers vary widely here. The large powered fretsaws are very expensive, and the smaller versions – e.g. the Dremel scroll saw – are not all that accurate for the type of work required, although the price is attractive. For example, it is not possible to cut strips precisely with them. If used as a simple motorised fretsaw, they can, however, be extremely useful. However, a circular saw and perhaps a lathe are more important and more useful for the serious modelmaker.

Special tools: In the course of this book I will mention a few special tools, which are used for particular jobs.

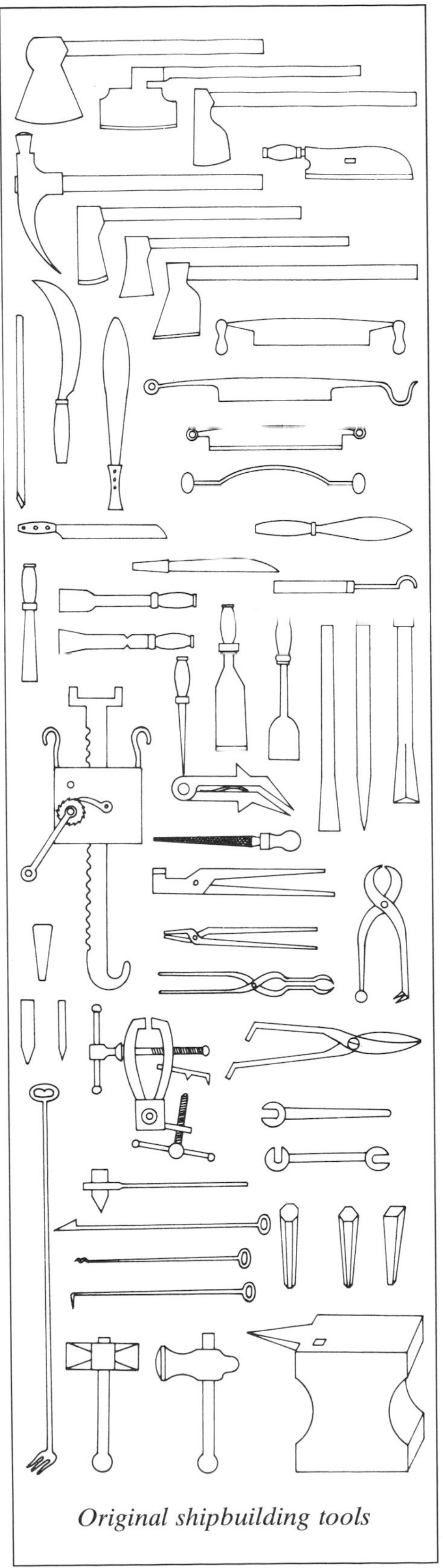

Original shipbuilding tools

Chemicals

International warning symbols:

Inflammable

Poisonous

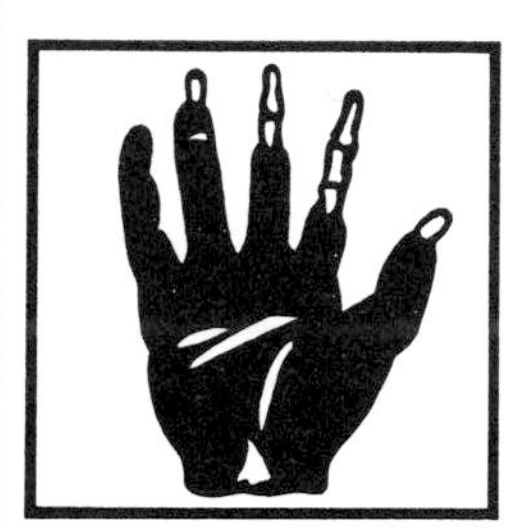

Corrosive

Dangerous fumes

Harmful (to the health)

"Caution!" "Read very carefully!" "Failure to heed this warning may result in danger to life!"

It is virtually inevitable, at least for the advanced model builder, that he will have to work with a number of substances which are anything but harmless.

If you work with such materials, you must accept the highest level of personal responsibility for your actions. Not only your life and health are at stake, but also the life and health of your fellows. Any modeller who is careless in these matters proves himself to be the last word in immaturity and irresponsibility – and he could also end up in prison.

The range of these dangerous substances covers the relatively harmless stains and paints right through to the deadly poisonous cyanide-based adhesives and copper sulphate used for galvanizing (electro-plating); from the hydrogen peroxide used for bleaching, which is only unpleasant if used wrongly, to sulphuric acid, also used for electro-plating, which has a powerful corrosive action.

You don't need to be worried by all this. If you are a sensible, responsible person who thinks clearly, nothing at all will go wrong. Stick rigidly to the following 11 commandments, and *never* make an exception to any of them.

1. All chemicals, from the most harmless to the most dangerous, belong in securely sealed containers.
2. Every container must have a label of adequate size affixed to it, with the exact contents written on it in clearly legible type. E.g.:

   Sulphuric acid H_2SO_4
   Caution!
   Strongly corrosive!
3. Get hold of self-adhesive labels with the internationally accepted warning symbols (illustrated left), and stick the appropriate label on the container (rather three too many than one too few).
4. Store chemicals in a lockable cupboard, which is used *exclusively* for such things. The broom cupboard or part of a food cupboard are absolutely out. Lock this cupboard *always*, and never leave the key in the lock.
5. Children, animals or other people who know nothing of the perilous nature of these substances, must have *no opportunity* to come into contact with them.
6. Follow the measures prescribed for care and protection (rubber gloves, protective goggles, etc).
7. When you are working with these materials, make sure that neither children nor animals can come into your vicinity.
8. If you have to work with these substances, do so only when you have plenty of time and peace. Concentrate on what you are doing.
9. If possible, a person in whom you have confidence should be close to you while you carry out this work – just in case an accident should happen.
10. If, in spite of all your precautions, an accident should occur, immediately go to the doctor, to the nearest hospital, or call the emergency services. Every second counts!
11. Waste chemicals do not belong in the W.C. or in the rubbish bin. Ask the dealer from whom you obtained these substances what is the best way of getting rid of residues and waste. (Environmental protection!)

If you always heed these commandments, and *never ignore any of them*, these chemicals are not dangerous. If you *do not heed* these commandments, you run the risk of causing permanent injury to yourself or your family.

French 70-gun ship Le Lion *of 1780*

The work area

For the construction of period ship models you do not need a large workshop or an expensive workbench. A strong table with a wooden o chipboard surface is quite adequate. Melamine (e.g. Formica) is not recommended, as the surface is too slippery. Nevertheless there are a few requirements which your work area should meet.

1. Adequate space. You must be able to move. The model which yo are building must also have sufficient space, as also your tools and materials. You must be able to set up your machines and still have enough free space left to work comfortably. The table should therefor be at least 4ft 6in× 3ft in area.

2. Space for your tools. Whether you hang some of your tools on the wall or store them in drawers is largely a matter of your own preferences, and the space you have available. A box in which all you tools rattle about, and in which you have to rummage for half an hour t find the file or pliers you need, is not exactly ideal.

3. Order. Many people are of the opinion that constantly clearing up takes too much time. In fact, constantly searching for things takes muc longer. Of course, from time to time you will have to let everything li where it is temporarily, as long as it does not disturb other people. Fo this reason alone the kitchen table is only moderately suitable as a miniature shipyard.

4. Good lighting. Whether windows, fluorescent tubes, individual lamps, all this depends on the possibilities offered by your work area. I any case it is important that you have enough light – rather too much than too little. The main light should always be to the left of you, if yo are right-handed, and vice-versa, so that your hand does not throw a shadow on the work.

5. Peace and quiet. No matter how anti-authoritarian you may have been in bringing up your children, and regardless of the fact that Solomon the tomcat is accustomed to clamber over whatever takes hi fancy, and that Joey the budgie is free to flit round the house at will, your work area is strictly out of bounds to all of them. Insist on this – o give up model shipbuilding.

Working wood & metal

This book does not cover the basic methods of working wood and metal. The basic concepts of sawing, filing, sanding, rubbing down and painting really have to be mastered by anyone who wants to devote himself to this hobby. You do not need to be an absolute expert – practice makes perfect in the end – but you should have a pretty goo idea of these techniques.

I would also like to pass over more advanced techniques such as milling, turning brass and wood, etc. After all, you need the appropriate machinery, and the dealer from whom you buy your equipment should be only too pleased to show you the techniques and possibilities of the machines. In any case, comprehensive operating instructions are usually supplied. What you do not know by them you can find out by experiment. Theory is a very fine thing, and can be very useful now and then, but it is no substitute for practice.

I will try to explain a few special techniques in the following pages, which are particularly useful for period ship modelling.

Admiralty model (with fully planked hull) of the British 60 gun ship Achilles *of 1757. One of the most elegant ships of the mid-18th century, with finely balanced ornamental work*

Carving

Metal ornamental components, as offered for sale in good model shops

There are very many model builders who are scared stiff of carving. Of course, some patience and practice are needed – experts don't fall ready made from Heaven – but carving is by no means as difficult as many people think.
The tools you need are a set of small carving chisels with straight, curved, angled, V and U shaped blades, which must always be very sharp. Bear in mind that the blades are blunted more rapidly through working on soft wood than on hard. You will also need small files and the finest grade of emery or carborundum paper. A set of the smallest burrs that you can find (available in good model shops), which are driven by a flexible drive shaft connected to one of your machines, is also very useful.

Grooving: This is the simplest way of carving. Here you do little more than emphasise the line of the carving by cutting a V or U shaped groove along the lines. You can also round off the shape slightly with a file and emery paper. Decorative strips are often worked in this way, and for the beginner this type of carving is quite enough to start with.

Relief: This is a semi three-dimensional form of carving, as seen on sterns, head timbers or on the hull sides. These carvings are mostly almost flat. You begin by carving as in the grooving method described above, but the differences in height and the roundness of the carving are exaggerated. The head timbers of the *Le Capricieux* shown on the right illustrate such relief carving.

Three-dimensional sculpture: The most difficult method, but seldom required on model ships, except for the figureheads and perhaps a few figures at the stern. The principle of this type of carving is no different from that of relief carving, but you have to work entirely in three dimensions, and the figures are completely rounded. The greatest danger is that some parts will break off (arms, for example). The damage can, of course, be repaired with instant glue (cyano-acrylate), or you can avoid the problem by dividing the figure.

Division: One of the tricks of carving is not to try and carve too large a piece or a surface in one go. If, for example, you make only the body and head at first, then carve the arms separately and stick them on, you will often find the job easier. The wings of the mythical creature at the bow of the *Le Capricieux* have been clearly added on afterwards, and even the relief carvings on the head timbers are made individually and glued together. In this way the most complex stern can be assembled, consisting of several dozen individual components – and if you make a mess of one little part, then it does not matter.

Evasion: If, despite trying all these methods, you find carving simply beyond you, have a try with casting resin. For this method, you only need to carve plasticene, and if the final carving is to be painted or gilded, nobody will ever know what material is underneath.

Commercial alternatives: There is a wide variety of ready made "carved" parts available in model shops, most of them in metal. Do avoid complete sterns, however, as are sometimes seen advertised, as most are simply too awful for words. However, individual elements, decorative parts and bands can be a very useful aid – especially if you take them to pieces.

Head of the French 4th rate ship of the line Le Capricieux *of 1695*

Head of the French 1st rate ship of the line Dauphin-Royal, *1752*

Punching

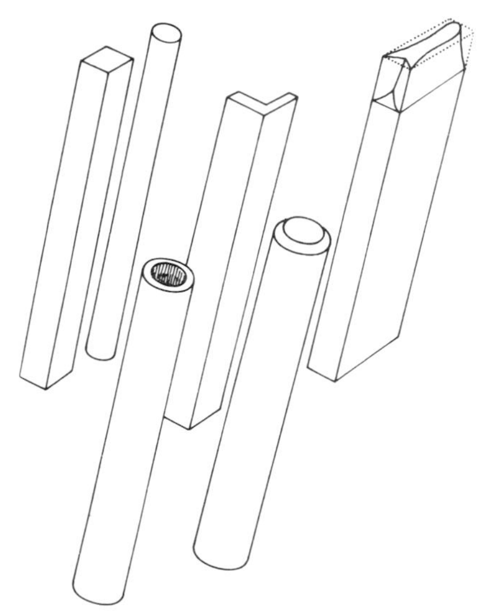

Punches: On the left, four types made from commercial section strip; second from right, embossing punch; right, punch filed to shape by hand (original section shown dotted)

There are a whole lot of tiny metal fittings components which, with the best will in the world, simply defy cutting out with the finest of tin snips; e.g. iron bands on gun mounts, angle brackets for skylights, the smallest hinge bands, base plates for ring bolts and much more besides. Now, if you know the trick, you do not have to omit these miniature details; details which make the final model particularly true to life and authentic in appearance.

These minute parts are struck from the thinnest copper sheet using a punch – a kind of metal stamp.

The most difficult part of this process is the manufacture of the punch itself. It is made from a piece of round or square section brass rod about 2-3in long, which is held in a vice. The top end of the brass rod is then carefully and very accurately filed to form the punch cutting end; it must be exactly the same size and shape as the fitting required, as shown in the drawing on the left. Take your time over this job, as the more accurately the punch is made, the cleaner and more accurate your miniature fitting will turn out. For the simpler shapes – round or rectangular plates, brackets, rings, etc, you can start with lengths of brass section, which are available in the railway department of model shops, as already mentioned. Once you have finished the punch, the rest is a piece of cake.

Take a sheet of hard rubber, at least ⅜in thick, to form a base. Lay on this a sheet of copper foil, ·004in thick at most. The punch head is now set on the copper foil, and the rear end struck with a hammer, very lightly and carefully. This will stamp a piece of metal from the foil which is exactly the shape of the punch head. Lead sheet is an excellent substitute for rubber, incidentally.

It is important that your punch head always remains sharp edged, and you will need to re-sharpen it from time to time. To do this, it is sufficient to pass a very fine file a few times over the outside surface of the punch head. You have to release the stamped-out metal part from the hard rubber sheet now, and this is done using a pair of tweezers and great care, otherwise you will damage it.

Once you have gained a little experience with this technique you will find that it is possible to impress recessed details, such as fake nail heads and similar effects, into the copper at the same time.

Etching

This method is not required on ships before 1820. It is not exactly cheap, as you cannot carry out the etching process yourself; instead you have to use the services of a commercial firm. Etching allows the reproduction of the finest lines in metal, as are seen in steps or metal ladder rungs. Whole words or sentences can be etched, and in this case the background is recessed, and the letters left proud, but it is also possible to etch right through the metal, leaving holes; the minutest gratings can be produced by this method, for example.

I do not wish to go into the details of the process here, as it is beyond the scope of this book; you only need to know that it can be done.

If you want to have metal parts etched, apply to an etching business, which makes printing blocks, for instance. Such a firm will give you the information you require. A wide variety of photo etchings in the form of gratings, mesh, etc, is available from most model shops under the trade name of Scale-Link.

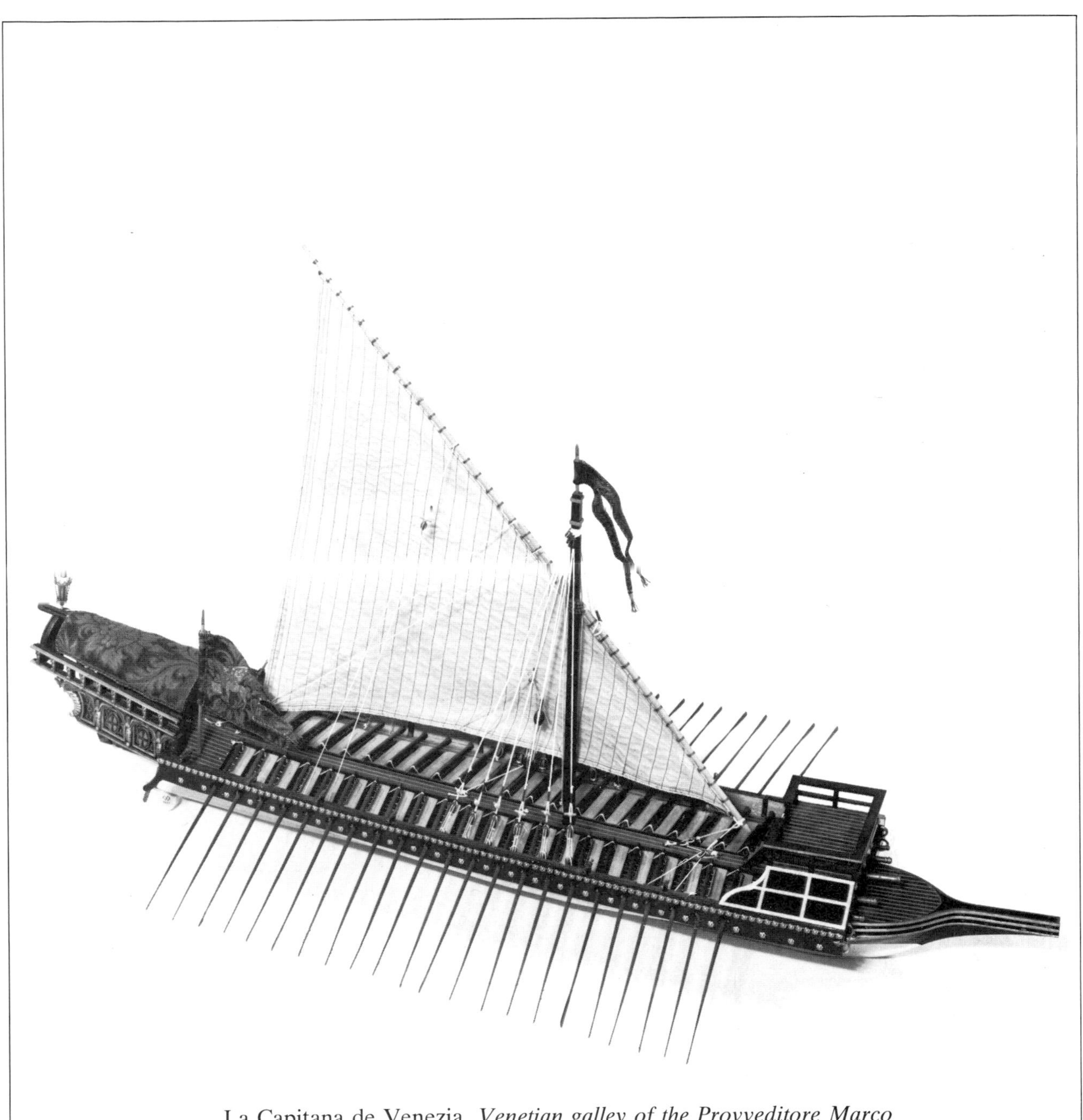

La Capitana de Venezia. *Venetian galley of the Provveditore Marco Quirini at the naval battle of Lepanto on 7th October 1571 (Model by the author for Aeronaut Modellbau)*

Joining materials

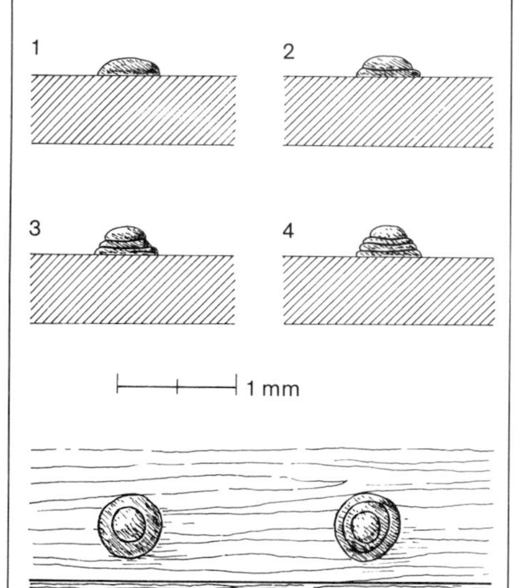

Imitation of iron nails or rivets in model building:
Using black, white and a little red distemper, mix a dark shade of grey. With a no. 0 paint-brush apply a not too runny droplet (1). When dry, add two to three more droplets (2, 3) until the desired height of the nail or rivet head is achieved. Finally add an even smaller droplet in a slightly lighter colour (4). When completely dry, carefully rub the finger-tip over this to create the 'metallic lustre'.

Glueing
The most important method of joining materials in period ship modelling is glueing. A vast range of special adhesives has been developed, and hardly any joining problems now arise which cannot be solved by glueing. The following is a list of the most important types of glue, and their applications in period ship modelling:
General-purpose glue: for rapid, transparent and flexible glue joints, e.g. for securing the ends of ropes and lashings. Has many uses, but cannot entirely replace specialist glues. Usually termed "general purpose" or "universal" glue, from all major manufacturers.
White glue: PVA resin wood glue for rigid, high-strength joints. Ideal for jobs where adjustment is required, as the glue is slow-drying, e.g. glueing and aligning frames on the keel. Most manufacturers. A similar glue preferred by some is aliphatic resin, which dries slightly yellow instead of clear but is easier to sand.
Cellulose glue: for hard, non-flexible, transparent joints, where glueing surfaces are small, and for spot-joints. Somewhat overrated for modelling purposes. Most balsa cements are in this category
Two-part epoxy resin glues: for strong, transparent joints capable of absorbing high loads, between wood and metal, e.g. frames, planking, channels, pin rails and bitts etc. Can also be used instead of solder for large-area metal joints. Two-part glues are available in a variety of versions, according to setting times, from 5 minutes to 24 hours. Capable of taking loadings of up to 2 tons per sq. inch when cured. From many manufacturers.
Contact cements: Instant joining of large area parts, which are difficult to hold in place while the glue dries, e.g. coppering hulls. Many manufacturers.
Plastic adhesives: for fast, transparent glue joints of plastic components (methyl-ethyl-ketone, polystyrene cement).
Cyano-acrylate glues: for small area joints involving metal and hardwood components. Sets in seconds, high strength. *Highly poisonous, dangerous to eyes. Goggles should be worn.*
Veneer glue: for hard woods, especially for light-coloured woods which must not be stained by adhesive residues, e.g. exterior and deck planking. (Balsa cement is used for fixing veneers in marquetry, so should provide a suitable alternative).

Pins
We have to differentiate between two basic uses here:
Invisible pinning to increase the strength of material joints in areas where they will not be visible after completion, e.g. fixing the frames on the keel. These pinned joints are not really needed nowadays, as there are special adhesives for every job, the use of which is preferable in every way. However, very thin steel pins are still used for the channels and the pin rails.
The other basic use is for visible pins, to simulate nails in the original, e.g. for planks and gunport hinges. For this the smallest brass or copper pins are used, the heads of which are blackened. These are available only in very good model shops. Take care over scale! The heads of these nails were originally no more than 3-5cm in diameter.
Here is one basic rule to remember: until some time after the introduction of coppered hulls in 1761 iron nails and bolts were used under water, the combined effect of the seawater and the tannin in the oak causing the iron to rust at an extraordinary rate. This phenomenon, known as nail sickness, was so accelerated by the electrolytic action between the iron and the copper plating that very soon all underwater metal fittings were being manufactured from bronze, brass or copper, and even above the waterline brass was preferred to iron until the 20th century, as long as the expense remained tolerable.

Screwing
This method of joining has no place in ship modelling. Use only in assembling the ship's display stand.

Soldering
Joints between metal areas of reasonable size are today often carried out using two-part adhesives. Very fine joints involving minute parts, e.g. soldering the cross-piece in stud chain used for anchor chains, are not done using ordinary soldering, but with solder paste (Fryolux paste, available in hardware stores). This solder paste is applied as a thin film, after which the parts are fitted together, and the soldering iron simply brought very close to the joint. Direct contact is not required. The joint is made instantly, and the solder paste runs so thinly into the joint that there is virtually no need to clean up afterwards.

Dowels
As long as ships had wooden frames and beams, planks were very often fixed in place with wooden dowels known as treenails instead of nails. In the Mediterranean and in wooden ships generally this is still common practice.
Treenails for modelling are usually made in bamboo. The first job is to cut the bamboo into pieces, and saw out the knots. The pieces are then split lengthwise into narrow strips of about $\frac{1}{8}$in diameter, using a strong knife. The hard outer skin is then cut off. Many modellers soften the bamboo in water at this stage. The strips are then pulled through a draw-plate (see drawing), which is held in a vice. Start with the largest hole through which the strip can be passed, and then gradually reduce it by pulling through smaller and smaller holes until the desired diameter is obtained. Originally treenails were $1\frac{1}{2}$-$2\frac{1}{2}$in. in dia. Down to $\frac{1}{32}$in diameter this drawing method works quite well, but from then on the work does become rather troublesome; however, a correctly treenailed hull looks so good that you can persuade yourself that the work is well worthwhile.
Treenails can be coloured very effectively by soaking for a long period in a suitable stain (up to a few weeks, if necessary). The best effect is obtained if light-coloured planks are fitted with darker dowels, and dark planks with lighter-coloured dowels.
Fitting the treenails is carried out as follows: Cut a piece of bamboo about $\frac{1}{4}$in long, and sharpen one end slightly. Now drill the hole for the dowel, using a drill of the correct diameter (a small electric drill is very useful here). Apply a tiny drop of glue to the point of the dowel (balsa cement is ideal for this), and plug the treenail into the hole, leaving about $\frac{1}{32}$in projecting. When the glue is dry, this projection is sanded off with great care.

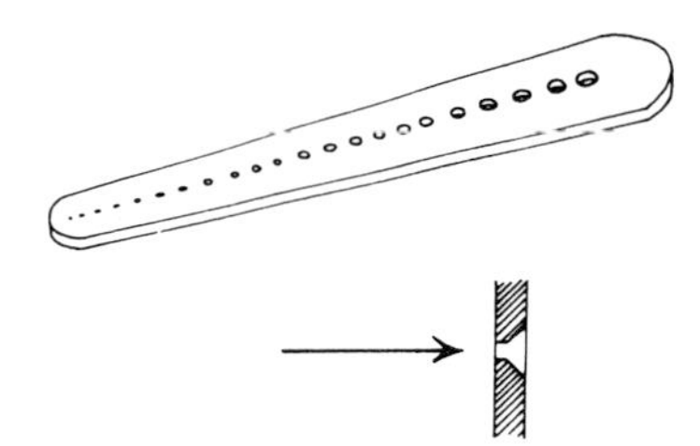

Drawplate (cross-section shown below). The bamboo is drawn in the direction of the arrow

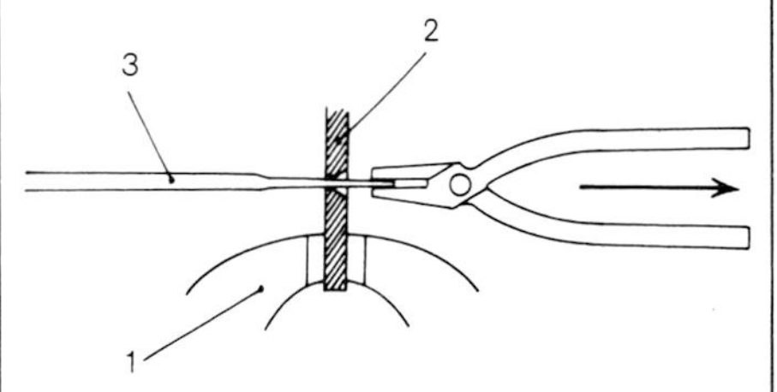

Drawing dowels: 1. Vice; 2. Drawplate; 3. Bamboo

Rivets
Real rivets are not needed in ship modelling. For an excellent method of imitating rivet heads on copper sheathing, funnels, boilers, etc, please refer to the sections on Coppering of hulls and Exposed machinery and engines.

Casting in synthetic resin and tin alloys

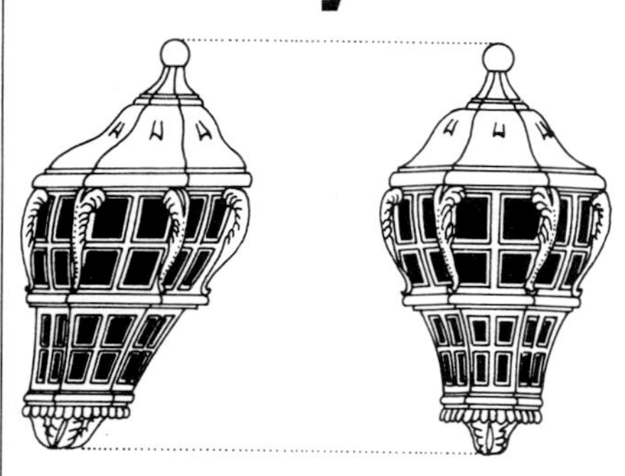

Plan of a poop lantern

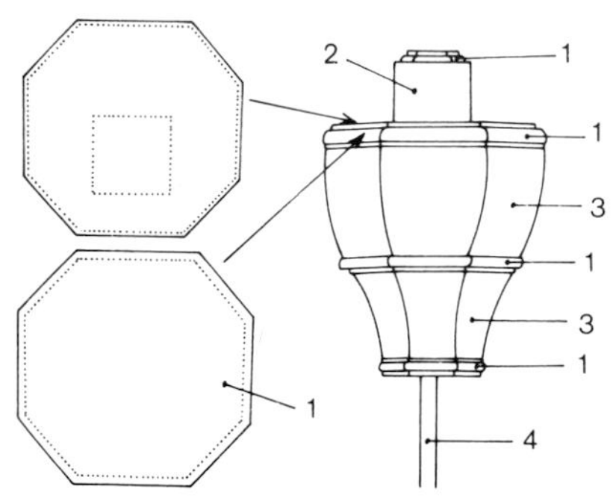

Pattern made of wood:
1. Rings; 2. Top support;
3. Cylinder; 4. Temporary stand

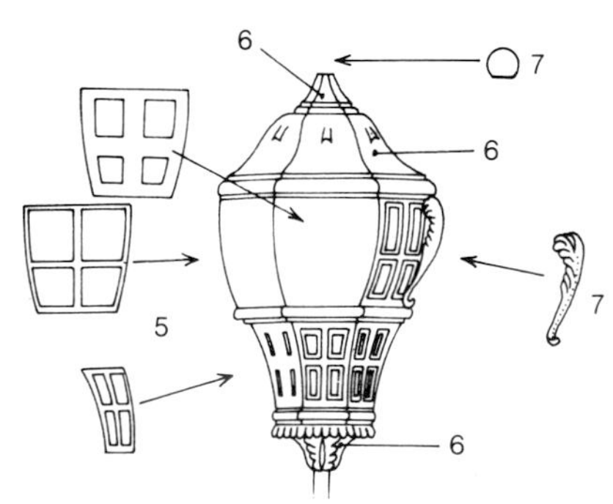

5. Window frame from very thin card, glued in place; 6. Roof and base from plasticene;
7. Decorative parts from plasticene (perhaps cast separately)

Casting resin and tin alloys
The introduction of synthetic resins has opened up manifold possibilities for ship modelling; indeed we have hardly scratched the surface yet. They are certainly useful for the production of curved glasses in poop lanterns and even in the production of carvings.
The materials required are unsaturated polyester or epoxy resin in a low viscosity, "pouring " grade, and silicone rubber for the mould. These are available from plastics suppliers.

The plug: for each cast component you will need an original – the plug – which can be of metal, wood, plastic, plaster, plasticene or even chalk. Plasticene offers great advantages, especially for all those modellers who have difficulty with carving. Plasticene (available in any toy shop) can be moulded into any shape without difficulty, it can be cut, scratched, kneaded, it sticks to itself without any glue, etc. Dental tools are ideal for this type of work.
Sometimes it is best to make up a "combination" original, e.g. a wood core, on which the fine details are applied in plasticene.

Casting mould: The ideal casting mould for modelling purposes is made of silicone rubber: it requires no separate release agent, i.e. the cast components do not stick to the mould, and it is flexible, which means that projecting parts of the casting can be eased from the mould without having to destroy the mould in the process.
Silicone rubber is a two-part material, grey, beige or whitish in colour, and fairly high in viscosity. The working time (the time in which the material remains fluid and hence pourable) and the setting time can be controlled by the proportion of hardener added.
2% hardener gives a working time of 25 minutes and a setting time of 2 hours; 5% hardener gives a working time of 8 minutes and a setting time of 15 minutes.
If the mould is to be made in two parts, the tendency of the two halves to stick to each other can be eliminated by coating the contact surfaces thinly with soapy water, or a thin film of oil, when the first part is fully hardened. To ensure that the parts of the mould fit together accurately, short metal register pins are incorporated into the mould components (see drawing). The mould should be at least ⅜in thick on all sides, to ensure adequate stability.
After the mould material has set, it should be left for 4 to 6 days at room temperature, after which it should be washed out twice with paraffin (kerosene) which improves the fidelity of repeat castings to a considerable extent.

Unsaturated polyester resin: Caution! Resin and hardener flammable. Hardener corrosive. Rubber gloves should be worn, and also goggles when working with the hardener. Open windows to clear the fumes. Polyester resin shrinks somewhat as it hardens, and becomes very brittle. It costs around £1 per kilo. It is used at room temperature, but it has proved a good idea to warm up the silicone rubber mould to around 60-80°C before casting. The working time and hardening time are strongly dependent on the temperature. The working time is around 30 to 45 minutes, and the casting can be removed from the mould in 20 to 30 hours. Although the material appears to be hard on removal from the mould, the hardening process continues, and it is best to leave the finished casting for a few days before continuing work on it.

Epoxy resin: Caution! Hardener poisonous! Wear rubber gloves and open the windows: dangerous fumes.
Epoxy resin hardly shrinks at all on hardening. It costs around £4 per

kilo, and is thus much more expensive than polyester resin, but this is of no account as the amounts used in modelling are so small. The resin is used at room temperature, and the mould does not need to be warmed before casting.
It is important to adhere to the instructions regarding the proportions of resin and hardener, as variations of as little as ±5% have a noticeable effect on the resin. The working time is about 40 to 50 minutes. Epoxy resin is more viscous than polyester resin, and is therefore less easy to cast. The finished casting can be removed after about 30 to 40 hours.

Mixing: The stated mixing proportions of resin and hardener should be adhered to as accurately as possible. Mix for the time stated, stir the mixture very thoroughly, but avoid stirring in air bubbles. Only mix up an amount which you can work within the resin's "pot life" without having to hurry. It is better to mix too little than too much.

Casting: Only small components should be cast in one piece. Larger parts should always be built up slowly in several layers. This has the advantage that any air bubbles in the resin can rise to the surface by the shortest route. Both types of resin amalgamate seamlessly and invisibly, so the individual layers of the casting will not be detectable later. The only thing to watch is that no dust or dirt can get on to the surface during the hardening period. Before you add a new layer, the previous one should be fully cured.
When working with polyester resin, bear in mind that the silicone rubber mould will swell slightly as it absorbs styrene from the resin. This is not important, as the styrene evaporates again if the mould is left for at least 24 hours between castings. If you cast several items in rapid succession, the swelling of the mould will reduce the accuracy of the castings.

Safety measures: Apart from the safety measures which apply to all chemicals, please note the following points:
No fire, no smoking, no naked flames;
Provide good ventilation of the work room, and keep windows open.

Tin alloys: Silicone rubber moulds can also be used to cast low melting-point metals, which can be useful for gun barrels, etc. The important point here is that the silicone rubber used for the casting mould must be a type which can withstand high temperatures. You will also need to provide a means of cooling after the casting has been poured. Casting temperatures of 300°C are already in the critical area, so lead cannot be used (melting point +327°C), but alloys of tin and lead where tin is the larger proportion are very suitable. Low melting-point alloys can be bought from military modelling suppliers. Modellers who do a lot of casting add a little antimony and bismuth to their alloys of tin and lead. The casting process is exactly the same as with synthetic resin, but the component is cast in one piece, instead of in layers. When making the mould, try and build in vent holes.
After casting, the tin component will need to be freed of all excess material, any irregularities smoothed off, and the finished item filed smooth.

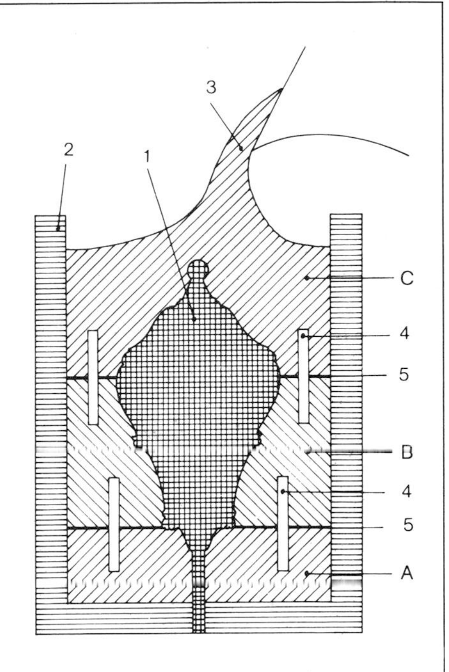

Silicone rubber mould:
1. Pattern; 2. Plaster bed;
3. Silicone rubber; 4. Register pins; 5. Division planes (divide at the broadest points); A. First layer of casting; B. Second layer of casting; C. Third layer of casting

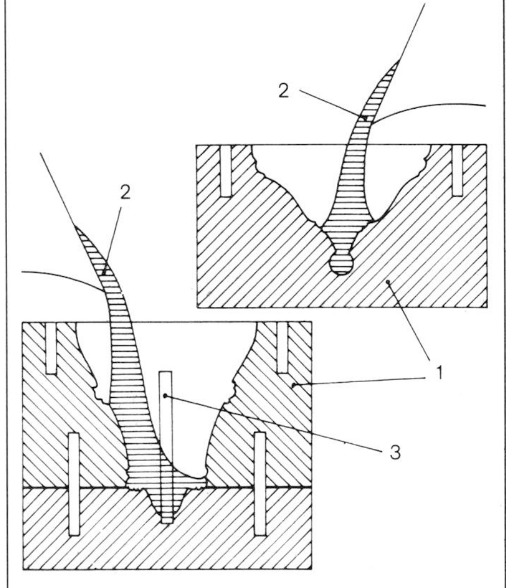

Casting in synthetic resin (cast in two parts):
1. Silicone rubber mould;
2. Synthetic resin; 3. Brass tube or pins cast in as wick holders

Electro-plating

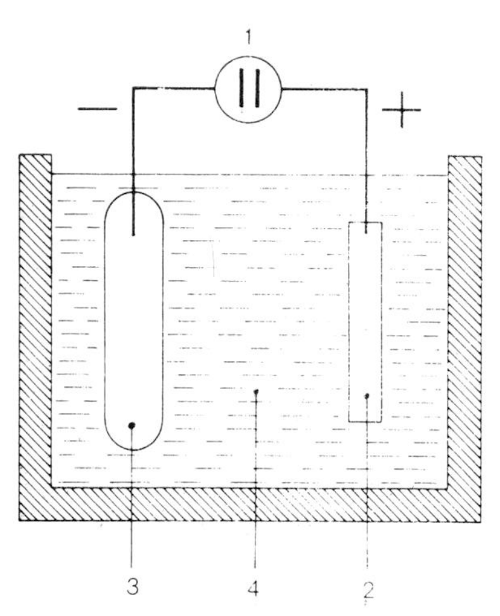

Electro-plating:
1. Power source: D.C. supply, 0·5 – 1·5 Volts, 1 – 2 Amps/dm²
2. Pure electrolytic copper sheet, positive pole (Anode)
3. Object, negative pole (Cathode)
4. Distilled water with copper sulphate and sulphuric acid. Temperature 25 – 40°C

Electro-plating

Electro-plating is a matter for advanced modellers and experts, not so much because of the complex method of working, but because of the equipment required:

Basin: Ideally of stone, with the following approximate dimensions: Length 8-12in, width 6-8in, depth 4-6in. Laboratory equipment suppliers should be able to supply these.

Direct current supply: i.e. a suitable transformer which transforms the A.C. mains supply to a D.C. supply. *Never* use the mains supply direct.

Adjuster (potentiometer): This enables the exact current level to be set, when used with the transformer.

Two things can be done by the electro-plating method:

1. Metal components made of copper or brass can be given an exceedingly thin layer of silver or gold (this is called electro-plating).
2. Complicated metal components, such as ventilator heads, compass binnacles and decorative work can be reproduced by the electro-plating itself, the deposited metal layer forming a self-supporting shell.

Electro-plating bath: Distilled water (*not* tap water), copper sulphate or other metal solvent, according to whether you want to add a coating of copper, silver or gold etc, and concentrated sulphuric acid (H_2SO_4). For making shells, the standard material used is copper. The mixture is 81% water, 16·5% copper sulphate, 1·5% sulphuric acid. The acid must be added (slowly) to the water, *not the water to the acid.*

Caution! Most chemicals are dangerous. Copper sulphate is poisonous, sulphuric acid is *extremely* corrosive.

Always wear rubber gloves when electro-plating. If using sulphuric acid, be sure to wear goggles.

Negative, or female mould: In order to produce an electro-plating shell, you again have to make an original out of plasticene or other material, and cast a negative mould in silicone rubber as already described under CASTING RESIN.

Electro-plating: To do this, connect the cathode (negative terminal) to the object, and suspend it in the bath. If using a silicone rubber mould, spray the inside first with "conductive silver". This material is available from dentists' suppliers. Make sure that the wire really makes contact with the conductive silver. The anode (positive terminal) always consists of pure electrolytic copper sheet. Voltage: 0·5-1·5V, 1-2 amp/dm².

Duration: This depends on the thickness of the metal layer required. For electro-plating shells, you can leave the object in the bath overnight at least.

Finally, switch the current off, remove the object from the bath, rinse it very thoroughly with clear, running water, and then remove the formed metal part from the silicone rubber mould.

N.B. With electro-plating, the first deposit is the cleanest and sharpest. The thicker the deposit, the less sharp and well-defined it becomes. When plating precious metals onto metal, the layer added should therefore be as thin as possible. A few hundredths of a millimetre are quite sufficient.

For three-dimensional shells you need a certain minimum material thickness to give the item some strength. Hence you should always work with negative (female) moulds, so that the first, most accurate deposit forms the external side, i.e. the visible surface.

Components made by this method should have a minimum material thickness of ·012-·020in. The chemicals required are obtainable from chemists and chemical suppliers.

Stern of the Russian two-decker The Holy Trinity *of 1760*

Stern of the Dutch two-decker Princess Carolina, *ex* Rotterdam *1770*

Colouring

There are as many opinions on the colouring of model ships as there are model makers, and ship modellers could argue about the matter all night long without ever agreeing. Which of the various lines of thought you adopt is largely dependent on your personal tastes. There are two fundamental trends: the one declines to use any colour at all, and the model shows nothing but bare wood and metal (bare wood models); the advantage of this approach is that the work of the modeller is displayed at its clearest. The other faction aims to show the ship as it really looked, with all colours and paint effects included. Between these two extreme approaches there are, of course, a whole range of compromises, e.g. the ship coloured above the waterline, and the underwater hull left as bare wood, etc.

Paints

Paints can be applied as an opaque layer or as a transparent glaze. The beginner should use opaque colours, as he will be working with less fine quality wood, and the paint can be used to cover up small mistakes. The advanced and expert worker should use transparent colours – especially on larger surfaces – as the wood's grain structure shows to good effect through them; this type of finish is also a closer representation of the original. Tempera paints are intended to be used as an opaque finish, but they can also be applied thinned down with a large quantity of water to produce the transparent effect. Artists' water colours can be used as transparent colours, and there are also special acrylic paints available. All of them are available from good artists' suppliers.

Humbrol enamels are the best paints for plastic components. Other types of paint do not adhere well to plastic, and they begin to peel off after a short while. These paints are available in model shops.

If the timbers of your ship have been artificially aged, the colours of the rest of the vessel should not be too fresh and vibrant. They can be toned down by mixing in tiny amounts of brown or black.

Colours used for large areas, or colours which are needed repeatedly for different parts of one model, should be applied directly from the tube or tin, i.e. unmixed, as it is almost impossible to mix up the same colour twice. The wide range of colours from the companies of Rowney, Winsor & Newton & Pelikan in water colours and tempera colours makes it quite easy to find the correct shade.

All paints should be applied with a fine paintbrush. Oil and enamel paints are basically unsuitable for period ship models.

Dutch and Northwest German rudder heads of the 18th/19th centuries

Staining

The colour of natural wood surfaces can be modified to the desired shade by application of stain. There are water stains – these include the Colron stains, which bring out the grain pattern of wood particularly well, wax stains, which have the great disadvantage that nothing can be glued to the stained surface, and spirit stains. Ask for details at a good specialist shop, and study the sample cards.

All stained surfaces should be brushed down thoroughly with an old toothbrush after the stain has dried, as this accentuates the wood structure. The stains are applied with a paintbrush or with a small sponge. It is a good idea to wear a pair of rubber gloves, otherwise you will have dark stains on your fingers for days on end.

Bleaching

In some cases, such as the decks, the light-coloured woods such as maple or boxwood are still too dark. The answer here is to bleach the wood, using hydrogen peroxide (H_2O_2). This material is best applied with a wad of cotton. Caution! Be sure to wear rubber gloves. Hydrogen peroxide is available from chemists.

Gilding

Carvings and ornaments can be gilded by two means: gold paint or gold leaf. The beginner should stick to gold paint, as the application of gold leaf requires a very expert touch (and is also very expensive).

The commercially available watercolour and Plaka gold bronze paints look poor, and are not suitable for our purpose. The Humbrol range includes an excellent gold. Very thin lines can be drawn with it, if it is applied by means of a ruling pen. Done this way, the lines will look much cleaner and more precise than if applied with a paintbrush.

Gold leaf is an exceedingly thin sheet of real gold. Carvings and embellishments which are to be gilded must first be treated with very thin woodworking glue. Paint or dip the component, and rub down when dry to obtain a sufficiently firm surface; this is repeated two or three times. When the final coat is thoroughly dry, apply a thin coat of a bonding agent (usually gold size) which has to be left to dry for several hours.

Ask at your dealer, from whom you obtained the gold leaf, exactly how long a drying time is required etc. There are simply too many different makes to be able to lay down a general rule.

When the bonding agent has dried to the required degree, the gold leaf is stuck in place in small pieces, using a paintbrush – never touch it with your hand! Tap it into place using a soft, short-haired brush. When the bonding agent is quite dry, brush down the whole object again with a soft paintbrush, to remove any loose ends.

It is essential to practise applying gold leaf on a test piece before working on your model. There is also what is known as "false" gold leaf, which is cheaper, and some of which is extremely good. Gold leaf and all the accessories are obtainable from good paint shops.

Varnish

All the exterior surfaces of a model ship should be protected with a varnish. This applies in particular to all the metal components and gilded surfaces (for gold leaf ask at your specialist supplier for a suitable protective lacquer). Use silk (semi-matt) or dead matt varnish – *never* glossy. The basic rule here is: the larger the model, the more matt the varnish.

Cellulose varnishes are suitable – there are many makes, and you should seek advice from a good specialist shop once again. Sealing lacquers, which are intended for sealing floors, have also proved to be highly suitable. The ideal varnish for metal parts – and on no account should metal surfaces be left unprotected – is Ronseal Mattcoat.

Always apply varnish thinly, otherwise you risk glossing over the fine details – quite literally.

Blackening metal

On period ships almost all metal parts were painted or tarred to provide protection against the effects of seawater and the weather. You could, of course, paint the metal black, but in my experience the effect is not good. This is the way to blacken metal:
The first stage is to remove absolutely all traces of adhesive from the surface. This is essential, because otherwise the parts protected by the glue will remain as bright copper or brass. The metal has to be cleaned with a glass fibre brush – larger areas can be cleaned up with the finest grade of steel wool. Take care not to touch the surface with your fingers after cleaning.
There are two methods for the actual blackening process:
1. Fixer bath. Ask a photographer for some *old, exhausted* fixer (the more "exhausted" it is, the more silver it contains, and it is the silver which does the work). Dip the metal in the fixer, and it will turn medium to dark grey. The reaction should occur in 10 to 20 seconds, otherwise there is not enough silver dissolved in the fixer.
2. Silver and sulphuric acid. If the grey tone obtained with the fixer is not dark enough for your purposes, this second method has to be used. Here the metal component is first silver plated (electro-plated to produce a very thin coating, or immersed in a concentrated silver solution). The prepared part is then placed in the sulphuric acid. The metal can now be left to turn the shade of grey required, almost black being possible, depending on the length of immersion. The chemicals needed for this are obtainable at chemists.

Ageing wood

You sometimes see models which are covered with an even, dirty grey-brown layer of "patina" – that is appalling! On the other hand, a model can look most attractive if it shows "natural" signs of wear and use. If, for example, the handrails are rubbed away slightly by the hands of the sailors, while a little dirt has collected along the waterway.
These ageing and patina effects should be applied with great care, and a sensitive hand. Always check your technique on a scrap piece, until you are confident, and then heed this warning: rather too little than too much, or you risk ruining your whole model.
Technically speaking, the ageing effect is very simple to obtain: after dampening the wood, a highly dilute black or dark brown wax stain is painted on, using a toothbrush. When dry, the result is a slightly "dirty" surface.
You now use a glass fibre brush to clean up this surface again. Rub the stain away gently, leaving those areas which have been weathered or worn a lighter shade, while the more inaccessible areas remain dark. On a mast, for example, the smooth surfaces are light in tone, while the corners round the mast bands and the wooldings are dark. On deck the large areas are light-coloured, while only the corners of the waterways and the coamings are left dark and "dirty" – where the sailors could not reach so well when scrubbing the decks. It is important to remember that the transitions from light to dark should be gradual.

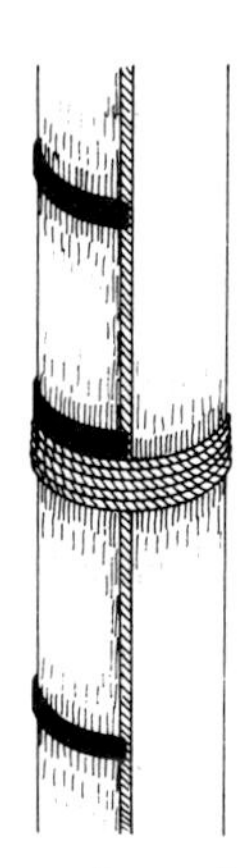

Artificial ageing of wood, using a mast as an example: darker at the mast bands and wooldings, lighter on the smooth surfaces. Take care with the transition areas

Le Sans-Pareil
French 108 gun 1st rate of 1757

The Hull

Hull · Reference points
Units of measurement
Recalculating dimensions
Plans · Frame construction
Jig · Keel · Stem and sternpost
Frames · Stern · Deck beams
Interior construction of fully planked hulls · Wales
Planking · Stern planking
Gun ports · Fenders · Deck
Marking the waterline
Underwater painting
Sheathing with lead
Coppering · Rails · Bulwarks
Stern windows · Galleries
Quarter galleries · Bulkheads
Head · Cathead · Gratings
Rudder

In comparison with the intricate tasks involved in making some of the tiny detail components, the construction of the hull is simple – although not as simple as many model makers would like to believe. As in all period ship modelling, the first commandment is that you work to a high standard of accuracy. A crooked hull, buckled planking and wavy decks cannot be rescued by the finest carving, the neatest fittings, or rigging of the utmost precision.

At the end of the introductory chapter I pointed out the necessity of making vital decisions at an early stage. Now, at the point of starting on the hull, the reasons become clear. You must have decided on the type of model, the fittings to be included, and the extent of the rigging. Basically you can choose between three types of model:

1. Frame models: the fittings on these models are limited to capstans, knightheads, bitts and pumps, while all the movable fittings, such as guns, ships' boats, etc are omitted. Frame models never carry masts and rigging.
2. Admiralty models: These can be fitted out to the same extent as frame models, or as complete models (excluding the ship's boats). They can be built with or without masts and rigging, but never carry sails.
3. Fully planked models – these can be fitted out as hull models in the same way as an Admiralty model. If the model is built with masts and rigging, the ship's fittings must be complete, and it can be rigged with or without sails. Fully planked models are not only the simplest to build, they also offer the widest range of possible variations. A very important decision on the hull is the subsequent treatment of the guns (see under ARMAMENTS). If the guns are to be shown run out, ready to fire, you have to plan and build the lower decks when building the hull – and even build in some of the guns at that stage. The main point, which I want to emphasize once more, is the great difference in difficulty between building a frame model or an Admiralty model on the one hand, and a fully planked hull on the other – as already discussed under TYPES OF MODEL. Frame and Admiralty models are exclusively the province of experts. In the course of this chapter you will be shown some details on the original construction of certain components – under the headings FRAMES, STERN and DECK BEAMS – which must be reproduced accurately in the case of an "open" hull. In the section on INTERIOR CONSTRUCTION OF PLANKED HULLS you will find details of the simplified technique which is adequate for the construction of "closed" hulls, and even the absolute beginner is unlikely to meet any problems.

There is a wide range of aids to construction on offer from the manufacturers of model kits as well as the modelling press: fully prefabricated hulls in balsa or obechi, bread-and-butter designs, moulded polyester resin hulls, and all possible combinations of these methods. I spent a long time considering whether to discuss these techniques, and finally decided against it. I have restricted myself to frame construction, because this method remains the best and simplest method – even for fully-planked hulls. Moreover this technique requires no great technical expertise, and remains the cheapest method. Frame construction has shown its value for period ship models a hundred thousand times over, to such an extent that I see little point in experimenting with new basic techniques.

French 104 gun 1st rate of 1692. Frame model (note the close spacing of the frames on a warship), with wales, planked poop and ribbands of the hull below the waterline

French 2nd rate Le Brillant *of 1690. A particularly finely worked hull model of a 64 gun ship*

Dimensions

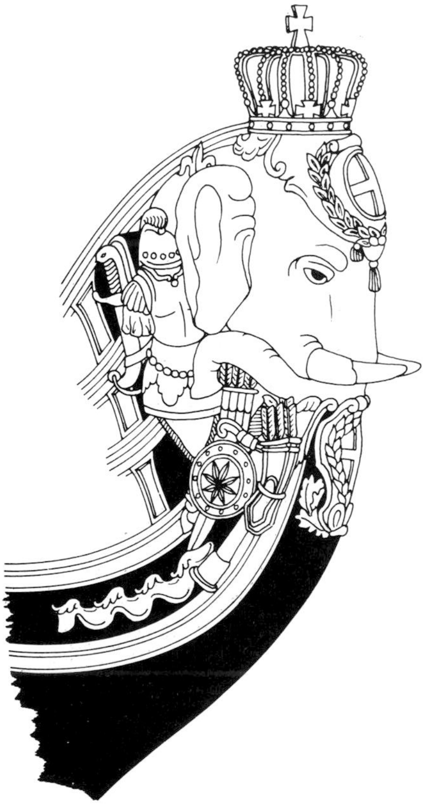

Figurehead of the Danish warship Elephant of 1741

Before we move on to the details of designing and constructing the hull, we must first deal with its basic dimensions, as these are crucial to the scale to which the model is built.
There is a wide range of dimensional information from which you can find the size of a ship:

Extreme length: the length from the aftermost part of the stern to the forward end of the figurehead. This is sometimes called the overall length but the true overall length is measured from the aftermost part of the stern, or driver-boom, if there is one, to the forward end of the jibboom (or flying jibboom where fitted). It is a dimension seldom quoted in full size practice but is useful to the modeller who wants to know if his finished model will fit on the sideboard.

Length between perpendiculars: the basic length of the merchant ship. Measured from the afterside of the sternpost at the height of the wing transom to the forward side of the stem at the same height. After the demise of the wing transom it became the practice to measure this length at the load water line. In vessels with no stern post the centre of the rudder stock is taken as the after datum point.

Length on the gun deck: the basic length of the warship. Measured from the forward side of the rabbet of the stern post to the after side of the rabbet of the stem at the height of the gun deck. The gun deck is the lower deck in a two or three decker. In a frigate, sloop or any other vessel where the gun deck is the upper deck the measurement is taken on the lower deck.

Moulded breadth: the maximum beam of the ship not including the external planking. In other words the breadth of the ship as drawn on the lines plan.

Extreme breadth: the moulded breadth of the ship plus twice the thickness of the bottom planking, *NOT* the wales.

Depth in hold: measured from the upper side of the limber strakes amidships to the upper side of the lower deck beams above.

Height at side: the height of the deck edge amidships above the rabbet of the keel.

Overall height: the height from the base of the keel to the highest point of the rigged ship, normally the mainmast truck. Like "extreme length" it is basically a modeller's term not used in full size practice.

Load waterline: the waterline at which the loaded ship floats. In theory it should coincide with the design waterline; in practice it seldom does. Sailing ships are normally trimmed by the stern (draught aft greater than draught forward) so that the load waterline is not usually parallel to the keel.

Draught: This is measured from the waterline to the lower edge of the keel. When the ship is trimmed by the stern (or the head) the mean draught is the average of the draught aft and the draught forward.

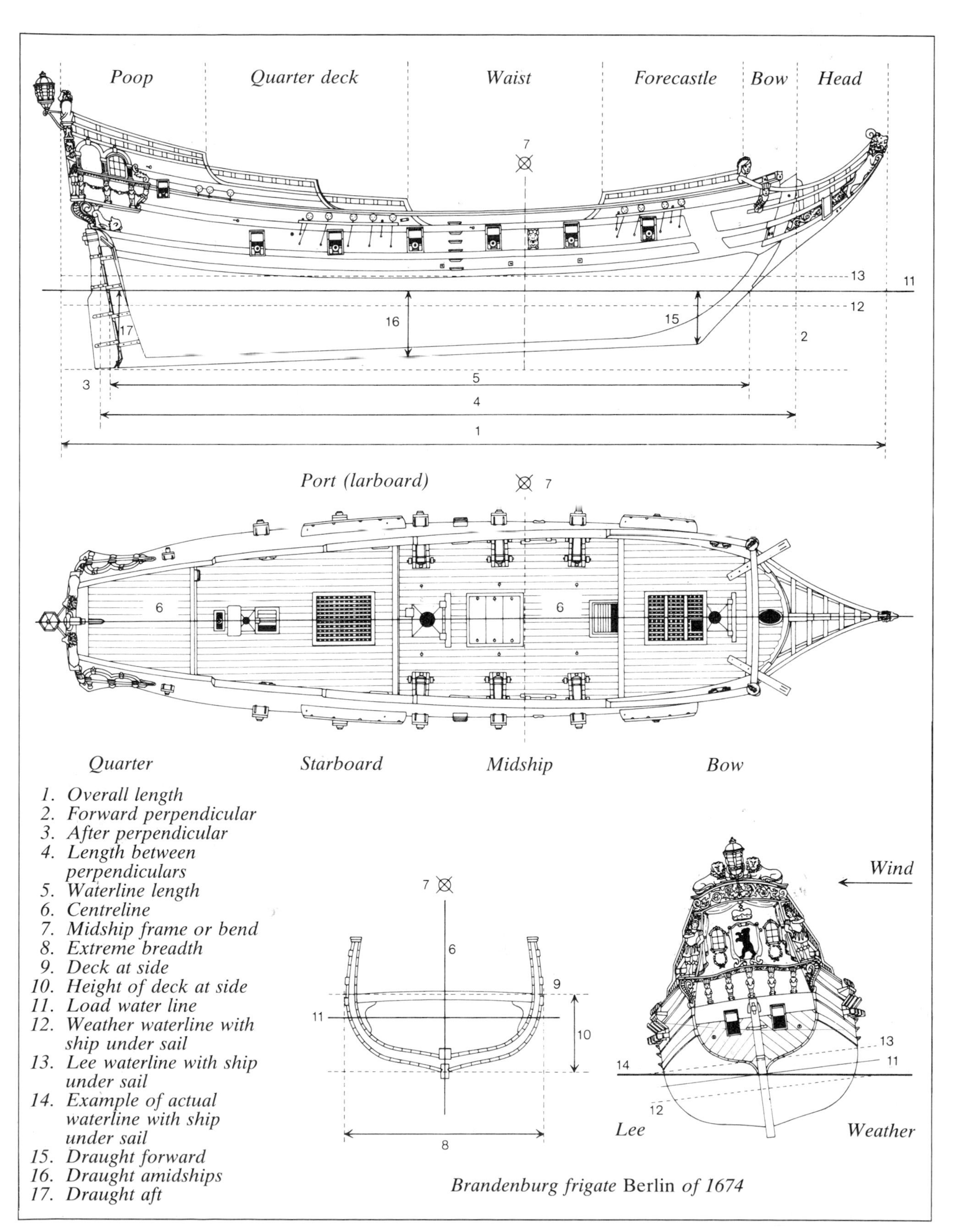

Brandenburg frigate Berlin *of 1674*

Units of measurement and conversion of units

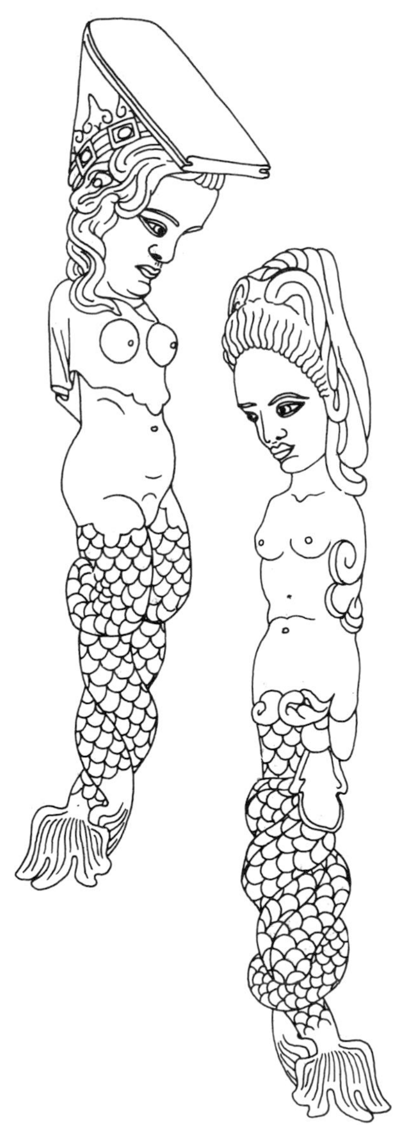

Two caryatids forming cathead supporters on the Swedish royal ship Wasa *of 1628*

Units of measurement and their conversion

If you build period ship models you will sooner or later come up against units of measurement which may appear quite alien to you, and which then have to be converted into other units.

Nautical units

These nautical units are still in use today, but they are of little importance to the model maker. Nevertheless, you should have a passing acquaintance with them:

1° of Latitude	= 60 nautical miles	= 111.111 km.
1 Nautical mile	= 10 cables	= 1.852 km.
1 Cable	= 100 fathoms	= 185.2 m.
1 Fathom	= 6 feet	= 1.852 m.

Old units

In Paris in 1799 the metre was laid down and defined as the basic unit of the metric system of weights and measures. Before this date each country – even each town in some areas – had its own system of weights and measures, and it took the whole of the 19th century before the metre eventually came to predominate in Europe. Even today this development is still not quite complete, as the English speaking countries continue to use Imperial units.

Here is a list of the most important old units of measurement, which crop up again and again in period ship modelling:

Amsterdam foot	= 11 inches	= 283·1 mm
Antwerp foot	= 11 inches	= 286·8 mm
Danish foot	= 12 inches	= 313·9 mm
English foot	= 12 inches	= 308·0 mm
French foot	= 12 inches	= 324·8 mm
Hamburg foot	= 12 inches	= 286·0 mm
Lübeck foot	= 12 inches	= 287·6 mm
Prussian foot	= 11 inches	= 313·8 mm
Rhenish foot	= 12 inches	= 313·9 mm
Russian foot	= 12 inches	= 308·0 mm
Swedish foot	= 12 inches	= 296·0 mm
Venetian foot	= 12 inches	= 348·0 mm

Imperial units

To the Continental modeller calculations involving English units of measurement are unfamiliar and complex. However, as Great Britain and the USA produce excellent specialist literature on the subject of sea travel and shipbuilding, as well as numerous plans, the period ship modeller will almost inevitably have to come to grips with feet and inches at some stage, and the table on the facing page will provide some assistance with his calculations.

The Continental modeller will also meet some confusing statements of scale on Anglo-Saxon plans, complicated by the fact that there are two methods of writing the scale down. Here is a summary in tabular form:

1″ = 1′	or	1′–1″	= 1: 12
¾″ = 1′	or	4′–3″	= 1: 16
½″ = 1′	or	2′–1″	= 1: 24
⅜″ = 1′	or	8′–3″	= 1: 32
¼″ = 1′	or	4′–1″	= 1: 48
6/25″ = 1′	or	25′–6″	= 1: 50
3/16″ = 1′	or	16′–3″	= 1: 64
4/25″ = 1′	or	25′–4″	= 1: 75
⅛″ = 1′	or	8′–1″	= 1: 96
1/16″ = 1′	or	16′–1″	= 1:192

English Feet and Inches – Millimetres

ft.	in.	0″	1″	2″	3″	4″	5″	6″	7″	8″	9″	10″	11″	12″
0	0	0	25	51	76	102	127	152	178	203	229	254	279	305
1	12	305	330	356	381	406	432	457	483	508	533	559	584	610
2	24	610	635	660	686	711	737	762	787	813	838	864	889	914
3	36	914	940	965	991	1 016	1 041	1 067	1 092	1 118	1 143	1 168	1 194	1 219
4	48	1 219	1 245	1 270	1 295	1 321	1 346	1 372	1 397	1 422	1 448	1 473	1 499	1 524
5	60	1 524	1 549	1 575	1 600	1 626	1 651	1 676	1 702	1 727	1 753	1 778	1 803	1 829
6	72	1 829	1 854	1 880	1 905	1 930	1 956	1 981	2 007	2 032	2 057	2 083	2 108	2 134
7	84	2 134	2 159	2 184	2 210	2 235	2 261	2 286	2 311	2 337	2 362	2 388	2 413	2 438
8	96	2 438	2 464	2 489	2 515	2 540	2 565	2 591	2 616	2 642	2 667	2 692	2 718	2 743
9	108	2 743	2 769	2 794	2 819	2 845	2 870	2 896	2 921	2 946	2 972	2 997	3 023	3 048
10	120	3 048	3 073	3 099	3 124	3 150	3 175	3 200	3 226	3 251	3 277	3 302	3 327	3 353
11	132	3 353	3 378	3 404	3 429	3 454	3 480	3 505	3 531	3 556	3 581	3 607	3 632	3 658
12	144	3 658	3 683	3 708	3 734	3 759	3 785	3 810	3 835	3 861	3 886	3 912	3 937	3 962
13	156	3 962	3 988	4 013	4 039	4 064	4 089	4 115	4 140	4 166	4 191	4 216	4 242	4 267
14	168	4 267	4 293	4 318	4 343	4 369	4 394	4 420	4 445	4 470	4 496	4 521	4 547	4 572
15	180	4 572	4 597	4 623	4 648	4 674	4 699	4 724	4 750	4 775	4 801	4 826	4 851	4 877
16	192	4 877	4 902	4 928	4 953	4 978	5 004	5 029	5 055	5 080	5 105	5 131	5 156	5 182
17	204	5 182	5 207	5 232	5 258	5 283	5 309	5 334	5 359	5 385	5 410	5 436	5 461	5 486
18	216	5 486	5 512	5 537	5 563	5 588	5 613	5 639	5 664	5 690	5 715	5 740	5 766	5 791
19	228	5 791	5 817	5 842	5 867	5 893	5 918	5 944	5 969	5 994	6 020	6 045	6 071	6 096
20	240	6 096	6 121	6 147	6 172	6 198	6 223	6 248	6 274	6 299	6 325	6 350	6 375	6 401
21	252	6 401	6 426	6 452	6 477	6 502	6 523	6 553	6 579	6 604	6 629	6 655	6 680	6 706
22	264	6 706	6 731	6 756	6 782	6 807	6 833	6 858	6 883	6 909	6 934	6 960	6 985	7 010
23	276	7 010	7 036	7 061	7 087	7 112	7 137	7 163	7 188	7 214	7 239	7 264	7 290	7 315
24	288	7 315	7 341	7 366	7 391	7 417	7 442	7 467	7 493	7 518	7 545	7 569	7 594	7 620
25	300	7 620	7 645	7 671	7 696	7 722	7 747	7 772	7 798	7 823	7 849	7 874	7 899	7 925
26	312	7 925	7 950	7 975	8 001	8 026	8 052	8 077	8 102	8 128	8 153	8 179	8 204	8 230
27	324	8 230	8 255	8 280	8 306	8 332	8 357	8 382	8 408	8 433	8 458	8 484	8 509	8 534
28	336	8 534	8 559	8 585	8 610	8 636	8 661	8 686	8 712	8 737	8 763	8 788	8 814	8 839
29	348	8 839	8 864	8 890	8 915	8 941	8 966	8 991	9 017	9 042	9 068	9 093	9 118	9 144
30	360	9 144	9 169	9 195	9 220	9 246	9 271	9 296	9 322	9 347	9 373	9 398	9 423	9 449
31	372	9 449	9 474	9 500	9 525	9 551	9 576	9 601	9 627	9 652	9 677	9 703	9 728	9 754
32	384	9 754	9 779	9 804	9 830	9 855	9 881	9 906	9 931	9 957	9 982	10 008	10 033	10 058
33	396	10 058	10 083	10 109	10 134	10 160	10 185	10 210	10 236	10 261	10 287	10 312	10 337	10 363
34	408	10 363	10 388	10 414	10 439	10 465	10 490	10 515	10 541	10 566	10 592	10 617	10 642	10 668
35	420	10 668	10 693	10 719	10 744	10 770	10 795	10 820	10 846	10 871	10 897	10 922	10 947	10 973
36	432	10 973	10 998	11 024	11 049	11 075	11 100	11 125	11 151	11 176	11 202	11 227	11 252	11 278
37	444	11 278	11 303	11 328	11 354	11 379	11 405	11 430	11 455	11 481	11 506	11 532	11 557	11 582
38	456	11 582	11 607	11 633	11 658	11 684	11 709	11 734	11 760	11 785	11 811	11 836	11 861	11 887
39	468	11 887	11 912	11 938	11 963	11 989	12 014	12 039	12 065	12 090	12 116	12 141	12 166	12 192
40	480	12 192	12 217	12 243	12 268	12 294	12 319	12 344	12 370	12 395	12 421	12 446	12 471	12 497
41	492	12 497	12 522	12 548	12 573	12 598	12 624	12 649	12 675	12 700	12 725	12 751	12 776	12 802
42	504	12 802	12 827	12 852	12 878	12 903	12 929	12 954	12 979	13 005	13 030	13 056	13 081	13 106
43	516	13 106	13 132	13 157	13 183	13 208	13 233	13 259	13 384	13 310	13 335	13 360	13 386	13 411
44	528	13 411	13 437	13 462	13 487	13 513	13 538	13 564	13 589	13 614	13 640	13 665	13 691	13 716
45	540	13 716	13 741	13 767	13 792	13 818	13 843	13 868	13 894	13 919	13 945	13 970	13 995	14 021
46	552	14 021	14 046	14 072	14 097	14 122	14 148	14 173	14 199	14 224	14 249	14 275	14 300	14 326
47	564	14 326	14 351	14 376	14 402	14 427	14 453	14 478	14 503	14 529	14 554	14 580	14 603	14 630
48	576	14 630	14 656	14 681	14 707	14 732	14 757	14 783	14 808	14 834	14 859	14 884	14 910	14 935
49	588	14 935	14 961	14 986	15 011	15 037	15 062	15 088	15 113	15 138	15 164	15 189	15 215	15 240
50	600	15 240	15 265	15 291	15 316	15 342	15 367	15 392	15 418	15 443	15 469	15 494	15 519	15 545

Plans

Sketches by Willem van der Velde for the carved decorations of the British three-decker St. Michael *1667*

Ship plans are simply the projection of the three-dimensional ship's hull on to two-dimensional paper.
Every hull can be defined in three dimensions: length, breadth, depth, – sheer plan, half-breadth plan and body plan correspond in each case with the projection of one of these dimensions: sheer plan the length, half-breadth plan the breadth, body plan the depth.
The drawing at bottom left on the facing page shows how these three projection planes are situated in relation to the ship's hull: the sheer plan through the centreline plane (shown by – – – – lines), the waterline or half-breadth plan through the waterline plane (shown by ----- lines), and the body plan through the plane of the midships section (shown by -·-·-· lines). Now, for the projection of an entire ship's hull these three main section planes are not sufficient, so a series of further sectional planes are drawn through the hull, which, however, must always lie parallel to the main section planes, as shown in the drawings on the far right. In this way a series of differently shaped areas is obtained, which would produce an accurate skeleton of the ship's hull, if, for example, they were bent to shape from thin wire and joined together.
In any of the drawings two projection planes run "parallel" to the observer, and are seen as a series of vertical and horizontal lines, while the third dimension lies "square on" to the observer, and hence appears as a curve or curves.
In practical terms, this can be expressed as follows:
Sheer plan: ship viewed from one side. The body plane (-·-·-·) is vertical to the observer, the half-breadth plane (---) is horizontal, while the lines of the centreline plane and the planes running parallel to it, called buttock lines, (– – –) are observed as curves.
Half-breadth plan: Seen from below and above the ship. The body planes (-·-·-·) are again vertical to the observer, the centreline and the buttock lines (---) are horizontal, while the waterlines (– – –) can be observed as curves.
Body plan: Ship viewed from ahead or astern. The buttock lines (– – –) now stand vertical to the observer, and the waterlines (---) horizontal, while the frame outlines (-·-·-·) are presented to the observer as curves, from the smallest (forward and aft) to the widest (the midships frame) in the centre. On ship plans, the body plan is always shown divided down the centreline, with the left-hand half showing the frames from the stern to the midships frame, and the right-hand half the frames from the bow to the midships frame. As a ship's hull is strictly symmetrical (almost without exception) the modeller only needs to fold a frame around its centreline to obtain the complete shape. In many shipbuilding plans, there are also other projections drawn in, but they are of little significance to the ship modeller. It is best not to bother at all about them, as every point on the ship's exterior hull can be precisely defined by using the co-ordinate of the sheer plan, half-breadth and body plan.

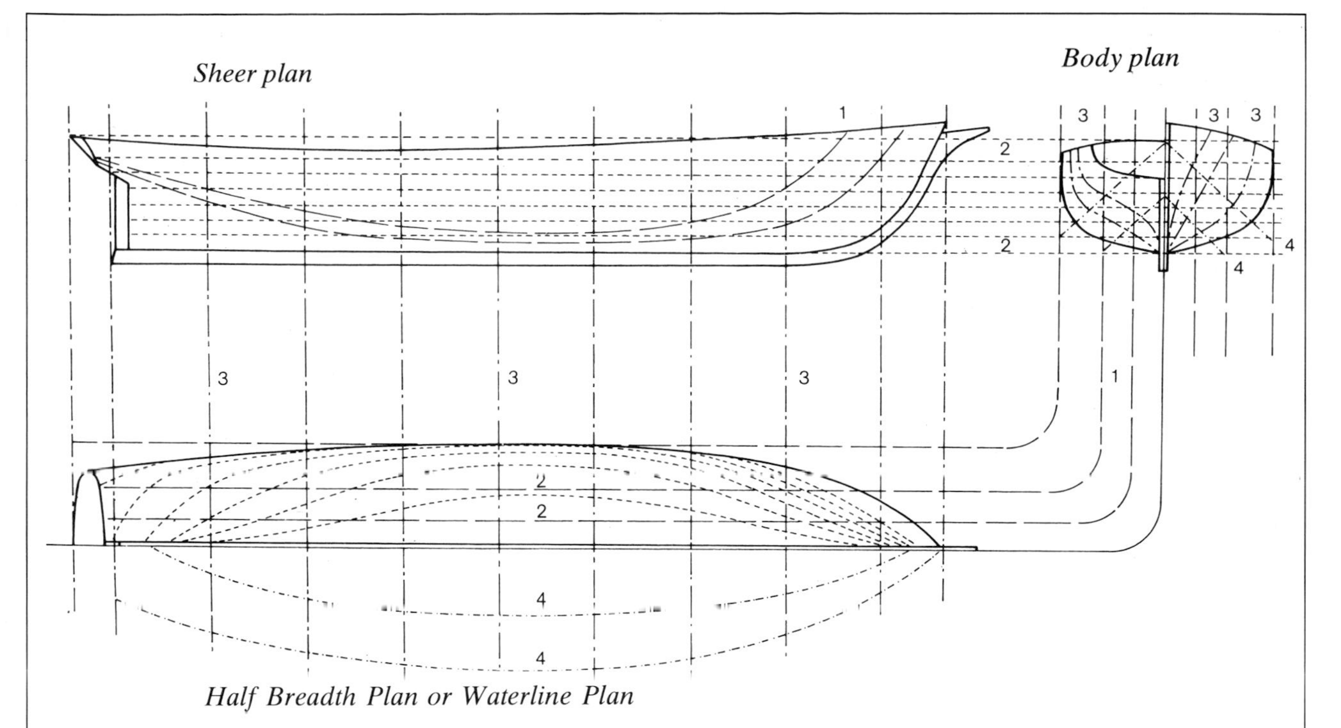

1. *Sheer plan – the sections run parallel to the midship plane*
2. *Half Breadth plan – the sections run parallel to the waterline plane*
3. *Body plan – the sections run parallel to the midships frame*
4. *Diagonals – of minor significance to the model maker*

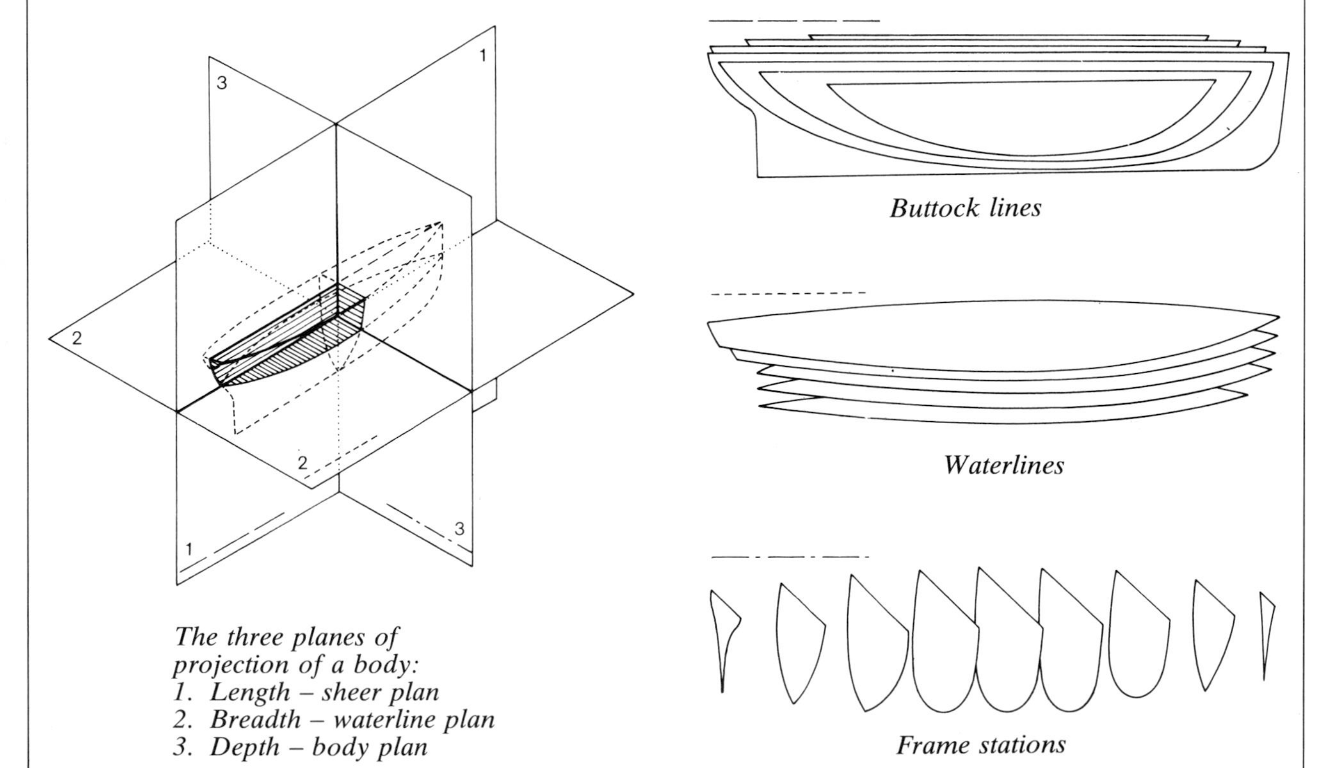

The three planes of projection of a body:
1. *Length – sheer plan*
2. *Breadth – waterline plan*
3. *Depth – body plan*

Construction of the frames

Look out for toy or model figures in the scale you are working at Many railway, soldier or even Red Indian figures can be modified without great difficulty to provide crew figures performing tasks which add interest and life to your model. However, if they are not exactly the right scale it is far better to leave them off

Figure too small for pump

Figure too large for capstan

One of the saddest aspects of historical model ship building is the fact that far too many model-builders, even those who are good at the job, base their models on highly dubious plans or even kits and thus programme completely unnecessary faults into their otherwise perfectly built models.

If you then ask these people why in heaven's name they work from such doubtful documents, the answer in 90 out of 100 cases will be that the model frames were all drawn up ready, whereas historically correct plans usually only give technical draughts and they didn't think they were capable of taking the model frames from these.

This is even more regrettable since with a little skill, accuracy and patience – without which a historical model ship cannot be built in any event – the drawing out of frames for the model is not so very difficult. In the adjacent drawings I have shown what is necessary for the construction of a model frame for a fully planked model. The principle is the same for Admiralty frame models, but slightly more complicated; anyone building models of this type must know so much about the construction of frames that the instructions given here are a matter of course for him and for this reason I have excluded the subject here for the sake of clarity.

Proceed therefore in the order of the adjacent drawings:

1. On a piece of transparent graph paper first draw the centre line and the load water line, or, alternatively, use the lower line of the keel as a base line. Now lay the graph paper onto the body plan and carefully trace the appropriate section line. In doing this you must check whether the section line gives the shape of the frame with or without planking. For each frame required make one such sheet.
2. Now lay the graph paper with the centre line on the corresponding frame line of the side view and transfer the location of the gun ports and wales onto your sheet.
3. In the same way the location of the deck beams can be taken from the centre longitudinal section. Here care must be taken, as the centre longitudinal section always shows the maximum height of the deck beams, since the deck beams slope outwards because of the curvature of the deck (see DECK BEAMS).
4. Finally the width of the frames is taken from the cross-sections and drawn in.

How you now produce or complete a model frame plotted in this way from the plans, to be able to transfer it, finally, to wood and cut it out for your model, you will find in the section on INTERNAL CONSTRUCTION OF PLANKED HULLS.

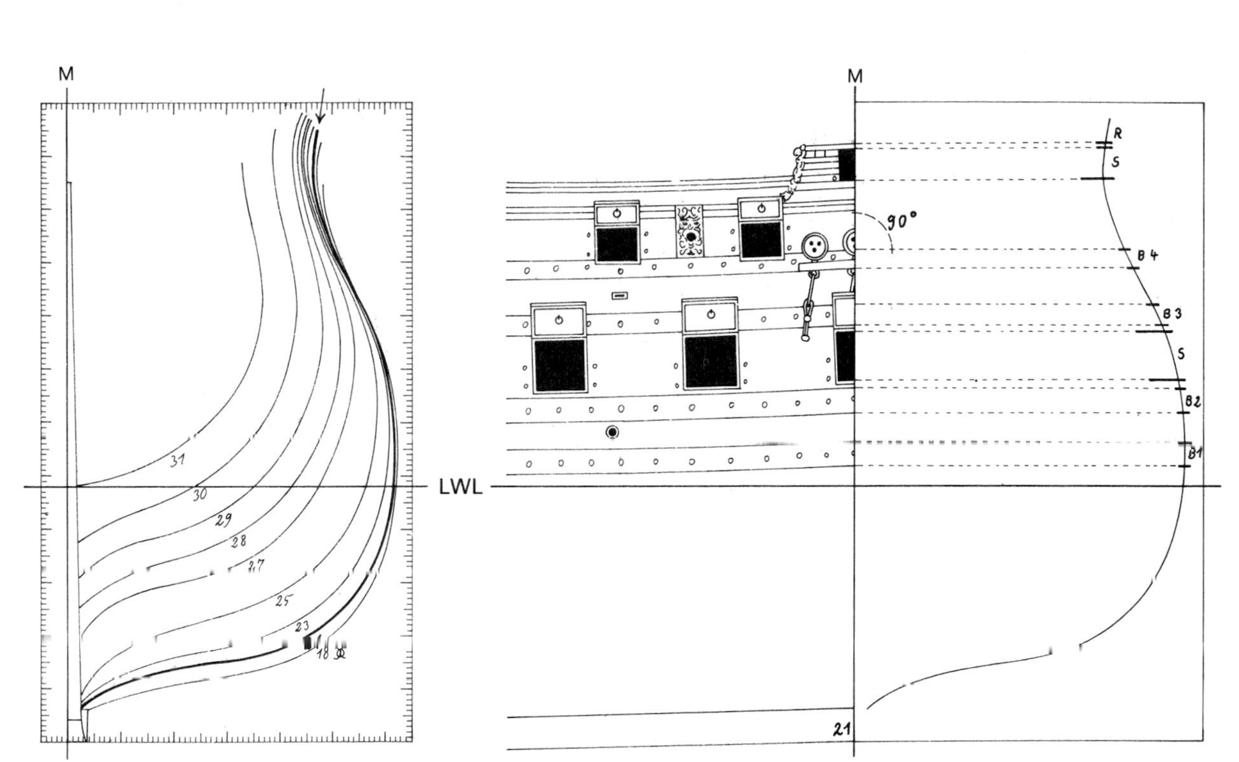

1. *Tracing a section from the body plan*

2. *Locating the gunport and wale positions from the profile*

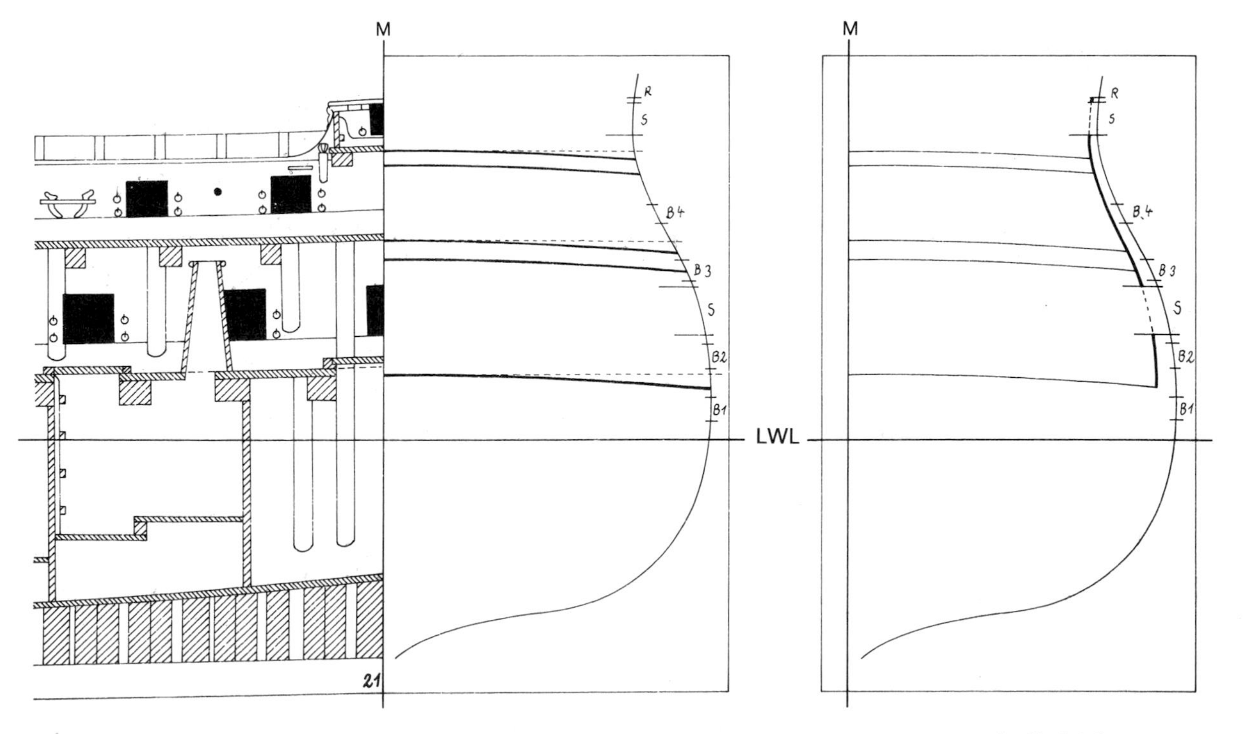

3. *Marking the deck centre points from the longitudinal section*

4. *Drawing in hull thickness etc.*

The Building jig

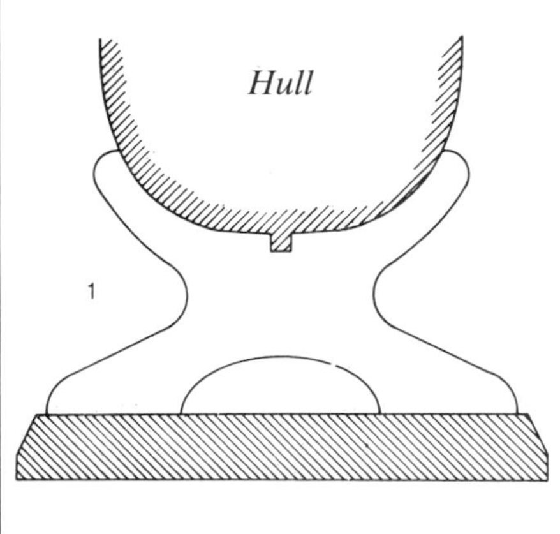

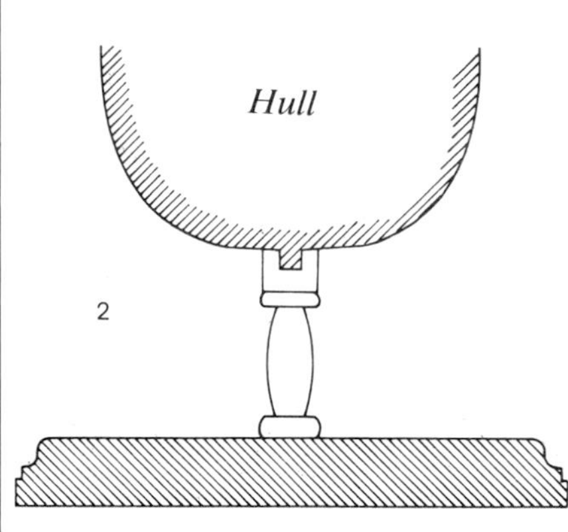

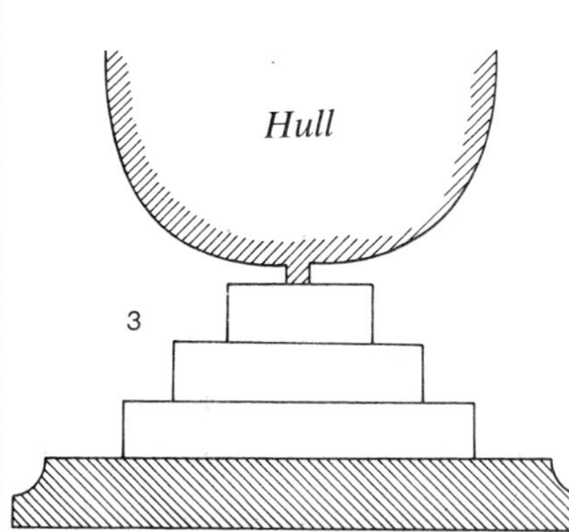

Model stands:
1. Keel blocks, or cradle stand
2. Column stand
3. Block base

Before the actual construction of the model starts, there is one more preparatory job to be carried out, although it is not a difficult one: the building of the jig. The jig's task is to provide the model with a stable base during construction, and to hold it still while the modeller carries out work on it. The base plate should be a sheet of chipboard about ¾in thick, somewhat longer and wider than the ship's hull. Glue paper or plastic film on to this base, and draw on it the exact centreline of the ship and the precise location of the frames – later on you will appreciate these lines: you will be able to tell whether the frames are exactly at right-angles to the keel by using a small plumb bob, without having to mess about with squares and straight edges. The supports for the stem and stern must be exactly at 90° to the base plate, to ensure that the keel, stem and sternpost are exactly vertical. This again allows you to check whether the centre of the frames and the centre of the deck beams are exactly on the midship plane, using a small plumb bob once more. These supports can be made of wood, or – better – from angle iron. The model will remain on this building jig until the wales are fitted, when the hull becomes quite rigid. At that stage – but not before – the model can be removed from the jig in order to plank it. After planking, staining, painting, and coppering the underwater hull (if appropriate), it makes sense to fix the model on its permanent display stand. The base plate of this stand should be made of a high quality hardwood, as appropriate to the model. The choice of wood, is, of course, a matter of taste, but it should certainly harmonise with the colouring of the ship. You could not go far wrong with a choice of walnut, pear or even oak. Mahogany can also look very fine, but the colouring of the timber tends to draw the observer's attention, and for this reason should only be used for the fairly dark ships of the 19th century with their clean-cut lines.

The base board is best left to a cabinet maker to construct – this will not cost the earth, and you can be sure that he will make a very nice job of it. There are two types of model display stand, one of them being the cradle, the other the column stand. Occasionally models are displayed on the keel blocks of a shipyard slipway – these are effectively multiple column stands. In all cases the stand must be securely attached to the base board, and the model itself should also be absolutely secure on its supports – glueing is good, screws are better.

The advantage of the cradle is that the model's security and the builder's peace of mind are ensured; the disadvantage is that in two places the lines of the underwater hull are interrupted. Incidentally, the support surfaces of the cradle must be an exact fit to the hull. The advantage of the column stand is that the hull form is shown off to its maximum effect; nevertheless, I don't care for column stands personally, as I can never get rid of the sneaking suspicion that the model might just tip over. Hull and frame models can also be set on blocks as in the original shipyard.

You should also bear in mind that the display stand should match the overall style of the ship. If in doubt, the general rule is this: rather too plain than too elaborate. Here is one little wrinkle worth remembering: a model ship always looks better if the stand supports are not too low. 1½ – 2ins between baseplate and keel represents a minimum figure for a medium-sized model.

To prevent the base plate suffering damage during further construction work, cover it with a sheet of thick plastic and secure the edges with sellotape.

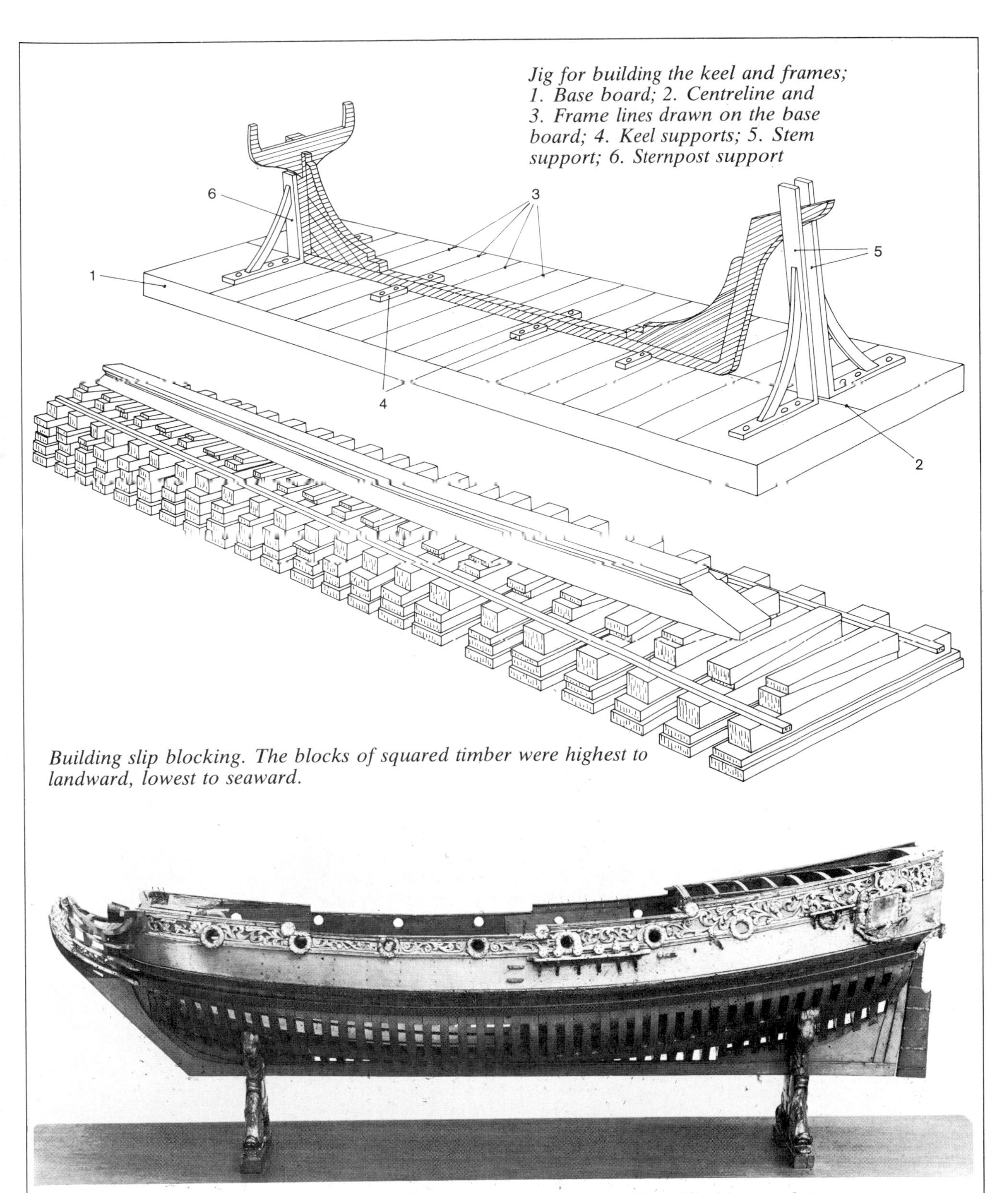

Jig for building the keel and frames; 1. Base board; 2. Centreline and 3. Frame lines drawn on the base board; 4. Keel supports; 5. Stem support; 6. Sternpost support

Building slip blocking. The blocks of squared timber were highest to landward, lowest to seaward.

Admiralty model of a British royal yacht around 1690. The ship stands in a finely carved cradle stand. It is important to note that the plane of the waterline is exactly parallel to the base board.

Keel, stem and sternpost

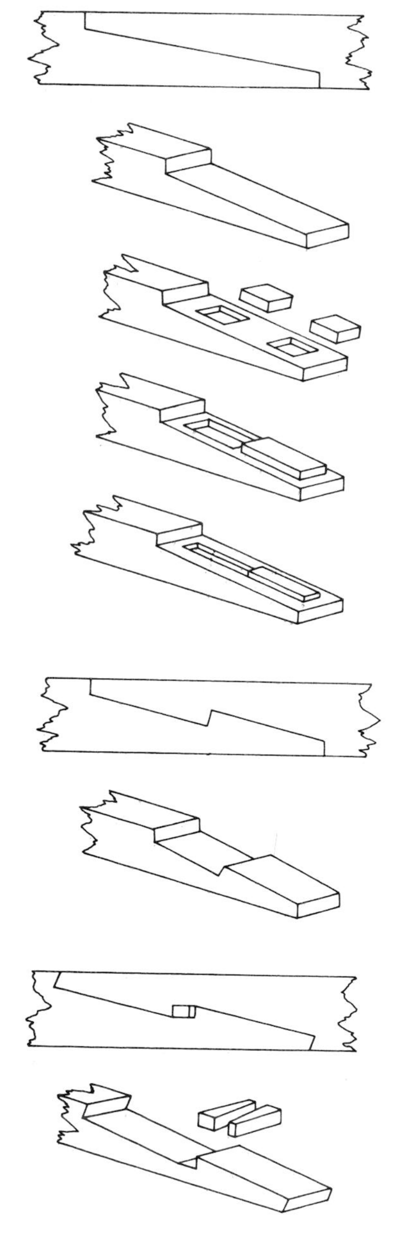

Methods of assembling the keel and stem components. Minimum length of scarf on larger ships was five feet

The keel, stem and sternpost form the backbone of the entire ship. Consequently it is essential to use well-seasoned, stable hardwood for their construction, to ensure that no warping creeps in.

The keel

Although you can usually find the length of the keel from the plans without difficulty, its thickness and height are often less reliably stated – for this reason I include the drawing at bottom centre on the facing page, which shows the usual proportions for ships up to the 19th century.

According to Nicolaes Witsen in 1671, the width of the keel would constitute 1/25 of the maximum breadth of the ship amidships. Hence a ship of 25ft beam would have a keel of 1ft wide amidships, which would taper to 10¼ins at the bow, and 9½ins at the stern. In the course of the 18th century the keel became slimmer, and from around 1770 onwards was about 1/30 of the maximum breadth; the remaining proportions were not changed.

As the keel was far too long a structure to be made from one piece, it was assembled from several components; four or five on a large ship. The individual parts were joined by scarphs. The most common types of scarphs are shown on the left. These scarphs were at least four times as long as the thickness of the keel, a distance of at least 5ft on larger ships.

A thick plank, called the false keel, was fixed under the keel for protection. If the ship ran aground, the false keel was designed to tear loose, leaving the actual keel undamaged.

The false keel probably emerged in the early 18th century in England and was soon adopted by continental shipbuilders.

A triangular groove, known as the rabbet, was cut along the whole length of the keel to provide a seating for the lower or garboard strakes.

Stem and sternpost

The construction of the stem and sternpost is best understood by studying the drawings; they were composed of a whole series of individual timbers. In the course of the centuries there was a very wide variety of methods used in their construction. The rabbet is continued up the stem and sternpost for the planking strakes.

Building up the stem and sternpost from the separate pieces of wood is extremely tedious, and you will also need a very accurate and reliable plan. If you wish to simplify matters, whilst still retaining virtually the identical effect, you can make the keel, stem and sternpost from a smaller number of larger pieces of wood, and then score the joints of the individual timbers with a knife. To ensure that the keel, stem and stern are joined absolutely flat, use a fairly thick glass plate as a base when glueing them together (two-part epoxy resin). This guarantees that the underside will be absolutely flat. When the adhesive has cured, the upper side can be sanded flat – check this with the glass plate again. When satisfied, the tapers towards bow and stern can be sanded in, and you should check at this stage that the transition from the thickest to the thinnest areas is as even and regular as possible. No bends, curves and buckles – the changes in thickness should be virtually invisible.

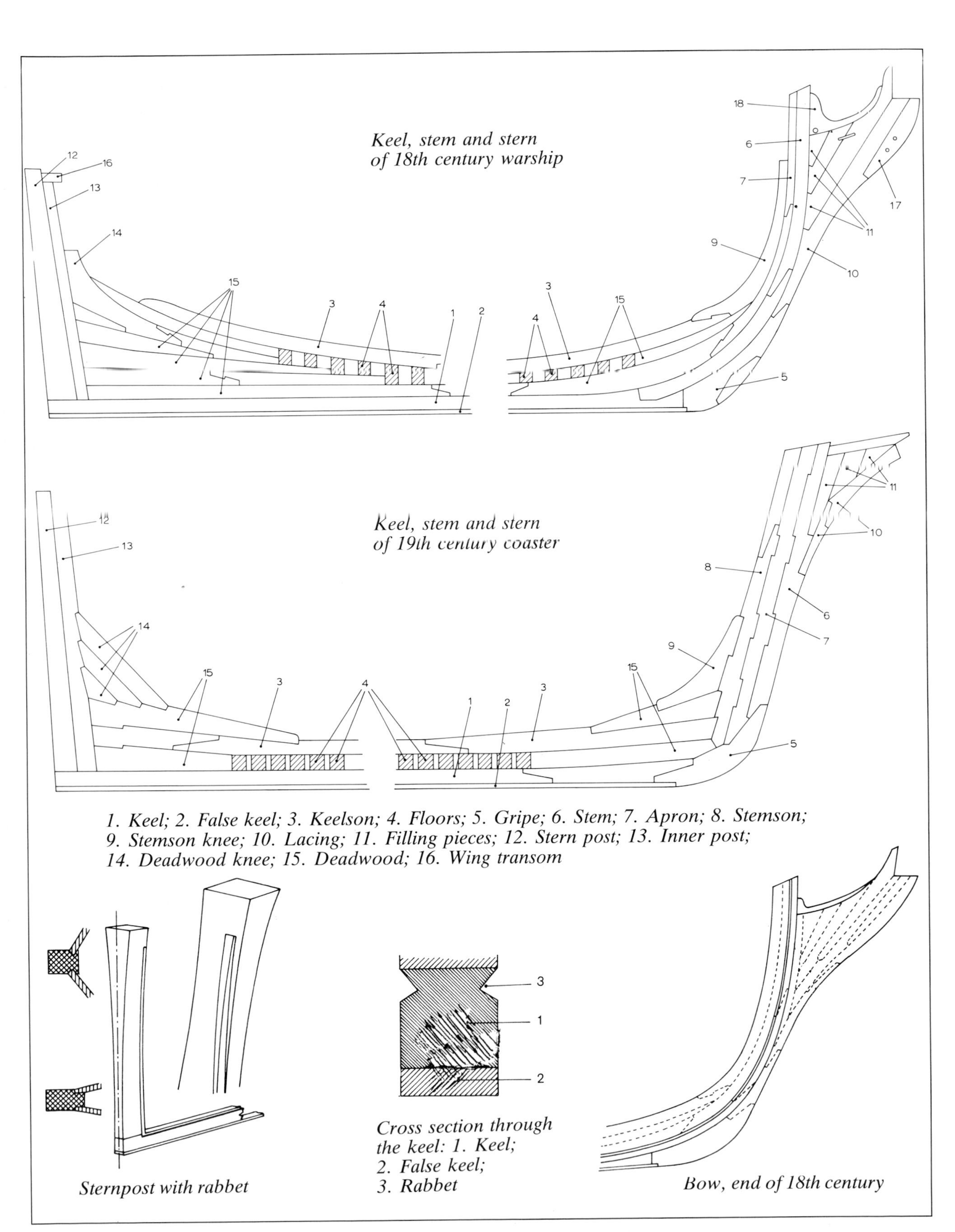

Sternpost with rabbet

Cross section through the keel: 1. Keel; 2. False keel; 3. Rabbet

Bow, end of 18th century

Frames

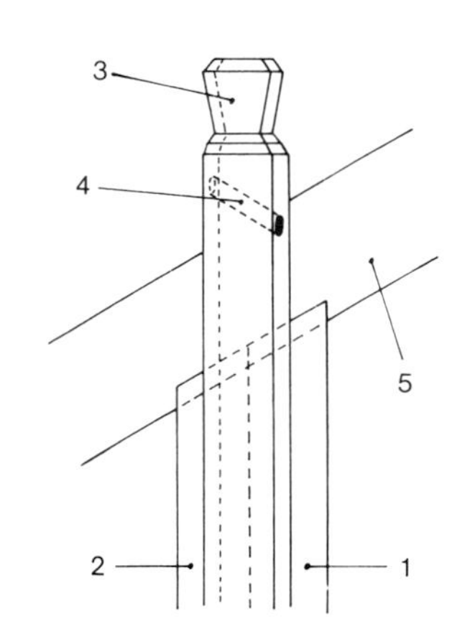

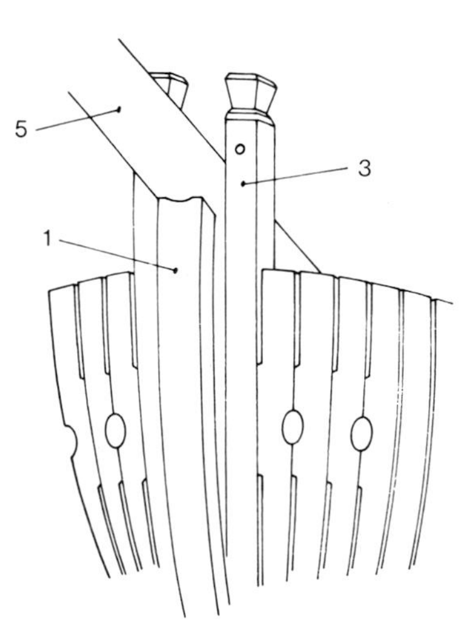

Knightheads:
1. Stem; 2. Apron; 3. Knightheads; 4. Hole for mainstay collar; 5. Bowsprit

Caution! The following stages of construction – frames, stern, deck beams and wales – are the most important in the whole of ship modelling. Whether they are cut accurately or not, and assembled carefully or not, dictates the subsequent appearance of the hull, and hence the overall quality of the whole model. Mistakes or carelessness at this point cannot be remedied at a later stage by any measure known to man. If you have patience, take your time, and work with the greatest accuracy you can muster.

Most of the information in the next pages, regarding the construction of frames, stern and deck beams, refers to the original shipbuilding methods, and is only of direct significance if you are constructing a frame or Admiralty model. If you intend fully planking the hull, you can save yourself much of the work described here. Your heading is INTERIOR CONSTRUCTION OF FULLY PLANKED HULLS.

Nevertheless, do not skip over these pages, as many specialized terms are only explained once, and many details – e.g. the round up of the deck beams and many others – are not described again. Furthermore, a little knowledge of historical construction methods will often prove useful when you are in doubt.

The frames, in conjunction with the keel, stem and sternpost, form the skeleton of the ship. The shape of the frames is found from the body plan. The first job is to draw each frame out individually onto squared tracing paper from the body plan. It is sufficient to draw half of each frame, as they are all absolutely symmetrical about the centreline.

It is a good idea to mark the position of the waterline, the deck beams, the wales and the gunports on the frames.

As the illustrations on the next two pages show, the frames were built up from several timbers. If you wish to assemble the frames in true scale fashion, it has proved best to cut the individual components to approximate shape initially, and join the parts – taking care over the grain direction. Once assembled, the final shape of the frame can be marked accurately and sawn out.

The drawing can either be traced using carbon paper, or – better – the frame drawing can be stuck to the wood with double-sided film and the wood and paper sawn out together – the paper and film can then be peeled off without any difficulty.

The frames at the bow and stern present particular problems. These frames have to be bevelled to ensure that the planking rests against their entire width. The amount of bevel should never be more than a quarter of the thickness of the frame. However, as this would not be possible with frames set parallel at the bow and stern, the frames in these areas were set at an acute angle to the keel, the last ones being filled out with hawse pieces running almost parallel to the keel. Frames of this type were termed cant frames.

Frame spacing varied considerably, depending on period and type of ship. The exact dimensions and spacing, and also the thickness of the frames themselves, have to be taken from your plans. An old rule of thumb says: rib thickness = rib interval.

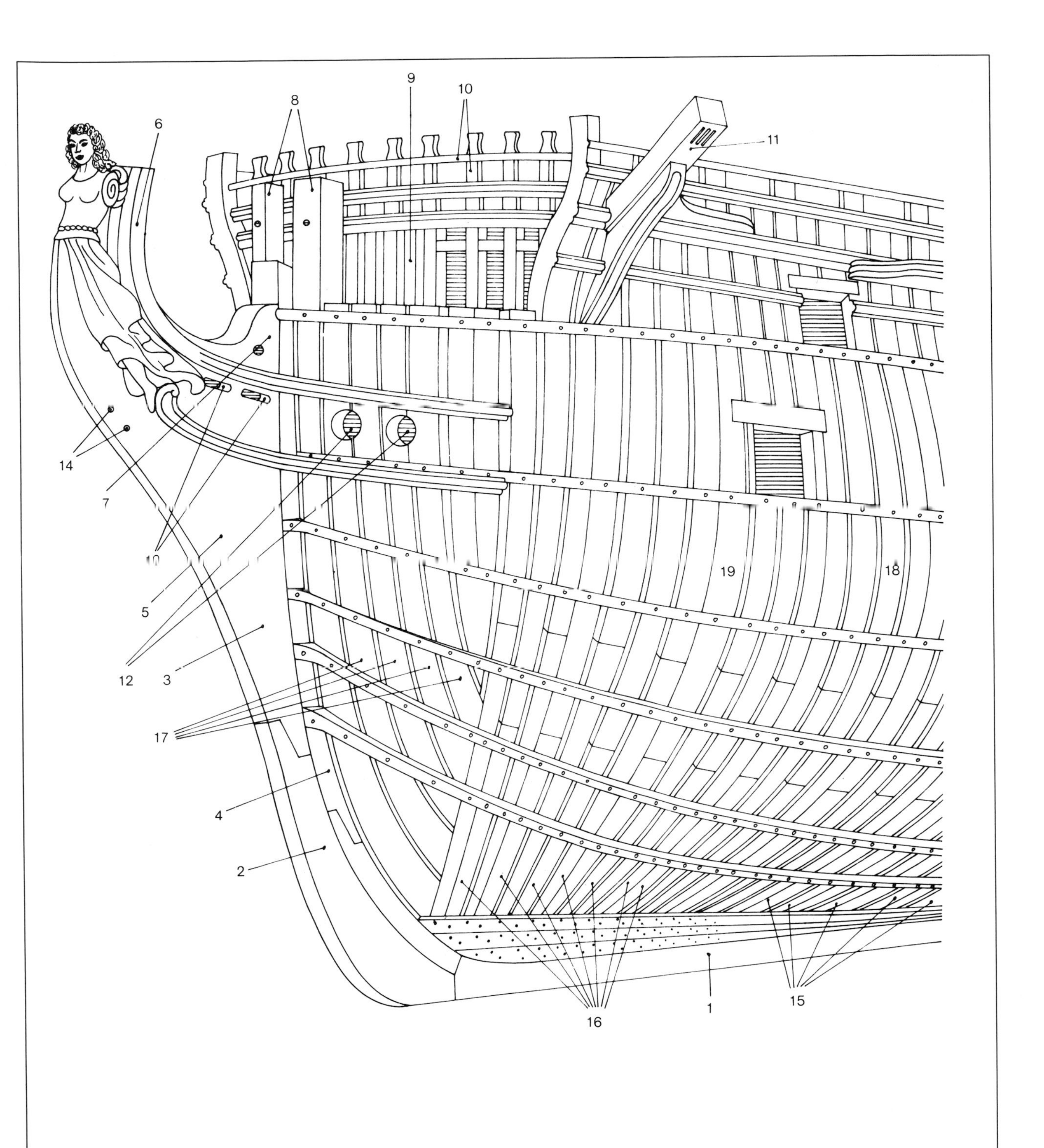

Bow of a warship of the late 18th century:
1. Keel; 2. Gripe; 3. & 5. Knee of the head; 4. Stem; 6. Hair bracket; 7. Gammoning knee; 8. Knightheads (also known as the bollard timbers); 9. Beakhead bulkhead; 10. Forecastle rail; 11. Cathead; 12. Hawse holes; 13. Gammoning holes; 14. Bobstay holes; 15. Square frames; 16. Cant frames; 17. Hawse pieces; 18. Filling frames; 19. Double frames

Frames

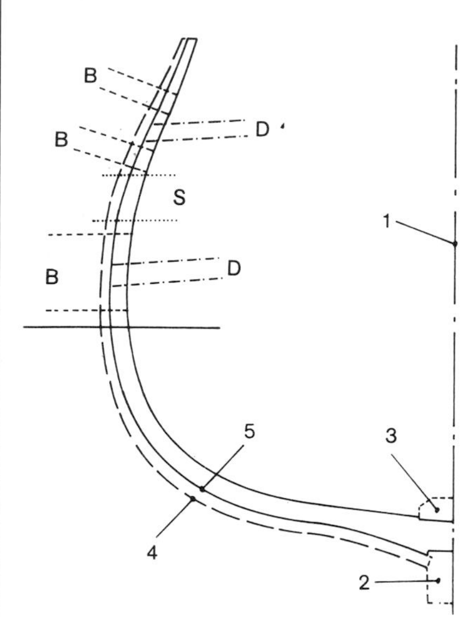

Drawing a frame:
1. Centreline; 2. Keel; 3. Keelson; 4. Line of planking; 5. Moulding line; (B) wales; (S) gunport; (D) deck beam

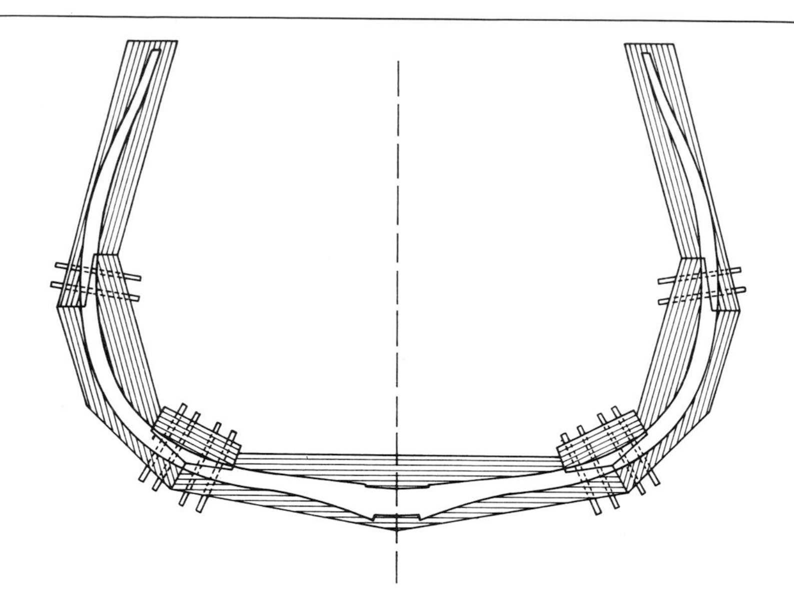

Construction of model frames: The frame must be built up as the original in order to obtain the correct grain direction (shown by hatched lines). To achieve this, rough-cut pieces of wood are cut, joined and dowelled, after which the exact shape of the frame can be sawn out.

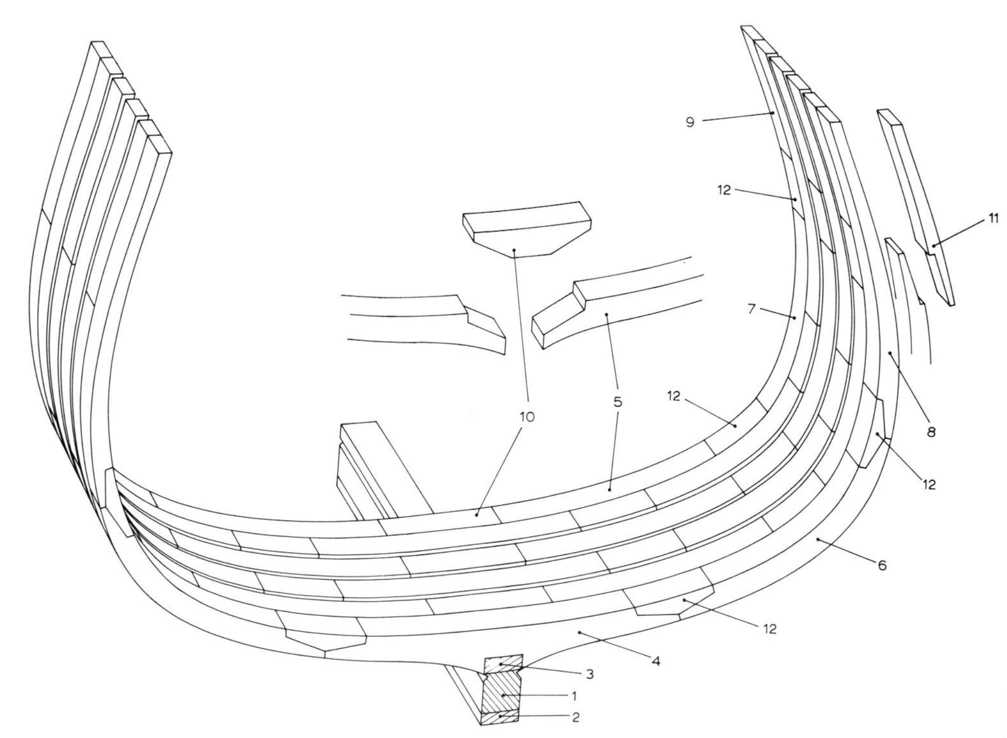

Construction of frames: 1. Keel; 2. False keel; 3. Deadwood; 4. Floor; 5. First futtock; 6. Second futtock; 7. Third futtock; 8. Fourth futtock; 9. Top timber; 10. Cross chock; 11. Alternative scarph for top timber; 12. Scarph chock

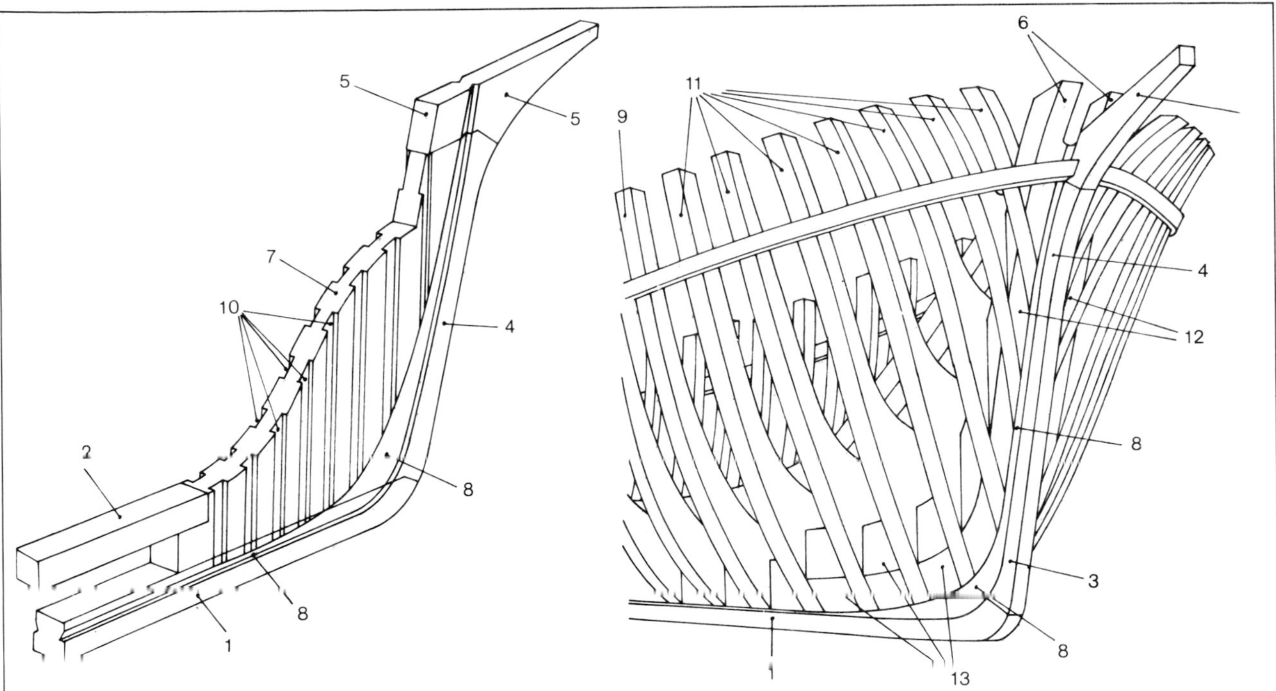

Fitting the cant frames at the bow of a model of a small 19th century merchant ship: 1. Keel; 2. Keelson; 3. Gripe; 4. Stem; 5. Stemhead; 6. Knightheads; 7. Deadwood; 8. Rabbet; 9. Square frame; 10. Grooves for fitting the cant frames; 11. Cant frames; 12. Stem doublers; 13. Filling pieces

Bevel of frames: 1. Keel; 2. Square frames; 3. Plank

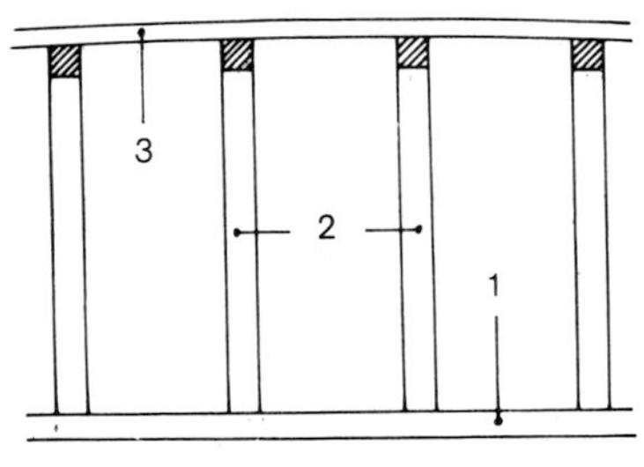

Amidships

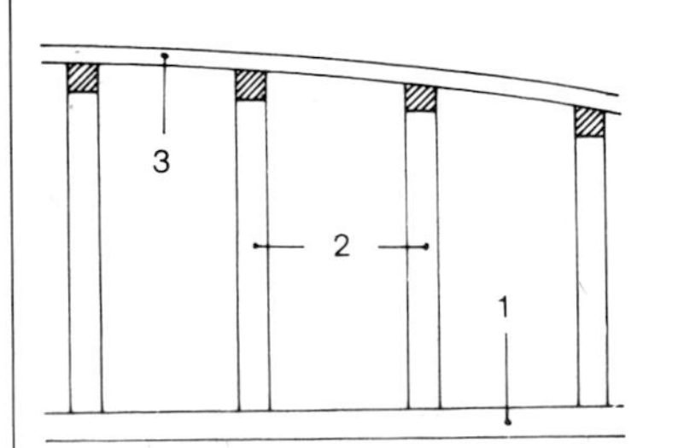

Slight bevel – bow fore and quarter

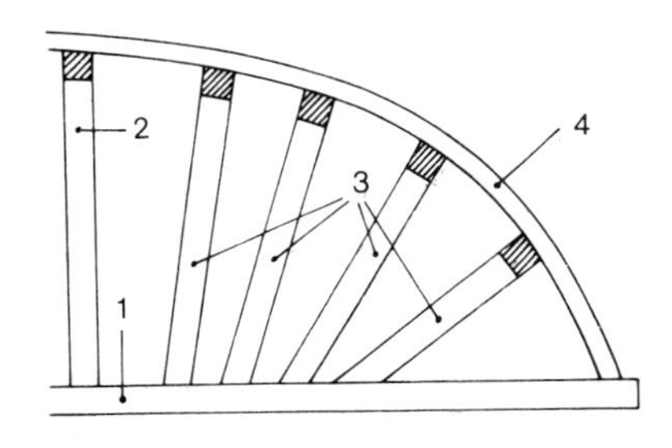

Bevel of frames at bow and stern: 1. Keel; 2. Square frames; 3. Cant frames; 4. Plank Correct use of cant frames

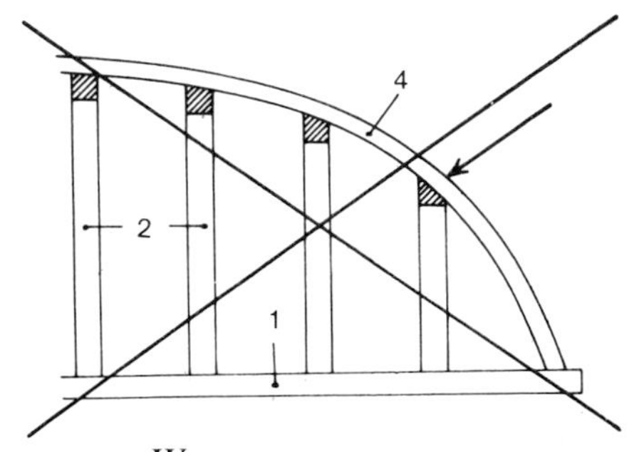

Wrong. Parallel frame bevelled too severely (arrowed)

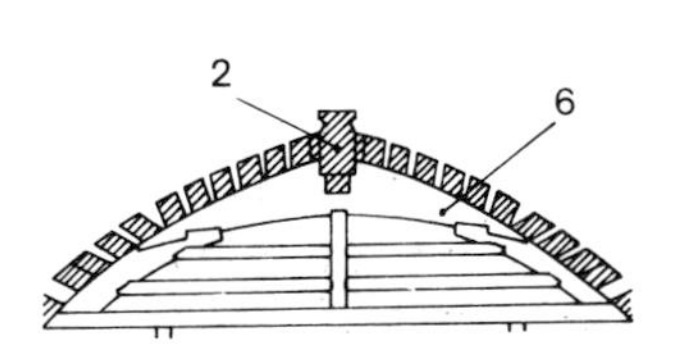

Bow with cant frames: 1. Keel; 2. Stem; 3. Square frames; 4. Cant frames; 5. Hawse pieces; 6. Breast hook

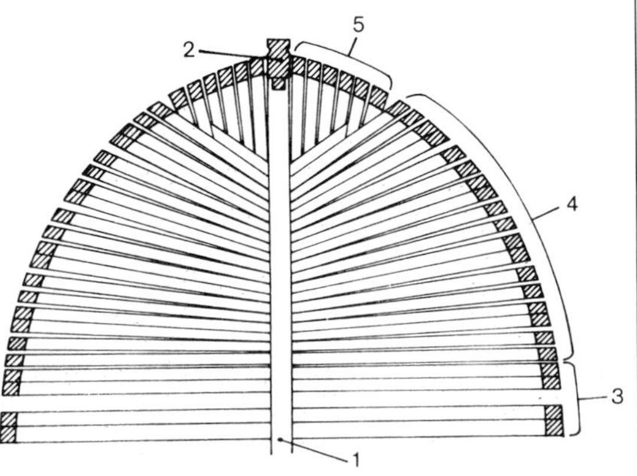

The Stern

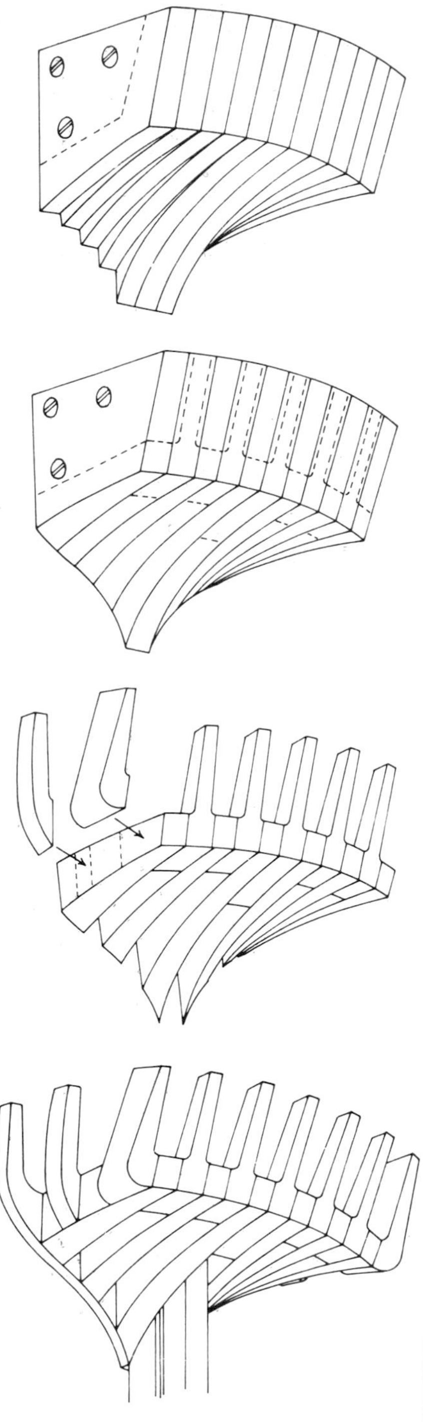

Construction of stern of model of small 19th century merchant ship

The stern, especially in the case of frame models, is an extremely complex part of the ship. Until the end of the 15th century the stern was more or less round, and built in a similar fashion to the bow with cant frames and hawse pieces. As early as the mid-13th century a small, trapezoid structure was fitted above the round stern, known as the stern castle, which was supported by a cross beam, attached to the sternpost – the wing transom.

This design altered little until the beginning of the 16th century, except that the stern or after castle became larger, and the wing transom stronger, and in a slightly modified form the round stern can still be found in some local Mediterranean craft today.

The introduction of the wing transom led to the development of the square tuck stern. In this type of stern the wing transom was supported at either end by an S shaped timber which faired into the sternpost and was known as a fashion piece.

Several horizontal filling transoms connected the fashion pieces to the stern post and served to support the planking, usually diagonal, which covered the triangular area created by the wing transom and the fashion pieces. This formed the lower part of the stern which nowadays is often erroneously called the transom. The ship's side planking terminated on the fashion piece.

It was usual for the wing transom to round up in a similar way to the deck beams and in later and more sophisticated ships it rounded aft as well. This resulted in a slightly convex rather than a flat lower stern.

Having now established a much stronger wing transom it was possible to use this as a foundation for the large and complex upper sterns with their ornate galleries which now began to appear. They were supported in a fore and aft direction by a series of counter timbers seated on the wing transom much in the same way that the frames sat on the keel in a transverse direction.

In the early part of the 19th century British shipwrights developed the round tuck stern. The lower ends of the fashion pieces were now brought forward on to the stern deadwood and the ends of the filling transoms moved forward with them. This resulted in much finer lines aft and apart from a few lower strakes it was possible to bring the ends of the hull planking up onto the wing transom itself. This round tuck soon became universal in British ships and was gradually adopted on the continent during the course of the next century.

By the middle of the 19th century ships' lines had become finer and the galleried stern and wing transoms were displaced by much simpler semi-circular or semi-elliptical sterns using lighter counter timbers radiating out from the stern post.

From about 1815 onwards warships in England were built with a rounded stern (Seppings); the rounded stern appeared in merchant ships from about 1850 onwards.

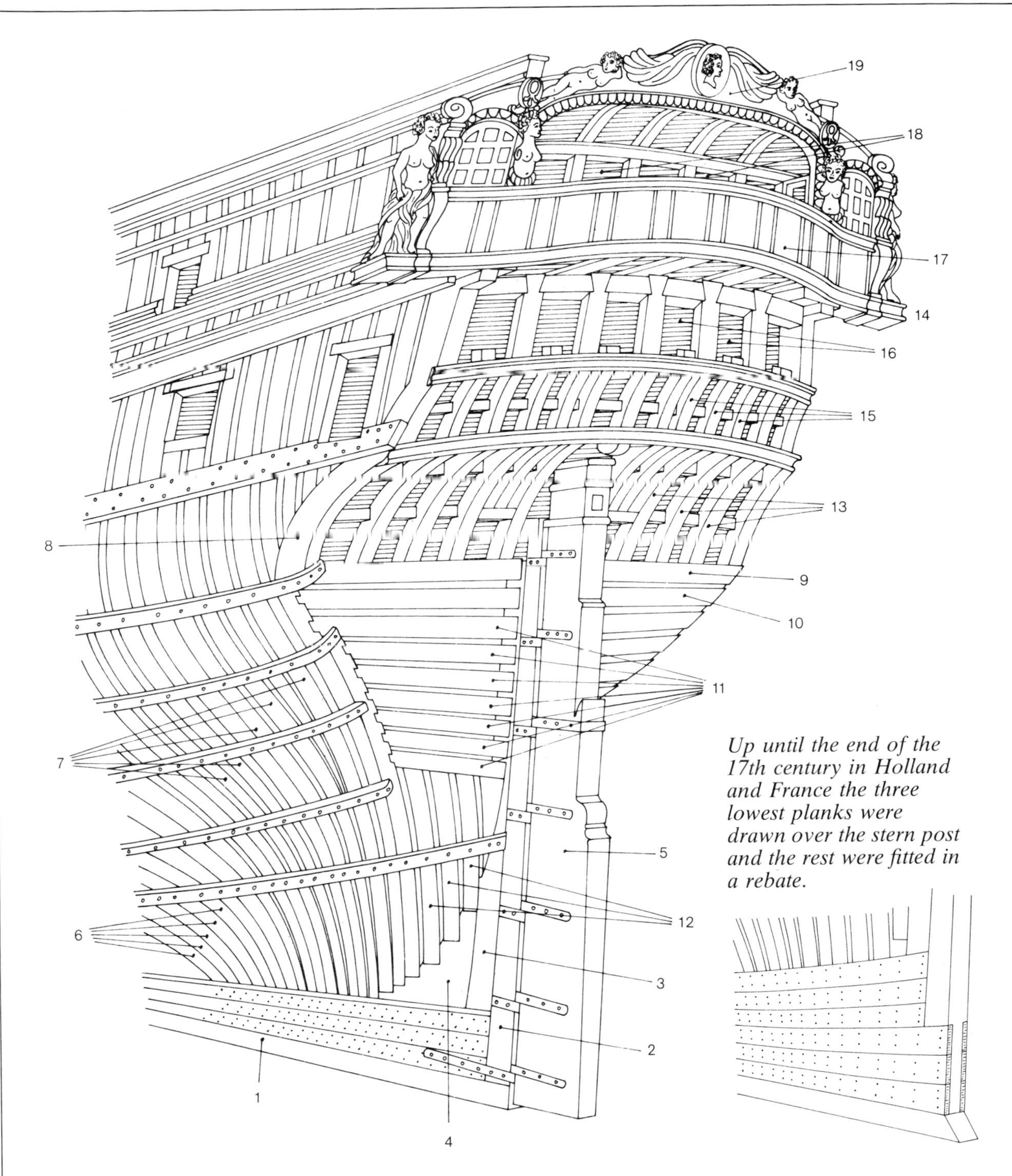

Up until the end of the 17th century in Holland and France the three lowest planks were drawn over the stern post and the rest were fitted in a rebate.

Stern of an English warship of the late 18th century:
1. Keel; 2. Stern post; 3. Inner post; 4. Deadwood; 5. Rudder; 6. Square frames; 7. Cant frames; 8. Outer counter timber; 9. Wing transom; 10. Deck transom; 11. Filling transoms; 12. Filling pieces; 13. Lower counter timbers; 14. Fool-rail; 15. Upper counter timbers; 16. Lower tier of lights; 17. Gallery; 18. Upper tier of lights; 19. Tafferel

The Stern

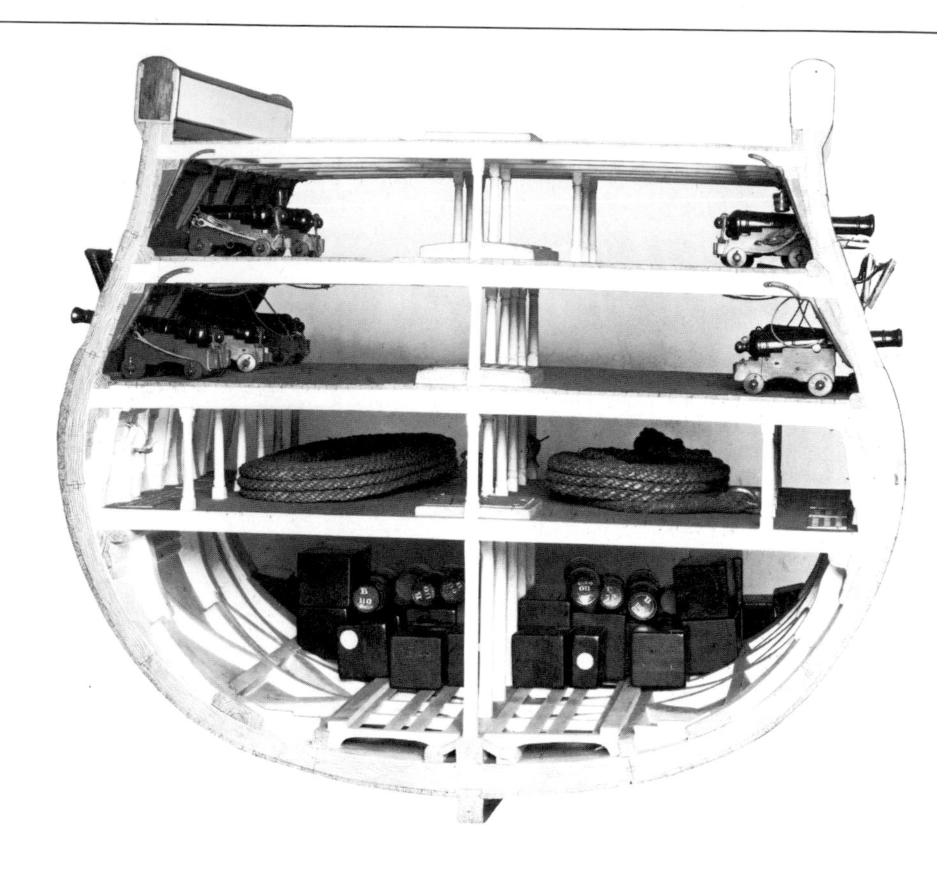

Right: HMS Rodney *of 1833*
Below: HMS Vanguard *of 1835*

Two models of midship sections of British warships. The interior construction and division of space are very clearly seen on these models. The accurate construction of such models is extremely difficult.

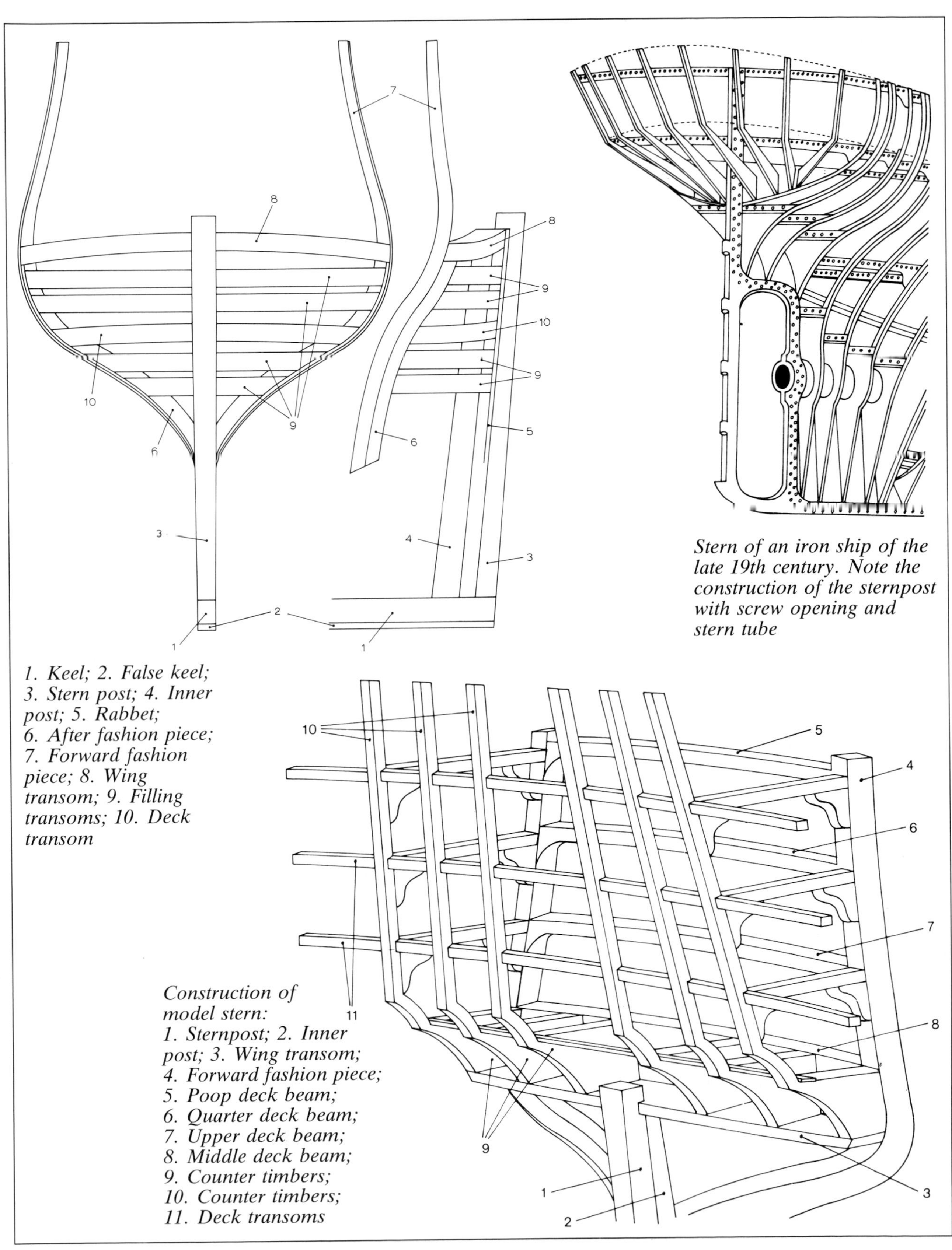

Stern of an iron ship of the late 19th century. Note the construction of the sternpost with screw opening and stern tube

1. Keel; 2. False keel; 3. Stern post; 4. Inner post; 5. Rabbet; 6. After fashion piece; 7. Forward fashion piece; 8. Wing transom; 9. Filling transoms; 10. Deck transom

Construction of model stern:
1. Sternpost; 2. Inner post; 3. Wing transom; 4. Forward fashion piece; 5. Poop deck beam; 6. Quarter deck beam; 7. Upper deck beam; 8. Middle deck beam; 9. Counter timbers; 10. Counter timbers; 11. Deck transoms

Deck beams

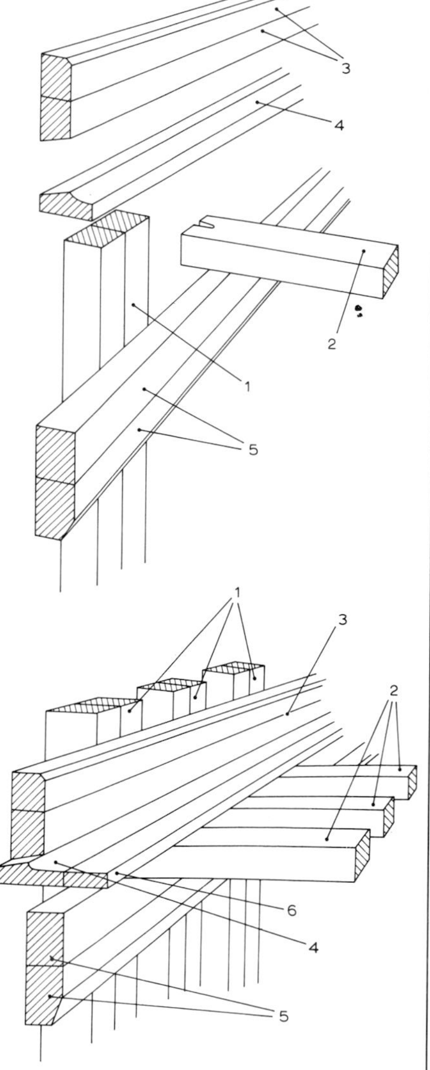

1. Frames; 2. Deck beams;
3. Spirketting; 4. Waterway;
5. Clamp and shelf; 6. Deck plank

The deck clamps acted as longitudinal stiffening members of the ship's hull. They supported the deck beams, which in turn acted as cross stiffeners to the frames. The depth of the deck beams was from 1/50 of their length in small ships and when supporting elevated decks (forecastle deck, quarterdeck), up to 1/35 for the lower decks (gun decks) of larger ships. The spacing between the beams varied considerably depending on the type and size of the ship but was generally about 4 to 5 feet.

Ships' decks are always rounded up or cambered to allow water on the deck to run off more easily. It is expressed as a height in inches and a general rule of thumb for the upper deck of a late 19th century ship is ¼in for every foot of moulded breadth. Earlier ships tended to have slightly more camber but it varied from deck to deck, the higher the deck the greater the camber. For all practical purposes the modeller can ignore this and should make up one template which can be used for all decks.

You will find a typical half-curve on the right at the very bottom. Trace it off, transfer it onto a piece of stout cartridge paper, cut it out cleanly, and you have a deck camber template 12ins wide – you will hardly ever find a model ship's deck wider than that – not that you would build, anyway. The deck beams were braced underneath by hanging knees, and laterally with lodging knees. These components were made in a very wide variety of shapes, as can be seen on the drawings.

Between the beams and notched into them were rows of lighter fore and aft timbers called carlings – two or three rows per side. Between the carlings, and in turn notched into them, were thwartship timbers called ledges.

The outboard ends of the beams were covered by a broad plank up to 24″ wide, known as a waterway, running the full length of the ship.

Now a few more words about the assembly of frames, stern and deck beams.

The basic method of joining these components is to glue them. The individual pieces of the frame, stern and deck beams should be stuck with two-part epoxy, or possibly with balsa cement, and small joints with instant glue. Butt joints and the joint areas of assembled parts should be strengthened by epoxy and fitting wood or bamboo dowels. Pins or nails, which are often recommended in modelling books, should not be used as far as possible, as dowels hold better as well as looking closer to scale.

For glueing the frames on to the keel, or attaching the stern, you should use p.v.c. glue, or a two-part resin with not too short a pot life. The advantage of these adhesives is that you have long enough to align the components precisely; take particular care that the frames are absolutely at right-angles to the keel and to the baseboard of the jig. The best way of checking this is to use a small plumb bob and a try-square.

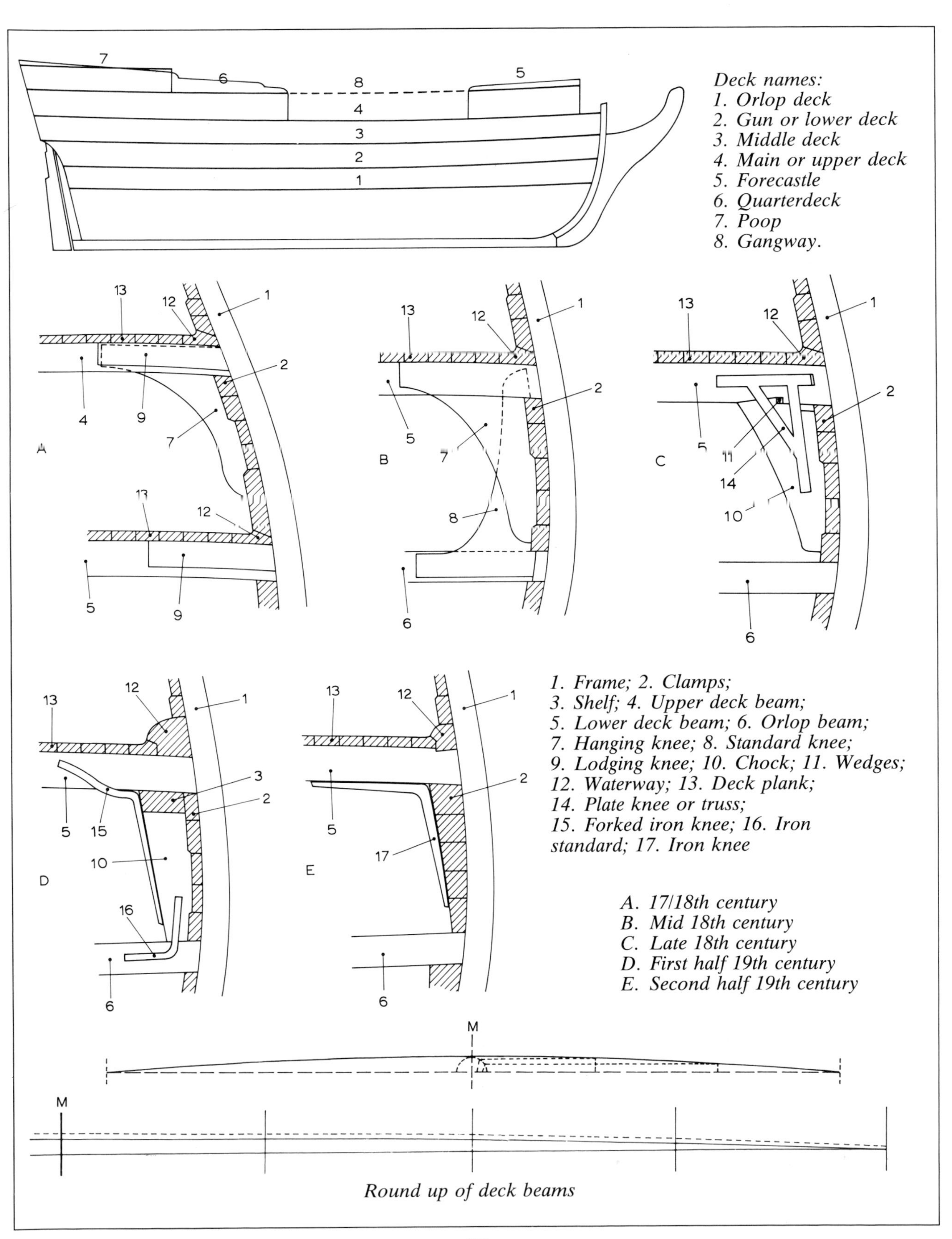

Round up of deck beams

Deck beams

Hull of the English Blackwall frigate True Briton *of 1861*

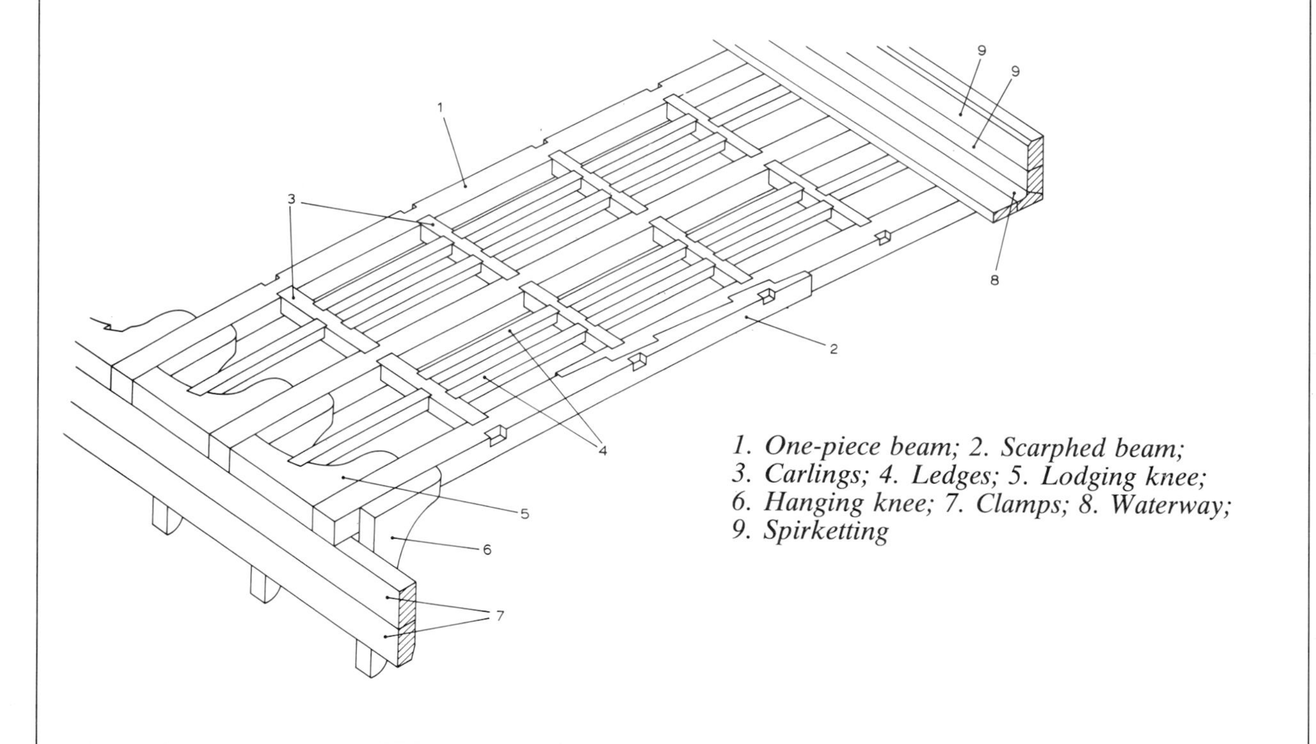

1. One-piece beam; 2. Scarphed beam; 3. Carlings; 4. Ledges; 5. Lodging knee; 6. Hanging knee; 7. Clamps; 8. Waterway; 9. Spirketting

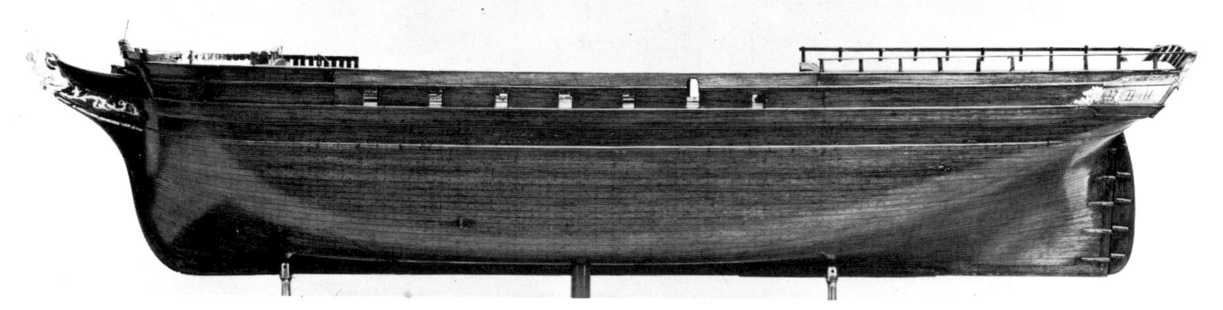

Hull of the English merchant ship Vimiera *of 1848*

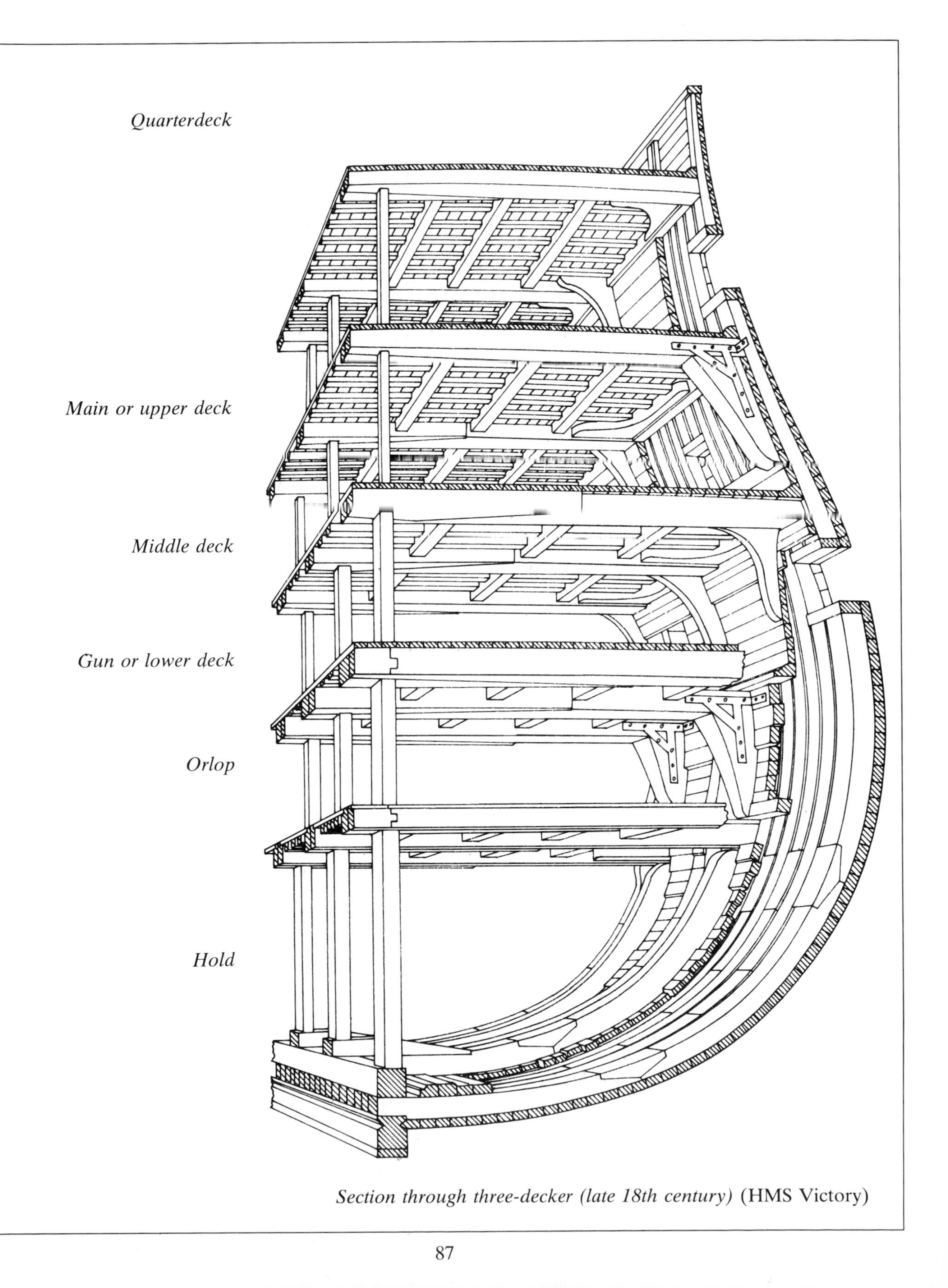

Section through three-decker (late 18th century) (HMS Victory)

Internal construction of fully planked hulls

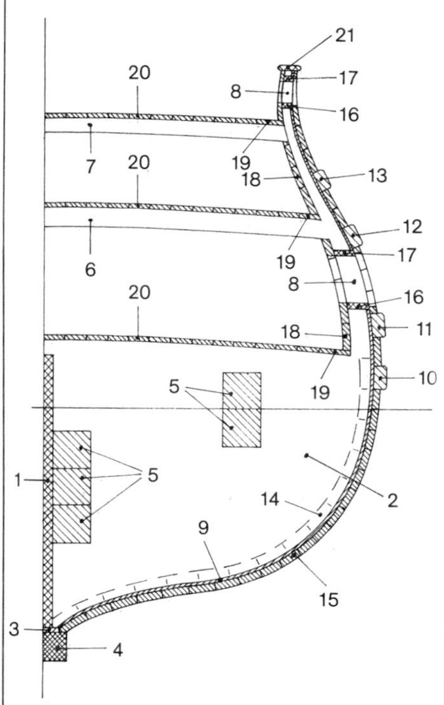

Cross-section through a fully planked model hull:
1. Hull plate (plywood); 2. Frame (plywood); 3. Rebate strip (pine); 4. Keel (solid wood); 5. Bracing rails (pine); 6. Deck beams of a lower deck (plywood painted dark brown); 7. Visible deck beams of an upper deck (solid wood); 8. Gun port; 9. Under-planking (veneer); 10. 1st wale; 11. 2nd wale; 12. 3rd wale; 13. 4th wale (all wales in solid wood); 14. Internal planking of underwater hull (pine); 15. External planking (solid wood); 16. Under stringer (solid wood); 17. Upper stringer (solid wood); 18. Internal planking (solid wood); 19. Scupper (solid wood); 20. Deck planking (solid wood); 21. Breastwork/railing (solid wood)

As already stated, if you intend to plank your ship's hull entirely, you can simplify the construction of frames, bow, stern and deck beams to a quite substantial degree.

Hull Plate
In the case of planked hulls a vertical hull plate takes over the supporting part of the construction – it can best be compared with a greatly enlarged keel hog. It stretches from the inside edge of the keel and stem-post to about 4mm below the lower deck. The hull plate is made from 5-8mm thick plywood (depending on the size of the ship). Obeche 8-10mm thick can be used which has the advantage of not warping, bending or buckling but, of course, the disadvantage that it splits and breaks more easily.
Suitably sized holes for the mast heels and, if necessary, at the stern for the rudder stock (see RUDDER) are drilled out. Slots for the frames are also sawn in. There is a trick here: put the thickness of the frames *ahead of* the main (largest) frame *behind* the construction line of the frame, and for frames *aft of* the main frame *in front of* this line. This has the advantage that in each case you have at your disposal a 100% exact frame line, which is otherwise easily lost when bevelling the frames; gaps between the rear edge of a frame and planks – they really only arise in the bow area – can be made good with filling compound. Finally the load water line is drawn accurately on the hull plate.

Keel and Stem-post
As these parts are visible, they must be made of solid wood as described earlier and fixed to the hull plate, using epoxy glue and dowels or nails. Since it is particularly troublesome to make the necessary rebate on the forward stem-post, work is considerably simplified by producing the rebate from an added strip. It should be about 2mm thick and 2-3mm narrower than the keel or stem-post. Initially, it is mounted on the hull plate and then the keel and stem-post are placed over it; its thickness must, of course, be subtracted from the height of the keel or stem-post.

Frames
Tracing out of frames from plans has been described in detail above. Now these frame drawings must be prepared for model building:
1. The lower part up to the lowest deck remains solid.
2. Draw in/mark slot for the hull plate.
3. Draw in/mark openings for the bracings – we will consider these shortly.
4. Enlarge gun ports by the thickness of the lining.
5. Deduct the thickness of the hull side.
6. Build in supports/stays where the gun ports cut through the frames. There are two methods for this: the first is a pair of 5-8mm thick supports which are later, after planking, carefully cut out. This method must be used for all decks into which one will be able to see on the finished ship. i.e. under the gangway and forecastle. The second method is a central support/stay about 30mm thick, which will be left in and painted dark brown. This method can be used in the dark, lower decks where these supports are then almost invisible.
Not to be recommended is the method described by some authors, of sawing out the gun ports after planking. This looks very easy on a drawing but is really troublesome in practice and seldom does a clean job.
7. Deck beams for the lower decks can also be left in plywood and painted dark brown since they too will hardly be visible later. Where the deck beams can be seen, again under the gangway and forecastle,

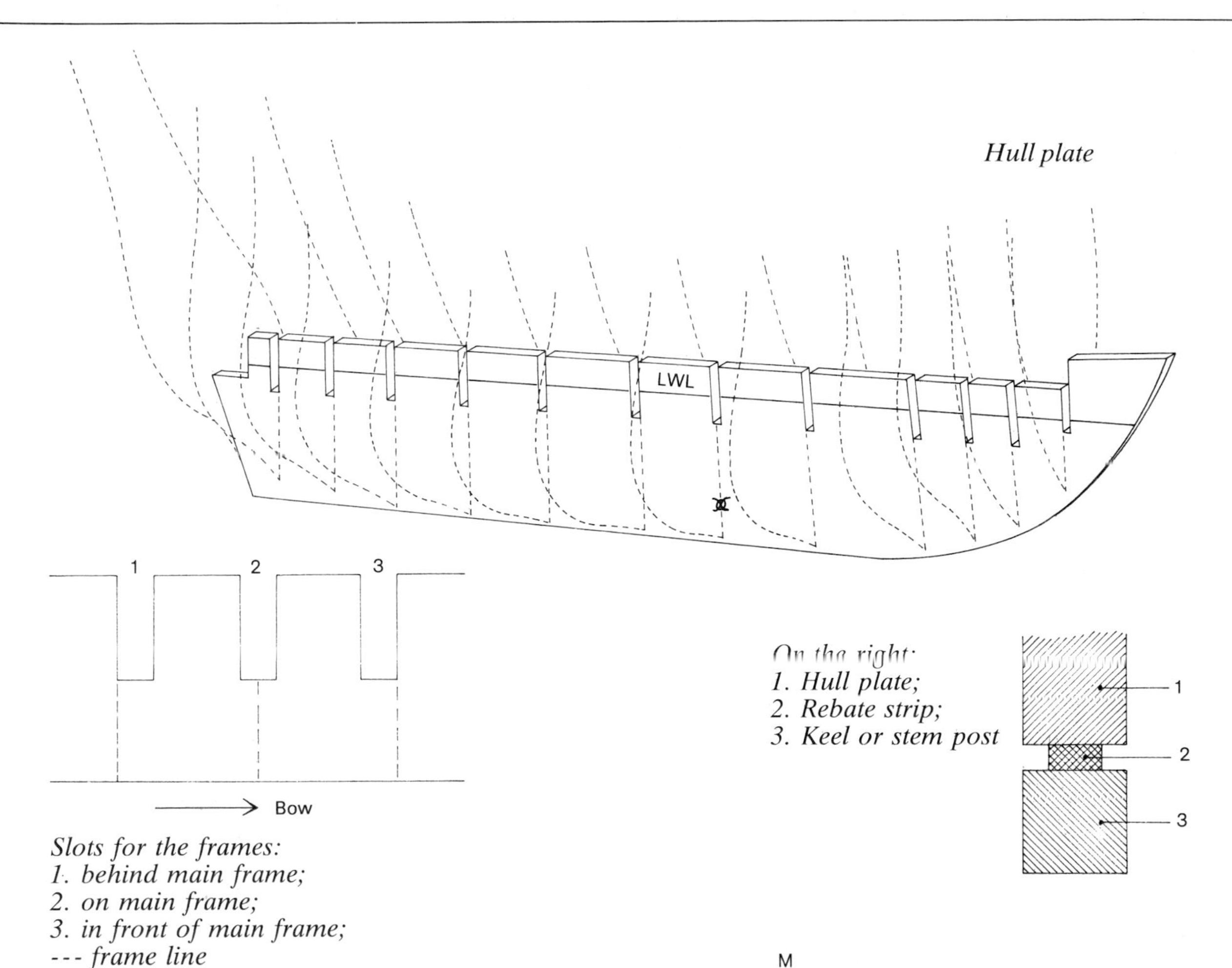

Hull plate

Slots for the frames:
1. behind main frame;
2. on main frame;
3. in front of main frame;
--- frame line

On the right:
1. Hull plate;
2. Rebate strip;
3. Keel or stem post

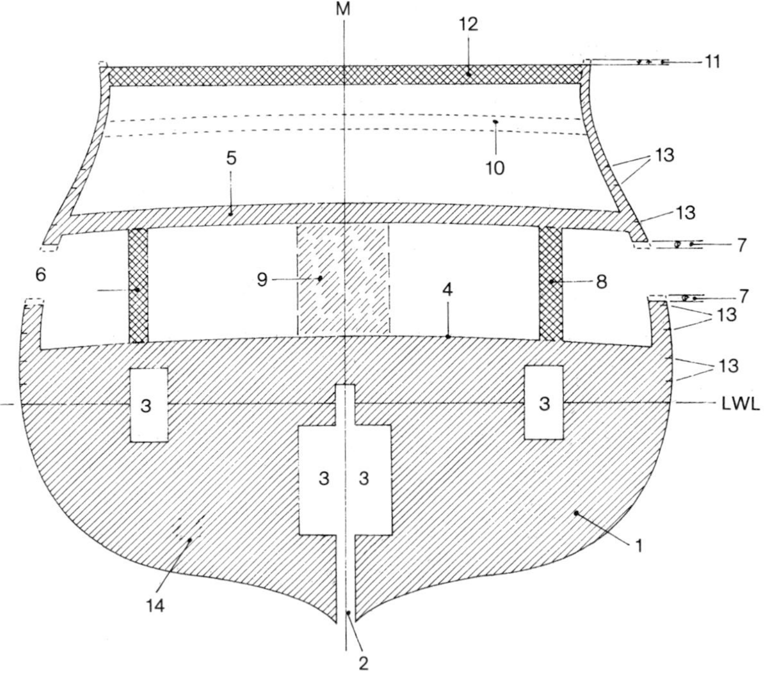

Model frame (plywood):
1. Frame; 2. Slot for hull plate; 3. Opening for bracing rails; 4. Upper edge of battery deck (without planks!); 5. Deck beams of a lower deck; 6. Intersecting gun port; 7. Thickness of lining is deducted;
8. Supplementary support (removed after planking);
9. Supplementary support in lower deck (remains and is painted dark brown);
10. Visible deck beam (installed later in solid wood); 11. Thickness of shipside/bulwark is deducted; 12. Cross-brace (removed after planking);
13. Marking of wales

Internal construction of fully planked hulls

Stern supports/structure of a model with a heavily raked stern. (End of 16th century)

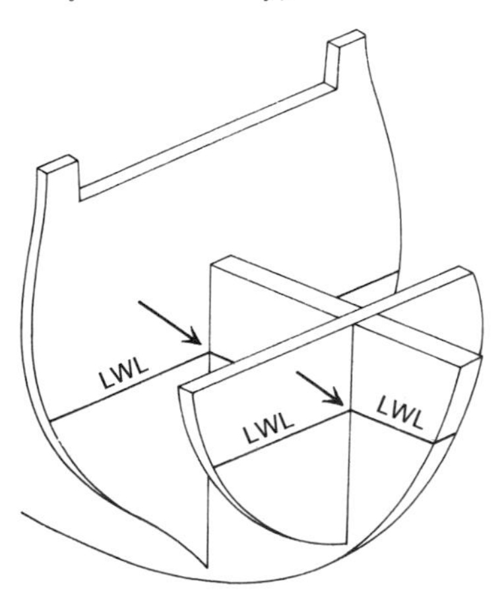

When putting together hull plate and ribs, care should be taken that the LWL coincides exactly in each case

they should be replaced later in solid wood, at the original intervals.
8. It is strongly advised that the frame is reinforced at the top with a cross-brace which will also be sawn out after planking because otherwise there is a danger that the relatively long upper parts of the frame e.g. in the waist, will be bent inwards during planking under the pressure of the timber.

The thus completed building frame is now traced onto a new piece of transparent graph paper, turned over on its centre line and then the other half is traced.

The transparent graph paper is now stuck onto 5-8mm (depending on size of ship) thick plywood with the aid of double-sided tape and sawn out. The drawing can, of course, be traced onto the plywood using carbon paper, but since this takes just as long and carbon paper always makes dirty streaks, I strongly advise the stick-on method!

After cutting out, the important lines – LWL, wale edges and centre line – are scored with a knife, the tape and graph paper are removed, and the lines are gone over again with a fine pen.

Installation of Frames

Now the frames are slotted in sequence into the hull plate and glued with white glue. Take care that the LWL markings on hull plate and frame match up precisely. Note that the utmost care must be taken with both the sawing out of the frames and their insertion into the hull plate. Mistakes and sloppiness here can never be rectified and can wreck your model for good in its early stages.

Bracings

In order to give the hull the necessary stiffness a number of pine battens or bracings 10×10mm are inserted: 2-4 of them directly onto the hull plate and two or three more on the outside to port and starboard respectively. These battens should ensure that the internal constructional members cannot buckle during planking or later.

The rule here is the more solid and stable the better!

Cant frames, filling transoms and hawse pieces

It goes without saying that you do not need to bother with cant frames, filling transoms and hawse pieces if the hull is to be fully planked. Their place is taken by solid in-fill blocks, which are best built up from obechi sheet, as shown in the drawing on the right, then sanded to correct shape. At the bow you should note that holes have to be drilled through the wood for the hawse holes. At the stern remember to cut the openings for the stern gunports and the rudder.

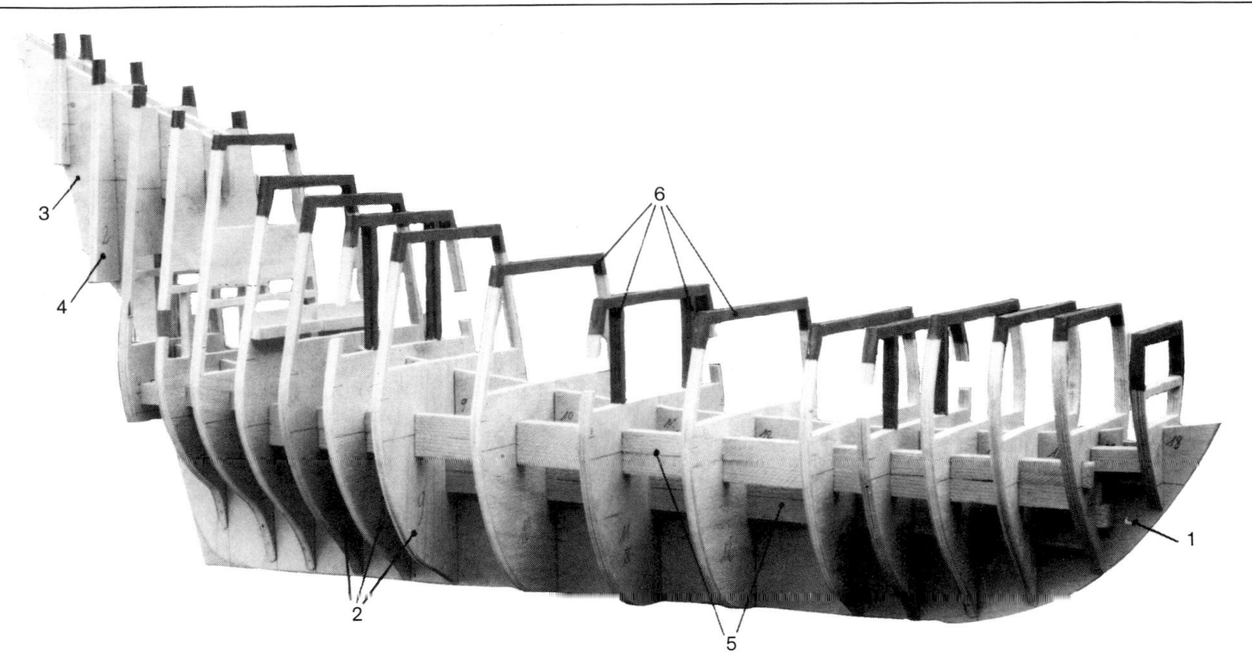

Internal construction of a model:
1. Hull plate; 2. Frames; 3. Stern supports/stays; 4. Ribs inserted into the stern supports/stays; 5. Bracing rails; 6. The dark pieces are supplementary supports and braces which are removed after planking

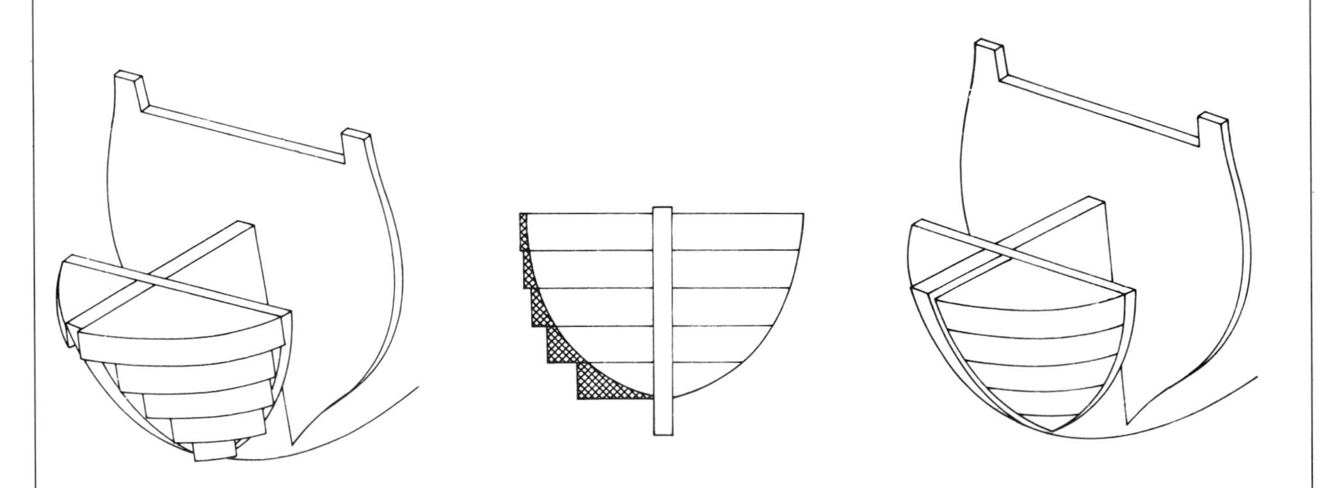

Solid filling pieces e.g. in obeche wood instead of cant frames and filling transoms

Wales

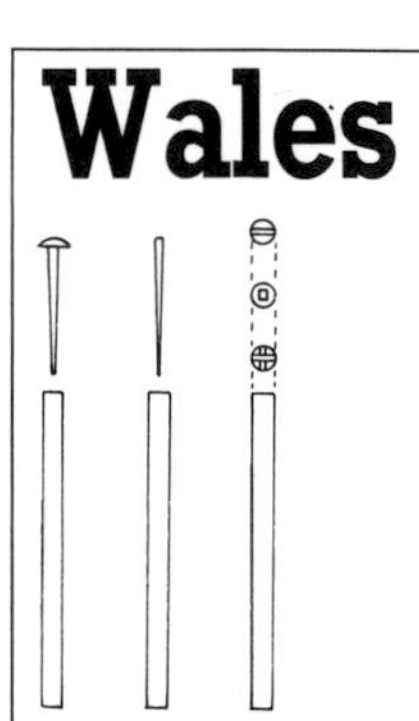

Wooden dowels were expanded using a wooden or iron splitting-pin or nail

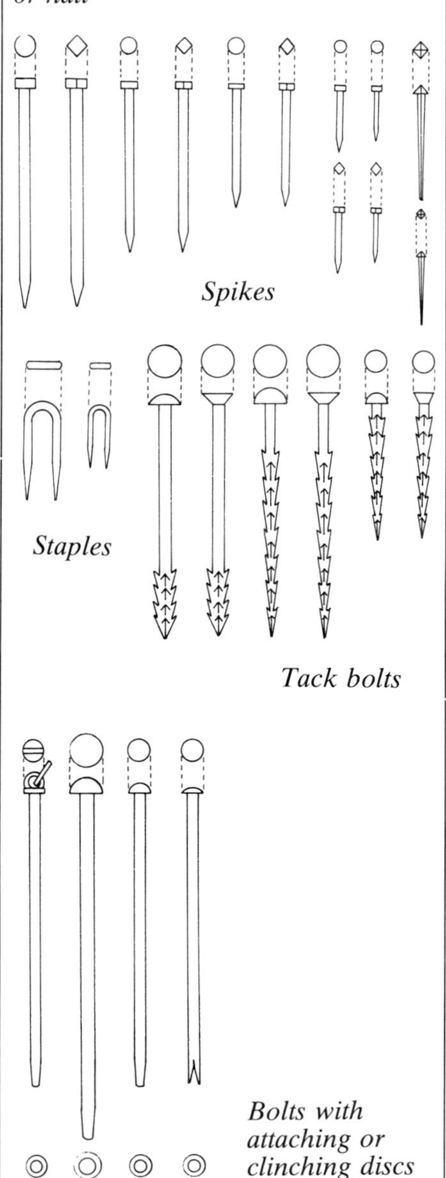

Bolts with attaching or clinching discs

Before the wales and the planks can be attached, all the frames have to be bevelled correctly. This means that the outside edges of all the frames are angled to a greater or lesser extent to follow the run of the hull, so as to provide a solid support for the strakes. This work is carried out with the aid of a thin bevel batten, which enables you to see clearly the angle required. The actual bevelling is done with a fine rasp or a file and glasspaper, and at the bow and stern a sharp knife or chisel, although you must be extremely careful not to remove any material inside the frame outline, otherwise the correct shape of the hull is lost. If you leave all the bevelling work until the frames have been fitted, you run the risk of loosening the entire hull framework, so the approximate angle is cut before the frames are assembled. With the frames in place the precise final angle can be sanded into them.

The angle of bevel is found on the waterline plan, and many modellers go to the trouble of drawing their own bevel plan, although my own view is that this is unnecessary effort except in the case of a frame model.

The wales were a series of heavy planks, the position of which is shown on the plan. They were about the same width as the hull planking, but were thicker, with the result that they projected 3-4ins beyond the planking on 16th and 17th century ships, and 2-3ins on 18th and 19th century vessels. Their top and bottom edges were very slightly rounded off. These wales were attached to the frames before the planking.

N.B. When fitting the wales – and this applies to all the other planking – never attach several strakes at one time on one side. Always work alternately: one strake to starboard and one strake to port.

The wales are fixed to the frames, following markings on the frames' edges. Take the greatest care that they have a regular and smooth run, without flat spots and sudden bends. The wales are pinned or dowelled in the same way as the planking (see PLANKING).

Special forms of planking were developed in England in the 17th and 18th centuries, which were later adopted by a few continental nations. These were anchor stock, top and butt and hook and butt planking and are illustrated on the opposite page.

Top and butt, hook and butt and anchor stock planks are best cut in a special jig. The planks are first cut to approximate shape, then clamped between two metal templates (brass, at least 3mm thick) and sanded to exact profile.

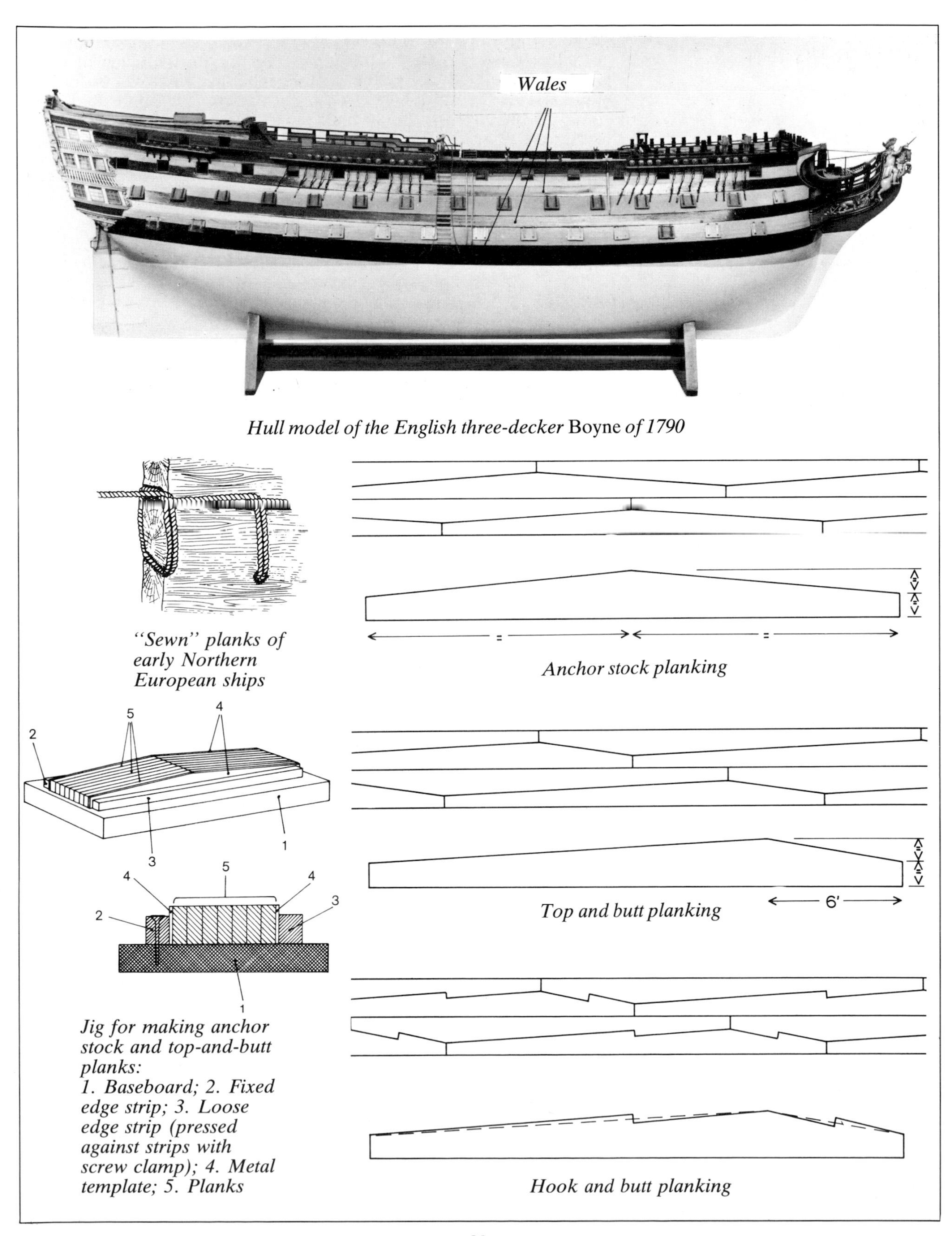

Hull model of the English three-decker Boyne *of 1790*

"Sewn" planks of early Northern European ships

Anchor stock planking

Jig for making anchor stock and top-and-butt planks: 1. Baseboard; 2. Fixed edge strip; 3. Loose edge strip (pressed against strips with screw clamp); 4. Metal template; 5. Planks

Top and butt planking

Hook and butt planking

Planking

Nailing or treenailing the planks

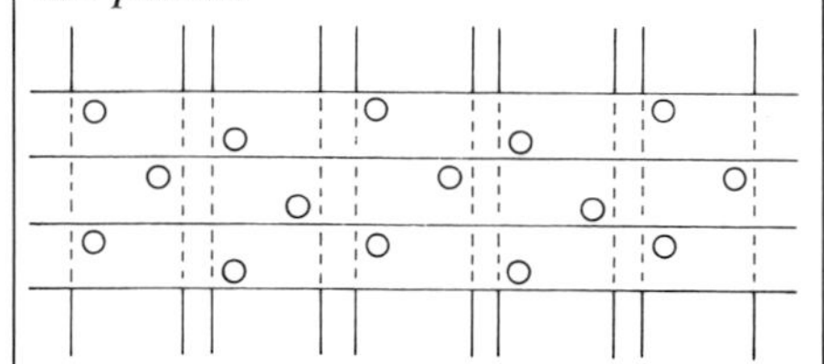

Planks narrower than 8″

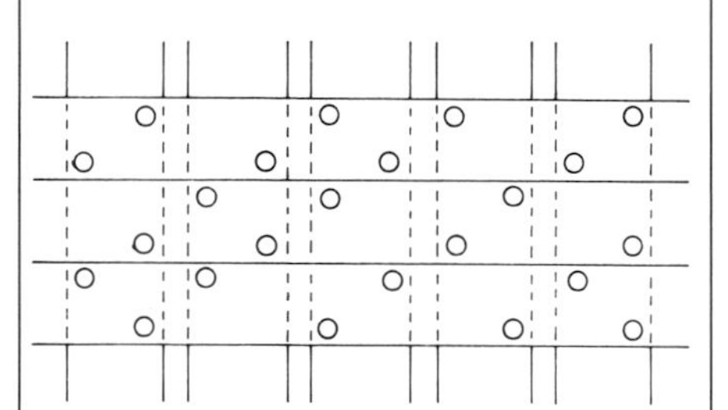

Planks from 8″-11″

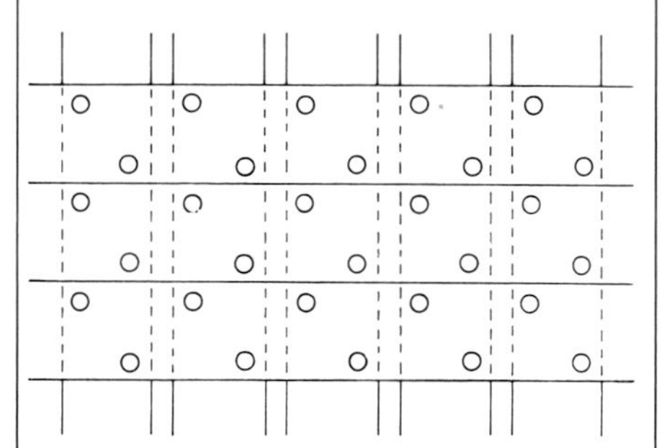

Planks wider than 11″

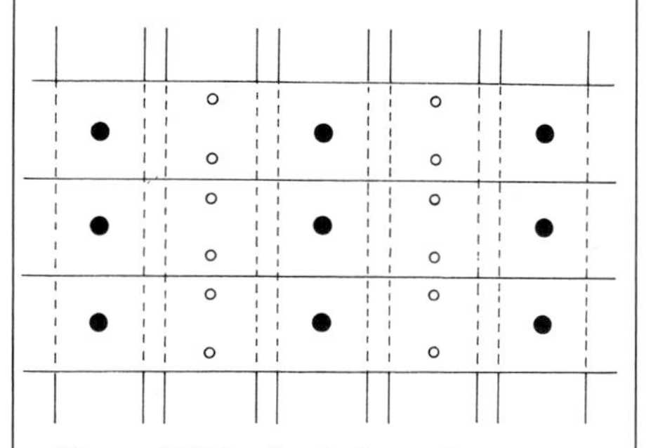

Up to 1700 plank fastening was often alternate iron bolts (black) and wooden dowels or iron bolts of different size

We have to draw a distinction between two systems of planking:
1. Clinker. In this case the planks overlap, with the higher always overlapping the lower. This system evolved from the North. Viking ships, the North European ships of the Middle Ages and some ships' boats to this day are clinker built.
2. Carvel. Here the individual strakes are butt-joined to each other. Carvel planking came from the Mediterranean, and came to predominate on larger ships in general during the 14th century.

Double planking

For modelling purposes, by far the most practical method of planking is to attach it in two layers. This does involve more work, but you will find it much easier to fit the planking really neatly and accurately.
The first stage is to fit a base layer of planking to the whole hull. For this use strips of obechi or lime, about 1/16in thick and 1/4-5/16in wide. As you do not need to worry about end joints in the strakes, each plank can be bent round the full length of the hull and attached to all the frames. To provide extra rigidity, balsa, pine or obechi strips can be glued between the frames on the inside of the hull. Strong curves in planks, e.g. on the bow, should be preformed. Some manufacturers offer all but useless machines for this and with steam, which is often recommended, it is all too easy to scald the fingers. The best method – it was used in original ship-building too – is water and fire: you wet your plank and then bend it as required over a candle flame.
At this stage wood filler paste is applied over the entire hull, and subsequently sanded off again. This is repeated until every crack, groove, dent and bulge has entirely disappeared. This is one of the great advantages of double planking: you can correct mistakes and irregularities without any difficulty.
The second advantage is that the actual run of the planks can be marked accurately on the hull. To do this, divide up the hull at the midships frame into divisions the same size as the width of the planks. You can now count the number of planks, and divide each frame in turn into the same number of divisions. If the points thus marked are joined with a thin bevel batten, you will obtain the exact run of the strakes. At their ends the planks should never be narrower than 0.5, nor wider than 1.5 times the midship width; instead you have to work in stealers which taper in one direction or the other, as drawn on the right. Once you have found the exact shape of the strakes, they can be cut from the genuine solid wood planking material or thin hardwood veneer, and glued in place, remembering to observe the butt joints now. The planks were originally about 20-24ft long, and were butted together according to the pattern shown on the right.
Until the end of the 17th century the width of the planks varied between 18ins and 13ins, (the older, the wider), in the 18th century between 14ins and 11ins, and in the 19th century the average was 12ins. The thickness of the strakes varied from 3 or 4 inches at the bilges to 5 or 6 inches on either side of the wales.

Nails and treenails

The various patterns of nailing and treenailing the planking are shown on the left. The rows of nails or treenails follow the line of the original frames, of course, hence many will need to be fitted between the model's frames. Wood nails (known as treenails) had a diameter of 1½-2ins. Metal nails in planking had a head diameter of about 5/8in and bolts had heads up to about 2½ins diameter with a height of the head about 5/8 of the diameter. Where washers were used with bolts, they had a diameter of 1.25 × the head diameter.

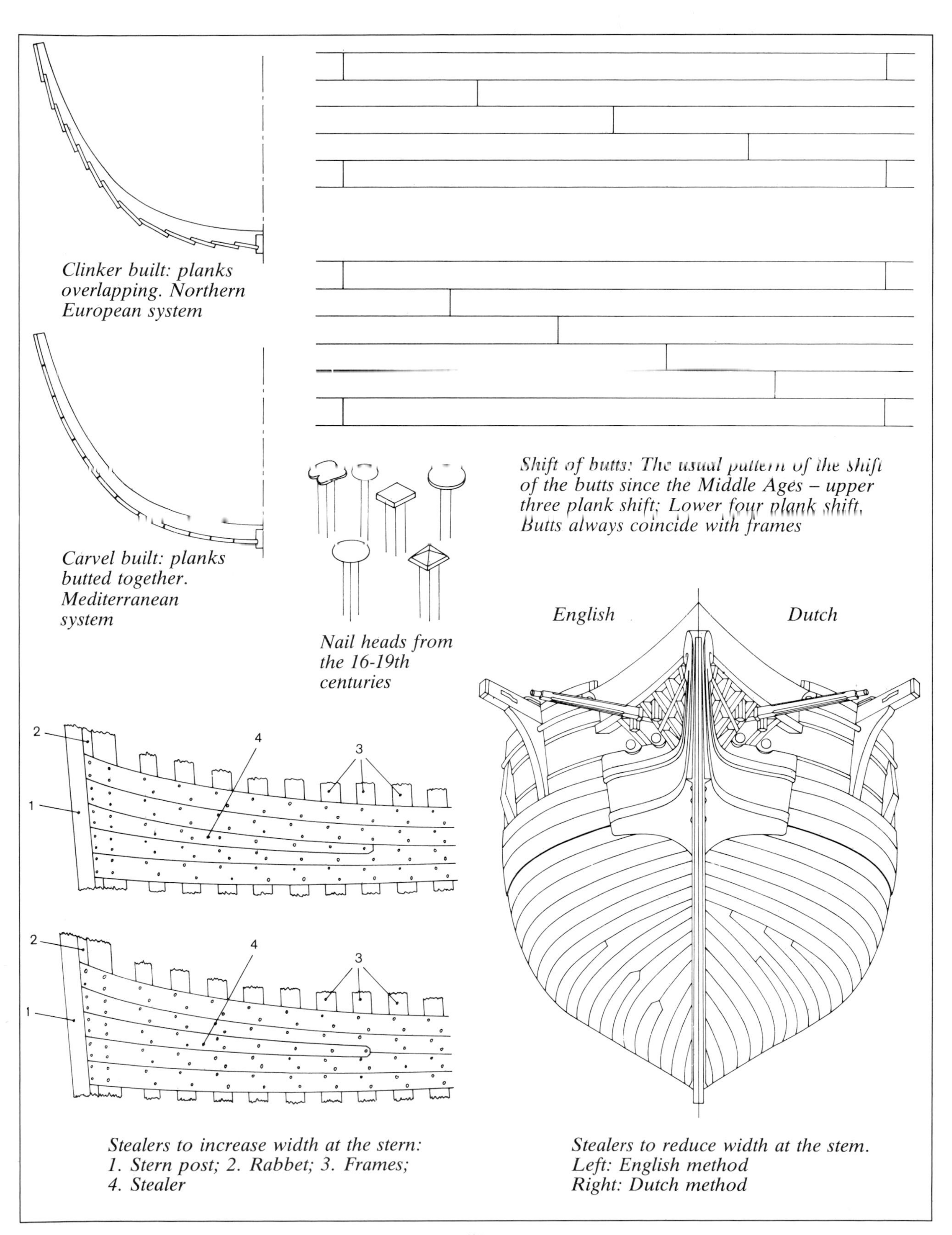

Clinker built: planks overlapping. Northern European system

Carvel built: planks butted together. Mediterranean system

Nail heads from the 16-19th centuries

Shift of butts: The usual pattern of the shift of the butts since the Middle Ages – upper three plank shift; Lower four plank shift. Butts always coincide with frames

Stealers to increase width at the stern: 1. Stern post; 2. Rabbet; 3. Frames; 4. Stealer

Stealers to reduce width at the stem. Left: English method Right: Dutch method

Stern planking

Right into the late 15th century a ship's hull ended in a more or less round stern, which was built on the same principle as the bow. In the Mediterranean and on many smaller ships this method of construction never varied. On larger ships the square tuck predominated after the end of the 15th century. This square tuck – it was slightly curved in the 17th century – is best made from obechi wood and attached to the final frame. It can then be planked with strips of veneer. The planks ran, as shown in the drawing, from the sternpost diagonally downwards on both sides at an angle of 30° to 45°, and were frequently pierced for gunports or loading ports.
After 1620 the British began to do away with the square tuck, and to replace it with a round tuck, which became flatter towards the top, where it blended into the counter. By about 1725 the other maritime nations had followed the English lead and this form of construction prevailed until well into the 19th century.

Gunports

The framing to the gunports was formed by the main frames at the sides, and the upper and lower cills, which were fitted between the frames.
On a fully planked model this work can be much simplified by constructing the gunport frames individually and glueing them behind the planking. Do check that they match the curve of the planking accurately. It is best to incorporate the gunport frames while you are planking the hull.
The size of the gunports varied according to the size and type of gun, those for carronades being roughly one and a half times the size of those for carriage guns. Actual sizes and spacings varied from ship to ship and should be taken from the drawings.

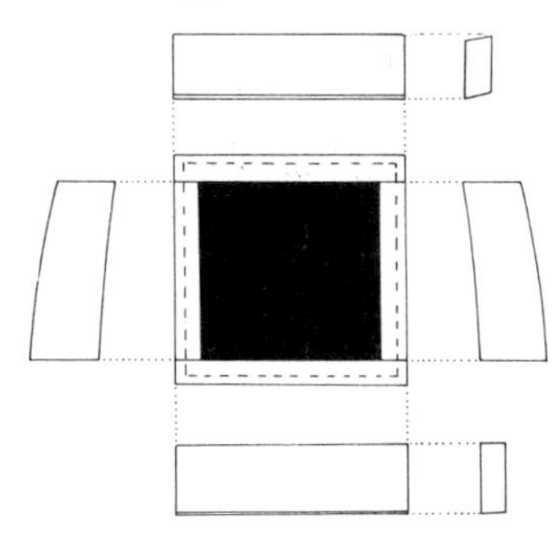

Gunport framing can be built quite simply from 2-3mm wood but make sure that the lining is flush with the hull planking. Note cills are parallel to deck camber.

Fenders

In the Middle Ages and until the middle of the 16th century vertical timber strips known as fenders were fitted to the hull to offer extra rigidity as well as to prevent damage to the outer skin when the ships lay side by side during boarding skirmishes. After the middle of the 16th century only two or three fenders remained; they were fitted abreast the main hatch and were designed to prevent damage to the moulded rails on the ship's side by boats or stores being hoisted inboard by the main yard tackles.
These fenders began to disappear in the latter half of the 18th century on the continent and in the early part of the 19th century in Britain.

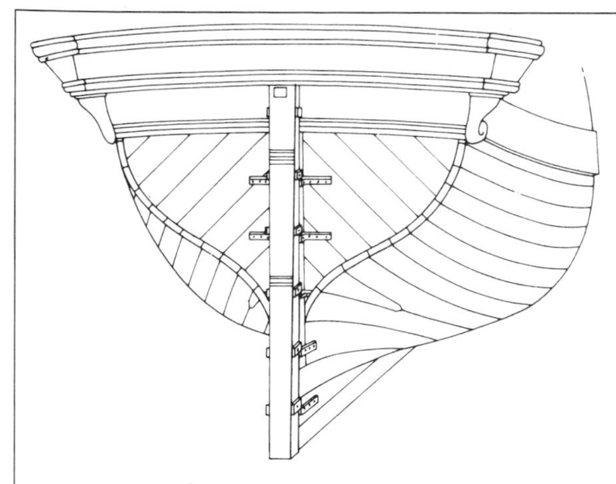

Square tuck stern

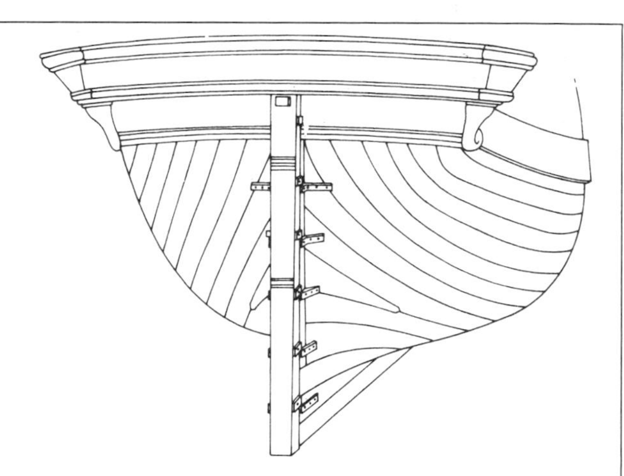

Round tuck stern after 17th century

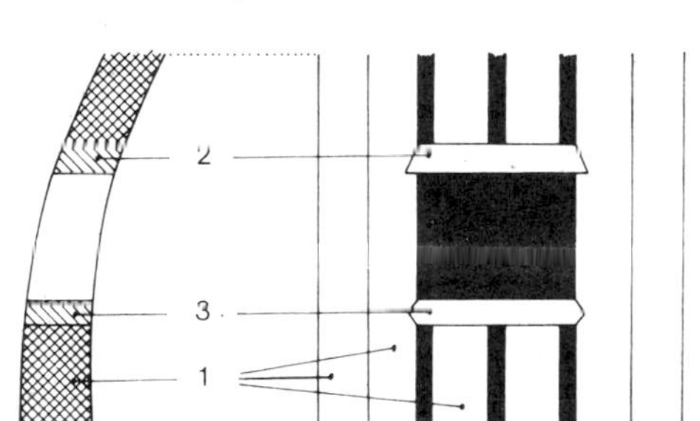

Gunport, frame construction

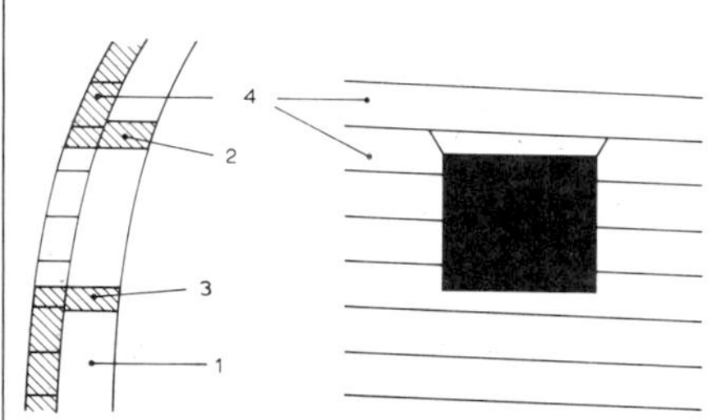

Gunport without port lid

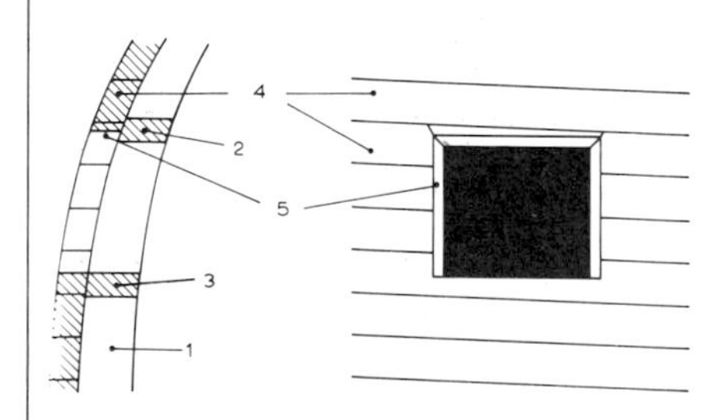

Gunport with port lid

1. Frames; 2. Upper cill;
3. Lower cill; 4. Planking;
5. Rebate for port lids

Original model of a Catalan Nao from the 15th century. The rounded stern and the fenders are clearly seen

Decks

Nails or treenails of the deck planking

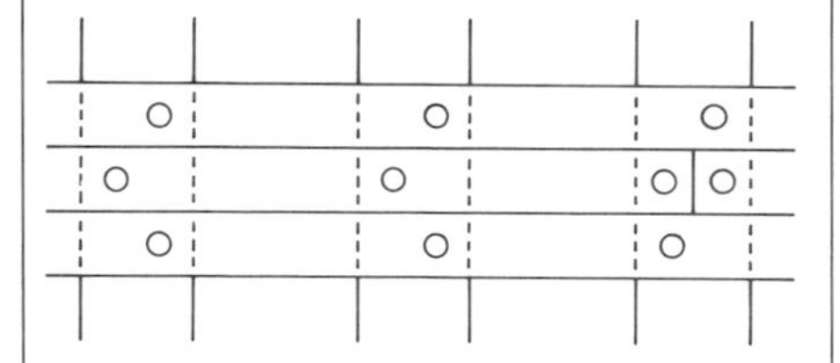

Planks narrower than 6″

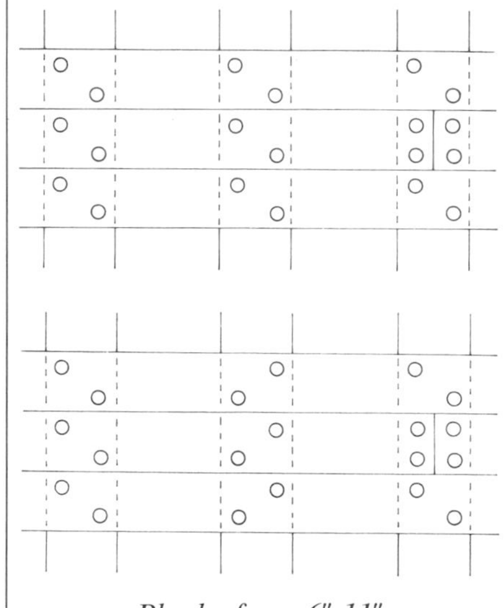

Planks from 6″-11″

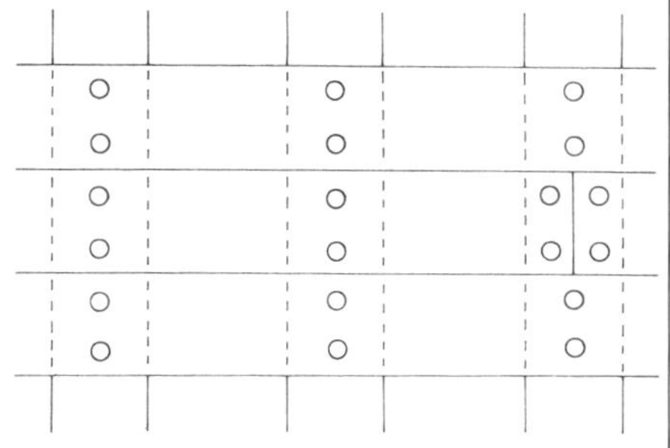

Planks wider than 11″

The fitting of the decks presents no great technical difficulties, but it is vital to make out a precise list of all those things which have to be fitted before a deck is sealed. Among the items most often overlooked are the lower deck guns, the port tackles (see GUNPORT LIDS), bitts, fixed blocks, hemp and chain cables, the main sheet (see SHEETS), etc. Study your plans with the greatest care, and read the chapter THE FITTINGS, if you wish to avoid experiencing unpleasant surprises!

Deck base

The first stage is to make a base, or underlay, for each deck from ·030-·040in (·8 or 1mm) thick plywood, and fit it to the hull. This has two advantages: the deck planking will be easier to fix, and the planks will lie flatter and more evenly.

Make a template from thin card and trim it to an exact fit before transferring the shape to the wood and sawing it out. Incidentally, you will often save much work, time and material if you start the construction of difficult parts by making a card template first, followed by the final wood part when the problems have been ironed out.

Do not forget the openings for the masts, hatches, gratings and companions.

Deck planking

As the decks were usually very light coloured, box or maple are suitable materials for the deck planking; the lower decks can be planked with spruce strips.

The width of the deck planks varied quite widely over the centuries. Before the beginning of the 16th century the width of the deck planks was 12 to 18ins, in the 17th century 10 to 16ins, in the 18th century 8 to 14ins, in the first half of the 19th century 6 to 8ins, and after the middle of the 19th century about 6ins.

The thickness of the deck planking varied slightly from deck to deck; the lower decks were up to 4ins thick, and the upper decks 3ins. The various systems of shifting the deck butts are shown in the drawings on the right.

A gap about ⅜in wide was left between the deck planks, to suit the caulking iron. These seams were caulked with oakum, and paid with tar. On a model the seams can be imitated in the following way: 8 or 10 deck planks are placed in a stack, clamped tightly together, and the narrow sides painted with black cellulose. When these planks are placed edge to edge, a thin black line will always be visible.

Plank joggling

On English and Dutch ships – but very seldom on French – the deck strakes were joggled, especially at the rounded edges close to the bow. The details of this feature are shown in the drawings. Such joggled ends are rather fiddly details to incorporate, but a well-built model should not lack them.

Nails and treenails

The size of nails and treenails followed the same rules as for the hull planking. Please note: on iron framed ships – that is, after 1850 – no treenails or nails should be visible on the model, but the wooden plugs covering the fixing bolts would be and would appear similar to treenails with a cross instead of an end grain.

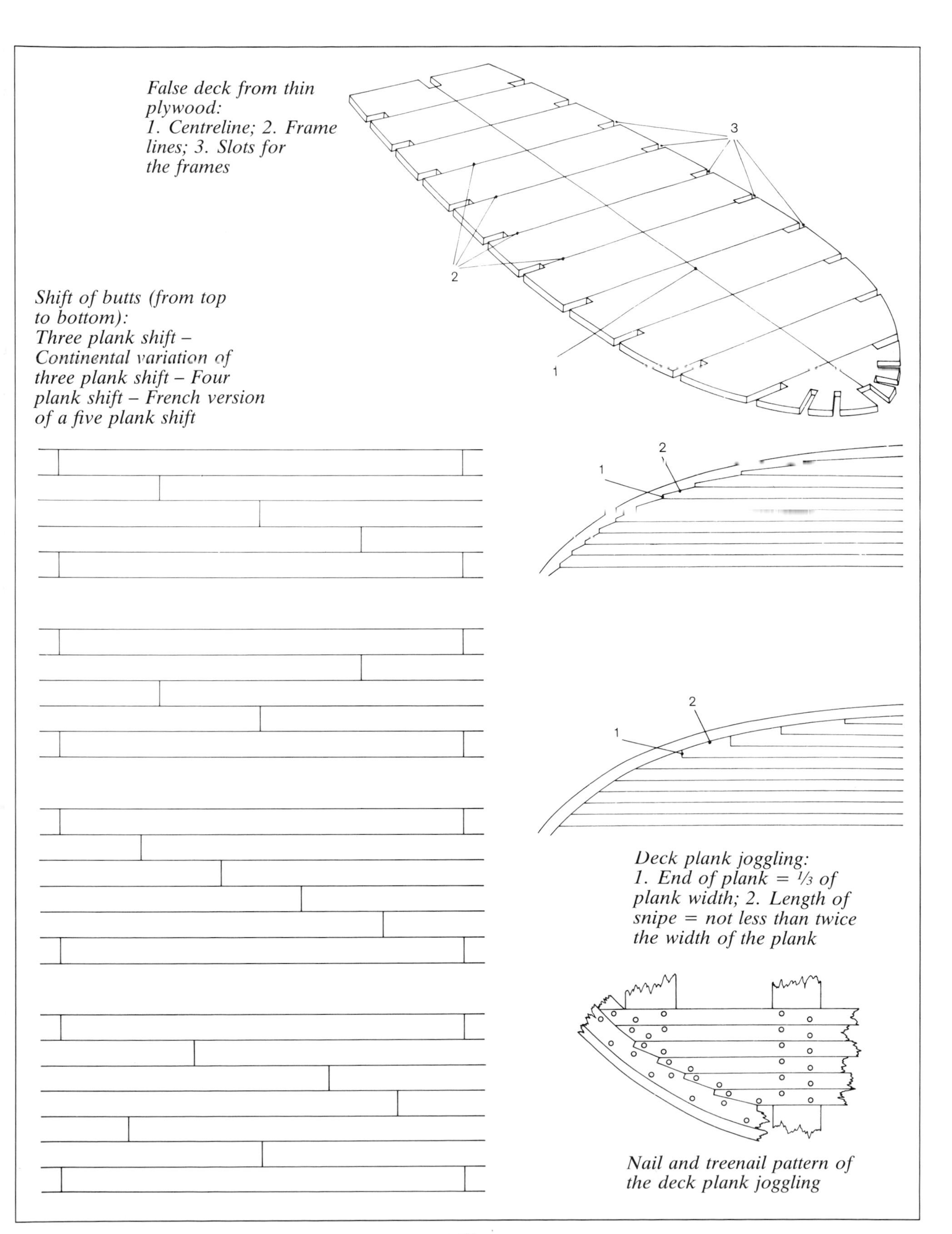

False deck from thin plywood: 1. Centreline; 2. Frame lines; 3. Slots for the frames

Shift of butts (from top to bottom): Three plank shift – Continental variation of three plank shift – Four plank shift – French version of a five plank shift

Deck plank joggling: 1. End of plank = 1/3 of plank width; 2. Length of snipe = not less than twice the width of the plank

Nail and treenail pattern of the deck plank joggling

Marking the waterline

Before the model ship's hull can be fitted to the display stand, the underwater hull has to be completed. The first task here is to mark the waterline on on the hull.
Set the model up in its jig in such a position that the waterline lies exactly parallel to the baseboard, i.e. raise the bow until this is so (see DIMENSIONS).
The waterline is marked on with a sharp pencil, which is attached to a wood block. Check that the point is exactly at the waterline (see drawing right). By carefully sliding the block along the baseboard and allowing the pencil to be pulled along, the waterline can be marked on the hull.

The underwater finish

Below the waterline the hull was usually painted with wood-coal tar, which coloured it a dark brown, or almost black. Sulphur was often added to the tar to offer protection against worm attack, and this was standard practice from the late 16th century on. This resulted in a yellowish-grey colouring. The alternative was to paint the underwater hull with white lead paint, which produced a dirty white finish.
As a further protective measure wooden sheathing in the form of elm or fir planks was nailed to the underwater hull (for modelling purposes it is best to use strips of veneer), and was fixed with a great number of large headed nails.

Lead sheathing

The Portuguese and the Spanish, whose ships were subject to attack by the teredo worm in tropical waters, experimentally sheathed the underwater hull with thin lead sheets from the early 16th century onwards, and these again were fixed with closely spaced, large-headed nails. These sheets were from 48×21ins to 86×64ins in size, and were butted up edge to edge, rather than overlapped. The model builder is advised to use ·012ins thick brass or copper sheets, which are blackened before fixing, then attached with contact cement. Thin tin sheet could also be used.

Coppering

Shortly after the middle of the 18th century the practice of sheathing the underwater hull with copper sheets began, the British 32 gun frigate *Alarm* being the first ship to be treated in this way, and by 1780 this method was predominant.
The copper sheets for the model are cut from ·004ins thick copper foil; the sheets were approximately 48×15ins in size in England and Holland, and slightly larger in France.
The best way of imitating the nails is by means of an embossing tool, or – even better – with a converted tracing wheel (available at sewing machine accessory shops), as shown on the right. The nail heads were from ⅜ to 1¼ins in diameter.
The copper sheets usually overlapped from the bow to the stern, and from the top to the bottom although there were occasional exceptions. Consequently when fixing them, you must proceed in the opposite sequence. The copper sheets are best fixed in place with contact cement. Finally clean them up *very* thoroughly with the finest grade of steel wool and a glass fibre brush, and immediately apply a coat of protective lacquer (cellulose clear lacquer). Take care – unlacquered copper will show every fingerprint after a few hours due to oxidisation. Do *not* try to age copper artificially – in 3 or 4 years it will acquire exactly the right patina, even under the lacquer.

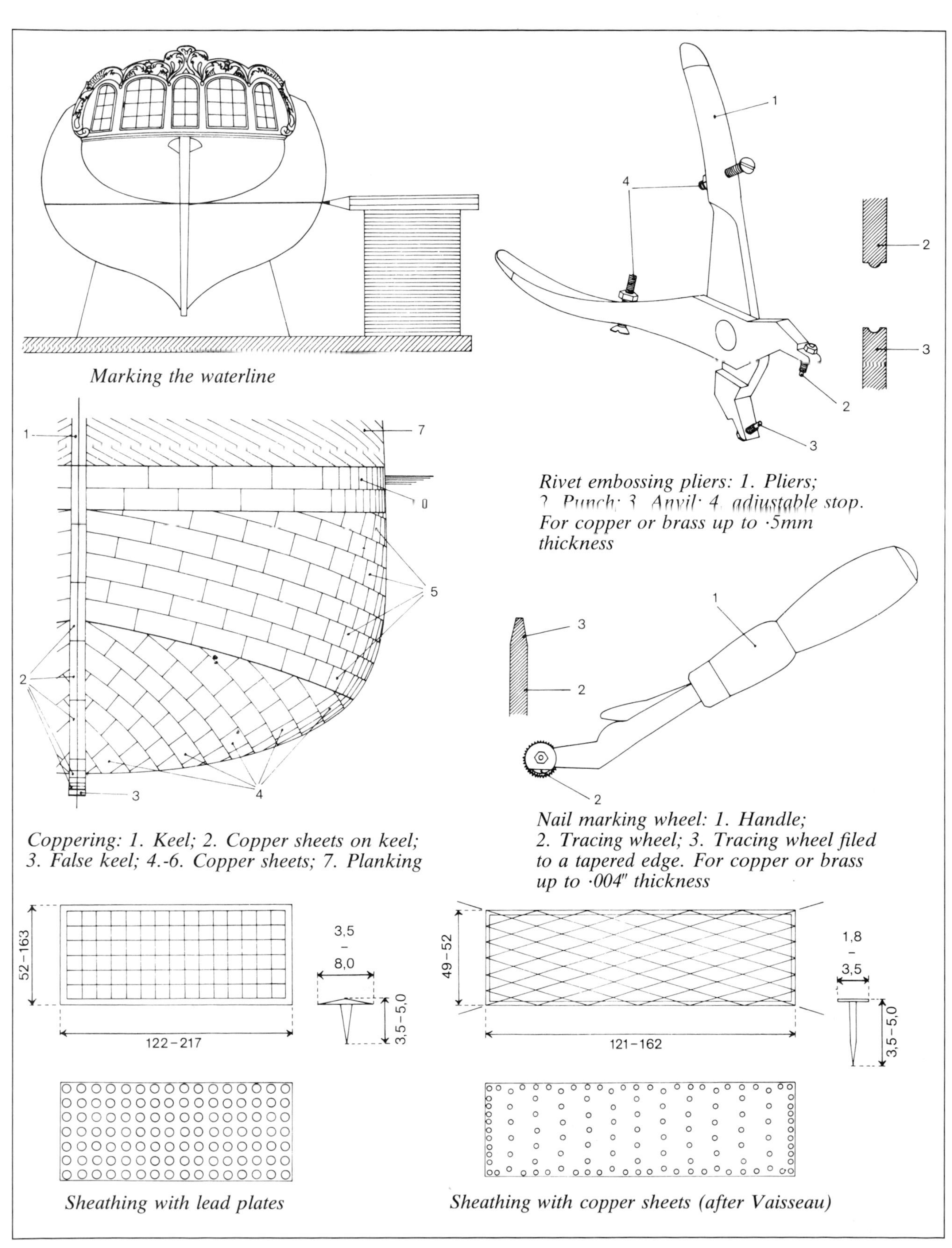

Marking the waterline

Rivet embossing pliers: 1. Pliers; 2. Punch; 3. Anvil; 4. adjustable stop. For copper or brass up to ·5mm thickness

Coppering: 1. Keel; 2. Copper sheets on keel; 3. False keel; 4.-6. Copper sheets; 7. Planking

Nail marking wheel: 1. Handle; 2. Tracing wheel; 3. Tracing wheel filed to a tapered edge. For copper or brass up to ·004" thickness

Sheathing with lead plates

Sheathing with copper sheets (after Vaisseau)

Rails and bulwarks

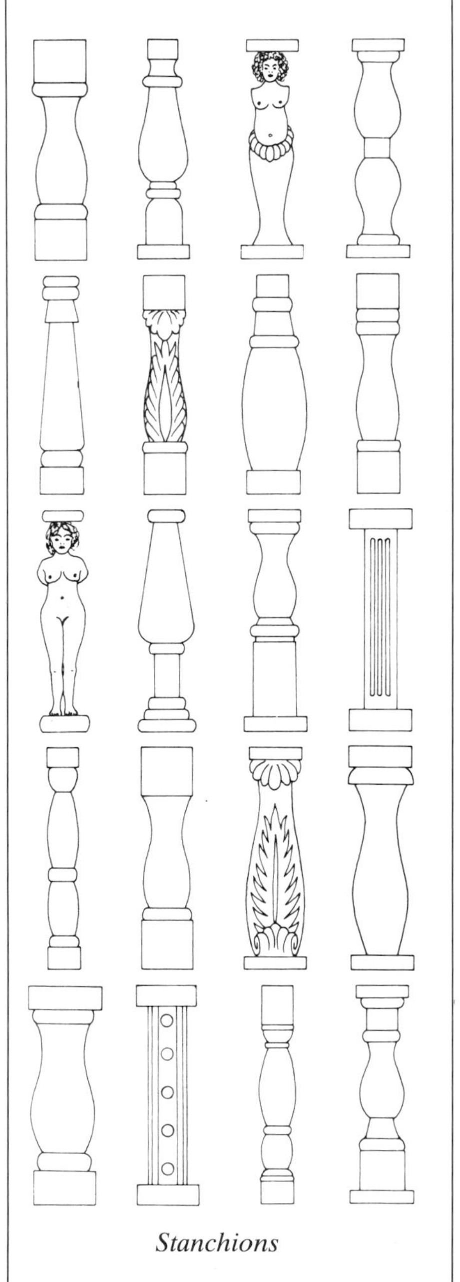

Stanchions

The upper part of the planking in the region of the weather decks (main deck at the waist, quarter deck, poop and forecastle) was termed the bulwark. The bulwark was finished off at the top by a rail. By the middle of the 16th century the top frame timbers were taken up as far as the rail and thus served as bulwark stanchions. The bulwarks were only a foot or two high and were not yet planked on the inside, so the upper part of the frame timbers remained visible in this area.
After the middle of the 16th century the Spanish, followed soon afterwards by other nations, began to plank the inside of the bulwarks. A further rail, the fife rail, appeared above the main rail and was supported on it by short wooden stanchions, frequently plain in small merchant ships and ornamentally turned in large merchant ships and warships.
By the 18th century the low quarterdeck bulwarks were surmounted by a waist high rail, the roughtree rail, and the bulwarks in the waist had risen almost to the height of the quarterdeck and forecastle. The waist bulwark, and in warships with their large crews the roughtree rail, were topped by nettings in which the crew's hammocks were stowed. The forecastle bulwarks had almost disappeared, leaving the timber heads exposed as belaying points.
In the last decade of the 18th century the quarter deck bulwarks of warships were planked or berthed up to a height of about 4ft, with a square forward end in place of the former elegant scrolls or volutes. Shortly after 1800 the forecastle followed suit. Shallow hammock nettings were then built into their tops and the nets in the waist were replaced by deep wooden "nettings" to the same height, giving the appearance of a continuous bulwark the whole length of the ship.
Although smaller merchant ships never had internally planked bulwarks, the development of the larger merchant ships ran parallel with that of warships until the middle of the 18th century. However, in the middle of the 18th century it became more and more common to omit the interior bulwark planking on merchant ships. In the 19th century a further development took place. The top frame timbers were extended only as far as the level of the waterway, and covered there with a covering board. At every second frame a separate bulwark stanchion was added, planked on the outside only, and capped with the main rail. Further small stanchions were fitted on top of the rail, supporting a fife rail, and this area was also planked on the outside.
For the modeller, there is little point in fitting separate bulwark stanchions, and it is best to extend the top frame timbers up to the level of the rail in all cases. On ships before the middle of the 16th century on small merchant ships, and on large merchant ships after the middle of the 18th century the only point to remember is that the bulwark stanchions were located over every second original frame, i.e. further bulwark stanchions have to be fixed between the bulwark supports which result from the model's own constructional frames, to correspond with the original frame spacing. This is best done by glueing in square strips of wood after planking is complete. The breaks of the quarter deck and poop were usually protected by a rail or barricade. It was unusual for the break of the forecastle to be fitted in this way except in large ships. This rail took the form of an open balustrade, supported by simple square or round columns until the early 17th century. After this time they were usually replaced by artistically turned or carved balustrade supports, some of which are illustrated on the left. In some cases they were gilded, and the spaces between the supports were quite often filled out with decorative latticework.

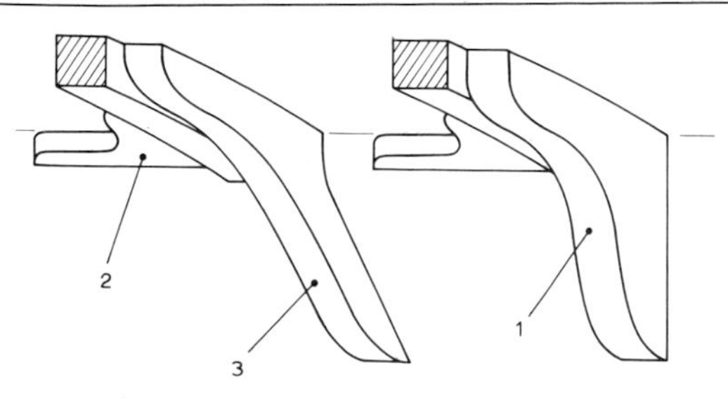

1. Hanging knee; 2. Lodging knee;
3. Cant knee

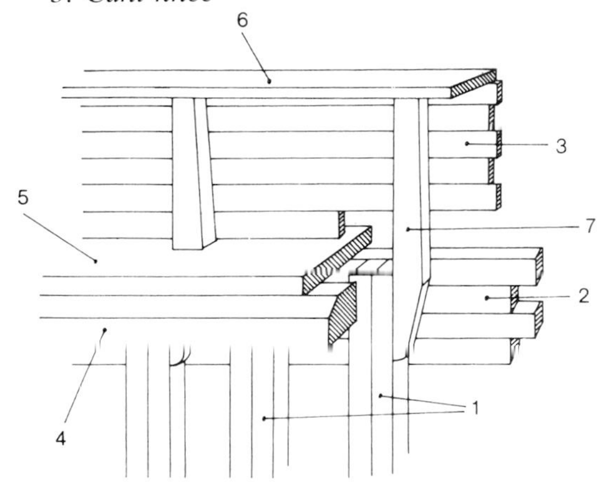

19th century merchant ship bulwarks:
1. Frames; 2. Planking; 3. Bulwark planking;
4. Waterway; 5. Covering board; 6. Rail;
7. Frame extension

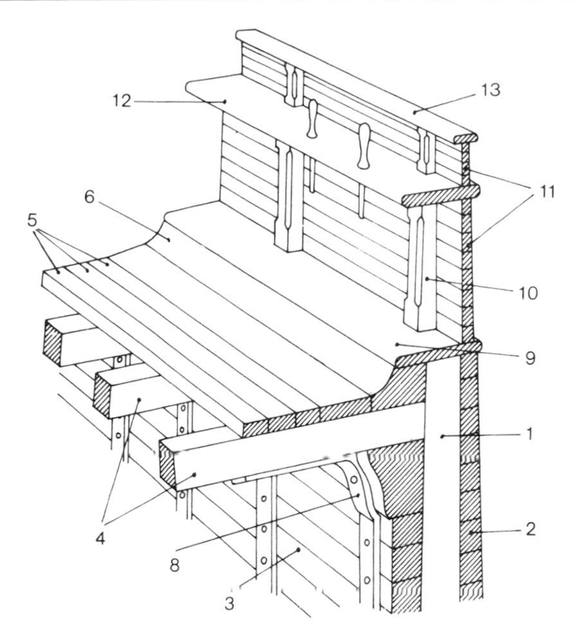

20th century merchant ship bulwarks;
1. Frame; 2. Outer planking; 3. Ceiling;
4. Deck beams; 5. Deck planks; 6. Waterway;
8. Iron knee; 9. Covering board;
10. Bulwark stanchions; 11. Bulwark planking;
12. Main rail; 13. Topgallant or fife rail

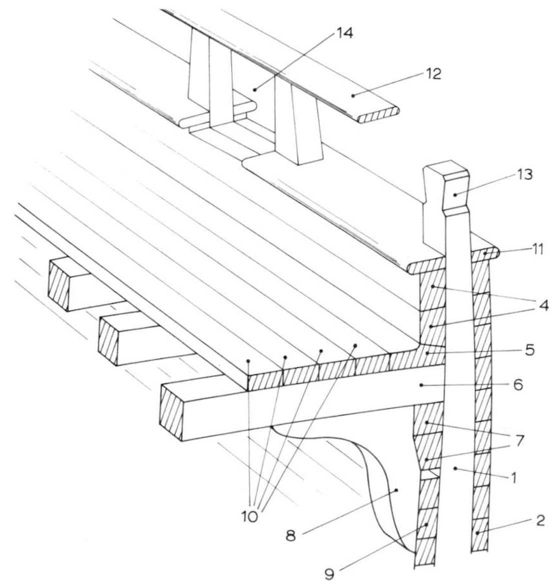

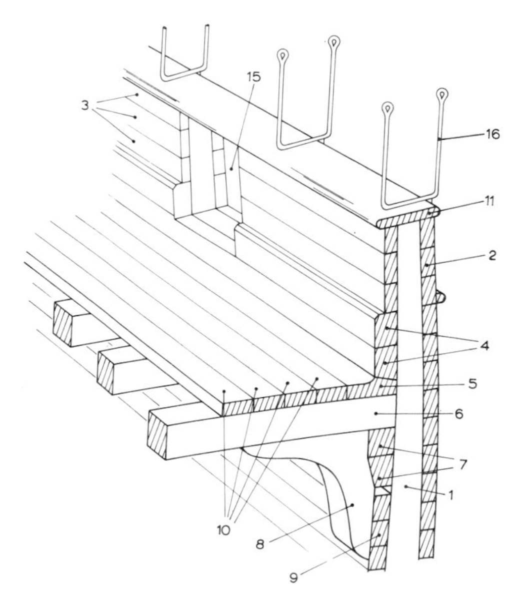

Quarterdeck of warship with open rail (left) and bulwarks (right): 1. Frame; 2. Outer planking; 3. Quickstuff; 4. Spirketting; 5. Waterway; 6. Beam; 7. Clamps; 8. Knee; 9. Upperdeck quickstuff; 10. Deck planks; 11. Planksheer; 12. Roughtree rail; 13. Timberhead; 14. Gunport; 15. Carronade port; 16. Hammock crane

The stern

The richly ornamented sterns which were for centuries a proud feature of any ship were a Spanish/Italian invention of the late 16th century, which was adopted so quickly and with such enthusiasm by all other sea-faring nations that soon the armament and protection of the after part of the ship became sadly neglected in favour of carved garlands and figures, galleries and balconies, and the stern became the most vulnerable area of the whole ship.

It was without doubt the baroque period which saw the pinnacle of this development. Pierre Puget, whom Louis XIV of France commissioned to add the final artistic flourish to the ships of his fleet, devoted himself to his task with an alarming passion. The story goes that Puget loaded down the stern of many ships with such a conglomeration of heavy, carved and richly gilded oak saints, ancient gods and goddesses scrollwork, emblems, coats of arms, balustrades, garlands and sea monsters, that the beleagured captains had most of the decoration torn down and thrown overboard shortly after launch, in order to make their stern-heavy ships seaworthy. The stories may well be true . . .

It was the French again who tried to hang on to the decorated stern right into the first half of the 19th century, until they too had to bow to the demands of stability and armament at the stern, finally relinquishing the richly decorated stern around 1840.

To the modeller the stern presents no major constructional difficulties but this is more than outweighed by the work involved in carving and similar tasks. The more glorious, the more richly decorated the stern, the easier it is to fall in love with a ship; however, when you come to reproduce it, it is a different matter!

The virtue of knowing your limitations is never more valuable than when you are struck by the sight of a glorious stern.

Lights

As already described in the section GLASS, there has alway been a wide variety of methods of representing this material on a model ship as real glass is very rarely suitable.

Until far into the 17th century the windows of ships were made up of fairly small glass panes linked by lead strips, the advantage of this arrangement being that the small panes were more flexible and less likely to break than large panes. These lead strips are an essential feature on every model ship.

The simplest method is either to draw them on the window with black Indian ink, or make them from thin, blackened copper or silver wire and glue them to the front of the window.

However, they certainly look best when the lead strips are embedded *in* the glass. To do this, the lead strips are made from thin, blackened wire, then placed in a silicone rubber mould, and the glass added in the form of clear casting resin. Try it once, and you will never bother with any other method.

The window frame is made up from thin wood strips, and glued on to the window.

In the case of transparent windows, it is as well to paint the area inside the ship a dark colour – black, dark brown, or dark blue, of which the latter looks most attractive.

Construction of lights: 1. Frame; 2. Pane; 3. Lead strips; 4. Square pattern; 5. Diamond pattern

Stern of the British ship of the line Boyne *of 1790*

Sterns

Dat Meerswin *Hamburg cog 1475*

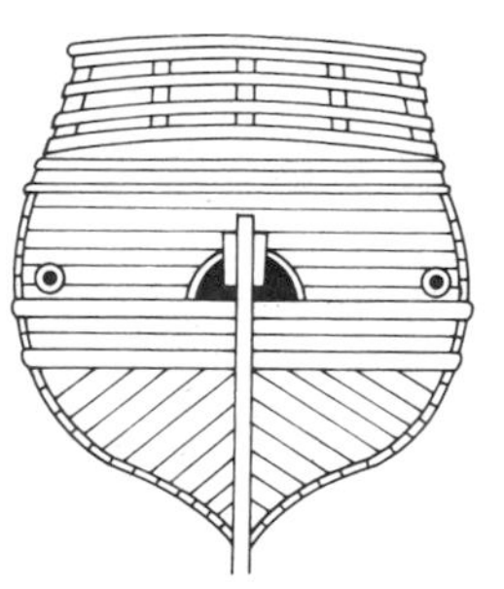

Niña *Spanish caravel 1492*

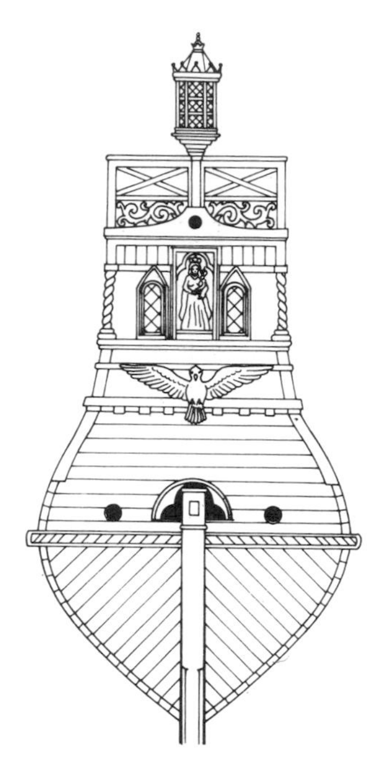

Santisima Madre
Spanish galleon 1500

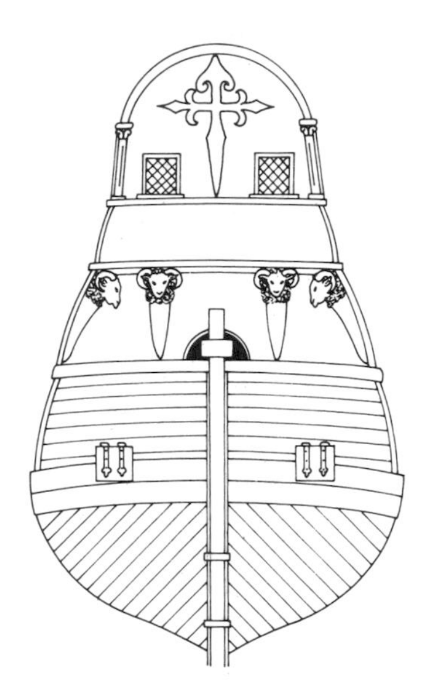

Sant Iago
Spanish galleon 1540

Elisabeth Jonas
English galleon 1580

Golden Harp
Irish galleon 1580

Corona Aurea
Spanish oared galleon 1585

San Michele
Genoan galleon 1600

Angelo
Neapolitan 1695

Halve Maen
Dutch two-decker 1666

La Couronne
French two-decker 1636

St. Michael
English three-decker 1667

Star
Dutch flute 1670

Grosse Jacht
Brandenburg yacht 1678

Sterns

Royal Caroline *English yacht 1749*

Royal George *English three-decker 1715*

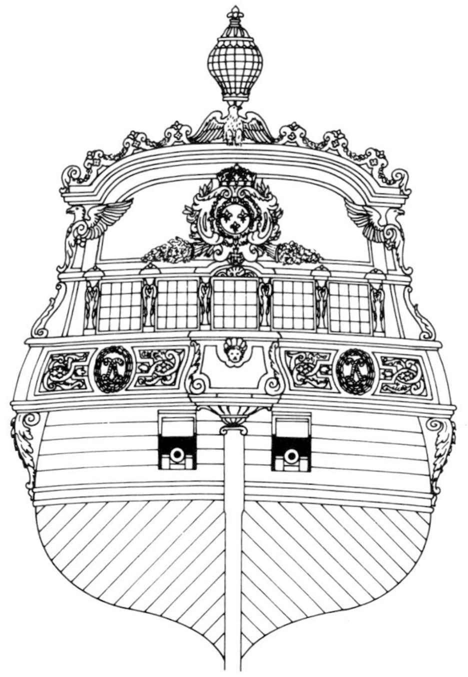

L'Aigle *French two-decker 1690*

Padmos *Dutch East Indiaman 1722*

Iydland *Danish two-decker 1739*

Jupiter *Swedish privateer frigate 1760*

Fürst Wladimir *Russian three-decker 1780*

Rattlesnake *American brig sloop 1780*

L'Achille *French two-decker 1790*

Le Sphinx *French paddlewheel driven corvette 1829*

Illustrous *British two-decker 1789*

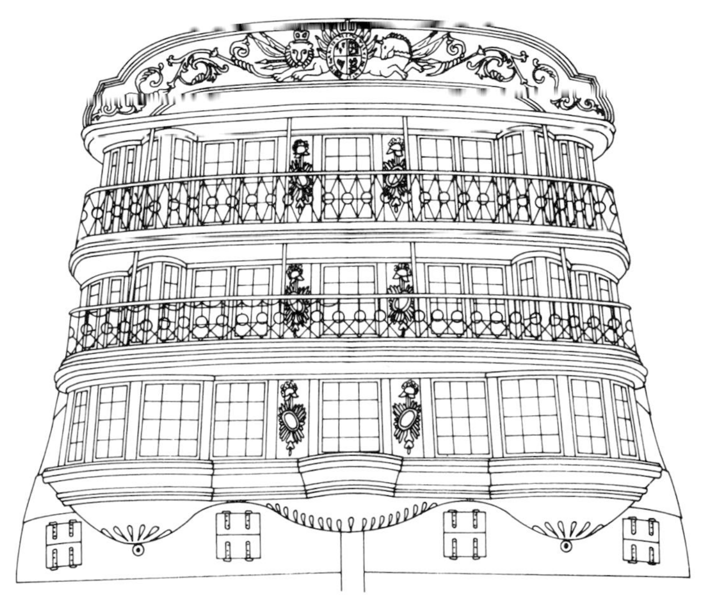

Royal Adelaide *British three-decker 1828*

La Belle Poule *French frigate 1834*

Galleries and quarter galleries

The French two-decker La Couronne *1636*

Around the middle of the 16th century the open balconies and galleries began to creep round the stern – this feature, together with the tall, narrow stern and the long, low head, provided the characteristic silhouette of the ships of this era.
At the beginning of the 17th century there was a trend towards covering these open galleries, a very good example of which is shown by the French *La Couronne,* shown on the left. By the middle of the 17th century these covered-in galleries had developed into what we now think of as quarter galleries, and were blended into the richly decorated stern, sharing its constructional and ornamental features.
As in the case of the stern, the quarter galleries varied widely in design from one country to another. Along with the stern and the head, they represented characteristic features by which the nationality of a ship could be recognized.
The English built enclosed quarter galleries with a semi-circular basic shape and one or two rows of rectangular windows; the Dutch (and also the Germans, the Danes, the Swedes and the Russians) had longish and fairly low quarter galleries, which curved strongly outwards, and sometimes had no windows; the French and the Spanish preferred theirs to have one open gallery (two in large ships) and one round or oval centre window. In the second half of the 18th century a hybrid French/English form became standard. The basic shape now was a quarter segment of an ellipse, and the quarter galleries featured one to three rows of angular windows, according to the size of the ship. The illustrations of *Victory* and the *Gulnara* show this feature. In the second half of the 19th century the quarter galleries disappeared with the introduction of the elliptical stern.
The construction of galleries and quarter galleries is somewhat more complex than the construction of the stern. As the plans usually show no constructional details, the modeller himself has to resort to the squared paper, straight edge and compasses. It is a good idea to make a base support, the roof (often coppered) and the parts between the rows of windows first, join them with the correct spacing maintained by small blocks, and only then install the windows complete with the window frames.
Be sure to fix them securely to the hull sides and the frames. If your model features complicated quarter galleries, it is often advisable to make a trial version first from obechi and/or plywood, which will enable you to obtain a good fit, and the correct shape, by trial and error.

Bulkheads

The athwartships walls of a ship are termed the bulkheads. They always included doors, often windows, and were frequently embellished with ornaments. The shape and appearance of the bulkheads is shown on your plans (see bow elevation and cross sections).
The bulkheads are cut from thin plywood and checked for precise fit – but do not fix them in place yet. The next stage is to add the planking to the bulkheads. The planking was always horizontal, and always clinker fashion during the whole of the 17th century on Dutch ships and during the first half of the 17th century on French ships. Then the doors, windows and decoration can be added. Finish off the bulkheads completely, down to the painting, before fitting them to the model.
The bulkheads were often crowned with a rail.

Brandenburg two-decker Friedrich Wilhelm zu Pferde, *1680*

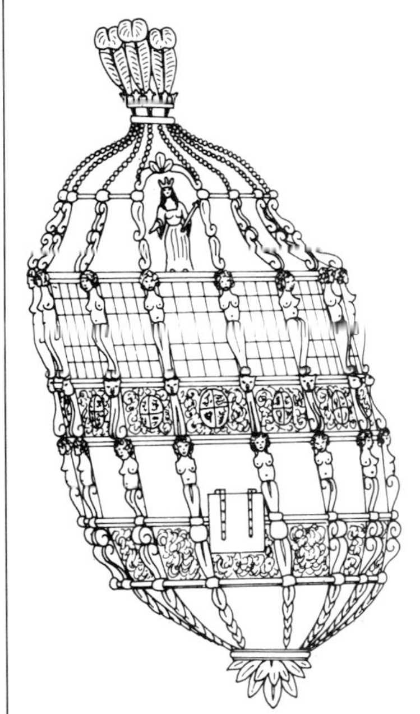

British three-decker Royal Katherine, *1664*

French three-decker Royal Louis *1690*

British three-decker Victory *after 1803 refit*

Dutch yacht around 1790

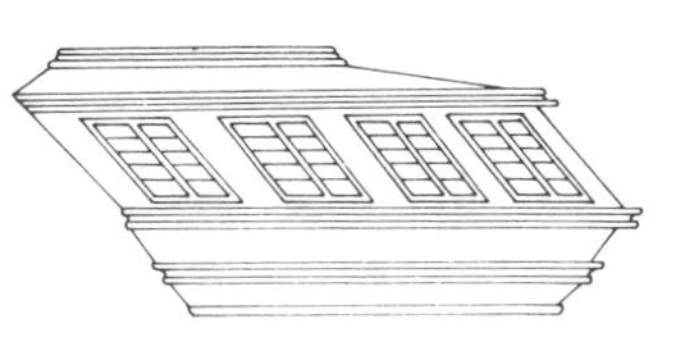

Sardinian paddlewheel corvette Gulnara *1832*

The Head

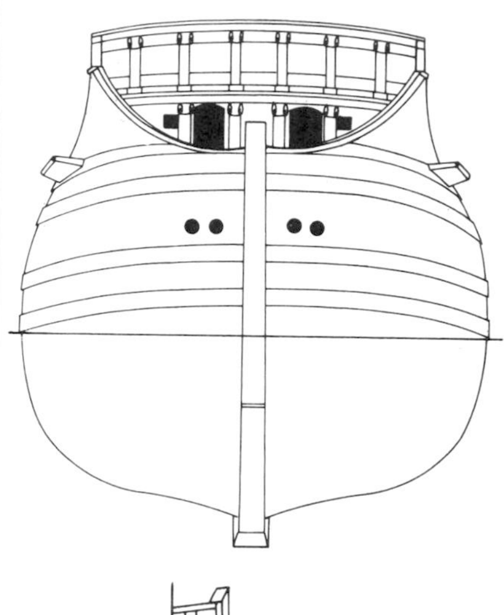

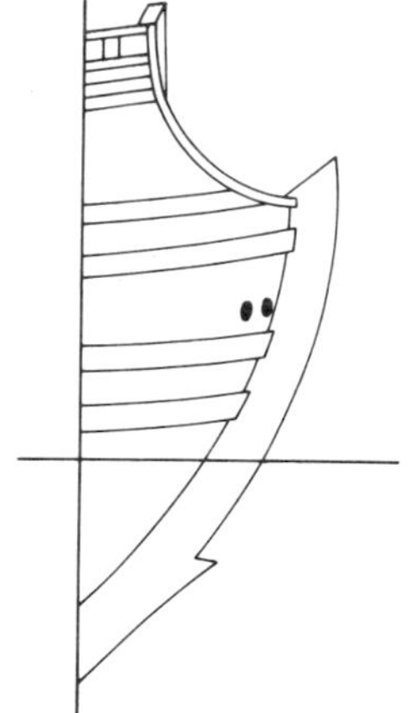

Bow without head

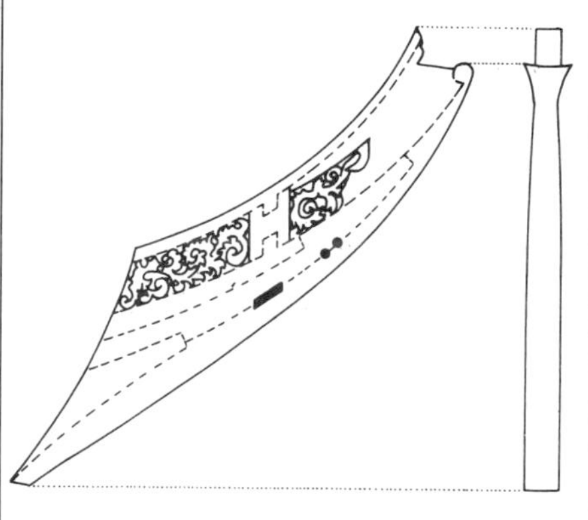

Knee of the head

Right up to the end of the 19th century the bow of a ship was secondary only to the stern as the place for elegant and ostentatious ornament. To the model builder the bow and stern have always represented a major headache, but at the same time they are a challenge, and they are two areas where he is able to show off his skill to the full.
The bow and stern are certainly among the areas which the modeller should study very carefully on the plans before deciding whether to build one model in preference to, perhaps, a simpler one. A poorly made, clumsy or over-simplified head, for example, can absolutely ruin the overall impression of a model ship.
On the other hand, I don't wish to put you off; after all, these things are not as difficult as they may at first sight appear. With careful forethought, some skill and plenty of patience you will be able to produce something acceptable.
The most splendid bow ornamentation dates from the 17th and 18th centuries – but it was also the most complex. Let us study a Dutch ship from the 17th century (on the facing page: sheer plan, body plan, profile, bow elevation, plan of the head and centreline section).
The most common problem is that the individual parts of the head are not shown on the plans, and the modeller has to work out and calculate the shapes. Once you know how and where to find the information, construction is no more difficult than a hundred other parts on your model ship.

The knee of the head
The knee of the head is the extension of the stem at the bow, and represents the load-bearing support for the whole head. The drawing on the left shows the bow of our Dutch ship, as it would look planked and with finished stem but without head.
The shape and dimensions of the knee of the head are found from the sheer plan, the body plan and the waterline plan, while its appearance is shown on the side elevation and sometimes the centreline section.
Like the stem, the knee of the head consists of a series of timbers fitted together (shown dotted in the drawing). This process of assembly is usually far too complicated for the modeller, and he will make the knee of the head from a single piece. The joints of the various timbers should nevertheless be scored on with a knife; if you wish to do this, check that your plans include the information – such plans are scarce. It is not exactly good practice to invent your own pattern!
Please note that the knee of the head is as wide as the stem at the point at which the two parts join, but it tapers towards the front. It is also very important that the knee of the head lies exactly in line with the keel, otherwise the whole head will be crooked.
Before the knee of the head is installed, the holes for the bowsprit gammoning must be sawn through, and also the holes for the fore tacks where necessary.
Once again, stick to the rule that every part must be completely finished before it is finally glued in place. Think through the sequence of construction very carefully; this applies in particular to the head, as if you try to drill a hole, saw out a slot or fit an overlooked part at a later stage, you will almost inevitably damage or break something.

The gammoning knee
At the top the knee of the head is secured to the stem by the gammoning knee. From the 18th century onward the gammoning knee is often integral with the knee of the head. The shape and dimensions of the gammoning knee are found from the sheer plan, the deck plan and the centreline section. The gammoning knee is sometimes slightly narrower than the stem to which it is joined. Before fitting the knee, check

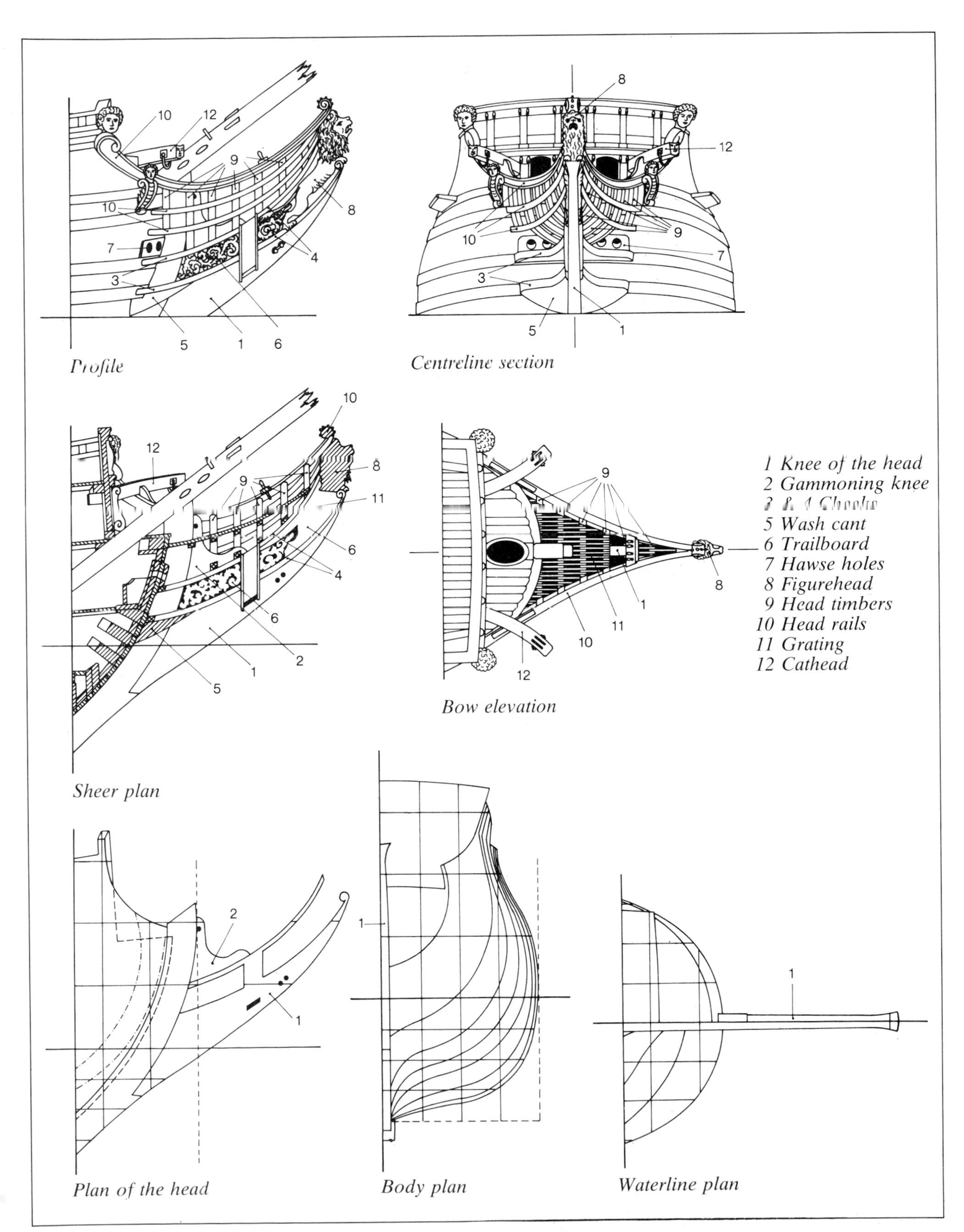

Profile

Centreline section

Sheer plan

Bow elevation

Plan of the head

Body plan

Waterline plan

The Head

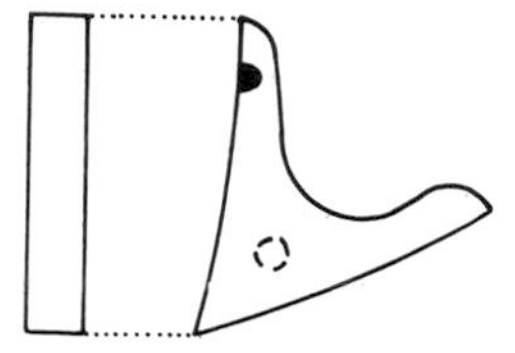

Gammoning knee with opening for the stay collar, standard in the 17th century, British pattern (shown dotted) usual until the beginning of the 19th century.

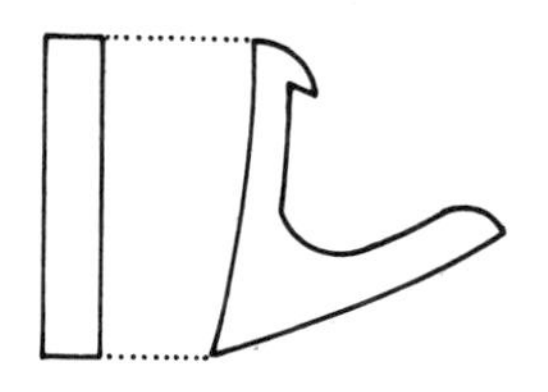

Gammoning knee with hook for the stay collar, particularly common in France.

whether the opening for the stay collar is cut through it, as it must be drilled beforehand.

The cheeks and the hair brackets
The knee of the head is supported laterally by two or more pairs of knees, the cheeks, one or more of which usually fair into the lower wales. The upper ones are extended to form a pair of ornamental mouldings, the hair brackets, and the lower pair generally end below the figurehead. The dimensions and exact location of the cheeks and the hair brackets can be found from the waterline plan, the bow elevation and the profile.
It is difficult to find the exact shape of the cheeks at the first attempt, and I would advise that you start by making a card template and trim this to fit. The cheeks can then be cut from wood to match the template. Leave a slight excess of material where they meet the wales, and then trim them to exact fit by careful sanding. This is a rather tricky job, but the alternative method, which is often seen on poorly built models, is to trim them to an approximate fit, then fill the gaps with filler paste – hardly in keeping with a high-quality model.
The hair brackets are somewhat easier to fit, as their dimensions can be found readily from the sheer plan and the side elevation. You just need to saw the pieces out and carve them. If these brackets are gilded or otherwise coloured, as is often the case, you *must* do this before fitting them to the model.

Wash cants
Below the lower cheek there is often a shaped timber, the wash cant, which is intended to prevent the rising anchor damaging the head timbers. The shape and dimensions of the wash cant are found on the waterline plan and the bow and side elevations, in the same way as the shape of the cheeks. The exact shape of the wash cant is extraordinarily difficult and complex to work out on paper, and this is one case where trial and error is really much more sensible than calculation and drawing.
The first stage is to saw out the two parts, leaving them much oversize, after which their approximate outside shape is carved and sanded. Their joint faces are then trimmed carefully to fit, in the same way as the cheeks. Only when the two wash cants seat really accurately should you go back to shaping their external contours accurately. If you finish the outside surfaces first, and then the fitting stage does not quite work right, you will have to remake the whole piece. This happens to the best of model makers now and then, and you will have wasted more work than you needed to.
It is important that the two wash cants are exact mirror images, and they should not be fitted to the model until you are absolutely satisfied with them. This whole task is rather troublesome, especially if you are working with the harder timbers; many modellers cannot resist the temptation to make these parts from soft, easy to work obechi or even balsa wood. Please let me warn you against such short-cuts – you will ruin the whole model!

Filling pieces
In the 18th century the upper part of the knee of the head was filled out between the cheeks of British ships with a carved trail board. These parts can be made in one piece, which is a difficult job, or – as in French ships – from short, vertical pieces. This method is shown in the drawing of a French 74 gunship of 1770 on Page 115, and is much easier to carry out. The only point to watch is that the edges of these pieces are always perpendicular to the cheeks and hence individual pieces are not

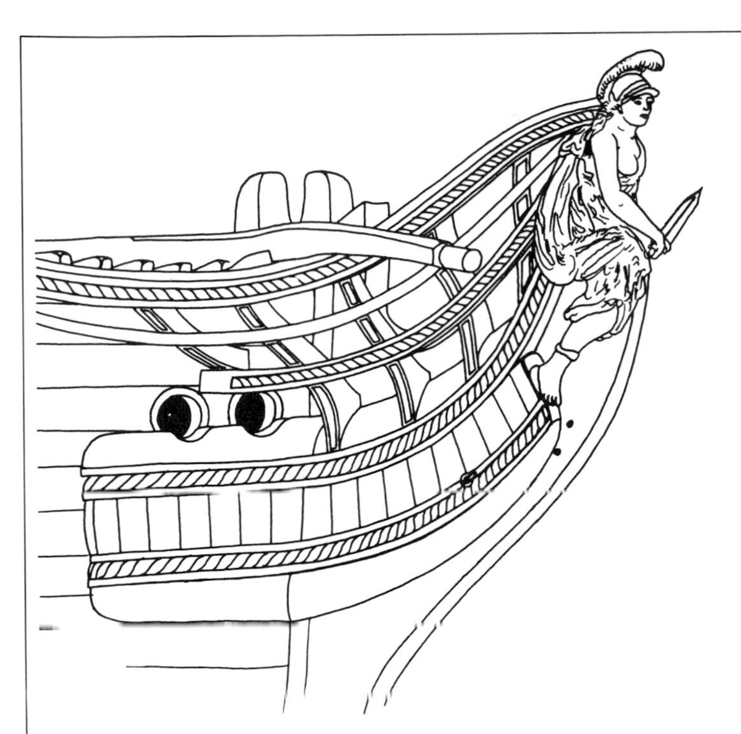

French ship's bow of 1770
(after Vaisseau)

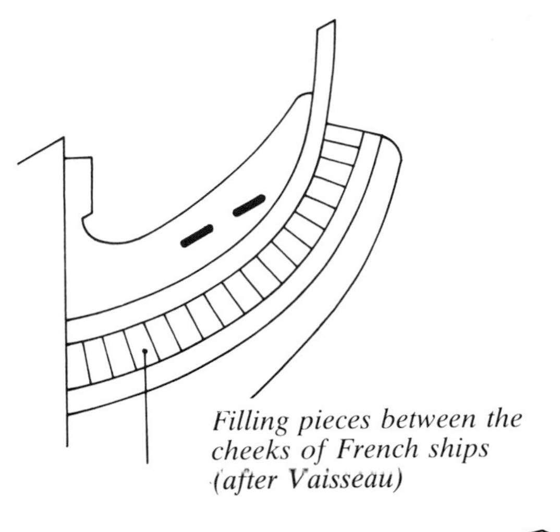

Filling pieces between the
cheeks of French ships
(after Vaisseau)

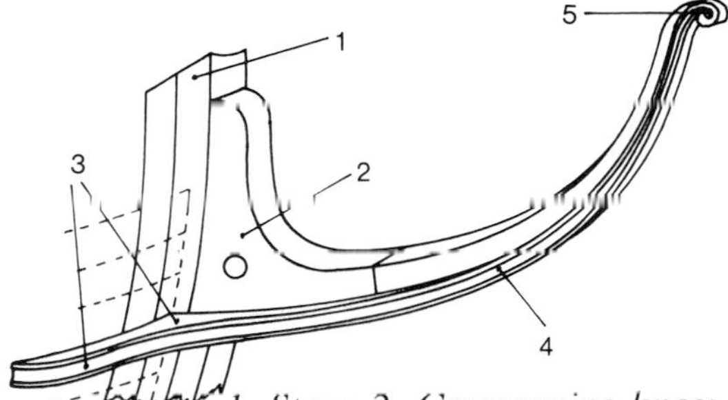

1. Stem; 2. Gammoning knee;
3. Upper cheek; 4. Hair bracket;
5. Scroll or volute

Bow of a paddlewheel frigate from
the middle of the 19th century

The Head

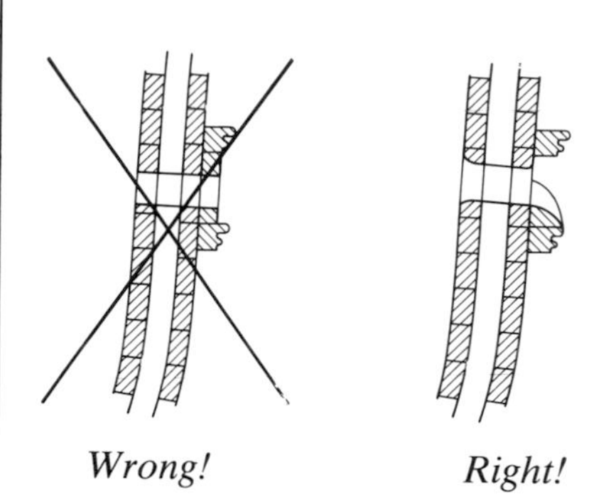

Run of the anchor hawses through the planking

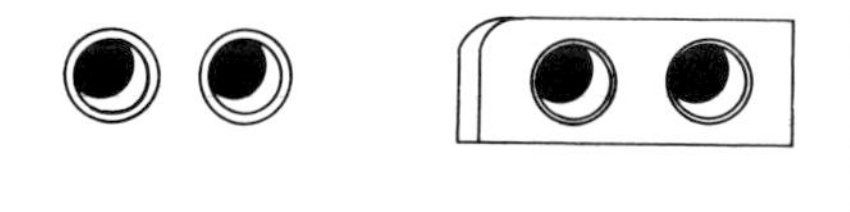

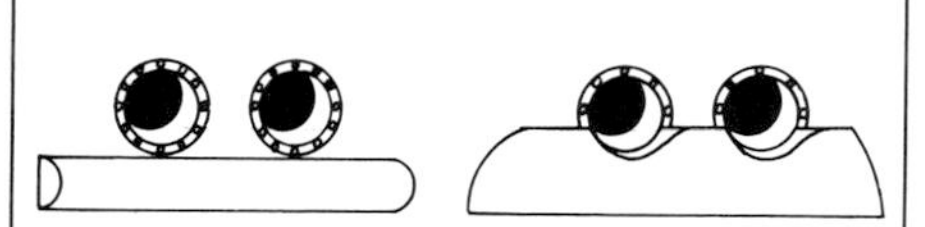

Hawse holes from the 15th to the 19th century. At bottom with bolsters

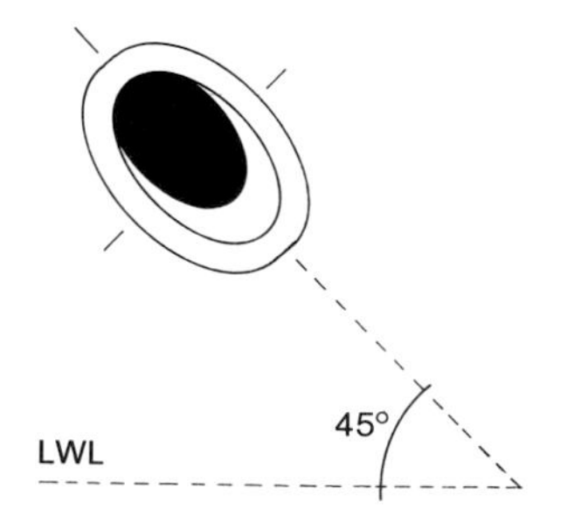

An iron hawse hole from the mid-19th century for use with anchor chain. Note the angle of 45° to the waterline

rectangular where the knee of the head curves, but are slightly trapezoidal in shape.

Hawse holes and hawse timbers

One of the things which regularly saddens me when I study an otherwise well-built model ship is the minor mistake which should really have been avoided, but which devalues the modeller's long hours of intricate labour.

One of the most frequent mistakes of this type concerns the hawse holes. The modeller just drills a hole straight through the hull, as shown in the drawing on the left, and passes the anchor rope through – and the crime is already committed!

The hawse holes were radiused at both their inner and outer ends. The lower part of the outer end was continued in a bolster as in the right-hand drawing, in order to give the cable a smoother run by minimising chafe. It also protected the cable from nipping on a sharp edge when riding at anchor.

The hawse holes themselves were lined with lead until the 19th century, to protect the hawse timbers from abrasion of the cables. From the 19th century onwards iron or steel hawse pipes came into use.

The middle drawings on the left show hawse holes from the time before 1500 until 1900, the bottom two of which are fitted with bolsters.

Take care! Bear in mind that the cables should be fitted at an early stage, before the decks are sealed and you still have access to the inside of the hull. Notes on appearance and dimensions of cables are to be found in the appropriate section of this book.

The figurehead

For centuries the figurehead represented the personification of the whole ship, and a corresponding amount of care and loving attention was bestowed upon its construction and finish. Please do not be frightened off by the task of making the figurehead, although obviously you should take very special care over it. The shape, dimensions and appearance of the figurehead are shown on the side and bow elevations; a photo of a good museum model can also provide valuable extra help.

The first stage is to take the piece from which the figurehead is to be made, and cut it to fit exactly over the upper part of the knee of the head. It is often helpful to assemble the figurehead from several pieces (in our example the dotted lines give an idea where the joins could be made). It is often sensible to carve projecting arms and weapons separately, and fix them to the figure when complete.

The next step is to saw out the basic profile of the figurehead and fix the whole thing temporarily onto a piece of wood of the same thickness as the knee, to make further work easier. As the drawing shows, this support piece is then clamped in a vice before you start carving, sanding and milling.

For the carving itself you should refer back to the appropriate section of this book, or it may suit you better to cast the figurehead in resin. Every modeller has to decide how best to produce any particular figurehead, but you can be sure that with some patience and one or two failures you will certainly be able to produce something acceptable.

The figurehead is finally carefully gilded and painted, removed from its support piece, and fitted onto the knee of the head.

Types of head

Before we turn our attention to the rails and head timbers, we have to make a brief study of the different types of head and their development. As early as the 13th century ships began to feature small turrets and platforms at the bow, intended to give soldiers a raised and therefore

The splendidly carved and gilded bow of the English 100 gun ship Prince *of 1670*

The Head

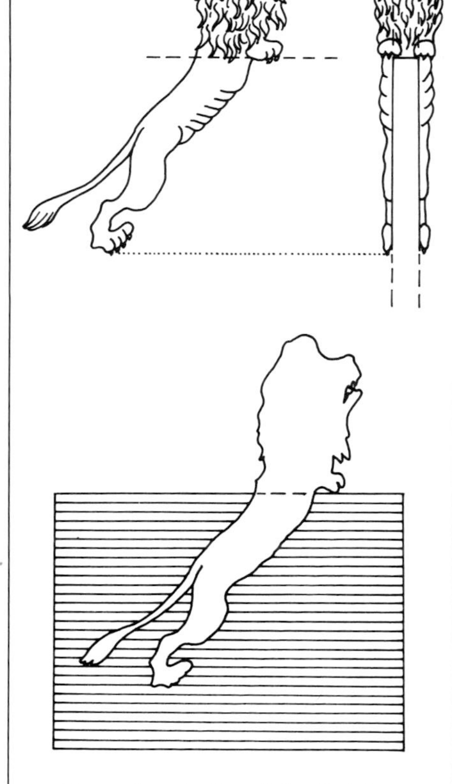

Figurehead. Possible divisions for model shown above; figurehead shown on carving support board below

strategically advantageous position in battle. It was not until the beginning of the 15th century that these platforms were integrated into the ship's hull, to produce the forecastle, as is seen in the drawing No. 1 on Page 120. These castles very soon grew into mighty, multi-storey structures (No. 2), which had the effect of making the ships more and more bow-heavy and hence awkward and slow.
The great turning point came with a development from Spain and Portugal, the leading naval powers of the first half of the 16th century. Undoubtedly influenced by the bow form of the galleys (No. 3), they cut the giant forecastle down to one raised deck (forecastle deck), and added to this a lower deck projecting over the bow, protected by a rail (No. 4).
In the major part of Europe, namely Spain, Italy, England (No. 5), Flanders (No. 6) and France (No. 11), nothing changed until 1640. At the beginning of the 17th century the English adopted a head which curved upwards slightly (No. 12), although nothing significant was altered, except that the shapes were simpler. The next new development came from Holland. The typical low, compact head up to that time had one unpleasant characteristic: it took in a lot of water in rough weather. Consequently the head was curved upwards more sharply, and when this also failed to have the desired effect, the plank rail was simply omitted, leaving only the FRAMEWORK of the head remaining (Nos. 7 and 8).
This development was complete in Holland by around 1640; it was immediately adopted by the Germans (No. 9), who were completely dependent on Holland for shipbuilding, then with only minor alterations by Denmark, Sweden and also, after Peter the Great, by Russia (No. 10).
Around 1650 England followed the trend, although with one important change compared with the Dutch original. The Dutch head frames were cut in a U-shape, but the English adopted V-shaped head frames, and reduced their number (14).
The last nations to adopt the new type of head were Spain and France around 1680, and they introduced a third variant. Their head was curved deeply downwards, and then rose up steeply. In Spain the design was rather more prominent (No. 13), while in France it was kept very compact (No. 15).
Until the late 17th century the various forms of the head retained national characteristics, but after this time the various types began to blend into a cross between the French and English head designs (No. 16), which then became the standard form.
The 19th century finally brought the end of the line for the head. Rudiments (Nos. 17 and 18) lingered on into the second half of the century, until about 100 years ago, when it was finally discarded as being an utterly superfluous piece of ornament.

The head timbers and head rails
The most fiddly part of the head is the assembly of the head timbers and the head rails. The position of the head timbers is found from the profile. The first, aftermost pair rested on the bow planking, while the remaining pairs rested on the knee of the head. Their shape – shown in the bow elevation – differed widely from nation to nation, from U-shaped in Holland to V-shaped in England. Please note that the edges of the head timbers are moulded.
The head timbers were linked by the head rails. As these are shown fore-shortened in the side elevation, you have to work out their actual shape from the side elevation and the deck plan, as shown in the drawing on the right (B, B′, B″-C, C′, C″-D, D′, D″), where the line of the centreline plane (M) and the waterline (A-A′) are

Figureheads from Germany, Denmark, France, England, America, Finland and Russia.

The Head

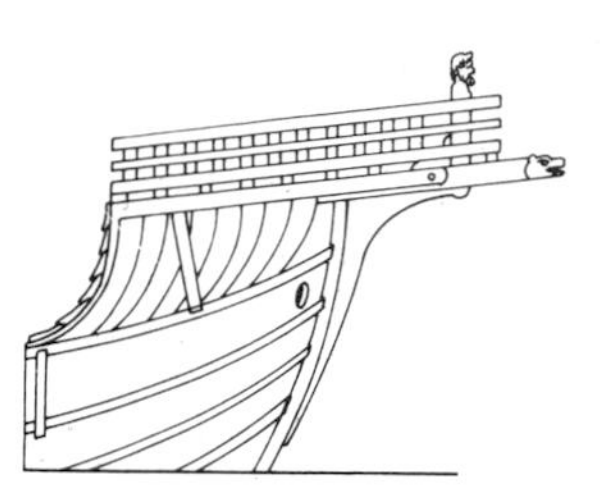

1. *Catalan Nao 1450, known as the Mataró ship*

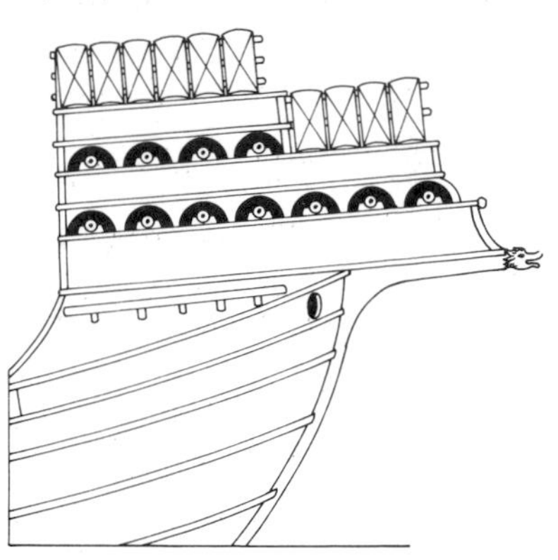

2. *Portuguese heavy carrack 1520* Santa Catarina do Monte Sinai

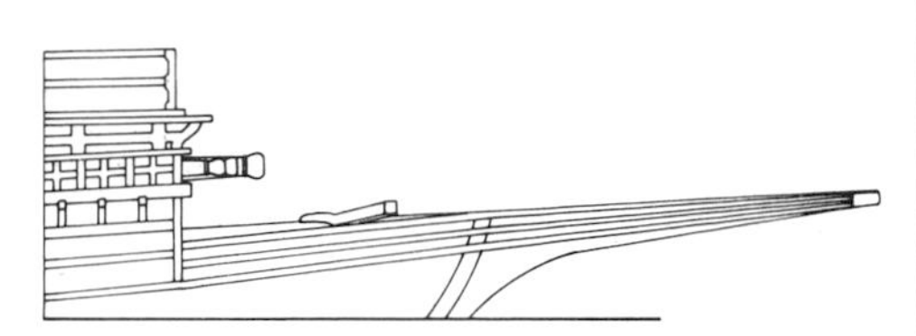

3. *Genoan galley (French type) 1620*

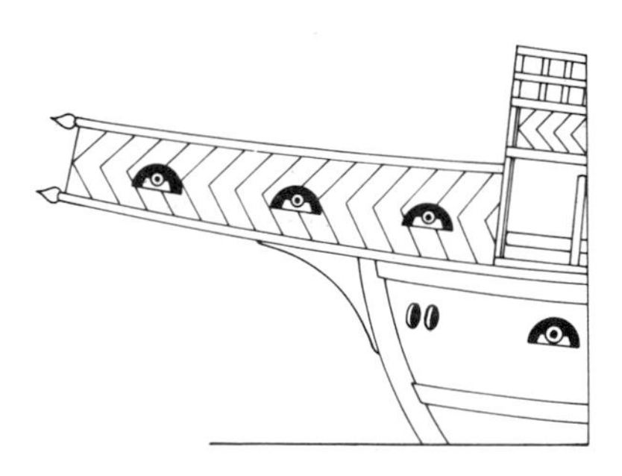

4. *Spanish galleon 1540* Sant Iago

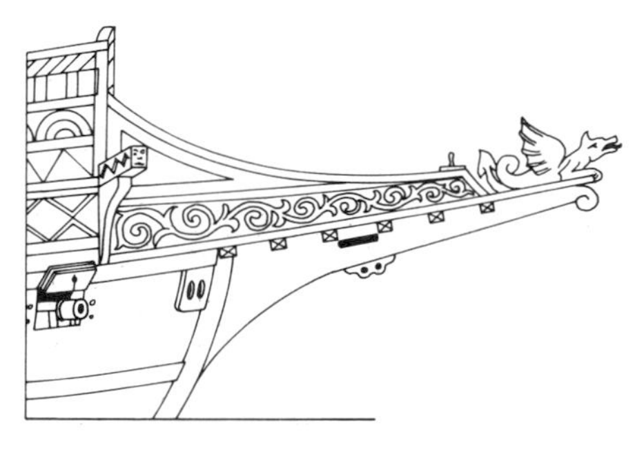

5. *English galleon 1580* Revenge

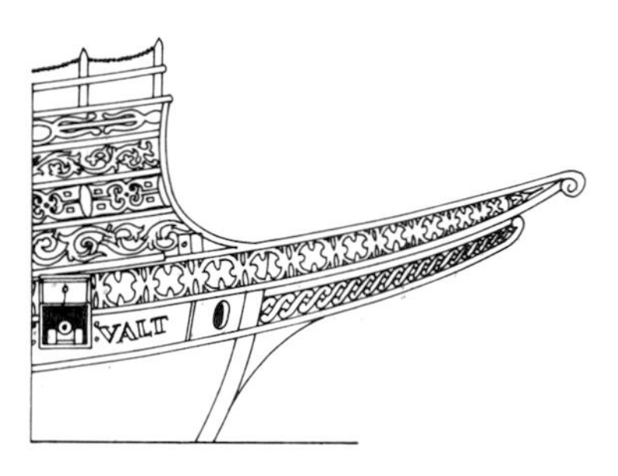

6. *Flemish galleon 1593*

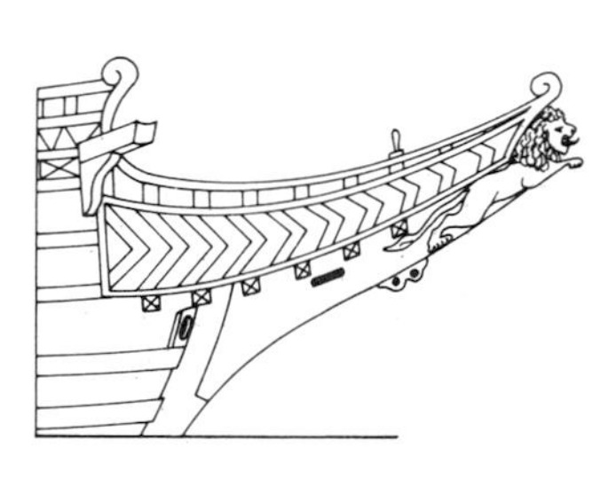

7. *Brandenburg frigate 1597* Roter Löwe

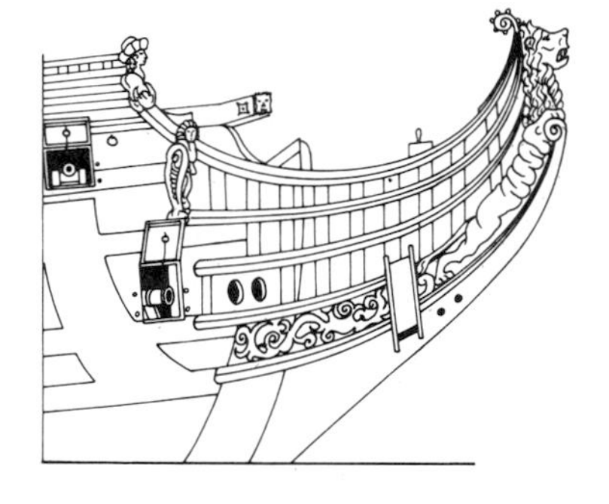

8. *Dutch two-decker 1660*

9. *Brandenburg two-decker 1680* Friedrich Wilhelm zu Pferde

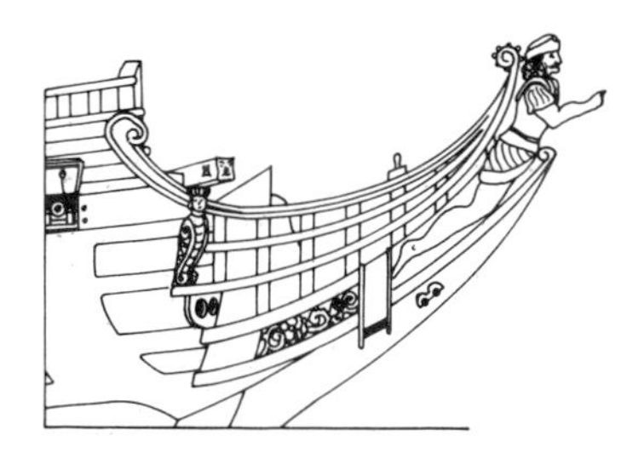

10. *Russian two-decker 1715* Moskva

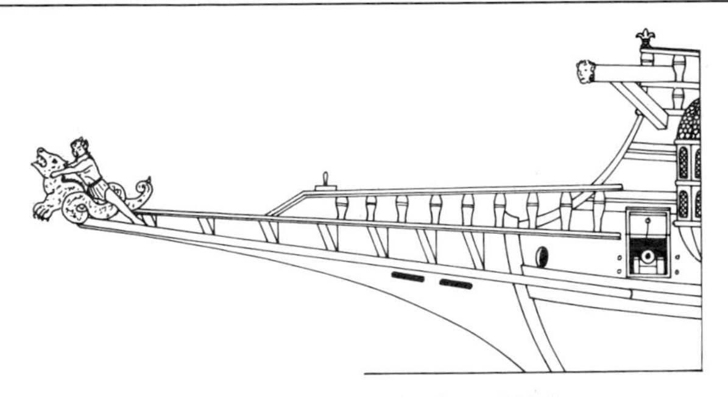

11. French two-decker 1636
La Couronne

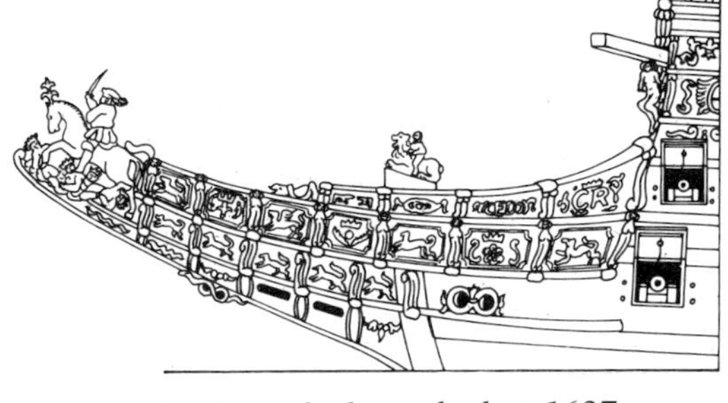

12. British three-decker 1637
Souvereign of the Seas

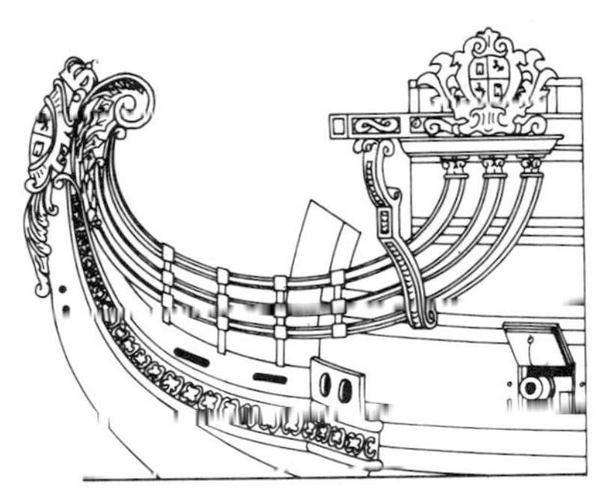

13. Spanish three-decker 1690
S. Felipe

14. British three-decker 1690
Prince

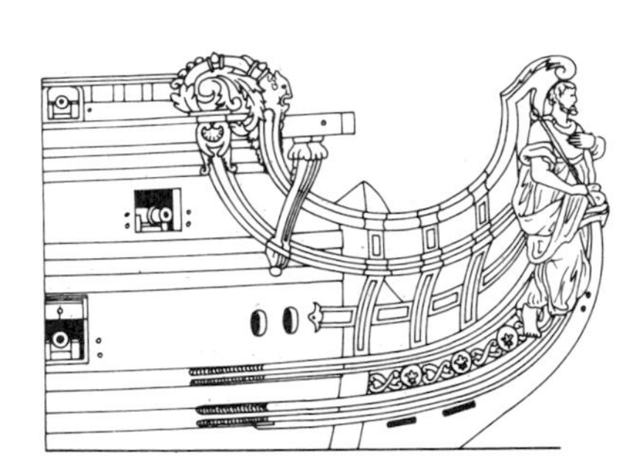

15. French two-decker 1690
St. Philippe

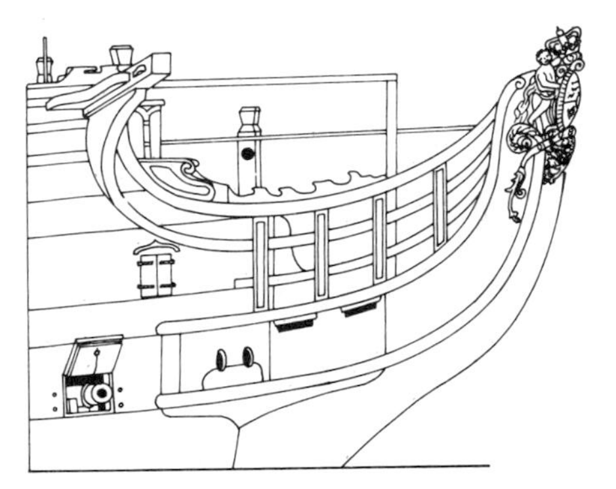

16. British three-decker Victory
after 1803 refit

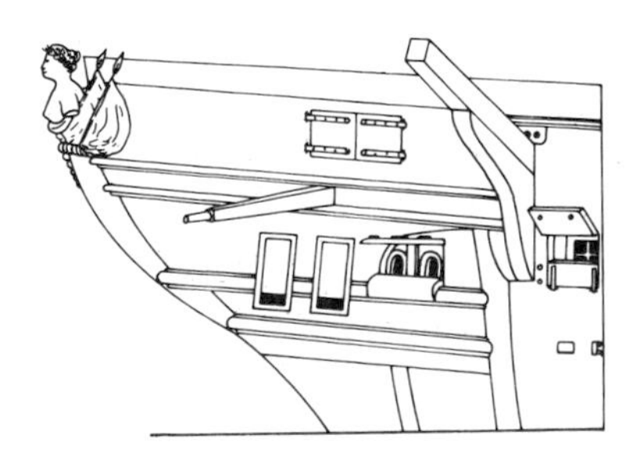

17. French heavy frigate 1834
La Belle Poule

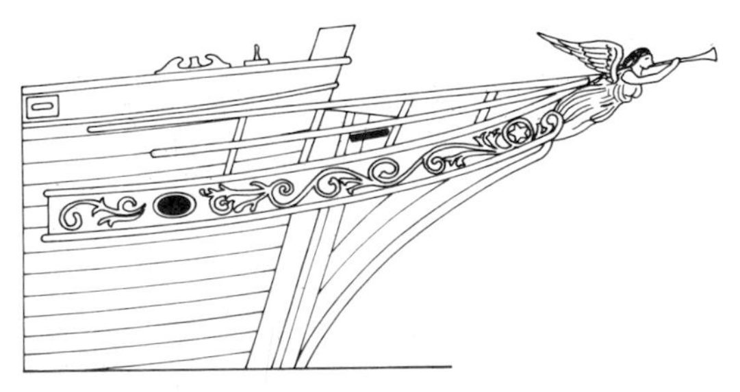

18. English clipper 1853
Star of Empire

The Head

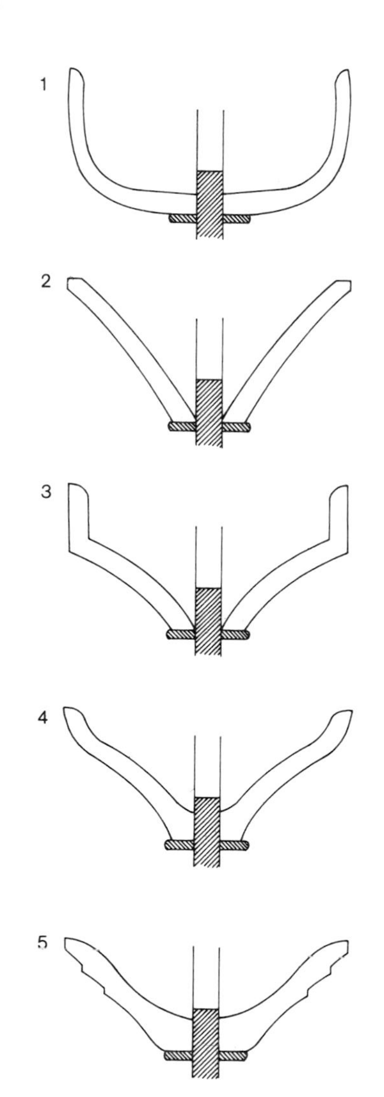

Head timber shapes:
1. Dutch
2. English, 18th century
3. French around 1700
4. French around 1750
5. Spanish

used as coordinates.
Unless you happen to have very good plans to hand, you will very quickly discover that, nine times out of ten, you can only obtain approximate dimensions using squared paper, ruler and compasses. For this reason you may as well accept that you will not get far without a little trial and error. The best method is to make the head timbers out of plywood first, and cut the head rails to fit from card and/or thin plywood. Only when everything fits perfectly should you dismantle your temporary head and use the individual parts as templates for the final head. This is a somewhat long-winded procedure, certainly, but it remains the only reliable method, and the one which is used by all the experts in modelling.

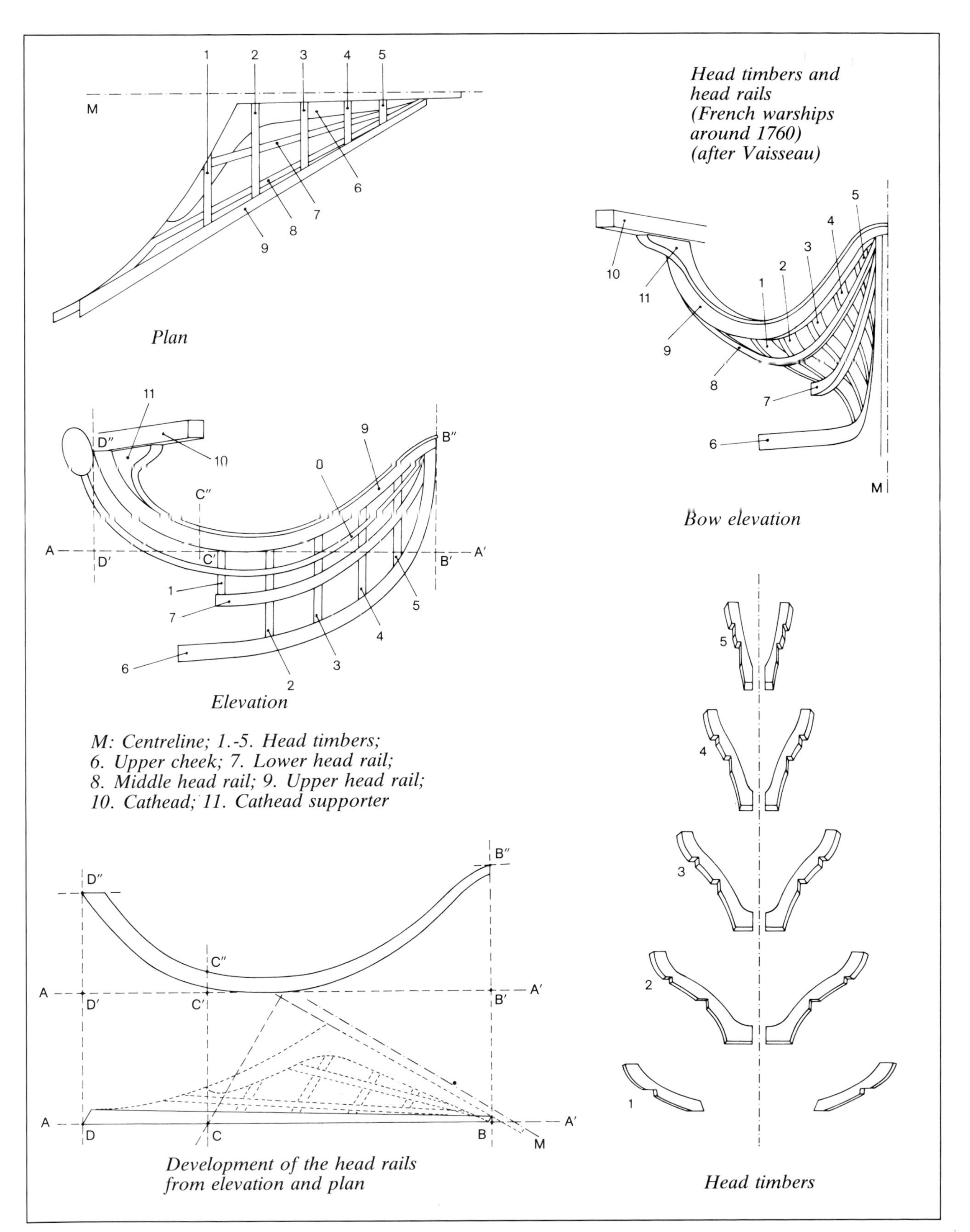
Head timbers and head rails (French warships around 1760) (after Vaisseau)
Plan
M
1
2
3
4
5
6
7
8
9
Elevation
D″
B″
C″
A
A′
D′
C′
B′
10
11
M: Centreline; 1.-5. Head timbers;
6. Upper cheek; 7. Lower head rail;
8. Middle head rail; 9. Upper head rail;
10. Cathead; 11. Cathead supporter
Bow elevation
Development of the head rails from elevation and plan
D
C
B
Head timbers

The Head

Have patience! Do not force any component into an unnatural shape. Sand and carve away until each part locates correctly without tension or pressure. The cross-sectional dimensions of the head timbers and rails are so reduced that if any of them are under permanent pressure or tension they will eventually bend – and then your whole head is crooked. The head rails must of course have an even, regular curve, without any sudden bends and bulges. They must also be symmetrical about the ship's centreline.

The head beams
The head timbers were fitted with beams in the same way as the deck beams, and here they supported the head platform (or the head grating). After 1730 the head timbers and beams were supported on either side by lodging knees.
For modelling purposes it is often best to make the head timbers in one piece with the cross beams (the joints are scored on with a knife), as they are then slightly stronger.

The head grating
As the head could easily be flooded in rough seas, the earlier solid deck was given up from the middle of the 16th century onward, to be replaced by gratings. There were various grating layouts, as the drawings on the right show. The standard square grating came into general use fairly late, and it was more common to find wood carlings running from one head timber to the next; the spaces between the foremost one or two pairs of head timbers were left open in many cases. Remember to leave space for the bowsprit gammoning in the head gratings.

The seats of ease
After the late 16th century the crews' latrines, or seats of ease, were accommodated in the head – those for the officers were usually in the quarter galleries or at the ends of the beakhead bulkhead. It is surprising how seldom these seats are to be found on good models – a large number of model builders seem to hold the opinion that such an immodest and unromantic fitting has no place on an otherwise decent period ship model. They were made of wood, usually with two seats next to each other. The discharge, when fitted, was also of timber, extending downwards next to the knee of the head, with its bottom edge at the upper cheek. For this reason the seats of ease are always located to one side of the centreline. Smaller ships usually had one, and larger ships two seats of ease either side of the knee of the head.

The pin rail
Until the beginning of the 18th century it was very common to find a pin rail in the forward part of the head, to which parts of the running rigging were belayed. This pin rail was fitted on the upper head rail.

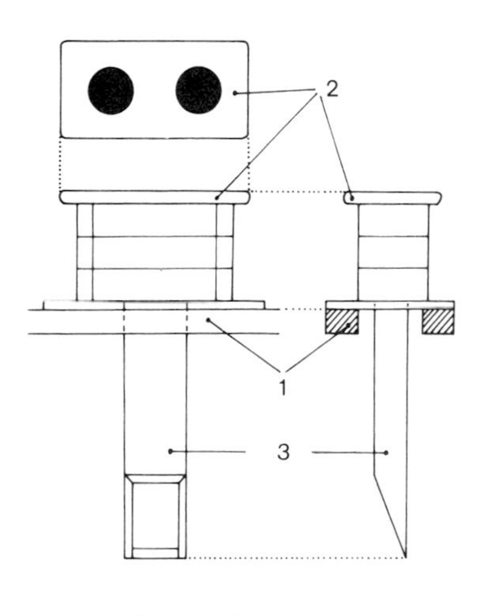

Seats of ease;
1. Carling; 2. Seat;
3. Discharge

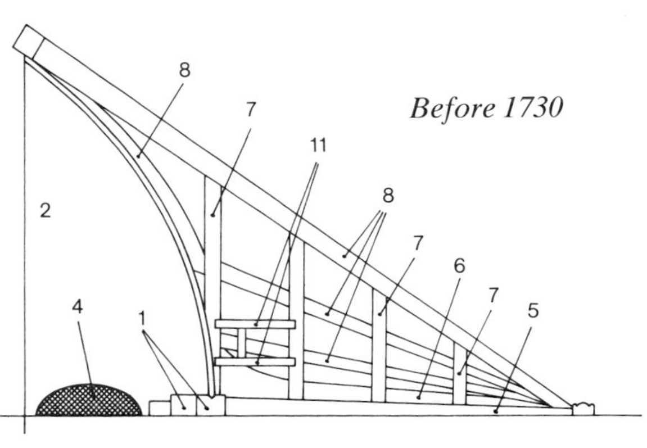

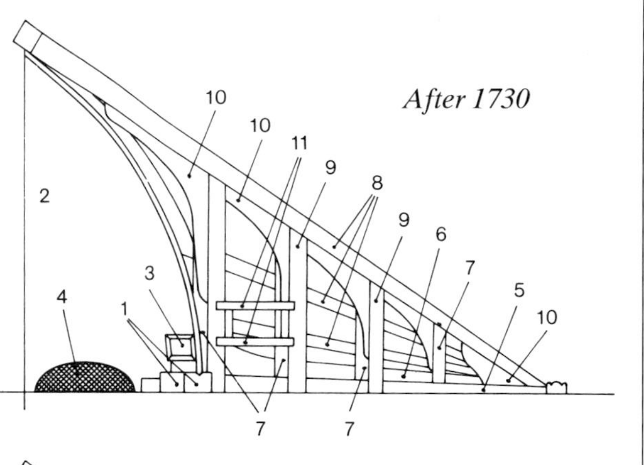

Head components: 1. Stem; 2. Head; 3. Knightheads; 4. Bowsprit opening; 5. Knee of the head; 6. Cheek; 7. Head timbers; 8. Head rails; 9. Beams; 10. Lodging knee; 11. Carlings

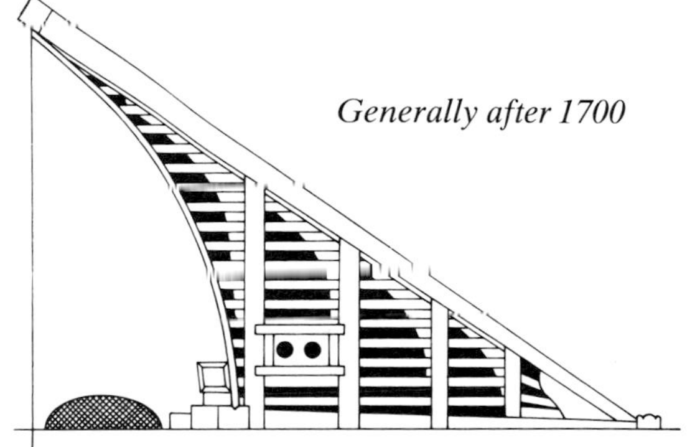

Head gratings after 1635

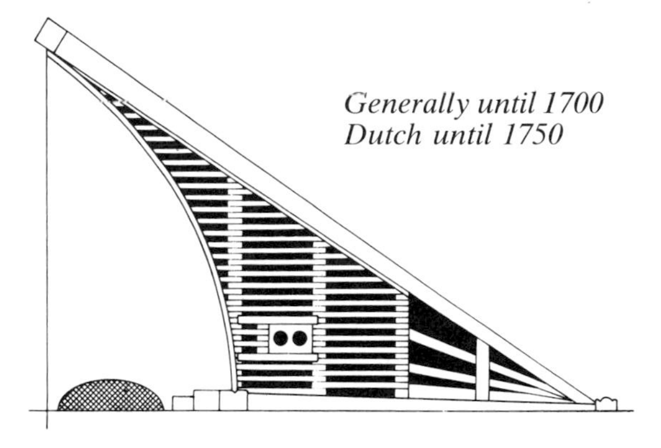

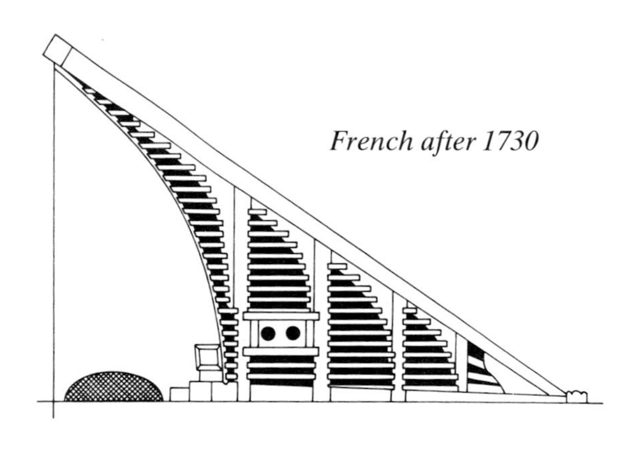

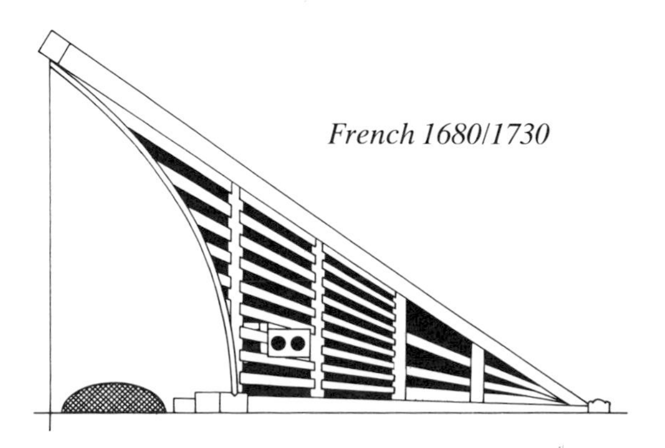

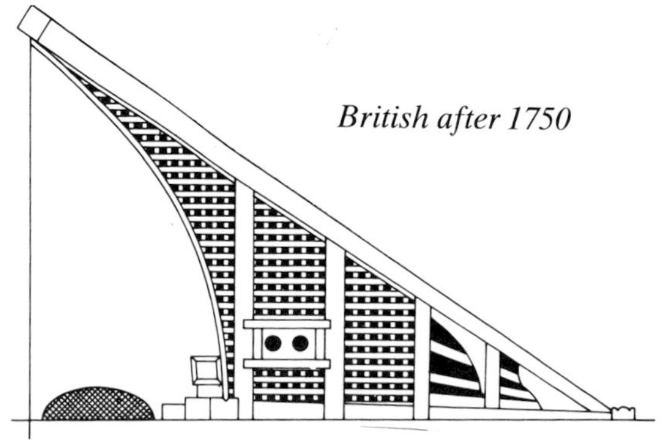

Catheads

As the anchors became increasingly large and heavy during the late Middle Ages, it became impossible to heave them over the rails on to the deck by hand. This method was superseded by the use of a heavy hook, spliced to a rope, which then passed inboard through a block. This was usually in the form of a D-block.

It rapidly became clear that this arrangement brought the anchors dangerously close to the hull as they were hoisted, making damage likely. For this reason the block was moved further outboard on a heavy beam – and the cat-head was born.

The cat-head remained unchanged in basic principle until close to the end of the 19th century: a heavy wooden beam, which carried two or three sheaves at its outboard end. The anchor cat tackle reeved through the sheaves and belayed to a cleat, or a timber head on the forecastle. The arrangement of the cat-head and the attachment of the supporter, a massive hanging knee which supported it underneath, varied from nation to nation, and from century to century to such an extent that it is impossible to list and describe them all in the scope of this book; in any case the variants should be shown clearly enough on your plans.

I will just mention here that in the 19th century the cat-head was often fitted with a whisker boom, over which the outer jib guys were passed (see THE JIB RIGGING).

Gratings

When and where gratings were invented is not known, but we do know that they were in general use from about 1500. Their purpose was to ventilate the lower decks, and they allowed gunpowder smoke and fumes to escape during battle. Until the 19th century they were always of wood construction, and thereafter metal gratings became more and more common. The construction of timber gratings is a rather time-consuming job, and many are the methods of manufacture which are recommended. To my mind the original method of fabrication, as shown in the drawings on the left, remains the most sensible and practical method. However, for this technique one tool is indispensable – a circular saw.

If you do not have access to a circular saw, you will have to rely on commercial offerings, which include complete assembled gratings as well as grating strip material. I have to say that these items are not very satisfactory, as they are hopelessly oversize for a model built to a scale of ¼in to 1ft – the holes are too big. The holes in the gratings – and this is an important point to note – were never larger than 2¾ins square. The reason for this was simply that the sailors' heels would otherwise get jammed in them. After assembling the gratings, carefully glasspaper the top surface to even out any irregularities in height.

Metal gratings, as were often used in the late 19th century, can either be made by punching out the holes – which is difficult and seldom turns out neat enough – or they can be etched. This is an expensive process, but the results look incomparably better.

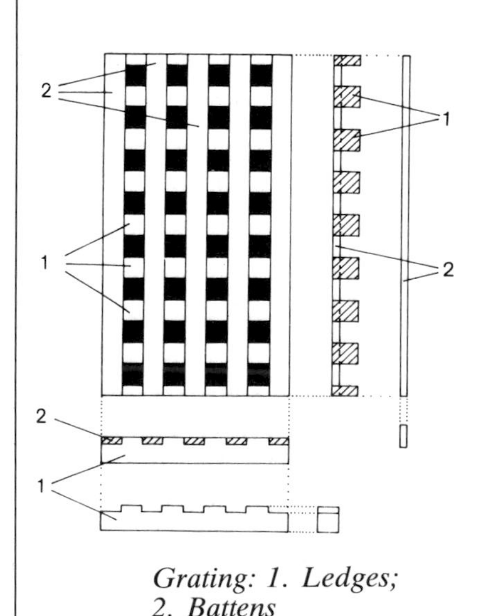

Grating: 1. Ledges; 2. Battens

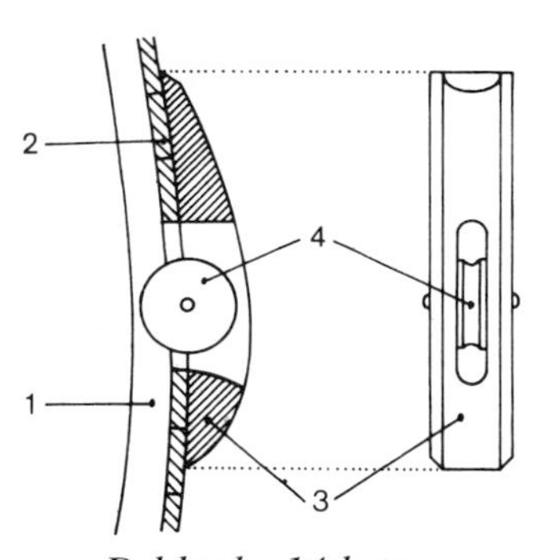

D-block, 14th to 16th century:
1. Frame; 2. Planking; 3. Block; 4. Sheave

Cathead with supporter, 16th/17th centuries

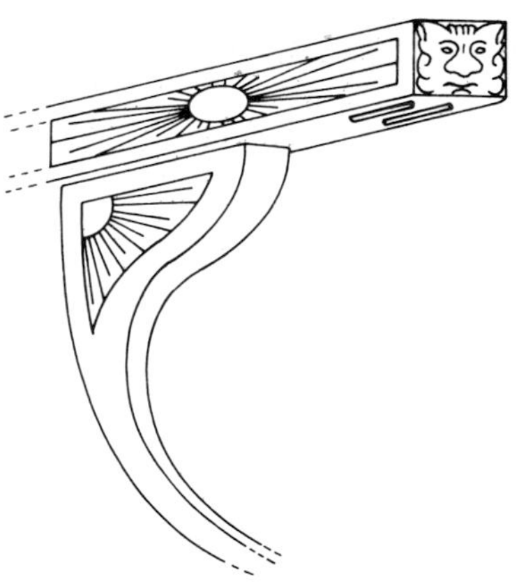

Cathead with supporter faying into head rails; 17th/18th centuries

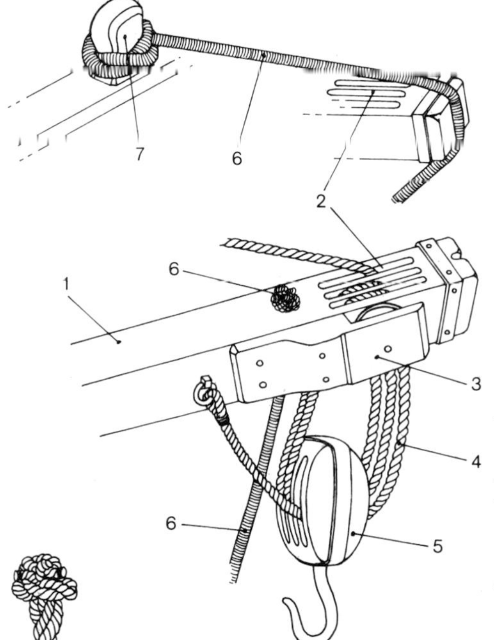

Cathead:
1. Cathead;
2. Sheaves for cat tackle; 3. Sheave for cathead stopper; 4. Cat tackle; 5. Cat block; 6. Cathead stopper;
7. Timberhead (after Vaisseau)

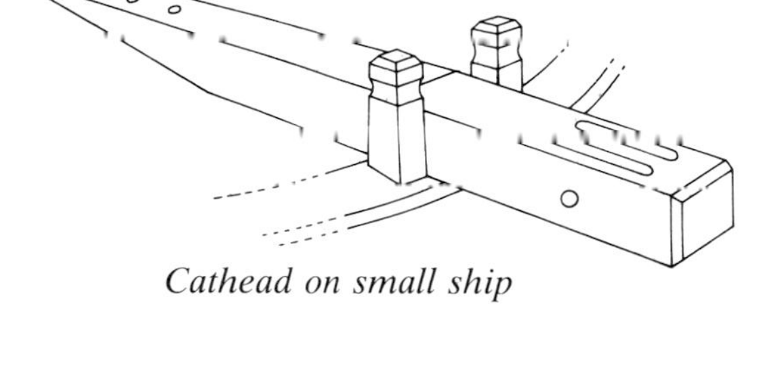

Cathead on small ship

Outboard end of cathead

The cat's face was a common decoration on the outboard end of the cathead in British ships

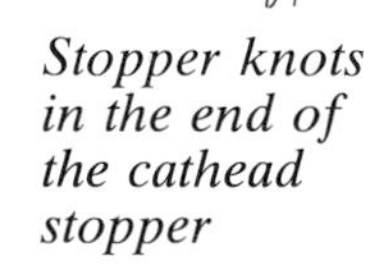

Stopper knots in the end of the cathead stopper

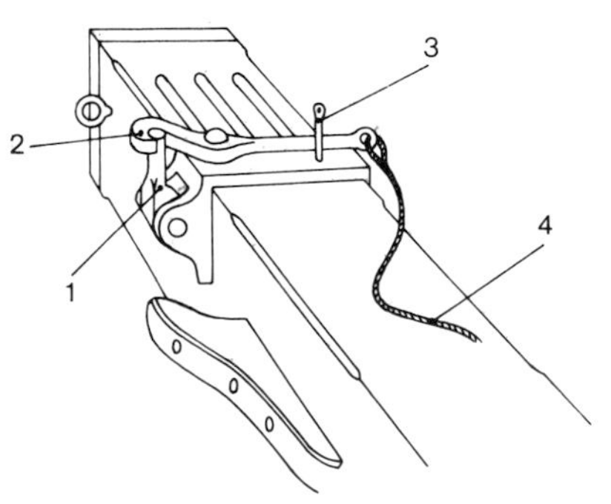

Cathead from about 1800:
1. Anchor release pin; 2. Release catch;
3. Preventer pin; 4. Release lanyard

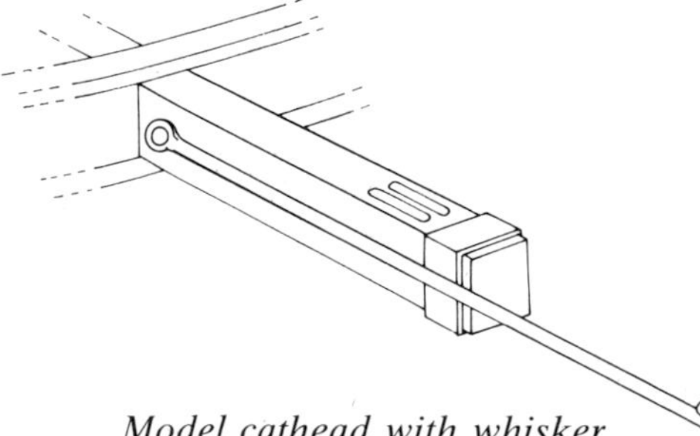

Model cathead with whisker boom, 19th century merchant ships

Rudders

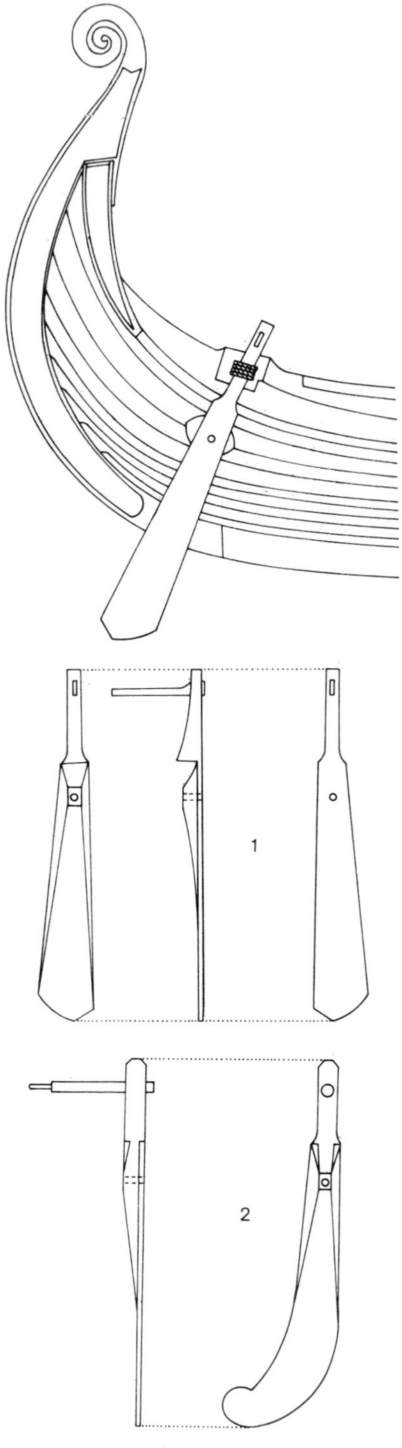

1

2

Viking rudders (starboard only): 1. Up to 980; 2. After 980

The purpose of the rudder was to steer the ship, and it consisted of three components: the rudder blade, the rudder stock and the tiller (see also STEERING GEAR), which passed into the ship through a hole in the counter.

Steering oars

The most common representative of the steering oar was the type used in ancient Egypt. The blade had a fairly long shaft which was attached to one side of the stern, or to the stern itself, and could be rotated.

Side rudders

The side rudder was developed by the Greeks and the Phoenicians around 1200 B.C. It was located to one side at the after end of the ship, and could usually be let down into the water and raised again by means of a rope. In the Mediterranean two side rudders were usually carried, while Northern ships only had one, which was always fitted on the starboard side (hence the term starboard – "steer board"). In the early and high Middle Ages the larger ships of Northern countries also adopted the double side rudder.

The stern rudder

The stern rudder, which is suspended at the stern by means of hinges known as rudder irons, seems to have been a Swedish invention, at least the oldest picture of one (early 13th century) is to be found in the church of Fide in Gotland. However, it took two centuries for the stern rudder to supersede the side rudder entirely.

Although steering oars and side rudders only changed slightly in the course of the centuries, there soon appeared a large number of variations on the stern rudder theme. Basically the shape of the rudder varied according to the speed of the ship, and, as a general rule, the slower the ship, the larger the rudder, and the faster the ship, the narrower. For this reason river and inland ships usually have much larger rudders than ocean-going ships. From the second half of the 18th century the lower part of the rudder was coppered, like the ship's hull. At the level of the top iron the rudder's leading edge was as thick as the stern post, and from there the thickness reduced downwards to the thickness of the keel.

The rudder irons

The rudder was hinged to the stern by means of rudder irons consisting of pintles on the rudder and gudgeons on the stern post. With the exception of small boats and Mediterranean vessels, there were always at least four pairs of rudder irons. After the introduction of coppering they were of bronze or copper under water, and of iron above the waterline. The spacing of the rudder irons was no more than 5ft. The forward edge of the rudder was bevelled up to 45° on either side to allow full movement.

The rudder pendants

The rudder tended to lift out of its irons in rough seas but was prevented from doing so by means of a wooden block known as a wood lock. Strong ropes and chains were fitted to the rudder as a secondary precaution and to provide a means of control in the event of damage to the tiller. These were attached to the rudder and the stern, and were known as the rudder pendants.

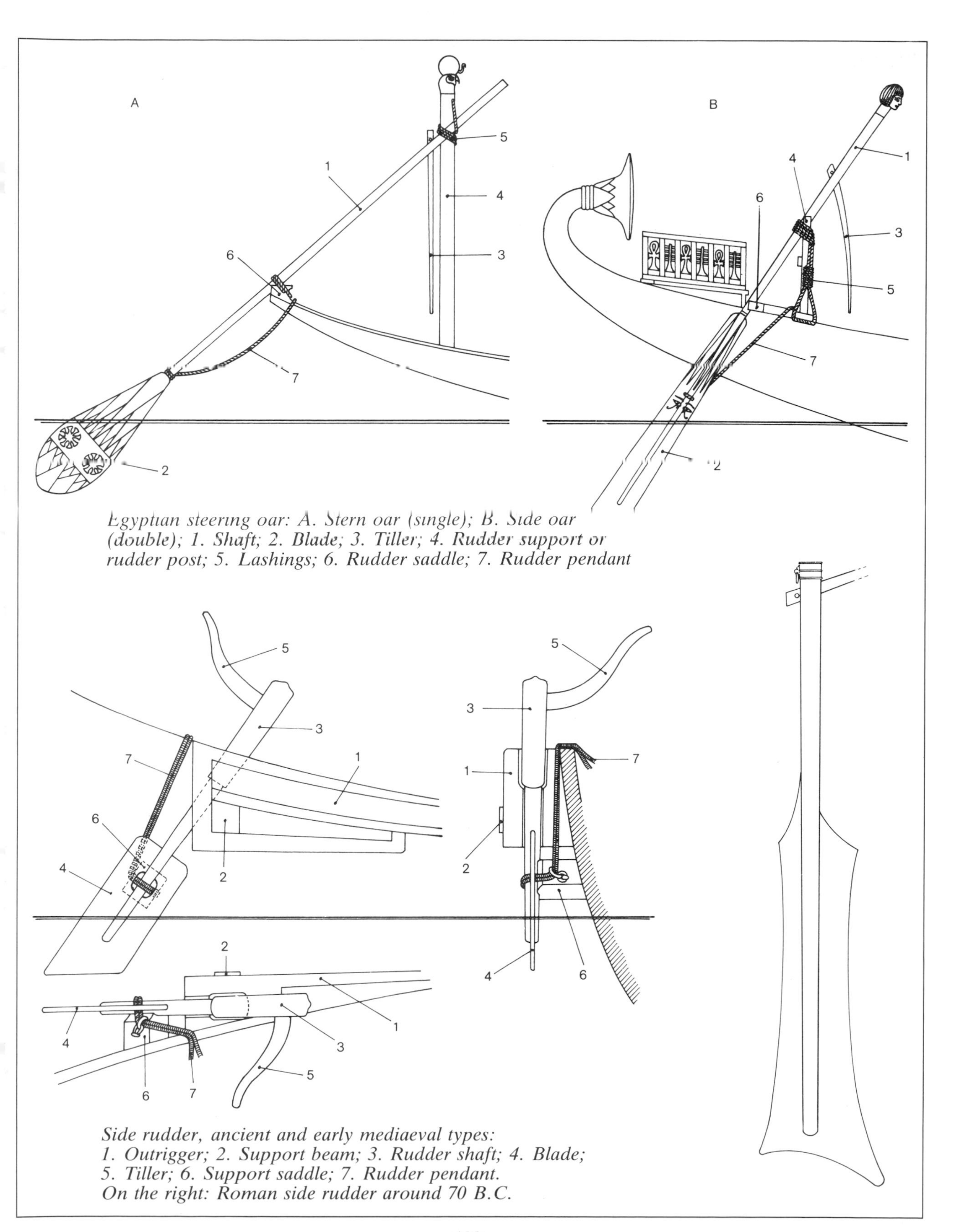

Egyptian steering oar: A. Stern oar (single); B. Side oar (double); 1. Shaft; 2. Blade; 3. Tiller; 4. Rudder support or rudder post; 5. Lashings; 6. Rudder saddle; 7. Rudder pendant

Side rudder, ancient and early mediaeval types: 1. Outrigger; 2. Support beam; 3. Rudder shaft; 4. Blade; 5. Tiller; 6. Support saddle; 7. Rudder pendant. On the right: Roman side rudder around 70 B.C.

Rudders

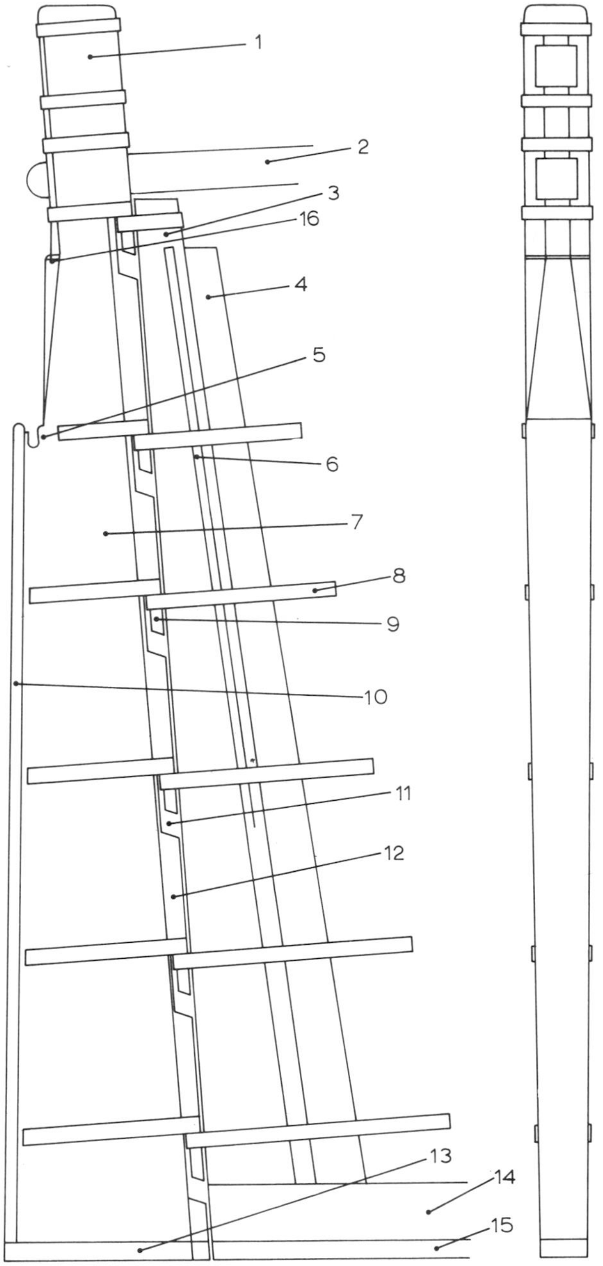

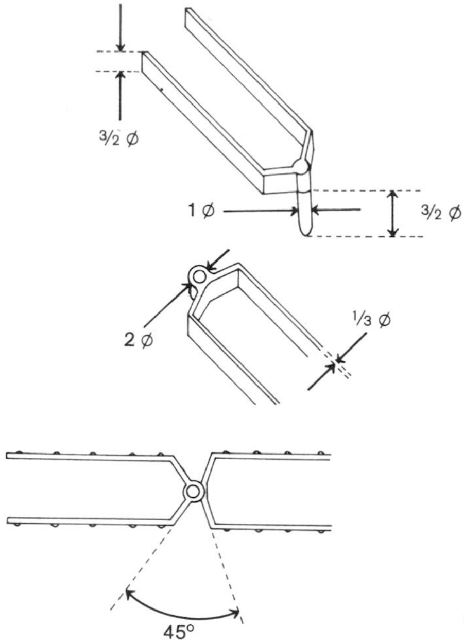

Rudder irons

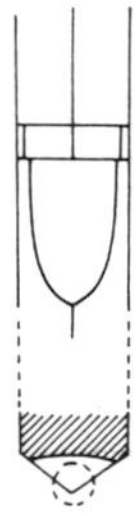

Score

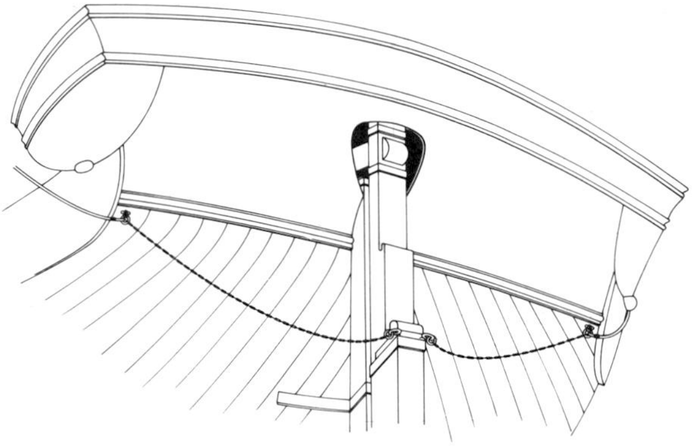

British rudder pendants

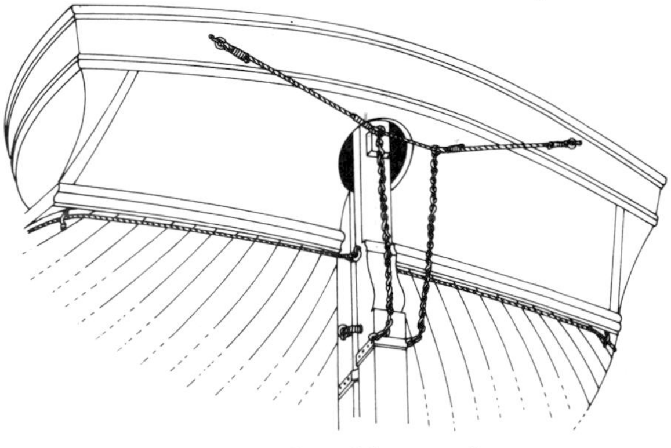

French rudder pendants

1. Head; 2. Tiller; 3. Stern post; 4. Inner post; 5. Lower hance; 6. Rabbet; 7. Rudder; 8. Brace; 9. Pintle; 10. Back; 11. Score; 12. Bearding; 13. Sole; 14. Keel; 15. False keel; 16. Upper hance

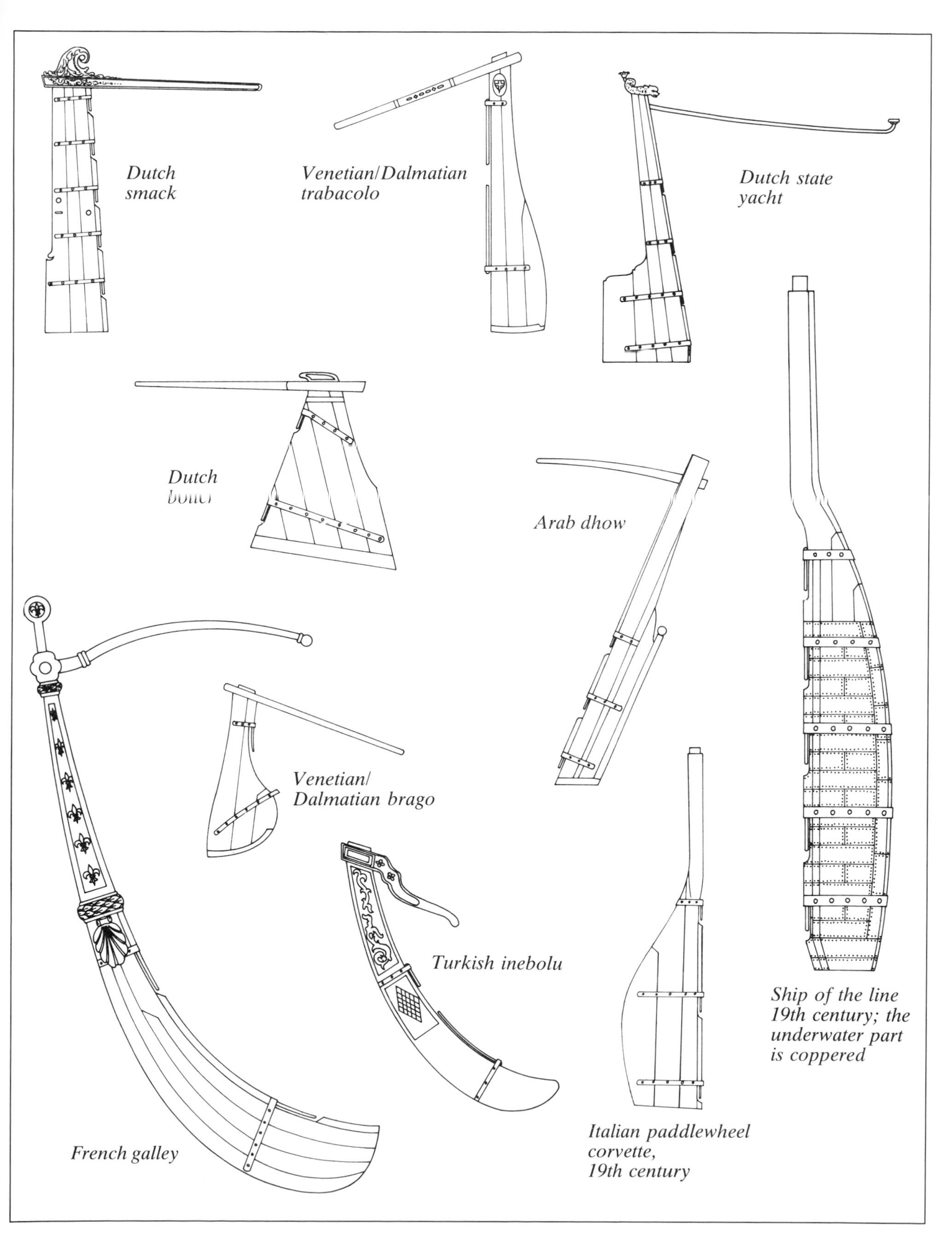
Dutch smack
Venetian/Dalmatian trabacolo
Dutch state yacht
Dutch
Arab dhow
Venetian/ Dalmatian brago
Turkish inebolu
Ship of the line 19th century; the underwater part is coppered
Italian paddlewheel corvette, 19th century
French galley

Fittings

Channels · Chain plates Sheaveholes · Scuppers Hatches · Hatch covers Portholes · Skylights Ventilators · Ladders Companions · Deckhouses Compass · Binnacle · Steering gear · Poop lantern · Galley and galley chimney · Ship's bell · Riding bitts · Fife rails Pin rails · Knightheads and kevel blocks · Tack cleats Staghorns · Armament Rating · Gunport lids Capstan and windlass Winches · Bollards · Anchors Pumps · Ships' boats · Boat chocks · Davits · Oars Boarding nets Hammock nettings

The feature which really brings the hull of a model ship to life is the hundreds of detail fittings: the hatches and poop lanterns, the companions, the skylights, the pin rails, the guns, the deck houses, the anchors, the capstans and the ship's boats.

A well built hull is the essential base for any high quality ship, but its real quality is only appreciated when the details are fitted. A badly proportioned anchor, a clumsily assembled capstan, a crudely constructed ship's boat can have a disproportionate effect on the model's overall impression. Consequently it is vital that you place jus as much importance on all these small components and detail fittings a you do on the large, major parts of your model, and construct them with just as much loving care. Even though many of these tiny parts ma be difficult to pick out on the finished model, you must not neglect them at least, you would be extremely ill-advised to do so, because you can be sure that somebody will notice them then!

Now, there is a great variety of these small fittings available commercially, from gun barrels and poop lanterns via anchors, capstans, portholes and ladders right to complete ships' boats. My advice is to view these offerings with a healthy dose of distrust. By thi I do not mean that everything on offer is bad, of poor quality and unusable. By no means; I just mean this: be critical. Study every iter carefully, and ask yourself whether or not it is of the same quality as th rest of your model.

To the beginner these commercial items are extremely tempting, and there is really no reason why he should not use them with a clear conscience until he has acquired the skill to construct the same parts himself. Nevertheless, he should also bear in mind that every item he purchases adds to the cost of the model.

There are also many items which the advanced modeller, and even th expert, should consider obtaining commercially, simply out of commo sense: because their fabrication is simply too time-consuming or too difficult. I shall return to this subject many times in the course of the book. And one more thing: when the hull is finally finished, many model makers are tempted to make a start – just a start, mind you, o the masts, yards and rigging, and then to make up and attach the man detail fittings subsequently. Banish such thoughts instantly! If you wis to make a proper job of installing the fittings, you will need as much space as possible in which to work. For instance, when it is time to fix the tiny eyebolts for the sheet blocks to the hull and fit the gun tackles, the decks simply cannot be empty enough. Any vestige of masts and rigging, even just the beginnings, robs you of space and freedom of movement. So take the sensible course and stick to the logical sequence. This dictates the fitting out of the hull as the next stage, even if a good friend should remark that "lately you don't seer to have made any progress at all with your model" . . . Just because he i incapable of recognizing the art of assembling a capstan or the steerin gear accurately.

Admiralty model of the English 74 gun ship Royal Oak *of 1769*

Channels and chain plates

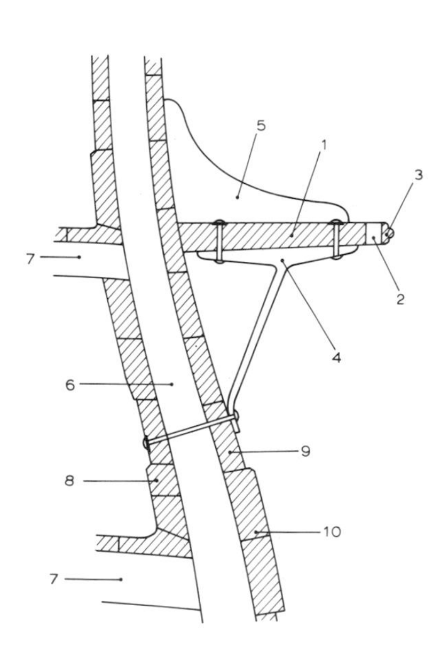

Cross-section of channel:
1. Channel; 2. Slot for chain;
3. Capping strip; 4. Tee plate;
5. Knee; 6. Frame; 7. Deck
beam; 8. Spirketting; 9. Outer
planking; 10. Wale

Channels began to appear on ships from the end of the 15th century, and they largely disappeared again in the second half of the 19th century. The channels were stout boards, attached to the sides of the hull, to which the lower ends of the shrouds were secured. The channels varied in design according to the masts to which they belonged, that is, fore, main and mizen channels, and there were also smaller backstay channels or stools on some vessels.

For the modeller the first important step is to check the dimensions of the channels: they must be wide enough to prevent the shrouds touching the rail. To check this, set each mast temporarily in place, and run a thread from the masthead to the outside edge of the channel – if the thread rubs on a rail, the channel must be extended to correct this.

The position of the channels was subject to many various changes, and was characteristic of particular periods in shipbuilding. In the case of three-deckers the main and fore channels were located below the gunports of the middle deck battery in the 17th century, and from the beginning of the 18th century they were fixed above these ports. In the second half of the 18th century they projected above the main deck gunports. On two-deckers the channels were situated under the main deck gunports until 1740, and thereafter above them. Frigates and smaller vessels carried their channels above the upper deck gunports. All these developments took place in England, but were adopted by the Continental naval powers after only a few years.

The channels occasionally cross the gunports, and in this case the channels are divided into two or three parts.

The mizen channels were noticeably smaller, and were usually situated one deck above the main channels. The chain plates or links were fitted in rectangular notches at the outboard edge of the channels. Before you cut these notches, check that they are not spaced evenly on the plan. In fact, if the shrouds are to be evenly spread, these spacings must increase steadily towards the stern; another point to watch is that the shrouds do not cross the gunports.

As the channels – even on a model – have to withstand considerable tension, they should be fixed very firmly to the wales and the hull, using long steel pins. The channels were often further supported with wood or metal knees and T-bars. When you have fitted the channels, it makes good sense to check their strength. Do not be too faint-hearted here – it is far better to tear a channel from the model now than to have it break off when setting up the rigging.

The lower deadeyes (construction of deadeyes is described in the chapter BLOCKS AND ROPES) are enclosed by a metal strap, which is held in turn by the chain or chain plate. The bottom end of each chain or chain plate is fixed to the hull with strong pins.

A wide range of chain plate designs was used over the centuries. They are made from wire and/or brass sheet, soldered together in the least conspicuous place, and blackened as described previously – painting them black usually looks awful.

On ships dating from the mid-16th century and later the channel is capped with a capping strip, after fitting the lower deadeyes and chains. The final job is to fit, where appropriate, the crutches for the studding sail spars and for the spare spars when these are carried on the channels.

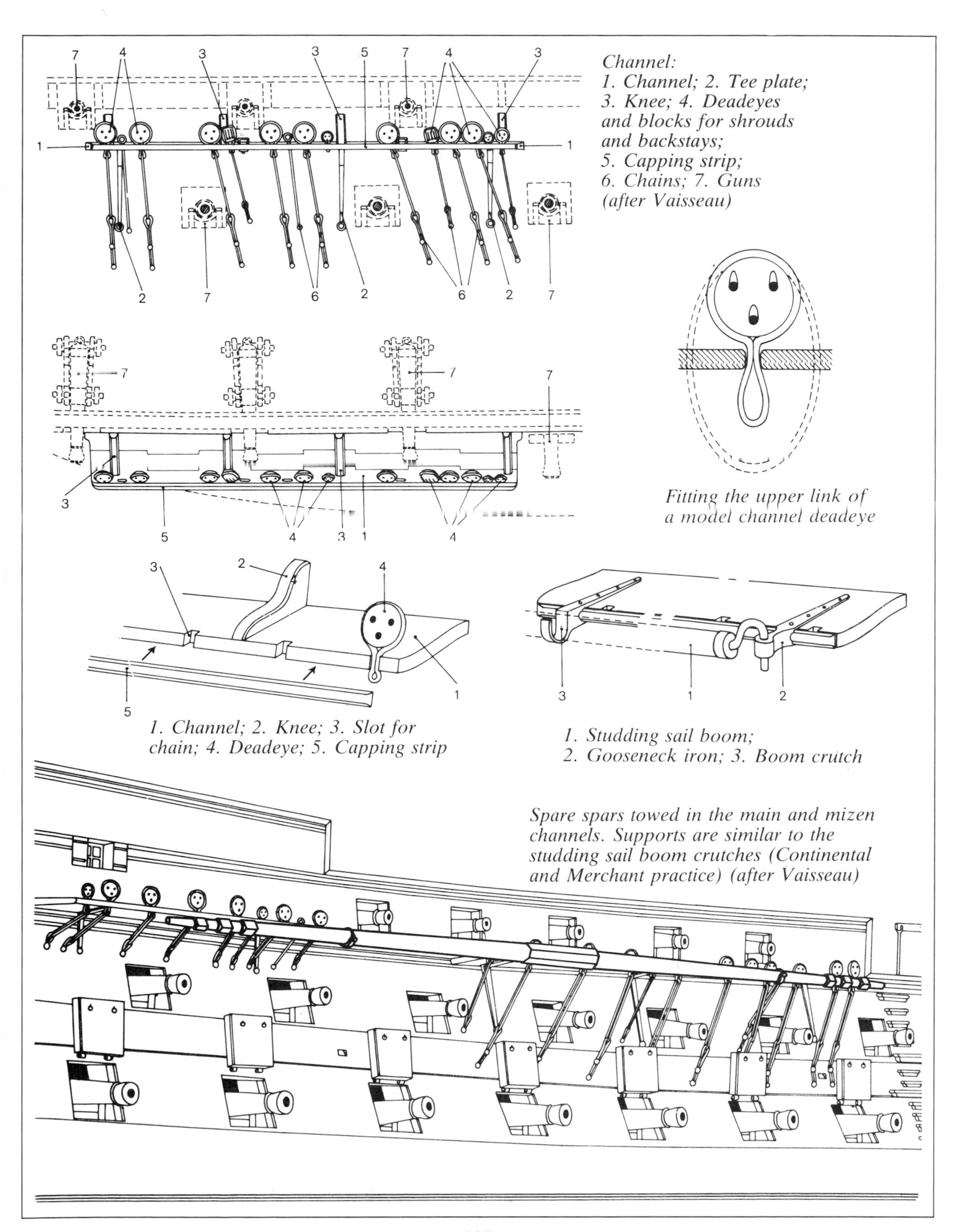

Channel:
1. Channel; 2. Tee plate; 3. Knee; 4. Deadeyes and blocks for shrouds and backstays; 5. Capping strip; 6. Chains; 7. Guns (after Vaisseau)

Fitting the upper link of a model channel deadeye

1. Channel; 2. Knee; 3. Slot for chain; 4. Deadeye; 5. Capping strip

1. Studding sail boom; 2. Gooseneck iron; 3. Boom crutch

Spare spars towed in the main and mizen channels. Supports are similar to the studding sail boom crutches (Continental and Merchant practice) (after Vaisseau)

Channels and chains

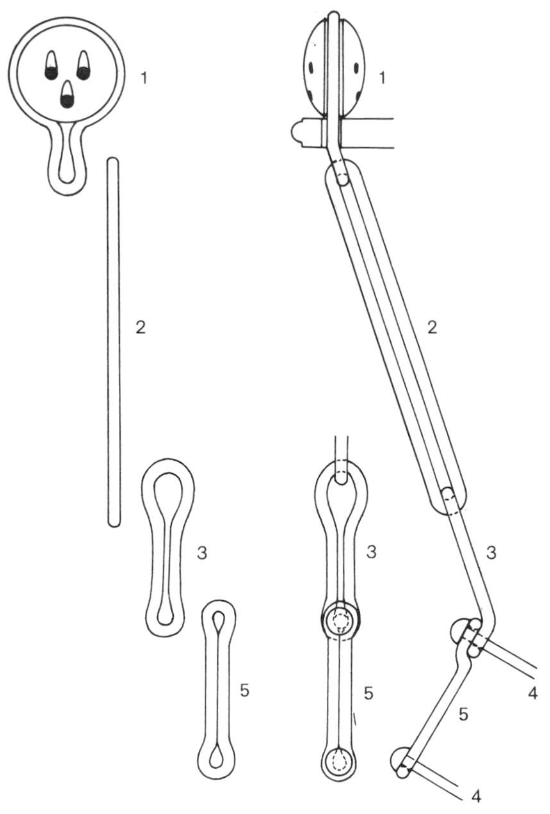

Chain plates: 1. Lower deadeye and upper link; 2. Middle link; 3. Toe link; 4. Bolts; 5. Preventer link

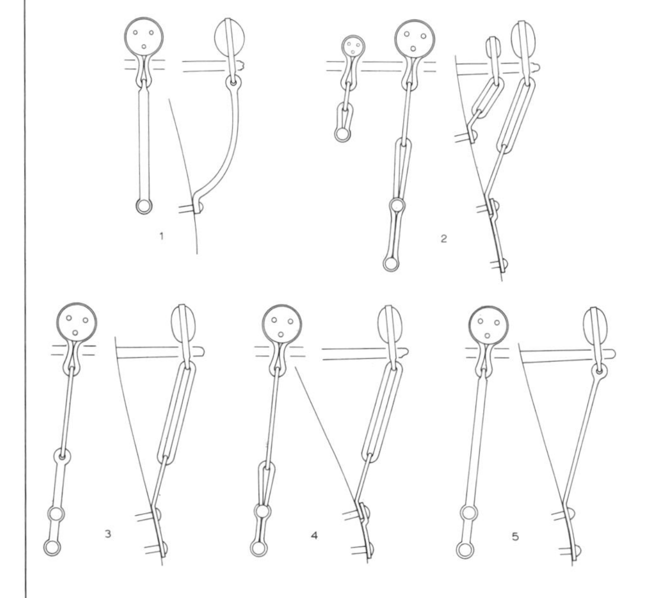

Chains:
1. 17th century;
2. British after 1760
3. British early 18th century
4. French late 18th century
5. Dutch late 18th century

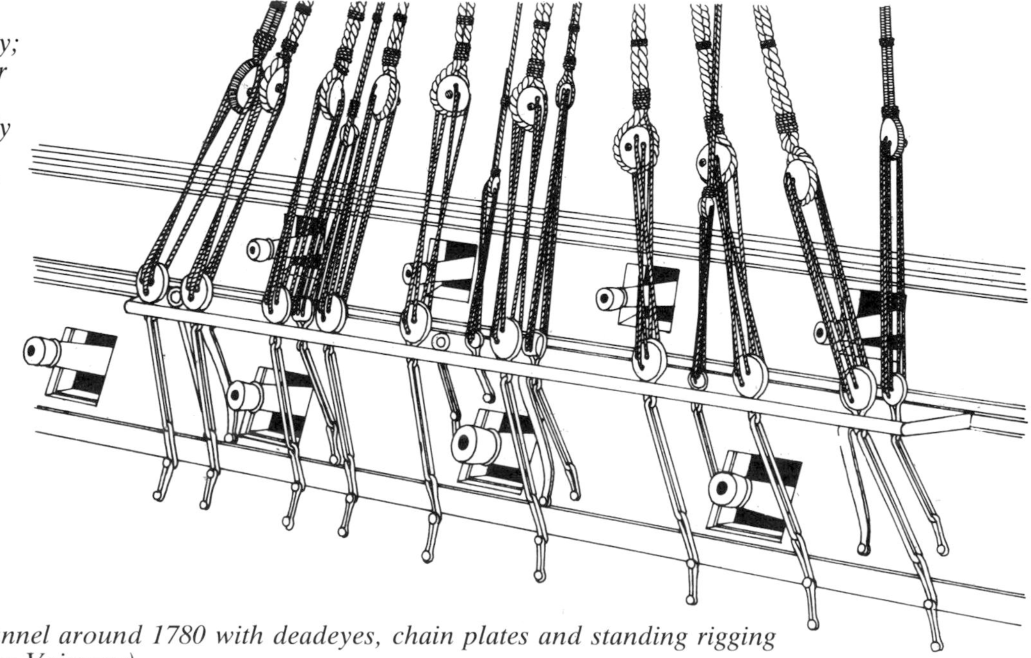

Channel around 1780 with deadeyes, chain plates and standing rigging (after Vaisseau)

Arrangement of chain plates and deadeyes on ships of the 19th century

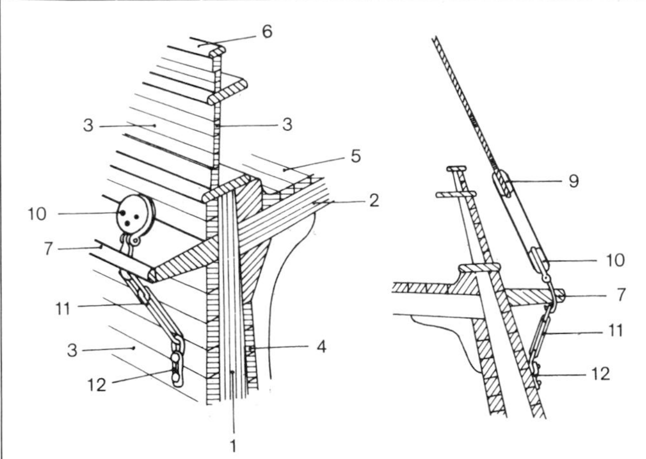

Warships and merchant ships of the early 19th century

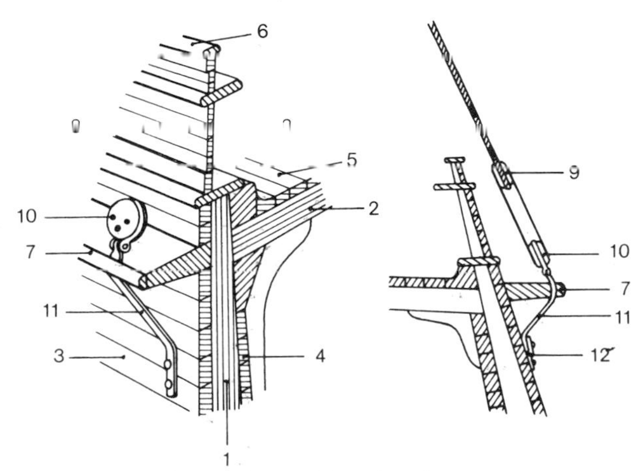

Warships and merchant ships by the middle of the 19th century, later on warships

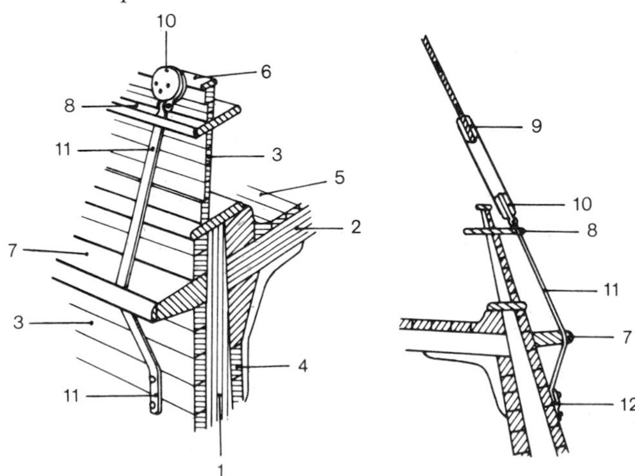

Large merchants ships and clippers after the middle of the 19th century

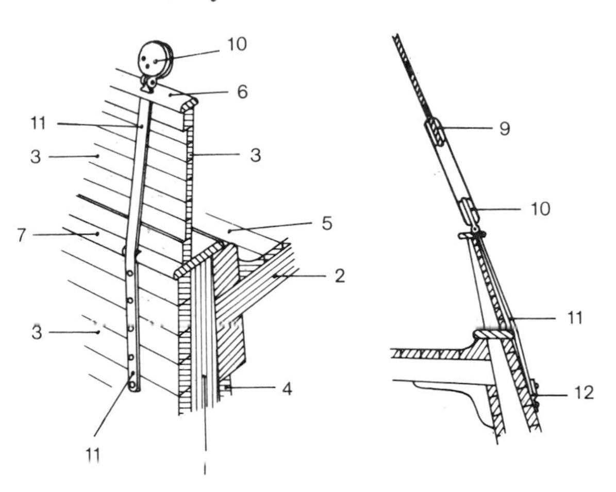

Smaller merchants ships after the middle of the 19th century

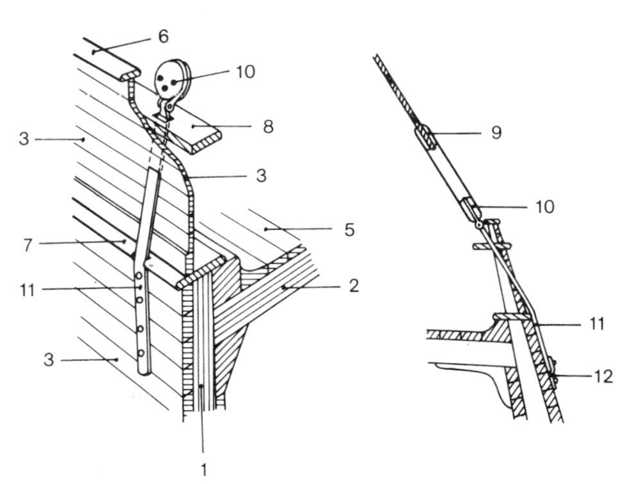

Merchant ships, especially schooners after the middle of the 19th century

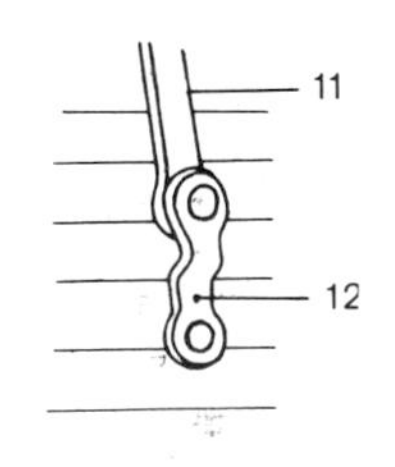

1. Frame; 2. Deck beam; 3. Outer planking; 4. Ceiling; 5. Deck planks; 6. Rail; 7. Channel; 8. Channel boards; 9. Upper deadeye (with shroud); 10. Lower deadeye; 11. Chain plate; 12. Preventer

Fixed blocks

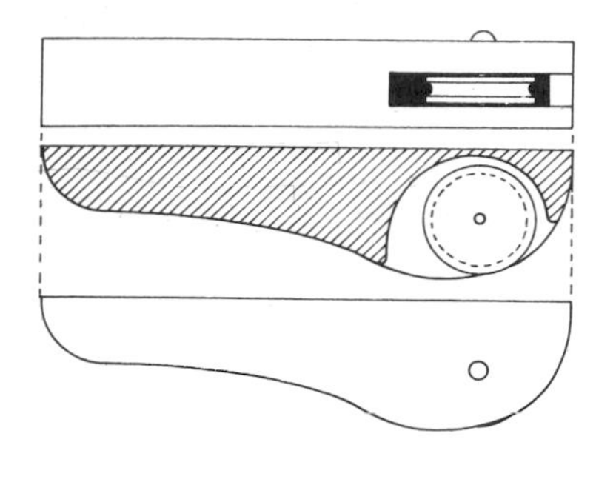

The lower sheets and some other ropes were led into the inside of the ship via fixed blocks.
In the Middle Ages and into the 16th century the forerunner of the fixed block was an opening in the hull which contained a sheave; from the 17th century onwards these openings began to be fitted with their own hardwood blocks, which accommodated the sheaves and their pins. This assembly was then fitted into the hull.
The fixed block swallow is sawn through the wood, and you should note that the edges of the swallow where the rope reeves through are sanded back and rounded.
The sheaves themselves can be turned on a small lathe, or cut from brass sheet (not too thin), and filed to section.
Steel pins of suitable diameter are used, but please note that the pins were never installed at right-angles to the waterline, but inclined aft by 6-10 degrees.
There were never more than three sheaves on one pin; when four sheaves were required, they were always arranged as two pairs in line.

Scuppers

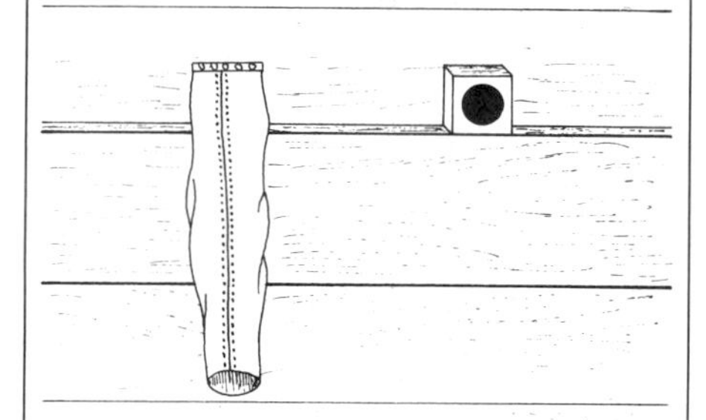

Scuppers are among those small details which are hardly ever included on models of indifferent quality. The purpose of the scuppers was to allow water to run off the deck, whether the water was from rough seas, from the bilge pumps, or was simply used for scrubbing the decks. For this reason two or three pairs of scuppers were arranged at the lowest point of the decks, i.e around midships at the waist, and a further pair was often located aft just ahead of the mizen mast. The scuppers were usually fitted on the middle and upper deck on three deckers, on the gun and upper deck on two-deckers, and on the upper deck of single deckers (frigates and similar vessels). The scuppers led from the deck waterway obliquely downwards through the planking to the outside. In the Middle Ages they were lined with hardwood, and from the 16th century sheathed with lead so that the water could not penetrate into the timbers.
Of course, scuppers can be home-made, but this is a case in which it might be sensible to have a look at what is commercially available.

Hatches and hatch covers

The hatches were designed to permit stores to be loaded into the ship. Their frame was formed by the hatch coaming, into which the hatch cover was set. On warships these covers consisted of gratings (see GRATINGS), while on merchant ships they were of solid timber. They could be flat, curved, half barrel-shaped, pitched like a roof, or like a school desk, and the modeller should not neglect the essential handgrips – rings, rods, hand brackets, recesses – which again are all too often omitted.
The hatch coaming and hatch cover were made of timber until the second half of the 19th century, and they remain so on many smaller ships to this day. On large ships the hatches and hatch covers were increasingly made of metal from about 1850 on.

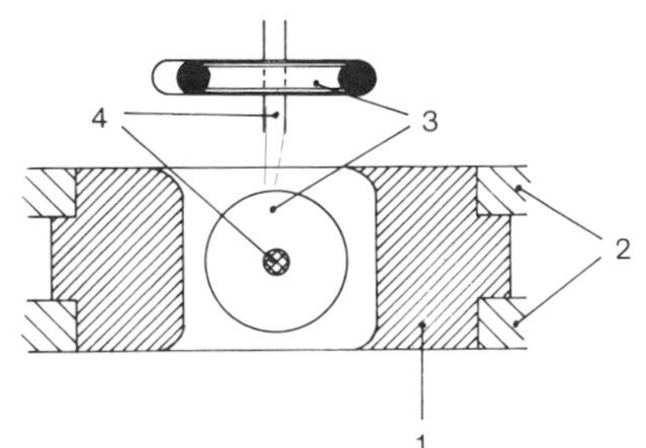

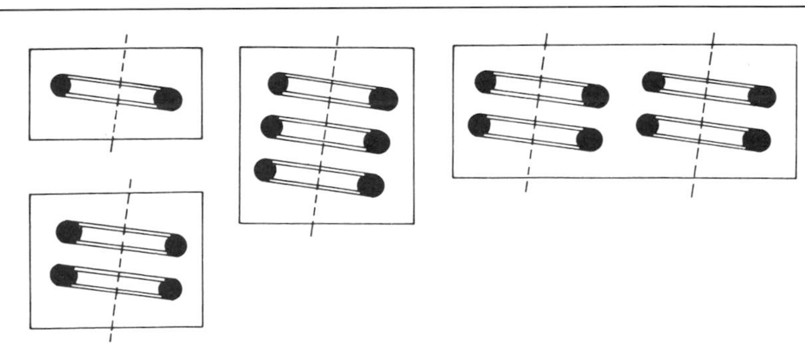

Fixed blocks:
1. Block; 2. Planking;
3. Sheave; 4. Pin;
Top right single, double, triple and quadruple blocks

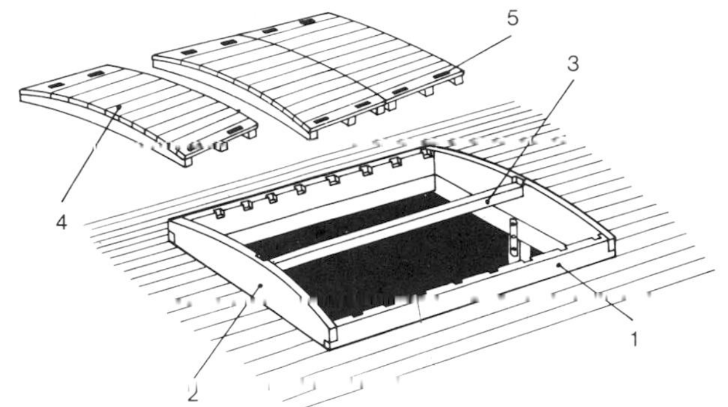

Hatch with hatch cover: 1. Coaming; 2. Head ledge; 3. Removable carling; 4. Section of hatch cover; 5. Hand hole (or bolt ring)

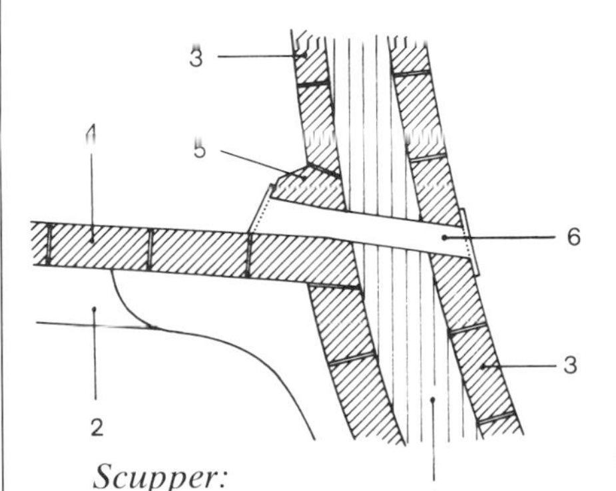

Scupper:
1. Frame; 2. Deck beam; 3. Planking;
4. Deck planks;
5. Waterway;
6. Scupper

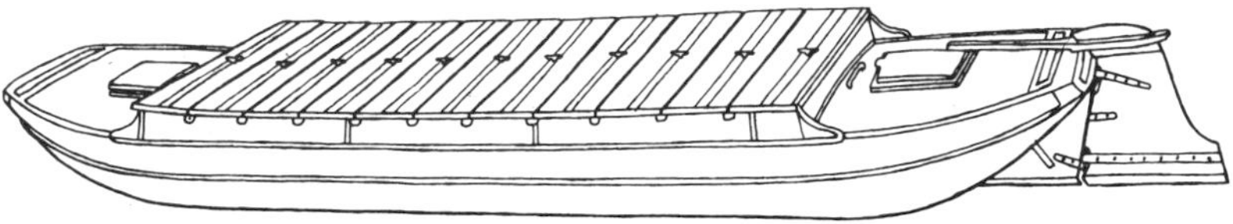

Dutch Schuitje (towing barge) of the 19th century. The loading hatches take up the large part of the ship; they were sealed with flat hatch covers

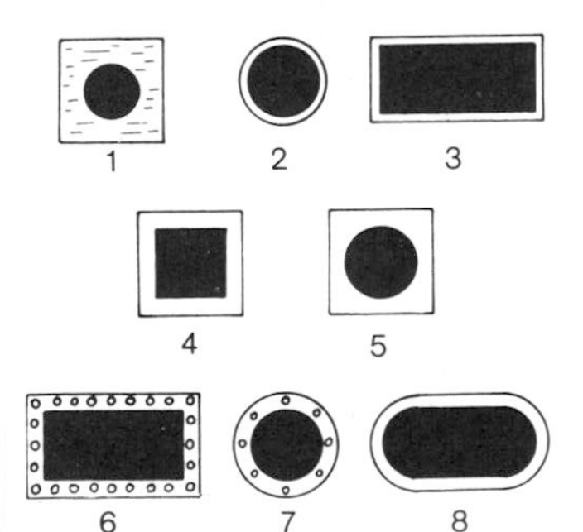

Scupper openings:
1. Hardwood, Middle Ages; 2.-5. Lead, 16th/19th century;
6.-8. Iron, 19th century

Dutch Tjalk (shown without mast) of the 18th/19th century. The loading hatches are arranged behind the mast and covered in a pitched-style roof. Some of the removed hatch covers are stacked up on the foremost hatch

Portholes or scuttles

The lighting and ventilation of the ship's interior was for many centuries of an extremely dubious standard. The glittering gilded splendour of the baroque ships emitted a terrible stink, and the elegant galleys were accompanied by such a pestilent vapour that the ships were directed to special anchorages far from the rest of humanity. Many ports refused them entry at all – and in those days the common people were by no means as squeamish about foul smells as we are in this refined age. Such conditions did not improve at all until the late 18th century, and not significantly until the 19th century.
Portholes came into use about the middle of the 19th century. The model maker has to decide again how he intends to represent the glass – either by the traditional "glass colours" of green, blue or black, or with small pieces of celluloid, which are glued into the portholes. It is, of course, essential that all the glass on a particular model is represented in the same way. Hence if you have made your stern windows from celluloid, you should not change to "glass colours" for the portholes or skylights, and vice versa. The portholes themselves can be turned from brass on a small lathe, although it makes more sense to purchase these items ready made. They are fitted into holes in the hull which should be drilled with the greatest care. Allow me to mention once more that you should never drill a hole to the required diameter in one go, but start with a pilot drill, and gradually open up the hole with a series of larger drills.

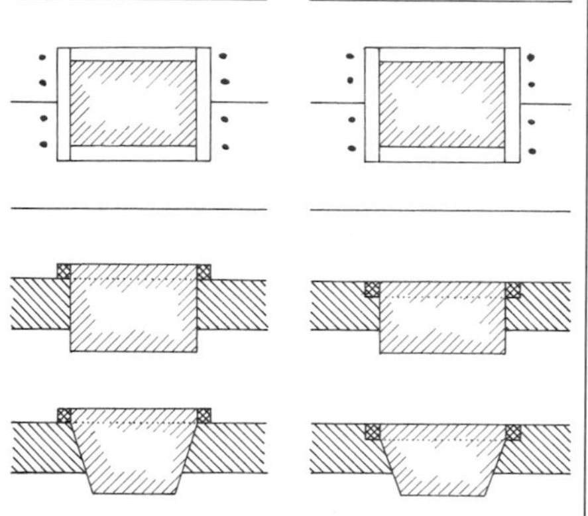

Decklights came into general use in about 1840. Three views of raised-frame and flush-frame versions are shown left and right respectively

Skylights

Skylights were not used widely until the first half of the 19th century, except on Dutch state yachts, which incorporated them as early as the 17th century, and British warships which fitted them in their quarter deck or poop companions. The frames were of wood until the last third of the 19th century, when metal skylight frames came into use. The glass is treated as described for the portholes. The protective grilles sometimes fitted are made of thin steel or brass wire, and inset into the frames. Skylights are sometimes offered as finished commercial units, but in this case it is much better to make them yourself, if you are keen to keep your model to a high standard of accuracy and historical fidelity.

Ventilators

Ventilators became necessary around 1825 with the introduction of steam engines and boiler rooms below deck. After the middle of the 19th century pressure and suction ventilators were developed, and they are still in use today – although suction types were very rarely used in the 19th century. Ventilators can be made from metal, wood or synthetic resin; it is also possible, with a little luck and patience, to find ready made items in model shops sufficiently true to scale to be usable. Please remember that the top of the airshaft should be visible at the back or bottom of the ventilator opening, and you may need to drill a short way into the unit to indicate the hole. The heads of pressure ventilators, which are extremely difficult to fabricate, are ideal for the electro-plating method of producing shells.

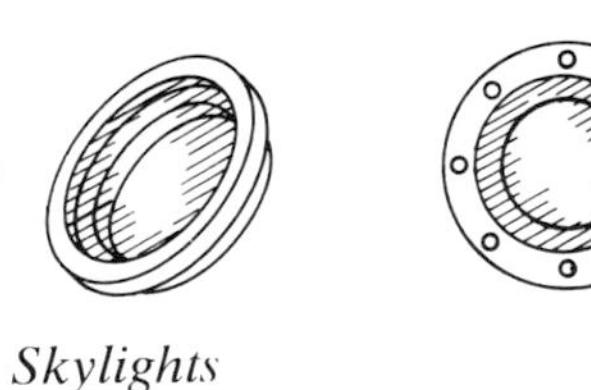

Portholes, metal-rimmed, as commonly used after the first half of the 19th century

Skylights

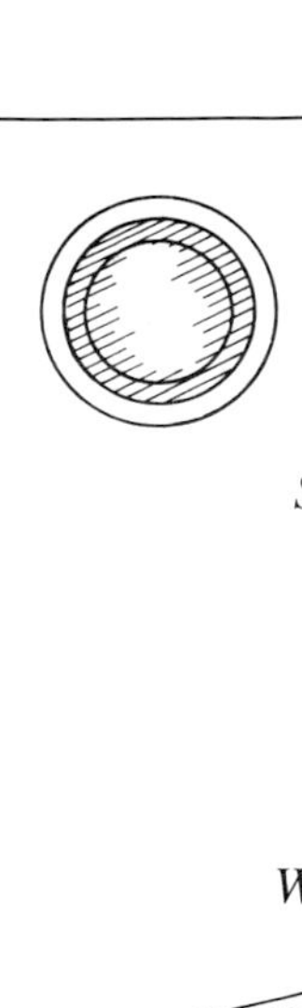

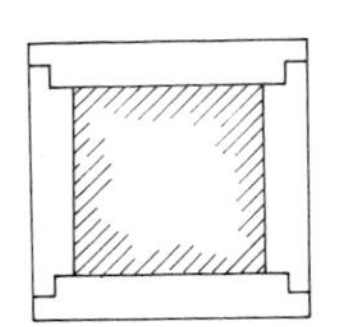

Wood-framed port

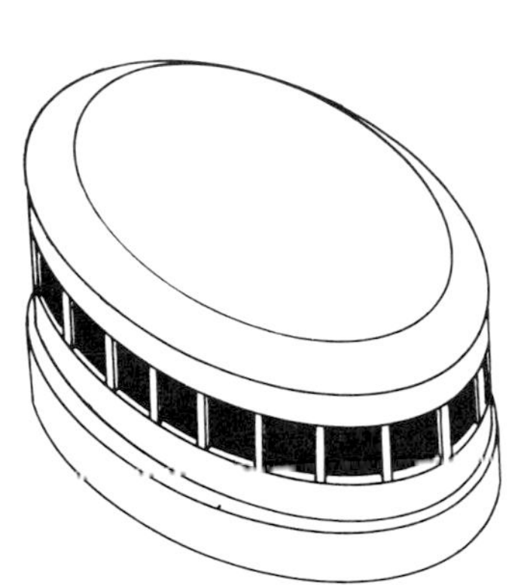

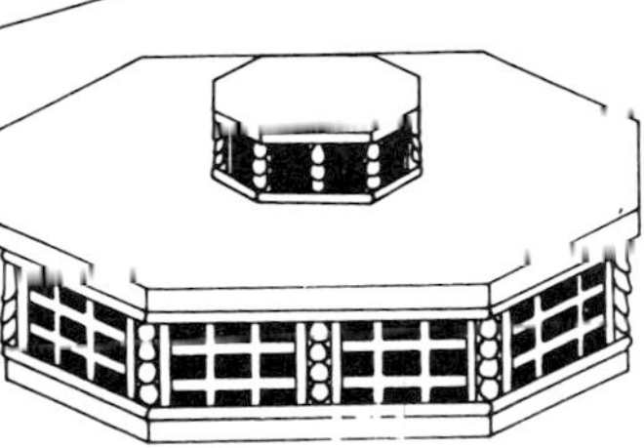

Skylights of the 18th and early 19th centuries

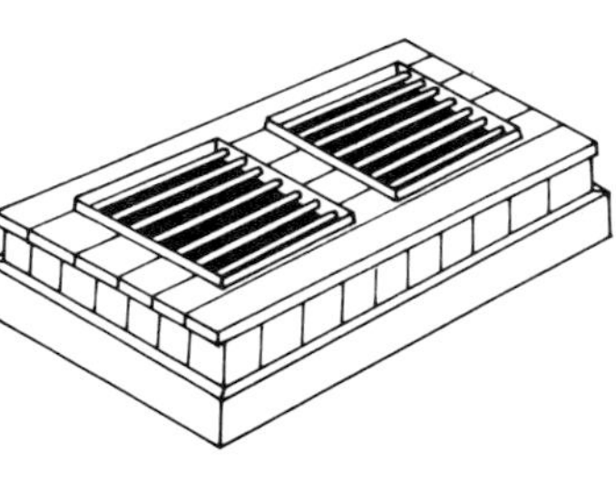

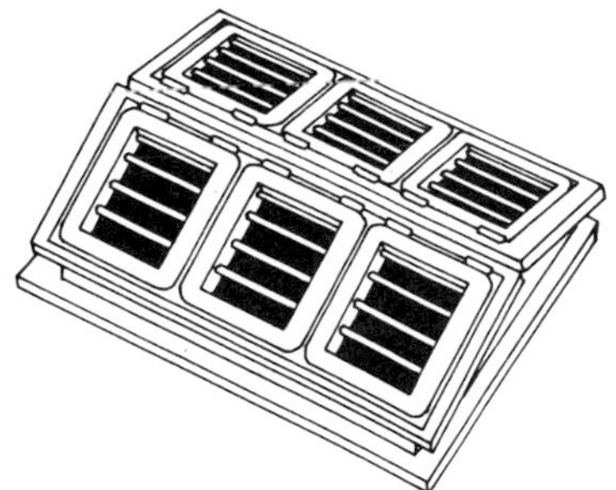

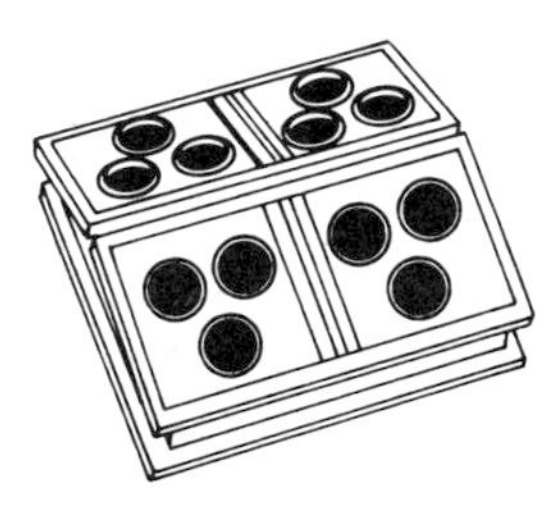

Skylights after the middle of the 19th century

Ventilators

Ventilators, in use since about 1830

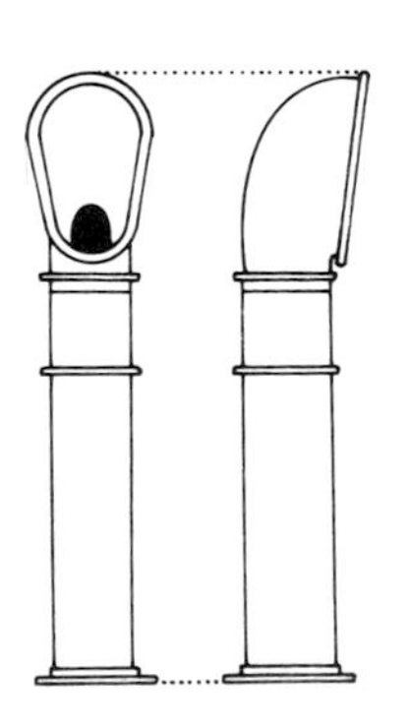

Pressure ventilators, the most common form of ventilator after the middle of the 19th century

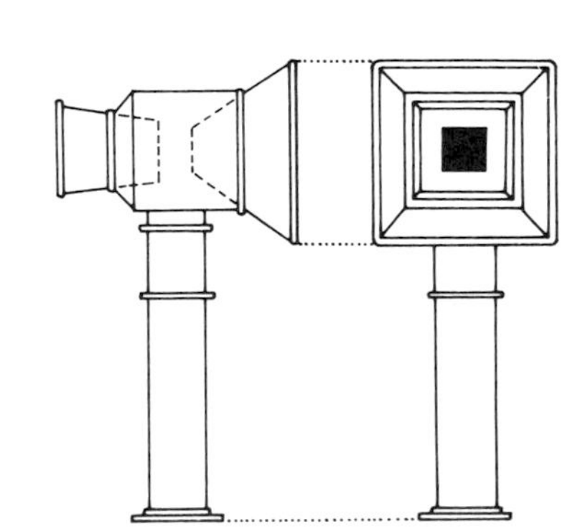

Suction ventilators, after the middle of the 19th century

Ladders

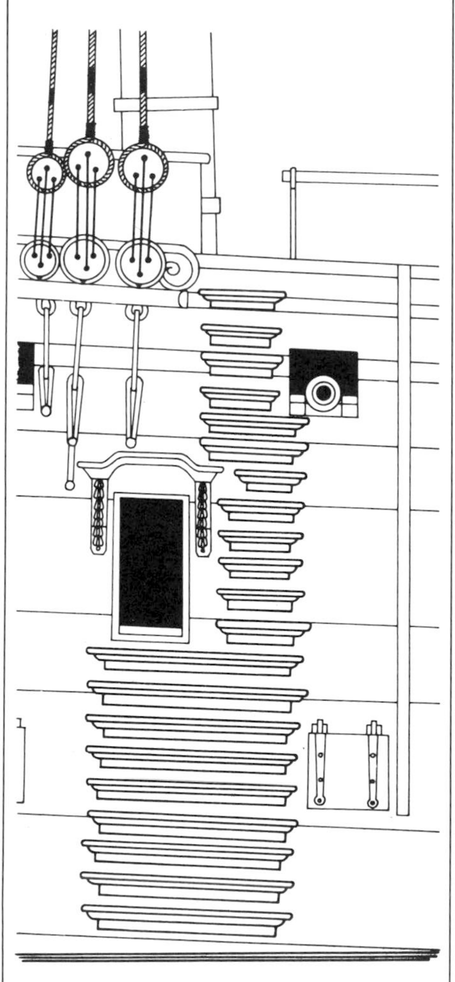

External ladder (may be fixed or rope) of a three-decker, 18th century. The port led into the middle deck

The various levels of the ship were connected by means of large numbers of ladders. Until well into the 17th century the ladders were of simple design, usually rather steep and awkward to use, with a handrail a rare luxury. In the baroque and rococo periods, when splendour and ostentation reached their zenith (from the middle of the 17th century to the middle of the 18th century), the ladders were fitted with splendidly carved, turned, and sometimes gilded balustrades – but they remained steep and inconvenient.

In the late 18th century a degree of sobriety and practicality returned and in the second half of the 19th century the strings and treads of the ladders began to be made of metal – but they remained, as ever, steep and awkward.

Ladders really have to be made by the modeller, as those available commercially are not up to much. This task is made much easier if you start by making a jig, as shown in the drawing. The treads are set between the individual wood blocks. The tread spacing on the original was about 8 or 9ins. The strings can then be glued to the tread ends. It would be enormous trouble to have to construct a jig of this type for each separate ladder. Fortunately, all the ladders in a particular ship usually shared the same tread spacing and also the same pitch angle – at least this is true of the exposed ladders on the upper decks. This allows the modeller to make virtually all the ladders for his model on the same jig.

Until the introduction of fixed outboard ladders in the 17th century (much later on small ships) a rope ladder or Jacob's ladder served the same purpose. The rope ladder consisted of round wood rungs tied between two ropes. Such a ladder was also fitted abaft the mast from the crow's nest to the deck until the late 15th century; i.e. in the period before the shrouds were fitted with their network of ratlines.

Fixed outboard steps had no strings, only treads. A long strip with the right cross-section for the treads is cut from a strip of wood (or you can use several strips from which the required number of small lengths are cut). These treads now just need to be trimmed square and to exact length before they are fixed to the hull.

Take care! Bear in mind that the top surface of the treads must be parallel to the waterline. This involves sanding the inner edge of the treads to allow for the curvature of the hull.

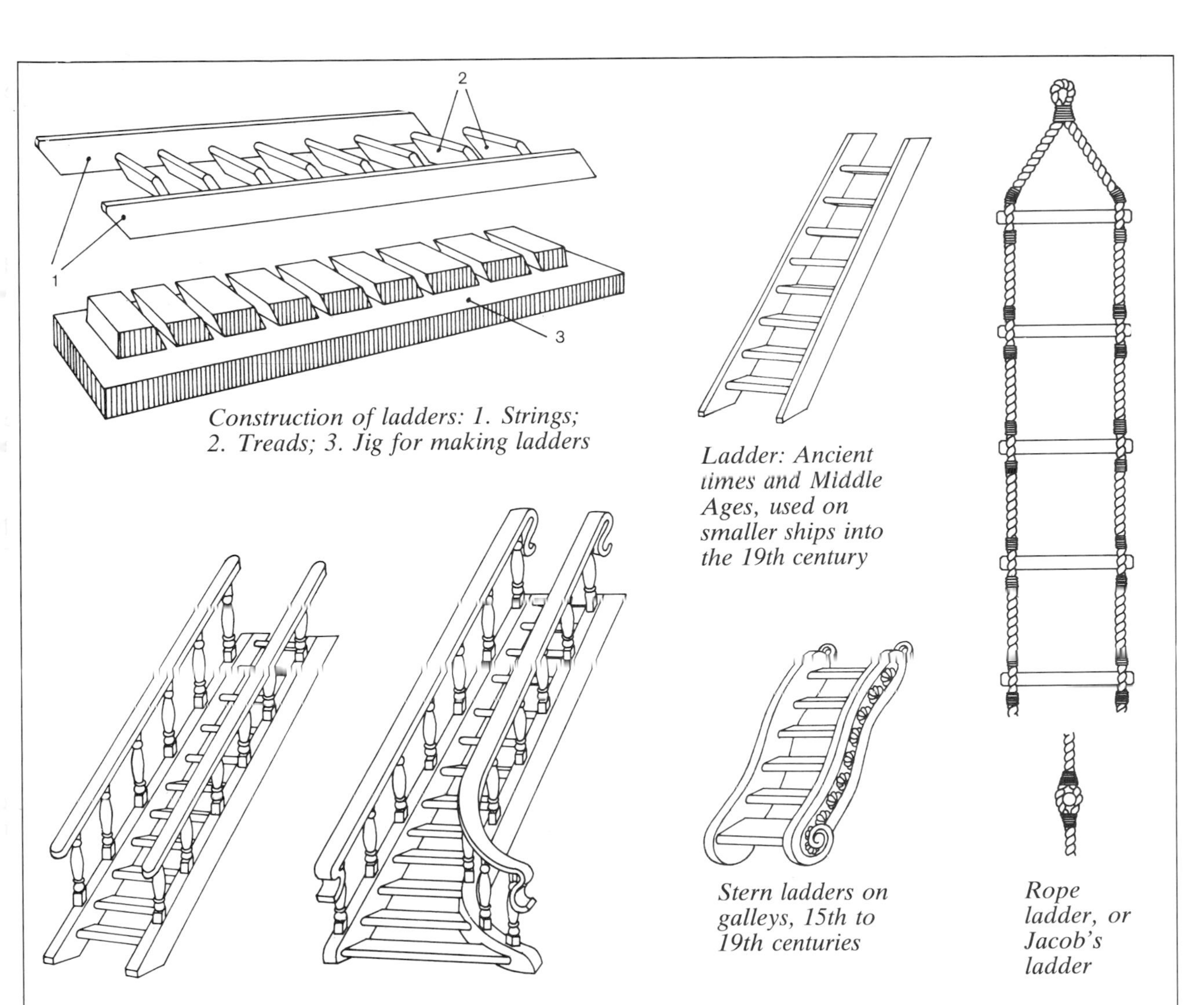

Construction of ladders: 1. Strings; 2. Treads; 3. Jig for making ladders

Ladder: Ancient times and Middle Ages, used on smaller ships into the 19th century

Stern ladders on galleys, 15th to 19th centuries

Rope ladder, or Jacob's ladder

Ladders in the 17th and 18th centuries

Companions and deckhouses

You are unlikely to encounter any major technical problems with these parts but there are still a few little detail points which you might like to note.

Companionways

The companionways in merchant ships are the ladderways which lead down from the upper to the lower decks, and until the 18th century the only surround was a coaming and a single guard rail. In the late 18th century a lattice of metal hoops was erected across this rail, over which a tarpaulin could be stretched so that rain did not reach the lower decks in bad weather. This development was soon superseded by the erection of a fixed timber structure over the companionways of merchant ships and the ladderways of small warships, with doors for weather protection. The word companion was used in warships to denote openings in the decks to provide light and air and normally covered by a removable skylight. They were not ladderways.

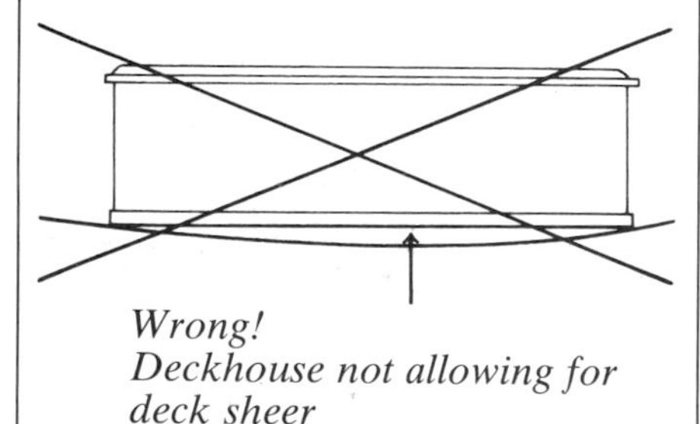

Wrong!
Deckhouse not allowing for deck sheer

Deck houses

Deck houses are, with some exceptions, fairly new, and date from the period shortly before the middle of the 19th century. Details on their appearance should be included on your plans. The only important point to note is that the base of the deckhouses must precisely match the convex or concave curvature of the deck, as shown in the drawing on the left. Several ships' boats were often stowed up on top of the deck houses (see BOAT CHOCKS).

The oldest form of deck house, if you can call them that, was the hen house, a variety of which was erected on the waist or the poop deck from the 18th century on. Pig, goat and sheep houses of similar types also occur.

The animal stalls themselves are built from wood strips, and the bars are fitted in the same way as the skylight grilles. The floor of the stalls should be given a very thin coat of glue (balsa cement is ideal, as this dries completely transparent), onto which a thin layer of sawdust is spread.

If you want to include true-scale hens, pigs, sheep or goats in the stalls, take a look around a model railway shop where such things are available. But do be sure that the animals are to the correct scale. There are firms which specialise in the manufacture of people and animals for model railways. The only difficulty is that the usual scales for model railways and model ships do not have much in common. As model railway people state their scales in "gauges", here are the most important equivalent scales:

O gauge	– 1:45	OO gauge	– 1:76
HO gauge	– 1:87	N gauge	– 1: 125

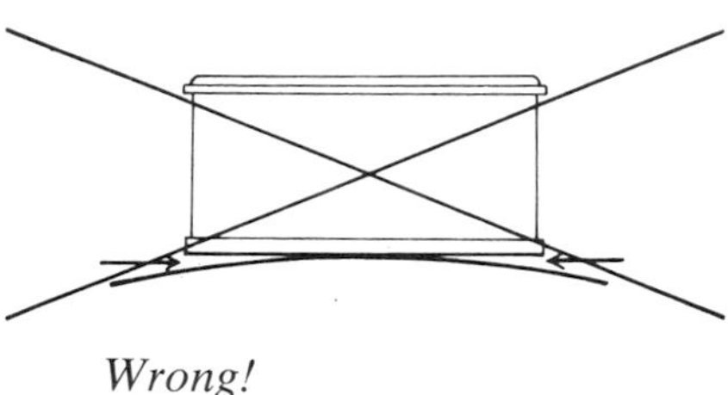

Wrong!
Deckhouse not allowing for deck camber

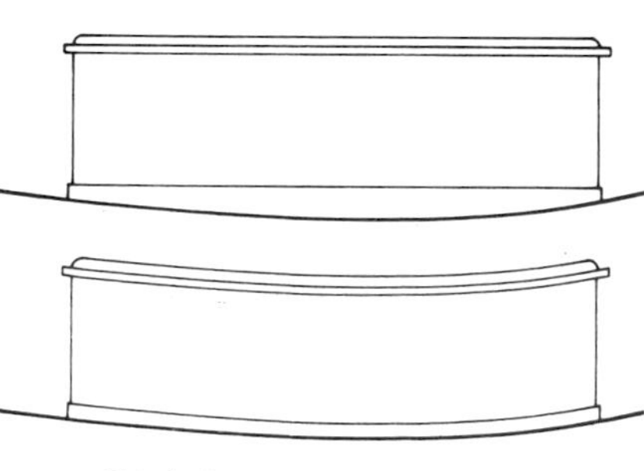

Right!
Base of deckhouse shaped to fit snugly to deck

Ornamental gondola with canopy used by the Imperial Ambassador to Venice

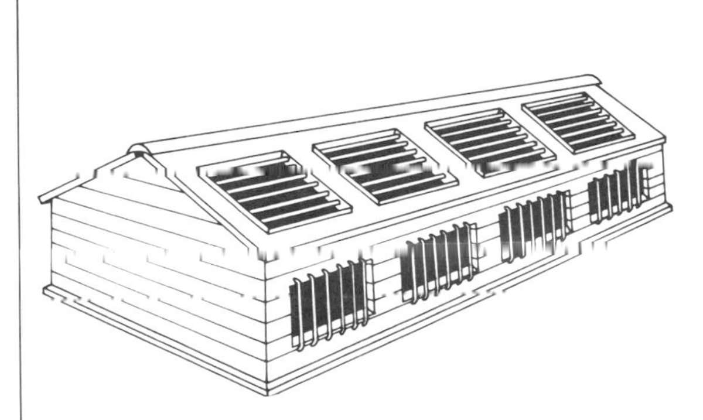

Chicken coop, 18th/19th centuries

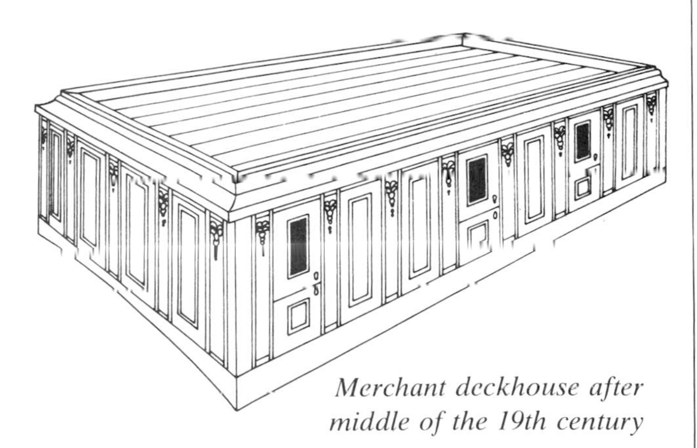

Merchant deckhouse after middle of the 19th century

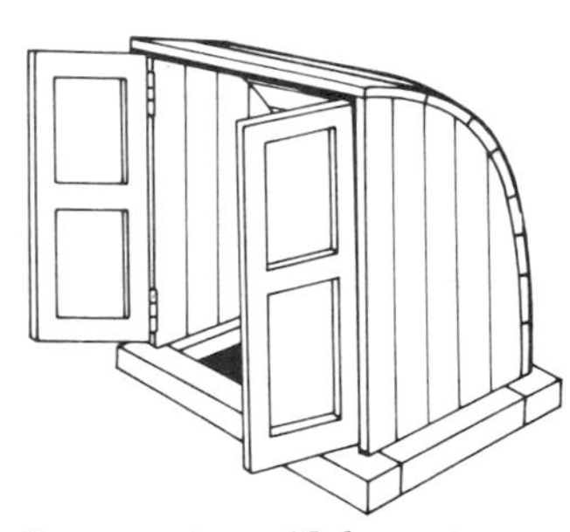

Companion, 19th century

The richly carved and gilded stern superstructure of La Capitana di Venezia, *a galley at the battle of Lepanto, 1571. The awning is of red damask. Model by the author for Aeronaut Modellbau*

The Compass

Since its introduction in the 13th/14th century the compass has remained the single most important navigation aid right through to the present day. Its essential value to the mariner is indicated by the richly decorated, painted compass dials, often inlaid with ivory, tortoise shell and precious metals which are often found. The modeller is unlikely to take upon himself the job of making a compass unless the scale of his model is extremely large, but nevertheless the instrument demands at least a few words in this book.

The Binnacle

It is only natural that this precious, vital and sensitive instrument should be deemed worthy of special protection. Since the beginning of the 17th century the compass was set up in its own binnacle in front of the helmsman. This binnacle, which remained largely unaltered in appearance during the whole of the 17th and 18th centuries, consisted of a wooden box with three compartments and glass windows. There were two alternative arrangements for the equipment inside: there were either two compasses, one in each of the two side compartments, the middle section containing a lantern for illumination at night – this was the usual form, especially in warships. Otherwise the compass was located in the central compartment, and the lamps were set up in the two side sections – this was the more common arrangement in merchant ships.

In 1820 H. Popham designed a compass binnacle with a virtually cube-shaped base and a low pyramid-shaped cap, which had glass panes on all four sides to allow observation of the compass. In 1835 the Englishman Preston patented his compass binnacle, and from this design all the variations in common use from 1860 to the present day have evolved. All ships used to carry – and still do carry – a whole series of compasses, such as the small bearing compass shown on the right. With the introduction of iron ships in England in 1880, the compass with deviation spheres was developed by Sir William Thompson (later Lord Kelvin) and this means of correcting deviation arising from magnetic influences of the ship's structure on the compass needle rapidly became universal.

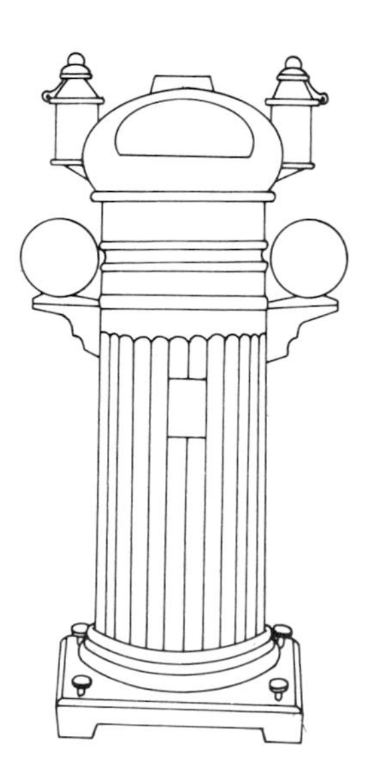

Binnacle, 19th/20th century type, with deviation adjustment

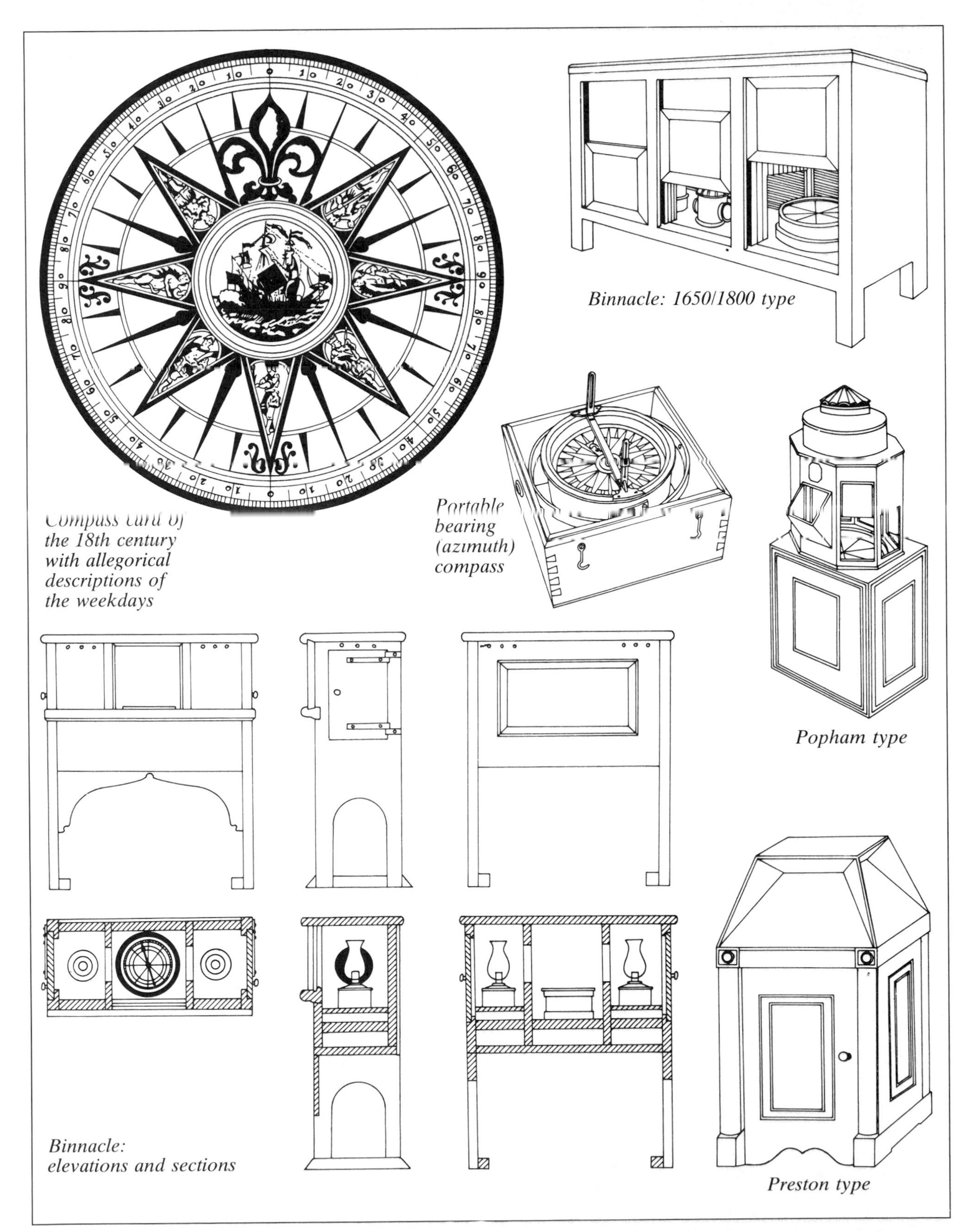

Compass card of the 18th century with allegorical descriptions of the weekdays

Binnacle: 1650/1800 type

Portable bearing (azimuth) compass

Popham type

Binnacle: elevations and sections

Preston type

Steering gear

Steering gear, 16th/17th centuries

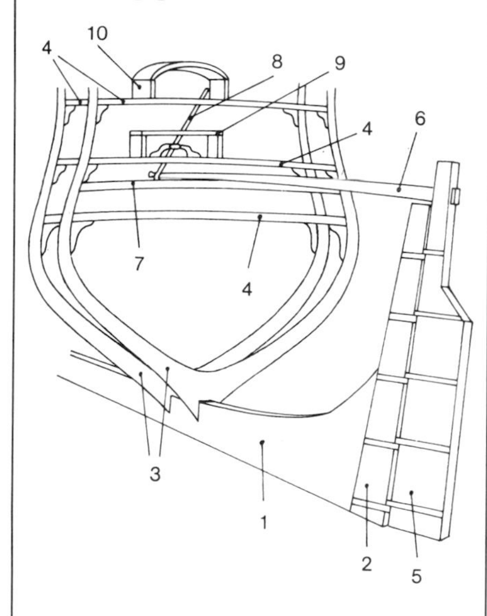

Steering gear, 18th/19th centuries

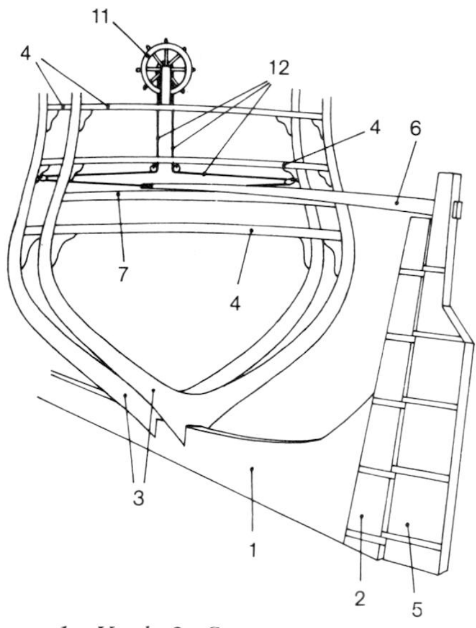

1. Keel; 2. Stern post; 3. Frames; 4. Deck beams; 5. Rudder; 6. Tiller; 7. Sweep; 8. Whipstaff; 9. Steering position; 10. Helmsman's shelter; 11. Ship's wheel; 12. Tiller ropes

There are three methods of operating the rudder:
1. The tiller;
2. The tiller and whipstaff;
3. The tiller and wheel.

The position from which the rudder is controlled is termed the steering position.

The tiller

We have already discussed this component in connection with the rudder itself, so there is no need to repeat the information here. Steering by means of the tiller was and still is the normal method on all smaller ships, and until the 15th century it was also the only known method.

In the 17th century two ropes were fixed to the tiller, which could be used either to hold the rudder in one position, or to operate the tiller in heavy seas, if it was feared that the strength of two or three men would not be sufficient. This arrangement was adopted by virtually all smaller warships in the 17th century (cutters, brigs, and sloops), and also by many merchant ships.

The whipstaff

In the 15th century ships began to grow larger and larger, and as the stern superstructure rose ever higher, the helmsman at the tiller found himself one or two decks below the level of the commanding officer. This meant that the helmsman was working blind, and had to steer by command only – an extremely insecure method in rough weather or in battle. For this reason the whipstaff was invented, which initially was a bar connected to the tiller and pivoting through a hole in the deck above. This permitted the helmsman to steer from a higher deck, as well as providing better leverage.

During the 16th century ships had been allowed to grow so large and heavy that the need arose for some additional assistance to operate the correspondingly large rudder and tiller. The sweep was introduced at this time; a heavy timber beam, which took the weight of the tiller. Its top surface was sheathed with metal, which was coated with grease and soap to reduce friction when the tiller was moved. The whipstaff was itself fitted with a swivelling bearing, again with the intention of improving leverage. The greatest disadvantage of the whipstaff was its small angular throw – this was 40 to 50 degrees, which correspond to a rudder movement of only 5 to 10 degrees.

On smaller ships the helmsman steered from the upper or quarter deck, while on larger ships he usually stood on the upper deck, but was able to see out through a hole in the quarter deck and steer by sight. Protection was provided by a shelter over the top; this was designed to provide the helmsman with the safest location possible even during a storm or in battle.

The ship's wheel

At the beginning of the 18th century the whipstaff was superseded by the ship's steering wheel. A barrel was supported on two pedestals, and fitted with one or two large handwheels.

The movement of the tiller was now effected by means of ropes, which offered the advantage of excellent transmission of power, as well as increased rudder throw, and hence manoeuvrability of the whole ship.

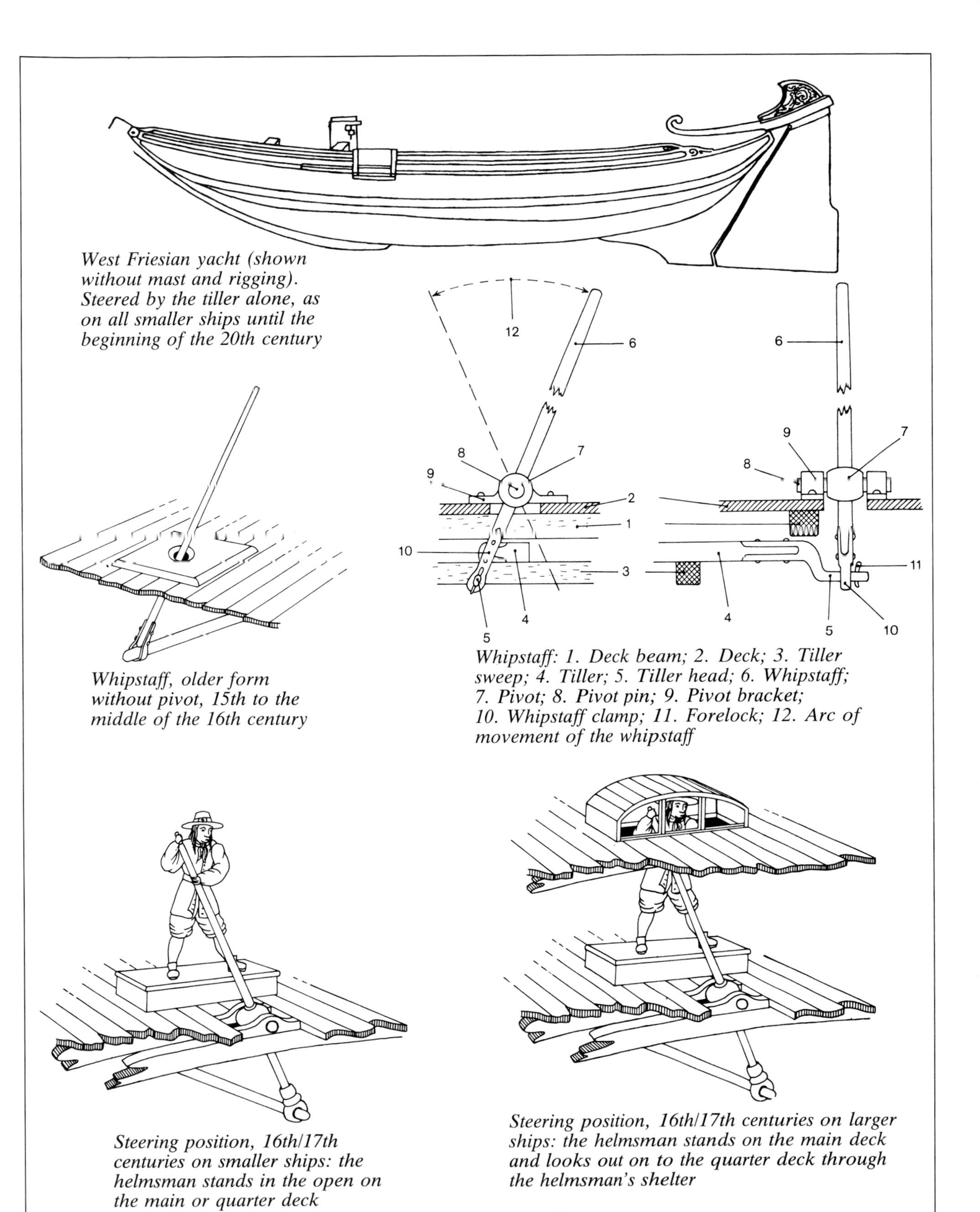

West Friesian yacht (shown without mast and rigging). Steered by the tiller alone, as on all smaller ships until the beginning of the 20th century

Whipstaff, older form without pivot, 15th to the middle of the 16th century

Whipstaff: 1. Deck beam; 2. Deck; 3. Tiller sweep; 4. Tiller; 5. Tiller head; 6. Whipstaff; 7. Pivot; 8. Pivot pin; 9. Pivot bracket; 10. Whipstaff clamp; 11. Forelock; 12. Arc of movement of the whipstaff

Steering position, 16th/17th centuries on smaller ships: the helmsman stands in the open on the main or quarter deck

Steering position, 16th/17th centuries on larger ships: the helmsman stands on the main deck and looks out on to the quarter deck through the helmsman's shelter

Steering gear

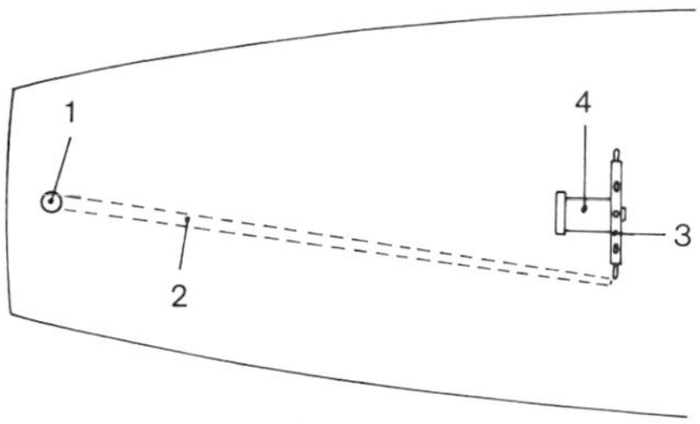

1720 to 1820

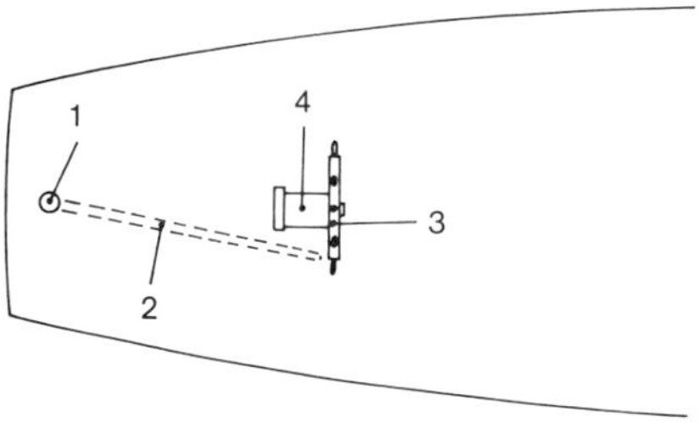

1800 to 1850

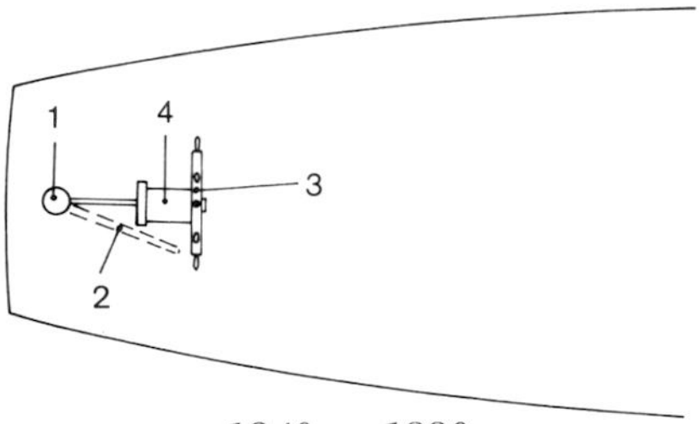

1840 to 1880

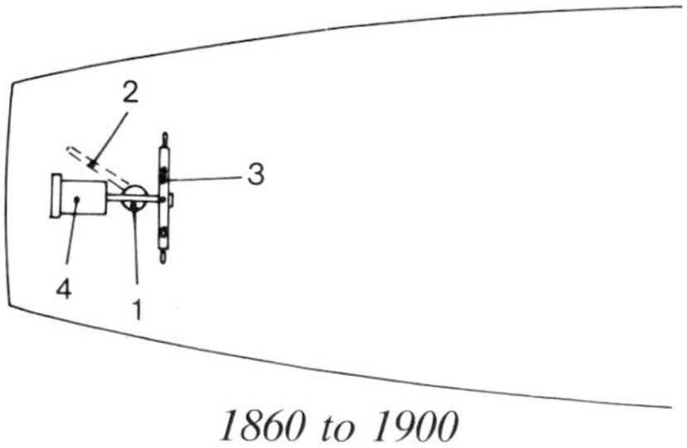

1860 to 1900

Arrangement of rudder, tiller and ship's wheel:
1. Rudder head; 2. Tiller;
3. Ship's wheel; 4. Barrel

The simplicity of construction of a model whipstaff dated before 1700 is in stark contrast with the patience and care required for the steering gear with a wheel in ships of later periods. There are some commercial items available here which offer some help – I shall return to them later – but the complete ships' wheels which are occasionally offered are not of much use.

The first job is to establish exactly where the steering position was located – the plans can usually be relied upon for this information. Until the early years of the 19th century the tiller was fairly long, and the wheel was situated just abaft the mizen mast in continental ships and ahead of it in British ships. When mechanical gearing replaced the tiller ropes in the mid 19th century the wheel moved aft until it was close to the rudder head.

The steering gear was sometimes mounted on a platform, which was usually composed of gratings. The two pedestals in which the barrel spindle was supported were fixed to this platform. The barrel itself was made of wood; it is best assembled from pieces of dowel, and the handwheels fixed to the ends. The construction of the ship's wheel itself is rather complicated, but the method used in the original, and which is shown in the drawing of the right, can only reasonably be used in models built to an appropriately large scale. In model ships built to 1:48 or smaller, the whole wheel is best sawn out of the closest grained timber you can find (boxwood for example), after which the spokes, wheel rim and hand grips are filed, carved and sanded to shape. Finally the metal parts are made from thin brass sheet and glued in place.

Ships' wheels as available commercially should certainly be subjected to critical appraisal. Do not under any circumstances use a plastic one (even a home-made resin casting), as it is impossible to make plastic look like timber afterwards. For the same reason, little can be done with metal.

Making metal ships' wheels yourself is an extremely tricky and thankless task, and this is one time when you really should turn to the model shop. If you insist on trying it yourself, you will find a method described in "Plank on Frame Models", by Harold A. Underhill.

Selection of the wrong diameter for the ship's wheel is a common mistake. On large to medium large ships the diameter across the handles was about 5ft, and on smaller ships around 4ft. The ropes to the tiller were arranged on the same principle on all vessels, except that on large ships they were led below deck through two slots, whilst on smaller ships the ropes were fitted above the deck, as shown in the drawings. Another important point to note is that the number of turns of rope round the drum was no more than 5 to 7, and for chains the figure was seldom more than 5.

In the course of the 19th century mechanical steering gear came to be covered by a housing – please note the nationality of the ship here, as there was a European and an American form of the housing, which are occasionally mixed up. From the first half of the 19th century many experiments were carried out to find the best method of transmitting power from the ship's wheel to the tiller, or directly to the rudder head, including steam assistance in the last third of the 19th century. The most important and most commonly found types are illustrated on the next pages.

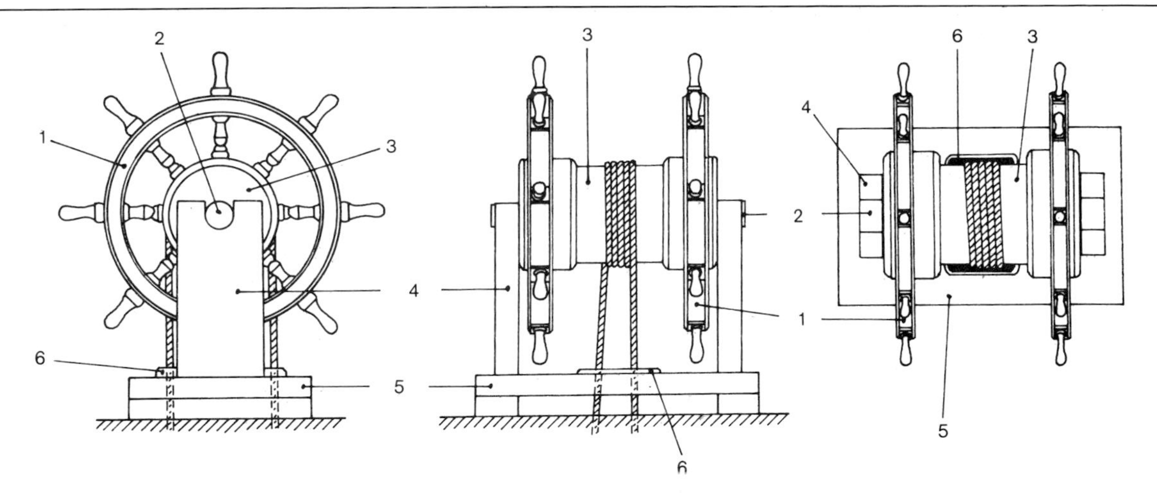

Steering gear, 18th/19th centuries: 1. Wheel; 2. Spindle; 3. Barrel; 4. Pedestal; 5. Platform (often in the form of a grating); 6. Tiller rope slots

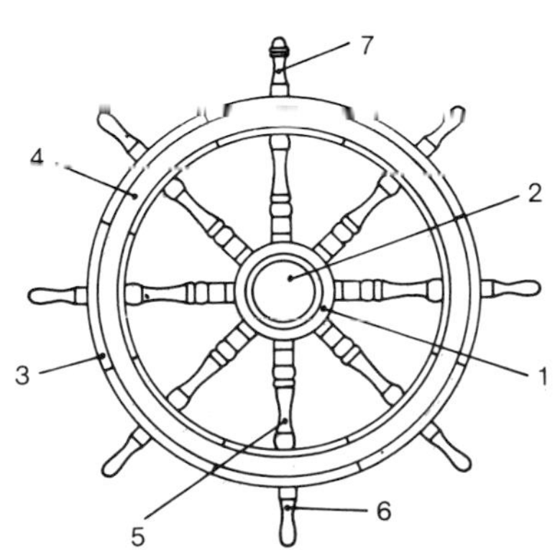

19th century ship's wheel: 1. Nave; 2. Nave plate (brass); 3. Wheel rim; 4. Brass rim plate; 5. Spokes; 6. Handles; 7. King spoke

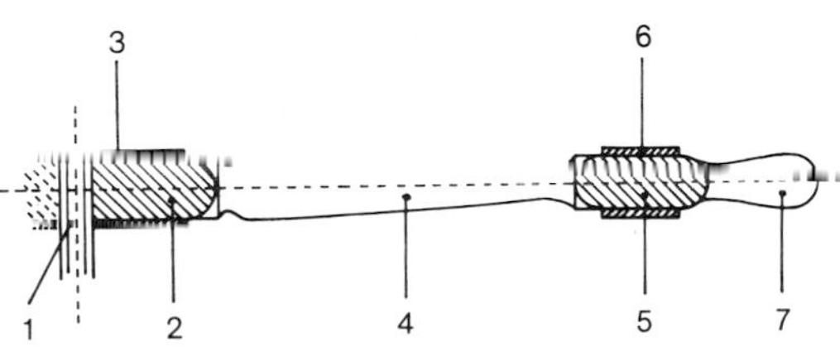

Cross-section through ship's wheel: 1. Spindle; 2. Nave; 3. Nave plate (brass); 4. Spoke; 5. Wheel rim; 6. Brass rim plate; 7. Handles

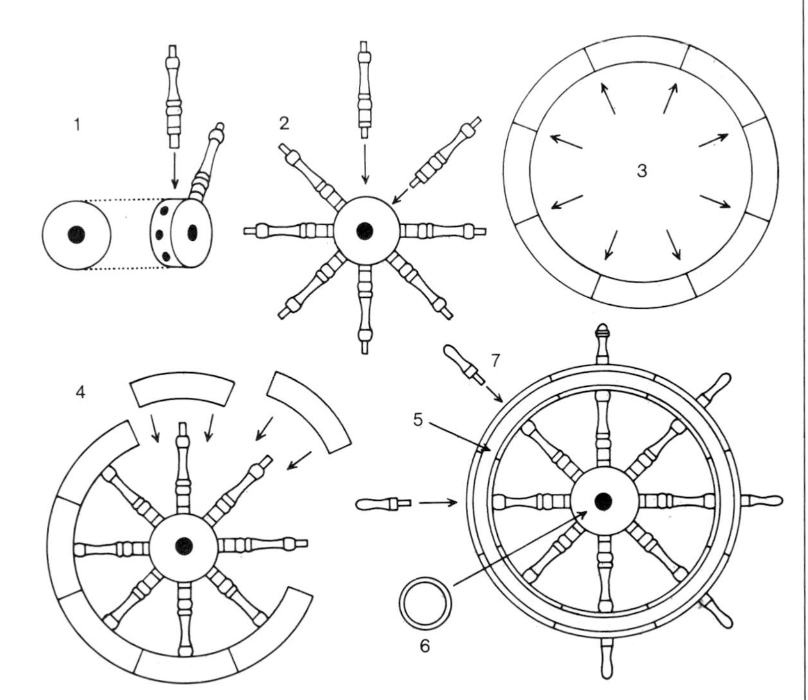

Construction of a ship's wheel from wood: 1. Nave; 2. Fitting of the spokes; 3. Wheel rim made up of felloes; 4. Fitting of the felloes; 5. Brass rim plate; 6. Fitting the nave plate; 7. Fitting the handles

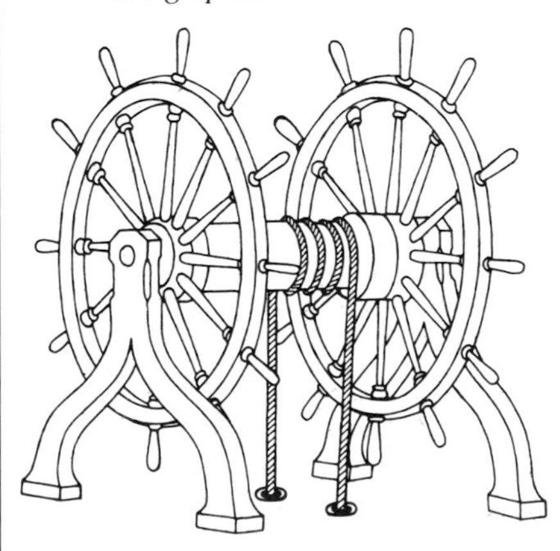

Large steering position with double wheel (French warship c1800)

Steering gear

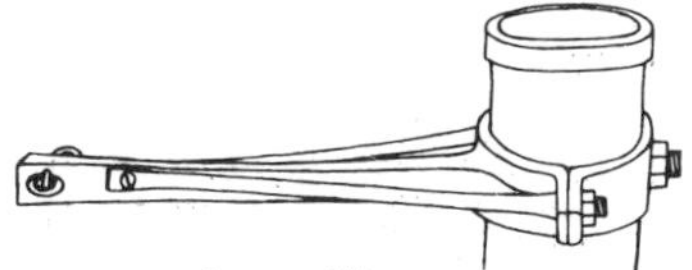

Iron tiller

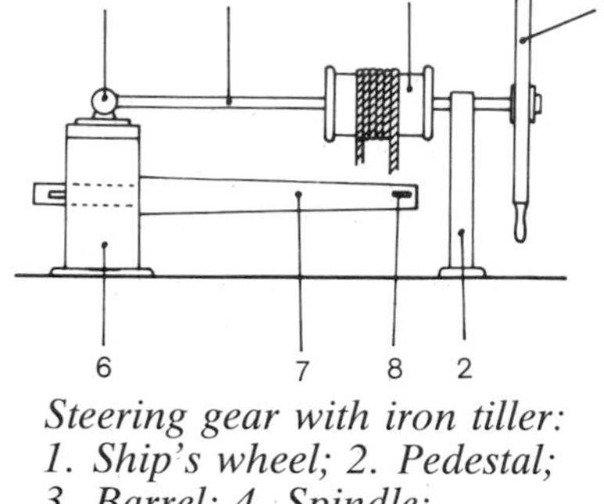

Steering gear with iron tiller: 1. Ship's wheel; 2. Pedestal; 3. Barrel; 4. Spindle; 5. Spindle bearing; 6. Rudder head; 7. Tiller; 8. Eyebolt for tiller rope

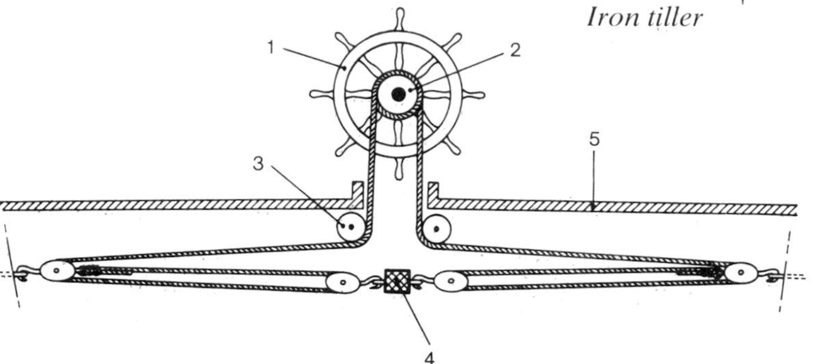

Tiller ropes on large ships: 1. Ship's wheel; 2. Barrel; 3. Sheaves; 4. Tiller; 5. Deck

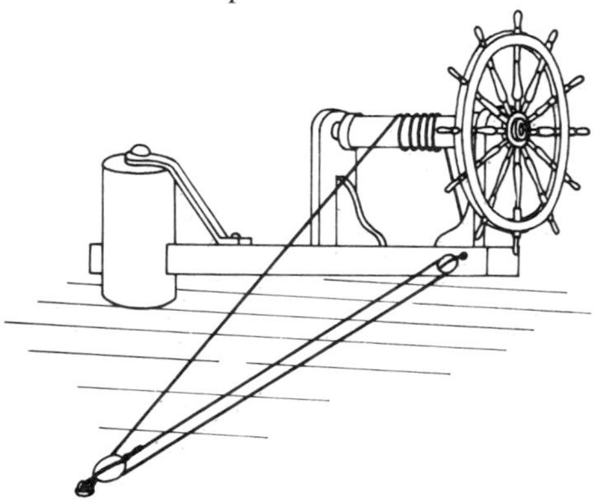

Steering gear of American coastal vessel, 19th century. The ship's wheel was fitted on the tiller and moved with it.

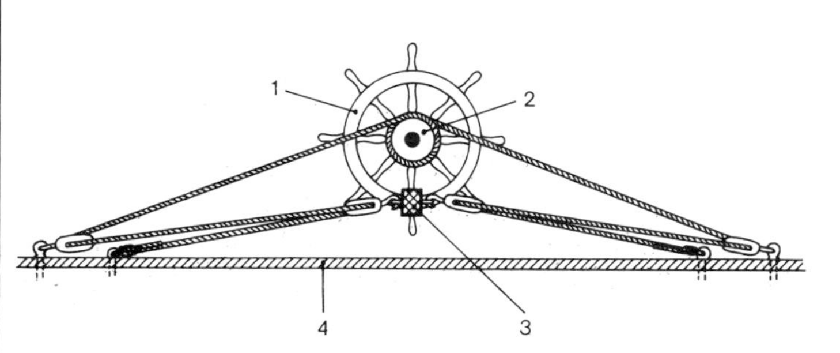

Tiller ropes on smaller ships: 1. Ship's wheel; 2. Barrel; 3. Tiller; 4. Deck

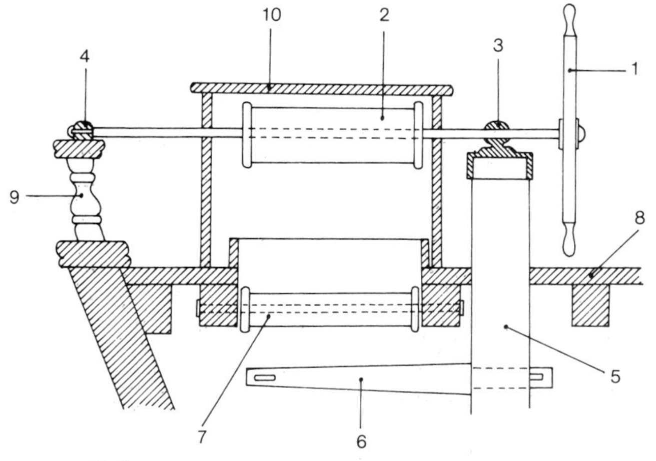

19th century steering gear housing: 1. Ship's wheel; 2. Barrel; 3. Front spindle bearing; 4. After spindle bearing; 5. Rudder head; 6. Tiller; 7. Roller; 8. Deck; 9. Taffrail; 10. American type of steering gear housing

Steering gear housing European type, late 19th century

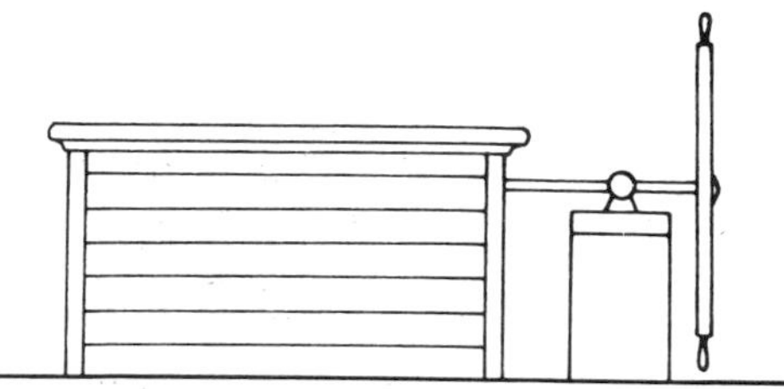

Steering gear housing American type, late 19th century

Steering gear from 1830 to 1890

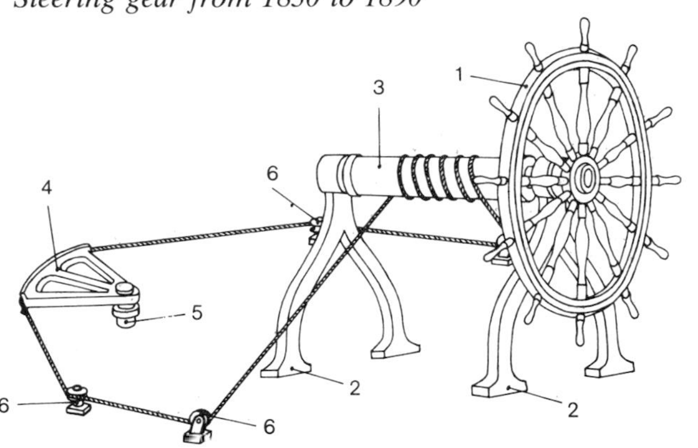

Steering gear with tiller rope running round quadrant: 1. Ship's wheel; 2. Pedestal; 3. Barrel; 4. Quadrant on the rudder head; 5. Rudder head; 6. Leading blocks

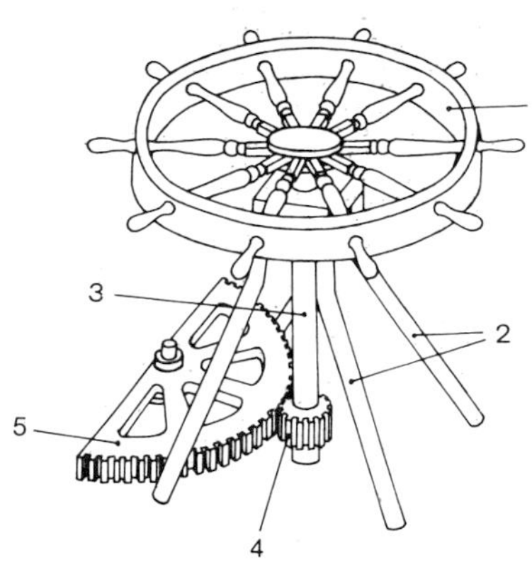

Steering gear with horizontal wheel (Rhine barges): 1. Wheel; 2. Pedestal; 3. Spindle; 4. Pinion; 5. Quadrant on the rudder head

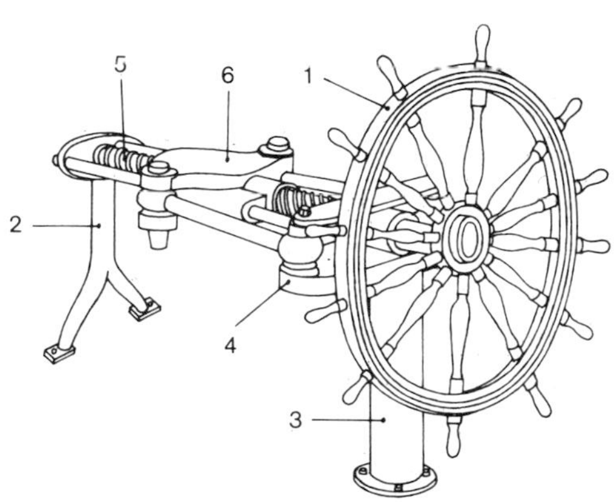

Steering gear with rigid transmission by means of worm and nut: 1. Ship's wheel; 2. Pedestal; 3. Rudder head; 4. Yoke; 5. Worm gear; 6. Travelling nut

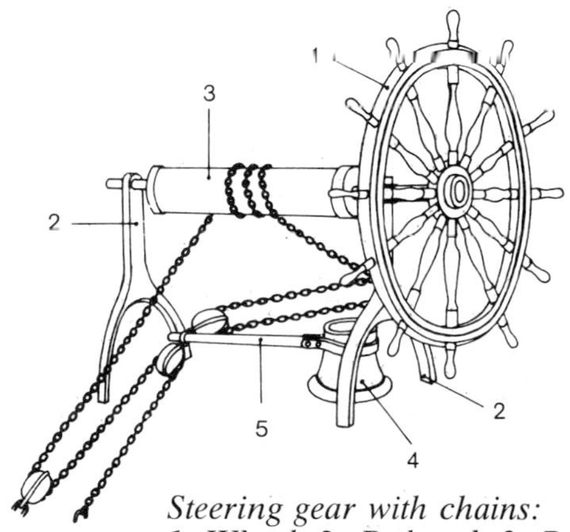

Steering gear with chains: 1. Wheel; 2. Pedestal; 3. Barrel; 4. Rudder head; 5. Tiller

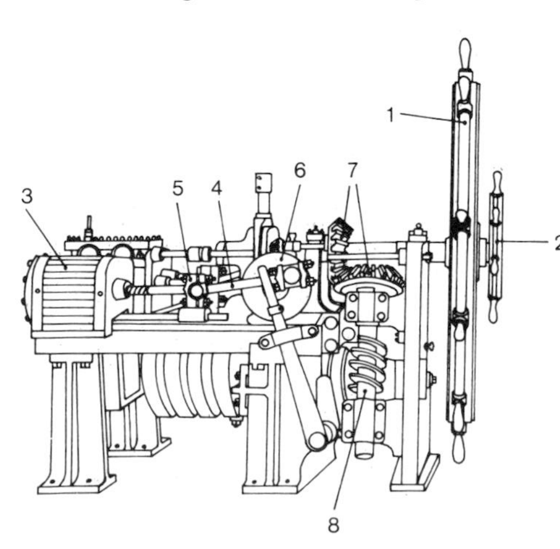

Two types of steam assisted steering gear: 1. Ship's wheel; 2. Handwheel for steam control; 3. Steam cylinder; 4. Connecting rod; 5. Little end; 6. Flywheel; 7. Bevel gears; 8. Worm gear; 9. Pinion gear; 10. Spur gear; 11. Chain drums

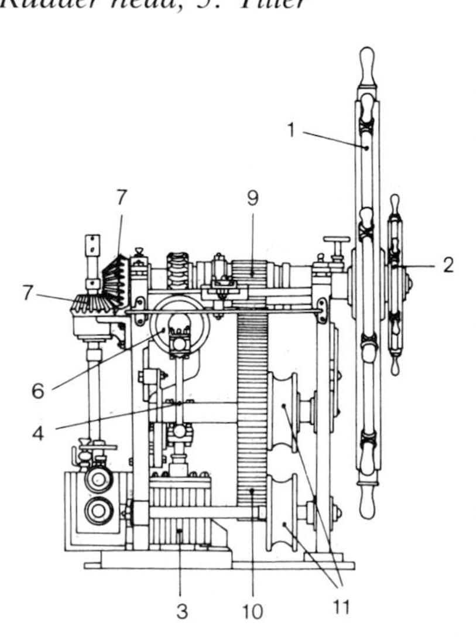

The Poop lantern

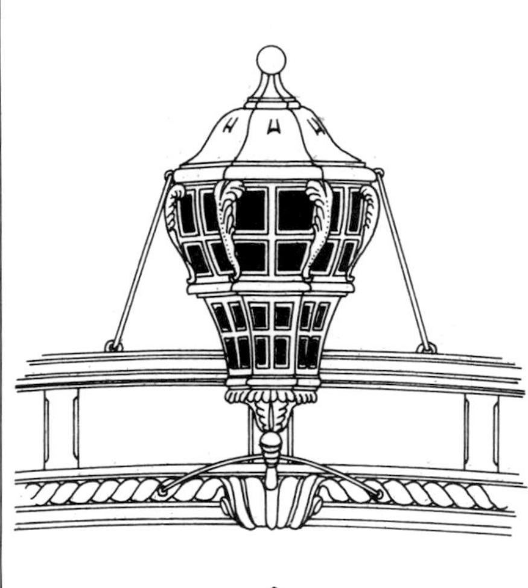

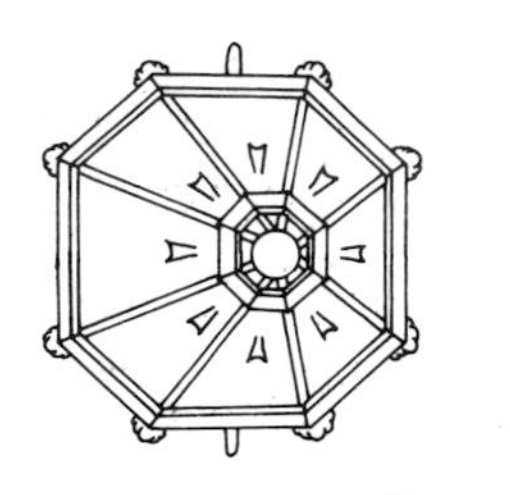

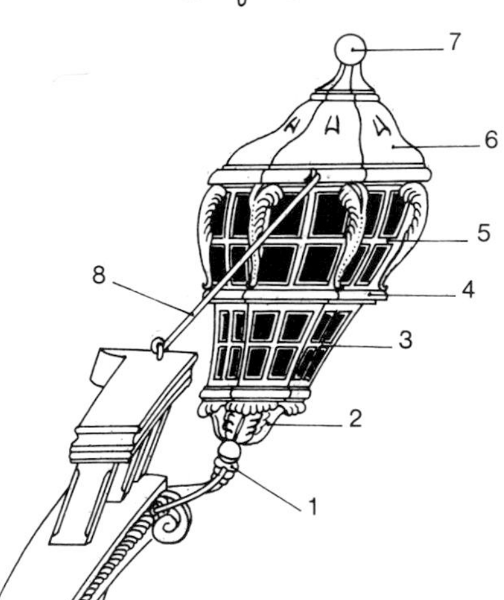

Asymmetrical poop lantern: 1. Bracket; 2. Base; 3. Lower section; 4. Middle ring; 5. Upper section; 6. Top; 7. Finial; 8. Stays (after Vaisseau)

The poop lantern is undoubtedly one of the most intricate items which you will have to tackle in the whole realm of period ship modelling. With their rounded, bulging, often asymmetrical shapes, and the rich ornamentation so beloved of the baroque and rococo periods, they place great demands on the modeller. Even if you succeed with the rings and struts, the garlands, the scrollwork, there remains one problem: the glass. Where are you going to get rounded, moulded glass? Have we finally found the insoluble problem?

By no means! Let's look at the possibilities; you can choose from the following:

The solid wood lantern with painted glass

This method is standard for Admiralty models, among others. The poop lantern is carved as a unit from a block of wood; the metal parts (i.e. the base, the rings, the ribs, the top, etc.) are gilded, and the glass parts are painted green, blue, black (sometimes with white spots), that is, the so-called "glass colours". Traditionalists in ship modelling use this method – in spite of the result, which is far from convincing.

The framed, unglazed lantern

Another traditional method. The lantern framework is made of wood and/or metal, but the glass is simply omitted. Poop lanterns of this type do look slightly more natural, but they can never be entirely convincing.

The framed lantern with glazing

A lantern assembled as described above, but with small pieces of glass or – better – celluloid glued inside before fitting the top. Such lanterns look just right, but the method can only be used for poop lanterns with four, six and eight sides (or cylindrical types), i.e. in all lanterns which do not require double curvature glazing.

The solid lantern cast in resin

In cases where double-curved glass is required, i.e. for spherical, pear-shaped or asymmetrical poop lanterns, the best results are obtained by using transparent synthetic resin (the method of casting and working has already been described in the chapter MATERIALS AND TOOLS).

It is up to you whether the glazing only is made of resin, and the metal parts fabricated separately and added afterwards, or whether the whole structure is included in the casting, and the metal parts subsequently gilded. You will need to cast the poop lantern in several pieces, so that each piece can be removed from the mould without too much difficulty. Many modellers shy away from this method, "because it was only invented in the 20th century, and is not traditional", but that is no reason why you should reject it. If synthetic resin had been available in the 17th or 18th century, it would certainly have been used!

Commercial lanterns

You can forget this idea. I do not know of a single poop lantern available commercially which is of any use at all.

Portuguese, Spanish, Dutch, Venetian, Genoese, English, French, Danish and Swedish poop lanterns

Galley and galley funnel

Galley stove with Funnel, 19th century
Galley Funnels:
Top 17th century
Middle 18th century
Bottom 19th century

Ever since the first great voyages of discovery in the 15th century, the various log books and accounts of voyages have mentioned cooking arrangements on ship. There may well have been such facilities in the high Middle Ages, but where they were located, and what they looked like is not known in any detail. We only have specific information on the ship's galley since the 17th century. Until 1820 the galley – known to German sailors as the "Chamber of Horrors", and where the "Smutje" (literally "the dirty one") plied his trade – was usually established on the upper deck under the forecastle. Later in the 19th century it was often located on the middle or gun deck below the waist on warships, while merchantmen preferred to house it in its own deckhouse on the upper deck.

The stove position was walled in with bricks until the middle of the 18th century, which were often strapped round externally with thick boards and iron bands. At this stage metal stoves came into use and became a standard fitting in British warships.

Many galley stoves on warships were fitted with heavy iron rings – as shown in the drawing on the left – to enable them to be lashed down in heavy weather.

The model maker will have little to do as far as the galley itself is concerned, except on ships – especially 18th century vessels – which lacked a forecastle bulkhead, in which case the stove would be exposed.

One thing which was always visible was the galley funnel. Until the middle of the 18th century it was usually made of wood, and rectangular in section. Wooden funnels were sometimes left in their natural wood finish, but more often were painted black. If your plan does not give details and you are in doubt, you should stain the chimney black.

After 1750 metal funnels of a circular cross-section became increasingly common, and these were always painted black. The best way of fabricating them is to solder them up from thin-walled brass tubing, and blacken them as described earlier.

An important point to note whether the funnel is of wood or metal is that the inside of the chimney should be "sooty", that is matt black in colour, and this colouring extends out over the top edge of the chimney orifice, although it should be slightly lighter in colour there as a result of occasional "cleaning".

The American whaler Alice Mandell *of 1851.*
The walled stove with the two funnels of the blubber boiler are visible under the forecastle. Galley stoves looked similar, but were smaller

The Ship's bell

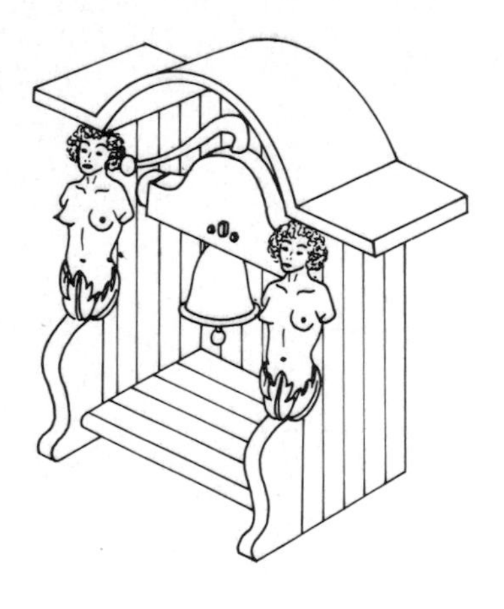

Ships' bells and belfries of the 17th and 18th centuries

If the figurehead was the personification of the ship, then the ship's bell was her voice. This may explain why for centuries the bell was the subject of loving care and considerable decoration, and was often suspended in an elaborate belfry. The bell was used to mark the beginning of the watches, to give the alarm, and to give audible warning signals in fog.

The English appear to have been the first to use ship's bells and an early indication of a separate belfry is in a painting by William van der Velde the Elder of the English second-rate *Rainbow* in 1650. A more elaborate belfry is shown in the photograph of the Science Museum's model of H.M.S. *Prince* of 1670 opposite.

Merchant ships only had one bell, which was originally located at the stern, but later – around 1600/1650 – it was moved to the forecastle. The belfry of merchant ships was usually kept rather plain, and in the 19th century the pawl bitts of the windlass often served as the belfry too.

Until the beginning of the 18th century warships also carried a single bell, but it was often suspended in an ornately decorated, carved and gilded belfry at the break of the forecastle. In the 18th century the bell and belfry were located at the after end of the forecastle deck.

In French two and three deckers of the 18th century a second, smaller bell was often carried at the break of the quarter deck, but this feature was not adopted in England nor on the Continent to any great extent, and it disappeared even from French ships in the early 18th century.

There are many possible methods of fabricating ships' bells: they can be turned from brass on the lathe – in this case the coat of arms or the ship's name, with which the bell was often decorated, have to be omitted. On models built to 1:48 or smaller you can hardly include such tiny details in any case. Turned brass bells are also available commercially.

A further possibility is to make ships' bells by the electro-plating shell method already described, or out of tin, on to which a thin layer of brass is electro-plated – both methods have the advantage that a coat of arms or lettering can be incorporated. For large-scale models one of these methods should certainly be preferred.

An important point in all cases is that ships' bells virtually without exception were cast in brass or bronze, and in one way or another the modeller has to show the brazen character of the material.

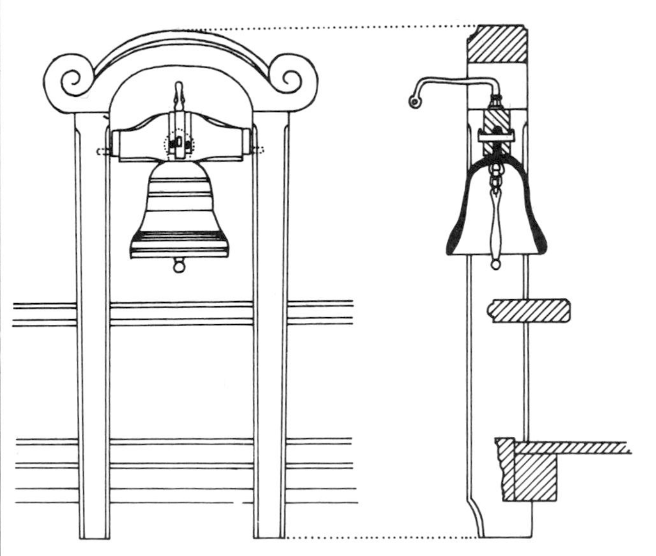

Ship's bell and belfry, front view and cross-section, of a French warship around 1760

Two ships' bells

Ship's bell of a 19th century merchant ship

Riding bitts

The massive riding bitts usually stood on the upper or middle deck below the forecastle, level with the hawse holes. Their task was to secure the cables; on larger ships there were usually two riding bitts, one behind the other.
The vertical posts passed down through the decks as far as the footwaling or ceiling into which they were stepped. They were linked by a heavy cross piece to which was attached yet another beam, known as the back. Towards the bow they were supported with two long, powerful knees or standards which were securely fixed to the deck beams by means of long bolts.
The anchor cables were turned round these bitts, and made fast to ring bolts with a number of stoppers, so that the anchor cable or chain could not rush out uncontrollably. This form of riding bitts disappeared towards the middle of the 19th century. On smaller ships the riding bitts were exposed on the main deck, and were often combined with the windlass (See CAPSTANS AND WINDLASSES).

Fife rails

At the base of the masts there were smaller bitts, whose bases extended down at least as far as the next deck. They were fitted with sheaves, through which, for example, the topsail sheets were reeved and then belayed at the bitt heads.
Until about 1660 these bitts were linked by simple cross pieces, but after that time these cross pieces began to be fitted with a number of belaying pins, to which further ropes of the running rigging could belay. The cross timbers were now termed fife rails.
In the first half of the 18th century a series of blocks was fitted at the base of the fife rails, through which the ropes coming down were led, before they were made fast to the belaying pins.

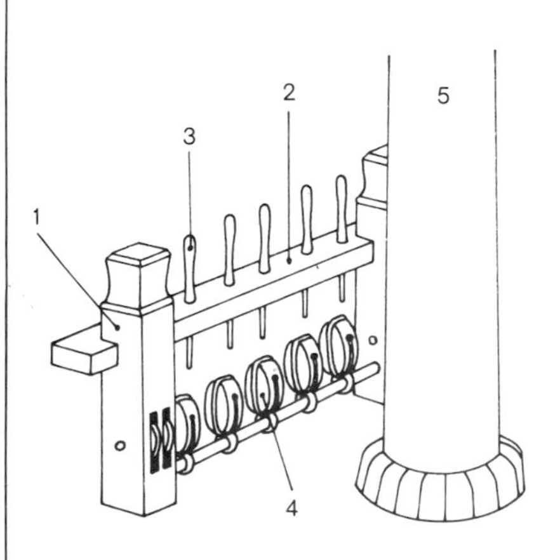

Fife Rail: 1. Bitts; 2. Cross piece or fife rail; 3. Belaying pins; 4. Blocks; 5. Mast

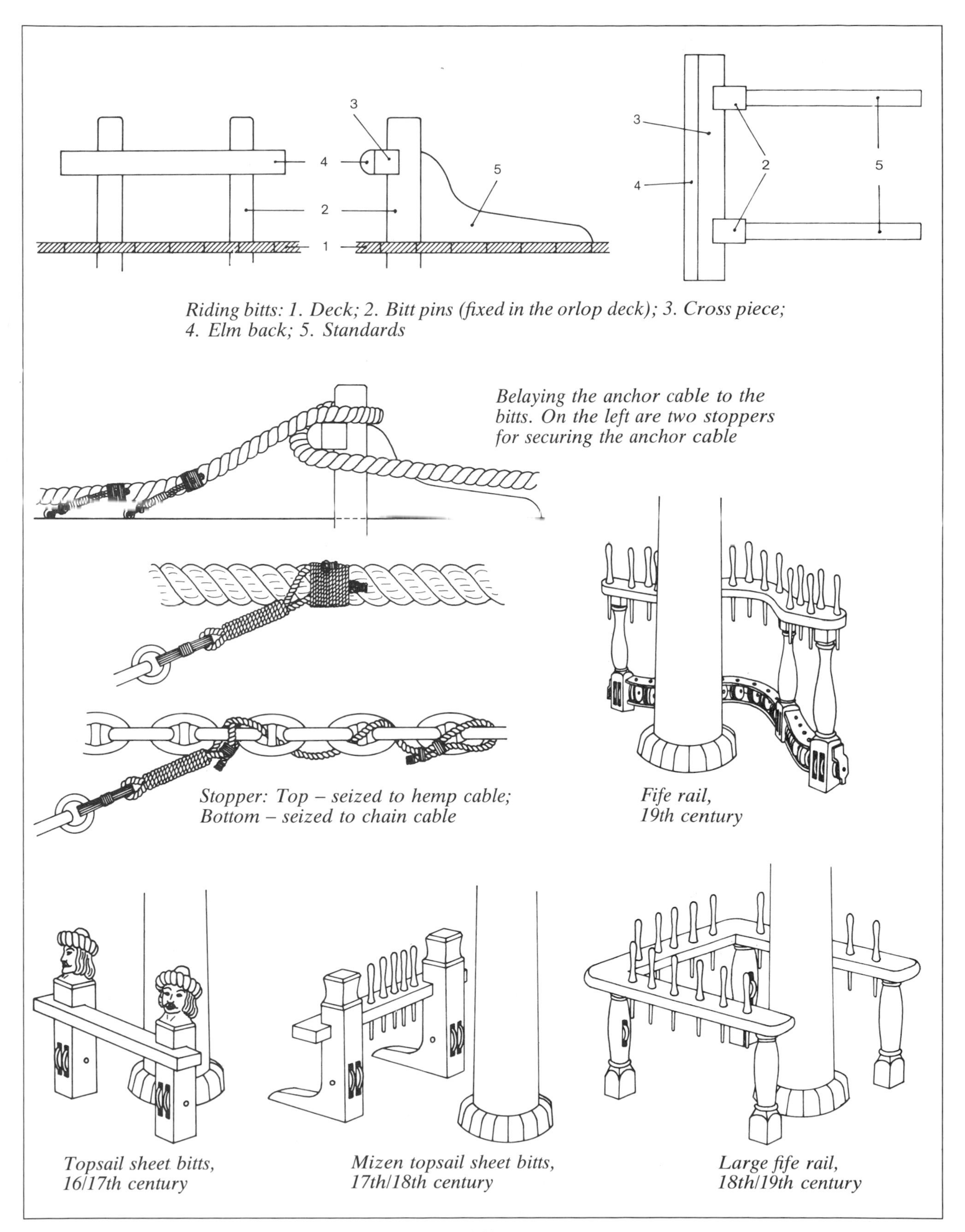

Riding bitts: 1. Deck; 2. Bitt pins (fixed in the orlop deck); 3. Cross piece; 4. Elm back; 5. Standards

Belaying the anchor cable to the bitts. On the left are two stoppers for securing the anchor cable

Stopper: Top – seized to hemp cable; Bottom – seized to chain cable

Fife rail, 19th century

Topsail sheet bitts, 16/17th century

Mizen topsail sheet bitts, 17th/18th century

Large fife rail, 18th/19th century

Pin rails

The smaller diameter ropes of the running rigging were belayed to the pin rails, which were fitted with a row of belaying pins, like the cross pieces of the fife rails. As in the case of the channels, it is important to fix the pin rails to the hull very securely, using steel pins, so that they do not fail when under the tension of the ropes.
Of course, there was insufficient space for pin rails and fife rails for the over 150 ropes of a three-mast ship, and consequently a series of belaying pins was placed in the bulwark rails and the rails of the forecastle, quarterdeck and poop decks, and the ropes belayed there; it did not become normal to make fast all ropes to pin rails until the 19th century.

Knightheads and kevel blocks

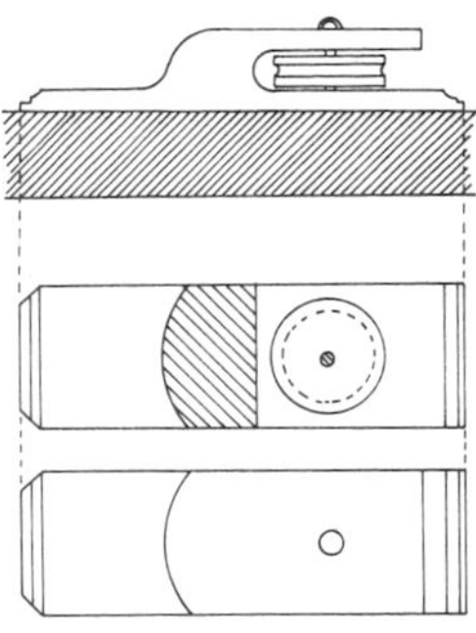

The Dutch are generally believed to have introduced kevel blocks in the mid 17th century

The knightheads formed the lower block of the halliard tackles of the lower yard tyes. The feet of the main and foremast knightheads extended right down to the ceiling into which they were stopped.
The fore and mainmast knightheads were fitted with four sheaves, three of which were used for the lower yard tye halliard tackles which attached to eye bolts on the sides of the knightheads. The fourth sheave was used to lead the top rope to the capstan. While the main and foremast knightheads were located abaft their respective masts, the mizen mast knighthead was ahead of its mast. This knighthead was very much smaller, and only had two sheaves.
Further small knightheads, known as kevel blocks, were fixed to the timberheads as belaying points for the lower braces.

Chesstrees

Until the middle of the 17th century the main tacks rove through a hole or a sheave in a vertical piece of timber fayed to the ship's side (fenders were also sometimes used for this), and led inboard a little further forward through another hole or fixed block in the hull. In the 17th century the chesstree was almost always decoratively carved, and was located between the rail and the top wale. Around the middle of the 17th century it became usual to lead the mainsail tacks directly inboard through a block in the ship's side, and this block was generally decorated with a gilded plate bearing a lion's head or a caricature. In the first half of the 18th century English ships reverted to the older method, while on continental ships chesstrees were given up altogether.

Staghorns

Heavy ropes of the running rigging were belayed to staghorns, which were fixed to the hull wall. The large staghorn served as belaying point for the main tack, which passed inboard through a block between its posts.
The smaller staghorns were belaying points for the sheets and fore tacks. The appearance and disposition of the staghorns will be shown clearly on the plan from which you are working.
British ships used large cleats (range cleats) to belay sheets and tackle

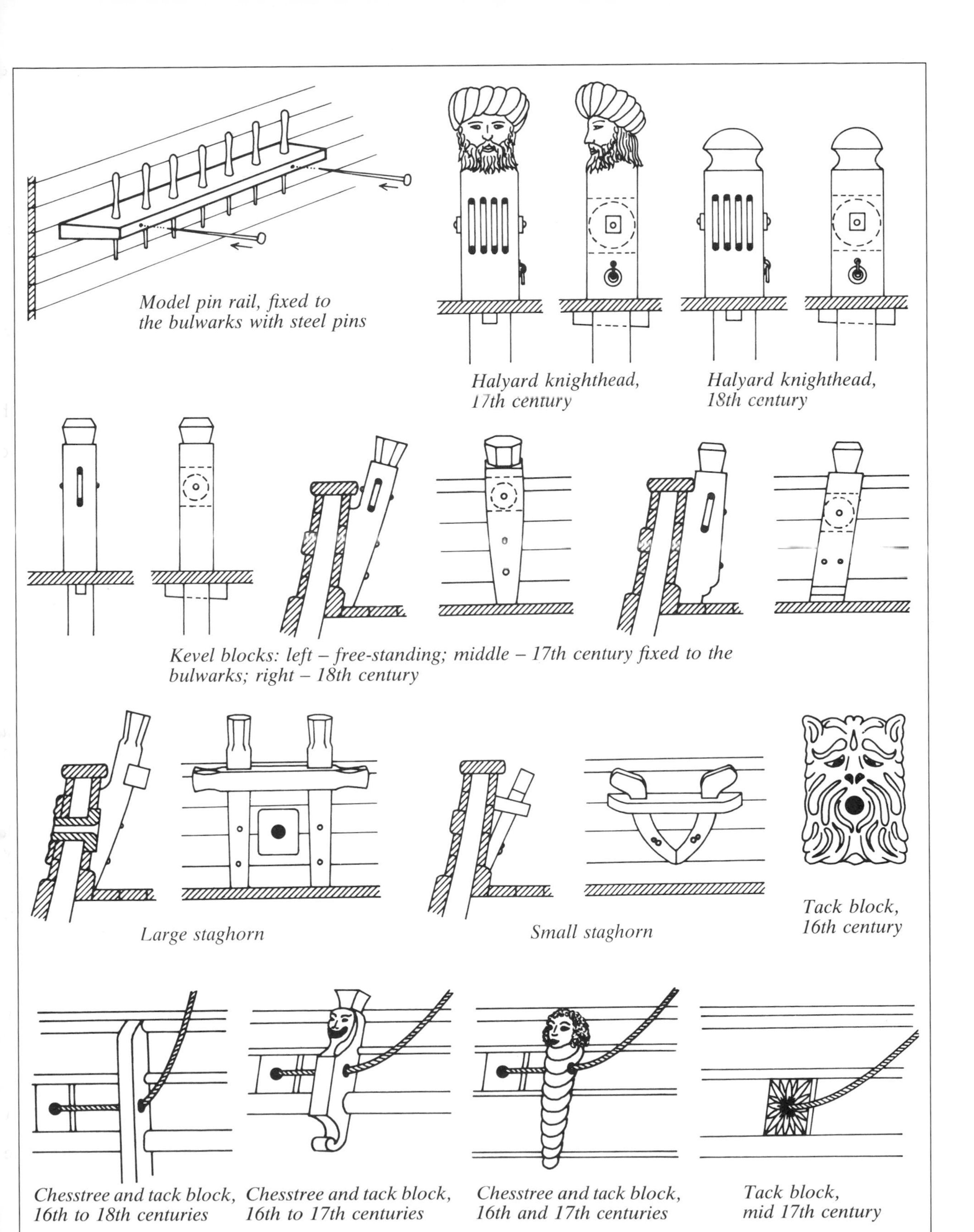

Model pin rail, fixed to the bulwarks with steel pins

Halyard knighthead, 17th century

Halyard knighthead, 18th century

Kevel blocks: left – free-standing; middle – 17th century fixed to the bulwarks; right – 18th century

Large staghorn

Small staghorn

Tack block, 16th century

Chesstree and tack block, 16th to 18th centuries

Chesstree and tack block, 16th to 17th centuries

Chesstree and tack block, 16th and 17th centuries

Tack block, mid 17th century

Armament

Bow of a Greek warship with ram

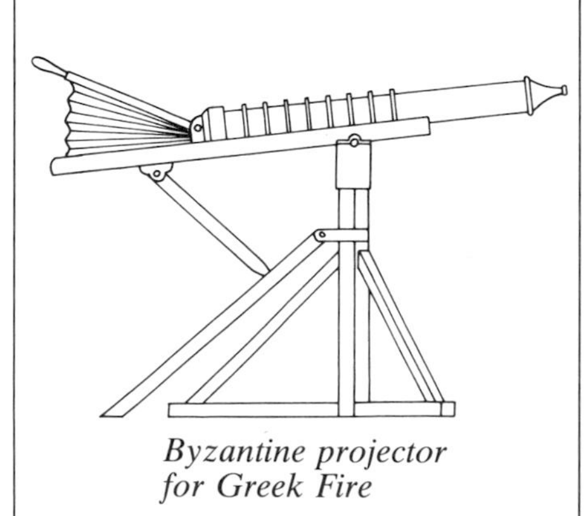
Byzantine projector for Greek Fire

Whether warship or merchant ship, every vessel carried a more or les complete range of arms as a fundamental item of equipment if it dare to travel more than a few miles from the protection of the home port and this situation prevailed for a period of thousands of years.
The oldest form of ship's weapon was the ramming bow, which was invented around 1200 B.C. by the Greeks. If this bronze or iron sheathed spike tore its way into the hull of an enemy ship, the battle was as good as over. The ramming bow turned the whole ship into a weapon.
The later development, in which a ship became not a weapon itself, but a carrier of weapons, began around 300 B.C., when the warships of the Greeks (and later also of the Romans) became too large and awkward for the tactic of ramming. The ships' battle power now resided in catapult devices, of which a wide variety of sizes and design was used. Three basic types can be distinguished:
Catapults:
These were a type of double-armed bow for arrow-type missiles, as illustrated on the right. The size of catapults ranged from the persona weapon "Gastraphetes" to the medium heavy "Chalkotonon" and "Euthytonon". The power of the bow arms was created by tightly stretched bundles of rope. There were even multi-shot catapults (polybolon), which were the heavy "machine guns" of the ancient world.
Ballista
These were catapults with two bow arms, used for hurling stone balls Designed on a similar principle to the catapults, they were of medium t heavy calibre (palintonon). They could not be used for direct shooting like catapults, instead hurling their stone balls towards the target in an arc.
Scorpion or Onager:
These were the heaviest of the slingshot machines used to project stone balls or whole lumps of rock. They had only one arm, which was tensioned by bundles of ropes, as before.
It would certainly be beyond the scope of this book to illustrate all the different types of catapult of the ancient world individually. If yo are interested in the ships and armament of this period, I can recommend the book "The Roman Fleet", by H.D.L. Viereck.
Many of these catapult machines, in particular those on Roman warships, were mounted on a rotating platform, which was supported on tapered rollers or balls, and which served the same purpose as the revolving base of modern gun turrets. A particularly dangerous weapo was developed in Byzantium in the late period of ancient history:
Greek fire:
This was not the least of the methods by which Ostrom was able to withstand the Mohammedan assault for so long. The Syrian Callinicus had invented "Greek fire". It worked on a similar principl to the modern flame thrower: a naphtha-sulphur-saltpetre mixture was packed into a metal tube, the rear end of which was connected to powerful bellows. The mixture was ignited and sprayed at the enemy The exact recipe for "Greek fire", which even burned when sprayed on water, was strictly secret, and was lost when Constantinople fell.
In Northern Europe ships' armament was unknown until the 11th century, after which catapults and ballista of the ancient type began to be installed on ships – although they were even then not widespread. To the model builder the fabrication of ancient and mediaeval catapult machines presents few technical problems, provide he has accurate drawings and a good supply of patience.
A major change in the armament of ships came about with the inventio of gunpowder. At the end of this section you will find a short summar

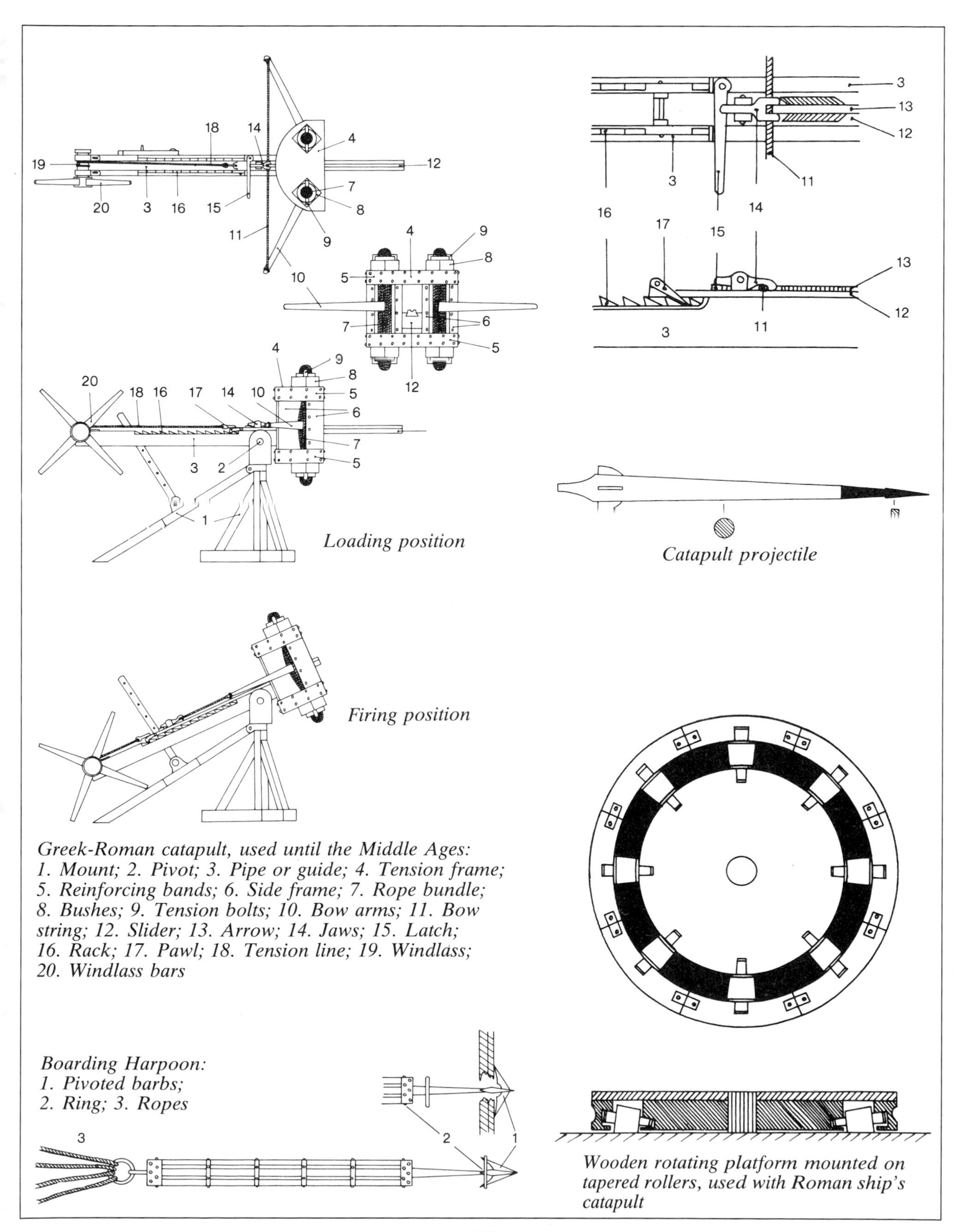

Greek-Roman catapult, used until the Middle Ages: 1. Mount; 2. Pivot; 3. Pipe or guide; 4. Tension frame; 5. Reinforcing bands; 6. Side frame; 7. Rope bundle; 8. Bushes; 9. Tension bolts; 10. Bow arms; 11. Bow string; 12. Slider; 13. Arrow; 14. Jaws; 15. Latch; 16. Rack; 17. Pawl; 18. Tension line; 19. Windlass; 20. Windlass bars

Boarding Harpoon: 1. Pivoted barbs; 2. Ring; 3. Ropes

Wooden rotating platform mounted on tapered rollers, used with Roman ship's catapult

Armament

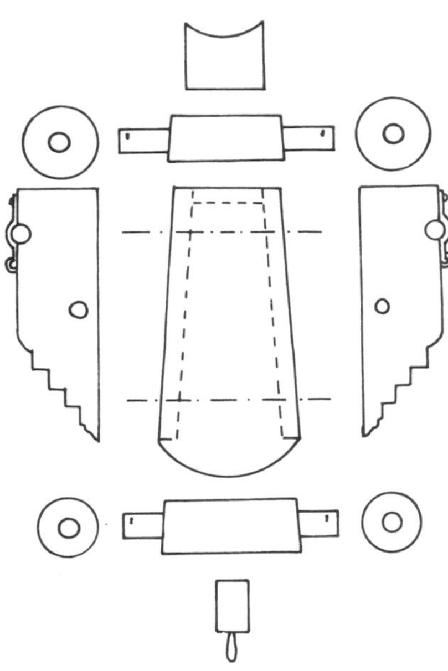

Parts of a Continental gun carriage. From above: transom, front axle tree with trucks, bed with side cheeks, rear axle tree with trucks, quoin

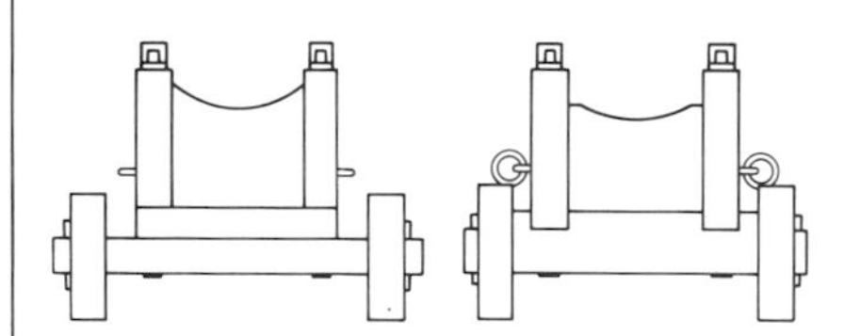

Gun carriages from the front: Left – Continental; Right – British

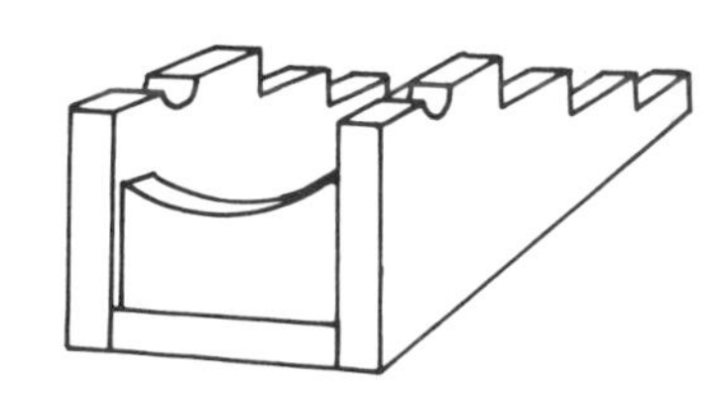

Much simplified model carriage for lower deck guns

of the most commonly used types of ship's artillery from the 13th to the 19th century. Of course, types and developments can only be enumerated in approximate terms, as there were innumerable variations. The drawings are only intended to give you a reference point, by which you can deduce whether the information on your plan is possible or not for its time. For instance, I know more than one model of Christopher Columbus' *Santa Maria* which is fitted with bronze gun barrels, which did not appear until a good half century later. Here again I must repeat: if in doubt, bury your head in the specialist literature on guns in general and ships' artillery in particular.

The carriage

The construction of gun carriages is no real problem for the model maker; the only point to watch is the that the right type is made, from the point of view of nationality and period. Many plans are extremely unreliable in this area. There were basically two types of carriage, which were used with minor variations from the late 16th to the first half of the 19th century. The Continental and early British type with straight cheeks and one-piece bed, and the later 18th century British type (also used in America) with no bed. The carriages of model lower deck guns, only a small part of which is visible, can be built without axles and wheels, with the bed glued – or even screwed – directly to the deck.

Barrels

Making the barrel is considerably more difficult. Gun barrels of plastic or of wood (which are occasionally seen) do not look right, and you should avoid these materials from the start. That leaves brass – in many cases the original material – and tin alloy. The following methods of manufacture are possible:

1. Turning from brass. Turned brass barrels look very neat and true to scale. Of course, you need a lathe for this, and this method has the disadvantage that the coat of arms, ornamentation etc., as often cast into the barrels from the 16th to the 18th century, cannot be incorporated.
2. Tin Alloy casting. This method will be used by all modellers who do not have access to a lathe. The first stage is to make a pattern – the best method of doing this is again a lathe, but as you will need a maximum of 2 to 4 sizes of gun barrel, you can either do the job quickly on a friend's machine, or get a friend to make them for you. If all else fails, you can make your pattern from wood with a lot of filling and sanding etc. The decorations, coats of arms and the rest are added in plasticene, and a silicone rubber negative mould cast. The barrels themselves are cast in tin alloy as described previously. This method can be used for all gun barrels which are to have a black finish – and that is most of them. Iron barrels were either blackened or painted black, and bronze barrels were often blackened, which made them less susceptible to corrosion from seawater. Cannon were usually black until the second half of the 16th century, and then again from the early 18th century onward.
In the 17th century, however, gun barrels were commonly left as bare brass or bronze in certain areas.
3. Commercial barrels. For the modeller who has no access to a lathe, it makes sense to check on what is available commercially. The large fittings suppliers include brass barrels in their ranges, although the carriages supplied with them should be consigned to the rubbish bin without delay, as they are no use at all. If you cannot find suitable sizes – for lower deck guns at 1:48 scale it is difficult – you have to make the barrels yourself.

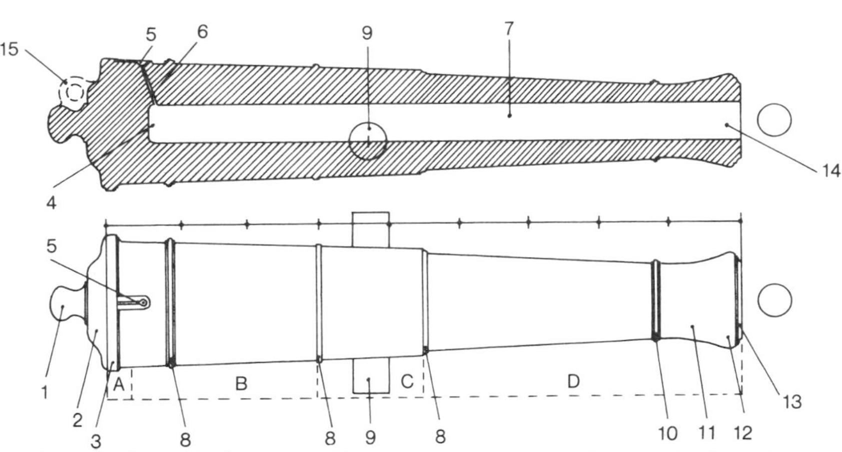

Cannon barrel of the 16th to the 19th century. Cross-section and plan view with scale of proportions. A. Breech; B. First reinforce; C. Second reinforce; D. Chase. 1. Pommelion or cascabel; 2. Breech mouldings; 3. Base ring; 4. Chamber; 5. Flash pan; 6. Vent; 7. Bore; 8. Reinforce ring; 9. Trunnion; 10. Muzzle astragal; 11. Throat; 12. Muzzle swelling; 13. Muzzle moulding; 14. Bore; 15. Breeching ring on English cannon, late 18th and early 19th centuries (after Vaisseau)

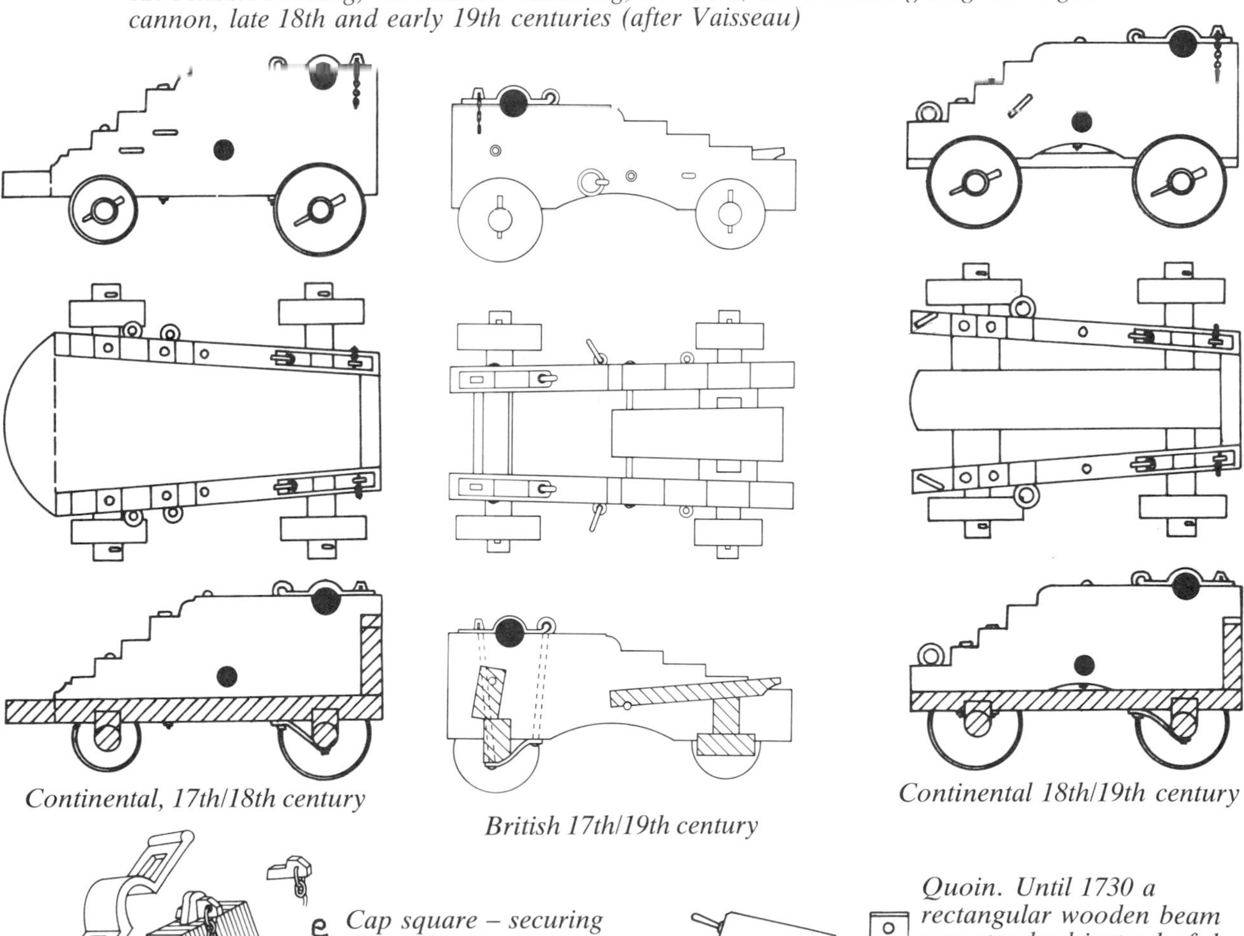

Continental, 17th/18th century

British 17th/19th century

Continental 18th/19th century

Cap square – securing clamp for the trunnions; hinged, to enable the barrel to be removed

Quoin. Until 1730 a rectangular wooden beam was standard instead of the quoin in Holland and Germany

Length of the breeching (French)

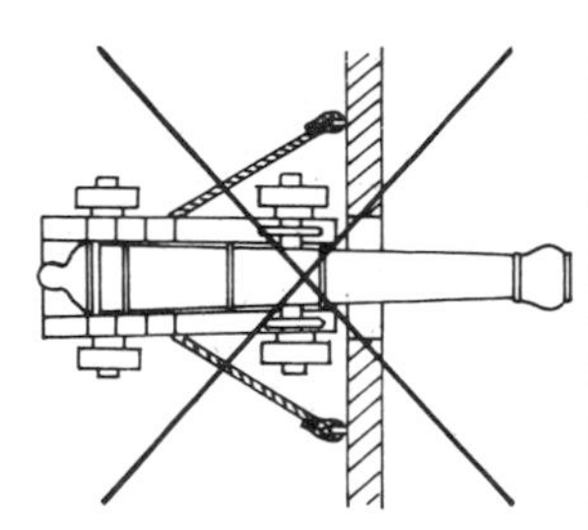

Wrong!
Under tension with the gun run out

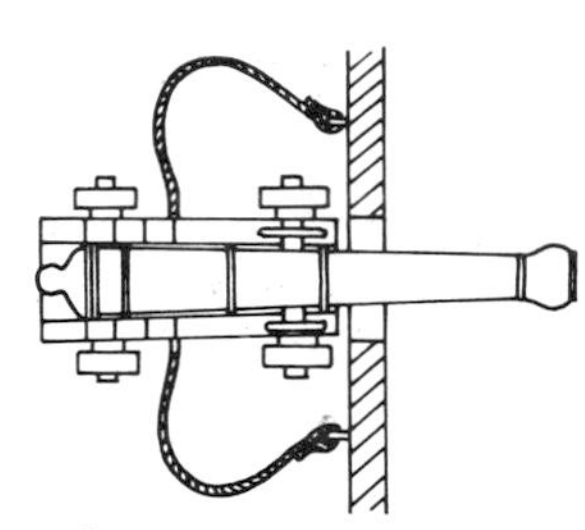

Correct!
Lying loose with the gun run out

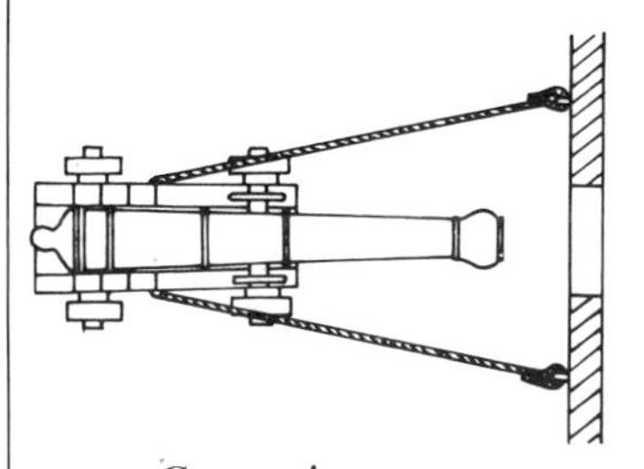

Correct!
Under tension after firing, ready for loading

4. Electro-plating. To do this, you first make a negative mould in silicone rubber, as already described. A brass coating is then plated on to the mould surface, after which the extremely thin-walled barrel thus formed is carefully filled with tin alloy to give the barrel strength. Many model builders fill the barrels with resin instead. The finished barrel is very carefully clamped in a vice, and the muzzle drilled to a depth of 3/16 to 3/8ins. The inside of the hole is then painted matt black. The finished barrel is placed on its carriage, and secured with the cap squares. The cap squares are punched from thin copper sheet and blackened (see MATERIALS AND TOOLS).
Finally the whole gun is attached to the deck, the quoin is glued to the carriage under the breech and at the same time the barrels are adjusted so that all of them are parallel to the waterline, or possibly with the muzzles slightly raised.

The location of the guns

This is one of the most common sources of error on period model ships, even though I still find this hard to believe. Before we begin setting up and rigging the guns, we have to decide precisely in what situation the ship is to be shown.

1. In action in fair weather – normally gunports open and the guns run out. It is possible, however, that the ship may only be fighting one side or that some guns are run in for reloading. (In this condition the ship should be under fighting sails only – i.e. topsails and some staysails).
2. In action in heavy weather – in this case it may be impossible to open lower deck ports on one or both sides. (In this condition the ship should be under reefed topsails and fewer staysails).
3. At sea but not in action – ports closed and guns secured (sails carried dependent upon the weather).
4. In port – ports closed and guns secured (sails furled or clewed up drying).

(N.B. Quarter deck and forecastle gunports and upper deck gunports in the waist seldom have lids and the guns were frequently secured in the run out position).
For a realistic model it is essential for the model builder to choose the state that he wishes his ship to be in and to conform to it in all aspects. For example, models are frequently seen with no sails set but with all guns run out – an unreal situation – but no more unreal than a ship with all sails set sitting on two brass pedestals. It is up to the individual to choose what he wants – realism or what might be termed a demonstration model.

Breeching

The breeching was a heavy rope, which was fixed to ring bolts in the ship's side; on French ships it was passed through the carriage, while on British ships it ran through ring bolts on the carriage, and finally, after the end of the 18th century, through a ring on the breech of the barrel. Up to the end of the 18th century the breeching had a cut splice seized to the cascabel. The purpose of the breeching was to absorb the recoil of the gun when it was fired. Another common mistake crops up here: the breeching being shown taut with the gun run out. This does look neat, certainly, but it is wrong!
The breeching must always be slack enough for the muzzle of the barrel to be brought back inside the ship for loading, as the bottom drawing on the left shows. With the gun run out the breeching lies slack on the deck. On a model the loose breeching sometimes tends to form a loop in the air, which does not look right – hence so many model makers leaving them taut – but a tiny drop of glue on the decks stops this trouble immediately.

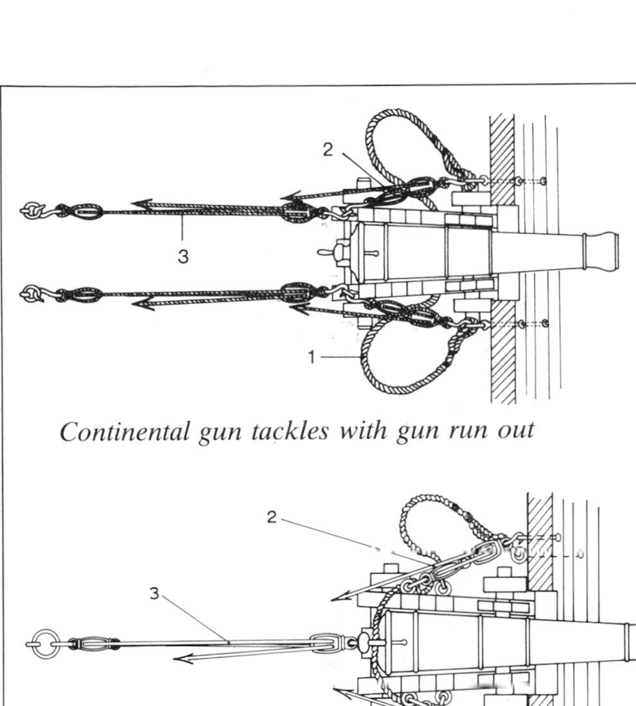

Continental gun tackles with gun run out

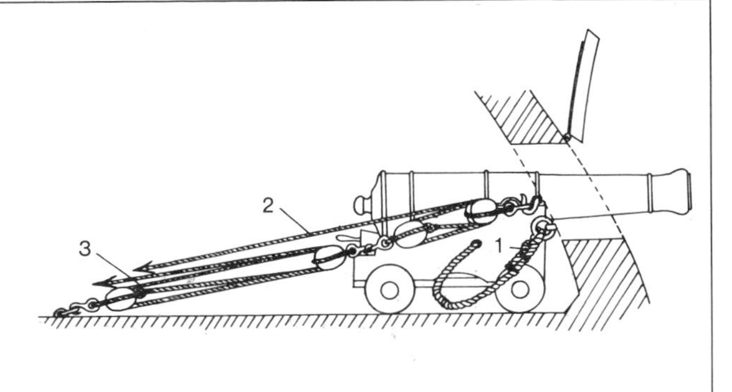

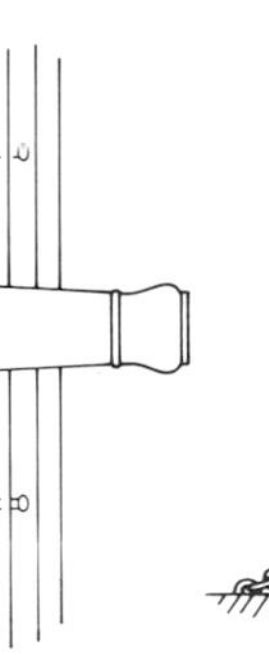

British gun run out

1. Breeching; 2. Gun tackle; 3. Train tackle*; 4. Muzzle lashing; 5. Breech strop; 6. Frapping (usually taken round the gun breeching and tackles*); 7. Quoins*

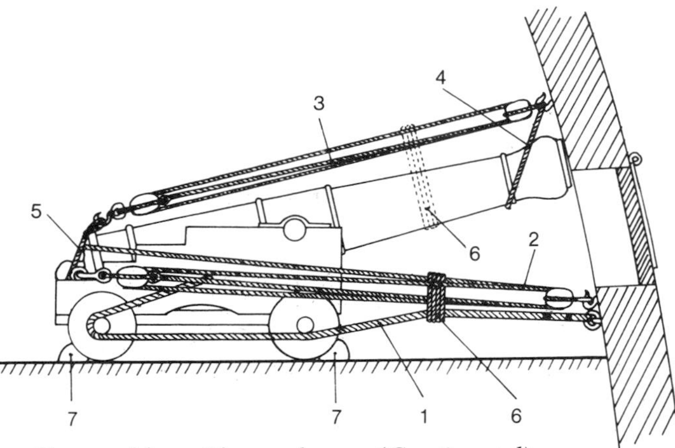

Gun tackles with gun house (Continental)

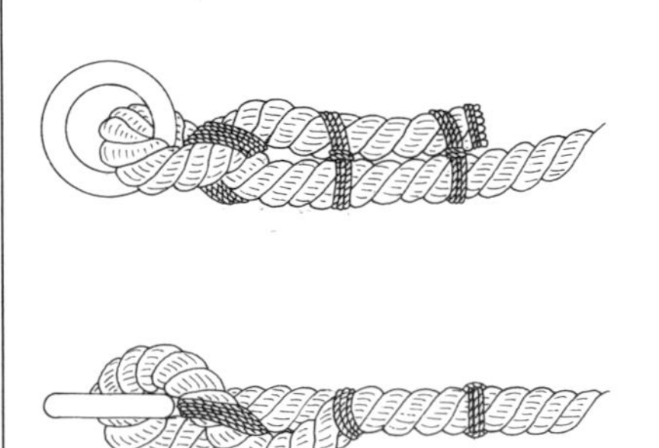

Breeching seized to ring bolt

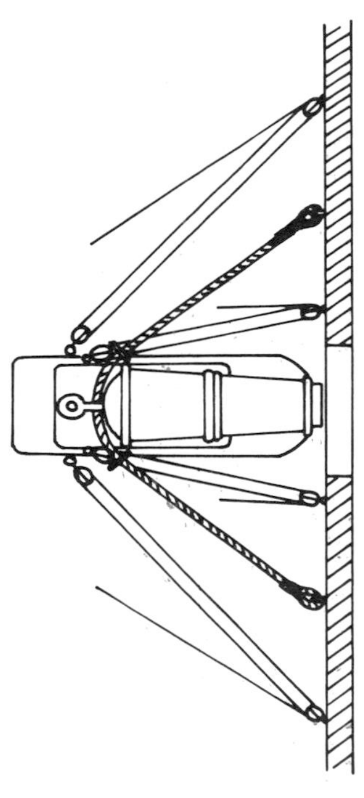

Tackle for a carronade

Armament

Guns carried by a British 64 gun ship:
Quarterdeck and forecastle – 9 pounder
Upper deck – 18 pounder
Gun or Lower deck – 24 pounder

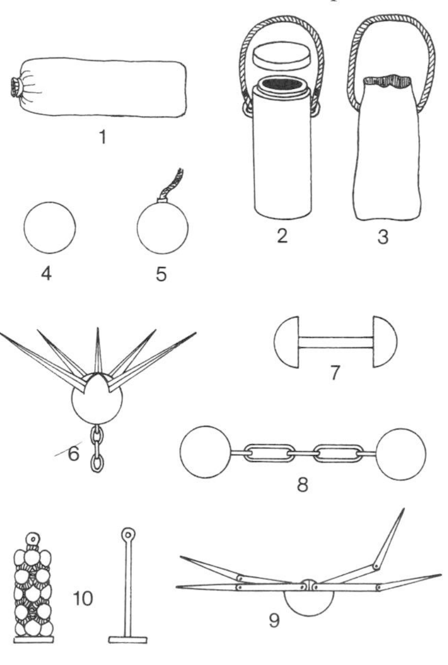

1. Powder cartridge; 2. Cartridge box; 3. Cartridge bag; 4. Ball; 5. Bomb or Shell; 6.-9. Various chain bar and anti-rigging shot; 10. Grapeshot with stand

The train tackle
The arrangement of the rest of the gun rigging is clear from the drawings, and the only point you should watch is that the correct form is chosen – either French or British. In fact, many plans are very imprecise in this area, and tend to mix up the two forms.

Loading and firing
Loading and firing a ship's gun was (and still is) a rather complicated procedure.

The first step was to load the powder cartridge – a cloth bag with a measured charge of powder sewn into it – into the barrel. (Prior to the introduction of cartridge bags in the 17th century the powder was loaded loose with a copper scoop). After this the ball and a wad of tow or rope were added, everything being packed tight together by the use of the rammer.

The gunner now pierced the powder cartridge with a priming iron passed through the vent, and shook highly inflammable fine powder on the pan. The cannon was now ready to fire.

The gunner then ignited the fine powder with the linstock around which a burning fuse was wrapped; the charge exploded and the ball was hurled out of the barrel. After the shot the barrel had to be cleaned. The worm was used to remove the glowing residue of the powder cartridge out of the barrel, after which the barrel was swabbed out with the sponge. Only after this could the loading process be repeated. In the latter half of the 18th century the British navy introduced the far more efficient flintlock to fire its guns, a system gradually copied by the other navies.

A practised crew could clean, charge and fire a 6 or 9 pounder in 1 to 1½ minutes, but with heavier calibres it took correspondingly longer. The handspike was used to push the carriage to one side as well as to raise the breech, if the quoin was to be moved, in order to alter the elevation of the gun.

The usual ammunition consisted of iron balls, which were aimed at the hull of the enemy ship. Chain and bar shot were used against the rigging. Grapeshot was often used against the deck crew; this consisted of 1-2lb iron balls tied to a wood mount with ropes, which broke after firing, producing a wide spray of fire over the enemy deck. Hollow iron balls filled with powder were known as shells. When shooting at land targets, they were fired from mortars, but they were little used for other purposes until the invention of the impact fuse, as they so often failed to explode.

On small scale model ships (1:72 and smaller) it is hardly possible to represent loading equipment and ammunition, but on models to a scale of 1:48 and larger you should at least show ammunition stowed in boxes or in the shot garlands. On large scale models the loading equipment should be shown, part of which was stowed close by the guns under the deck beams or inside the bulwarks.

Diorama of two gun crews in battle on the main deck of a model of the Swedish frigate Josephine.

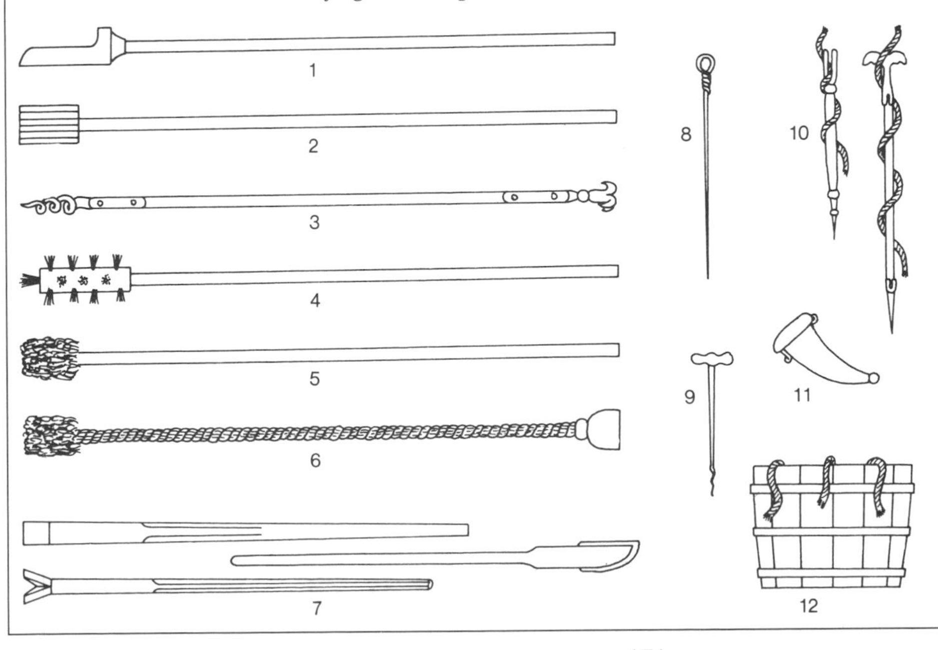

1. *Powder ladle*
2. *Rammer*
3. *Worm*
4. *Brush*
5. *Sponge*
6. *Flexible rammer and sponge*
7. *Handspikes*
8. *Priming iron or vent pricker*
9. *Vent auger*
10. *Linstocks*
11. *Powder horn*
12. *Tub with slow matches*

Armament

Falconet. 14th century. Breech loader which shot burning arrows as well as balls. Iron fork mount fitted on the bulwark. Oldest known ship's gun using powder

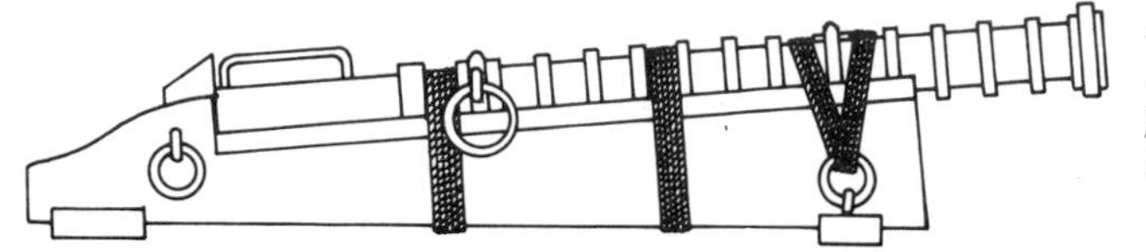

Chamber gun, 14th and 15th centuries. Breech loader assembled from forged iron bars and hoops, set in block mount

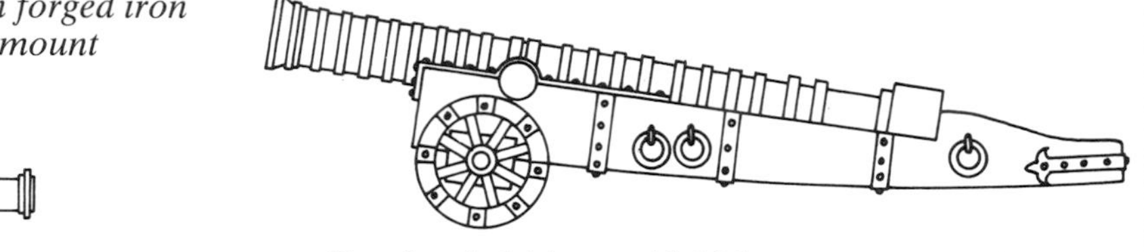

Bombard. 14th to mid-16th century. Breech loader on two-wheeled carriage

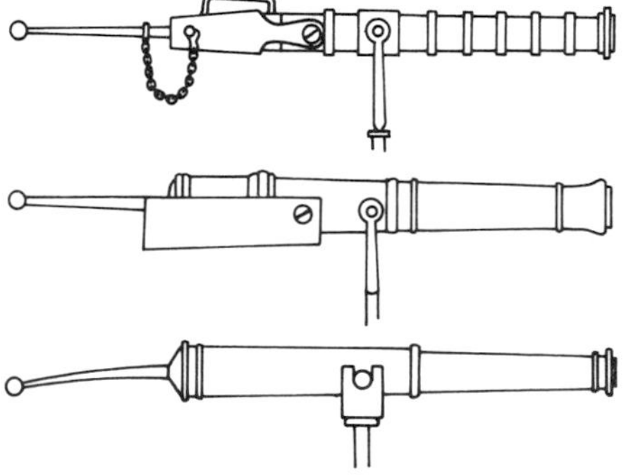

Swivel guns (small bulwark cannon) from 14th to 18th century

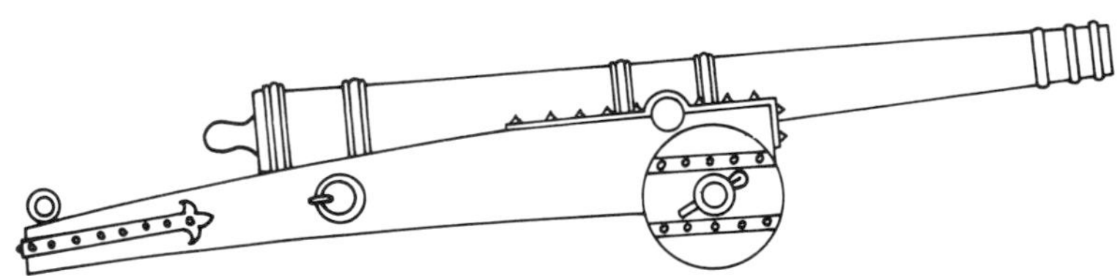

British Demi-culverin, 16th century. Muzzle loader. Cast bronze barrel on two-wheeled carriage.

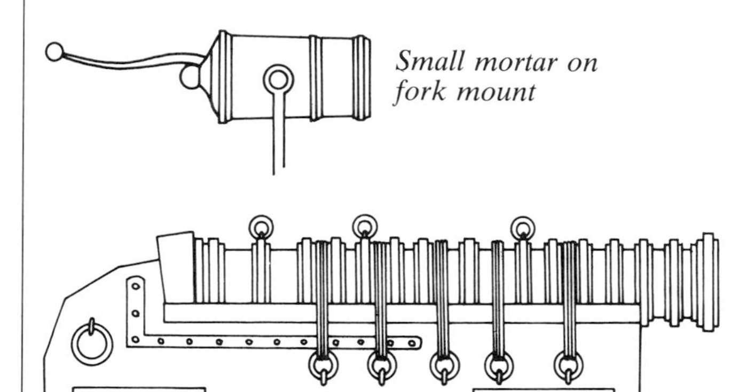

Small mortar on fork mount

Large calibre bombard, 14th and 15th centuries. Breech loader on heavy block mount. Also frequently used as galley gun

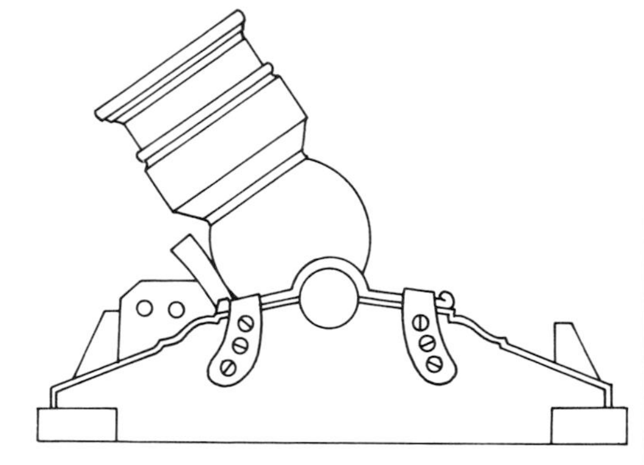

Heavy mortar. High-elevation gun for bombs. 18th and 19th centuries. Fired from special ships (bomb vessels) with reinforced decks

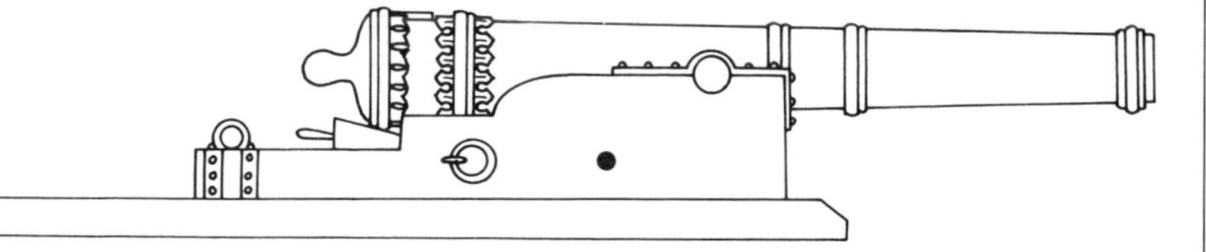

Galley gun, 16th to 18th century. Sliding mounting running between heavy rails

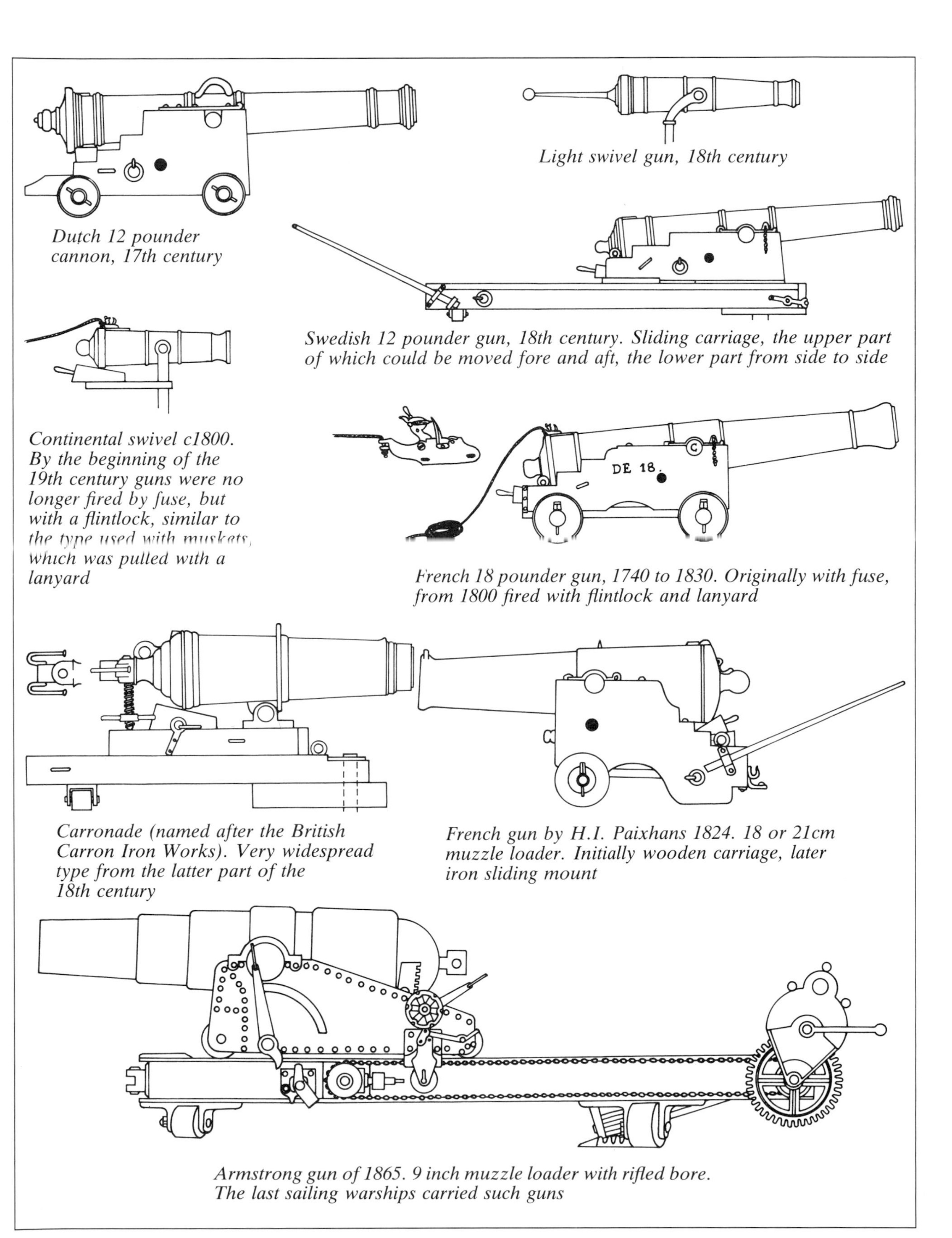

Dutch 12 pounder cannon, 17th century

Light swivel gun, 18th century

Swedish 12 pounder gun, 18th century. Sliding carriage, the upper part of which could be moved fore and aft, the lower part from side to side

Continental swivel c1800. By the beginning of the 19th century guns were no longer fired by fuse, but with a flintlock, similar to the type used with muskets, which was pulled with a lanyard

French 18 pounder gun, 1740 to 1830. Originally with fuse, from 1800 fired with flintlock and lanyard

Carronade (named after the British Carron Iron Works). Very widespread type from the latter part of the 18th century

French gun by H.I. Paixhans 1824. 18 or 21cm muzzle loader. Initially wooden carriage, later iron sliding mount

Armstrong gun of 1865. 9 inch muzzle loader with rifled bore. The last sailing warships carried such guns

Rates

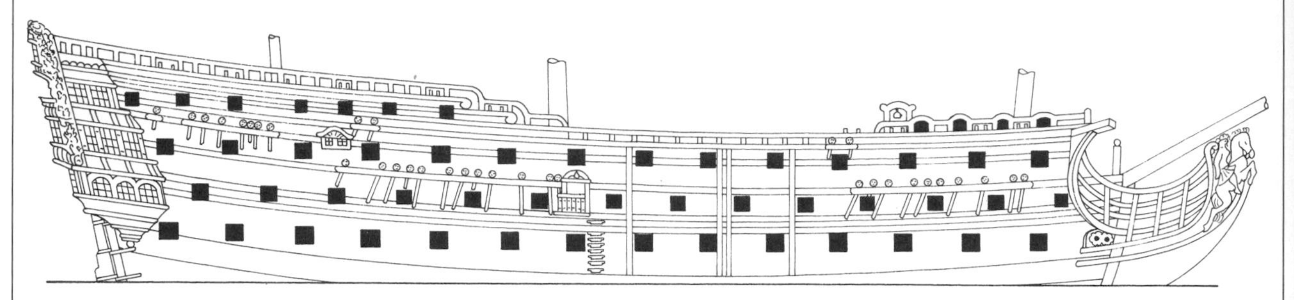

Ship of the line of the 1st rate, 100 and more guns

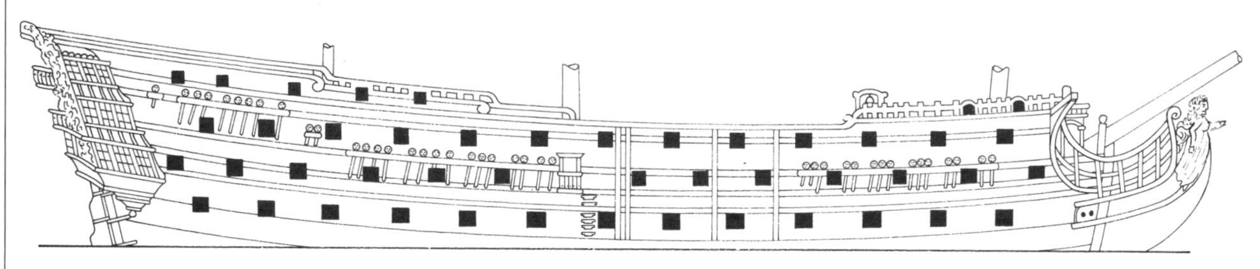

Ship of the line of the 2nd rate, 90 guns

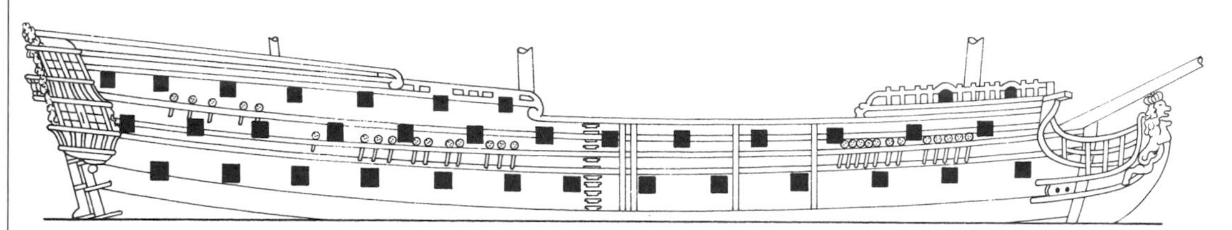

Ship of the line of the 3rd rate, 80, 70 or 60 guns

In the 17th century when sea battles developed into artillery duels, it was necessary to divide warships into classes or "rates" in order to set ships of roughly equivalent armament against each other. The system developed by the English in the middle of the 17th century, which was soon adopted with minor variations of the continent, remained valid until the early 19th century. The illustrations show the rates of the English fleet in the middle of the 18th century.
Only the large ships of the line of the 1st to 3rd rates were used in the actual battle line (hence the name 'ship of the line').
Ships of the 4th to 6th rate served as escorts to merchant convoys and above all in the colonies. They were later replaced by frigates to a large extent.
Frigates and corvettes, built with a good armament but particularly for speed, were initially used as fleet scouts but were soon trusted with their own independent duties as convoy escorts, sea raiders and expedition ships. Brigs, schooners and cutters were used mainly for coastal protection duty.

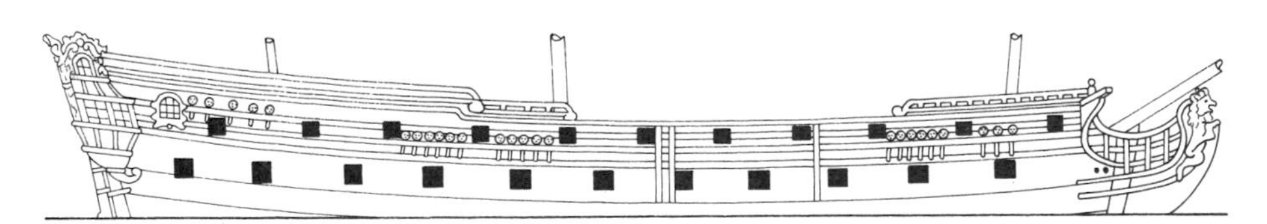

4th rate, 50 guns

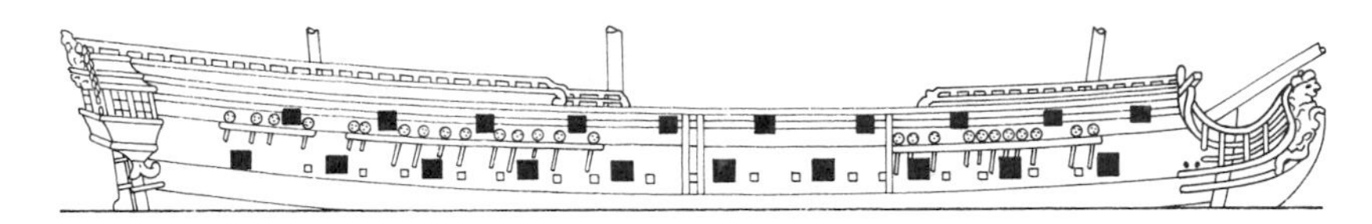

5th rate, 40 guns

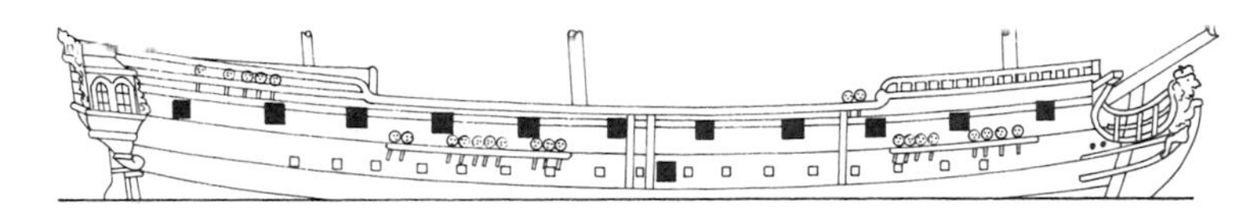

6th rate, 24 guns

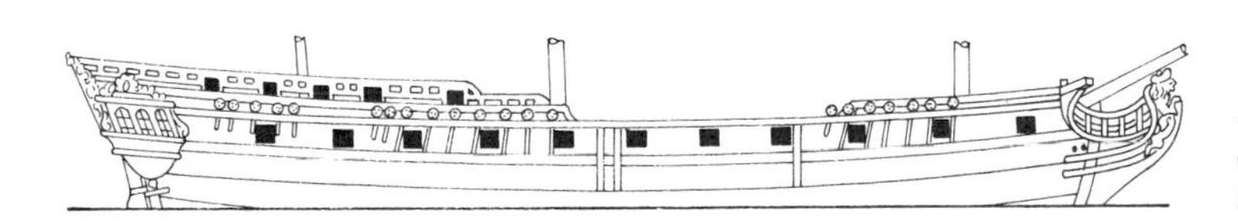

Frigate, 32 guns (the number of guns was often substantially increased later)

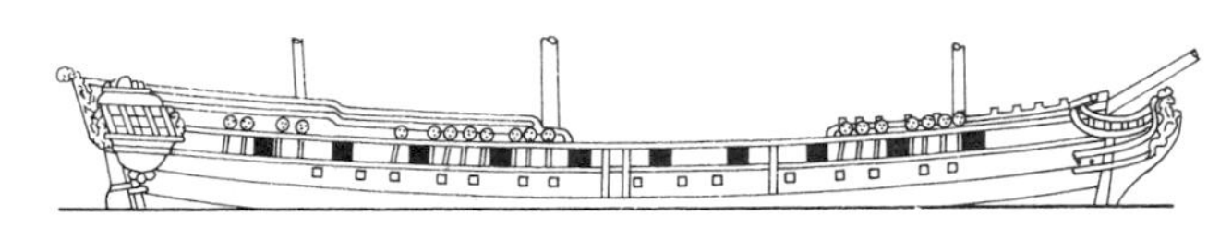

Corvette, 20 guns

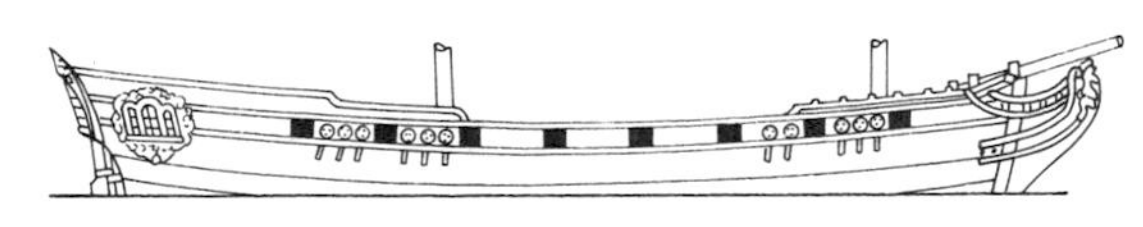

Brig, 10 to 18 guns

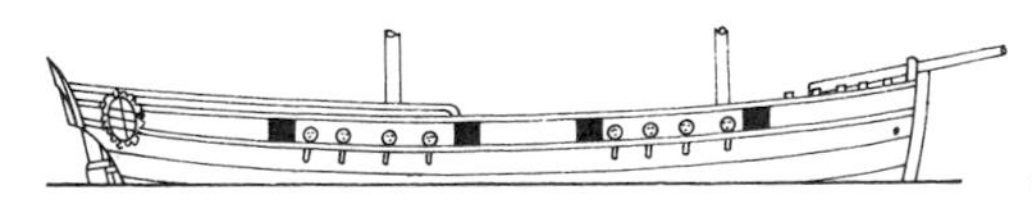

Schooner, 8 to 16 guns

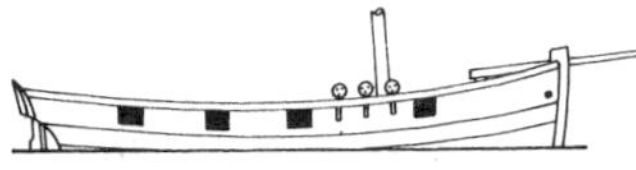

Cutter, 8 to 12 guns (later equipped to a large extent with carronades)

Gunport lids

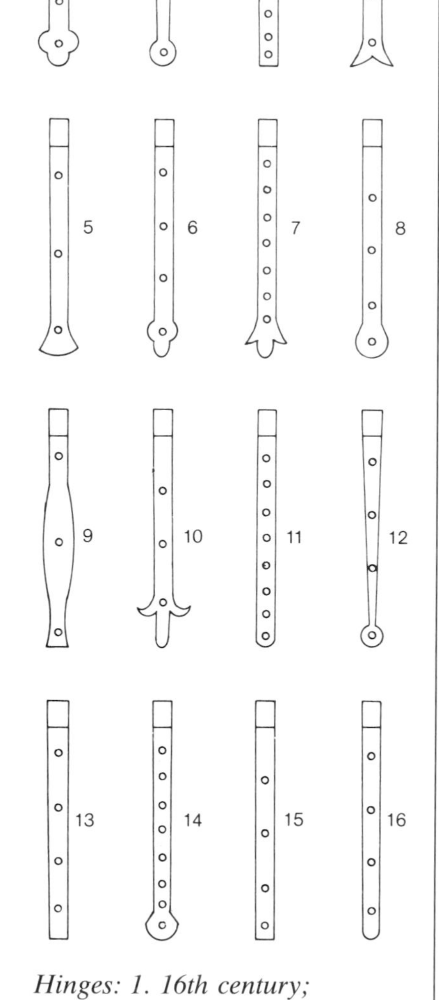

Hinges: 1. 16th century; 1.-8. 17th century; 9.-14. 18th century; 15. and 16. 19th century; 1. Spanish, Italian; 2., 3., 6., 10., 13. and 14. British; 4., 7., 9. and 12. French; 5. and 8. Dutch; 11. American

The gunports were sealed by the gunport lids. In the 15th century these were simple timber boards, which were placed over the ports on the inside, and secured with a locking bar. The invention of the gunport lid suspended on hinges and closed with a lanyard dates from the early 16th century and is ascribed to French master shipwrights.

The gunport lid consisted of two layers of wood, of which the outside larger piece exactly sealed the port opening in the hull and the inner, smaller piece fitted exactly in the opening of the port frame.

It is important to note that the gunport lids always followed the curvature of the hull; if they were crossed by the wales, corresponding strips were attached to the gunport lids, so that there was no apparent interruption of the hull when the ports were closed. The strips for the hinges are cut from thin brass or copper sheet, and for small-scale models they can be punched out. Finally the hinge strips are thoroughly blackened. Whether you actually pin them in place, or just emboss the bolt heads (the latter is easier in any case) depends on the scale of the model.

One problem for the model maker is the attachment of open gunport lids. They can be left supported on the hinge strips (such hinges are available commercially), but this method cannot be recommended as the gunport lids can be torn off or damaged so easily.

In my experience it is more sensible to fix the outer component of the gunport lid to the hull wall and the port frame with two thin steel pins, and then glue the inner component on top, thus concealing the pin heads – this is by no means a historically accurate method of fixing but it allows you to occasionally touch a port lid without ripping it from its mounting in an instant.

The last stage is to fix the port tackle spans to the ring bolts and run them inboard. In the 19th century thin chains were sometimes used as spans. Take care! Remember to fit the spans for the lower deck batteries before sealing the next higher deck.

The shape, appearance, and direction of opening of the gunports, and whether single or double spans were fitted, all this information can be gleaned from the plan, usually without any problems. The so-called "false gunports" are a special case; they were very widely used on merchant ships in the 19th century. These false ports could not be opened. They were just a timber frame with a small porthole and later they were just painted on to the white or yellow port frame in black. The original purpose of gunports was to attempt to deceive pirates into thinking the ship was more heavily armed than was the case; later they were retained for the sake of tradition.

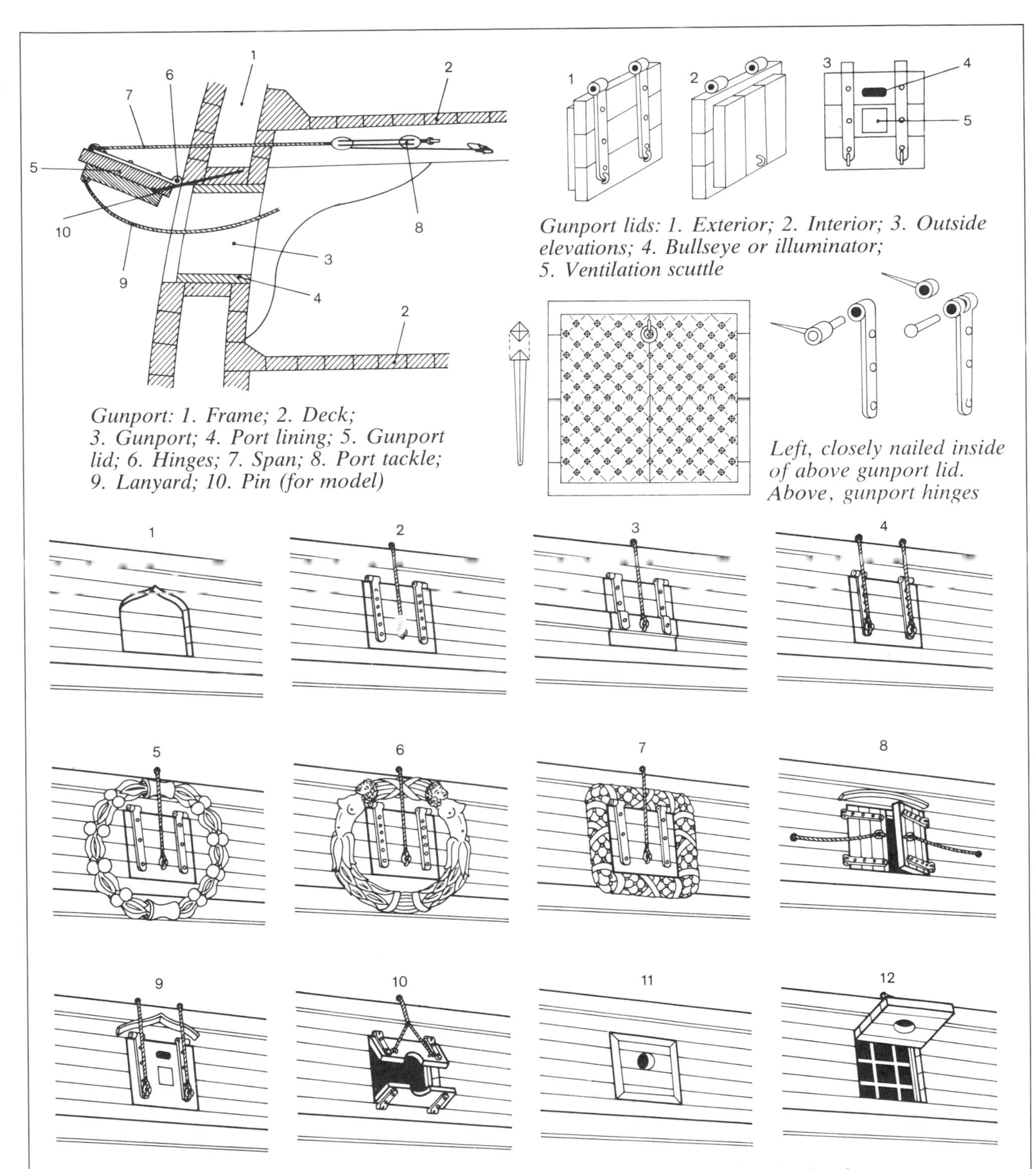

Gunport: 1. Frame; 2. Deck; 3. Gunport; 4. Port lining; 5. Gunport lid; 6. Hinges; 7. Span; 8. Port tackle; 9. Lanyard; 10. Pin (for model)

Gunport lids: 1. Exterior; 2. Interior; 3. Outside elevations; 4. Bullseye or illuminator; 5. Ventilation scuttle

Left, closely nailed inside of above gunport lid. Above, gunport hinges

Gunport lids: 1. Spanish, Portuguese up to 1550, closed with locking bar. 2. Single span 1520-1830; 3. Crossing the wale, 1600-1830; 4. Double span 1550-1830; 5. and 6. English 1640-1720; 7. French 1640-1720; 8. Vertical port lids 1650-1780; 9. Illuminator and ventilation scuttle 1800-1850; 10. Half ports 1820-1880; 11. False port 1830-1890; 12. False port with glass window behind 1750-1890

The Capstan

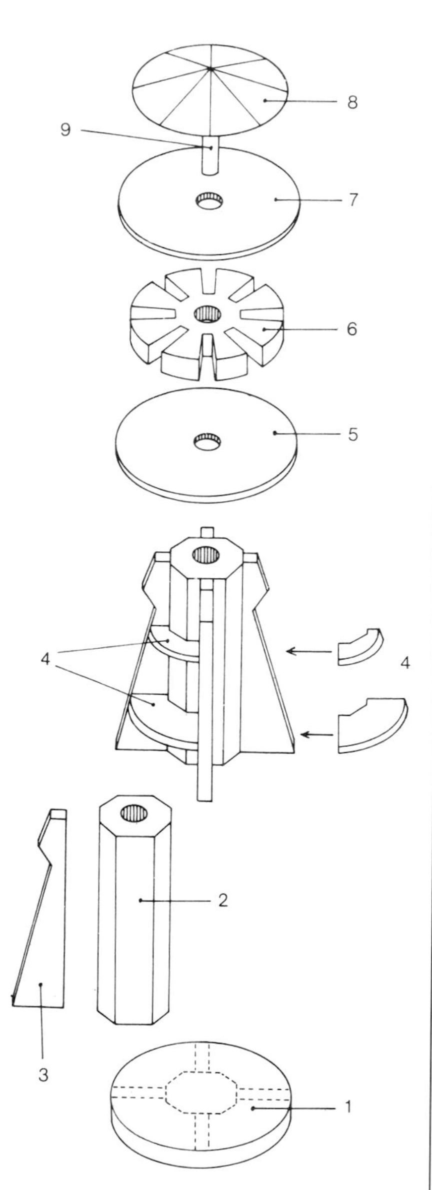

Construction of a model capstan:
1. Base plate; 2. Spindle; 3. Whelps; 4. Chocks; 5. Lower head disc; 6. Slotted disc for bars; 7. Upper head disc; 8. Cap; 9. Spigot for holding head together

The capstans were employed for weighing the anchors, hoisting the yards, and for hoisting the boats in and out. There are two main types: the capstan with a vertical spindle, and the windlass with a horizontal spindle, from which the very widely used pump-type windlass was developed in the 19th century.

The capstan
Capstans have been known since the middle of the 14th century. Initially they were fairly small and light, but very rapidly grew much larger and heavier.
Warships generally had one capstan, until the beginning of the 17th century, after which time two were carried, although there were exceptions, such as the *Wasa* which had three. Normally, with two, one was located abaft the foremast on or under the forecastle, the other abaft the mainmast on the main deck, and was often of double-capstan design, i.e. there were two barrels fitted on the same spindle, situated on two adjacent decks, which allowed double the number of men to man the bars. The capstan consisted of a barrel around which the whelps were distributed, the purpose of which was to prevent the rope slipping. Strengthening chocks were fitted between the whelps. The head was fitted above the barrel, and featured a number of square holes to take the bars by which the rotating force was applied. To prevent the capstan running backwards, Continental and early ships featured pawls which engaged in square holes in the base plate; after the mid 18th century British ships had the pawls set directly on the capstan base plate, which then engaged in a toothed pawl rim. The appearance of the capstan altered only in minor ways in the course of the centuries, except that the number of bars was increased.
The bars could be removed and were stowed against the ship's side, round the mast, or on the bulkheads of a deck house. A common error on models is capstan bars shown fitted in the capstan with the ship meant to be under way or engaged in battle; in fact the bars were only fitted immediately before using the capstan, whereafter they were immediately removed.

The windlass
Smaller ships in general and merchant ships in particular, since the 13th century, carried a horizontal windlass. This consisted of a barrel, either hexagonal or octagonal in section, which included the bar holes, and which was supported at the ends in the carrick bitts. Centrally ahead of the barrel there was a timber framework – often combined with the belfry or a pin rail – from which one or two pawls engaged in a pawl rim let into the surface of the windlass barrel, in order to prevent it running back. Large ships' boats were sometimes fitted with a windlass for laying out and recovering the ship's anchor.

The pump-type windlass
This was a further development of the windlass, and was also employed on merchant ships. Ahead of the windlass stood a column supporting a cross head into which bars could be inserted. The pumping up-and-down movement of the cross head was converted into rotary movement by means of connecting rods and pawls on two coaxial gearwheels mounted on the windlass spindle. These windlasses were often driven by a small steam engine in the late 19th century.

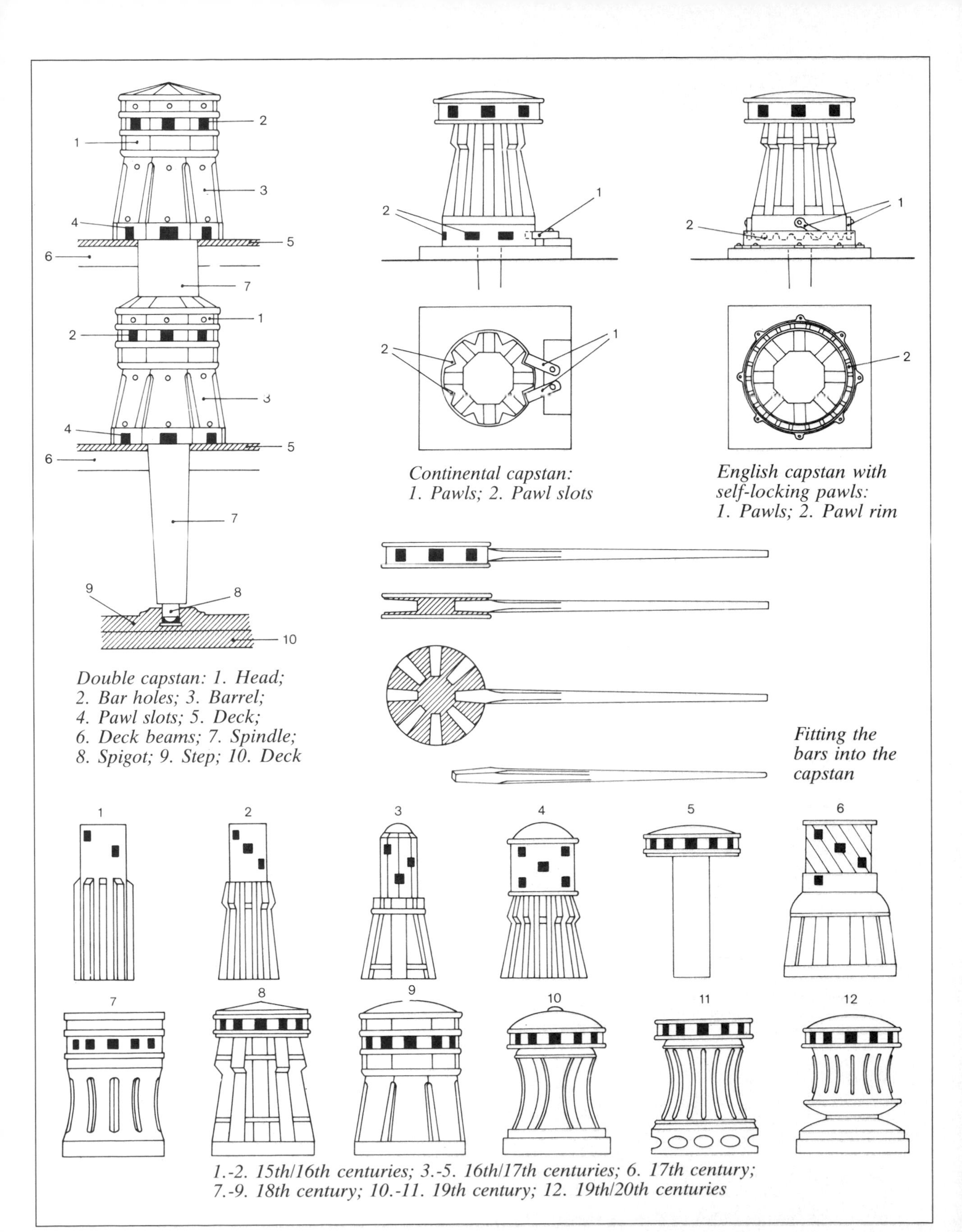
1
2
3
4
5
6
7
8
9
10
Double capstan: 1. Head; 2. Bar holes; 3. Barrel; 4. Pawl slots; 5. Deck; 6. Deck beams; 7. Spindle; 8. Spigot; 9. Step; 10. Deck
Continental capstan: 1. Pawls; 2. Pawl slots
English capstan with self-locking pawls: 1. Pawls; 2. Pawl rim
Fitting the bars into the capstan
11
12
1.-2. 15th/16th centuries; 3.-5. 16th/17th centuries; 6. 17th century; 7.-9. 18th century; 10.-11. 19th century; 12. 19th/20th centuries

The Capstan

A warship capstan around 1860
1. *Hawse pipe*
2. *Compressor*
3. *Bitt*
4. *Capstan*
5. *Spindle*
6. *Barrel*
7. *Pawls*
8. *Roller*
9. *Compressor*
10. *Navel pipe*

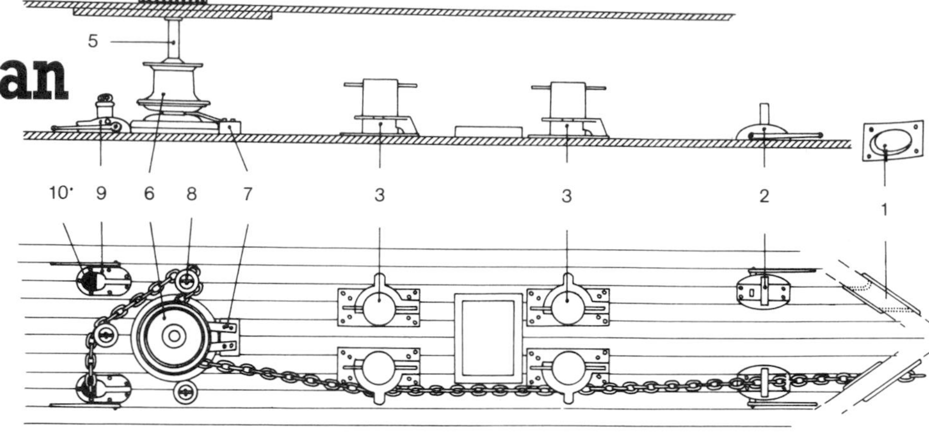

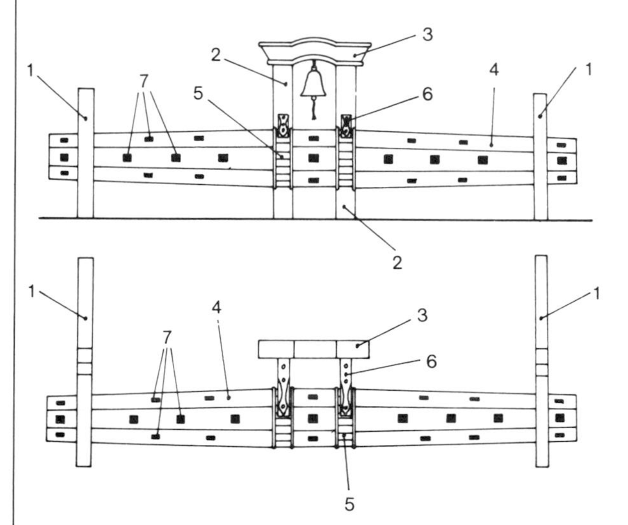

Large windlass: 1. Carrick bitts; 2. Pawl bitts; 3. Cross piece with belfry; 4. Barrel; 5. Toothed wheel; 6. Pawls; 7. Bar holes

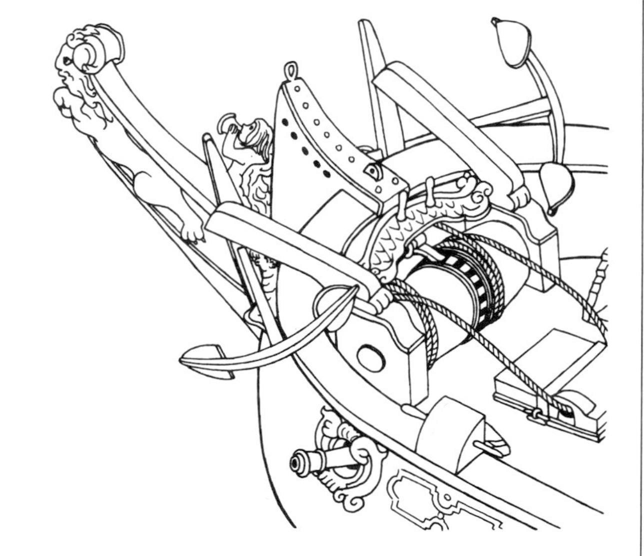

Bow of a Dutch state yacht around 1700, showing windlass

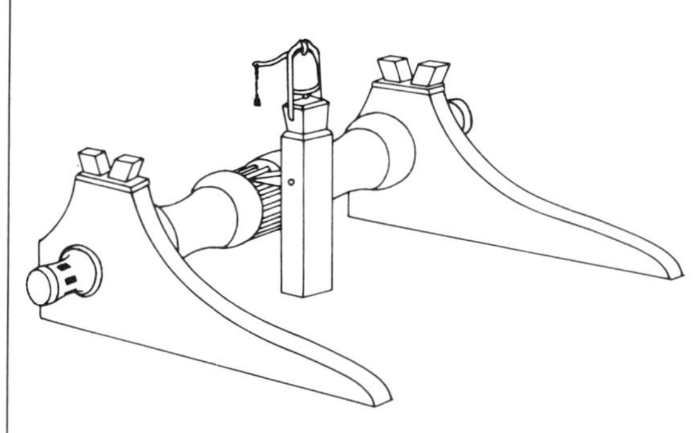

Early 19th century windlass

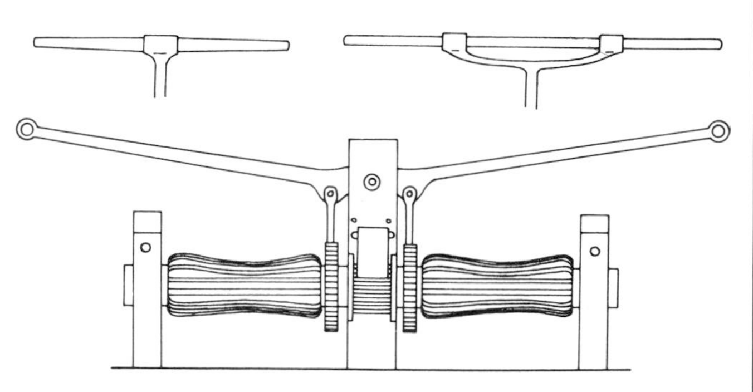

Pump-type windlass of American design

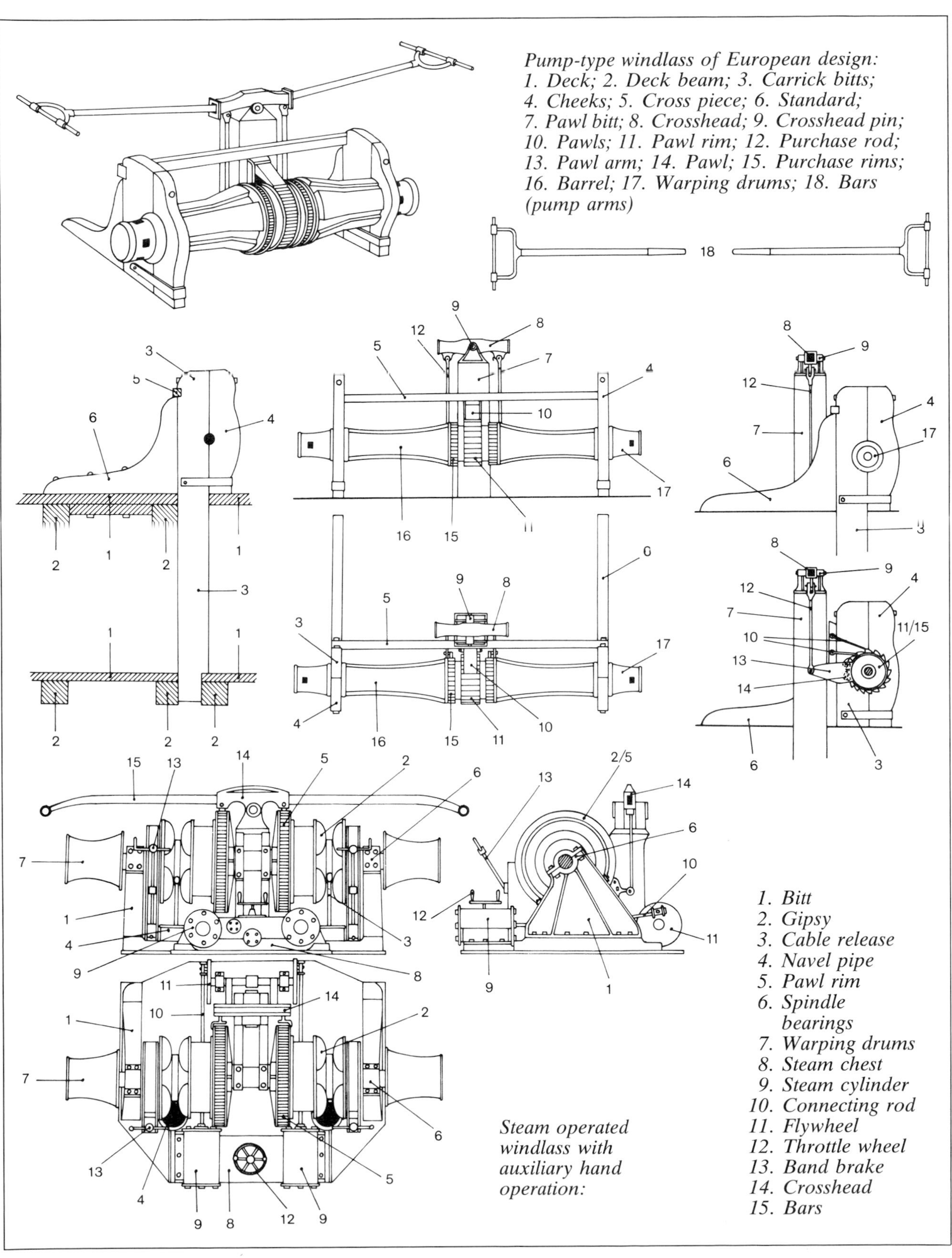

Pump-type windlass of European design: 1. Deck; 2. Deck beam; 3. Carrick bitts; 4. Cheeks; 5. Cross piece; 6. Standard; 7. Pawl bitt; 8. Crosshead; 9. Crosshead pin; 10. Pawls; 11. Pawl rim; 12. Purchase rod; 13. Pawl arm; 14. Pawl; 15. Purchase rims; 16. Barrel; 17. Warping drums; 18. Bars (pump arms)

Steam operated windlass with auxiliary hand operation:

1. *Bitt*
2. *Gipsy*
3. *Cable release*
4. *Navel pipe*
5. *Pawl rim*
6. *Spindle bearings*
7. *Warping drums*
8. *Steam chest*
9. *Steam cylinder*
10. *Connecting rod*
11. *Flywheel*
12. *Throttle wheel*
13. *Band brake*
14. *Crosshead*
15. *Bars*

Winches

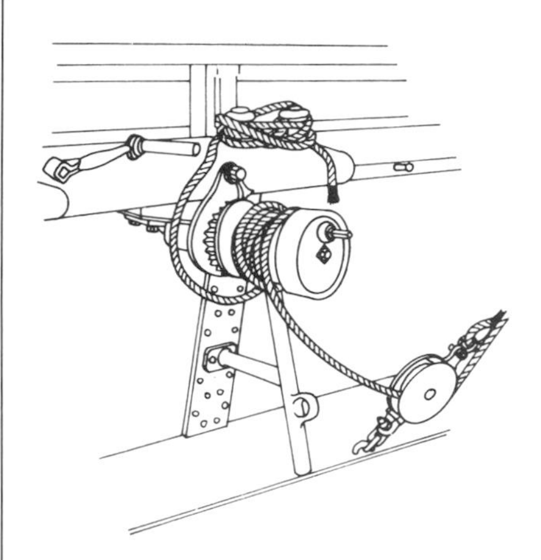

Small bulwark winch (English c.1860)

From the middle of the 19th century, winches of all sizes became increasingly common, especially on merchant ships, for raising loads, setting up the ropes of the standing rigging, hauling the ropes of the running rigging (brace winches, halyard winches). They were operated by hand cranks, which transmitted power to a drum via reduction gears. In the late 19th century the larger winches were coupled to steam engines.

If we disregard the capstan – although it is really a member of the same family – winches on ships are a very recent development. They came into use during the 19th century as a result of the increasingly bitter rivalry between sailing and steam ships: the shipowners had to save money, to rationalise. There was nothing to be saved in the building costs of a ship, so the savings were made in the crew. A steam ship required only a small number of specialist workers, viz. well-paid mechanics and engineers, plus a group of poorly paid labourers in the coal bunkers. Sailing ships, on the other hand, needed a fairly large number of trained sailors – cheaper than engineers, it is true, but more expensive than the stokers. The only way of reducing their number was to give the men mechanical assistance, and in particular by fitting a wide variety of winches, which allowed one or two men to do the work which previously required perhaps six or ten. The greatest achievement in this quest for rationalization was represented by the American gaff-rigged schooner *Thomas W. Lawson,* which had 7 masts, a displacement of 5000 tons, and a waterline length of 384ft but which was sailed by a crew of just 16 men.

For model purposes the winches are fabricated from brass sheet – thick sheet for the gearwheels, thin for the housing – brass strip, brass tubing and brass wire of various thicknesses, which are then blackened or – in the case of the housings and bitts – painted. Usable items can also be made by the tin alloy casting method for the larger and thicker parts, such as gearwheels and drums.

There is a very wide variety of winches available commercially, and if you are lucky, you will find the right one for your vessel, although you cannot depend on it. Under no circumstances should you be tempted to fit a non-scale winch (usually too modern) on your model, simply because you were able to obtain it ready-made. As I have already said, if you have problems working with metal, you should give preference to modelling ships from the period before 1820.

Bollards and fairleads

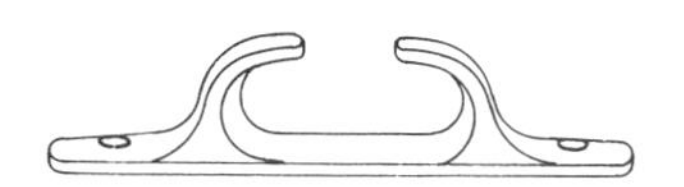

19th/20th century fairlead

Bollards – except in Holland, where they have been in use since the 17th century – are a comparatively recent feature on ships. They are principally used for making heavy ropes fast, when the ship is moored at the quayside.

Various bollards are illustrated in the drawing on the right. The first three were made of wood, the others from iron. The Dutch bollard (No. 1) was fixed at the top of the bulwark, the double bollard (No. 2) on or in the bulwark, while all the others stood unsupported on deck. The making of the wooden bollards should not present any difficulties at all. The metal bollards can be turned from brass, or cast from tin alloy and then blackened.

Virtually all model fittings manufacturers carry brass bollards of usable quality in their ranges.

Metal fittings for securing or leading cables became customary in the second half of the 19th century.

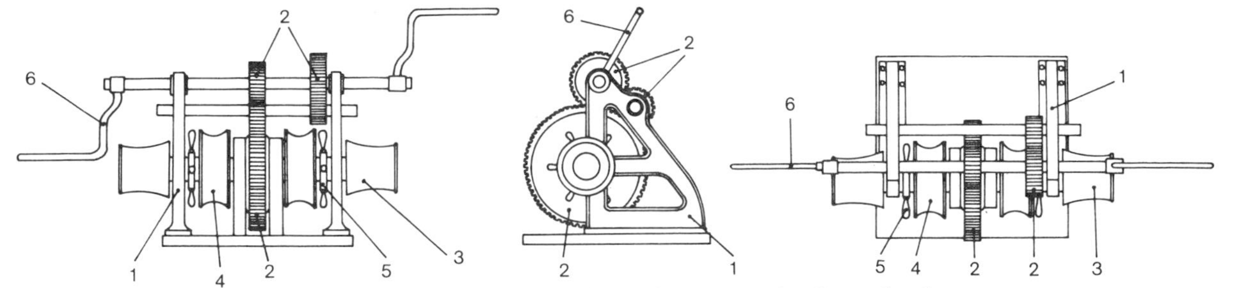

Multi-purpose winch with double hand crank: 1. Bitt; 2. Gearwheels; 3. External drums; 4. Internal drums; 5. Clutch handwheel; 6. Hand cranks

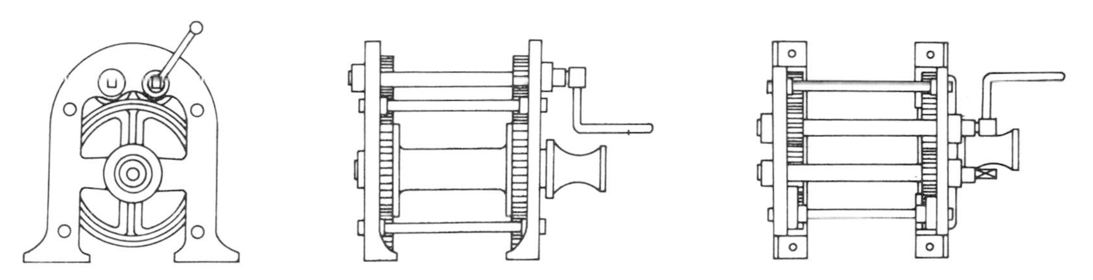

Brace winch with hand crank and additional external drum (British coastal craft)

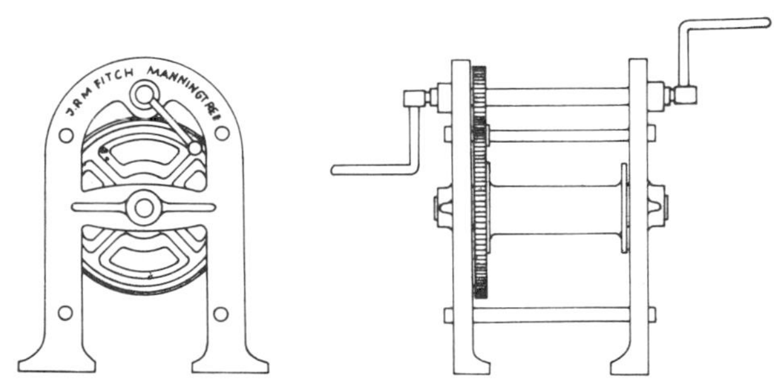

English halyard winch with double hand crank

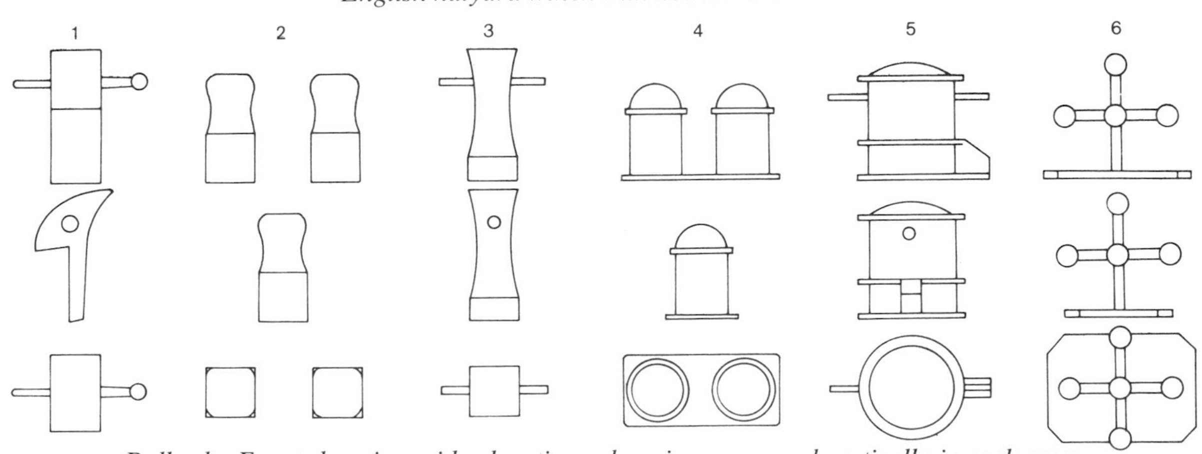

Bollards: Front elevation, side elevation, plan view, arranged vertically in each case: 1. Dutch bollard (fixed to bulwark), 17th/20th century; 2. Double bollard, 18th century; 3. Single bollard, beginning of 19th century; 4. Double bollard from middle of 19th century; 5. Large bollard, after middle of 19th century; 6. Staghorn, 19th century

Anchors

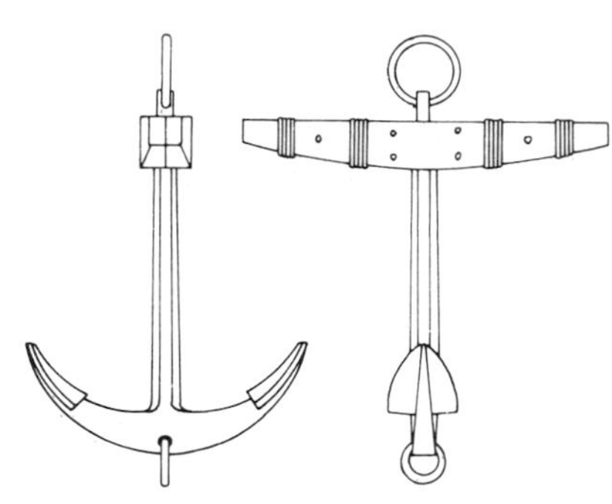

18th century Continental anchor

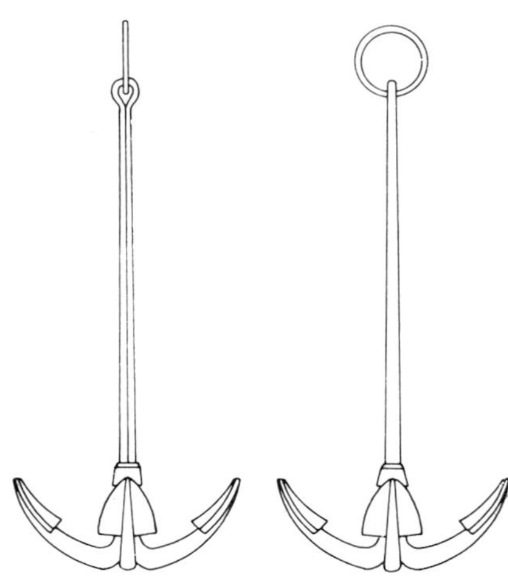

Boat's grapnel

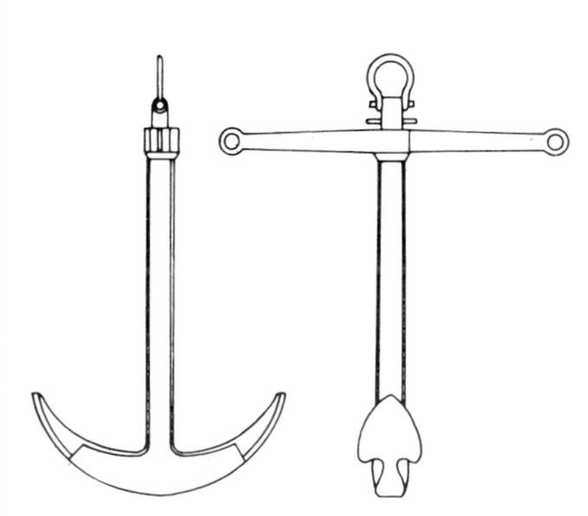

Rodger's anchor, after 1830

The anchors are amongst the most important items of the ship's equipment. Even on good plans it is unusual to find more than two anchors shown, even though ships carried at least four as early as the Middle Ages. In the 17th and 18th centuries this figure rose in some instances to as many as six, and the relative properties became standardised.

Anchors were categorised by weight and in the British Navy the weight of anchor for each ship was laid down by the Admiralty. The proportions were based on three basic dimensions:

1. The length of the arm from the inside of the throat to the bill.
2. The thickness at the trend. (This is the point on the shank which is distant the length of the arm from the inside of the throat).
3. The thickness at the small which is where the shank taper meets the square at its upper end. It is from 1½in to 3in less than the trend depending on the size of the anchor.

From these dimensions:
Length of shank = 3 × length of arm
Length of square = 4 × trend + ¾ small
Hole for the ring is ¾ small from the upper end
Outer diameter of ring = 4 × trend
Thickness of ring = ½ small
Width of base of palm = 4 × trend
Length of palm = base + 1in to 1¼in
Angle between arm and shank = 60°
Length of stock = shank + ½ diameter of ring
Width + depth of wooden stock at middle – number of inches that the stock is long in feet
Depth of wooden stock at ends = ½ depth at middle.

Establishment of Bower Anchors:

Guns	Weight (Cwt)	Shank (ft. ins)	Trend (ins)
100 & 110	81	19·8	10
98 & 90	73	18·8	9⅜
80 & large 74	71	18·5	9¼
small 74	67	18·2	9
64	57	17·4	8½
60	53	17·0	8⅜
50	49	16·8	8⅛
44 & 38	40	15·10	7¾
36	39	15·9	7¾
32	33	14·10	6⅞
28	31	14·4	6⅝
24	29½	13·8	6⅜
20	25	13·0	5⅝

A typical set of anchors and their location would be as follows: Best Bower anchor carried to starboard and fixed to timber heads and the fore part of the fore channel. Small bower anchor carried to larboard and fixed to timber heads and the fore part of the channel. Sheet anchor carried to starboard and fixed to the channel abaft the best bower anchor. A spare anchor was carried to larboard abaft the small bower anchor. The stream and kedge anchors were stowed below. Despite their names the best bower, small bower, sheet and spare anchors were all the same size. Stream and kedge anchors were approximately ¼ and ⅛ respectively of the weight of the bower anchors. After the first decade of the nineteenth century the arms were formed as part of a circle and a shackle type ring was used in conjunction with chain cable.

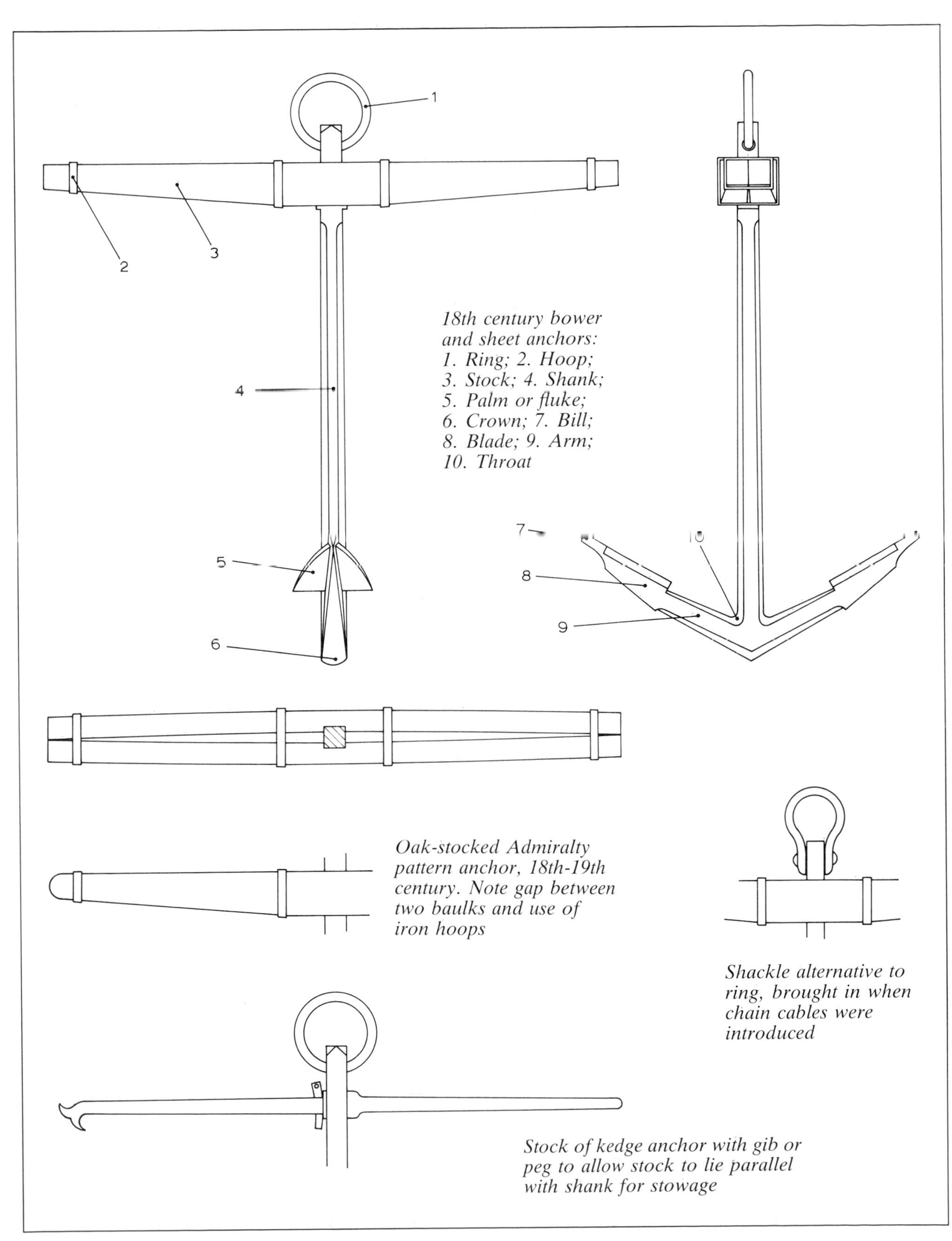
1
2
3
4
5
6
7
8
9
10
18th century bower and sheet anchors: 1. Ring; 2. Hoop; 3. Stock; 4. Shank; 5. Palm or fluke; 6. Crown; 7. Bill; 8. Blade; 9. Arm; 10. Throat
Oak-stocked Admiralty pattern anchor, 18th-19th century. Note gap between two baulks and use of iron hoops
Shackle alternative to ring, brought in when chain cables were introduced
Stock of kedge anchor with gib or peg to allow stock to lie parallel with shank for stowage

Anchors

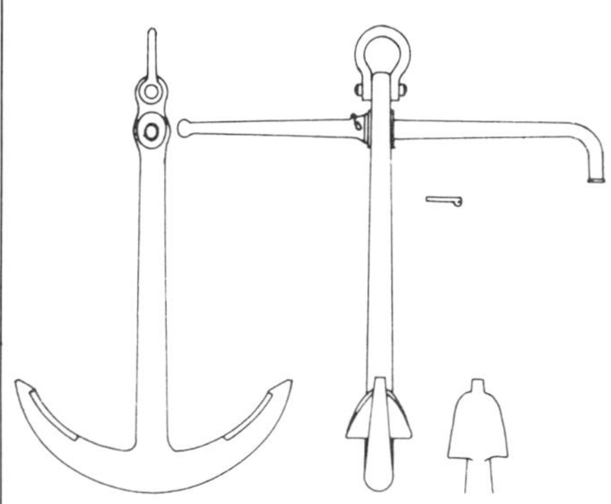
Admiralty pattern anchor from 1840

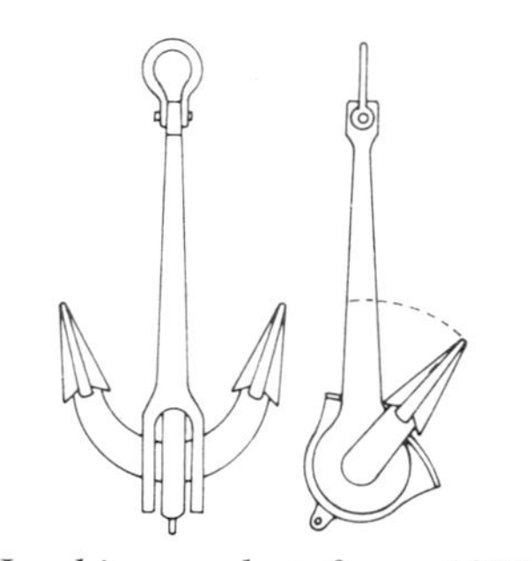
Hawkins anchor from 1820

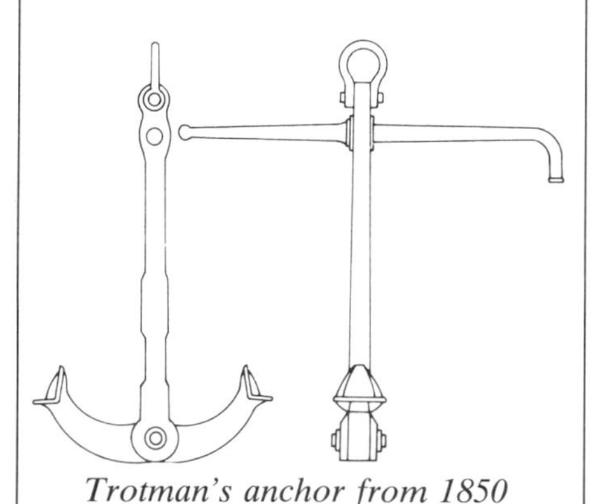
Trotman's anchor from 1850

Anchors are best made by sawing the shape out of thick brass copper sheet, with the flukes of thin sheet soldered in place. The stock is made of two pieces of wood fastened together with iron hoops with iron bolts in the centre section and wooden treenails in the outer sections.
All the metal parts of the anchor should be blackened. Virtually all model manufacturers supply anchors made of lead and/or brass. Be very careful here, as these anchors are seldom correctly proportioned, and they are rarely offered in the correct sizes for a specific model.
Making your own anchors is rather difficult, it is true, but the effect is incomparably better.
Until the introduction of chain cable the anchor rings were puddened first with tarred canvas, then served over with rope, secured with four snaked seizings. The modeller can, of course, omit the canvas, but the rope and seizings should certainly be fitted.
There were three different methods of attaching the anchor rope:
1. Round turn and one or two half hitches with the end stopped. This was used with the hawsers for smaller anchors, i.e. generally in the Middle Ages and for stream and kedge anchors later.
2. The inside clinch. This was used for large anchors (bower, and sheet anchors) as it was easier to form in heavy cables than the round turn and two half hitches.
3. The fisherman's bend. This was used for the four-armed grapnel anchor as traditionally used on galleys, but also carried on many Mediterranean vessels. It was also used on small anchors in preference to the round turn and half hitches, being less liable to jam when wet.
Anchor buoys served to indicate where the anchors were when they were on the seabed. They were made of light wood or cork, and covered in tarred yarn. The buoy rope was clove hitched to the crown of the anchor with its end stopped to the shank, its length coiled up, and the coil hung next to the buoy at the foot of the foremast shrouds.
In the Middle Ages the anchors were stowed at the waist rail when the ship was under way, but from the early 16th century on the channels were used. Purpose-made anchor stowages were used from the first half of the 19th century onwards.
The best bower (starboard) and small bower (larboard) anchors were secured with shank painters to the timber heads and to the catheads with stoppers or to special fittings, as shown in the drawings on the next page. The sheet anchor (starboard) and spare anchor (larboard) were stowed at the after ends of the fore channels with the stream and kedge anchors on the spare anchor or down below. On smaller ships the anchors were often simply heaved aboard or fixed to bollards on the rail. On galleys the large grapnel anchors were kept either side of the guns in the forecastle.

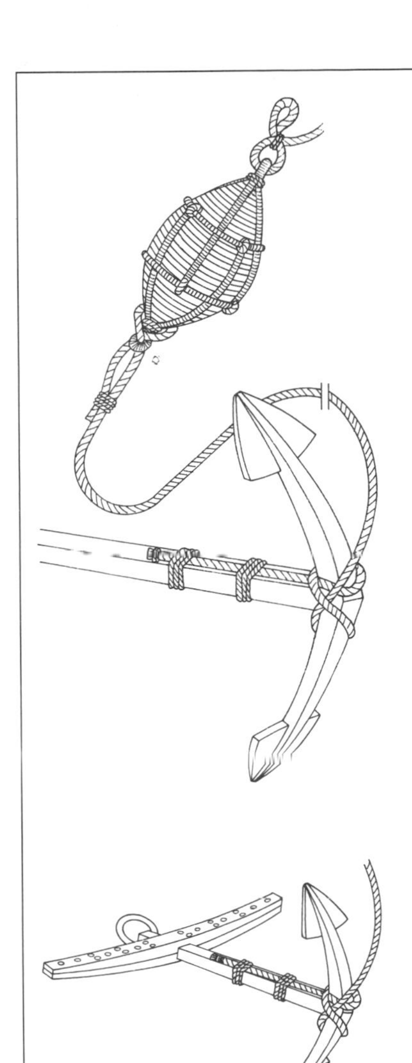

Anchor buoy

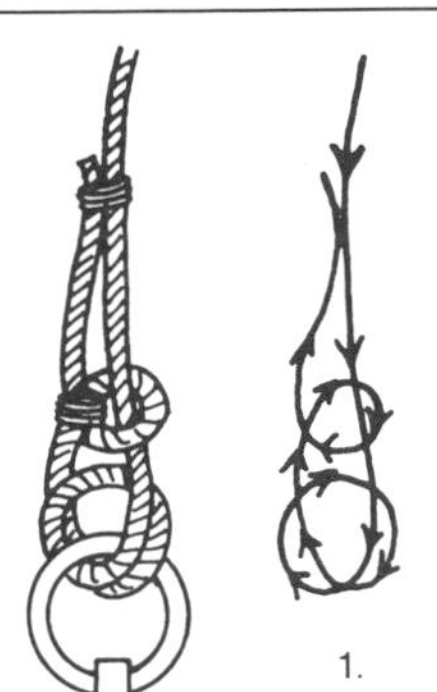

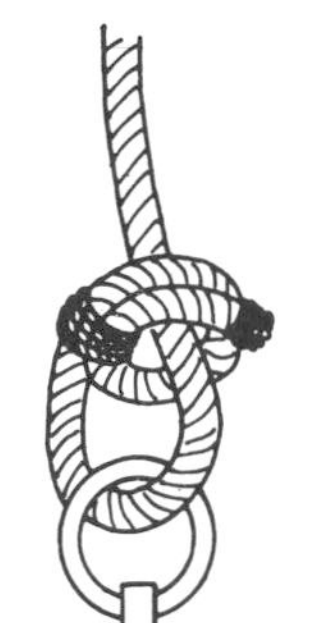

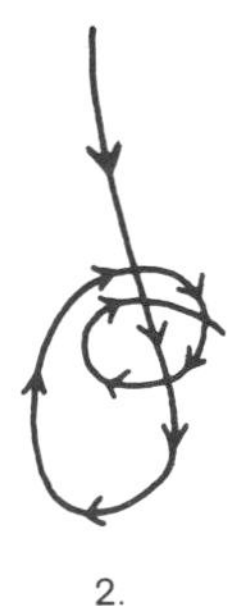

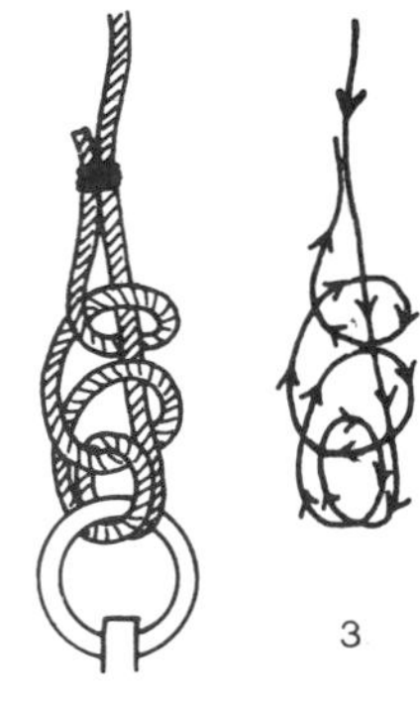

Anchor knots:
1. Round turn and a half hitch;
2. Inside clinch for large anchors;
3. Fisherman's bend

Puddening the anchor ring with tarred cloth, rope, and yarn

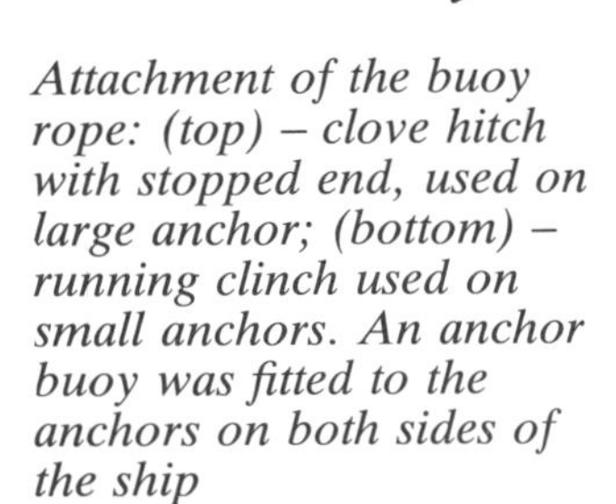

Attachment of the buoy rope: (top) – clove hitch with stopped end, used on large anchor; (bottom) – running clinch used on small anchors. An anchor buoy was fitted to the anchors on both sides of the ship

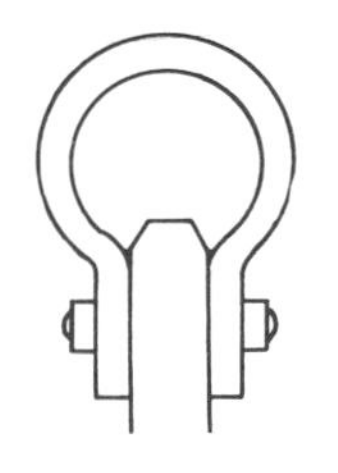

Anchor ring and shackle, 19th century

Stowed anchor on the French 1st rate ship of the line Royal Louis *around 1700*

Anchor stowage

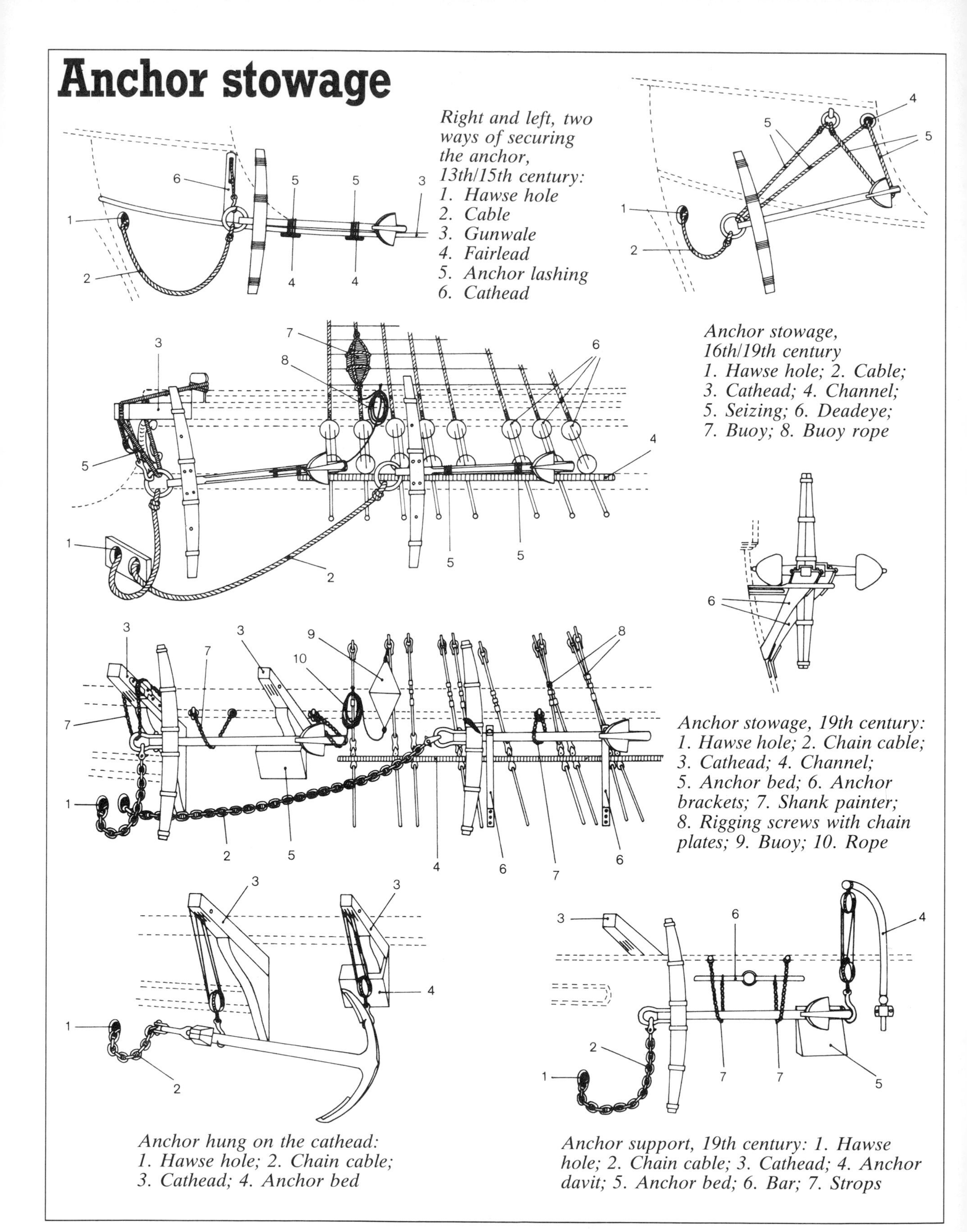

Right and left, two ways of securing the anchor, 13th/15th century:
1. Hawse hole
2. Cable
3. Gunwale
4. Fairlead
5. Anchor lashing
6. Cathead

Anchor stowage, 16th/19th century 1. Hawse hole; 2. Cable; 3. Cathead; 4. Channel; 5. Seizing; 6. Deadeye; 7. Buoy; 8. Buoy rope

Anchor stowage, 19th century: 1. Hawse hole; 2. Chain cable; 3. Cathead; 4. Channel; 5. Anchor bed; 6. Anchor brackets; 7. Shank painter; 8. Rigging screws with chain plates; 9. Buoy; 10. Rope

Anchor hung on the cathead: 1. Hawse hole; 2. Chain cable; 3. Cathead; 4. Anchor bed

Anchor support, 19th century: 1. Hawse hole; 2. Chain cable; 3. Cathead; 4. Anchor davit; 5. Anchor bed; 6. Bar; 7. Strops

In the 17th and 18th centuries a portable beam or fish davit was sometimes used instead of a secondary cathead or anchor davit for hoisting the anchor into position for fishing.

Anchor fishing

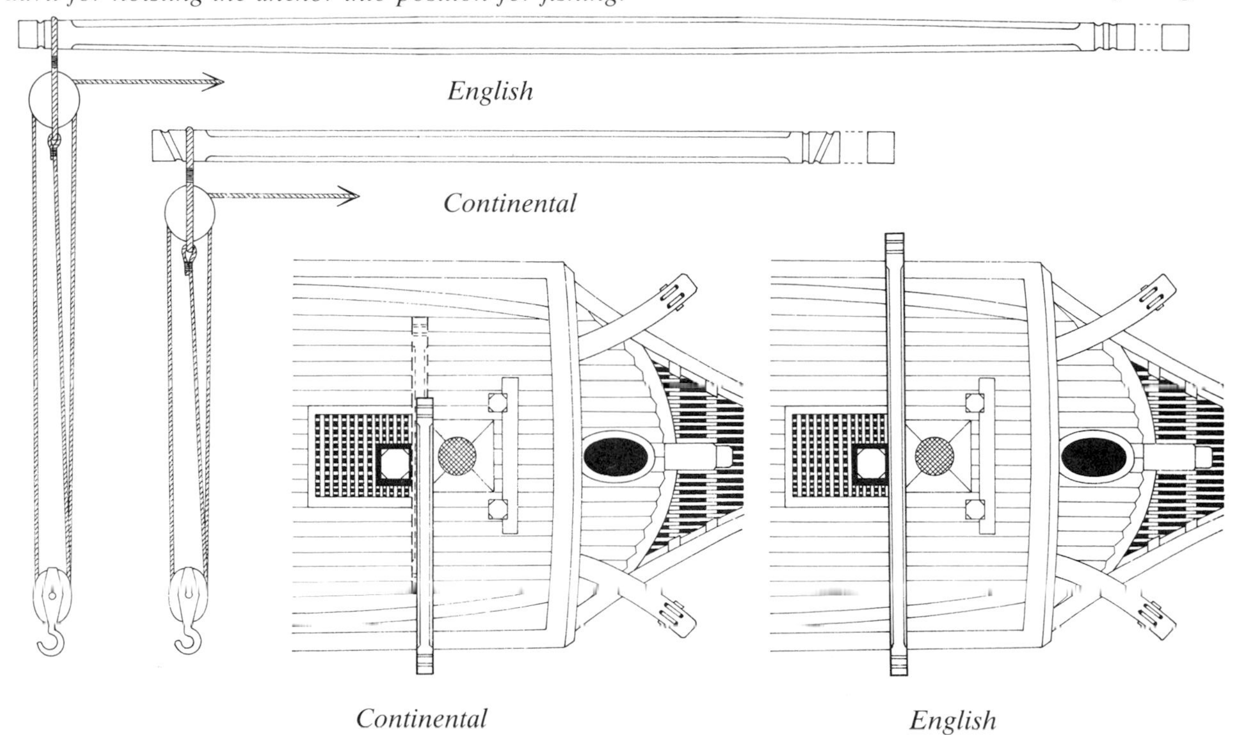

Fishing the anchor, after Willem van der Velde the Younger

Pumps

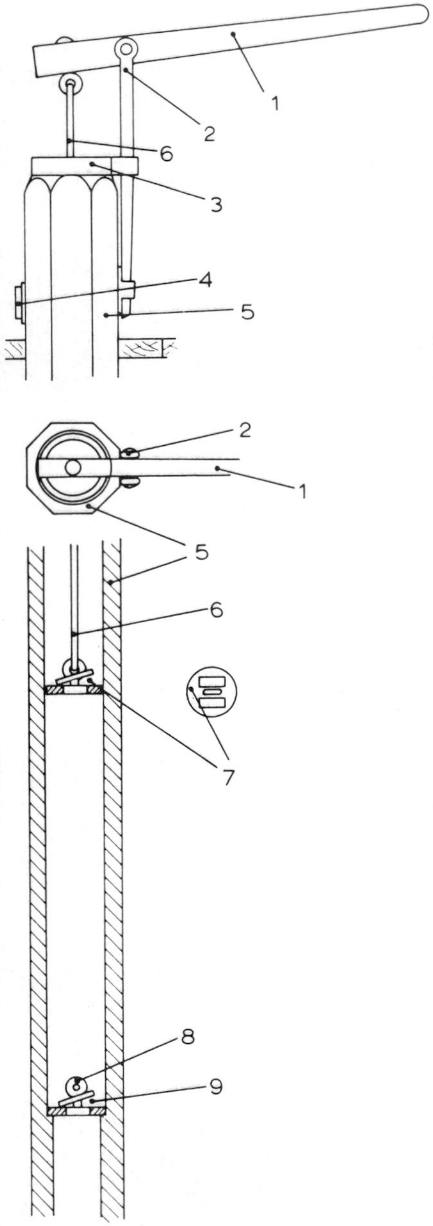

Elm tree pump: 1. Brake; 2. Forked pivot; 3. Iron hoop; 4. Outlet; 5. Barrel; 6. Operating rod; 7. Upper (moving) valve; 8. Lifting eye; 9. Lower (fixed) valve

It was not only rain and seawater which gathered inside the ship – all ships leaked to a greater or lesser extent. The water collected in the lowest part of the hull cavity, the bilges, whence it had to be pumped out at least once a day.

Hence the pumps were always located above the deepest part of the hull between the mizen and the main masts. On smaller ships in the Middle Ages one pump sufficed, while on the larger ships of the 16th century there were two to four. From the 17th century onward large ships usually had at least four. The pumps were located on a deck above the waterline and slightly to one side of the centre line, so that the suction tube avoided the keelson, which would have prevented it reaching far enough down. Their position is indicated by the pumpdale scuppers, which were larger than the other scuppers, and were fitted abreast of the pumps. Conversely, you can also find the position of the pumpdale scuppers if they are not shown on the plan, from the position of the pumps.

The oldest type of pump was made of four boards, and had a rectangular piston with valves made of thick leather plates. From the 14th century onward the pump shafts were round in section and being made from the trunk of an elm tree were known as elm tree pumps. They were operated by a handle or brake, a method which survived into the 19th century.

In the early 18th century chain pumps were introduced into the British Navy. These consisted of an endless chain with circular leather discs at about 3ft intervals. The chain passed over a wheel on an above water deck (usually the deck where the cables were worked), down through a protective trunking to the bilges where it passed over another wheel or roller and returned to the deck – this time through a circular pipe which was a close fit to the leather discs. The lower end of this pipe was below the bilge water level and consquently the water was lifted up by the discs and discharged into a cistern surrounding the upper wheel, which in turn discharged to the scuppers. The upper wheel was driven by long cranks which could be operated by as many as a dozen men in a large ship.

A chain pump manned by six men could discharge 1 ton of water per minute which was far in excess of the amount that the same number of men could discharge using elm tree pumps. The latter were retained but, except in an emergency, they were mainly used as wash deck pumps. Despite their undoubted efficiency chain pumps did not find favour on the Continent although in Britain they lasted to the end of the sailing navy.

In the 19th century crosshead pumps and wheel-driven plunger pumps came into use, the rotary action of the latter being changed to an oscillating movement by a double cranked axle.

The construction of pumps used until the 19th century presents no technical problems at all, although the building of crosshead and plunger pumps does demand some familiarity with metal-working techniques, as is true of many components of ships of this period. The pumps available commercially usually look so unnatural that you really have no choice but to rely on your own skill.

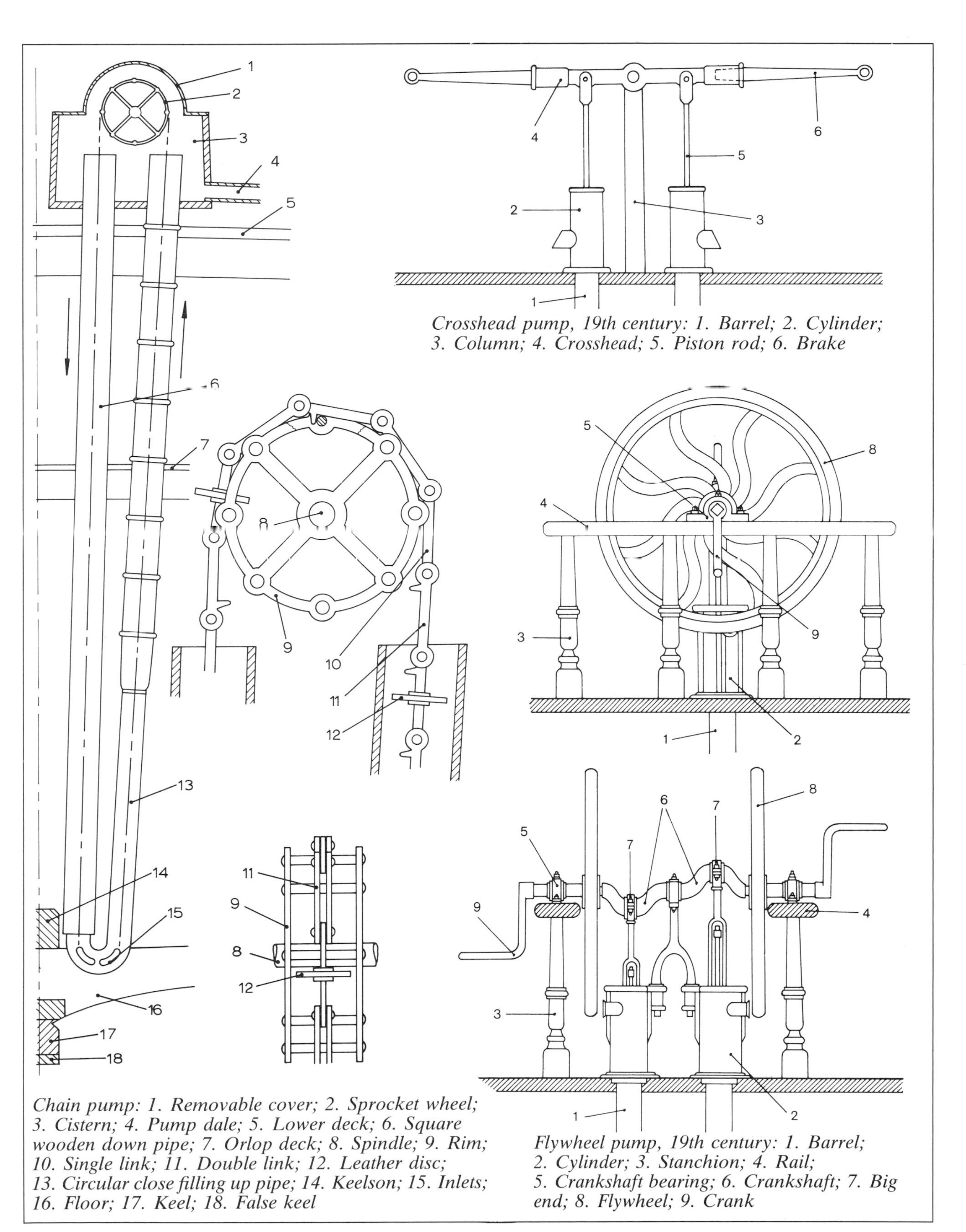

Crosshead pump, 19th century: 1. Barrel; 2. Cylinder; 3. Column; 4. Crosshead; 5. Piston rod; 6. Brake

Chain pump: 1. Removable cover; 2. Sprocket wheel; 3. Cistern; 4. Pump dale; 5. Lower deck; 6. Square wooden down pipe; 7. Orlop deck; 8. Spindle; 9. Rim; 10. Single link; 11. Double link; 12. Leather disc; 13. Circular close filling up pipe; 14. Keelson; 15. Inlets; 16. Floor; 17. Keel; 18. False keel

Flywheel pump, 19th century: 1. Barrel; 2. Cylinder; 3. Stanchion; 4. Rail; 5. Crankshaft bearing; 6. Crankshaft; 7. Big end; 8. Flywheel; 9. Crank

Ships' boats

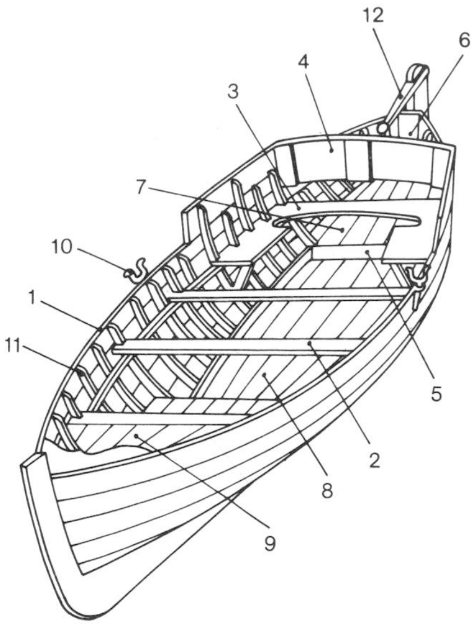

Parts of a ship's boat
1. Gunwale; 2. Thwarts;
3. Stern bench;
4. Backboard; 5. Step in bottom boards;
6. Coxswain's dicky;
7. Stern sheets; 8. Bottom boards; 9. Head sheets;
10. Crutches; 11. Frames;
12. Tiller

Since ancient times larger ships carried at least one small boat with them. Originally this boat could be towed, but on large Roman merchant ships it could be taken on board and stowed on deck. Throughout the Middle Ages the boats were towed, and it was not until the 15th century that the boats began to be taken on board again during a voyage.
Then in the 16th century it became common practice to stow the boats on the main hatch gratings, and from the middle of the 18th century on a series of skid beams which rested on the main rail or between the gangways over the waist. In the late 18th century davits were introduced from which the ship's boats were hung; they were fitted at the stern and on the bulwarks of the quarter deck. However, the larger boats were still stowed on the skid beams or on the top of the deck houses. Smaller ships towed their boats until far into the 19th century – still to this day in some areas of the Mediterranean – and basically all boats were lowered and towed when an engagement was imminent, as the boats would only have obstructed the crew on deck. The ships' boats were intended for use in harbour, for landings on shelving beaches, for personnel and load transport, and for communication between the ships of a squadron. However, it was not until the end of the 19th century that they served in the more narrow sense of lifeboats, as they would have been far too few to carry all the crew. In the 17th century, for example, a three-decker with more than 600 crew carried only three boats, and when the mighty passenger liner *Titanic* collided with an iceberg in 1912 and sank, it turned out that the lifeboats available only catered for less than half the passengers.

The long boat
Sometimes known as the sloop or the great boat. The largest ship's boat carried. Fitted out for 8 to 14 oars, up to 45ft long and including fittings for sailing. It was intended as a cargo and personnel transport boat, but was sometimes used to handle the anchor, and in such cases was fitted with a windlass. The following double page includes full drawings and perspective views of a long boat. It was replaced in the late 18th century by the launch in British warships.

The Barge
Used as a cargo and personnel transport boat with 10 or 12 oars, and fitted for sailing. From the middle of the 19th century on they were sometimes fitted with small steam engines. The pinnace and yawl were of similar form but with not more than 8 or 6 oars respectively.

The cutter
A clinker built general purpose boat with up to 12 oars and fitted for sailing – introduced in the latter part of the 18th century. The carvel built yawl of 4 or 6 oars was the smallest ship's boat on board until the late 18th century, when it was superseded by a small 18ft cutter pulling 4 oars, known colloquially as a "jolly boat"

The gig
A long, narrow, fast boat for personnel transport with 6 to 8 oars. The gig was used for carrying the Captain and usually his private property. With its introduction in the late 18th century the gig took over part of the duties of the pinnace or barge. Only one gig was normally carried.

The dinghy
The smallest ship's boat for oars; 12 to 14ft long. The dinghy came into use in the early 19th century.

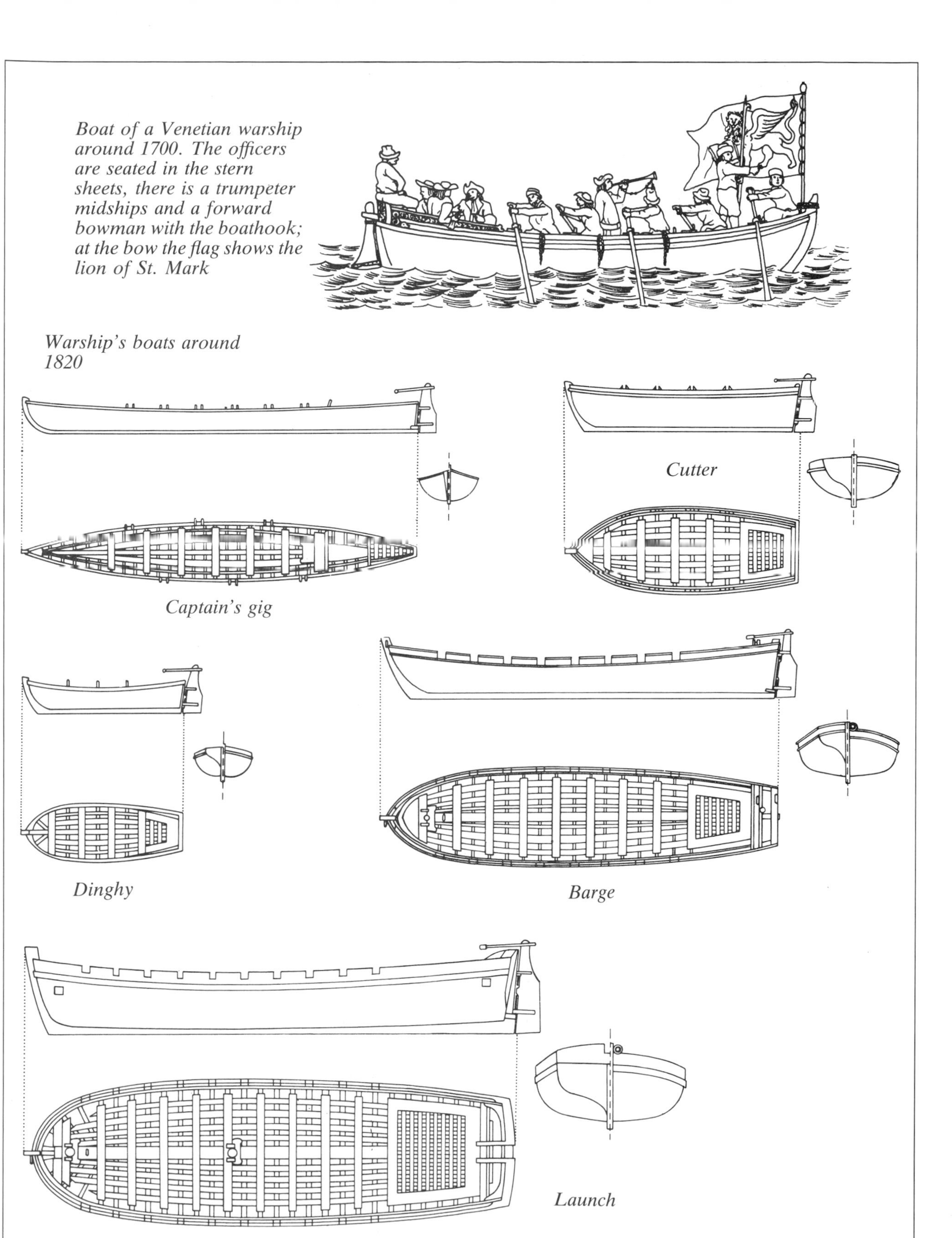
Boat of a Venetian warship around 1700. The officers are seated in the stern sheets, there is a trumpeter midships and a forward bowman with the boathook; at the bow the flag shows the lion of St. Mark
Warship's boats around 1820
Cutter
Captain's gig
Dinghy
Barge
Launch

Ships' boats

Oar

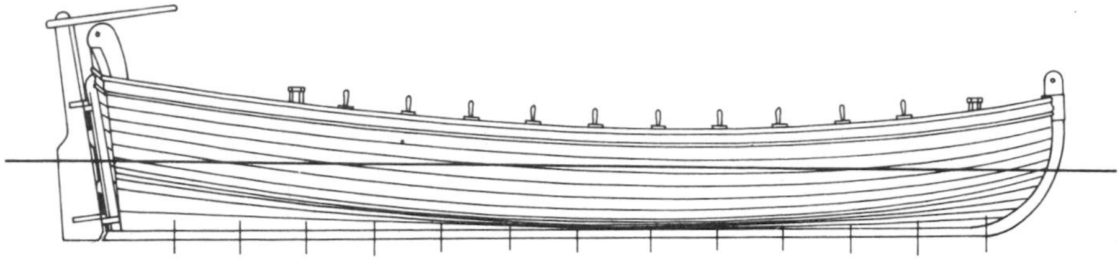

Sheer

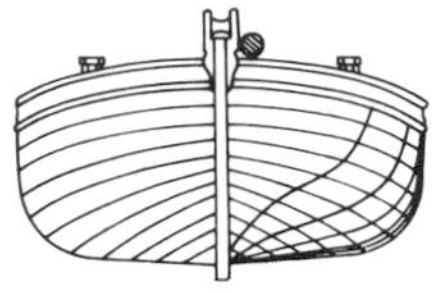

Bow elevation showing frames

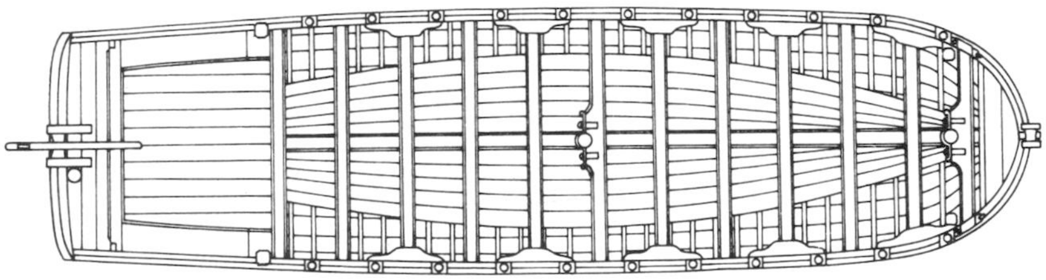

Plan

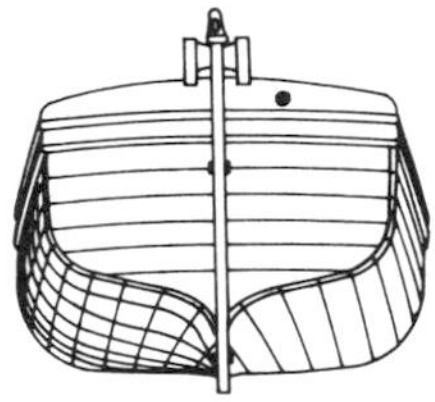

Stern elevation showing frames

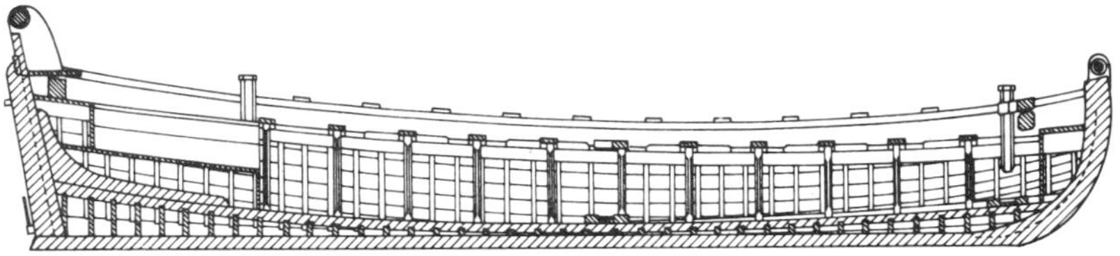

Profile

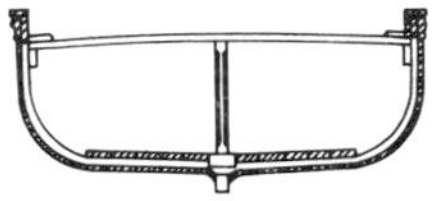

Midships section

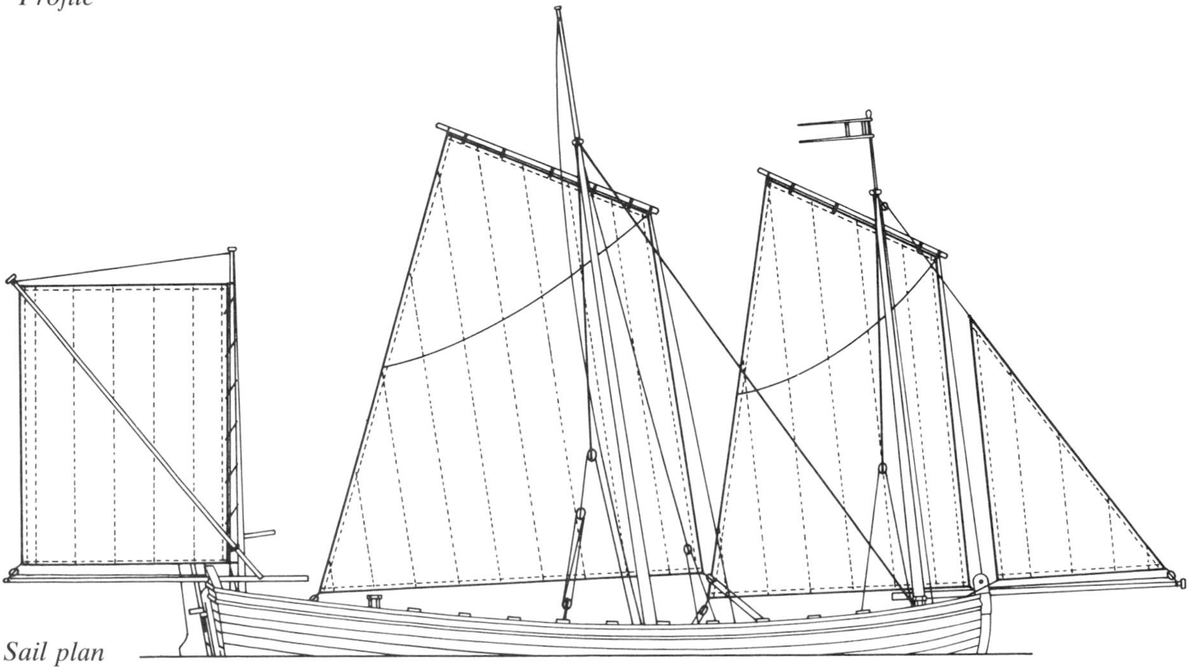

Sail plan

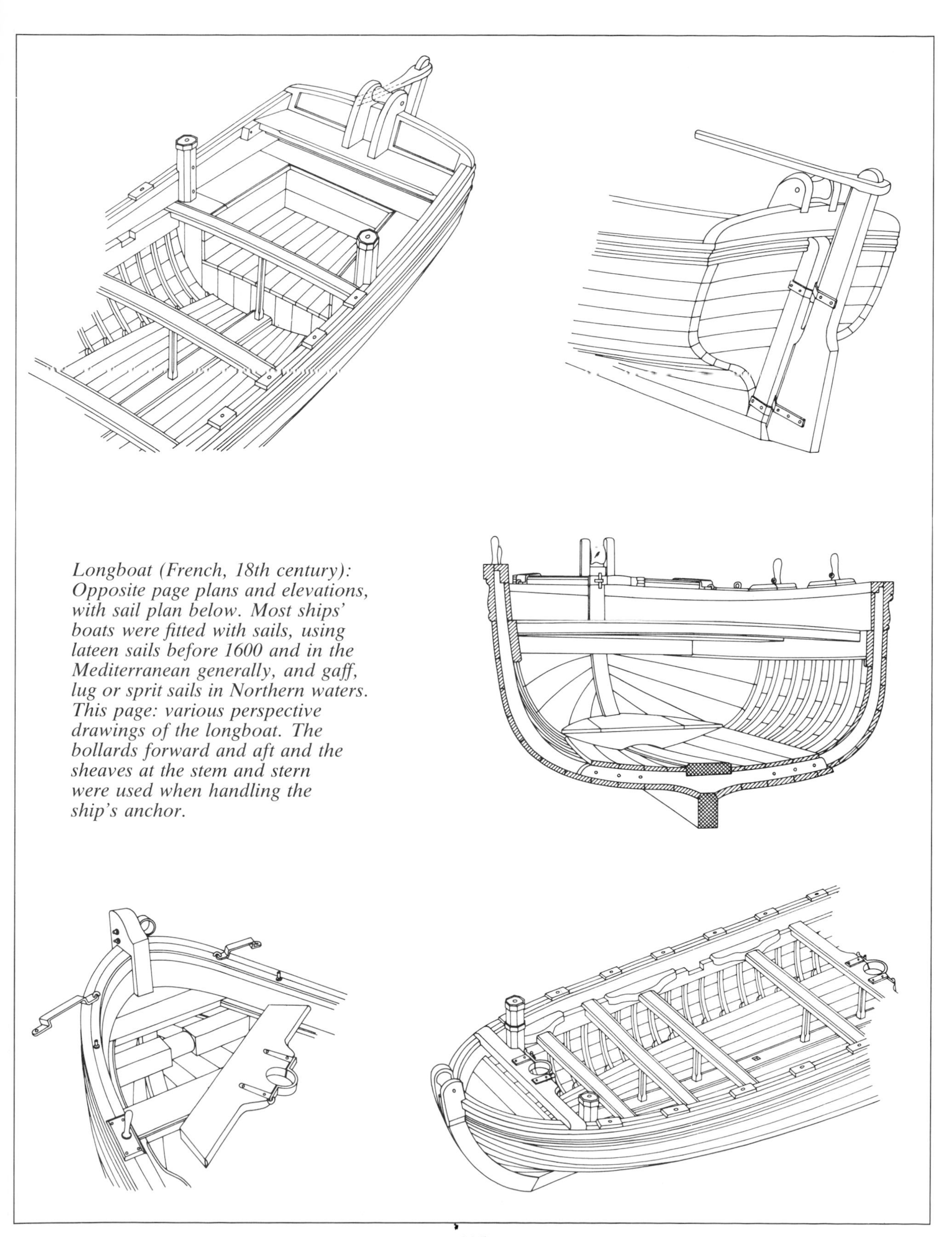

Longboat (French, 18th century): Opposite page plans and elevations, with sail plan below. Most ships' boats were fitted with sails, using lateen sails before 1600 and in the Mediterranean generally, and gaff, lug or sprit sails in Northern waters. This page: various perspective drawings of the longboat. The bollards forward and aft and the sheaves at the stem and stern were used when handling the ship's anchor.

Ships' boats

The construction of ships' boats is the trickiest and most trying job in the whole of period ship modelling. For this reason don't despair if your first attempt does not turn out quite as you imagined. Nor you second, or even your third. Building ships' boats takes time, patience and some experience and practice. By the way, I can save you the trouble of visiting the model shop, as the small boats offered fo sale there are suitable only for the rubbish bin – except that they are too expensive to throw away.

Many methods of making ships' boats have been suggested by variou specialist books and magazines, and I have tried them all. They are all unsatisfactory, with just two exceptions. These two methods are:

The conventional method of construction

This is shown in detail in the drawing on the right. One point to note here: it is essential to leave the framework on the jig for *at least* 14 day after fitting the frames, and dampen the frames every day for the first 10 days with sal ammoniac, so that they adapt to their new shape Do the same after the boat has been planked, but before removing it from the jig and fitting the gunwales, the thwarts, the gratings, the inner planking etc.

The electro-plating method of construction

I have obtained the best results of all using this method, and I canno recommend it too strongly. The first step is to make a male mould, bu in this case it can be made of plasticene over a wooden core. A femal mould can then be made by pouring silicone rubber (as described in the section on ELECTRO-PLATING), which is then sprayed with conductive silver, and a layer of copper, preferably not too thin, electro-plated onto this. This copper boat is then planked inside and ou with thin veneer strips, the frames added and the remaining fittings installed.

Boats' equipment

Even on a model to 1:48 scale the modeller should at least show the most important parts of the boat's equipment, such as the freshwater barricoe, the boathook and the oars. Here are a few dimensions for these items of equipment. A barricoe holding 5 gallons, as commonly used in English ships between 1750 and 1820 (in Continenta ships they were roughly the same size): length 21 inches, diameter 8½ins at the middle, diameter at the ends 7ins. Boathooks should be about 10ft long. Oars varied according to the size of the boat. British practice in the early 19th century is shown in the following table:

Breadth of boat		Length of oar		Handle	Loom		Body or shank		Blade	
ft	ins	ft	ins	ins	ft	ins	ft	ins	ft	ins
7	0	20	0	10	6	0	6	10	6	4
6	0	19	0	10	5	0	7	2	6	0
5	0	18	0	10	4	0	7	6	5	8
4	6	17	0	10	3	6	7	4	5	4
4	0	16	0	10	3	0	7	2	5	0

Boats' gear:
1. Rudder with yoke and lines for steering; 2. Rudder with wood tiller; 3. Bucket; 4. Oilcan; 5. Compass; 6. Emergency supplies; 7. Medicine chest; 8. Bailer; 9. Boat hook; 10. Thole pin; 11. Crutch; 12. Freshwater barricoe

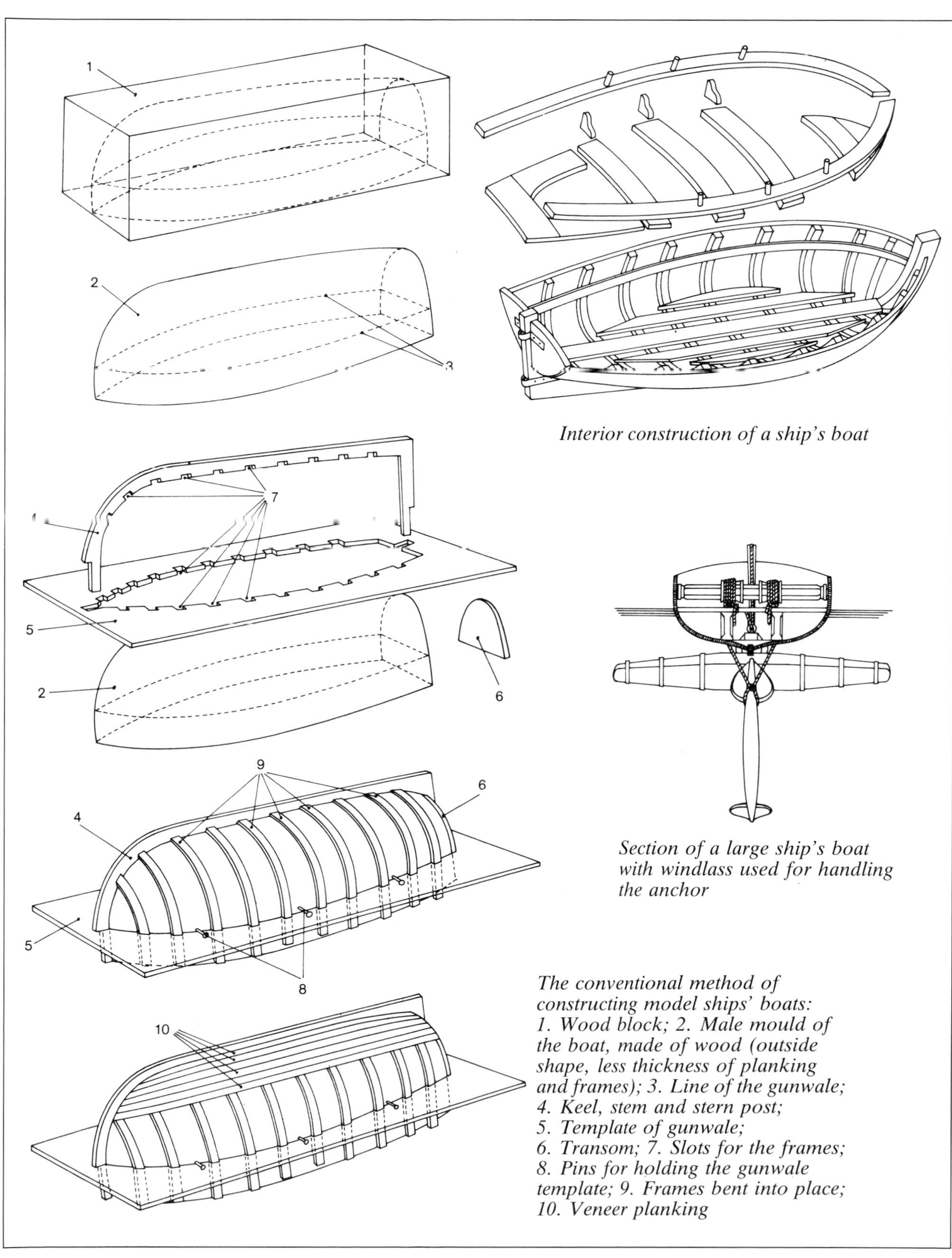

Interior construction of a ship's boat

Section of a large ship's boat with windlass used for handling the anchor

The conventional method of constructing model ships' boats: 1. Wood block; 2. Male mould of the boat, made of wood (outside shape, less thickness of planking and frames); 3. Line of the gunwale; 4. Keel, stem and stern post; 5. Template of gunwale; 6. Transom; 7. Slots for the frames; 8. Pins for holding the gunwale template; 9. Frames bent into place; 10. Veneer planking

Boat crutches and davits

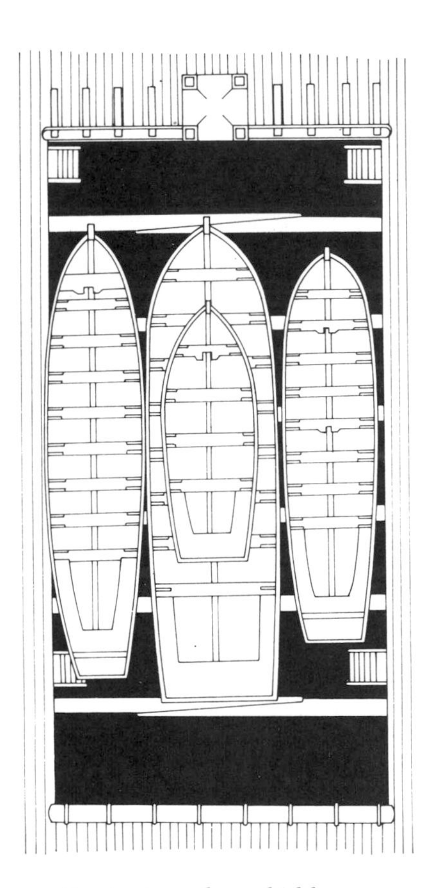

Boats stowed on skid beams over the waist. In the middle the launch, right and left two pinnaces, and in the longboat the cutter. Often all the boats were stowed inside one another in descending order of size.

Boat chocks have been known since ancient times, while davits are a very recent invention, dating from the turn of the 19th century. The fact that they very rapidly gained universal popularity is not surprising, as the task of raising a ship's boat from the boat chocks, which were fitted amidships in most cases, and of hoisting it over the side using stay tackles and yard tackles was a complex one, while lowering and hoisting davit boats although requiring the same amount of effort was simpler and quicker.

Boat crutches

These were a pair of wooden stands on which the boat rested which were mounted on the main hatch gratings or on the skid beams over the waist. Later they were mounted on the tops of the deck house of merchant ships. Smaller boat crutches were also set on the thwarts of larger boats, so that the ship's boats could be stacked up in sequence. The boat was held fast on the crutches with gripes. The gripes were almost always parcelled from the 17th century onwards, and were stretched across the boat at one third and two thirds of its length.

Davits

We must first differentiate between stern and side davits. The stern davits were rigid beams, which projected over the stern of the ship. The side davits were attached to the bulwark on the starboard or port side, and sometimes on the deck, and were almost always hinged. The first davits were made of timber, but from 1820 metal davits came into use.

The side davits were always supported laterally with davit guys, and sometimes hoisted with a topping lift which was led to the mizen mast, and reeved through a leading block. The head of wooden davits was always fitted with sheaves, and metal davits occasionally had them too. It was more usual to fit head blocks to metal davits. The running part consisted of the boat's falls and a lower block incorporating a hook, which could be engaged in heavy ring bolts at the bow and stern of the ship's boat when being hoisted.

There were pairs of small davits to carry one boat, and pairs of larger davits for two boats, and in the latter case the modeller should note that the heavier boat was always inboard (i.e. closer to the ship), and the smaller one outboard.

Fenders were attached to the davits to avoid the boats suffering damage. These fenders were made of old rope and canvas encircling a griping spar. The griping spar should be attached to the davits in such a way that the fenders are abreast the boat's rubbing strake when the boat is secured. With the ship under way the boats were held in to the davits with gripes which crossed over the boat diagonally. These were made not of rope – a common mistake on models – but of canvas strips, or, in the Royal Navy, sword matting.

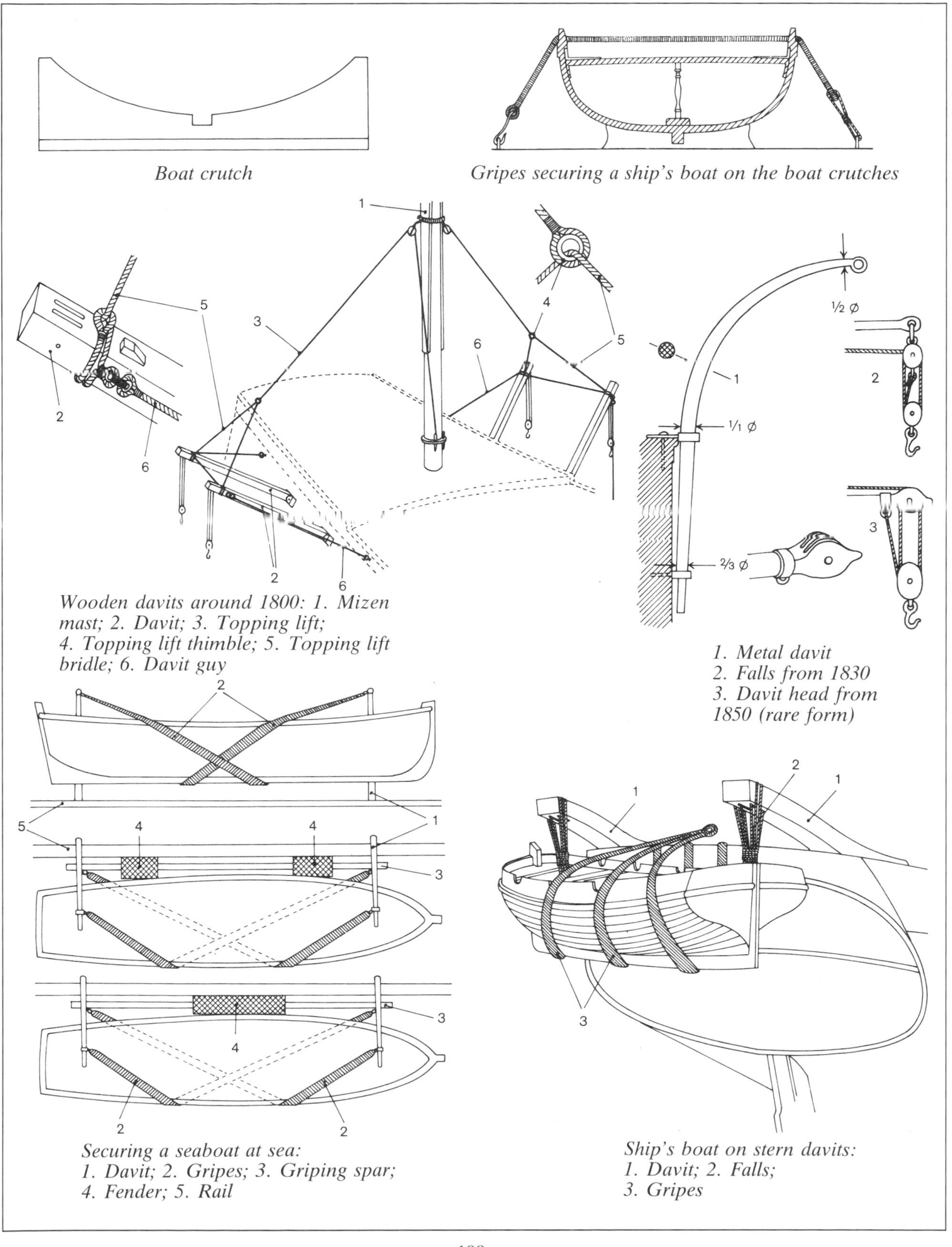

Boat crutch

Gripes securing a ship's boat on the boat crutches

Wooden davits around 1800: 1. Mizen mast; 2. Davit; 3. Topping lift; 4. Topping lift thimble; 5. Topping lift bridle; 6. Davit guy

1. Metal davit
2. Falls from 1830
3. Davit head from 1850 (rare form)

Securing a seaboat at sea: 1. Davit; 2. Gripes; 3. Griping spar; 4. Fender; 5. Rail

Ship's boat on stern davits: 1. Davit; 2. Falls; 3. Gripes

Oars

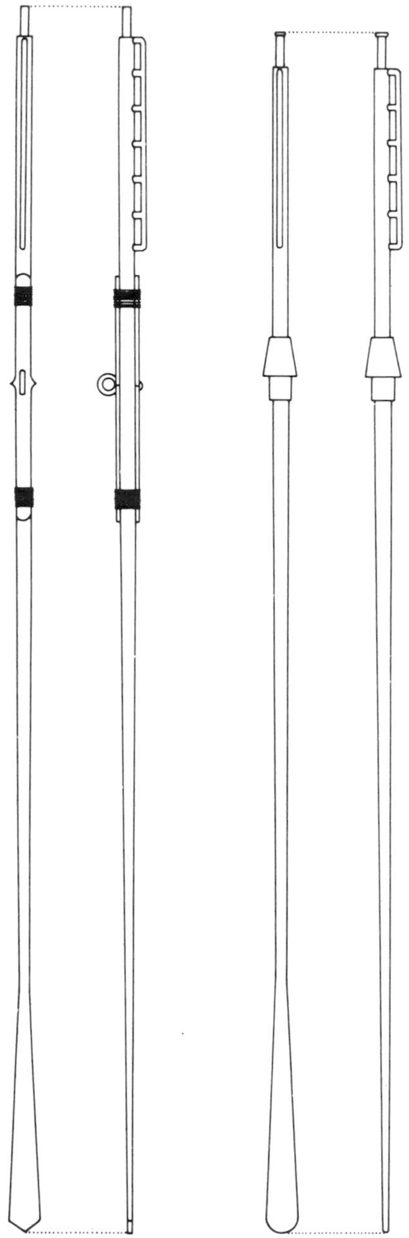

Galley sweeps:
Each of these heavy sweeps was worked by 5 to 7 men; the outside 4 to 6 held the handles, while the innermost held the grip.
Left: French and Spanish type; Right: Italian type

An oar consists of the following parts: a loom with a handle, and a one-piece shaft and blade, which is flat on ocean-going boats, and curved on inland water boats. The oars can again be subdivided into paddles, oars, sweeps and sculls.

Paddles
This is the oldest form of oar, and its development is lost in the mists of pre-history. Paddles usually have a flat blade, curved blades being fairly rare. The handle and shaft are not differentiated. The paddler sits or kneels in the boat facing the bow, and has no mechanical aid to help guide the paddle.

Oars
The loom of the oar or sweep is roughly as long as the beam of the boat (oar) or the height of a man above deck (sweep). There are five methods of using oars:
1. The oarsman stands in the boat, facing the bow, and uses a rowlock, crutch or thole.pins fixed to the gunwale as a pivot for guiding a single oar (Venetian gondola). Barges and lighters were frequently worked with a single sweep either pushed or pulled.
2. The oarsman stands in the boat, facing the bow, and guides the oars in pairs using rowlocks, crutches or thole pins as pivots, operating the starboard oar with the left hand, and the port oar with the right hand i.e. crossed over. (Chinese sampan).
3. The oarsmen are seated one to a thwart facing aft and each operates one of the oars, which are alternately starboard, port, starboard, port, etc., using rowlocks, crutches or thole pins as pivots. This method, known as 'single banked', was the usual one in gigs or whalers.
4. The oarsmen were seated as in 3, but two to a thwart, each with his own oar. This is known as 'doubled banked' and is the normal practice in ship's boats.
5. The oarsman sits on the centre line of the boat, facing aft, and has two oars. This is sculling and is confined to dinghies, small harbour boats and inland craft.

Galley oars
These were heavy oars on large oared ships (galleys), which were operated by 3 to 7 men each, and were guided by heavy rowlocks at the pivot points. As the shaft was too thick for a hand to grasp, strips were attached to it to provide a handhold. The galley oars of ancient ships were smaller, and arranged in groups of two or three (biremes, triremes). Similar arrangements were used in the Mediterranean until the mid-16th century (Fusta, Galia, sottil).

Sweeps
Sweeps are located near the stern when there is only one, and one at the bow and one at the stern on opposite sides when there are two. The oarsmen in this case stand facing forward. The oars of Venetian gondolas are typical small sweeps.

Sculls
The loom of the scull is roughly half as long as the beam of the boat, which means that they can be used in pairs. A pair of sculls is normally operated by one man, who sits in the centre of the thwart, but occasionally by two men sitting side by side, in which case the left-hand man operates the port scull, and the right-hand man the starboard scull.

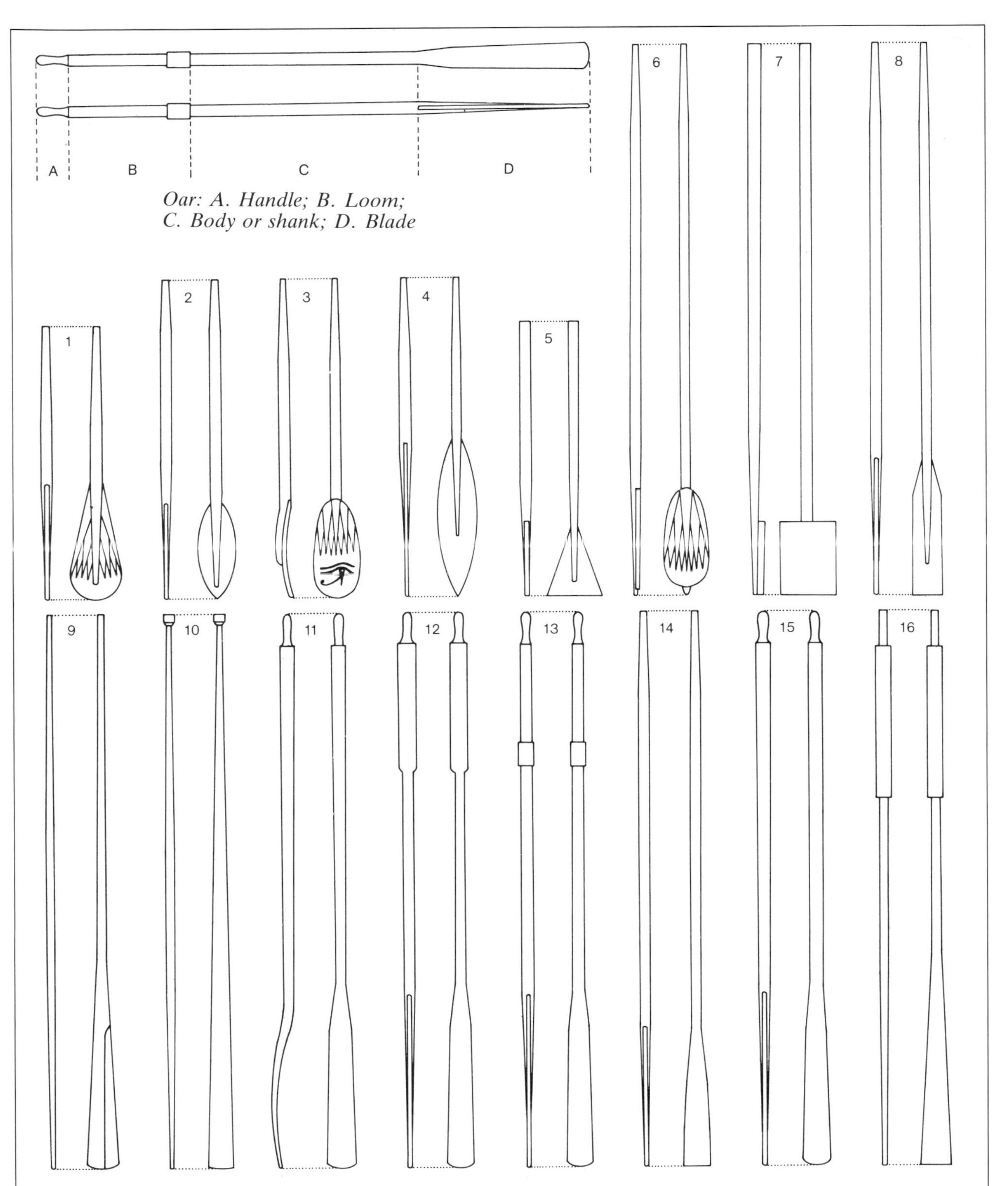

Oar: A. Handle; B. Loom; C. Body or shank; D. Blade

Ancient times: 1., 2. Egyptian paddles; 3. Egyptian scull; 4. Cretan paddle; 5. Phoenician paddle; 6. Egyptian oar; 7. Phoenician oar; 8. Greek oar.
Middle Ages and later: 9. Venetian gondola oar; 10. Oar; 11. Scull for inland water boats; 12., 13., 14. Oars for merchant ships' boats; 15., 16. Oars for warships' boats.

Boarding nets

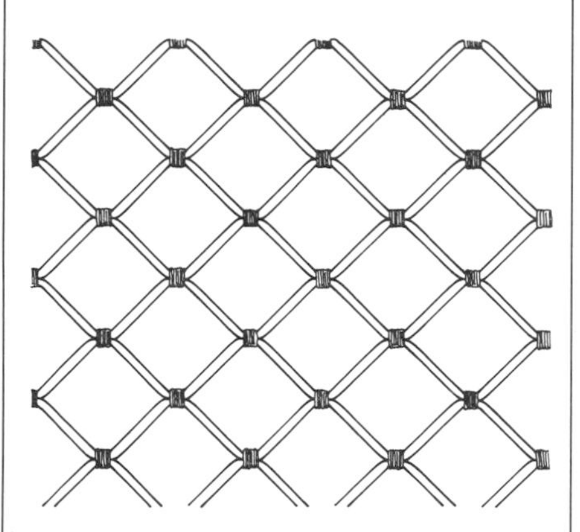

Boarding nets: Ropes seized together to make netting

In the 15th and 16th centuries nets were stretched across the waist to prevent enemy soldiers and sailors jumping across on to the ship. The waist was the lowest part of the ship and hence the most vulnerable to such attacks, but occasionally nets were also fitted over the quarter deck and the forecastle deck. There were three methods of attaching the boarding nets:

1. Free-hanging nets. In this case a strong rope was stretched from the after forecastle rail to the main mast or to the forward quarter deck rail. The boarding nets were pulled over this rope and lashed down on both sides to the waist rail – the Portuguese caravel shown on the right features such an arrangement.
2. A net stretched out over a framework. Here a roof-shaped structure of wooden spars was erected over the waist, over which the boarding net was pulled. The carack *Santa Elena* in the first chapter of this book shows a spar framework of this type.
3. A fixed net. This was stretched between the gangway which connected the quarter deck and the forecastle, and the waist rail.

On small-scale models the modeller can use open-weave tulle for the boarding nets, while for larger models the best method is to weave the nets yourself from thin thread. For a large-scale model you should also attach the lashings, made of thin thread, which were wrapped round each weave of the net. In the first half of the 17th century the boarding nets were superseded by massive boarding protection roofs made of gratings, and then finally disappeared around the middle of the 17th century.

Boarding nets reappeared in the middle of the 18th century. They hung loosely in bights from the yard arms and were secured to the rails.

Hammock nettings

These were also intended to protect the crew in battle, and came into use in the middle of the 18th century. They consisted of iron forks, stanchions or cranes mounted on the rail, into which an open topped net was secured. These nets were then densely packed with the crew's hammocks, which provided a good protection against musket balls and caseshot fire.

In the first half of the 19th century long wooden boxes replaced the nets on the rail, which were packed with the crew's hammocks in the same way, and which served the same purpose.

The hammock nettings are again best made from tulle, and the hammocks themselves from cotton cambric. Roll up the cambric in long strips before cutting suitable lengths for each hammock; each hammock is then folded over in the middle, as shown in the drawing on the left.

The colour of the hammocks is obtained by staining with tea, as are the sails (see SAILS), but in this case it should be slightly darker and rather patchy. In the Royal Navy each man had two hammocks and ships' standing orders ensured that they were scrubbed regularly. So for models of British ships the hammocks should be slightly off-white with a greyish tinge.

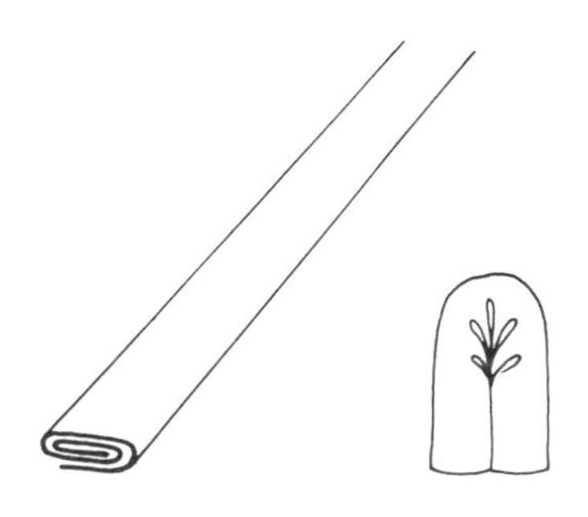

Folding the model hammock: Left – fabric rolled up, right – hammock bent double

Portuguese caravel around 1536.
The suspended net over the waist is clearly visible

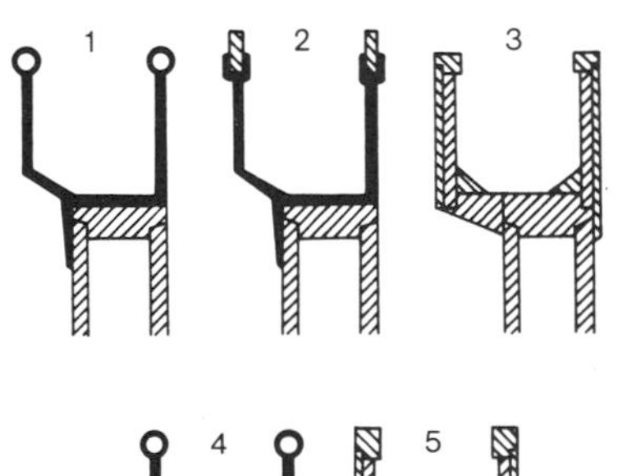

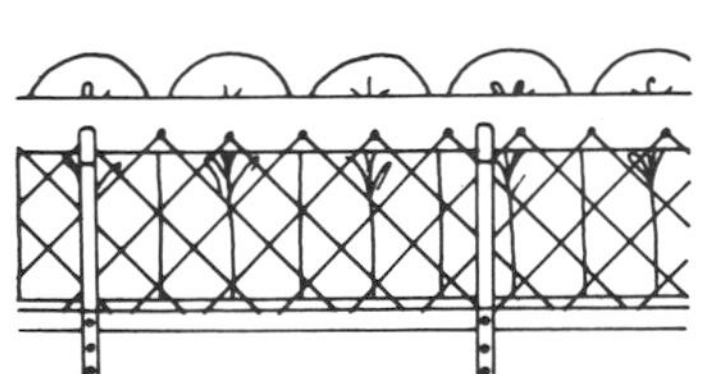

Left: hammock netting (with iron cranes or stanchions and net); right: wooden hammock netting with stowed hammocks

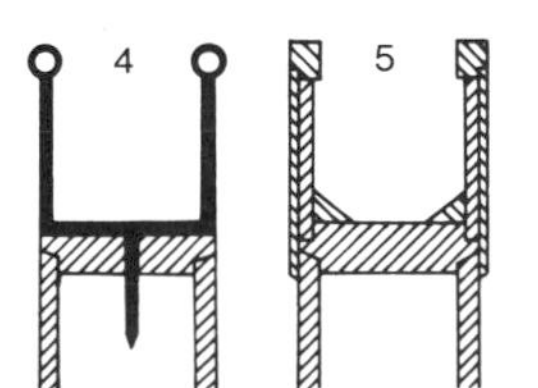

Hammock nettings (cross-section): 1., 2., 3. on small ships; 4., 5. on large ships; 1., 2., 4. with iron cranes; 3., 5. made of wood; 1., 4. rope rail; 2. wood rail; 5. built into the rail

Exposed machinery

Boilers · Engines · Funnels
Paddlewheels · Screws

On the 17th August 1807 the steam ship *Clermont,* designed by the American inventor Robert Fulton, covered the 150 miles from New York to Albany in 32 hours. After several earlier attempts by the Marquis de Jouffroy d'Abans, and by Lord Dundas and Fulton, the voyage of the *Clermont* finally ushered in the age of the steam ship. In 1819 the *Savannah* became the first ship to cross the Atlantic under steam and sail, and in 1838 the *Sirius* was the first ship to complete the same voyage under steam power alone. However, until about 1870 steam ships still carried rigging and sails in the interests of economy and safety. This period of hybrid propulsion offers the model maker a large number of extremely interesting ships.

I have deliberately omitted any discussion on the various methods of propulsion which can be employed on working model ships, using paddles or propellers. These are problems which do not touch the period modeller, or not, at least, for the type of model this book embraces. For information on this area of modelling please refer to a book which covers working models and the more modern type of scale ship.

In the present book I have restricted myself to describing how boilers, funnels, exposed engines, paddle wheels and propellers are best made to look how they should on an accurate static model.

If you are tempted to tackle a model ship with mixed propulsion, there are two points which you should consider:

1. You must be able to manage a wide variety of metalwork without too many problems, as you will need these skills not only for the engines, but also for the multitude of other parts of these ships which were made of metal – the later the date of the ship, the more metal parts.
2. Paddle wheel propulsion may look complex, but it is considerably simpler to represent in model form than screw propulsion. The reason for this is the screw itself, the accurate modelling of which is a difficult and complicated matter – the offerings by model manufacturers are suitable for modern ships only.

The French frigate L'Audacieuse *with auxiliary steam engine, 1854*

Boilers, Engines, Funnels

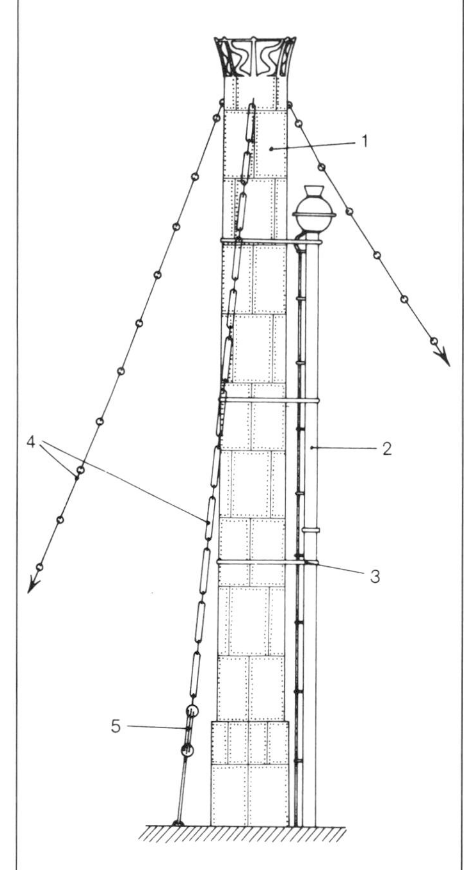

*The funnel around 1830:
1. Funnel; 2. Safety valve outlet pipe; 3. Hoops;
4. Funnel stays;
5. Deadeyes and lanyards*

It is very fortunate for many model builders that steam engines, with their cylinders, pushrods, levers, valves and other components were extremely heavy as well as sensitive to weather and water, and so they were fitted below decks, well protected and out of sight. This relieves the modeller of the exceedingly complex task of modelling all these items. Only the funnel and sometimes parts of the boiler remained visible above deck.

Boilers
Exposed boilers are made initially from a wood block (e.g. obechi), which is sawn, rasped and sanded to final shape. This wood core is then sheathed with thin copper plates, attaching them exactly as when coppering a hull. The rivets are imitated as described in that section. Metal sections suitable for this work are available commercially, and the rivets are embossed into the metal with rivet pliers, as described earlier. However, very little, if any, of the metalwork of a boiler would be visible as it would be lagged with wood.

Engines
If you intend making a model with an exposed engine, it is absolutely essential to get hold of a detailed and reliable plan of this engine before you start work. Such plans are not easy to obtain, the best sources being the large technical museums, e.g. the German Museum in Munich and the Science Museum in London.

Funnels
Until well past the middle of the 19th century ships' funnels were rather tall and slim, and it was only later that they became fatter and more squat. Brass tubing of suitable diameter is used for the funnel. Steps in diameter are achieved by sliding succeeding sizes of tube inside each other.
The inside of the funnel was always a deep, matt black (soot). Externally it was blackened or left as bare metal, and was made up from plates riveted together. These are best imitated as described for coppering boilers or the hull. The safety valve outlet, which was almost always left as bare brass or copper, was retained by several hoops. The outlet itself is made from brass or copper rod. A second pipe, surmounted by a whistle, was attached to the outlet pipe and the whistle can be turned from brass, or made by the electro-plating method.
The retaining hoops are best made from copper wire. The half-round section is formed by cutting a round channel in a block of brass, and hammering the copper wire into the channel. Please remember to leave the ends of the copper wire projecting out of the end of the channel, so that you can pull the wire out again with a pair of pliers.
A number of eyes were riveted to the top of the funnel to which the funnel stays were attached. These were intended to prevent the funnel breaking off or collapsing, and they were set up with tensioning arrangements (deadeyes, hearts, rigging screws, etc.) to the rail or to the deck.

A heavy side lever steam engine for paddlewheel drive, built around 1840. Such engines were usually located below deck, in order to protect them from the weather and salt water and to keep the weight low

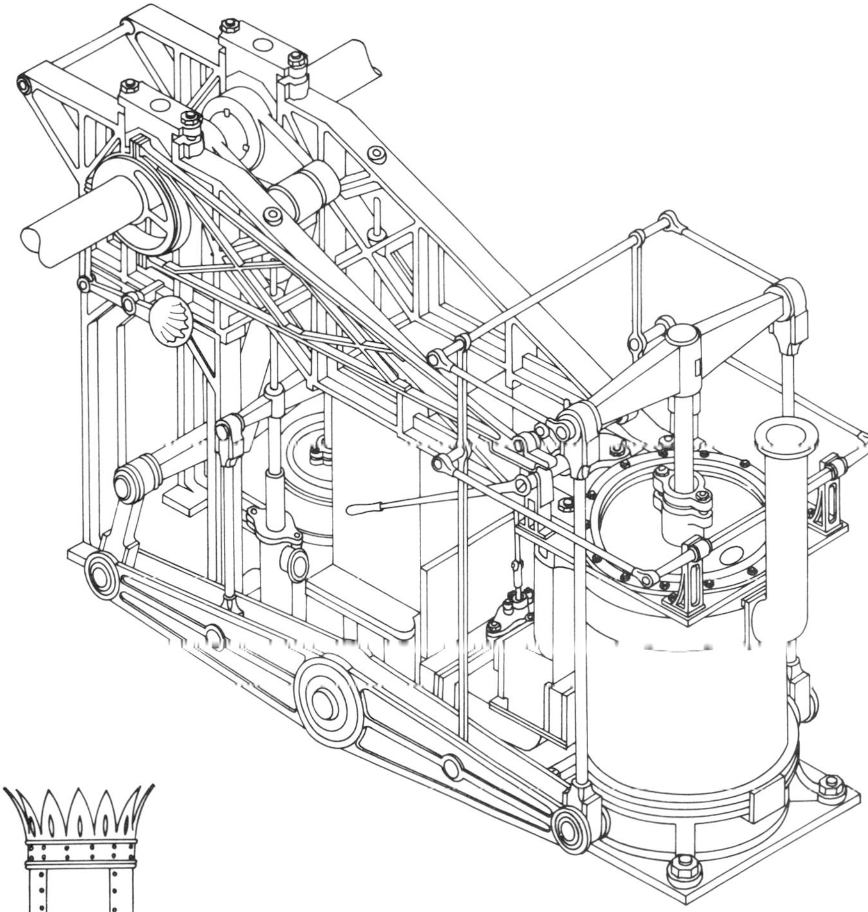

Boiler and funnel of the paddlewheel vessel Gulnara *of the Sardinian navy, built in 1832, parts of which were exposed on the main deck. Front elevation, side elevation, rear elevation and plan view*

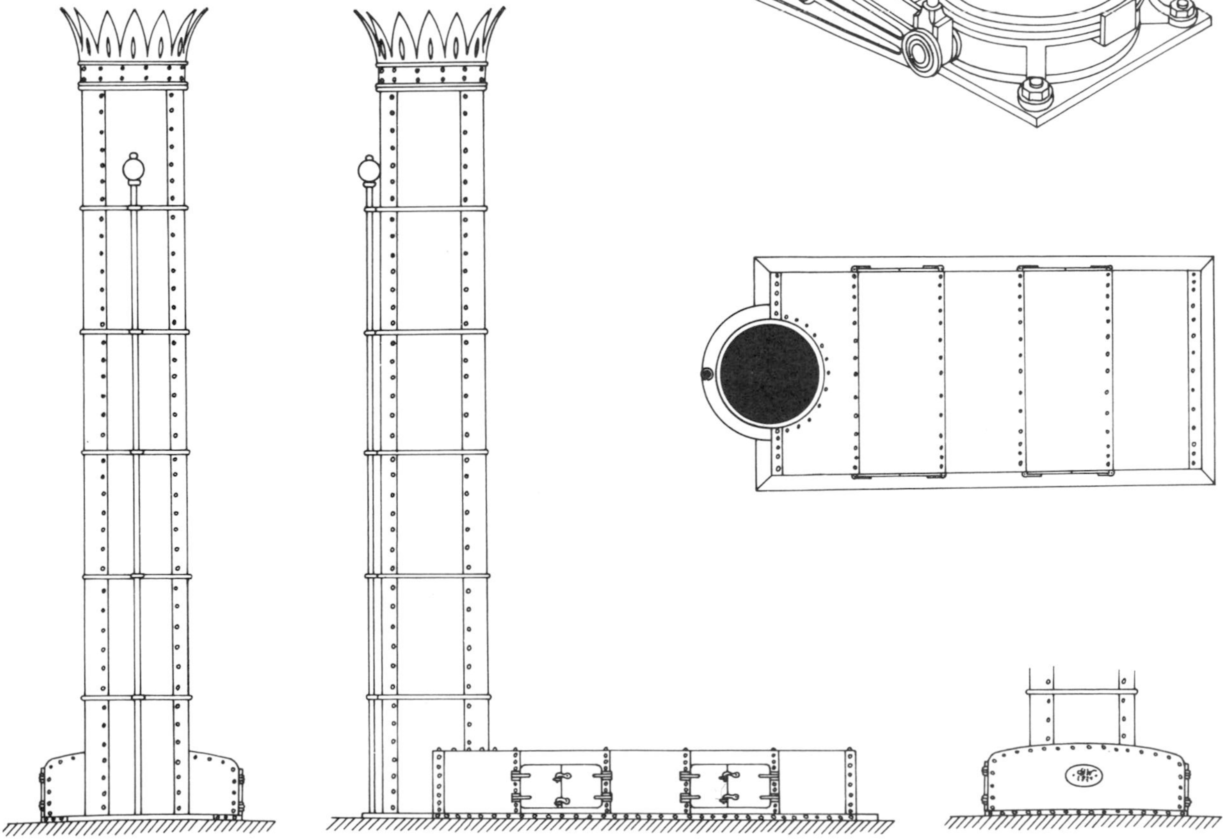

Paddlewheels

When dealing with paddle wheels, we have to differentiate between the type with rigid floats and the type with feathering floats. The rigid float type is the older version, and it was used in the whole of the first half of the 19th century. The type with feathering floats, although invented as early as 1807, did not make much headway until about 1850. The manufacture of paddle wheels is quite a test of patience to the model maker, but it presents no real technical difficulties.
Until about 1820 paddle wheels, with the exception of the shaft and fittings, were made completely of wood. After this time the frames – the rings and spokes – were made of metal. The floats themselves were almost always made of wood until the middle of the 19th century. It was only after 1850 that most paddle wheels came to be built entirely out of metal. Paddle wheels with feathering floats were generally made entirely of metal.
The frame was often stiffened by metal struts, and the modeller can make these from thin copper or brass wire, soldered to the frame with solder paste. From about 1820 on it was almost standard to paint the paddle wheels of merchantmen and warships red.

Screws

Although a paddle wheel may look complicated and a ship's screw simple, the truth is quite the opposite!
Making a paddle wheel calls for little more than patience.
Making a historically accurate screw calls for considerable technical expertise.
Until about 1880 ships' screws were almost always left as unpainted brass. For a model too, the only material to use is metal – gold-painted wood or plastic does not look very convincing.
On four or six-bladed screws the blades were usually fixed to the boss as shown in the drawing on the left. In this case the boss is turned from brass or cast in tin alloy. The blades are cut from brass sheet, filed to the correct section, with sharp outside edges, twisted to obtain the correct pitch and finally soldered to the boss. The boss can also be slotted to accept the bottom end of the blades, and this makes the finished screw much stronger.
Matters become much more difficult with two and three-bladed screws, on which the blades and the boss flow into each other with no definite join lines. In this case the only feasible method of manufacture is to cast the whole screw from tin alloy. Here it has proved best to cast the blades somewhat thicker and larger than required, and then file them back to size. The tin alloy tends to solidify too quickly when being cast, with the result that it does not run into the outermost sharp-edged portions of the blades – and you can count on one or two failed attempts in any case.
The centre of the boss must now be very carefully drilled to take the shaft.
If it proves impossible to produce the screw from brass, then you will need to add a thin layer of brass to the tin alloy casting by the electro-plating method – I know model builders who gold-plate their screws in this way; this process is not exactly cheap, but the results are very beautiful. The finished screw is fixed to the shaft with epoxy – rotating screws are simply out of place on static period models.

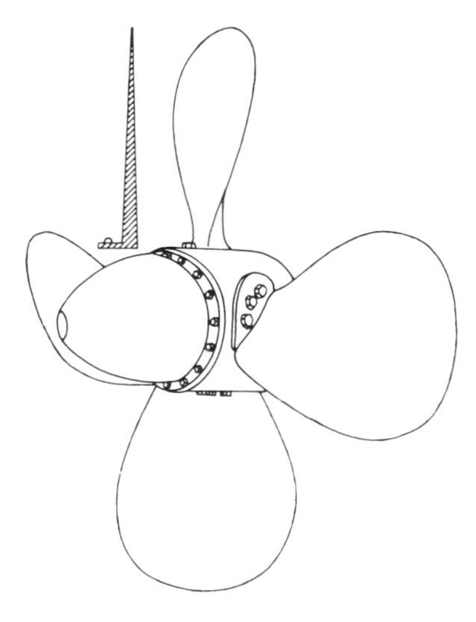

Ship's screw with aerofoil section blades

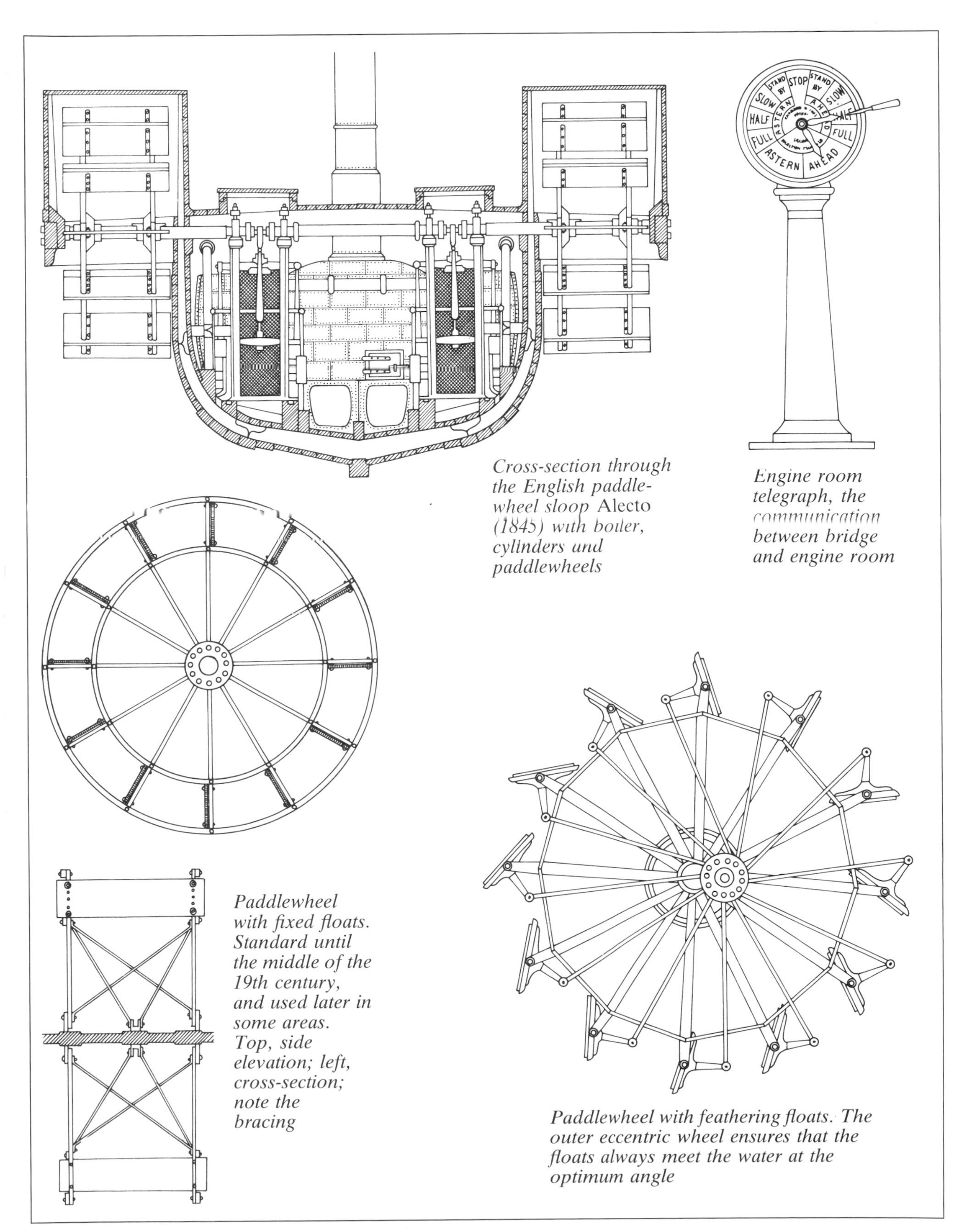

Cross-section through the English paddle-wheel sloop Alecto *(1845) with boiler, cylinders and paddlewheels*

Engine room telegraph, the communication between bridge and engine room

Paddlewheel with fixed floats. Standard until the middle of the 19th century, and used later in some areas. Top, side elevation; left, cross-section; note the bracing

Paddlewheel with feathering floats. The outer eccentric wheel ensures that the floats always meet the water at the optimum angle

Paddlewheels and screws

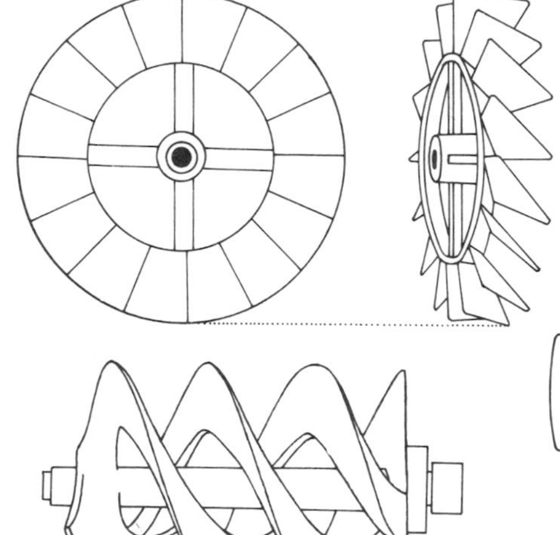

Two experimental types

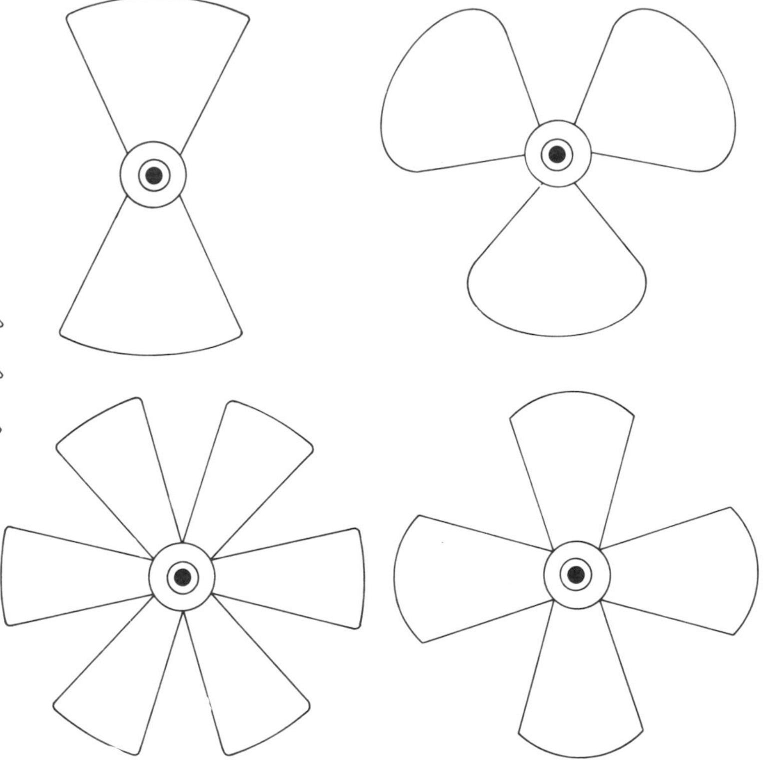

Ships' screws, 19th century

Charlotte Dundas. *One of the early experimental steam ships, built in 1802*

French paddlewheel corvette La Véloce *of 1838*

The French armoured frigate La Gloire *of 1859.*
Protected by 5 inch thick iron plates from the waterline to the gunports,
La Gloire *was the first European armoured ship.*

Masts and yards

Masts and yards · Names of masts and yards · Proportions of masts and topmasts · Mast Position of the masts Wooldings · Crosstrees · Cap Top · Topmast · Bowsprit Sprit topmast · Jib boom Proportions of yards · Yard Foot ropes · Jackstay · Spare spars · Studding sail yard Studding sail boom · Boats' masts · Lateen yard · Gaff Driver boom

I should really have finished off the previous page with a thick red line. Why?

Because that was the end of the first part of this book, which concerned the hull and its fittings. In this second part we have to leave the safety of the deck to climb up into the lofty heights of the masts, sails and rigging, with the vast number of spars and ropes which looks so baffling at first sight, some of them reaching up to a height of 200ft above deck.

You may occasionally be surprised at the sequence of construction advised in the next chapters – for example, the fact that the sails are discussed before the chapter RUNNING RIGGING tells you how to attach a yard to a mast. Now, this sequence is no accident. It is the pooling of the experience of generations of ship modellers. Masts, yards and rigging are not half as confusing and obscure as they may appear to the beginner, but they are certainly confusing enough to make the work considerably easier or more difficult depending on whether the modeller sticks to the wrong or the right sequence of work. One way or another, if you have patience and determination, you will finish the job in the end, but why make yourself unnecessary work?

Let us return to the masts and yards for now – what we might call the skeleton of the rigging as a whole. It is the purpose of the standing and running rigging to support or move these items. The selection of the right materials is of the utmost importance here. More than any part of the hull, the masts, topmasts and yards are subject to bending, warping and twisting. The following timbers are the most satisfactory: lancewood, degame (lemon wood) and spruce. In each case be sure to use knot-free and thoroughly seasoned timber only.

The masts and yards were natural brown in colour until the beginning of the 17th century, the only exceptions to this being Mediterranean and Spanish ships, with their black and red masts and yards. In the 17th century mastheads and topmast heads, crosstrees, tops (until then often brightly painted) and caps were painted black, as were the yards of English and French ships. The masts, topmasts and yards of Dutch ships remained natural brown. None of these colours changed in the 18th century, except that from the middle of the century the lower masts, bowsprit and topmast head of French ships were usually painted white, and in Holland more and more black yards came into use.

From the first half of the 19th century the lower masts complete with mastheads were white overall, while the masts of clippers and sometimes of warships were painted black. The yards were often white on merchant ships, but the yardarms were always black. The topmasts generally remained natural brown, often with white mastheads, although occasionally they were white or black overall. The tops, crosstrees and caps of some merchant ships were also white, while clippers and warships and also many merchant ships preferred the more sombre black.

The British cutter Comet *of 1809*

Names of masts and yards

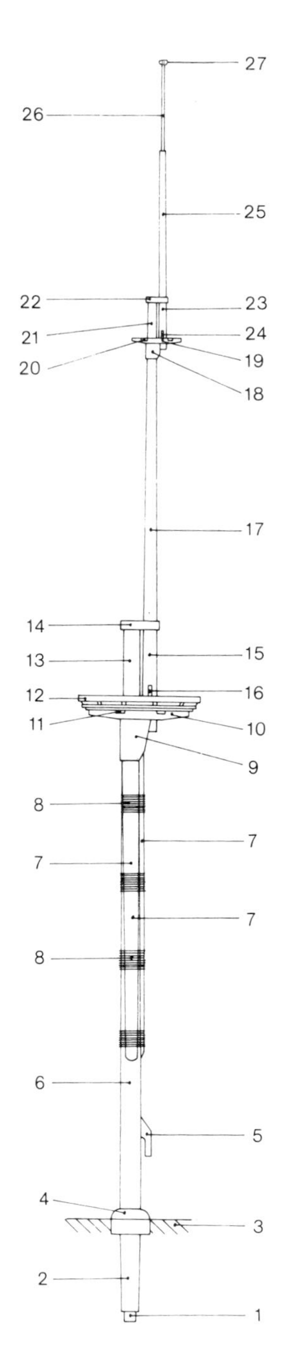

Terminology of mast components

Our first task here is, of course, to become acquainted with the names of the masts, topmasts and yards. The following lists contain all possible masts and spars, not all of which would necessarily appear on any one ship.

Components of the mast:
1. Heel tenon; 2. Mast heel; 3. Deck; 4. Mast wedges and coat; 5. Mast cleat; 6. Lower mast; 7. Fish; 8. Wooldings; 9. Mast cheeks; 10. Lower mast trestle trees; 11. Lower mast cross trees; 12. Top; 13. Mast head; 14. Cap; 15. Topmast heel; 16. Fid; 17. Topmast; 18. Topmast cheeks; 19. Topmast trestle trees; 20. Topmast cross trees; 21. Topmast head; 22. Topmast cap; 23. Topgallant mast heel; 24. Fid; 25. Topgallant mast; 26. Royal mast or pole mast; 27. Truck.

Masts, topmasts and yards on a ship before about 1830:
A. Bowsprit; B. Foremast; C. Main mast; D. Mizen mast;
E. Bonaventure mizen mast.
1. Bowsprit; 2. Sprit topmast knee; 3. Sprit top; 4. Sprit topmast; 5. Jack staff; 6. Martingale or Dolphin striker; 7. Jib boom; 8. Spritsail yard; 9. Spritsail topsail yard; 10. Foremast; 11. Foretop; 12. Fore topmast; 13. Fore topmast hounds; 14. Fore topgallant mast; 15. Fore topgallant hounds; 16. Fore royal mast; 17. Flag pole; 18. Fore yard; 19. Fore topsail yard; 20. Fore topgallant yard; 21. Fore royal yard; 22. Main mast; 23. Main top; 24. Main topmast; 25. Main topmast hounds; 26. Main topgallant mast; 27. Main topgallant hounds; 28. Main royal mast; 29. Flagpole; 30. Main yard; 31. Main topsail yard; 32. Main topgallant yard; 33. Main royal yard; 34. Mizen mast; 35. Mizen top; 36. Mizen topmast; 37. Mizen topmast hounds; 38. Mizen topgallant mast; 39. Flagpole; 40. Mizen yard; 41. Crossjack yard; 42. Mizen topsail yard; 43. Mizen topgallant yard; 44. Mizen topsail yard; 45. Mizen topgallant yard; 46. Bonaventure mizen mast; 47. Bonaventure mizen top; 48. Bonaventure mizen topmast; 49. Flag pole; 50. Bonaventure mizen yard; 51. Bonaventure mizen topsail yard; 52. Ensign staff; 53. Outrigger.

Masts, topmasts and yards on a ship after about 1830:
A. Bowsprit; B. Foremast; C. Main mast; D. Mizen mast;
E. Jigger mast.
1. Bowsprit; 2. Dolphin striker; 3. Jib boom; 4. Flying jib boom; 5. Foremast; 6. Fore top; 7. Fore topmast; 8. Fore topmast hounds; 9. Fore topgallant mast; 10. Fore royal mast; 11. Fore yard; 12. Lower fore topsail yard; 13. Upper fore topsail yard; 14. Lower fore topgallant yard; 15. Upper fore topgallant yard; 16. Fore royal yard; 17. Fore skysail yard; 18. Main mast; 19. Main top; 20. Main topmast; 21. Main topmast hounds; 22. Main topgallant mast; 23. Main royal mast; 24. Main yard; 25. Lower main topsail yard; 26. Upper main topsail yard; 27. Lower main topgallant yard; 28. Upper main topgallant yard; 29. Main royal yard; 30. Main skysail yard; 31. Mizen mast; 32. Mizen top; 33. Mizen topmast; 34. Mizen topmast hounds; 35. Mizen topgallant mast; 36. Mizen royal mast; 37. Mizen yard; 38. Lower mizen topsail yard; 39. Upper mizen topsail yard; 40. Lower mizen topgallant yard; 41. Upper mizen topgallant yard; 42. Mizen royal yard; 43. Jigger mast; 44. Jigger top; 45. Jigger topmast; 46. Gaff; 47. Spanker boom; 48. Signal gaff.

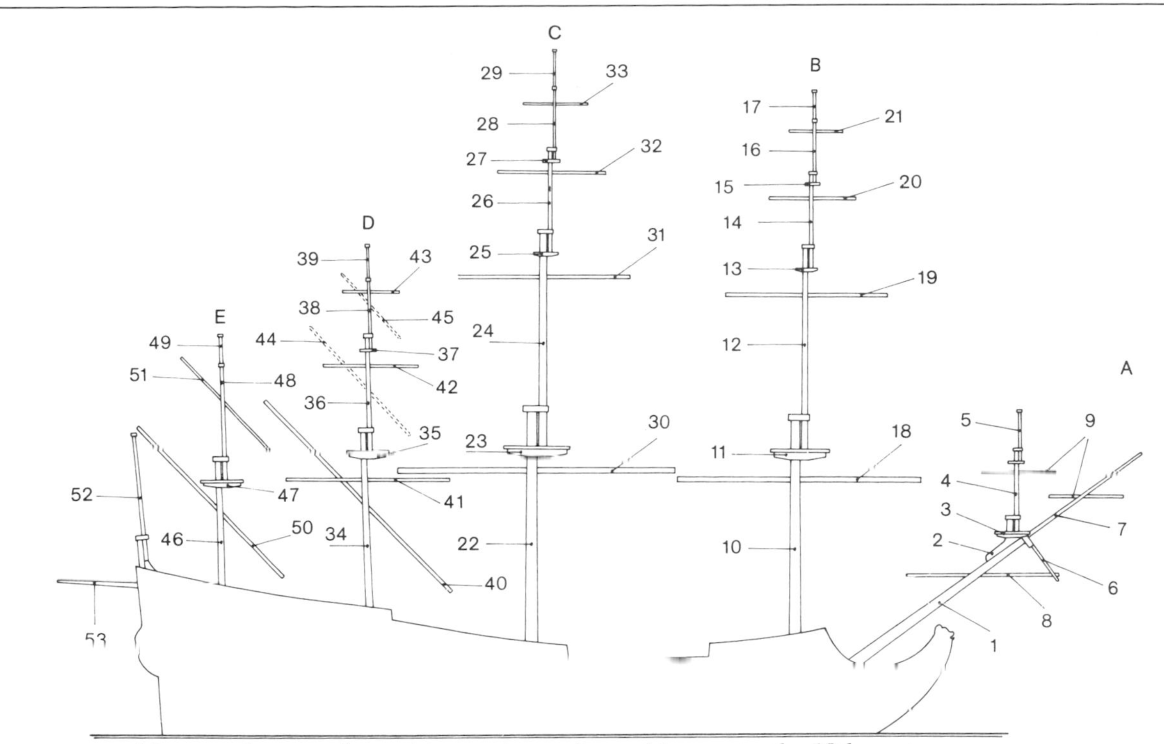

Names of spars of warships and merchant ships up to the 18th century. Many of these spars are from different periods and would not be carried together.

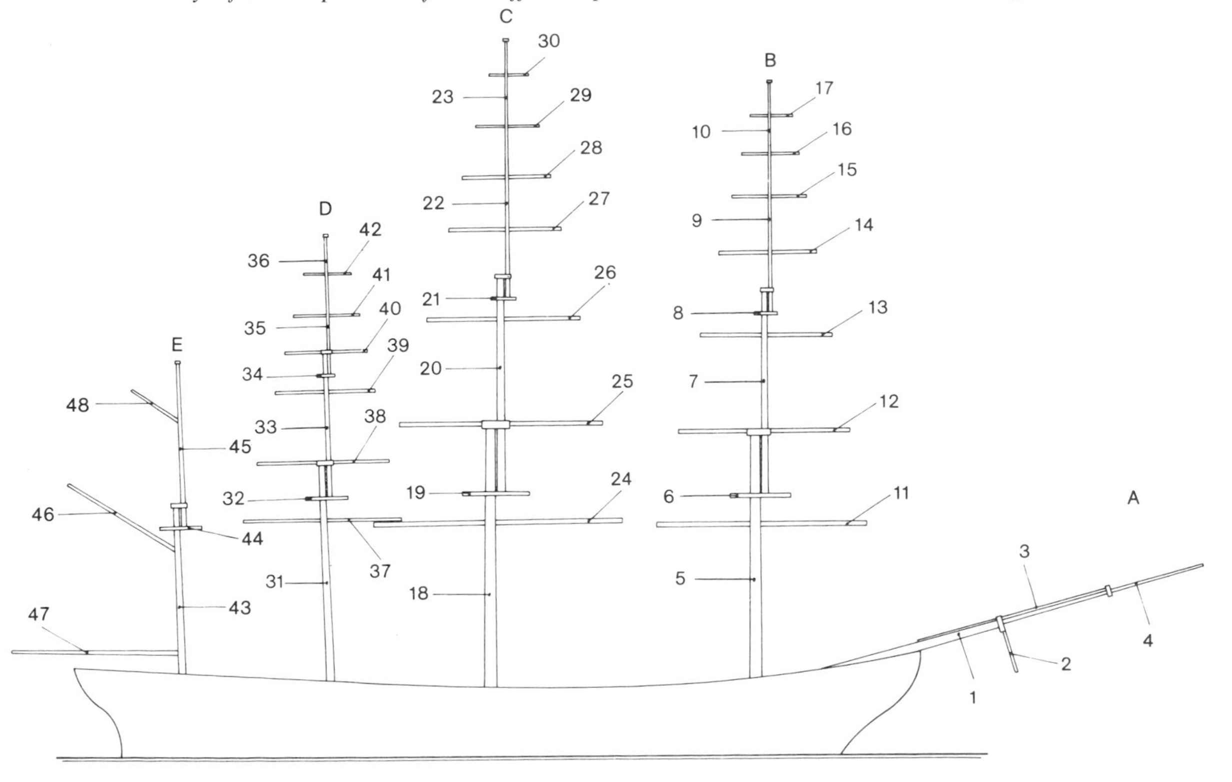

Names of spars of a merchant barque after the introduction of double topsails in the mid 19th century.

Proportions of masts and topmasts

B = Breadth amidships

Wrought iron flagstaff holders from Holland, 18th century

	German 1470	Spanish 1480	Spanish 1550	English 1570
Bowsprit length	1,100 B	1,480 B	2,650 B	2,235 B
Ø deck	0,028 L	0,026 L	0,014 L	0,028 L
Ø cap	0,600 Ø	0,500 Ø	0,600 Ø	0,330 Ø
Sprit topmast length				
Ø at foot				
Length of top				
Length of jack staff				
Length of jib boom				
Ø of cap				
Length of flying jib boom				
Ø of cap				
Length of foremast	1,874 B	2,000 B	2,140 B	1,990 B
Ø at deck	0,022 L	0,022 L	0,024 L	0,029 L
Length of top	0,030 L	0,058 L	0,095 L	0,100 L
Ø at top	0,550 Ø	0,570 Ø	0,750 Ø	0,660 Ø
Length of top			1,060 B	1,150 B
Ø at foot			0,028 L	0,028 L
Length of top			0,110 L	0,100 L
Ø at top			0,500 Ø	0,660 Ø
Length of fore topgallant mast			0,830 B	0,660 B
Ø at crosstrees			0,020 L	0,034 L
Length of fore royal mast				
Length of flagpole				0,470 B
Length of main mast	2,924 B	2,760 B	2,470 B	2,610 B
Ø at deck	0,023 L	0,030 L	0,024 L	0,029 L
Length of top	0,036 L	0,040 L	0,095 L	0,087 L
Ø at top	0,570 Ø	0,420 Ø	0,750 Ø	0,660 Ø
Length of main topmast		0,810 B	1,060 B	1,340 B
Ø at foot		0,060 L	0,028 L	0,034 L
Length of top		0,120 L	0,110 L	0,100 L
Ø at top		0,750 Ø	0,500 Ø	0,660 Ø
Length of main topgallant mast			0,870 B	0,680 B
Ø at crosstrees			0,020 L	0,034 L
Length of main royal mast				
Length of main flagpole				0,530 B
Length of mizen mast	1,500 B	1,750 B	2,140 B	1,765 B
Ø at deck	0,027 L	0,025 L	0,016 L	0,027 L
Length of top		0,090 L	0,100 L	0,075 L
Ø at top	0,500 D	0,500 Ø	0,500 Ø	0,660 Ø
Length of mizen topmast			0,830 B	0,620 B
Ø at foot			0,020 L	0,020 L
Length of mizen topgallant mast				
Length of flagpole				0,440 B
Length of jigger mast			1,630 B	1,653 B
Ø at deck			0,020 L	0,020 L
Ø at masthead			0,500 Ø	0,500 Ø
Length of flagpole				0,410 B

Spanish 1600	Italian 1600	Dutch 1600	French 1630	Dutch 1650	British 1650	French 1680	British 1710	French 1740	British warship 1800	British merchant ship 1810	French warship 1820
2,000 B	1,970 B	2,110 B	2,366 B	1,600 B	1,660 B	1,000 B	1,500 B	1,380 B	1,410 B	1,000 B	1,400 B
0,040 L	0,022 L	0,026 L	0,030 L	0,030 L	0,035 L	0,033 L	0,040 L	0,043 L	0,043 L	0,027 L	0,053 L
0,400 Ø	0,600 Ø	0,450 Ø	0,500 Ø	0,400 Ø	0,550 Ø	0,500 Ø	0,500 Ø	0,580 Ø	0,900 Ø	0,800 Ø	0,720 Ø
			0,570 B	0,450 B	0,730 B	0,464 B	0,400 B				
			0,030 L	0,030 L	0,030 L	0,035 L	0,040 L				
			0,110 L	0,090 L	0,120 L	0,110 L	0,100 L				
			0,320 B	0,150 B	0,500 B	0,600 B	0,350 B	0,410 B	0,325 B		0,415 B
								0,980 B	1,100 B	1,100 B	1,080 B
								0,020 L	0,020 L	0,022 L	0,025 L
									1,250 B	1,250 B	1,000 B
									0,010 L	0,010 L	0,020 L
2,225 B	1,740 B	2,000 B	1,900 B	2,136 B	2,400 B	2,280 B	2,250 B	2,130 B	2,110 B	2,135 B	2,279 B
0,030 L	0,032 L	0,030 L	0,030 L	0,027 L	0,027 L	0,027 L	0,026 L	0,028 L	0,027 L	0,027 L	0,028 L
0,100 L	0,100 L	0,100 L	0,110 L	0,120 L	0,110 L	0,100 L	0,100 L	0,120 L	0,150 L	0,150 L	0,170 L
0,800 Ø	0,730 Ø	0,700 Ø	0,700 Ø	0,750 Ø	0,660 Ø	0,660 Ø	0,660 Ø	0,690 Ø	0,700 Ø	0,660 Ø	0,680 Ø
1,040 B	0,950 B	1,050 B	1,085 B	1,200 B	1,430 B	1,330 B	1,375 B	1,330 B	1,250 B	1,250 B	1,270 B
0,034 L	0,045 L	0,038 L	0,026 L	0,030 L	0,022 L	0,024 L	0,022 L	0,028 L	0,027 L	0,027 L	0,028 L
0,110 L	0,120 L	0,100 L	0,110 L	0,140 L	0,110 L	0,100 L	0,110 L	0,110 L	0,130 L	0,150 L	0,170 L
0,700 Ø	0,700 Ø	0,700 Ø	0,700 Ø	0,700 Ø	0,660 Ø	0,660 Ø	0,660 Ø	0,500 Ø	0,700 Ø	0,660 Ø	0,680 Ø
0,610 B	0,670 B	0,530 B	0,575 B	0,530 B	0,950 B	0,610 B	0,786 B	0,573 B	1,043 B	0,714 B	1,225 B
0,040 L	0,028 L	0,026 L	0,033 L	0,030 L	0,023 L	0,023 L	0,023 L	0,022 L	0,027 L	0,027 L	0,028 L
										0,444 B	
0,550 B	0,420 B	0,550 B	0,330 B	0,320 B	0,500 B	0,500 B	0,500 B	0,290 B			
2,585 B	1,988 B	2,287 B	2,210 B	2,290 B	2,620 B	2,480 B	2,625 B	2,275 B	2,343 B	2,330 B	2,450 B
0,033 L	0,034 L	0,030 L	0,030 L	0,027 L	0,027 L	0,027 L	0,025 L	0,028 L	0,027 L	0,027 L	0,028 L
0,078 L	0,100 L	0,100 L	0,110 L	0,120 L	0,110 L	0,100 L	0,100 L	0,120 L	0,150 L	0,150 L	0,170 L
0,800 Ø	0,730 Ø	0,700 Ø	0,700 Ø	0,750 Ø	0,660 Ø	0,660 Ø	0,660 Ø	0,690 Ø	0,700 Ø	0,660 Ø	0,680 Ø
1,200 B	1,050 B	1,300 B	1,380 B	1,430 B	1,583 B	1,400 B	1,500 B	1,416 B	1,362 B	1,360 B	1,415 B
0,045 L	0,038 L	0,026 L	0,033 L	0,030 L	0,022 L	0,024 L	0,022 L	0,028 L	0,027 L	0,027 L	0,028 L
0,110 L	0,120 L	0,100 L	0,110 L	0,140 L	0,110 L	0,100 L	0,100 L	0,110 L	0,130 L	0,150 L	0,170 L
0,700 Ø	0,700 Ø	0,700 Ø	0,700 Ø	0,700 Ø	0,660 Ø	0,660 Ø	0,660 Ø	0,500 Ø	0,700 Ø	0,660 Ø	0,680 Ø
0,620 B	0,750 B	0,670 B	0,660 B	0,670 B	1,048 B	0,660 B	0,625 B	0,600 B	1,227 B	0,776 B	1,360 B
0,050 L	0,040 L	0,026 L	0,033 L	0,030 L	0,023 L	0,023 L	0,023 L	0,022 L	0,027 L	0,027 L	0,028 L
										0,485 B	
0,550 B	0,450 B	0,600 B	0,400 B	0,270 B	0,610 B	0,620 B	0,600 B	0,300 B			
2,450 B	1,500 B	1,675 B	1,380 B	1,850 B	1,940 B	1,740 B	1,750 B	1,583 B	1,950 B	1,940 B	1,500 B
0,022 L	0,030 L	0,030 L	0,030 L	0,027 L	0,020 L	0,027 L	0,020 L	0,025 L	0,025 L	0,020 L	0,028 L
0,075 L	0,100 L	0,100 L	0,110 L	0,120 L	0,100 L	0,100 L	0,100 L	0,120 L	0,150 L	0,120 L	0,170 L
0,800 Ø	0,700 Ø	0,700 Ø	0,700 Ø	0,700 Ø	0,660 Ø	0,660 Ø	0,660 Ø	0,690 Ø	0,700 Ø	0,660 Ø	0,680 Ø
0,695 B	1,180 B	0,680 B	0,570 B	0,680 B	0,950 B	0,770 B	0,750 B	0,870 B	1,030 B	0,970 B	0,980 B
0,045 L	0,030 L	0,026 L	0,030 L	0,030 L	0,022 L	0,022 L	0,022 L	0,022 L	0,027 L	0,020 L	0,028 L
					0,640 B	0,500 B	0,400 B	0,400 B	0,846 B	0,640 B	0,680 B
0,430 B	0,380 B	0,460 B	0,410 B	0,260 B	0,400 B	0,400 B	0,250 B				
1,300 B	1,520 B										
0,033 L	0,022 L										
0,540 Ø	0,700 Ø										
0,600 B	0,350 B										

The Mast

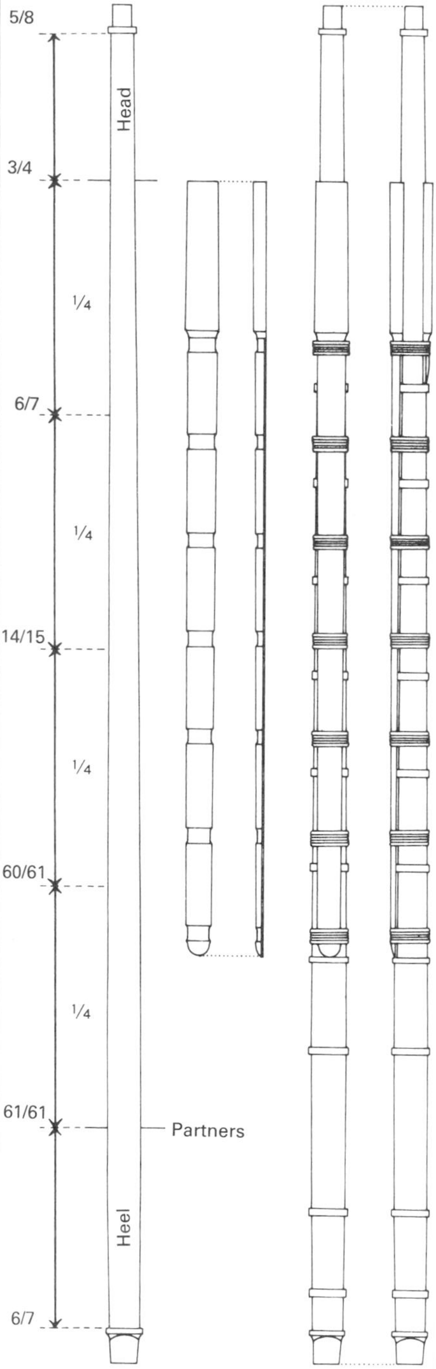

5/8
3/4
Head
¼
6/7
¼
14/15
¼
60/61
¼
61/61
Partners
Heel
6/7

Mast proportions, wooden fishes and mast

Before you begin building the masts, topmasts and yards, it is advisable to compare the dimensions and proportions shown on your plans with the tabular information on proportions in this book, as a top-heavy model is a lamentably common sight.
The tables of proportions for masts, topmasts and yards can only provide average values for individual countries and periods, and slight variations are possible. However, the proportions of spar diameters, as listed on pages 216, 218, 224, 226, 228 and 230, did not vary at all.

The positions of the masts
The main mast should be located at the mid length of the keel, or at the mid length of the main deck, that is 0·04 to 0·05 of the length between perpendiculars abaft the midships frame. The foremast was situated about ⅓ of the length between the forward end of the keel and the fore side of the stem until 1630, then moved to the halfway position around 1660, and to ⅔ of this distance around 1700; until 1630 it was ahead of the beakhead bulkhead, and after 1630 abaft it. The bonaventure mizen mast was located exactly over the sternpost, and the mizen mast midway between the main and bonaventure mizen masts. On three-masters the mizen mast stood ⅓ to ½ of the distance between the stern and main mast ahead of the stern.

Construction of the masts
Originally the masts were assembled from a series of square timbers jointed to each other. Model masts are made from a square strip of wood, which is first cut to the appropriate diameters. Using a small plane, this strip is then planed to an eight-sided section, then a sixteen-sided section, and finally sanded round.

Wooldings and mast hoops
Rope wooldings and iron hoops were fitted round the masts to hold the component timbers of the masts together. Wooldings were fitted on the main mast from the Middle Ages, on the foremast from the late 15th century, on the bowsprit from the 16th century, and on the mizen mast since the late 18th century. Rope wooldings were made from one inch tarred rope, and the width of the wooldings was the same as the mast diameter. After 1580 wood hoops were fitted above and below the wooldings, and in the 18th century wood fishes were fitted to reinforce the masts. They were originally fixed in place with rope wooldings, but by the end of the 19th century iron hoops had taken their place.

Mast wedges
To fix the mast firmly in the deck, a series of wooden wedges was driven in between the mast and the deck, which were then covered over with a fairing of canvas known as the mast coat. The model maker can fabricate the wedges from a single piece of obechi or lime, and then glue cloth on top.

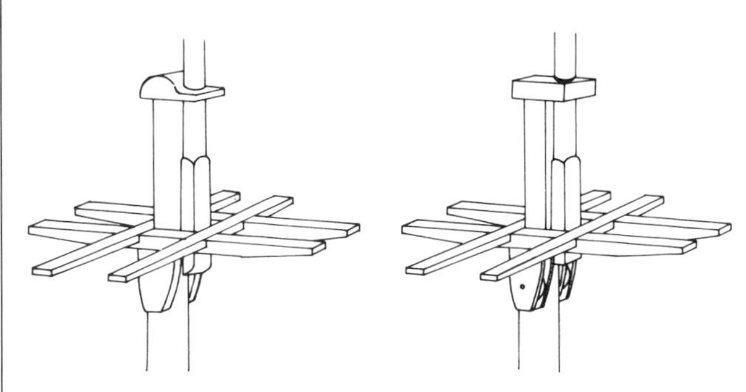

Masthead, 16th/17th century: Left, round Continental mast cap; right, square British mast cap

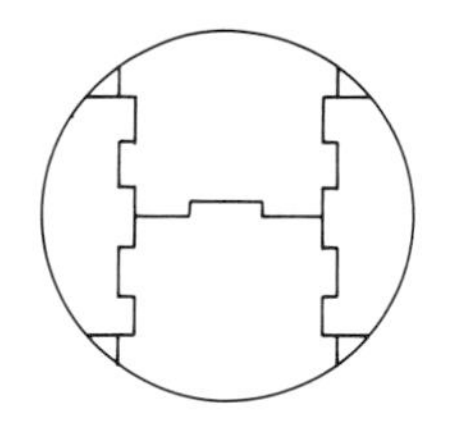

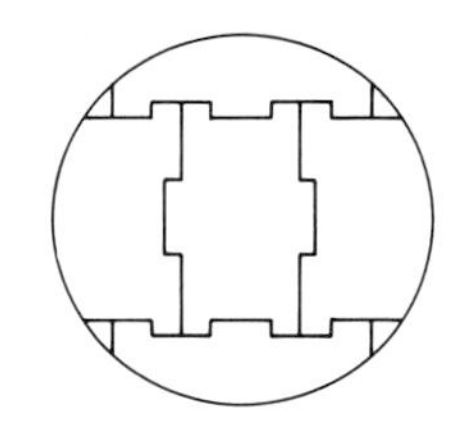

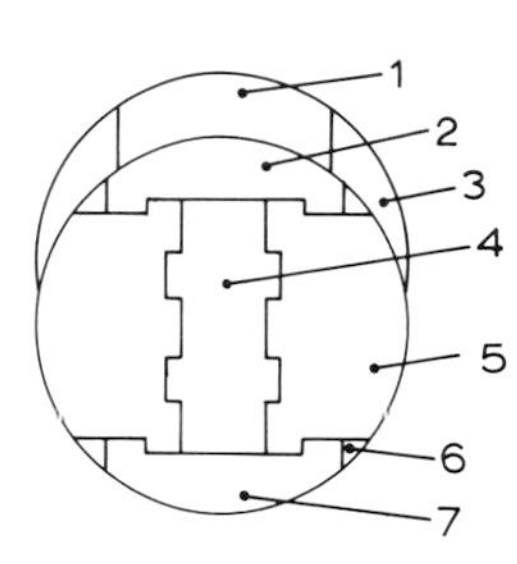

Made masts:
1. Front fish;
2. Fore side tree;
3. Filling;
4. Spindle;
5. Starboard side tree; 6. Cant piece;
7. After side tree

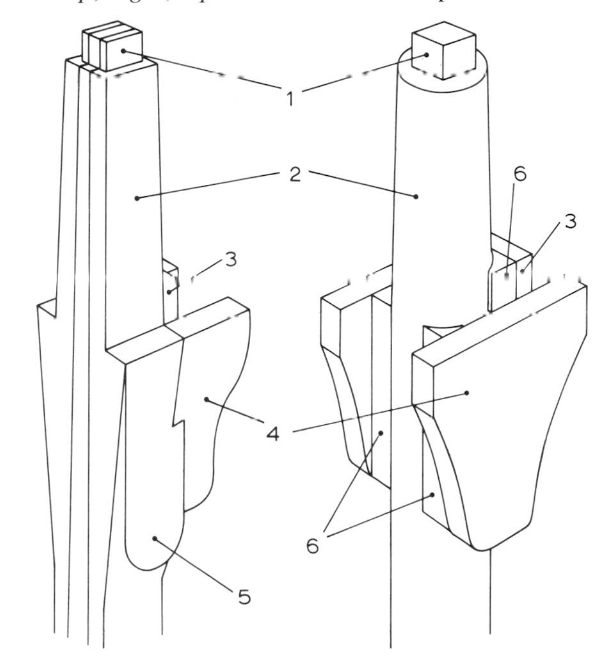

18th century lower mast head: Left, English; Right, Continental: 1. Tenon; 2. Head; 3. Chock for trestle tree; 4. Bibb; 5. Cheek; 6. Filling Chocks

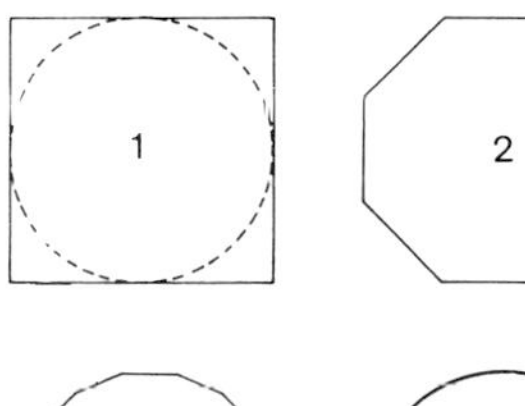

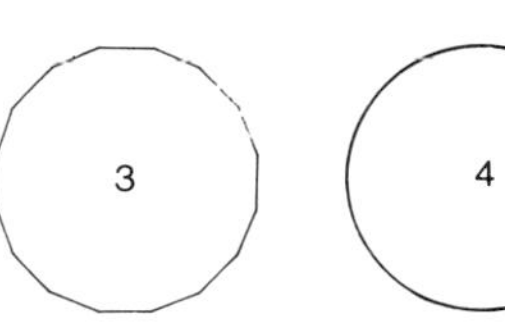

Construction of model mast: 1. Square section strip; 2. Octagonal section; 3. Planed to 16 sides; 4. Sanded round

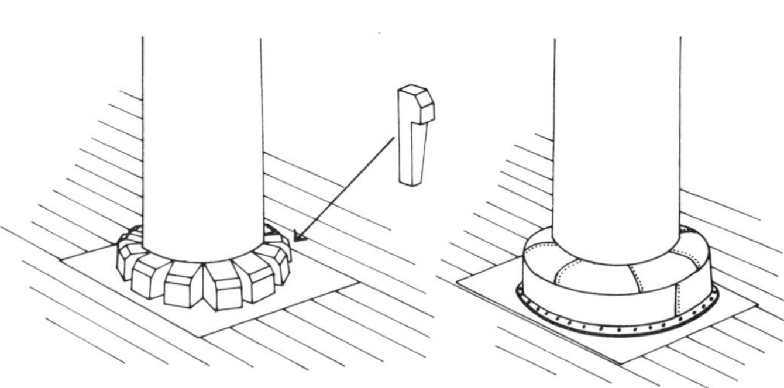

Mast partners at deck: Left, ring of wedges; right, mast coat

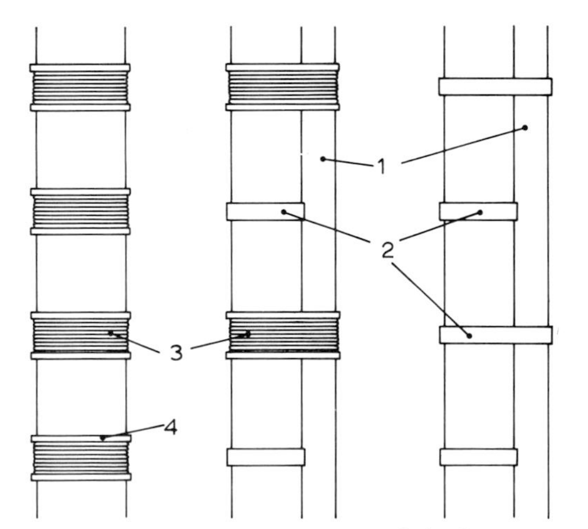

Mast bands: 1. Front fish; 2. Iron hoops; 3. Rope woolding; 4. Wooden hoops

Crosstrees and caps

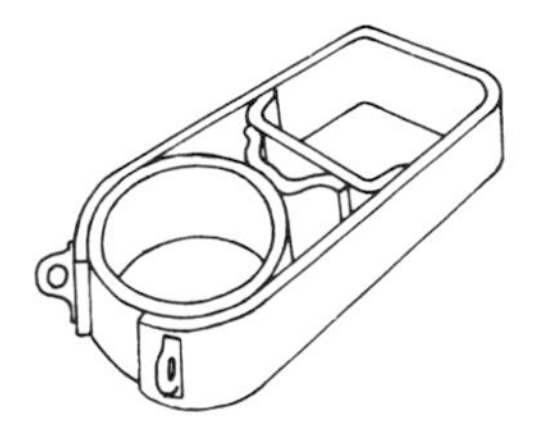

Iron cap, 19th century

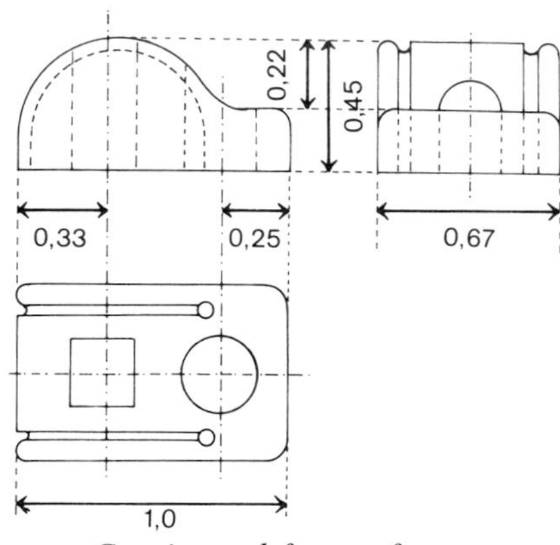

Continental form of cap

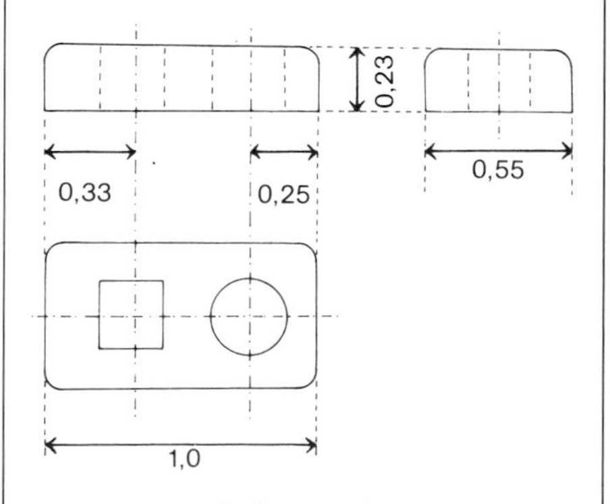

British form of cap

Mast cheeks

The lower crosstree supports were the mast cheeks, strong timbers the same width as the trestletrees, which were fixed to the mast with hoops, bolts, and nails. On British ships from 1560 to 1720 the mast cheeks were fitted with sheaves over which the halyards reeved (see HALYARDS).

The crosstrees

The length of the main trestletrees was 0·3 to 0·35 of the width at the top of the main frame, the height 0·08 of the length, the width 0·9 of the height in the 16/17th centuries, reducing to 0·45 of the height by the middle of the 18th century.

The crosstrees were as long as the trestletrees in the 16/17th centuries, as broad in section, but only half the height, and let into the trestletrees. In the 18th century the length of the crosstrees rose to 1·3 times the length of the trestletrees, they were then twice as broad in section, but still only half the height, and again let into them. The size of the crosstrees on the fore and mizen masts were in the same proportion to the main crosstrees as the masts were to each other.

The topmast crosstrees were similar in design to the main tops, except that they were usually three in number to support the topgallant and royal shrouds. In their proportions they corresponded to the crosstrees of the lower masts.

The topmast crosstrees were often curved aft slightly, and in the 16/17th centuries were the same length as the trestletrees, while by the middle of the 18th century they were sometimes almost twice as long. In the 19th century spreaders were sometimes fitted to the crosstrees over which the backstays ran. (see BACKSTAYS).

All the crosstrees were fitted with wooden bolsters at the masthead, which were rounded off on the outside edges; their purpose was to prevent the shrouds chafing on the edges of the trestletrees.

The cap

The purpose of the cap was to provide a support for the topmasts. There were two basic forms, an English form – which was widely adopted on the Continent after the middle of the 18th century – and a Continental one. In the 19th century caps were made of wood and iron, and there were no national differences.

The length of the caps was 0·5 to 0·45 of the length of the masthead. The rectangular hole fitted over the mast head cap tenon, and the round hole in front accepted the topmast heel. The holes and grooves in the Continental type of cap were designed to guide the halyards (see HALYARDS). They disappeared at the beginning of the 18th century. The cap did retain its basic shape, but became considerably flatter, until it was completely superseded by the English type around the end of the century.

In the 18th and early 19th centuries the caps were very often reinforced with iron bands. Until the middle of the 16th century the cap's front end was often just cut back to form a U-shaped recess. The topmast was located in this recess, and fixed in place with a rope lashing round the cap.

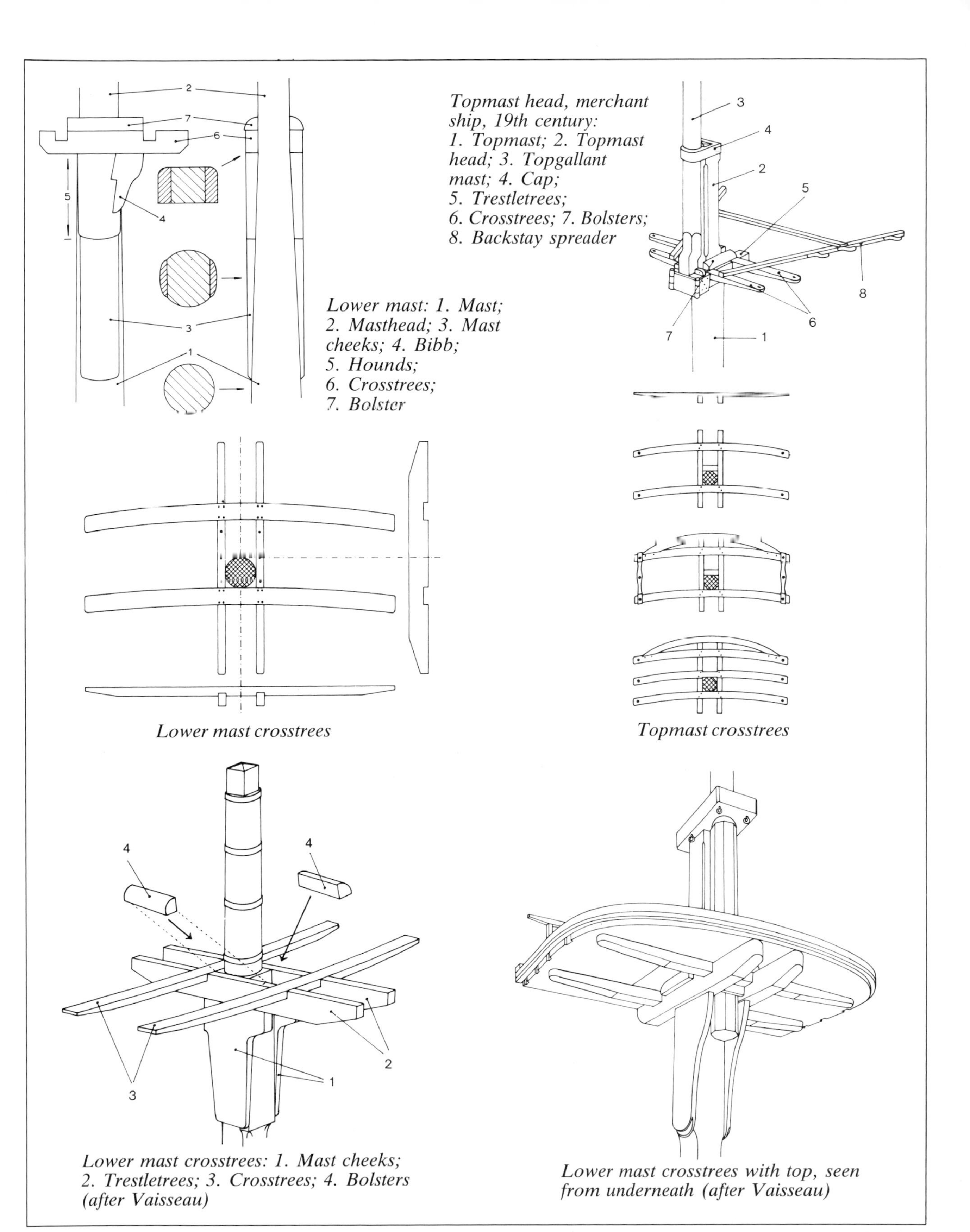

Topmast head, merchant ship, 19th century: 1. Topmast; 2. Topmast head; 3. Topgallant mast; 4. Cap; 5. Trestletrees; 6. Crosstrees; 7. Bolsters; 8. Backstay spreader

Lower mast: 1. Mast; 2. Masthead; 3. Mast cheeks; 4. Bibb; 5. Hounds; 6. Crosstrees; 7. Bolster

Lower mast crosstrees

Topmast crosstrees

Lower mast crosstrees: 1. Mast cheeks; 2. Trestletrees; 3. Crosstrees; 4. Bolsters (after Vaisseau)

Lower mast crosstrees with top, seen from underneath (after Vaisseau)

Tops

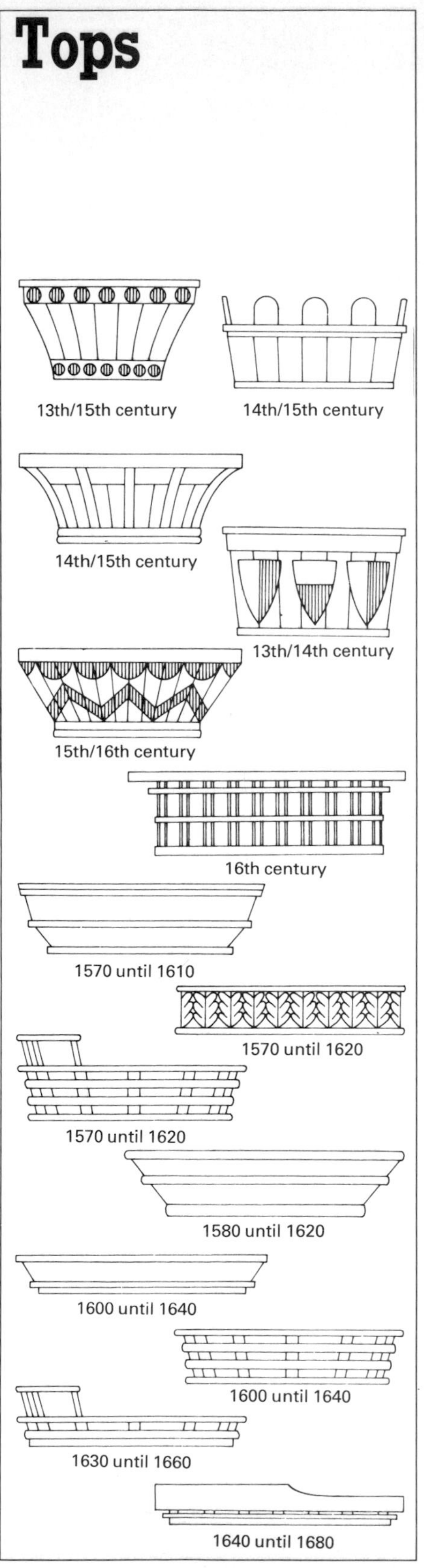

Platforms were fitted on top of the crosstrees and they were known as the tops. Until the end of the 17th century their basic shape was circular, and it was not until the beginning of the 18th century that the rear edge began to be straightened out, and in the first half of the 18th century the rear edge became quite straight, and the sides equally so, only the front third remaining elliptical in outline.

From the 13th to the 16th century the tops possessed fairly high guard rails, and were therefore often termed crow's nests. These rails were sometimes made of massive wooden boards, sometimes from a wooden latticework, and they were usually brightly painted.

From the middle of the 16th century onward the rails of the tops grew steadily lower, until by the last quarter of the 17th century they consisted of only a narrow ring. Even the bright colours disappeared, and from the middle of the 17th century the tops were uniformly black in colour.

Until the middle of the 17th century tops were carried on all crosstrees (lower mast, topmast, topgallant and bowsprit). Thereafter only the lower mast crosstrees and the sprit crosstrees were fitted with a top, and the latter also disappeared with the abolition of the sprit top mast around 1720.

The construction of the tops remained fairly well unchanged through the centuries. The top decking was about 1·16 × the crosstree in size, and was assembled from two layers of planking (forward and aft athwartships, sides fore and aft). For the model maker this procedure is, of course, too complex. He should cut his top decking from a sheet of wood, and score the joints with a knife. The thickness of the top decking was about 3ins to 4ins. The lubber's hole was 0·4 × the width. The sprit top only had a small opening, just large enough for the bowsprit knee and the heel of the topmast.

The ring which surrounded the top was supported by a number of ribs, which were distributed radially at even spacings. The ribs were rectangular and had a thickness of 3ins to 4ins at the ends.

The ribs, always even in numbers, were spaced 12 to 18ins apart at the edges of the top. The holes for the topmast shroud chain plates have to be drilled and filed out to a rectangle with radiused corners. On round tops the foremost hole is located slightly ahead of the forward edge of the lower mast, and the after hole midway between the forward hole and the middle of the after half of the top; in the case of angular tops it was about 8 to 12ins ahead of the after edge. The remaining holes were spaced out between them at regular intervals.

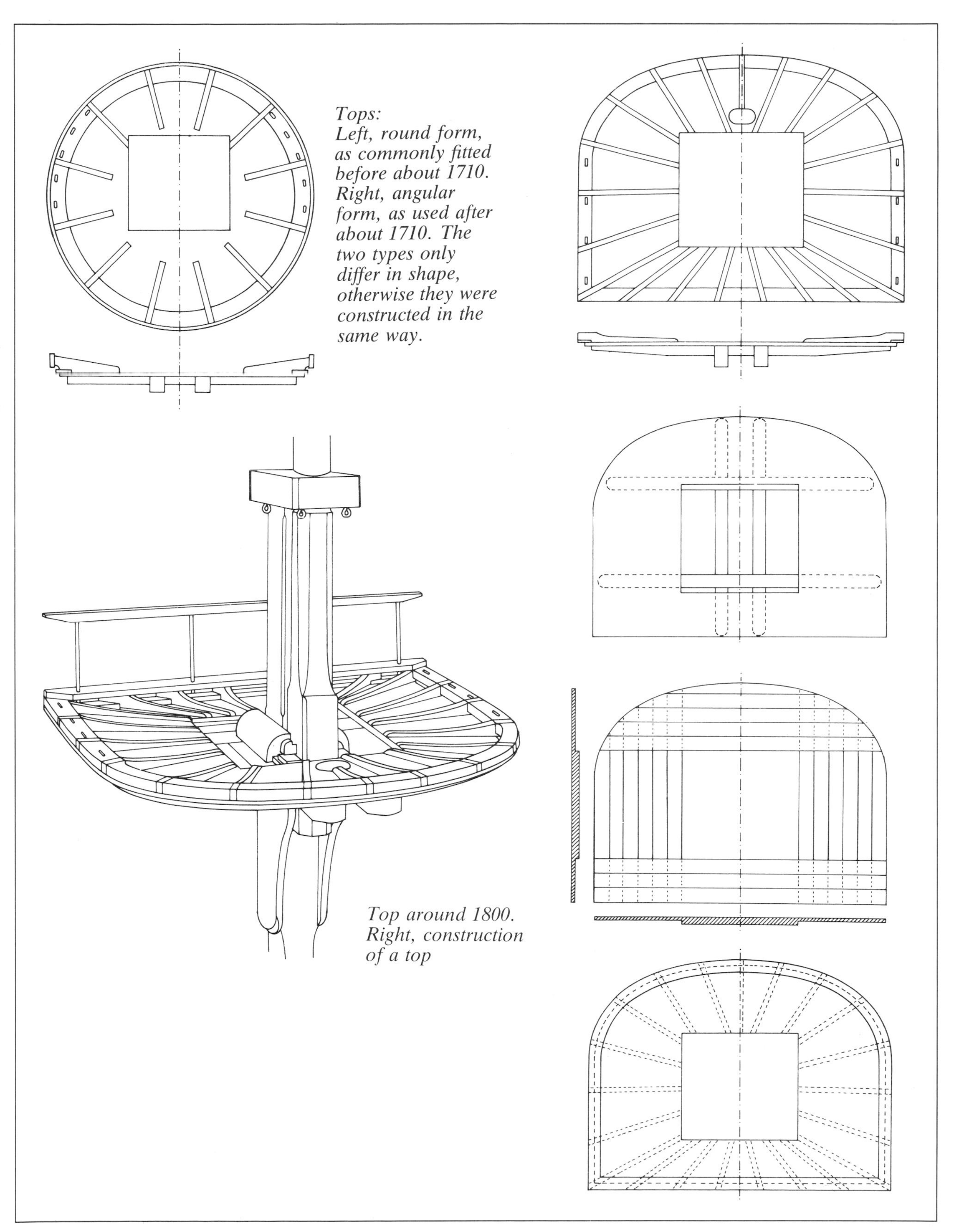

Tops:
Left, round form, as commonly fitted before about 1710. Right, angular form, as used after about 1710. The two types only differ in shape, otherwise they were constructed in the same way.

Top around 1800. Right, construction of a top

Topmasts

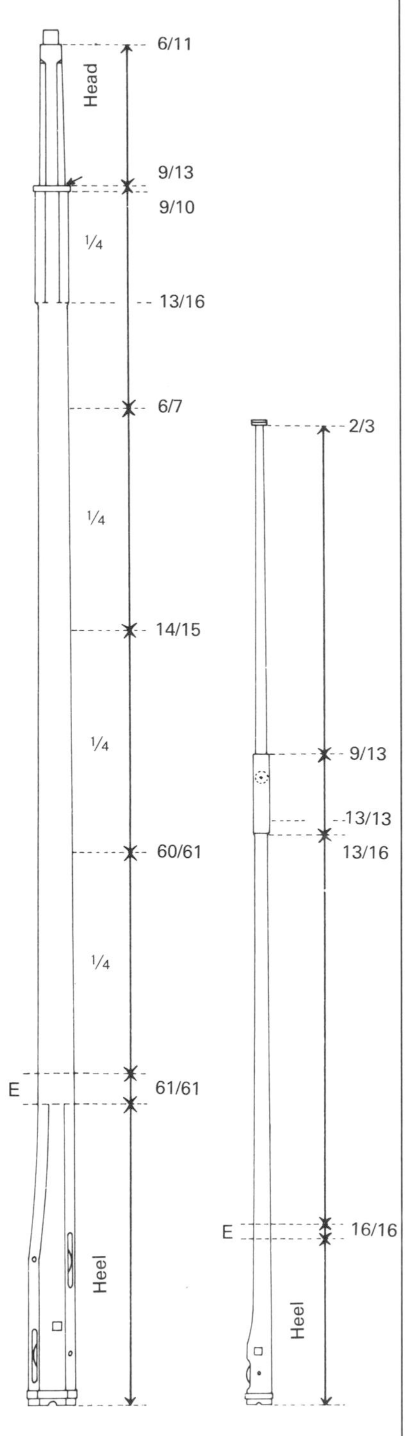

Topmast and topgallant mast

When topsails were introduced in the late 15th century, the masts had to be extended to carry them. However, the masts themselves were not lengthened; instead separate topmasts were added to them. The first half of the 16th century saw the addition of topgallant masts, and in the 17th century royal masts were introduced, ending in small flagpoles. In the 18th century the number of upper masts was reduced again to two, the topmast and the topgallant mast, the upper part of which was still termed the royal mast, if royals were carried. If not, the upper part became the flagpole.

Topmast construction

The topmasts are made up exactly like the masts, that is, a square section strip planed down to 8 and then 16 sides, and finally rounded off with glasspaper.

Many model kits include dowelling for masts, topmasts and yards – do not use them! Dowelling has to be tapered to the correct degree, and in practice this is much more difficult with round section material than with square section. Of course, you could use the dowels without tapering them at all, (i.e. upwards and outwards) – that looks clumsy on masts and topmasts, and downright terrible on the yards.

The topmast heel

The topmast heel was square in section from the end of the 15th century (eight-sided in England in the 18/19th centuries), and was frequently slightly thicker than the nominal maximum diameter of the topmast at the lower cap. It should be a snug, but not loose, fit between the trestletrees, so that the whole of the top mast neither wobbles nor leans to one side.

To prevent the topmast sliding through the top a wood or iron bar termed the fid was passed through the heel of the topmast, resting on the trestletrees. The lower edge of the fid hole should always be located twice the thickness of the topmast heel from the foot of the topmast.

There is a trick worth knowing for making the fid hole neatly: saw the foot of the topmast off square at the bottom of the fid hole, cut a groove of the appropriate width and depth using a circular saw, and glue the lower piece back on, using cyano-acrylate glue for preference.

A single sheave was fitted in the topgallant mast heel, and also in the topmast heel in the 16/17th centuries. In the 18/19th centuries a double sheave was fitted – please note the differences in the English and Continental forms. These sheaves served to take the topropes, when the topmast was to be hoisted or sent down.

The topmast head

The topmast head was octagonal in section on Continental ships, and square on English ships; those on English ships were fitted with sheaves, those on Continental ships were not. The topsail tyes (see HALYARDS) reeved through holes below the crosstrees, the sheaves of which were the same diameter as the topmast to which they were fitted.

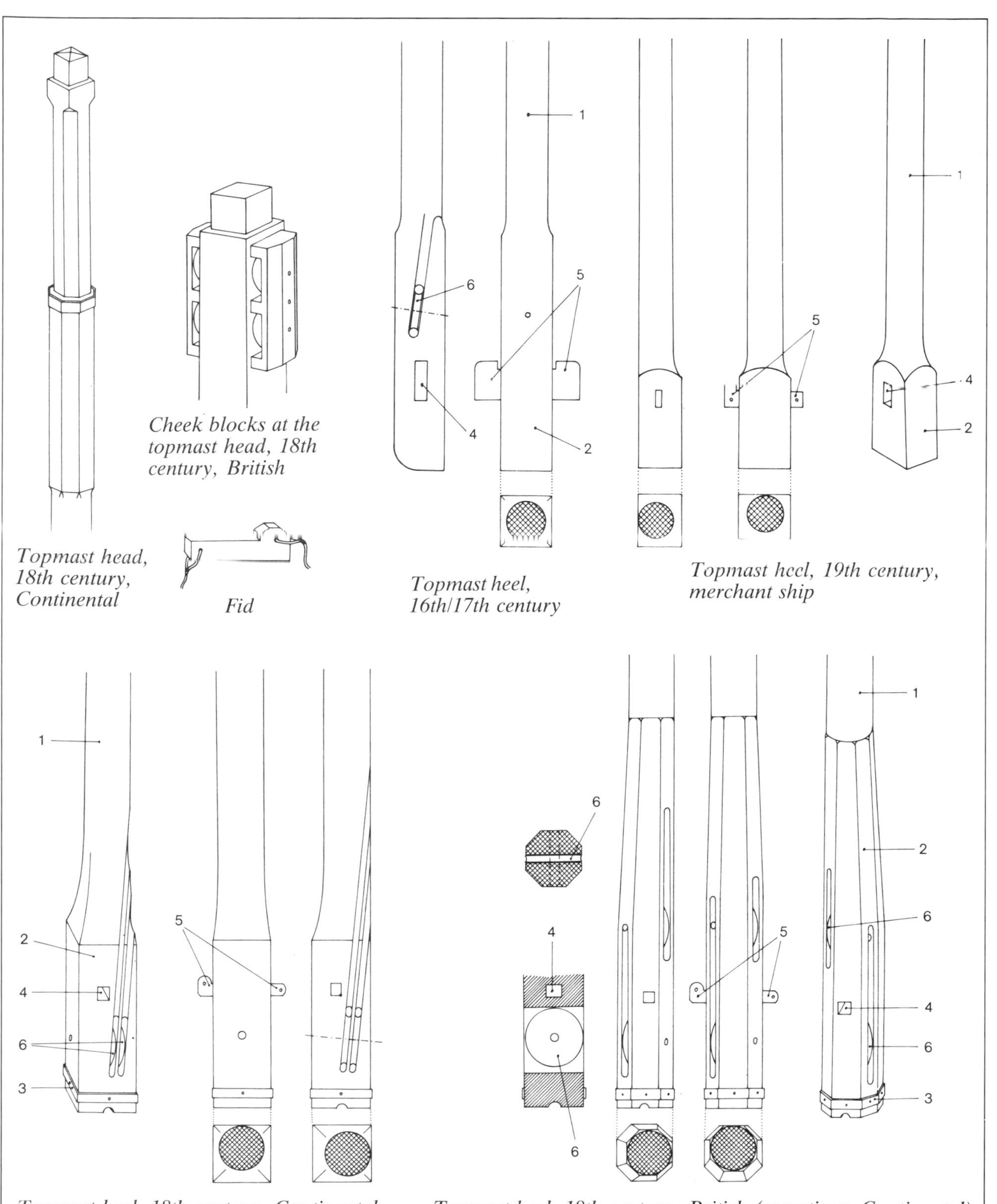

Cheek blocks at the topmast head, 18th century, British

Topmast head, 18th century, Continental

Fid

Topmast heel, 16th/17th century

Topmast heel, 19th century, merchant ship

Topmast heel, 18th century, Continental

Topmast heel, 18th century, British (sometimes Continental)

1. Topmast; 2. Topmast heel; 3. Iron hoop; 4. Fid hole; 5. Fid; 6. Sheaves for top ropes (after Vaisseau)

Bowsprit, sprit topmast, jib boom

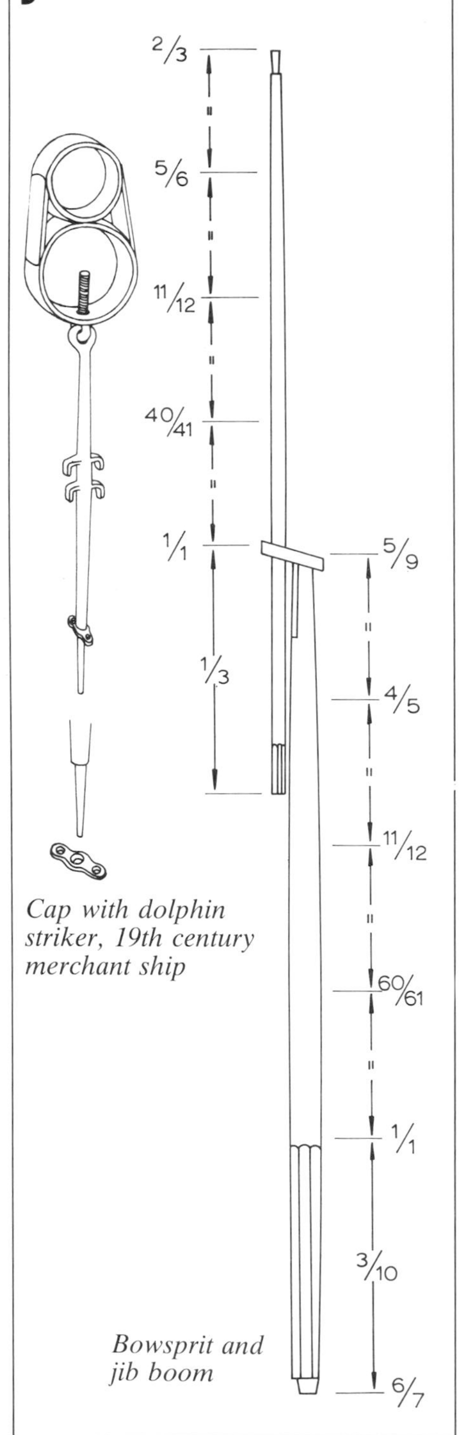

Cap with dolphin striker, 19th century merchant ship

Bowsprit and jib boom

The bowsprit
The bowsprit is really nothing more than a mast canted forward; it appeared from the 13th century onwards. Its angle to the horizontal varied quite considerably: in the Middle Ages it was 50° to 60°, in the 15th century around 50°, in the first half of the 16th century 30 to 35°, in the second half of the 16th century 25-30°, around 1630 20°, around 1650 30°, around 1665 40°, around 1675 35°, in the 18th century 25 to 30°, in the first half of the 19th century 20 to 25°, in the second half of the 19th century 14 to 18°. Naturally, these angles are only approximate.
Like the lower masts, the bowsprit featured wooldings and hoops. From the early 16th century until about 1650 (occasionally as late as 1670), the bowsprit was routed past the foremast on the starboard side. It did not lie parallel to the keel, but at an angle, so that the head of the bowsprit was on the centreline of the ship. After this time the bowsprit's heel was stepped in line with the foremast, and supported by the stem – thus it was situated with all its length exactly on the centreline, like all the other masts and topmasts.

The sprit topmast
From the late 16th century until about 1720 a small mast was carried on the bowsprit, known as the sprit topmast. At the head the upper surface of the bowsprit was flattened off slightly to provide a support surface for the sprit topmast knee. The lower arm of this knee was the same length as the fore masthead, the other leg arm was 2/3 of it. This knee carried the crosstrees and the cap.
The sprit topmast itself was similar to a topgallant mast, but without a sheave for the topmast tye. It was vertical or very slightly inclined forward (up to about 5°). Take care here. The sprit topmast must be firmly attached, and clamped securely to the knee. The stays and sprit topmast backstays exert a powerful pull on the sprit topmast when the rigging is set up, and it must not bend back further than the vertical.

The jib boom
Around 1715 an extension of the bowsprit came into use – the jib boom. For a short period it was carried below the sprit topmast then the sprit topmast disappeared. The bowsprit was then fitted with a cap through which the jib boom passed. At its after end it rested on a saddle and was lashed with a chain. The jib boom was either fitted on the centre of the bowsprit, or displaced to starboard. Two timbers, the bees, to right and left of the head of the bowsprit, served to attach the fore topmast stay, and the fore topmast preventer stay (see Stays). The dolphin striker was fitted under the bowsprit cap, and the martingale stays (see Bowsprit Rigging) passed under this. In the late 18th century a flying jib boom was introduced, which, supported on the bowsprit cap, passed through an iron cap on the forward end of the jib boom, and thus extended the latter even further.

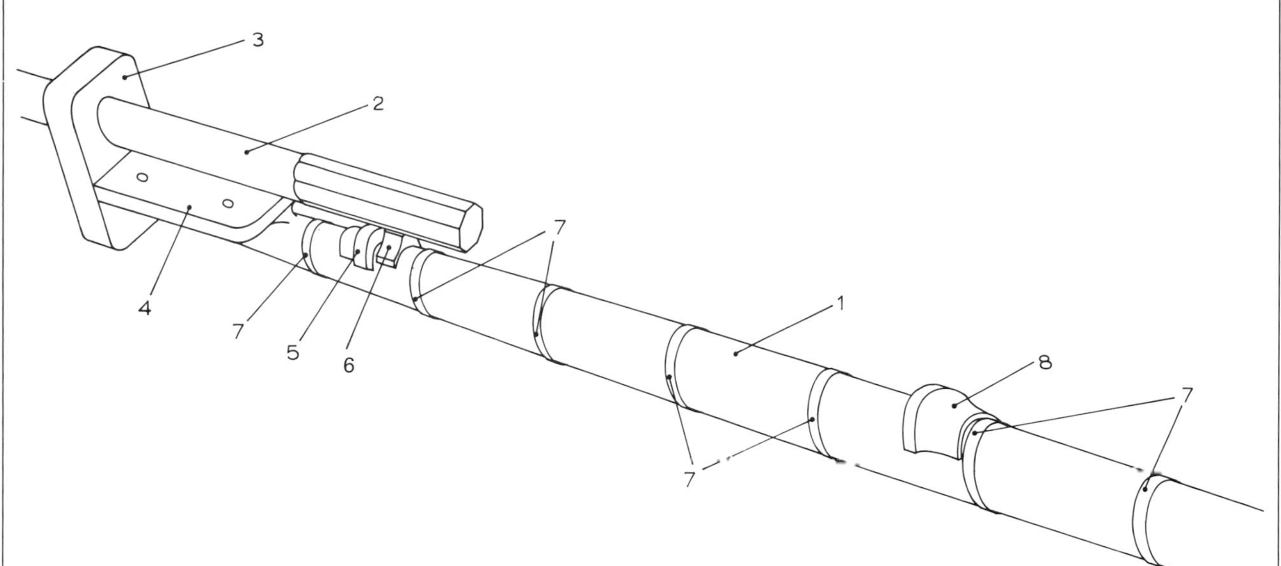

Bowsprit in late 18th century: 1. Bowsprit; 2. Jibboom; 3. Cap; 4. Bees; 5. Spritsail sling saddle; 6. Jibboom saddle; 7. Iron hoops; 8. Gammoning saddle (or cleats)

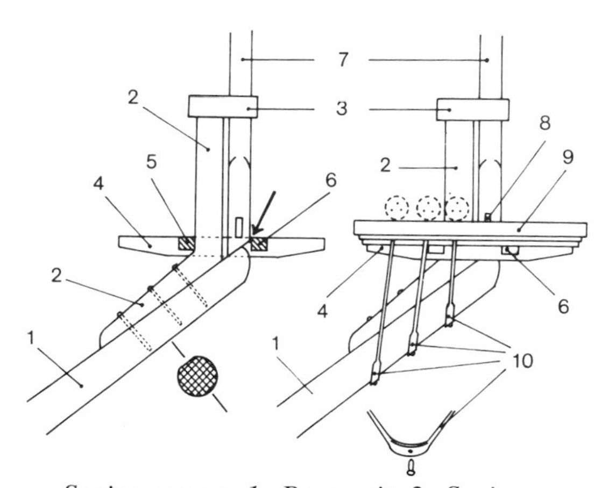

Sprit topmast: 1. Bowsprit; 2. Sprit topmast knee; 3. Cap; 4. Trestletrees; 5. After crosstree; 6. Forward crosstree; 7. Sprit topmast secured very firmly to the crosstree (arrowed); 8. Fid; 9. Top; 10. Special chain plates

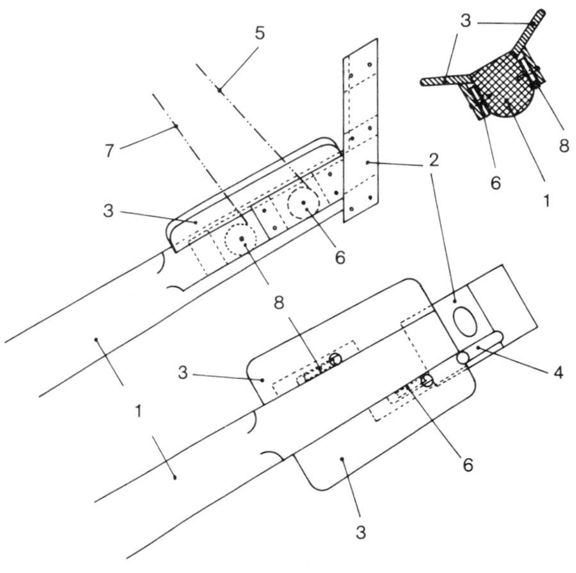

Bowsprit head (after 1780): 1. Bowsprit; 2. Cap; 3. Bee block; 4. Groove for Jackstaff; 5. Fore topmast stay; 6. Fore topmast stay sheave, starboard side forward; 7. Fore topmast preventer stay with 8. Sheave on port side, aft

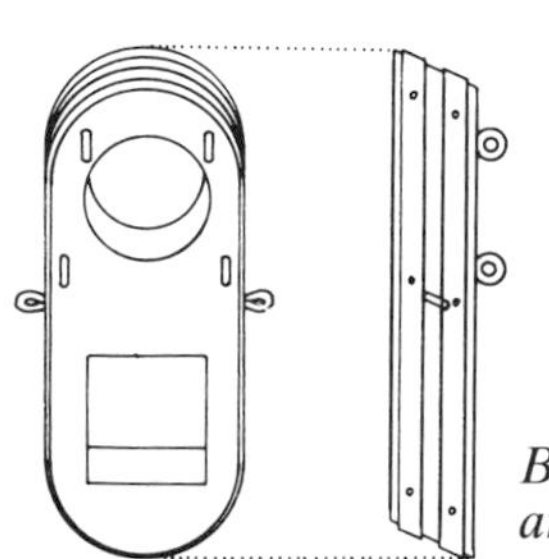

Iron cap

Bowsprit cap around 1800

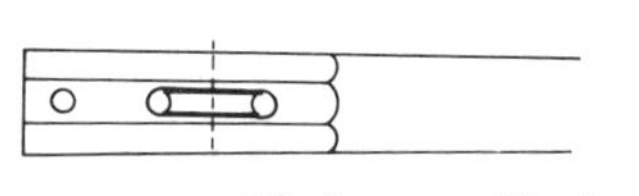

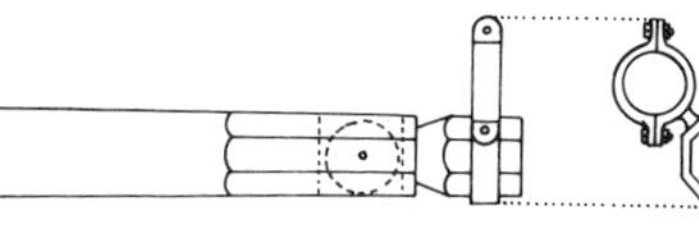

Jib boom: Heel and head with boom iron for the flying jib boom

Proportions of yards

B = Breadth amidships

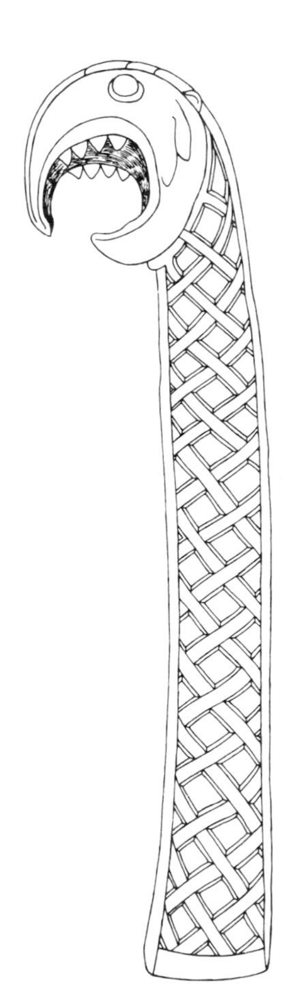

Dragon figurehead of a 19th century Viking ship

	German 1470	Spanish 1480	Spanish 1570	English 1570
Length of spritsail yard		1,230 B	1,235 B	1,184 B
Ø		0,032 L	0,022 L	0,025 L
Length of sprit topsail yard				
Ø				
Length of fore yard	1,025 B	1,395 B	1,788 B	2,000 B
Ø	0,029 L	0,023 L	0,021 L	0,020 L
Length of studding sail boom				
Ø				
Length of studding sail yard				
Length of fore topsail yard			0,780 B	1,060 B
Ø			0,019 L	0,024 L
Length of studding sail yard				
Length of fore topgallant yard			0,318 B	0,500 B
Ø			0,020 L	0,020 L
Length of studding sail yard				
Length of fore royal yard				
Ø				
Length of main yard	1,736 B	2,360 B	2,015 B	2,490 B
Ø	0,033 L	0,027 L	0,022 L	0,020 L
Length of studding sail boom				
Ø				
Length of studding sail yard				
Length of main topsail yard		0,935 B	0,894 B	1,245 B
Ø		0,027 L	0,019 L	0,024 L
Length of studding sail yard				
Length of main topgallant yard			0,326 B	0,633 B
Ø			0,020 L	0,020 L
Length of studding sail yard				
Length of main royal yard				
Ø				
Length of crossjack yard				
Ø				
Length of mizen topsail yard				
Ø				
Length of mizen topgallant yard				
Ø				
Length of mizen topgallant yard				
Ø				
Length of mizen lateen yard	1,435 B	2,500 B	2,000 B	2,082 B
Ø	0,017 L	0,018 L	0,019 L	0,015 L
Length of driver boom				
Ø				
Length of gaff				
Ø				
Length of jigger lateen yard			1,370 B	1,530 B
Ø			0,019 L	0,015 L

Spanish 1600	Italian 1600	Dutch 1600	French 1630	Dutch 1650	British 1650	French 1680	British 1710	French 1740	British warship 1800	British merchant ship 1810	French warship 1820
1,234 B	1,180 B	1,238 B	0,954 B	1,193 B	1,310 B	1,575 B	1,250 B	1,345 B	1,286 B	1,554 B	1,483 B
0,030 L	0,024 L	0,025 L	0,023 L	0,020 L	0,023 L	0,021 L	0,021 L	0,018 L	0,015 L	0,015 L	0,022 L
			0,595 B	0,664 B	0,714 B	0,565 B	0,750 B	0,926 B	0,841 B		
			0,022 L	0,017 L	0,025 L	0,021 L	0,020 L	0,018 L	0,015 L		
1,930 B	1,546 B	1,588 B	1,700 B	1,872 B	1,870 B	2,000 B	2,000 B	1,842 B	1,707 B	1,942 B	1,816 B
0,028 L	0,021 L	0,026 L	0,023 L	0,021 L	0,024 L	0,021 L	0,021 L	0,022 L	0,021 L	0,020 L	0,022 L
				1,030 B	1,100 B	1,100 B	1,100 B	0,920 B	0,854 B	0,971 B	0,908 B
				0,023 L	0,023 L	0,021 L	0,021 L	0,018 L	0,018 L	0,018 L	0,018 L
				0,358 B	0,655 B	0,700 B	0,700 B	0,553 B	0,512 B	0,583 B	0,545 B
1,016 B	1,000 B	0,800 B	1,137 B	1,024 B	1,000 B	1,500 B	1,166 B	1,345 B	1,232 B	1,294 B	1,496 B
0,030 L	0,024 L	0,025 L	0,022 L	0,020 L	0,024 L	0,021 L	0,021 L	0,018 L	0,018 L	0,018 L	0,020 L
						0,525 B	0,408 B	0,403 B	0,396 B	0,388 B	0,449 B
0,540 B	0,560 B	0,400 B	0,694 B	0,536 B	0,523 B	0,750 B	0,666 B	0,857 B	0,848 B	0,906 B	0,918 B
0,028 L	0,021 L	0,025 L	0,022 L	0,018 L	0,023 L	0,021 L	0,020 L	0,018 L	0,018 L	0,017 L	0,018 L
								0,257 B	0,254 B	0,272 B	0,275 B
										0,600 B	0,680 B
										0,017 L	0,015 L
2,440 B	2,062 B	1,938 B	2,137 B	2,088 B	2,262 B	2,100 B	2,125 B	2,020 B	1,963 B	1,942 B	2,040 B
0,028 L	0,021 L	0,026 L	0,023 L	0,021 L	0,024 L	0,021 L	0,021 L	0,022 L	0,021 L	0,020 L	0,022 L
				1,148 B	1,244 B	1,155 B	1,169 B	1,010 B	0,981 B	0,971 B	1,020 B
				0,023 L	0,023 L	0,021 L	0,021 L	0,018 L	0,018 L	0,018 L	0,018 L
				0,428 B	0,792 B	0,735 B	0,744 B	0,606 B	0,590 B	0,583 B	0,612 B
1,273 B	1,298 B	0,975 B	1,374 B	1,224 B	1,250 B	1,575 B	1,250 B	1,458 B	1,390 B	1,294 B	1,632 B
0,030 L	0,024 L	0,025 L	0,022 L	0,020 L	0,024 L	0,021 L	0,021 L	0,018 L	0,018 L	0,018 L	0,020 L
						0,551 B	0,438 B	0,437 B	0,417 B	0,388 B	0,489 B
0,688 B	0,714 B	0,487 B	0,800 B	0,632 B	0,645 B	0,787 B	0,750 B	0,926 B	0,963 B	0,971 B	1,040 B
0,028 L	0,021 L	0,025 L	0,022 L	0,018 L	0,023 L	0,021 L	0,020 L	0,018 L	0,018 L	0,018 L	0,018 L
								0,278 B	0,289 B	0,290 B	0,312 B
										0,647 B	0,735 B
										0,017 L	0,015 L
			0,855 B	1,056 B	1,286 B	1,130 B	1,666 B	1,345 B	1,268 B	1,424 B	1,619 B
			0,020 L	0,015 L	0,014 L	0,019 L	0,015 L	0,018 L	0,018 L	0,018 L	0,021 L
			0,542 B	0,592 B	0,726 B	0,565 B	0,666 B	0,970 B	0,939 B	1, 035 B	1,108 B
			0,022 L	0,018 L	0,021 L	0,021 L	0,020 L	0,018 L	0,018 L	0,018 L	0,018 L
								0,616 B	0,622 B	0,647 B	0,735 B
								0,018 L	0,018 L	0,017 L	0,015 L
										0,517 B	0,524 B
										0,016 L	0,015 L
1,953 B	1,963 B	1,713 B	1,412 B	1,700 B	1,490 B	2,000 B	2,000 B	1,852 B			
0,022 L	0,020 L	0,015 L	0,021 L	0,013 L	0,016 L	0,015 L	0,016 L	0,016 L			
									1,415 B	1,186 B	1,353 B
									0,013 L	0,013 L	0,015 L
									1,158 B	0,971 B	1,100 B
									0,010 L	0,011 L	0,013 L
1,445 B	1,366 B										
0,022 L	0,020 L										

The Yards

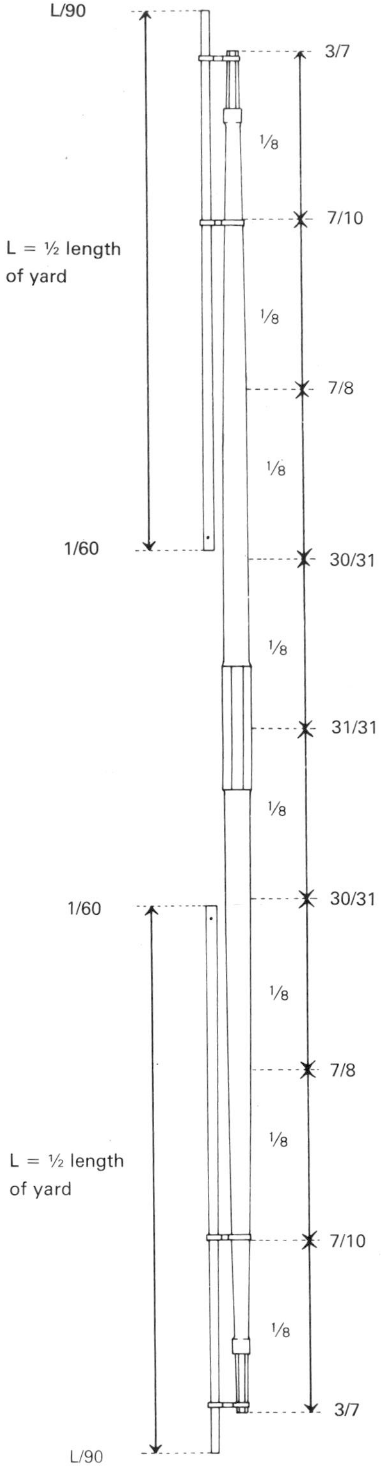

The design of the yards remained virtually unchanged for thousands of years. Small yards were made of a single length of wood, while longer yards were assembled and lashed together. One reason for this method of construction was that timbers sufficiently long, straight and knot-free were difficult to obtain and another was that they were less susceptible to breakage. Between 1400 and 1550 yards assembled from square-section timbers were introduced, initially lashed together with rope wooldings. Around the same time yard arms began to appear; that is, the extreme ends of the yard were stepped down to prevent the braces, lifts and clew earings of the sails sliding inwards. Between 1450 and 1550 the yard arms of large warships were sometimes fitted with sickle-shaped iron hooks, with which attempts could be made to cut down and tear the enemy's rigging during close combat. After 1530 wooldings disappeared, and in the late 16th century wooden cleats were fitted on the front of the lower yards, and sometimes on the topsail yards, to prevent the tyes and truss parrels sliding off. The yard cleats were made either in one piece or in two halves with a slot in the centre. The overall length of the yard cleats was 0·1 to 0·13 × the yard length, and the thickness 0·25 × the yard diameter. With the introduction of the studding sail the lower and topsail yards were fitted with studding sail boom irons. At the same time the yard arms of the topsail yards were lengthened considerably. Until that time the yardarms of the spritsail and crossjack yards had been 0·05 × the yard length, while the remaining yard arms had been 0·04 × that length; they were often round in section. Now all the yard arms were eight-sided in section, and the yard arms of the topsail yards were extended to 0·08 × the yard length with the introduction of reefs; they were also fitted with a sheave for the reef tackle. Around 1730 an octagonal battening was introduced in the centre of the yard. In the 19th century the yard cleats were discontinued.
The yards are made in the same way as the masts and topmasts; all the metal fittings are blackened.

The foot ropes
The foot ropes are strong ropes which led along the yard about 30ins below it, and provided the crew with a foot rest when reefing the sails. The foot ropes of the lower yards were about 3ins circumference. Footropes came into use on the lower yards after 1640, on the topsail yards after 1680, and on the remaining yards around 1700, with the exception of the crossjack yard, and also all the lateen yards and gaffs. A spliced eye in one end was fitted over the yard arm with the other end made fast behind the mast cleat on the other side of the mast, so that the two ropes crossed over at the mast. In the 18th century it became standard in some areas to fix the foot ropes at the centre of the yard, without crossing them over. Small foot ropes were also attached to the extreme ends of the yard, known as the "Flemish horses". The foot ropes hung behind the yard, and were held by vertical ropes known as stirrups.

The jackstay
1830 saw the introduction of ropes which ran along the yard through a series of ring bolts, and were attached to the yard arms with an eye splice and to the centre with a lanyard. These ropes, the jackstays were those to which the sails were bent. Initially hemp ropes were used then steel wire ropes, and from 1835-1840 metal rods.

Yard with studding sail booms

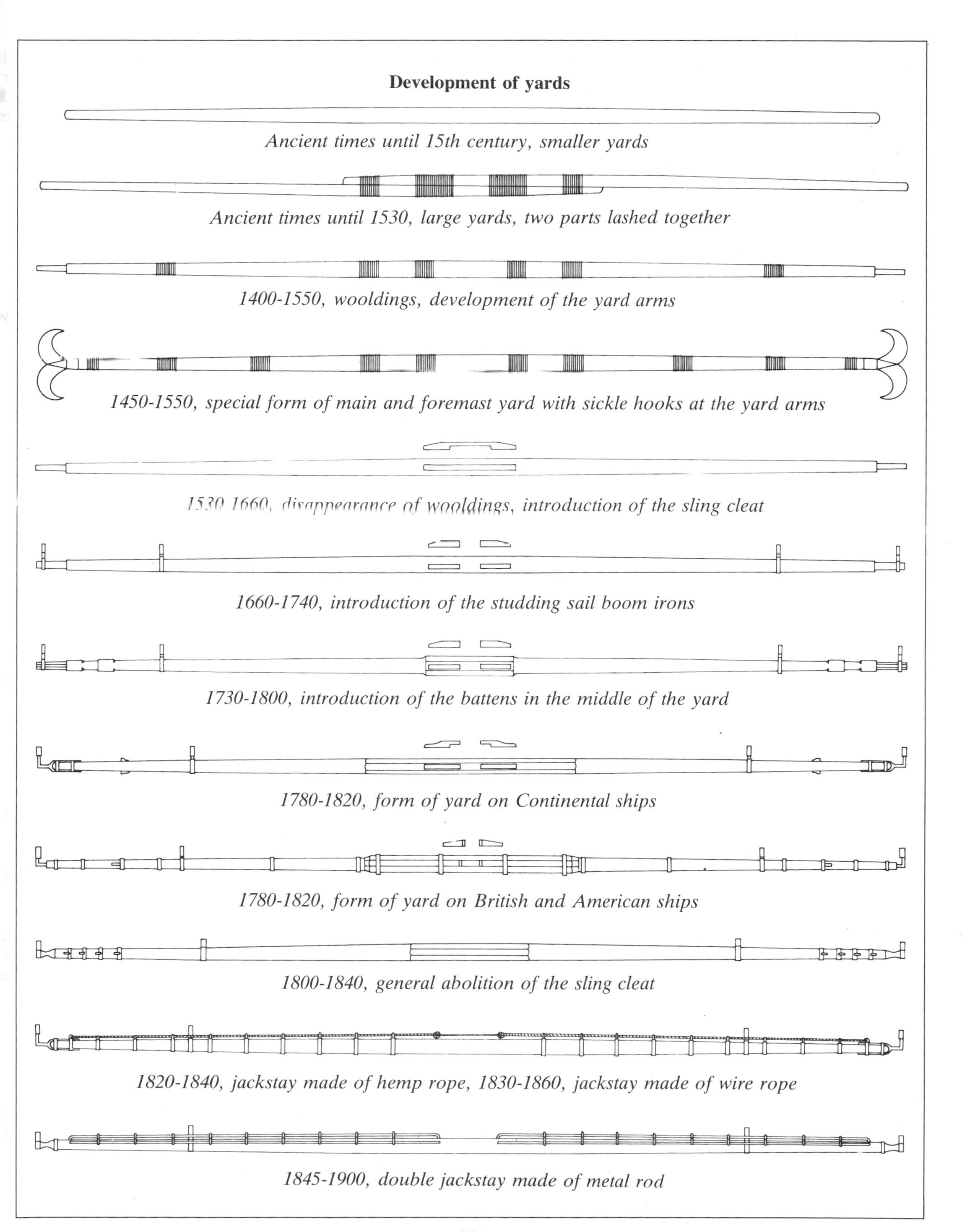
Development of yards
Ancient times until 15th century, smaller yards
Ancient times until 1530, large yards, two parts lashed together
1400-1550, wooldings, development of the yard arms
1450-1550, special form of main and foremast yard with sickle hooks at the yard arms
1530-1660, disappearance of wooldings, introduction of the sling cleat
1660-1740, introduction of the studding sail boom irons
1730-1800, introduction of the battens in the middle of the yard
1780-1820, form of yard on Continental ships
1780-1820, form of yard on British and American ships
1800-1840, general abolition of the sling cleat
1820-1840, jackstay made of hemp rope, 1830-1860, jackstay made of wire rope
1845-1900, double jackstay made of metal rod

Spare spars

Every ship carried a large number of spare spars, and it is really surprising how seldom they are seen on models. It is not known which spare spars were carried until the beginning of the 18th century, but it can be assumed that they were little different from those of the 18th and 19th centuries, perhaps one or more spars fewer.
Here is a list of the spare spars usually carried in the 18th and 19th centuries:
Warships: 1 main topmast, 1 fore topmast, 1 main yard, 1 fore yard, 1 fore topsail yard, 1 main topsail yard, 1 jib boom, 1 upper topsail yard (where fitted).
Long distance merchant ships: 1 main topmast, 1 topgallant mast, 1 lower yard, 1 topsail yard, occasionally 1 jib boom, 1 upper topsail yard (where fitted), 1 gaff.
Atlantic merchant ships: 1 main topmast, 1 lower yard, 1 topsail yard, occasionally 1 jib boom, 1 topgallant mast, 1 gaff.
Coastal merchant ships: 1 topmast, 1 yard (usually a topsail yard).
The main topmasts and yards were stowed on crutches or skid beams. In the 18th century in France most of the spare yards were stowed on the main channels (see CHANNELS). Smaller spars were also stowed in the waist until the first half of the 19th century, then later on the top of the deck houses.

Studding sail yards and booms

Studding sails were mentioned as early as around 1625, but seem to have been a temporary measure taken by individual captains. They came into general use on the Continent on the fore yard and the main yard around 1650, on the topsail yards around 1675, while in England main studding sails appeared around 1660, fore studding sails around 1690, and topmast studding sails not until around 1700. In the first half of the 18th century topgallant studding sails were added by all nations.
The studding sail booms were held by two iron bands, the boom irons, one of which was located on the yard arm, the other ⅛ to ⅙ of the yard's length further inboard.
Warships of all nations usually fitted the studding sail spars diagonally in front of the yard, with the exception of the Dutch, who fitted them diagonally behind the yard. 19th century merchant ships carried them below the yard. Studding sail booms were carried on the lower and topsail yards, and also the crossjack yard. The studding sail booms, on which the lower studding sails were hauled out, featured a hook which engaged in a heavy ring bolt on the channel or on the ship's side. They were either stowed on the channels, or hauled inboard and kept next to the waterway on merchant ships. See also THE STUDDING SAILS.

Boats' masts

Ships' boats were almost all fitted with sailing equipment. The following list gives the proportions of the boats' masts. The spars belonging to the masts bore the same dimensional relationships to the boats' masts as the corresponding spars on large ships.
Length of main mast = 2 to 3 x boat's beam;
Length of foremast = 0·8 to 1·0 x length of the main mast;
Length of mizen mast = 0·5 to 0·7 x length of the main mast;
Length of bowsprit = 0·25 to 0·42 x length of the boat.
The boats' masts and spars, and also the oars, were usually stowed in the boat.

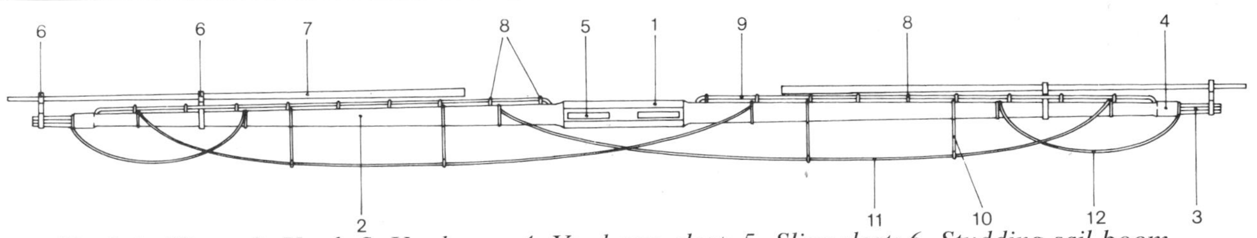

Yard: 1. Slings; 2. Yard; 3. Yard arm; 4. Yard arm cleat; 5. Sling cleat; 6. Studding sail boom irons; 7. Studding sail boom; 8. Ring bolt; 9. Jackstay; 10. Stirrups; 11. Foot rope; 12. Flemish horse; 13. Jackstay; 14. Wood peg

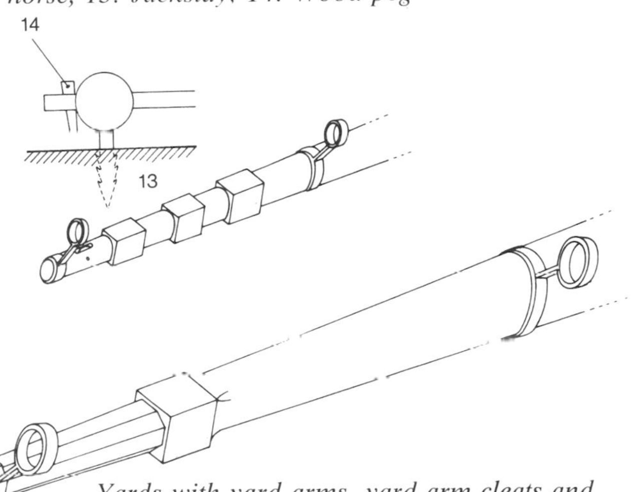

Yards with yard arms, yard arm cleats and studding sail boom irons; Top – topsail yard; Bottom – lower yard (after Vaisseau)

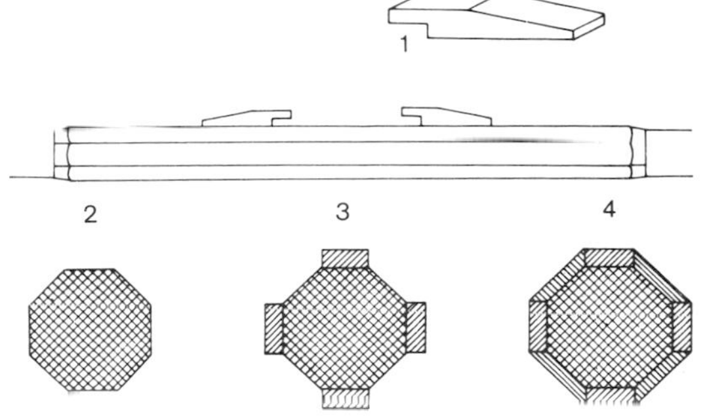

Yard slings: 1. Sling cleat; 2. Yard with 3. Partial battening; 4. Full battening

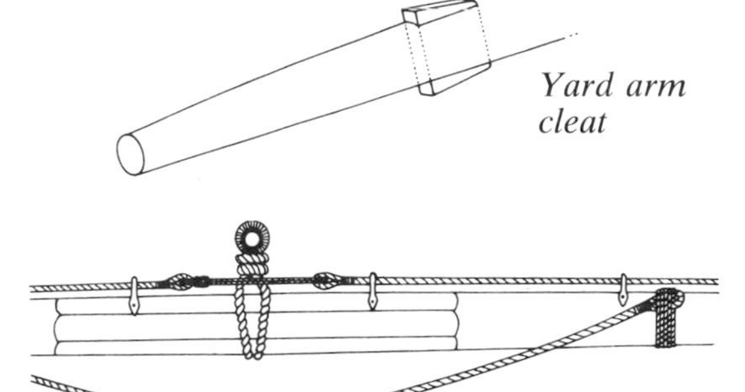

Yard arm cleat

Setting up the rope jackstay and attachment of the foot rope around 1830

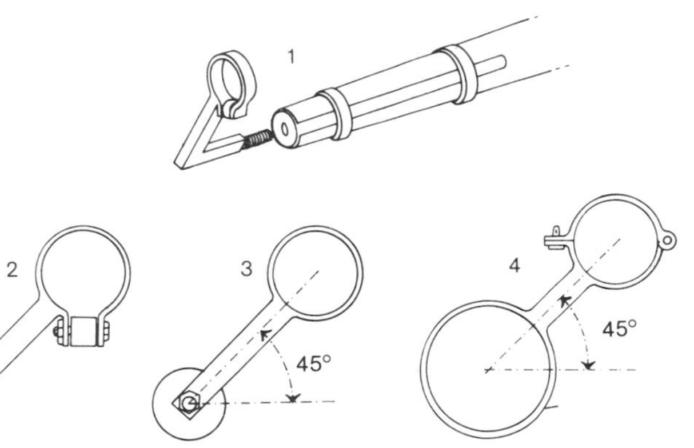

Studding sail boom iron: 1. Yard arm, 18th/19th century with outer studding sail boom iron screwed in; the threaded iron fitting at the yard peak is retained by two iron bands; 2. Outer studding sail boom irons with roller; 3. Outer studding sail boom iron without roller; 4. Inner studding sail boom iron

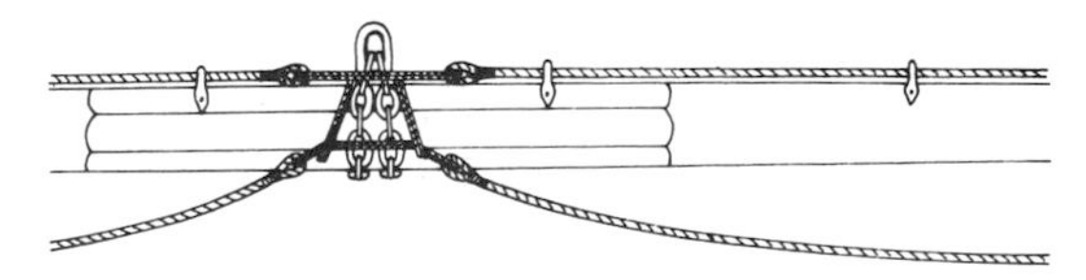

Setting up the rope jackstay and attachment of the foot rope around 1850

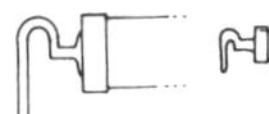

Studding sail boom, hooked to a ringbolt on the channel or hull

The Lateen yard and gaff

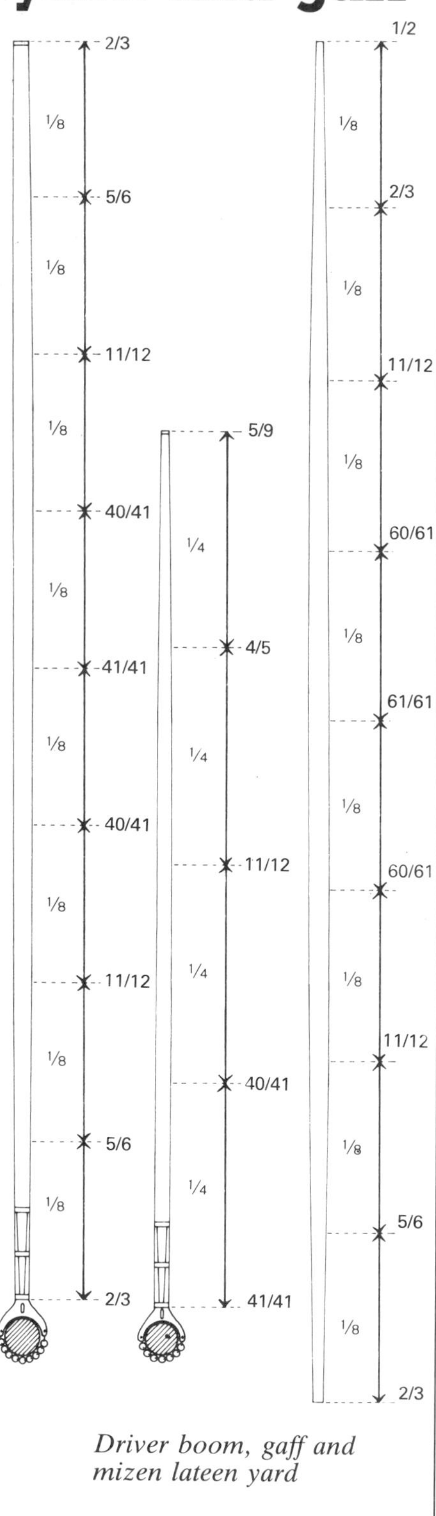

Driver boom, gaff and mizen lateen yard

It is rather difficult to hold a heading to any great degree of accuracy with square sails only, and in the late 14th century a small mast was erected at the stern which was fitted with a triangular lateen sail, in order to improve this situation.
The lateen sail evolved in the Mediterranean, and was adopted in Northern Europe generally at the beginning of the 15th century; in this case it was termed the mizen course.

The lateen yard
The yard of a lateen sail is termed the lateen yard. In the Mediterranean, where the lateen sail was often the only one carried right to the end of the 19th century, the sail assumed gigantic dimensions and the yard consisted of 2 or 3 spars lashed together with wooldings. The upper end was called the head while the lower, thicker end was the foot. Ships which were otherwise square-rigged often carried very large lateen yards in the form of the mizen lateen yard up to 1550, sometimes lashed together from two spars, but after that time, and indeed on other ships before that time, it was made in one piece like the other yards, or was made up from square-section timbers without wooldings.
In the 16th century lateen top and topgallant sails were also introduced on the mizen and bonaventure mizen masts of large ships, but they very quickly disappeared again because they proved to be impractical. The mizen lateen sail was retained until the early years of the 18th century when the fore part was removed and the leech lashed to the mast. The lateen yard was replaced by a gaff in small ships in the middle of the 18th century. Large ships retained the lateen yard until the end of the 18th century, a few surviving into the early years of the 19th century. The lateen yard was not symmetrical around its thickest section, like the other yards, but was slightly thinner at the head than at the foot (see drawing on the left).

Gaff and driver boom
In the second half of the 18th century the mizen yard was cut short at the mast, and the remaining upper part was fixed to the mast with a fork known as the jaws. A horizontal boom was then fitted at the bottom of the mast to enable the gaff sail to be fully deployed. This also ended in jaws, which rested on a saddle on the mast. The gaff and the driver boom jaws were held to the mast with a simple parral with trucks. In the 19th century the jaws were superseded by goosenecks. The driver boom sometimes carried foot ropes, and various means of fitting a studding sail or ringtail were also tried. Like the lateen yard, the gaff and driver boom were not symmetrical around their thickest point, which is a point worth noting if you are aiming at an outstandingly accurate model.

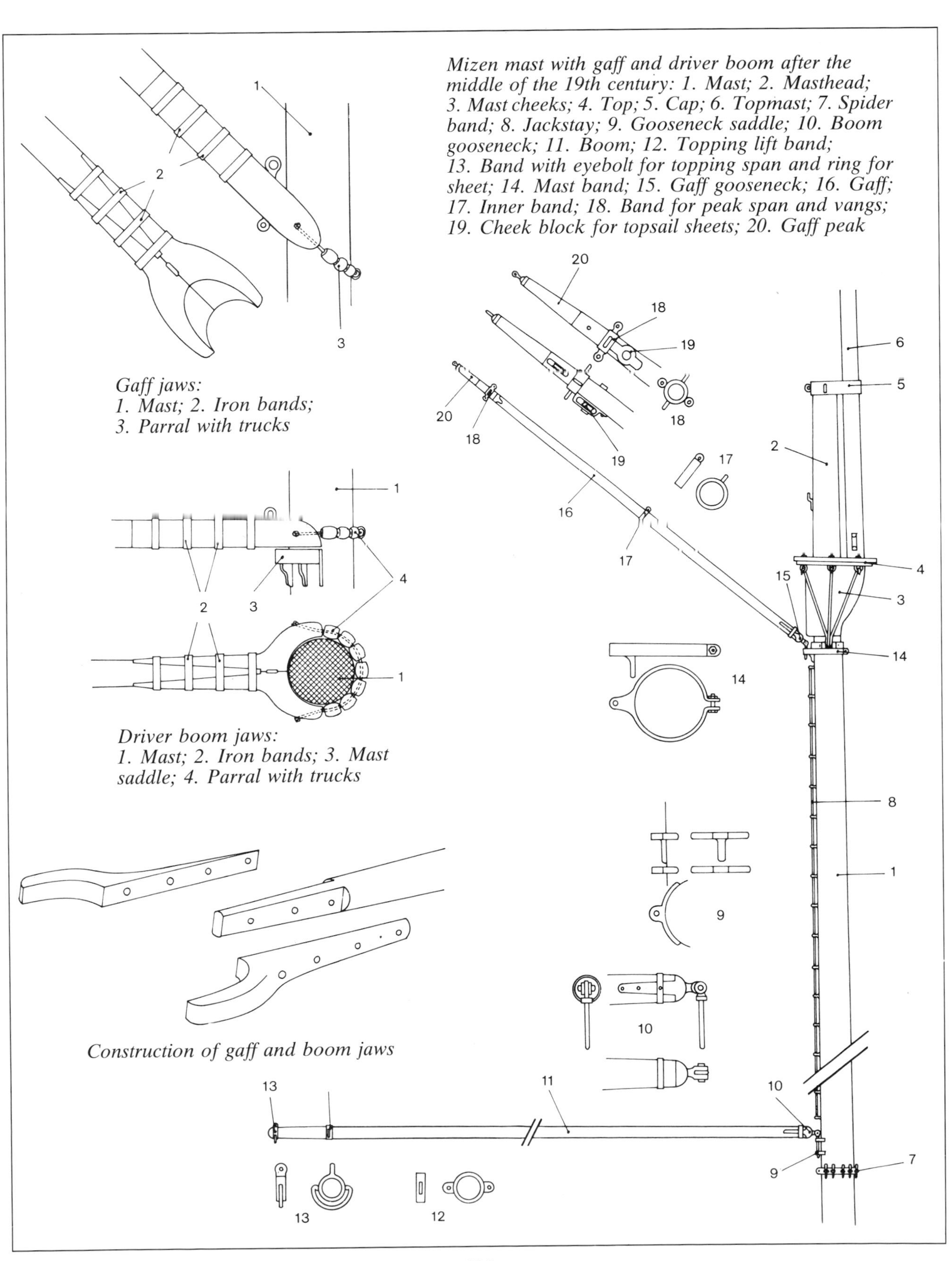

Mizen mast with gaff and driver boom after the middle of the 19th century: 1. Mast; 2. Masthead; 3. Mast cheeks; 4. Top; 5. Cap; 6. Topmast; 7. Spider band; 8. Jackstay; 9. Gooseneck saddle; 10. Boom gooseneck; 11. Boom; 12. Topping lift band; 13. Band with eyebolt for topping span and ring for sheet; 14. Mast band; 15. Gaff gooseneck; 16. Gaff; 17. Inner band; 18. Band for peak span and vangs; 19. Cheek block for topsail sheets; 20. Gaff peak

Gaff jaws: 1. Mast; 2. Iron bands; 3. Parral with trucks

Driver boom jaws: 1. Mast; 2. Iron bands; 3. Mast saddle; 4. Parral with trucks

Construction of gaff and boom jaws

Ropes and blocks

Blocks and ropes · Ropes
Cables · Chains · Blocks
Block strops · Deadeyes
Hearts · Fiddle block
Belaying pins · Cleats
Thimbles · Rigging screws

I find it astounding how many ship modellers will take almost infinite pains to construct their model's hull, all the minute detail fittings and all the intricate strops and lashings, only to ruin the rigging by using the first length of thread they find, in conjunction with ill-proportioned commercially-made blocks – perhaps even made of plastic.

The manufacturers of model kits of otherwise high quality must take their share of blame here. One well-known modelling company currently supplies a total of three different sizes of block. . . It is not this book's purpose to tell horror stories and hurl brickbats, but we have to say to the modeller working from kits that he should at the very least submit the rigging plans and the materials supplied by way of thread and blocks to a thorough going over. For reasons of rationalization commercial firms nearly all tend to make the rigging for the lower masts and yards too light, and that for the topmasts and yards too heavy. The beauty of a model ship depends to a considerable extent on the correct gradation of rope thicknesses and block sizes, which become thinner and smaller from bottom to top, following a strict code of proportions.

Now, you have to obtain your thread somewhere. And the prospect of making your own blocks and deadeyes (300 to 500 of them) plus 100 to 150 belaying pins – as would be needed to rig a three-master – leads many a modeller to hope that commercial sources will be able to offer some help. So let us look at the possibilities:

The "rigging thread" at present offered by the modelling companies – with the exception of the Graupner type – is not at all suitable for a high-quality model. The best source of supply for model ropes is a bookbinder, a furrier (skin processor) or a jeweller (cords for pearl chains). Crochet threads (needlework stores) are also highly suitable, as they are available in a wide range of accurately calibrated diameters. Take care! Never use synthetic threads (nylon etc.), and never use plastic blocks. Wooden blocks are offered by several firms, but they all have in common the fact that the number of sizes of block offered is too limited, and that their blocks are too angular for ships earlier than about 1815; this means you will have to modify them all (see BLOCKS).

Things look better with round deadeyes – thank goodness, for they are almost impossible to make if you don't have a lathe – but this path unhappily leads to a dead end if you are searching for triangular deadeyes, hearts and all the special forms of block – sheet blocks, ramshead blocks, clew-line blocks, fiddle blocks etc. – and the only way out is to make them yourself.

Wooden belaying pins are often slightly too thick, and need to be slimmed down, although brass belaying pins of good quality are obtainable. They can only be used for ships after 1830.

Blocks, deadeyes, cleats, belaying pins etc. were almost always a medium to dark brown in colour (not black), which can easily be obtained by staining. One little tip here: thread the blocks, deadeyes etc. onto a thin thread and dip the lot in the stain. Then hang up the thread and let them dry out before using them.

Contemporary model of an early 17th century ship, possibly of Continental origin, in the Ashmolean Collection at Oxford

Ropes

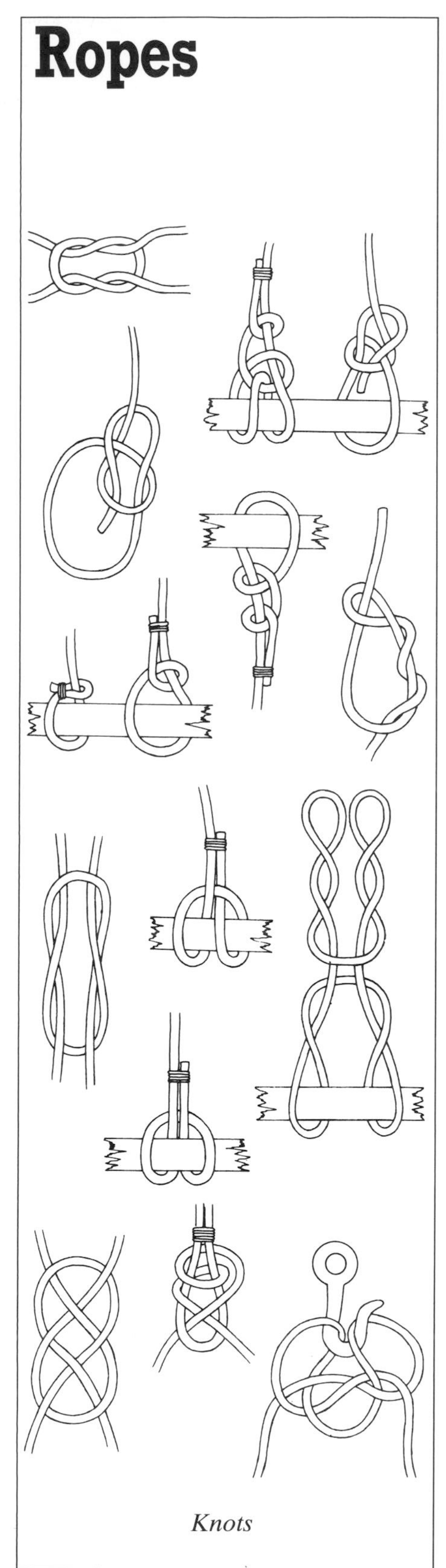
Knots

When dealing with ropework the first distinction we have to draw is between hemp ropes and wire ropes. All ropes were laid up from three or more strands which were in turn laid up from a number of yarns. With right-handed ropes the strands are left-handed and the yarns right-handed – and vice versa. The dimensions for ropework in old books always refer to the circumference of the rope – not the diameter.

Right hand lay – left hand lay

Here is a list of the most important types of cordage:

Yarns: strands twisted up right handed – whippings, light seizings, worming, etc.

Lines: ropes under 1 inch circumference – heavy seizings, worming, ratlines, etc.

Ropes: 1. 3 stranded right handed (hawser laid) – general purpose cordage.
2. 3 stranded left handed – alternative to 1. but more flexible – main use gun tackles.
3. Cable laid (left handed) – sometimes used for starboard side standing rigging.
4. Shroud laid (right or left handed) – 4 stranded with a centre core – sometimes used for shrouds – the term was also used to denote right handed rope used for larboard or port side standing rigging when cable laid rope was used for the starboard side.

Cablets: 3 right handed ropes laid up left handed – under 9in circumference – stays, towlines, hawsers, small anchor cables.

Cables: as cablets, but over 9in – anchor cables.

Commercially available threads are invariably laid right, and the conscientious model builder will find it necessary to build his own small rope walk, as shown on the right, or buy one from a good specialist shop, so that he can lay his own ropes. The trouble and expense are certainly worth it, since the crux of building a model to a high standard of fidelity is taking the trouble to get the small details right – such as the direction of laying his ropes.

From the 16th century on, parts of a rope which were subject to heavy wear were wrapped with three separate layers; this is another fine detail, like worming, which is only to be found on really good model ships. The rope would first be wormed, then wrapped round with tarred cloth (parcelling) – for modelling purposes the cloth can be omitted – and finally "served" by wrapping round tightly with yarn. The small jig shown on the right is not difficult to make, and makes this task far easier.

Wire ropes

Wire ropes came into use for the standing rigging after 1850, and for the running rigging not before 1870. The thickness of the metal ropes was always ⅓ of the thickness of the corresponding hemp rope. For modelling purposes metal ropes should not be represented by hemp cords.

Material for cordage

Hemp was the basic material, the best coming from Russia, and later from India. From 1830 Manila hemp was often used. All ropes with a few exceptions, such as tiller ropes and signal halliards, were tarred and therefore appear dark brown in colour. Running rigging would not normally be tarred again after manufacture and over a period of time, exposed to the elements, it would lighten in colour. Standing rigging however was re-tarred or "blacked down" at fairly frequent intervals and consequently darkened with time becoming almost black. The best way of colouring the ropes is to use a suitable stain, in which the rope is left for a few days, and then allowed to dry out thoroughly – at least a week.

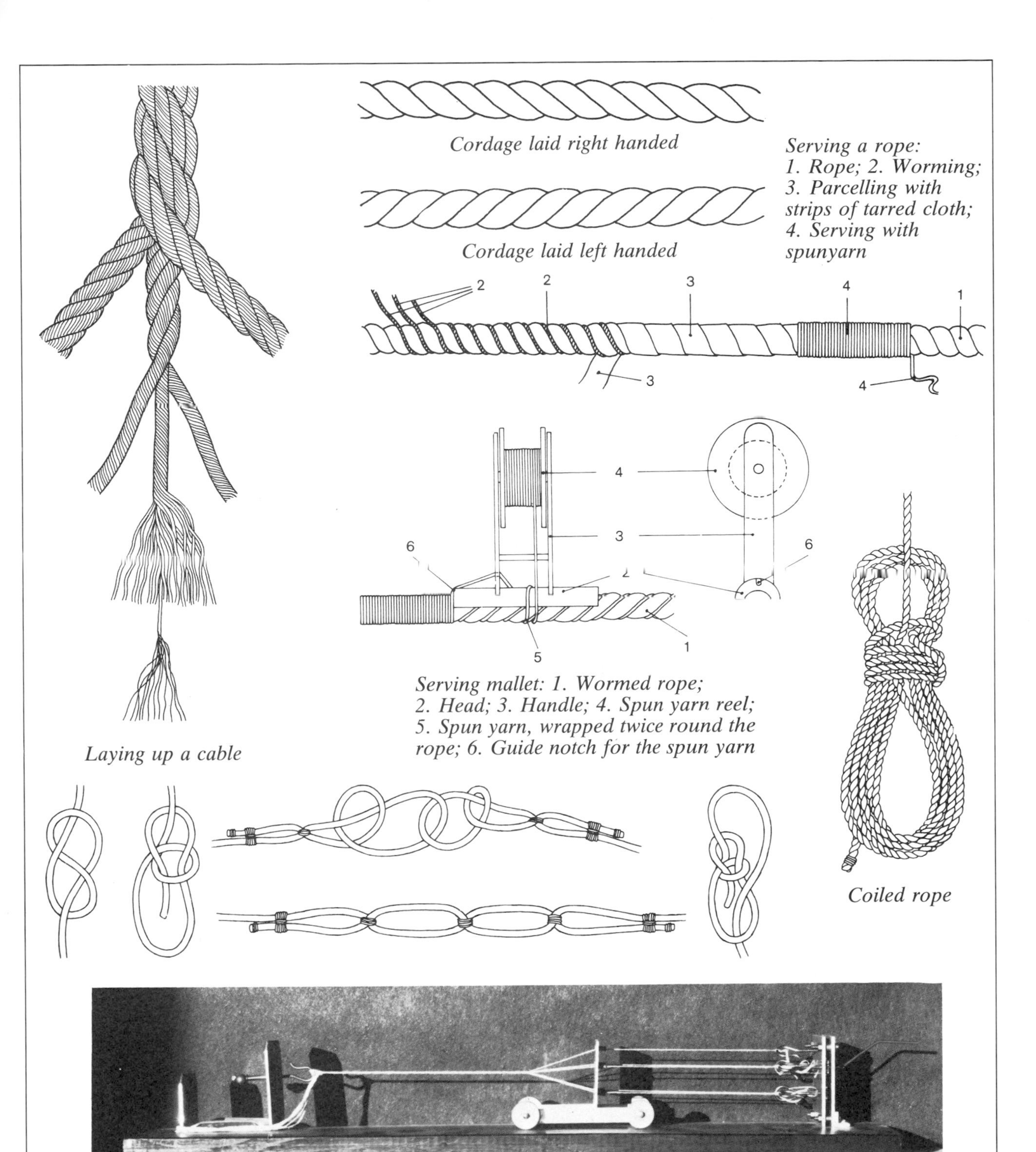

Cordage laid right handed

Cordage laid left handed

Serving a rope: 1. Rope; 2. Worming; 3. Parcelling with strips of tarred cloth; 4. Serving with spunyarn

Laying up a cable

Serving mallet: 1. Wormed rope; 2. Head; 3. Handle; 4. Spun yarn reel; 5. Spun yarn, wrapped twice round the rope; 6. Guide notch for the spun yarn

Coiled rope

Rope walk (rope-making jig) for modelling. The components have been placed close together for the photograph; the length of the rope track should be at least 4 to 5 feet. On the right are the rotating hooks (whirls) for the individual strands (fixed). On the left the hook to hold the rope (must be able to move, as the rope contracts in length when being laid). In the middle is the traveller, which ensures that the strands are wound together evenly

Anchor cables

The anchor cables were clinched to the anchor ring and led inboard through the hawse holes. (see CORDAGE).
One point to remember is that the cables have to be secured inboard, and have to be led out via the hawse holes before the main deck is sealed, if the model depicts the ship in harbour. At sea the cables were unclinched from the anchors and stowed below, the hawse holes being plugged from inboard by wooden bucklers.

Stoppers

In the 19th century the anchor cables and various other ropes of the standing and running rigging were replaced by chains. For the standing and running rigging (bobstay, bow stay, sheets etc.) plain chains (i.e. not stud-link chains) were always used. The thickness of the chains was 0·6 x the corresponding rope. From 1840 anchor chains were of the stud-link type. Their thickness varied according to the ship's tonnage – see table.
Chains were manufactured in specific lengths: 25·00m Continental, 12½ fathoms British. Each length ended in a plain link, which was attached to the next length by means of a shackle. To avoid the chain getting knotted up when the ship swung round at anchor, swivels were added at both ends of complete cables.
Brass chains are available in model shops, and silver chains from jewellers. The studs have to be soldered in by the modeller (use solder paste). The chains should be thoroughly blackened.

Stud-link anchor chains

Sailing ships tons	Chain thickness mm	Max. Load tons	Chain length fathoms (m)	Steam ships tons
50	17·5	8,500	120 (222·24)	75
100	20·6	11,885	135 (256·02)	150
150	23·8	15,800	165 (305·58)	225
200	27·0	20,300	165 (305·58)	300
300	30·2	25,375	195 (361·14)	450
400	33·3	31,000	210 (388·92)	600
500	36·5	37,125	240 (444·48)	750
600	38·1	40,500	240 (444·48)	900
700	39·7	43,900	270 (500·04)	1050
800	41·3	47,500	270 (500·04)	1200
1000	44·4	55,150	270 (500·04)	1500
1200	46·0	59,125	270 (500·04)	1800
1400	47·6	63,250	270 (500·04)	2100
1600	49·2	67,500	270 (500·04)	2400
1800	50·8	72,000	270 (500·04)	2700
2000	52·4	76,500	270 (500·04)	3000
2500	55·6	86,125	300 (555·60)	3750
3000 and more	58·7	96,250	300 (555·60)	4500 and more

(Table based on details from Lloyd's Register circa 1860).

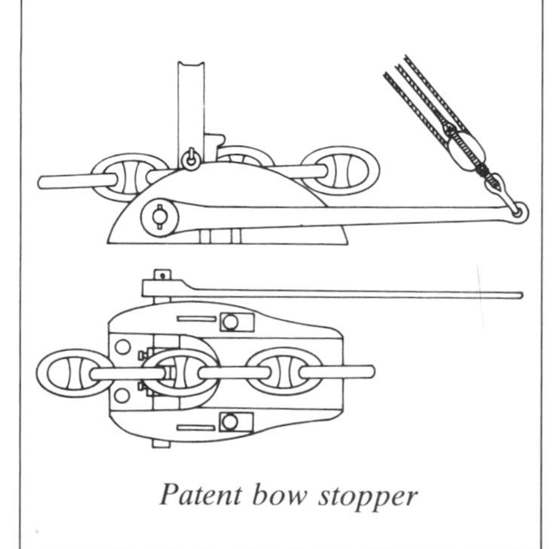

Patent bow stopper

Algerian Xebec,
18th century

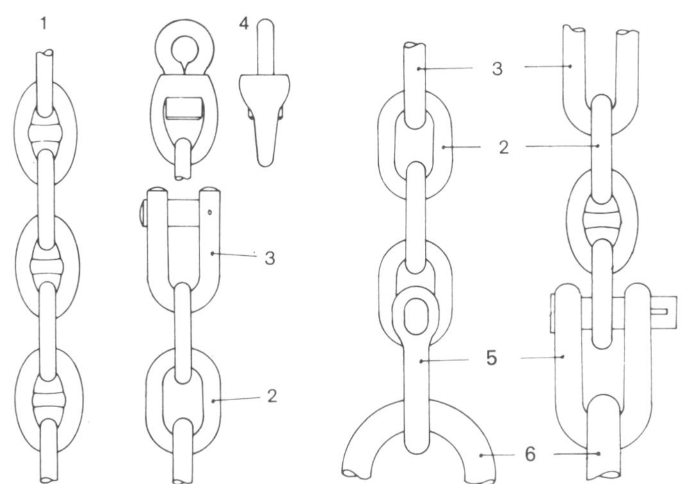

Chain cables: 1. Stud-link chain; 2. End link; 3. Shackle; 4. Chain swivel; 5. Anchor shackle; 6. Anchor ring

Blocks

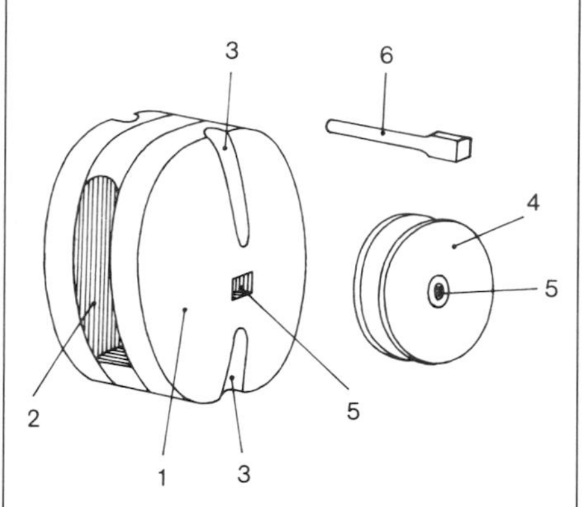

Block: 1. Shell; 2. Swallow; 3. Score; 4. Sheave; 5. Bush; 6. Pin

The rigging of a sailing ship is operated with blocks and tackles. For a three-master around 1,000 blocks were required, of which the largest (the Voyol blocks) was up to 5 feet long in a three decker, and the smallest (the signal halliard block) only 3ins.
A block consists of a shell – this could be made in one piece or assembled from several components – which was always made of wood until the middle of the 19th century. After this time the shell was occasionally made of metal. The shell contained a pulley, or sheave, over which the rope ran, and which rotated on a pin. The manufacture of blocks with rotating pulleys is hardly to be recommended – except for very large-scale models – and is technically well-nigh impossible in any case.
The drawing on the right illustrates how model blocks are made: they are first cut from a strip of very hard, dense wood (box, walnut, perhaps pear or olive) to the width and thickness of the blocks. Using a circular saw (indispensable for making blocks) cut crosswise grooves spaced out along the length of the strip (do not cut right through). The grooves for the swallows and for the strops are cut next, again using the circular saw, and the holes for the ropes drilled. The edges are rounded off with glasspaper, and the cross-cuts between the blocks widened with a triangular file. The individual blocks can now be separated from the strip, and sanded to a more rounded shape.
Until 1815 blocks were generally rounded in shape; on merchant ships they remained so until later, while warships after 1815 preferred a more angular shape of block. There were also a whole series of special block shapes:
Ramshead blocks (see HALYARDS), lift blocks (see LIFTS), shoe blocks, sheet and shoulder blocks (see SHEETS), clew-line blocks (see CLEW LINES) and snatch blocks (see BOWLINES).
Sheet blocks and lift blocks were only used on the Continent, British practice was to use individual blocks stropped together instead (see RUNNING RIGGING).

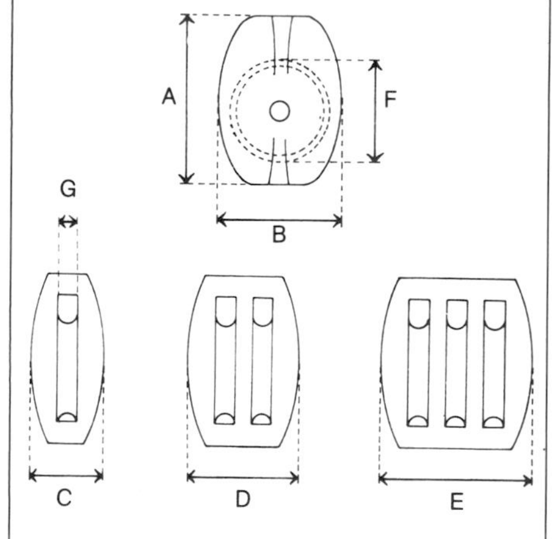

Block sizes
Sizes of blocks are given in mm.
The information given here is an approximate guide as variations temporal and national have not been included. There was also a certain tendency to make blocks for rope thicknesses of 6 to 13mm rather larger, and from 38 to 76mm rather smaller, than stated.

Rope dia.	A Height	B Width	C Thickness 1	D Thickness 2	E Thickness 3	F Sheave dia.	G Swallow	Strop dia.
6	72	60	40	53	66	33	7·2	6
8	96	80	53	70	88	44	9·6	8
11	132	110	73	97	121	61	13·2	11
13	156	130	86	114	143	72	15·6	13
16	192	160	106	141	176	88	19·2	16
19	228	190	125	167	209	105	22·8	19
25	300	250	165	220	275	138	30·0	25
32	384	320	211	282	352	176	38·4	38
38	456	380	251	334	418	209	45·6	44
51	612	510	337	449	561	281	61·2	57
63	756	630	416	554	693	347	75·6	76
76	912	760	502	669	836	418	91·2	89

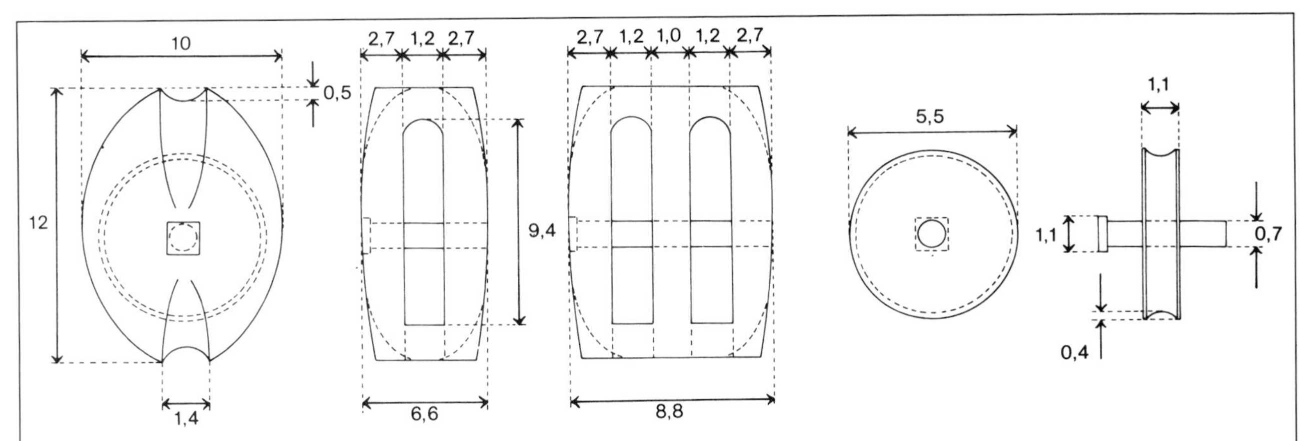

Proportions of a block (Continental practice). The dimensions refer to a rope thickness of 1.

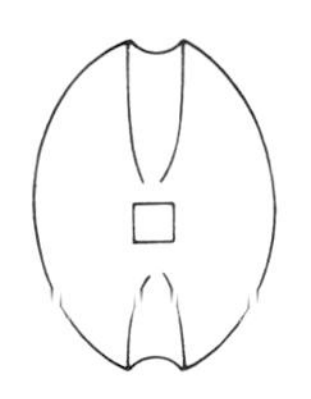

Block with strop score

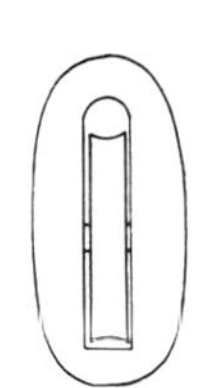

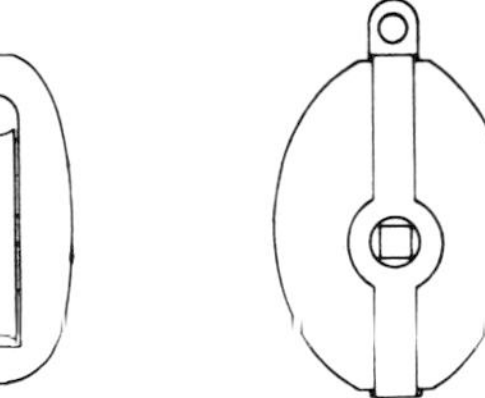

Standard until 1815, thereafter on merchant ships (Continental)

Block with metal strop

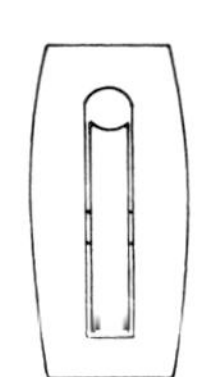

19th century warships (Continental)

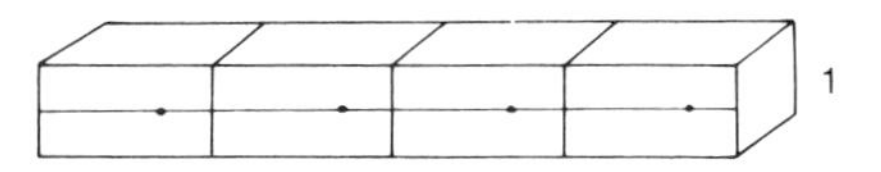

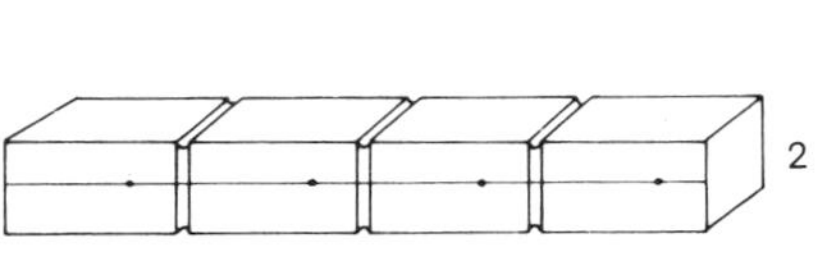

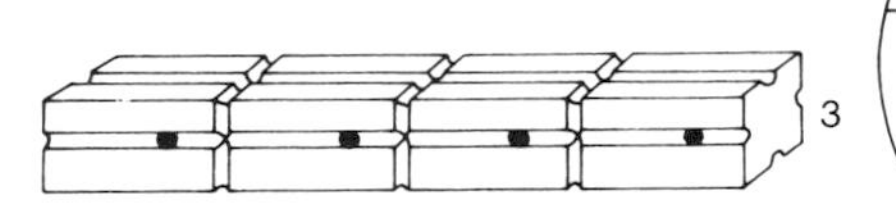

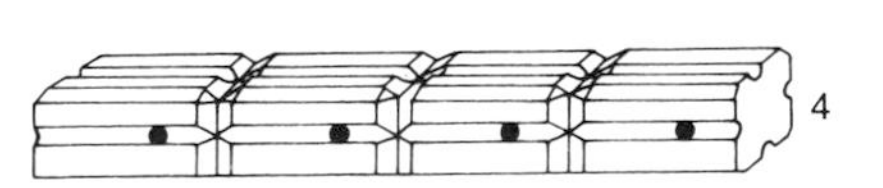

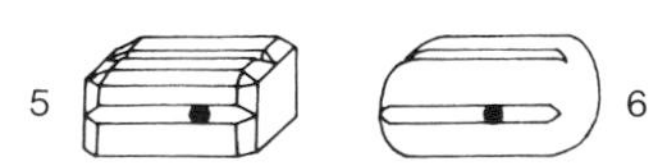

Making model blocks:
1. Wood strip; 2. Cut across grooves; 3. Drill holes and cut swallows and scores; 4. Chamfer the edges; 5. Separate blocks; 6. Round off all edges

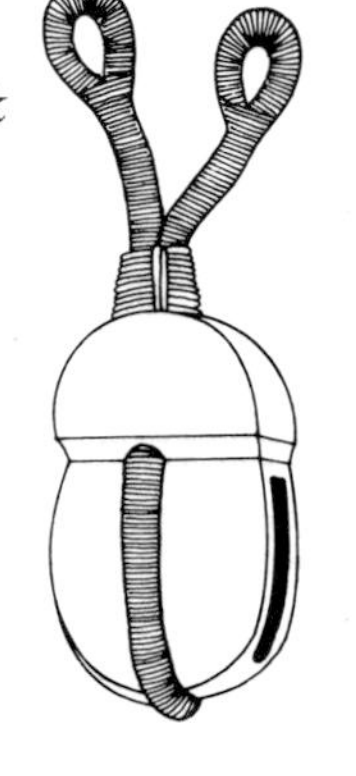

Clew-line block

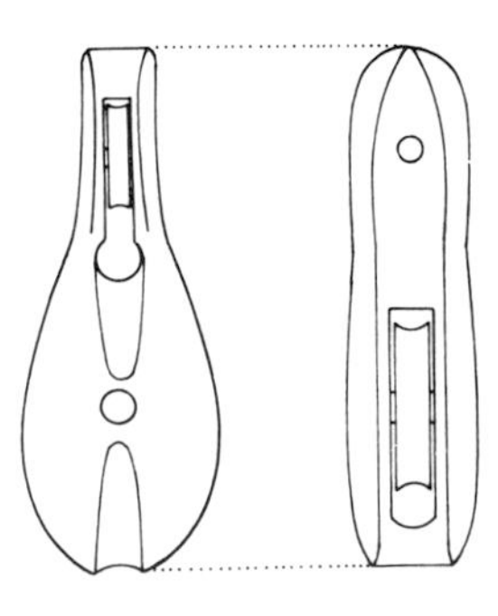

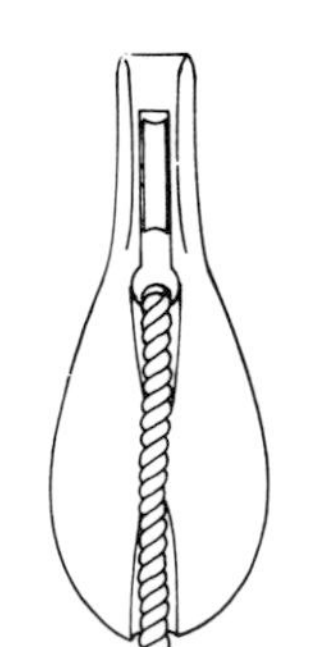

Sheet block (after Vaisseau)

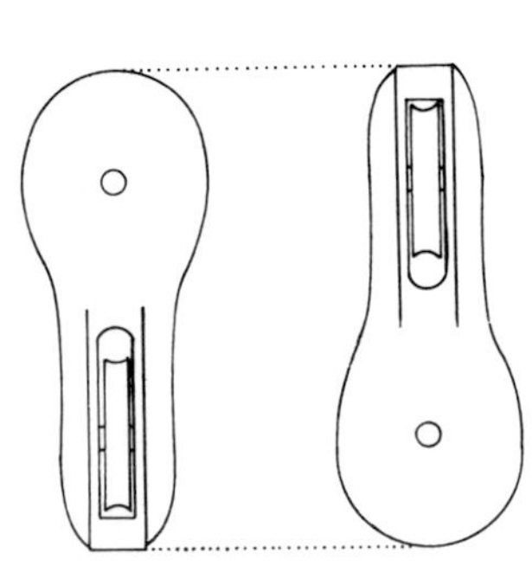

Shoe block (after Vaisseau)

Block strops

Almost all blocks were stropped, i.e. they were bound in a spliced loop of rope, which formed an eye above the block by which it was fixed. If the standing end of a tackle started at a block, then either the block was fitted with a second strop eye, or the standing end was eye spliced round the strop. Heavily loaded blocks were fitted with double strops.
The strops are impossible to splice neatly, owing to their small size, so the best method is to lay the rope loop out so that its ends are twisted into each other slightly, and then glue the ends together. The glued area is then carefully situated so that it is concealed by the seizing. If the strop is served, be sure to do this before binding the block. After placing the block in the loop, the excess is bound together with a seizing to form an eye.

Deadeyes

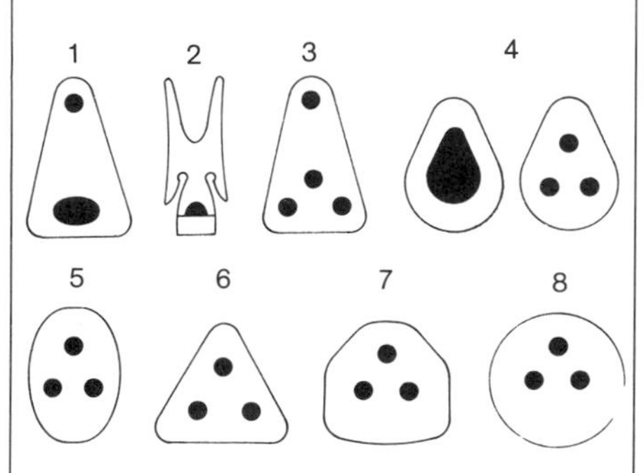

Deadeyes: 1. Ancient Roman; 2. 9-/10th century Viking; 3. 11-/13th century; 4. 12-15th century; 5. 12-15th century; 6. 15-16th century; 7. First half of 17th century; 8. After mid-17th century

All shrouds, and some backstays and stays, were set up, or tensioned, by means of deadeyes. In ancient times the deadeyes were longish in shape, and looked very similar to hearts. In the Middle Ages they were of similar shape, with an opening at the top for the shroud, and three holes at the bottom for the tackle lanyard. In the 15th century the deadeyes were triangular and rather flat, and the shroud was laid in a groove called the score round the deadeye. From the middle of the 17th century on round deadeyes came into use; they were also more curved in profile.
The diameter of the deadeyes was half as great as that of the masts to which they belonged, and sometimes slightly larger. Triangular deadeyes are made in a similar fashion to blocks. Grooves are cut in a triangular sectioned wood strip, using a circular saw, and then filed out slightly. The deadeyes are then cut off and hand sanded to final shape.
Round deadeyes can be made from round dowel, using a similar method, although the use of a lathe makes the job much easier.
If this machine is not available, your first recourse should be to the model shop for suitable items. The holes in the deadeyes are best drilled using a jig. The method of turning in the shrouds in the deadeyes is described in detail in the section SHROUDS.

Hearts

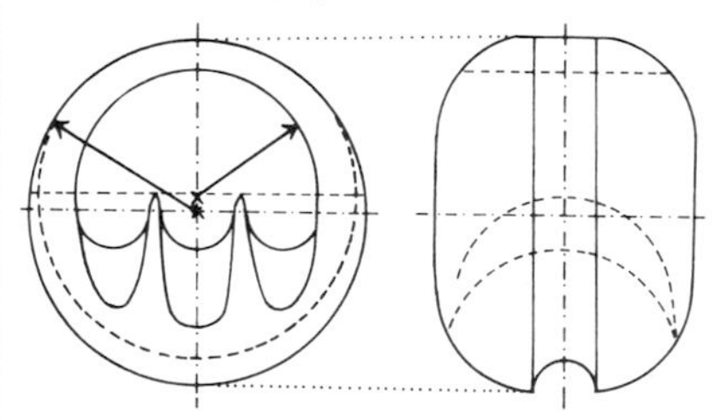

Hearts have been in use since the Middle Ages, if not since ancient times, if you include the earliest form of deadeye. From the late 17th century on they enjoyed increasing popularity. Until the early 19th century the hearts were heart-shaped, but thereafter mostly round. Their diameter corresponded to that of deadeyes. Hearts have a large opening in the middle, and usually 4 grooves to guide the lanyard; from the end of the 18th century hearts began to appear with 6 or 7 grooves to take the same number of lanyard turns. The hearts were stropped in a similar manner to the deadeyes.

Fiddle block

In some cases fiddle blocks were used instead of double blocks. Alternatively two single blocks were stropped together, one larger and one smaller, and one above the other. The running part always ran first through the smaller, then through the larger block.

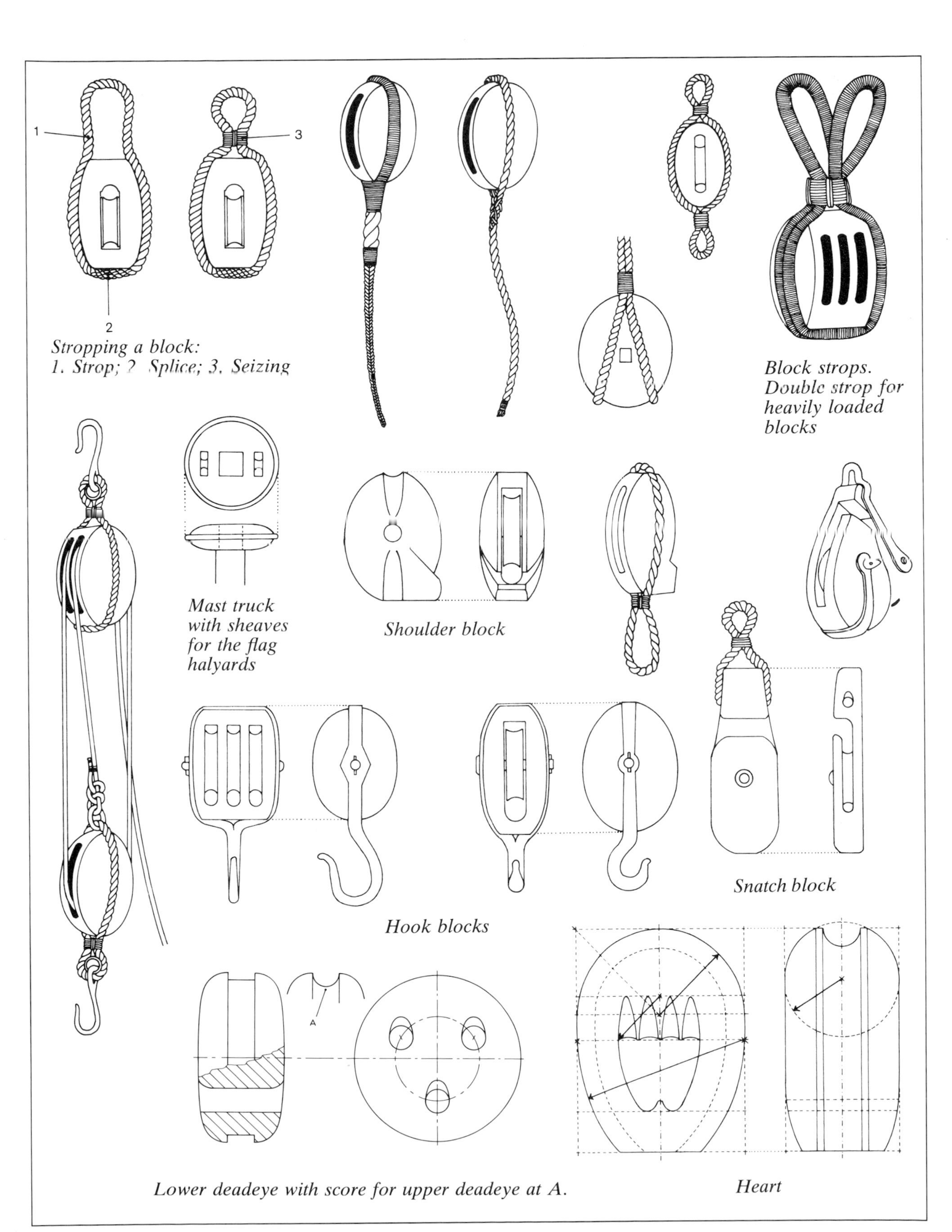

Stropping a block: 1. Strop; 2. Splice; 3. Seizing

Block strops. Double strop for heavily loaded blocks

Mast truck with sheaves for the flag halyards

Shoulder block

Hook blocks

Snatch block

Lower deadeye with score for upper deadeye at A.

Heart

Belaying pins

All the smaller sizes of rope were made fast to belaying pins, which were plugged into pin rails, the fife rails, or the rails. Until 1830 shouldered belaying pins were always made of wood, and thereafter sometimes of metal. Metal belaying pins which were a force fit in the pin rails and which tapered slightly towards both ends were in use in the British Navy in the late 18th century.
Generally speaking, the lower diameter of a belaying pin was never less than the diameter of the rope which was to be belayed. As only one size of belaying pin was kept on board, its diameter was that of the thickest rope to be belayed. The proportions of the pins and the method of belaying the rope are illustrated on the right; excess rope was coiled up and hung over the pin – for the model builder it is often the best idea to make this coil of rope separately and then hang it over the pin.

Cleats

The ends of thicker ropes were belayed on cleats, but in ancient times, in the Middle Ages and in the Mediterranean, cleats were used exclusively, as belaying pins were unknown. The cleats were fixed to the deck and to the bulwark. After 1720 very long cleats were often attached to the masts, and other cleats were lashed to the shrouds with seizings.
The dimensions of the cleats given in the following table are in mm, and again the figures represent a guideline, and do not take possible variants into consideration.

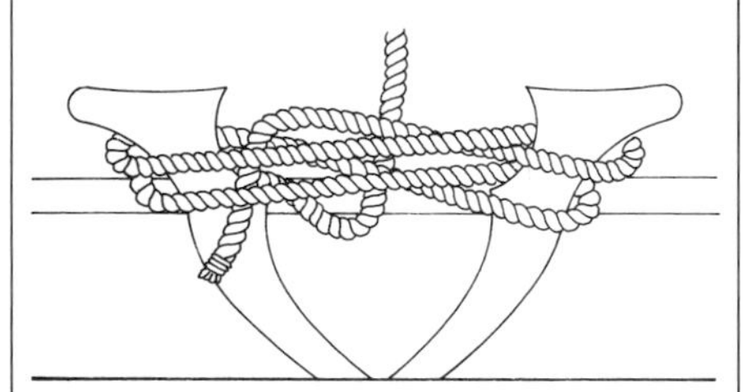

Belaying to a kevel

Rope dia.	A Length	B Height	C Width	Rope dia.	A Length	B Height	C Width
6	120	40	30	32	355	117	89
8	160	53	40	38	380	125	95
13	220	73	55	51	463	153	116
19	270	89	68	63	525	173	131
25	312	103	78	76	584	193	146

Thimbles

Trucks were used to guide ropes. They were lashed to the shrouds with a seizing. The hole was always big enough for the rope to run through it easily, and the outside diameter was three times that of the hole. The height was the same as the outside diameter.
From the 17th century onward, strop eyes generally incorporated a thimble. These thimbles were round and made of wood until the beginning of the 19th century, and after that time they were sometimes heart-shaped and made of metal.

Euphroes

The euphroes were long wooden rods or flat blocks which had drilled holes instead of sheaves. They served as guide blocks for the crow's feet. (See Stays, Back Stays, Topping Lifts, Clew Lines).

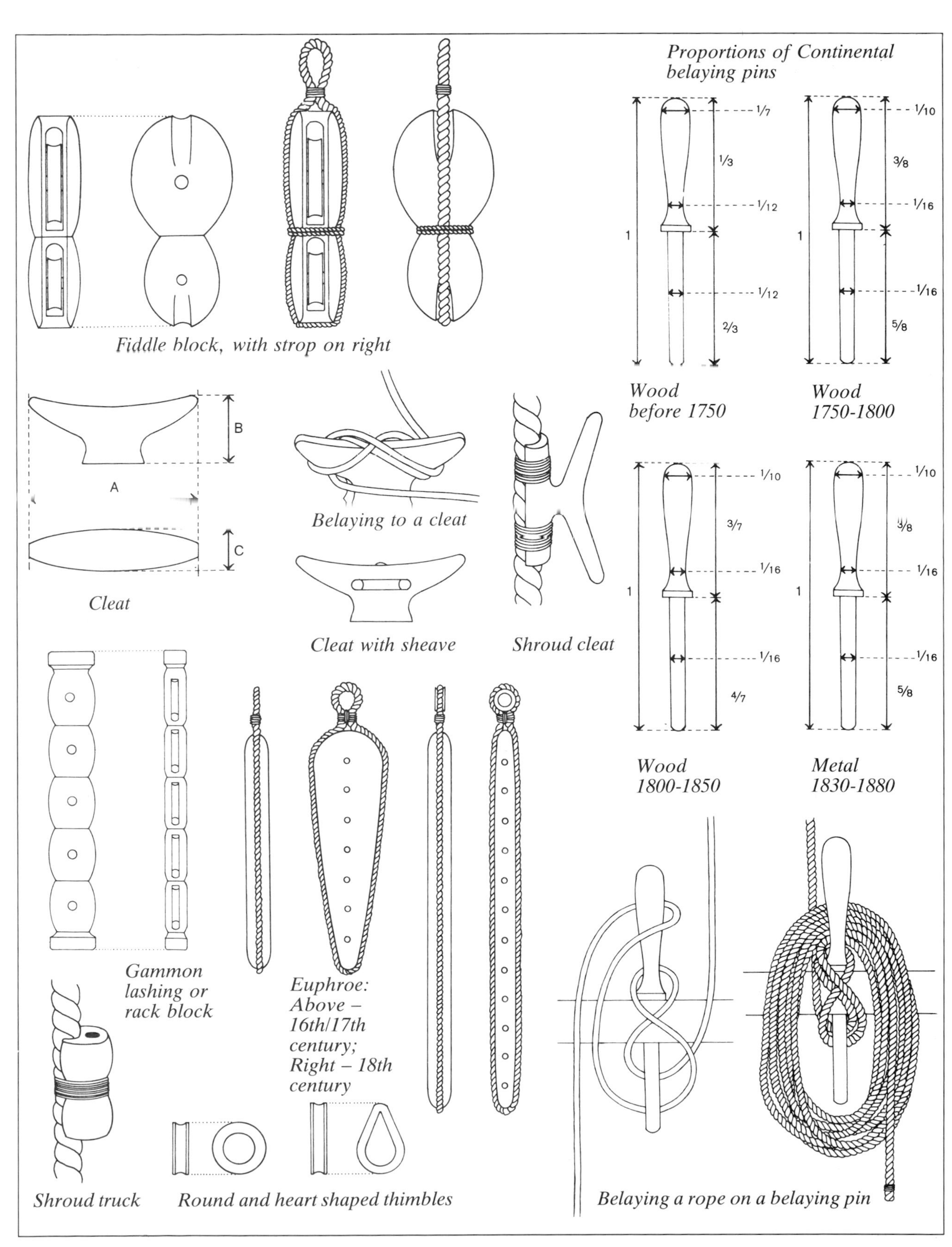
Fiddle block, with strop on right
Proportions of Continental belaying pins
1/7
1/3
1/12
1
1/12
2/3
1/10
3/8
1/16
1
1/16
5/8
Wood before 1750
Wood 1750-1800
B
A
C
Cleat
Belaying to a cleat
Cleat with sheave
Shroud cleat
1/10
3/7
1/16
1
1/16
4/7
1/10
3/8
1/16
1
1/16
5/8
Wood 1800-1850
Metal 1830-1880
Gammon lashing or rack block
Euphroe: Above – 16th/17th century; Right – 18th century
Shroud truck
Round and heart shaped thimbles
Belaying a rope on a belaying pin

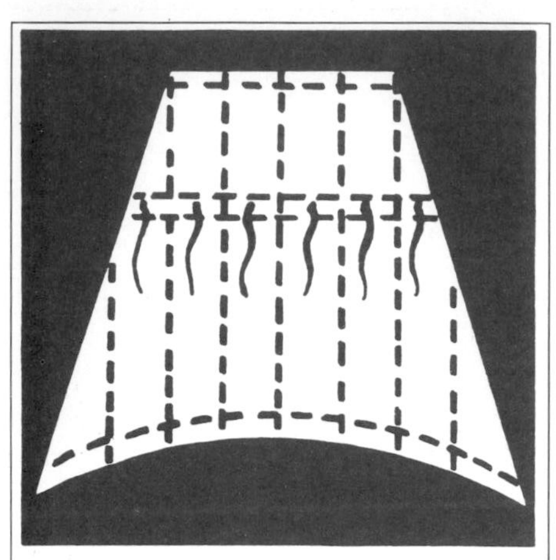

Sails

Sails · Names of sails · Sail colours · Sewing sails · Bolt ropes · Bonnets and reefs Bending · Gaff sails Staysails · Sprit sails Furled sails · Set of sails

As already mentioned at the beginning of this book in the section TYPES OF MODEL, there are many detail parts of the rigging which can only be shown if the model is fitted with sails. It is an unfortunate fact that the appearance of many model ships is made very much worse by their sails, and as they are very large items, the overall effect is even more disastrous. Hence the first commandment: take extra special care with the sails!

One of the main errors is the use of material which is too thick and too coarse – many model makers then claim that it was their intention to indicate the coarse structure of the woven sailcloth of genuine sails. In the section MATERIAL SCALE I have already mentioned that this is complete nonsense. If you reduce the woven structure of genuine sails by 48 or 72 times, it can hardly be seen at all. The best material to use for model ships' sailcoth is white cotton cambric, or some other very thin, lightweight, closely woven type of material, with as matt a surface as possible, but nevertheless not transparent. Buy plenty of the material, as you will use up a great deal of it cutting the sails to shape, not forgetting the seams and tabling. You will also need the sail linings and bands, which are often forgotten. Don't count your pennies here, as a few more shillings spent will save you a lot of trouble.

The dressing of the material can be washed out with warm water, which will also make the material more pliable. If you intend showing the sails furled on the yards, you should still remove the dressing. For small models, incidentally, Japanese tissue will be found to give a good effect.

The next stage is to tie the yards temporarily to the masts at the correct positions, and cut paper templates for the shape and profile of the sails. If one of your sails has a bonnet, cut the template to include this, and trim the whole sail to shape. When it fits correctly, you can separate the bonnet part.

When checking the size, the first thing to get right is the width of the sails. The head of the sail was always slightly less than the distance between the yard arms. In the case of the lower sails the shortfall was about 12ins on each side, and for the topgallant sails it was about 6ins on either side.

The foot of the sail, i.e. the distance between the clews, was the same length as the head of the sail immediately below it. The foot of the sail itself had the shape of an arc of a circle, so that it would not chafe against the deck erections, the rail, the stays or the top crow's feet. The height of this arc or roach was 0·04 to 0·05 x the width of the foot of the sail. British warship sails, other than courses, in the 18th and early 19th century had no roach.

Until the beginning of the 19th century the sails were quite markedly bellied – the older the more so – then after 1830 they became rather flat. Check the belly of your sails with the paper profile templates, and please note that a sail was less bellied the higher up on the mast it was located.

If the sails are to look right, it is important to get the direction of the material's weave correct. It always runs parallel to the length of the individual cloths, to which we will return shortly. On square sails the weave always runs perpendicular to the yard (i.e. vertical).

In the case of lateen, stay, gaff and lug sails the weave always ran parallel to the leach, i.e. parallel to the side of the sail facing the stern.

Cutter of the British navy around 1780

Sail names

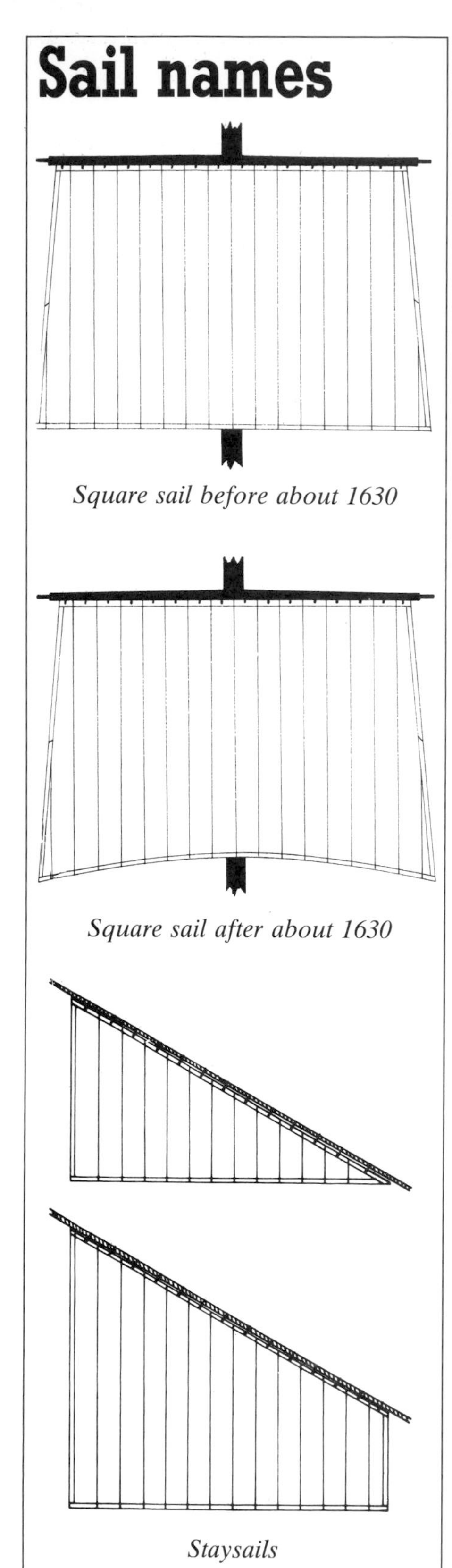

Square sail before about 1630

Square sail after about 1630

Staysails

One of your first tasks is to learn the names of the various sails, otherwise you will end up in a state of hopeless confusion – especially when you tackle the running rigging.
The two drawings on the right show the sails of ships before and after about 1830, with all the possible sails. This does not mean, of course, that all these sails were carried on every ship. The studding sails are only drawn in on the port side, although of course they were also fitted to starboard and they were differentiated by the prefix starboard or port.

Names of the sails on a ship before about 1830:
1. Spritsail course; 2. Spritsail topsail (on the right the arrangement commonly used before 1715).
3. Outer jib; 4. Inner jib; 5. Fore topmast staysail.
6. Forecourse; 7. Fore topsail; 8. Fore topgallant sail; 9. Fore royal sail; 10. Fore lower studding sail; 11. Fore topmast studding sail; 12. Fore topgallant studding sail.
13. Main staysail; 14. Main topmast staysail; 15. Middle staysail; 16. Main topgallant staysail.
17. Main course; 18. Main topsail; 19. Main topgallant sail; 20. Main royal sail (studding sails as fore studding sails).
21. Mizen staysail; 22. Mizen topmast staysail.
23. Mizen course; 24. Mizen topsail; 25. Mizen topgallant sail.

Names of the sails on a ship after about 1830:
1. Flying jib; 2. Outer jib; 3. Inner jib; 4. Fore topmast staysail.
5. Fore course; 6. Fore lower topsail; 7. Fore upper topsail; 8. Fore lower topgallant sail; 9. Fore upper topgallant sail; 10. Fore royal sail; 11. Fore skysail; 12. Fore lower studding sail; 13. Fore topmast studding sail; 14. Fore topgallant studding sail; 15. Fore royal studding sail.
16. Main staysail; 17. Main topmast staysail; 18. Middle staysail; 19. Main topgallant staysail; 20. Main royal staysail.
21. Main course; 22. Main lower topsail; 23. Main upper topsail; 24. Main lower topgallant sail; 25. Main upper topgallant sail; 26. Main royal sail; 27. Main skysail; 28. Main moonsail (studding sails as fore studding sails).
29. Mizen staysail; 30. Mizen topmast staysail; 31. Mizen topgallant staysail; 32. Mizen royal staysail.
33. Mizen course; 34. Mizen lower topsail; 35. Mizen upper topsail; 36. Mizen lower topgallant sail; 37. Mizen upper topgallant sail; 38. Mizen royal sail; 39. Mizen skysail.
40. Mizen staysail; 41. Mizen topmast staysail; 42. Mizen topgallant staysail.
43. Spanker; 44. Gaff topsail.

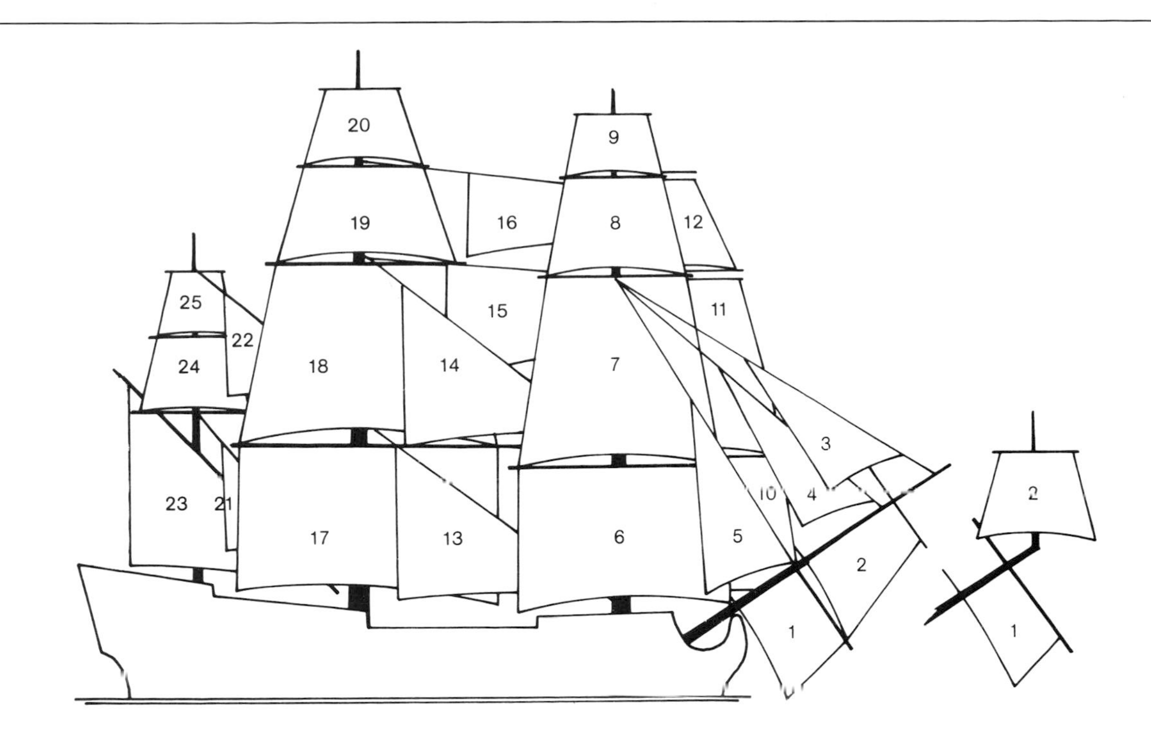

Names of sails on a ship before 1800 (right: bowsprit before 1715)

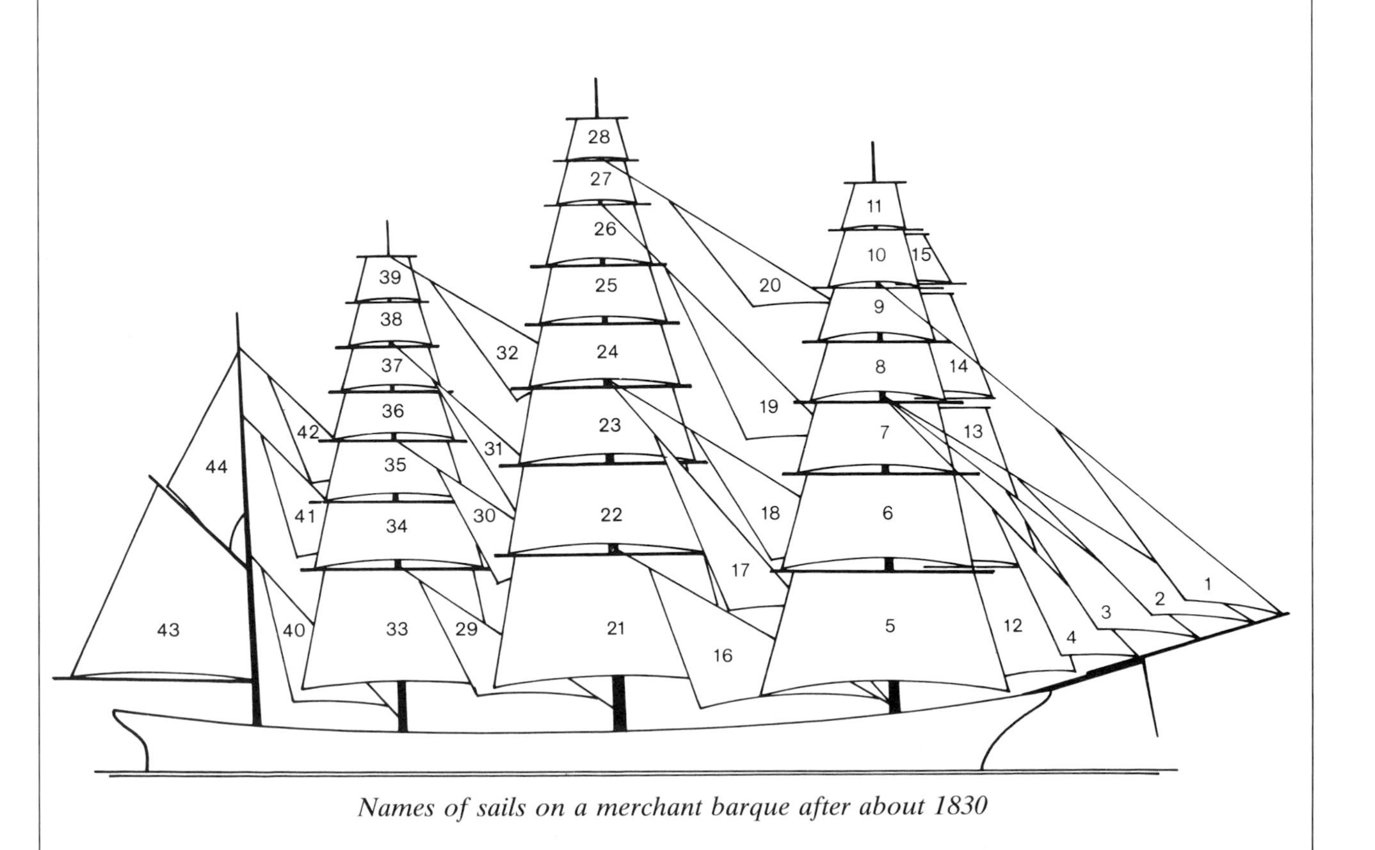

Names of sails on a merchant barque after about 1830

Sail colours

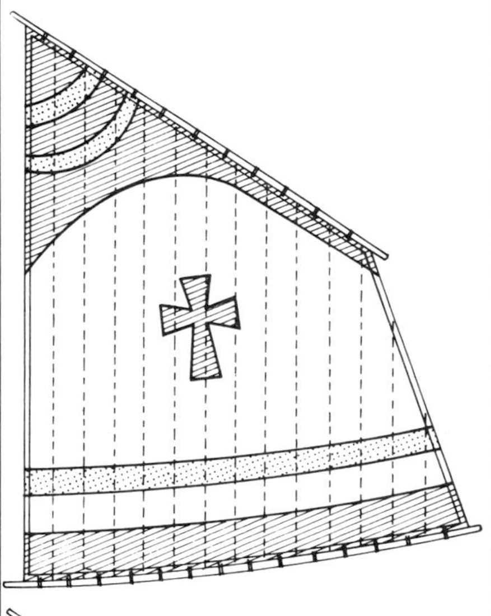

Colourful lug sails. Native to the North Adriatic, the Venice area, and the Dalmatian coast from the Middle Ages to the present day.

White sails on the horizon are an almost indispensable component of any adventure story involving sea travel.
Alas, with the exception of modern sport sailing boats and luxury yachts, sails have never been white! The colours range from the very light yellow ochre of unbleached linen via an infinite variety of greyish and yellowish ochres right up to more or less strong red, including the red-brown to medium brown of tanned sails. For a period it was not uncommon to find multi-coloured sails; in the Mediterranaean they can still be found to this day, although you should note that such decorations were very rarely woven into the cloth, dye or paint being the usual medium. It is a waste of time trying to obtain suitable sailcloth in exactly the right colour, unless you need real red or red/brown to brown sails. In all other cases it makes more sense to buy the fabric white, and dye it the desired shade yourself.
The ideal dyestuff for this purpose is tea. The best method is as follows: make the tea, and allow it to brew until it has acquired the desired colour; then pour it into a bowl through a sieve. The material intended for the sails is then placed in the liquid while the tea is still warm (it is more effective when warm). The material is then left in the dye bath for about 20 to 30 seconds, taking great care to saturate all the area. The material is then taken out of the bowl, and hung up on a clothes line while still dripping wet (do not wring). It can be ironed when it is almost dry, after which the sails can be cut to size and sewn up. Be sure to dye plenty of material for all the sails at one time, as each successive dyeing will inevitably produce a slightly different shade, which would spoil the appearance of the finished model. Which tea to use depends on the shade desired; there are many types, from Russian smoked tea via the green China teas to the various herb teas. There is only one method for establishing which type will produce the ideal shade for your sails: experiment.
If the sail is red and white, yellow and white, green and white or blue and white striped, as often on Mediterranean or Viking ships, or is painted with coats of arms, figures, ornaments and similar, as was popular on ships from the Middle Ages until the early 17th century, the sails are first dyed overall as described, then sewn up, and finally the other colours are applied.
The best paints to use are water colours or tempera paints. They are applied fairly thin, but no so thin that they run. If the paint is too dry, it will not penetrate the material, and will tend to flake off all too easily later. It is best to try out this procedure on a few scraps of material. If the colour does not run when you apply it, and does not flake off when dry if you flex the material, the proportion of water is just right.
If you have "aged" your ship's hull, the sails will also have to be given corresponding treatment. Chemicals are little use here. But if you subject your sails to the effects of sun, wind, rain and snow, they will soon acquire the right "age". Traces of soot on sails in the vicinity of funnels are applied very carefully by means of a sooty candle (hold a piece of metal in the flame). Hold the material far enough from the flame, to ensure that the soot is not too thick. Do not wipe or rub the material, but if there is too much soot, knock it off from the reverse side.

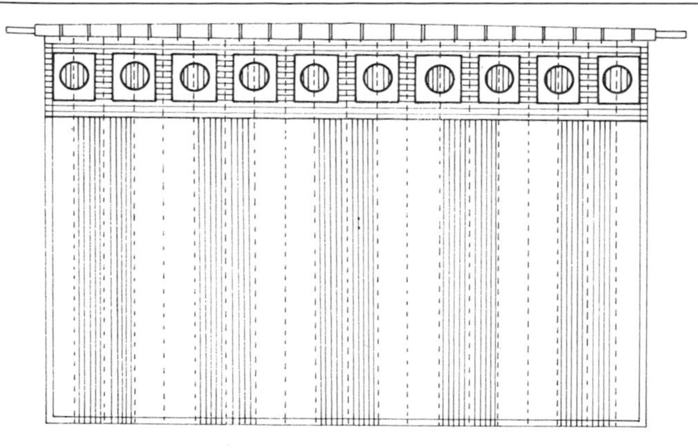

Norman Drakkar sail around 1066

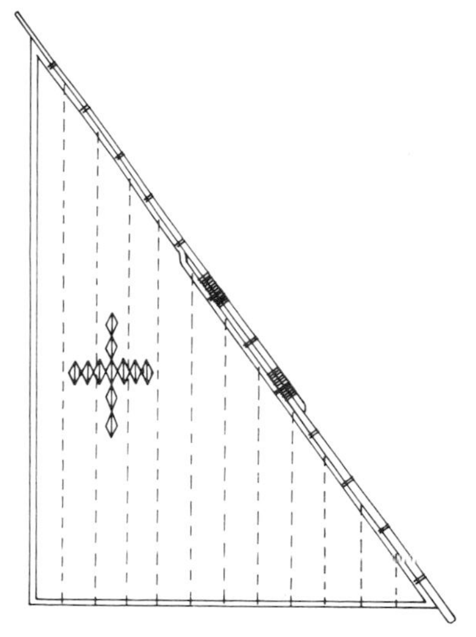

Sail from Pisa around 1350

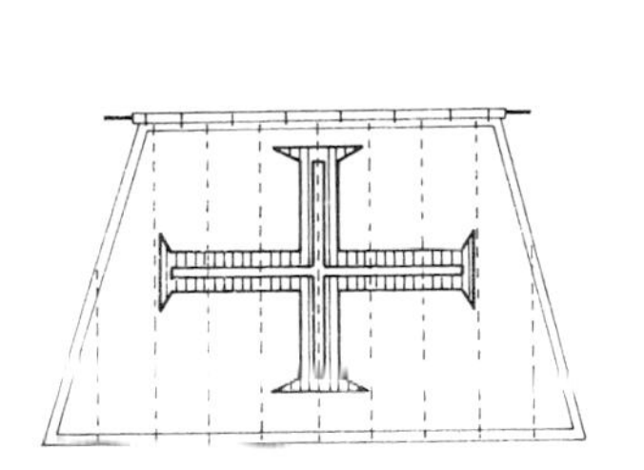

English heraldic display sail around 1426

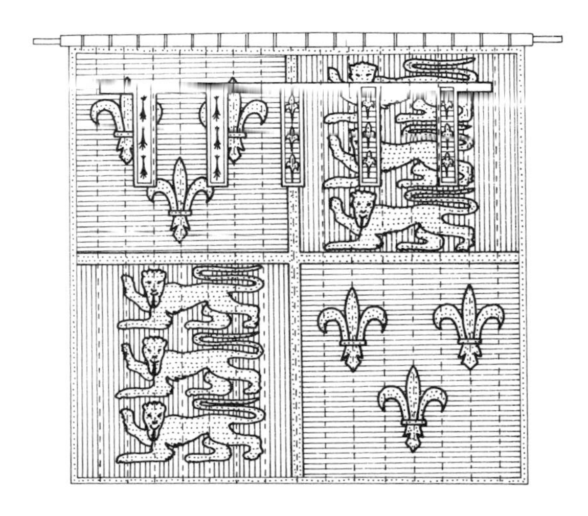

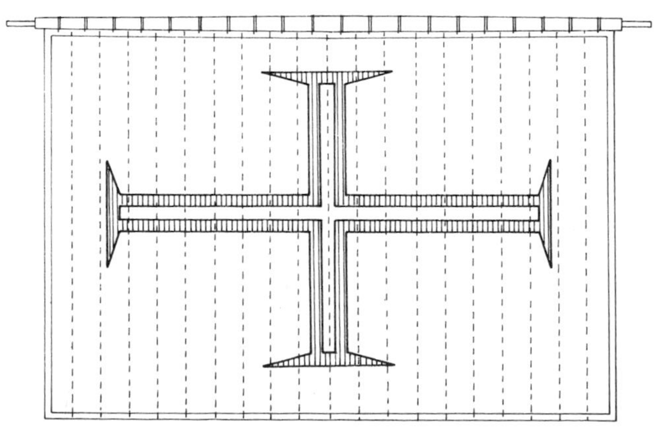

Portuguese main, top and topgallant sails of around 1500

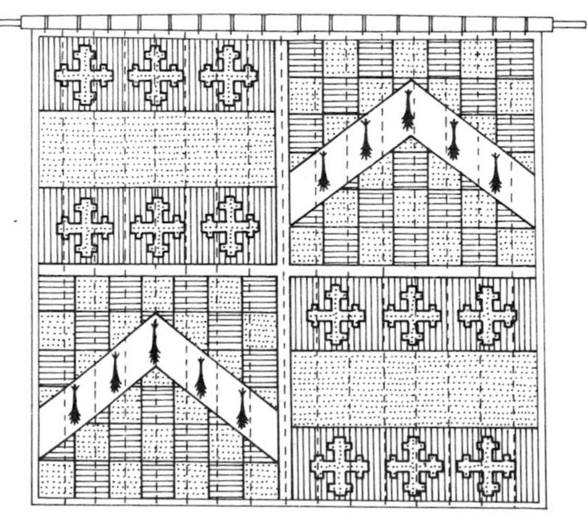

English heraldic display sail around 1485

Sail colours

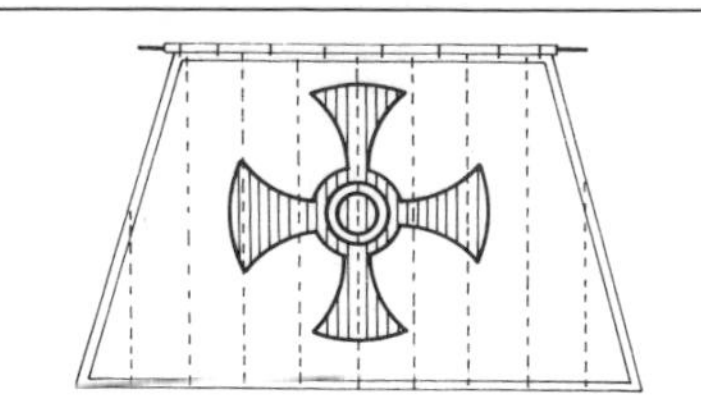

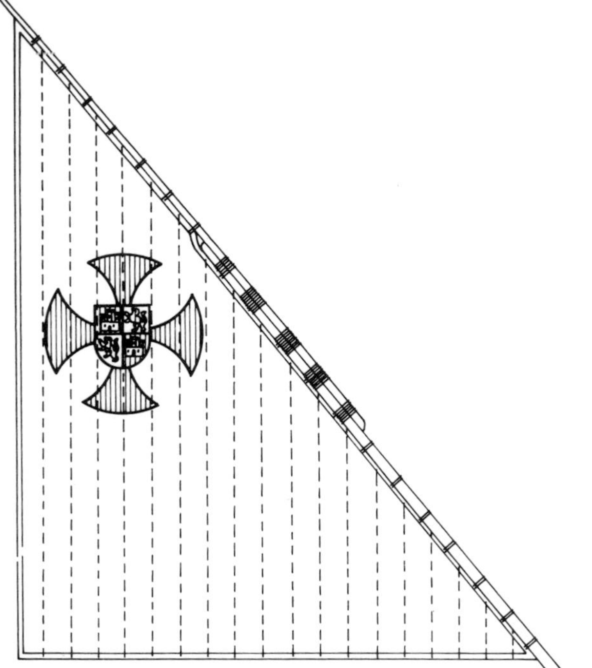

Spanish galley sail around 1550

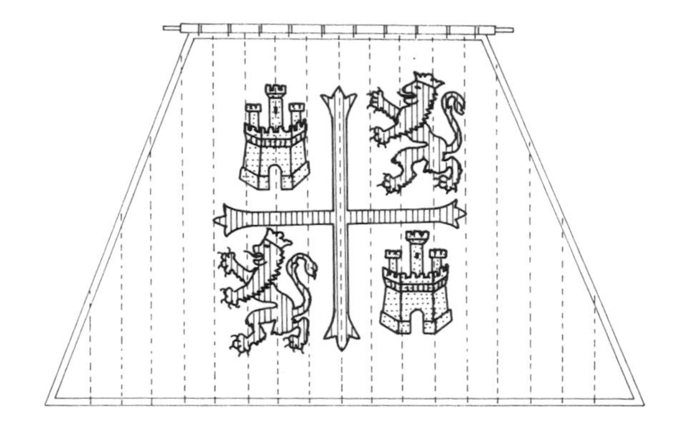

Spanish main, top and topgallant sails with coats of arms around 1540

English display sail of yellow damask around 1545

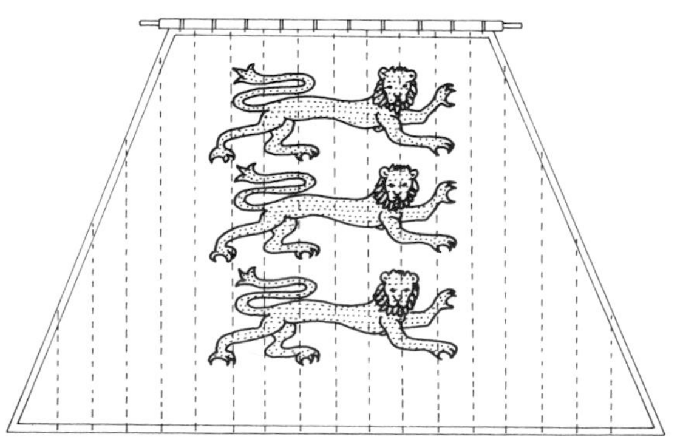

English heraldic sail around 1580

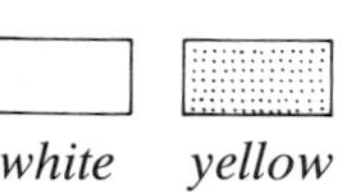 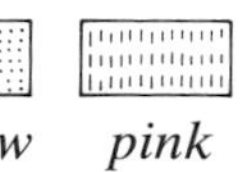 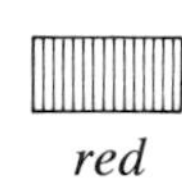 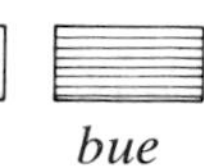  

white yellow pink red bue green black

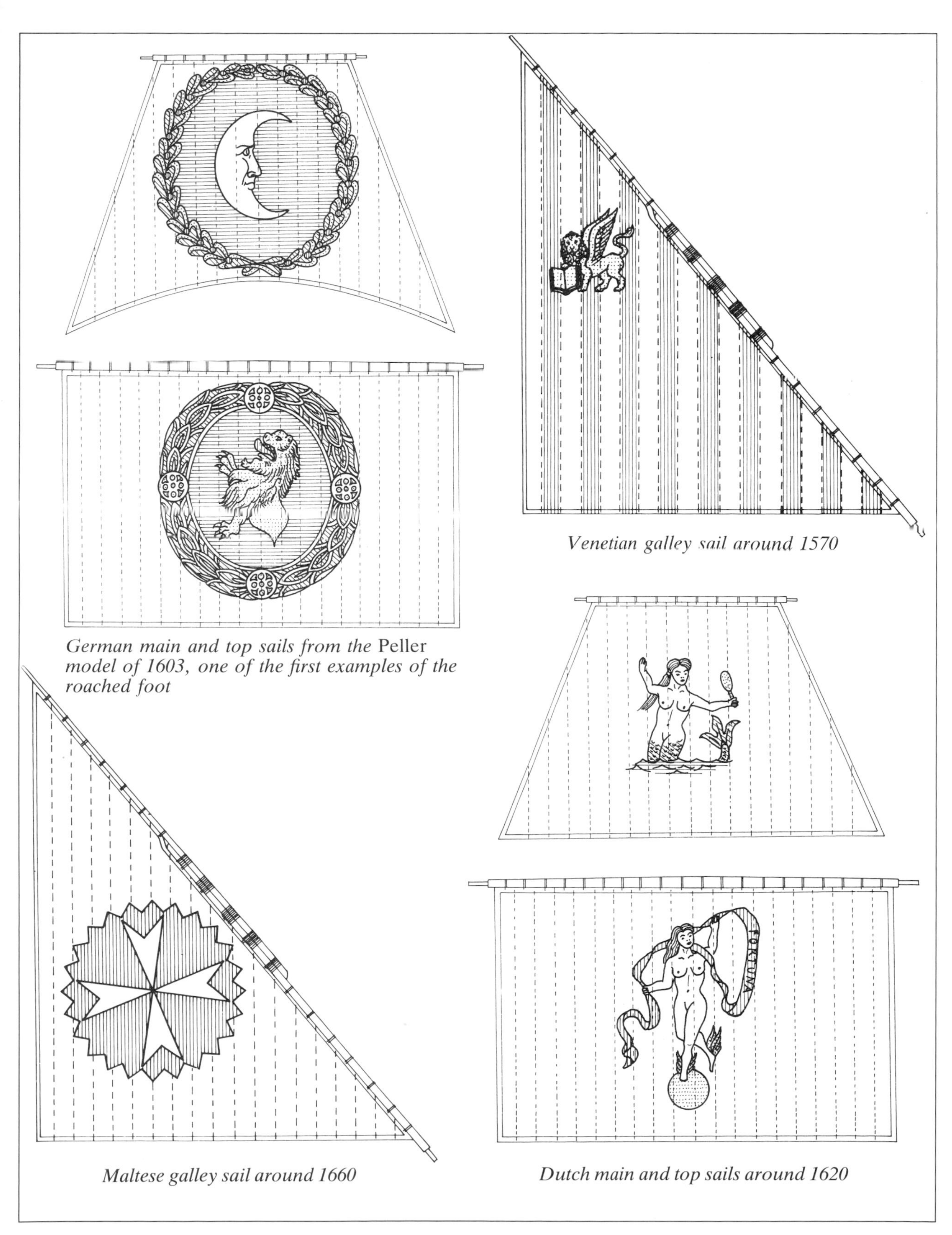

Venetian galley sail around 1570

German main and top sails from the Peller *model of 1603, one of the first examples of the roached foot*

Maltese galley sail around 1660

Dutch main and top sails around 1620

Sailmaking

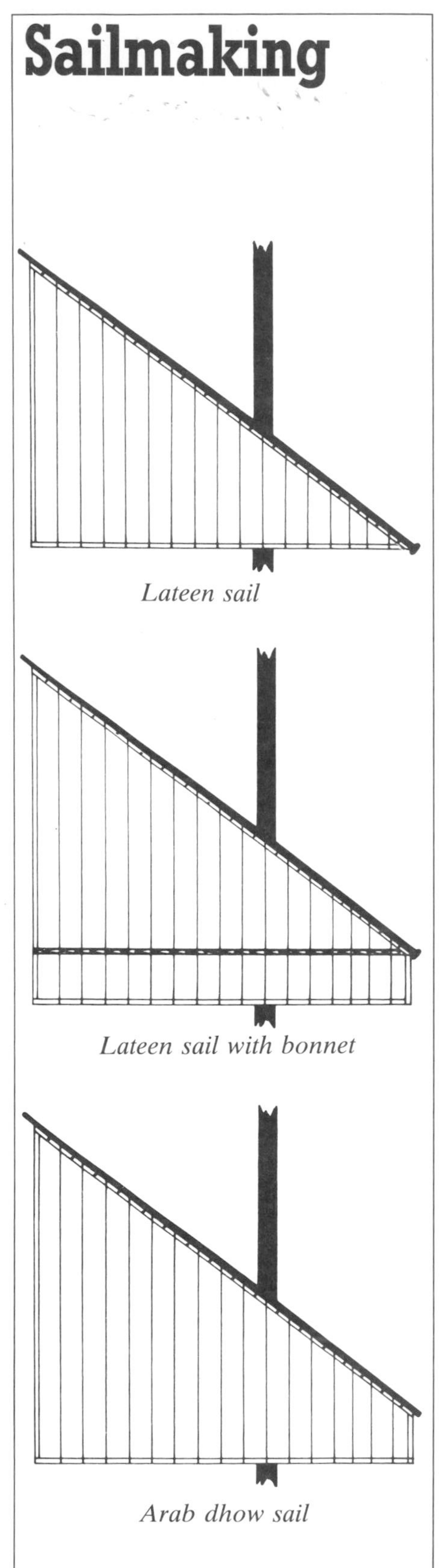

Lateen sail

Lateen sail with bonnet

Arab dhow sail

Except possibly in small craft in ancient times sails were not made out of a single piece of cloth, but were assembled from several strips, known as the cloths – this method produced sails which were considerably stronger and less liable to tear.
In ancient times the cloths were sometimes assembled crosswise, sometimes lengthwise, and some sewn up from rectangular pieces in both directions. Since the early Middle Ages the cloths have always been joined vertically, i.e. lengthwise.
When sewing up the individual cloths the traditional starting point was the extreme right-hand cloth – seen from the rear – with its left-hand edge taken upward to form the seam. The second cloth was laid on top of this, the right-hand seam at the bottom, the left-hand seam again taken upwards etc. Then the whole thing was oversewn from front and back to hold it all together. This procedure of making a sail from individual cloths is far too complex for the modeller, of course, especially as the same effect can be achieved by much simpler means. The material for the sail is cut with generous excess width, and the seams of the cloths are folded in an S-shape, noting that the visible seam edges always face the right. The cloths themselves were up to 4ft wide in the early Middle Ages, 32 to 36ins wide in the late Middle Ages, around 28ins wide from the middle of the 16th century to the beginning of the 18th century, and from then 24 or 18ins; the width of the seams fell over the same period from 1½ to 1in.
Sewing the seams is more difficult than laying out the strips. Start by pinning the seams in place, and ironing them. It is also advisable to glue the seams together carefully, although it is essential that the glue does not penetrate through the material. It does not matter whether there is a seam or cloth in the centre of the sail, but the strips should not become too narrow at the sides.
Originally the seams of the cloths were sewn with a double line of oversewing. However, as the seams of a 1:48 scale model are only 1/32ins wide, this process is not feasible for the modeller. He has the choice between just one row of oversewing or a double row of running stitch, as the drawing bottom right shows. However you do it, these stitches must be as even as possible (use a sewing machine!), and as small as possible. The sewing thread should be light brown, that is, a little darker than the sail itself, if the seams are to show up properly.
The next step is to cut the sail to the size of your template – do not forget the seam or tabling allowances. Fold the edges of the sail over, pin them, carefully glue them if desired, and finally sew them up with a double row of running stitches. The tabling was about 4ins wide. The leeches are sewn first, followed by the foot and head of the sail.
The linings are now sewn on the reverse side of the sail; they were themselves often made up from separate cloths. Oversewing is used again, as for the cloths. Only the foot lining was attached with running stitches, like the tabling. The last stage is to attach the reef bands, using running stitch.
All the eyelet holes – that is the holes through which the head lacing and reef points were passed – were sewn round. This task is unnecessary on a model, however, as the eyelets are hidden by the knots of the ropes. It is best to leave the eyelet holes out altogether at this stage.

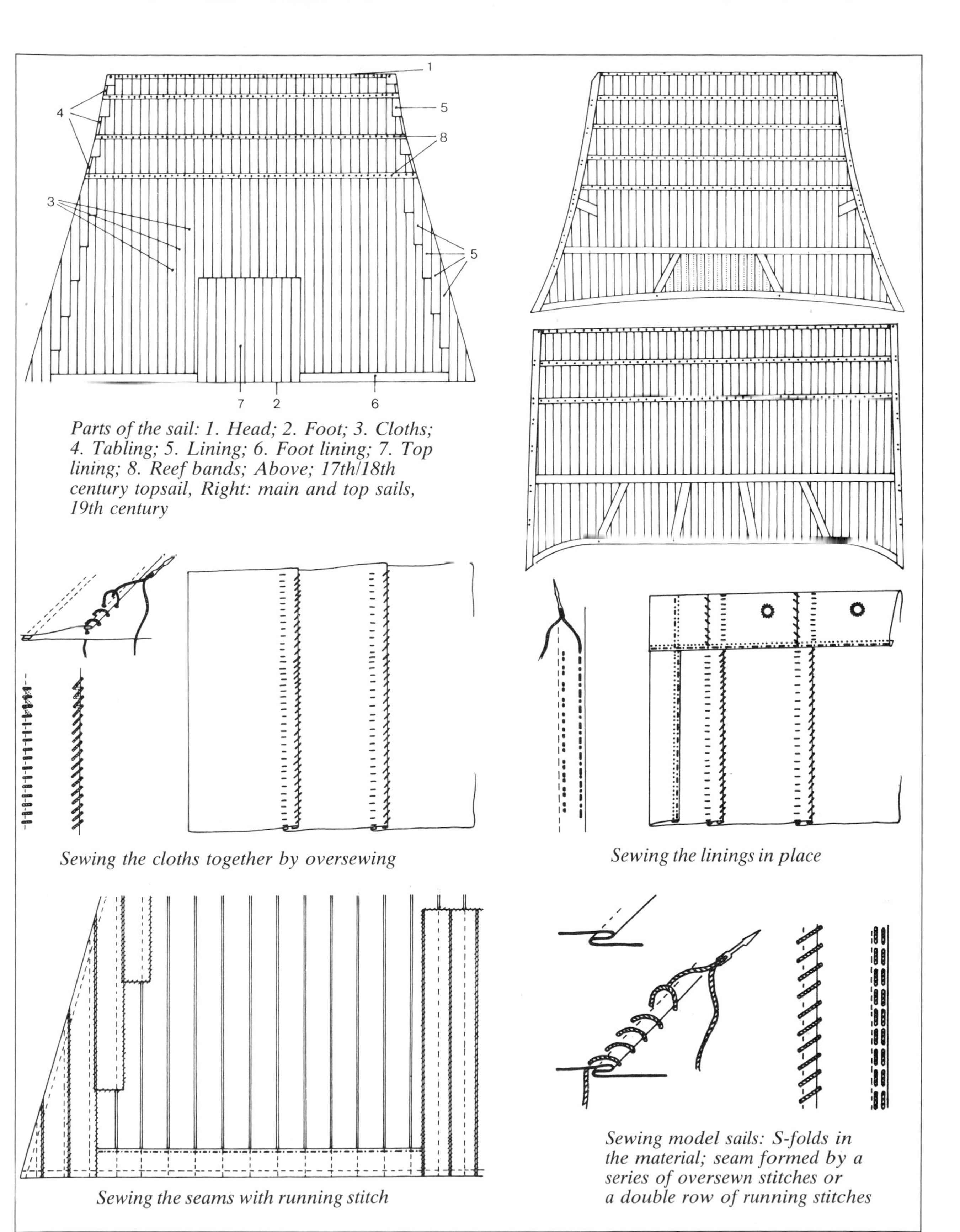

Parts of the sail: 1. Head; 2. Foot; 3. Cloths; 4. Tabling; 5. Lining; 6. Foot lining; 7. Top lining; 8. Reef bands; Above; 17th/18th century topsail, Right: main and top sails, 19th century

Sewing the cloths together by oversewing

Sewing the linings in place

Sewing the seams with running stitch

Sewing model sails: S-folds in the material; seam formed by a series of oversewn stitches or a double row of running stitches

The Bolt rope

Mizen course

Gaff top sail

Boom mizen or driver

All the sails were edged with a bolt rope; square sails on the after side, fore and aft sails on the port side. In the British Navy bolt ropes on courses were about ⅓ of the size of their respective stays, those on the topsails ⅔ of their respective stays and topgallant sails ½ that of their corresponding topsails. Head ropes on square sails were roughly half these sizes.

Lower staysail bolt ropes were roughly ⅖ of the main topmast stay, topsail and topgallant staysails ¼ and royal staysails ⅕. The bolt ropes on the heads of four sided staysails, and the luffs of triangular staysails set flying, were about twice the size of their leech and foot rope; those of other triangular staysails were the same all round.

The bolt ropes are fitted in the following way: start to right or left on the leech of the sail, leaving the rope a good inch overlength at the head of the sail. It is now taken downwards to the foot, and there forms the clew; it then runs along the foot of the sail to the second clew, and finally up the other leech, where it is again left a good inch overlength. The headrope is fitted as a separate piece, left 1½ to 2ins overlength at either end. The bolt rope is sewn to the sail with thin thread and small stitches. The thread should always lie in the lay of the bolt rope, in the same way as wormed rope. A very practical means of doing this job is to glue the bolt rope to the edge of the sail first, to prevent it shifting during the sewing process.

The ends of the bolt ropes at the sail head are now spliced together to form the earing cringles, as shown in the drawing on the right. The clews are then seized. If the bolt ropes are served at the clews and cringles, the best time to do this is when the bolt rope is already attached to the sail. In the 18th and 19th centuries it was also common to reinforce or double the bolt rope at the clews and parts of the foot bolt rope with a served rope of 60 to 75% thickness. The bolt rope was often fixed at these points with several seizings, so that it could not be torn off. The methods used are shown in the drawings on the facing page.

Finally, the cringles for the leech lines and bowlines are spliced into the leech and foot ropes. In the 19th century they were laid up independently of the bolt rope rather than spliced into it. Their exact location must be found from the rigging plan. These cringles usually consisted of a rope rather thinner than the bolt rope itself.

Example:
British 74 gun ship late 18th century.
Main stay 18½ins. Main topmast stay 8½ins.

	Bolt rope	*Head rope*
Main course	5¾″	2½″
topsail	5½″	2¼″
topgallant sail	2¾″	1½″
royal	2″	1¼″
staysail	3¼″	–
topmast staysail	2″	3½″

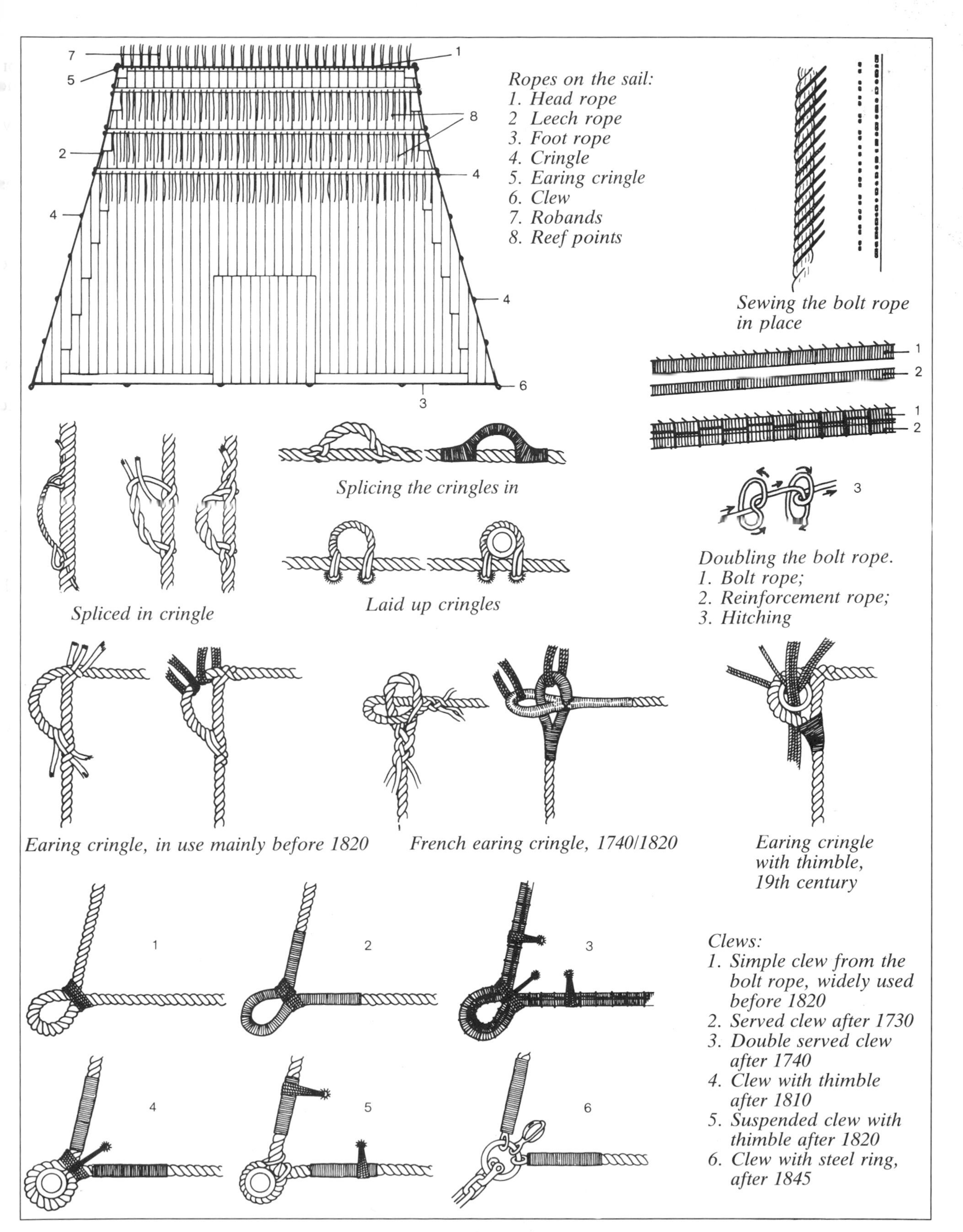

Ropes on the sail:
1. Head rope
2 Leech rope
3. Foot rope
4. Cringle
5. Earing cringle
6. Clew
7. Robands
8. Reef points

Sewing the bolt rope in place

Splicing the cringles in

Doubling the bolt rope.
1. Bolt rope;
2. Reinforcement rope;
3. Hitching

Spliced in cringle

Laid up cringles

Earing cringle, in use mainly before 1820

French earing cringle, 1740/1820

Earing cringle with thimble, 19th century

Clews:
1. Simple clew from the bolt rope, widely used before 1820
2. Served clew after 1730
3. Double served clew after 1740
4. Clew with thimble after 1810
5. Suspended clew with thimble after 1820
6. Clew with steel ring, after 1845

Bonnets and reefs

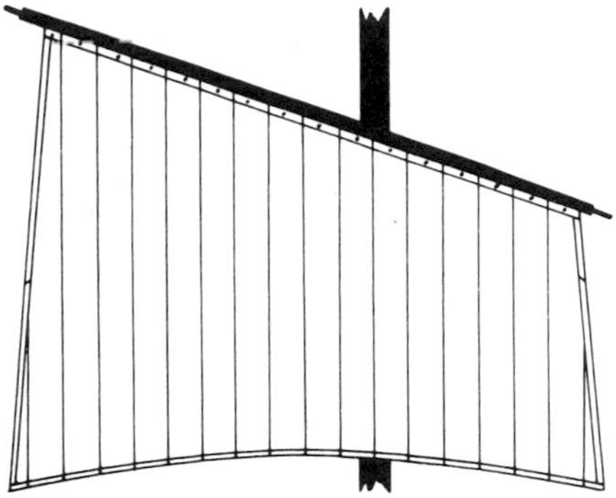

Standing lug sail

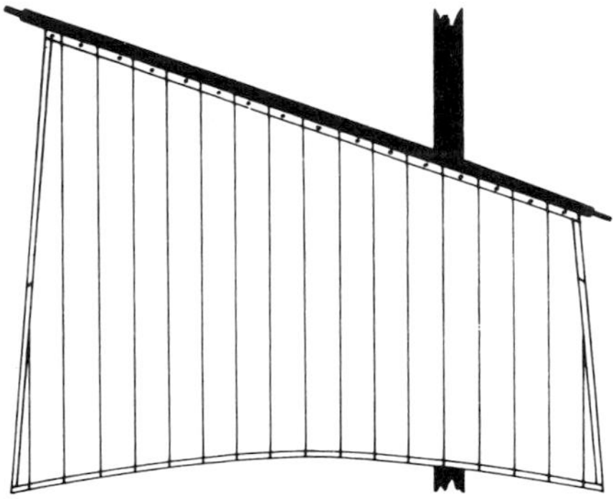

Dipping lug sail

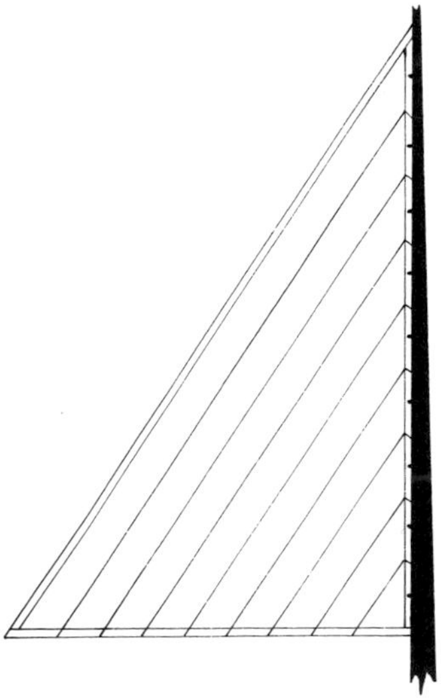

Bermuda sail

Any method of enlarging the sail area in light winds, and reducing it again in high winds, without having to change sails altogether (as is still done sometimes in the Mediterranean and the Arab area to this day) was a highly desirable feature, as can be imagined. Two fundamentally different systems were used to this end: the reef for reducing the sail area, and the bonnet for increasing it. The reef is the older method, being invented in the 12th century by the descendants of the Scandinavian Vikings, the Normans. The bonnet came from the Mediterranean area (whether from Italy, Spain or Portugal is not clear), and by the beginning of the 15th century it had displaced the reef. The latter was reintroduced in the middle of the 17th century, and had, in its turn, virtually superseded the bonnet by the end of the 17th century.

The bonnet

The bonnet was a strip of canvas – often two strips until the end of the 16th century on large ships – which was attached to the parent sail by a series of rope loops. The bonnet loops were pulled through eyelets at the foot of the parent sail, pulled across to the adjacent eyelet, and the next loop pulled through it. This produced a linked chain system, the last loop of which was made fast at the clew of the parent sail. If this seizing was loosened, all the loops were released, and the bonnet could be taken down.

For modelling purposes, it is advisable to "sew" the loops, as shown in the drawing, rather than to try to attach the loops to the bonnet first, and then pull them through, as per full-size practice.

Please note that the chain of loops was always situated on the fore side of the sail. To make it easier for the sailors to match the eyelet with the right loop when putting up the bonnet, it was a widespread practice on ships of Catholic nations (Spain, Portugal, Italy, and to some extent France) to write the first few words of the "Ave Maria" on the foot of the parent sail and the head of the bonnet, so that the sailors could align the same letters at top and bottom.

The reef

The reef points were short tapered lengths of flat plaited cordage which reeved though the sail and hung freely in front of and behind the sail, being knotted on both sides to prevent them pulling through. To avoid the sail tearing these points were reinforced with reef bands, sewn onto both sides of the sail.

On sails of the 13th to the 15th centuries the reef points were located in the lower part of the sail, but after their reintroduction in the 17th century they were fitted in the upper part – otherwise they were identical. Around 1655 a single row of reef point was introduced on the topsails, and around 1680 this was doubled; in the 18th and early 19th century up to four rows were used. When the topsail was divided into the lower topsail and the upper topsail in the middle of the 19th century, the reef points remained on the upper topsail, but were reduced to one or – at most – two rows.

A single row of reef points was used on the lower sails too from 1680 on, although it was common practice just to sew eyelets in the reef band until the middle of the 18th century, the reef points only being fitted when required. No reef points were carried on the topgallant sails; at best a reef band with eyelets.

All gaff sails also carried reef points, also the spritsail, often the fore topmast staysail, and occasionally the inner jib.

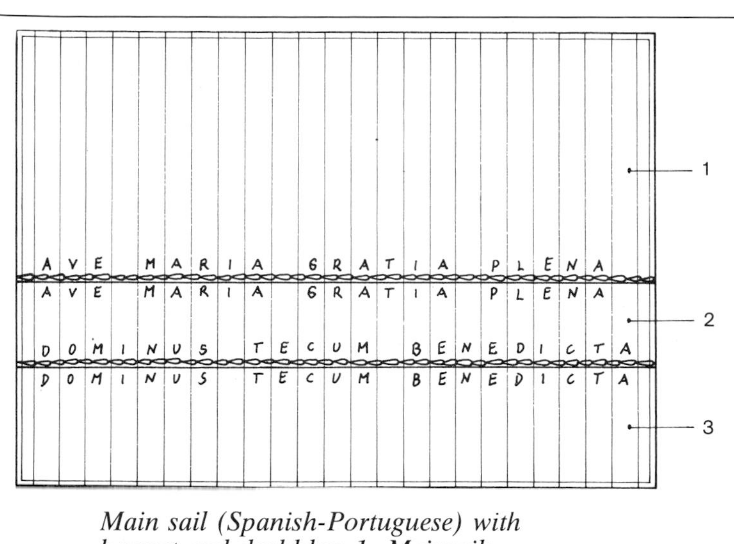

Main sail (Spanish-Portuguese) with bonnet and drabbler: 1. Mainsail; 2. Bonnet; 3. Drabbler

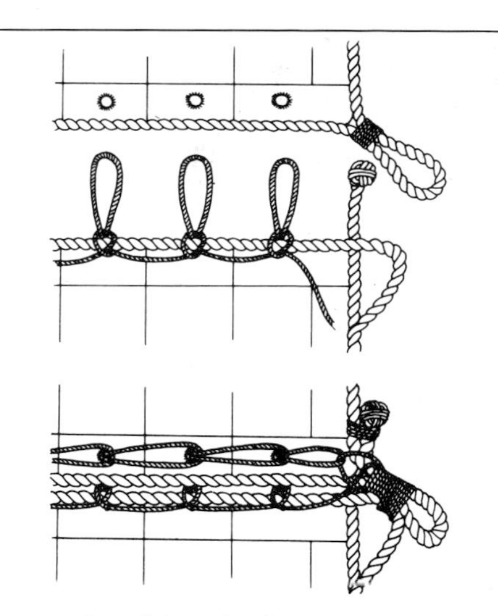

Attaching the bonnet: top detached, bottom attached by means of a lacing

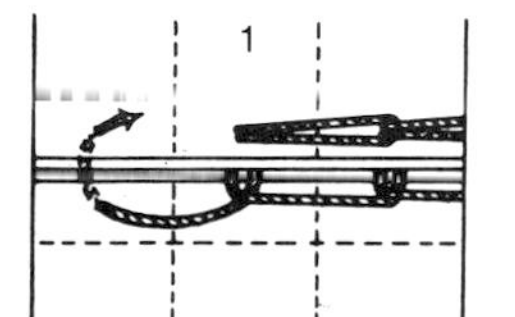

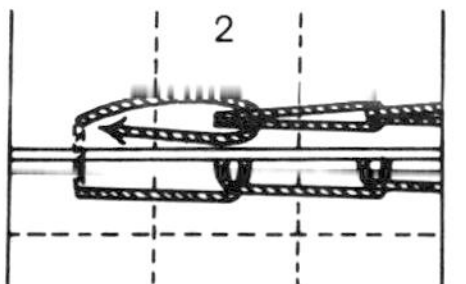

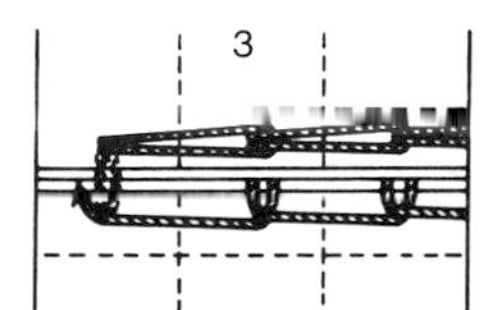

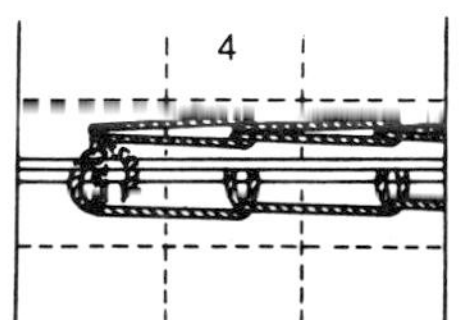

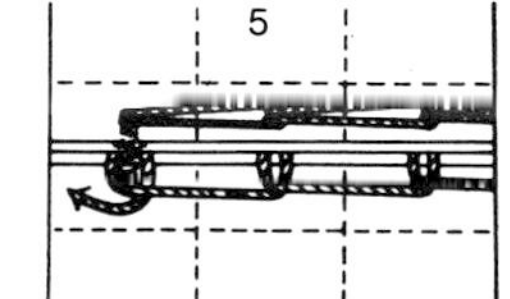

Method of sewing bonnet on models

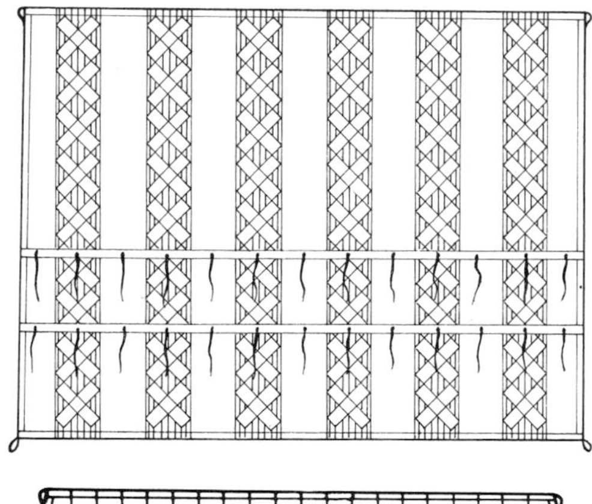

Reef points, 13th to 15th century. Up to 3 rows of reef points were fitted to the lower part of the sail

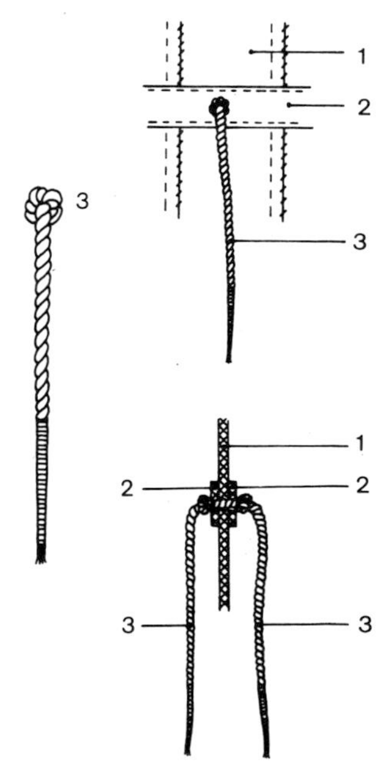

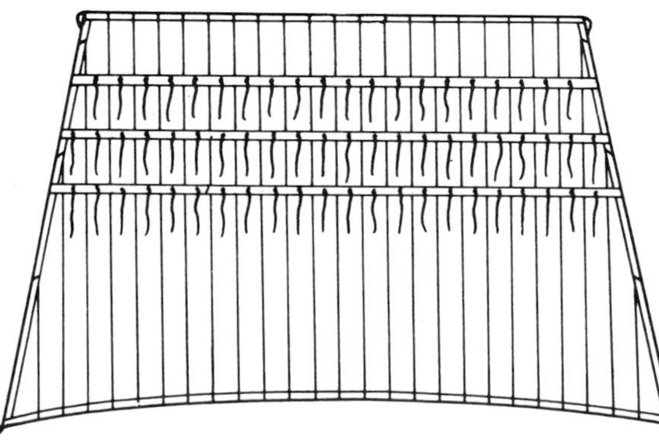

Reef points, 18th to 19th century. There was one row of reef points on the lower sail, and up to 3 rows of them on the topsail (4 after 1788 in the British Navy); they were located in the upper part of the sail.

Reef point: 1. Sail; 2. Reef band; 3. Reef point

Bending the sails to the yards

Spencer or trysail (Main and Fore): Spanker (mizen)

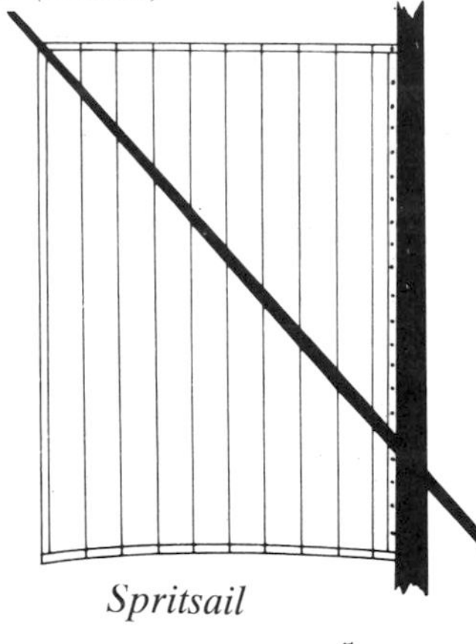

Spritsail

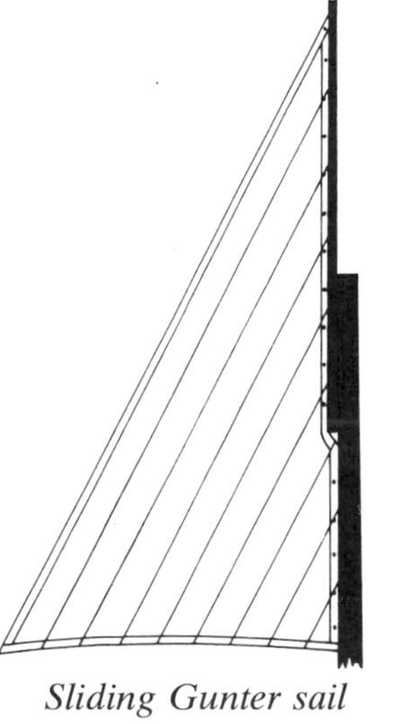

Sliding Gunter sail

With the sails now sewn up and fitted with bolt ropes all round, they are ready to be attached, or bent, to the yards.
To the less experienced model maker this may be somewhat surprising at such an early stage, as the yards are, of course, not yet attached to the masts. However, if you have a little experience in period ship modelling, you will know the reason: bending the sails to the yards is much easier to carry out if the yard and the sail are lying on the table before you, and you can turn them round and over to your heart's content. On the other hand, if you have to do this job with the complex ropework of the standing rigging and possibly even the running rigging in your way, you will find it well-nigh impossible.
At a later stage the yards complete with sails are mounted on the masts, which job is no more complicated than fitting the yards on their own.
On model plans the bending of the sails is generally either not shown at all, or if it is shown, then in most cases the method is inaccurate.
In the drawings on the right you will see the four standard methods:
1. Bending with a running lacing. This system was widely distributed in the early Middle Ages, and in the Mediterranean area in particular. From there it was adopted initially for the lateen sails of the late 14th century, and at the end of the 15th century for the first, very small, topsails. Incidentally, large lateen sails were never attached with a running lacing, but always with separate robands.
The running lacing disappeared completely from larger ships by the middle of the 16th century, but is still used to this day on small gaffed fishing vessels and coastal boats.
2. Bending the sails with robands. This was the usual method from ancient times onward, and was always much more widely distributed than the running lacing.
This older system used short lengths of cordage tied to front and back of the sail; the rear end was then wound once round the yard, and the two ends tied together on the yard, just in front of the centre. This was the standard method until the beginning of the 17th century, after which time it remained in use in some areas of the Mediterranean, where it lingered on until the 19th century.
3. In central and Northern Europe the start of the 17th century saw the introduction of a new method, by which several loops were passed round the yard and the head rope and then through the eyelets, before the robands were tied on the yard. There were two versions, one for the large sails of the lower and topsail yards, and a rather simpler one for the small sails of the topgallant and royal yards.
4. When jackstays were introduced, in the first half of the 19th century the sails were bent to the jackstays with either roband hitches or a round turn and a reef knot.
The earing cringles were lashed to the yard arms to prevent the sails pulling in towards the middle.
The sail should be taut on the yard, without being stretched very tight i.e. if you let it hang freely, there should be no folds. If the sail falls into vertical folds, then it is too loose, and the earings must be pulled somewhat tighter. If the sail falls into horizontal folds, it is too tight, and the earings must be loosened a little.

Bending with a running lacing. Used above all on smaller ships from the Middle Ages until the beginning of the 20th century on gaff and boom

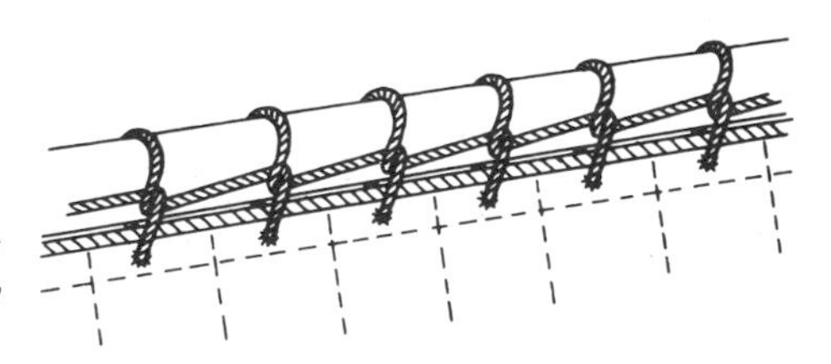

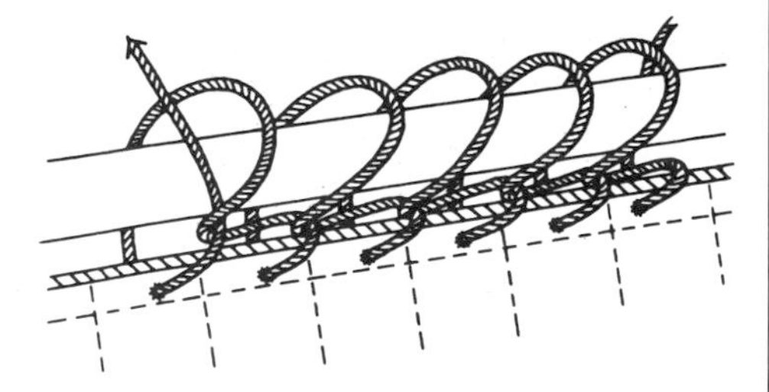

Bending with robands. Generally used from ancient times until late 18th century

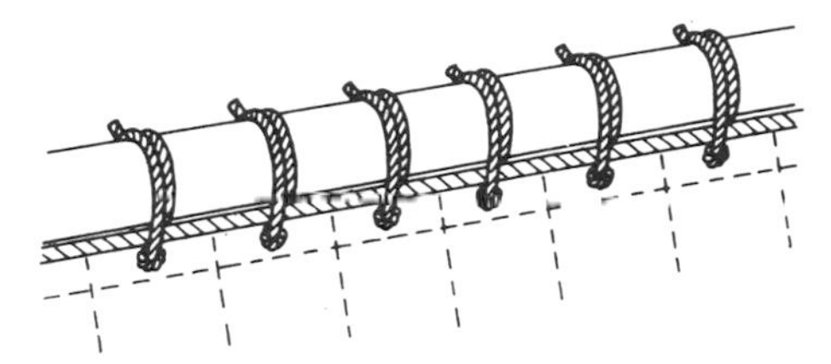

Bending with robands. Late 18th to mid-19th century. Right: method used on large yards; far right: method used on small yards

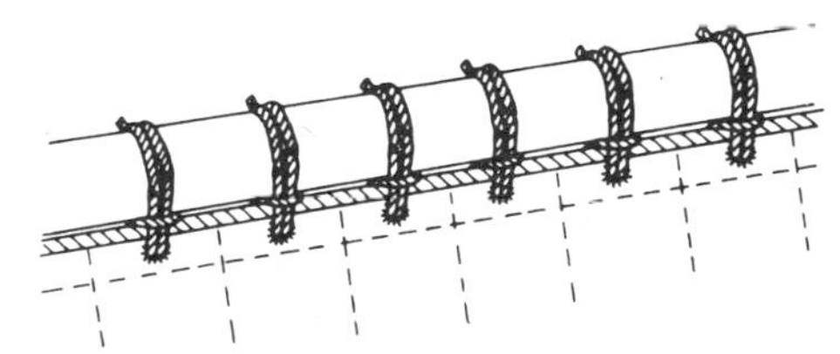

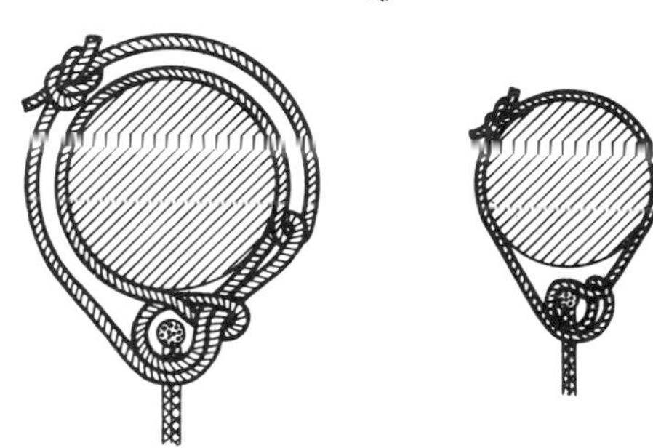

Bending with robands on the jackstay. The standard method used after the middle of the 19th century

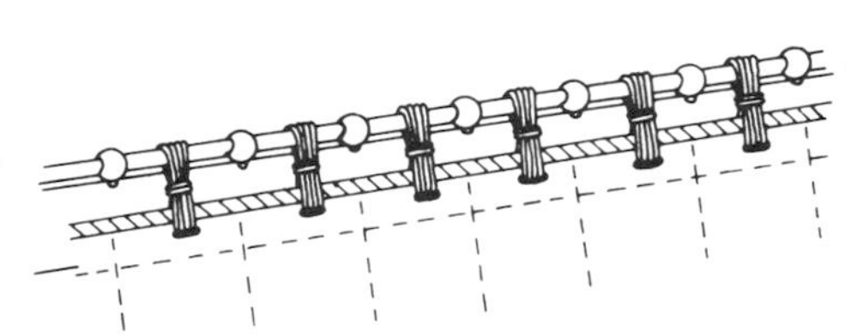

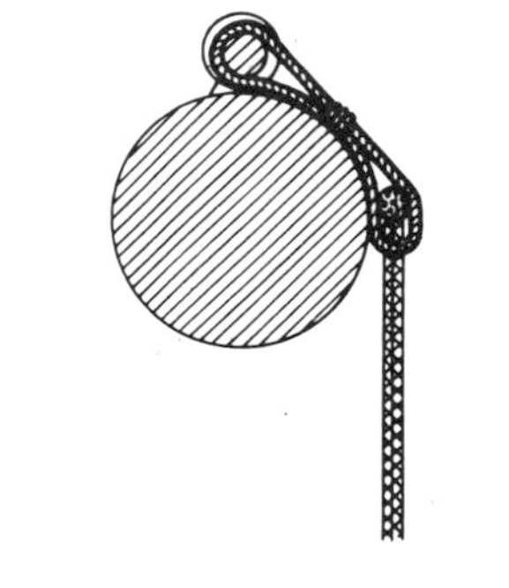

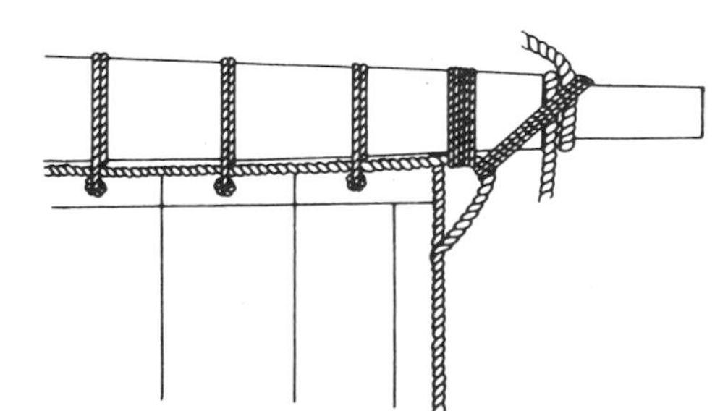

Head earing up to early 19th century

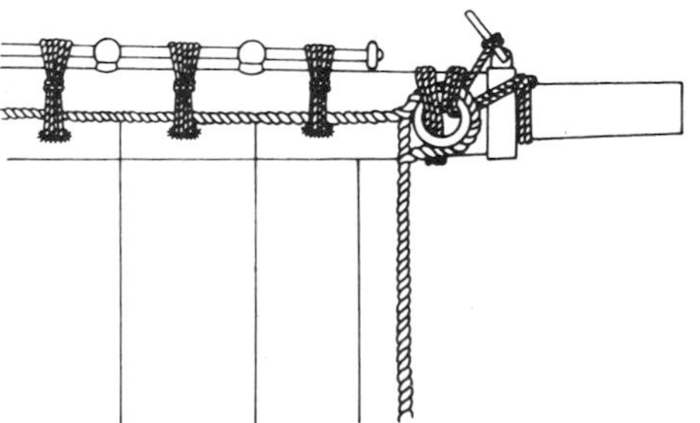

Head earing early 19th century

Gaff sails

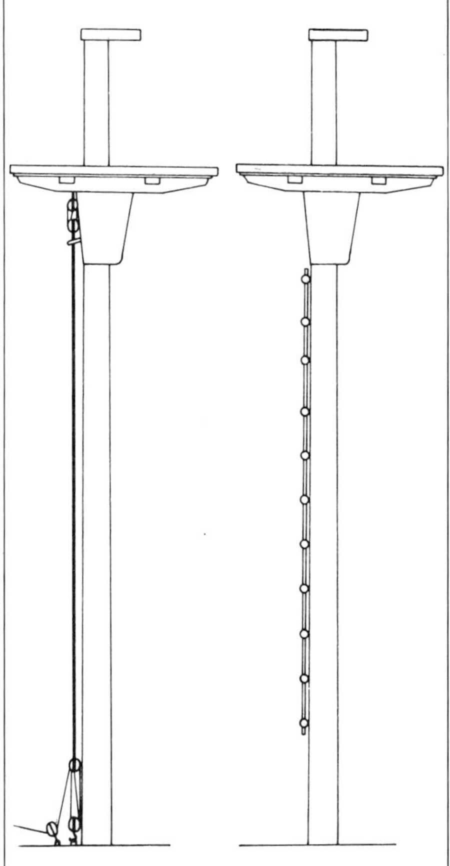

Gaff jackstay, 19th century: Left: older form with rope; Right: later type with metal rod

In the latter half of the 18th century the lateen sail, which had been carried on the mizen mast up to that time, was superseded by the gaff sail. One century later it became common to carry smaller gaff sails on the main and foremasts, as well as the large gaff sail on the mizen mast. Many ships were completely gaff-rigged, for example the schooners, and also cutters and yachts in some areas, the only square sails they carried being topsails.
The cloths of the gaff sails ran parallel to the leech – as is the case with all fore-and-aft sails. The gaff sails carried at least one row of reef points, and often two or three, occasionally as many as four.
The gaff sail was bent to the gaff with robands but there was a large number of different systems for attaching it to the mast. These various methods of bending the gaff sail to the mast are – once again – rarely indicated on any plan, and as they are also difficult to find in reference books, I have drawn them on the right-hand page in fairly full detail. Methods 1 to 5 were used in the 18th century. The trucks were intended to prevent the rope chafing on the mast. Methods 4 and 5 were used principally on smaller ships, and found favour until the beginning of this century, especially in Holland. Around 1800 rope hoops were introduced, although it took until about 1820 for these to oust the older types. Around 1820/1830 wood (ash) hoops came into use, either located in cringles (7), or with rope seizings through eyelets in the sail itself (8), to be supplanted soon after by metal hoops.
In the middle of the 19th century jackstays were introduced, as has already been mentioned. At first a rope was used abaft the mizen mast as the jackstay, and later a metal rod, to which the gaff sail was bent either with metal hanks (9) or with robands (10).

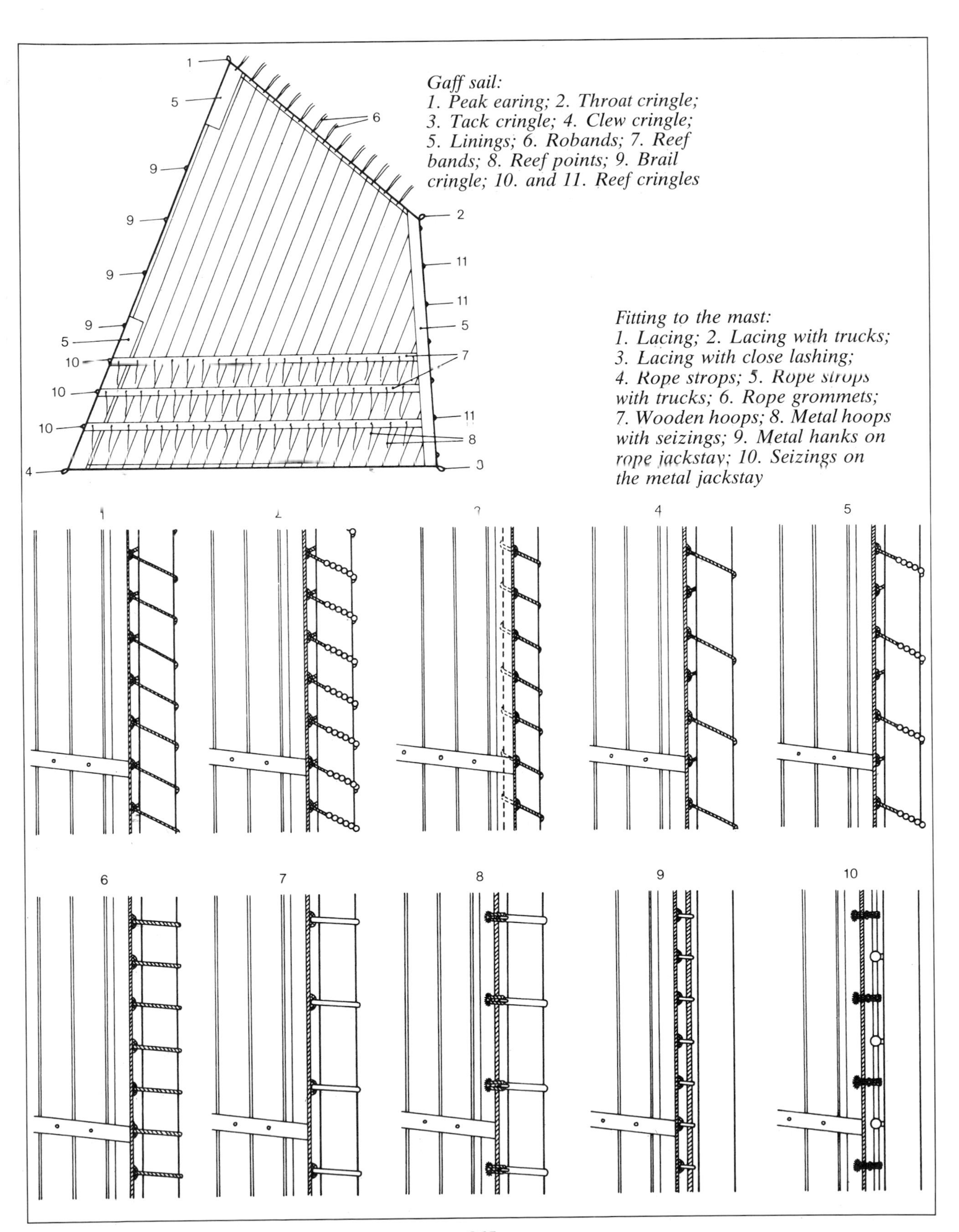

Gaff sail:
1. Peak earing; 2. Throat cringle; 3. Tack cringle; 4. Clew cringle; 5. Linings; 6. Robands; 7. Reef bands; 8. Reef points; 9. Brail cringle; 10. and 11. Reef cringles

Fitting to the mast:
1. Lacing; 2. Lacing with trucks; 3. Lacing with close lashing; 4. Rope strops; 5. Rope strops with trucks; 6. Rope grommets; 7. Wooden hoops; 8. Metal hoops with seizings; 9. Metal hanks on rope jackstay; 10. Seizings on the metal jackstay

Staysails

Staysails were already known on small ships and boats from the 15th century. On large ships they were not introduced until about 1660. The staysails are made up like all the other sails. Reef points were often carried on the fore topmast staysail, and occasionally on the inner jib also. There was a different arrangement of the cloths on the staysails from about 1830, and this is shown on the drawing on the right. This sail should also be made from two pieces with a central seam if your model is to be accurate.
The staysails were bent with a lacing or grommets until about 1820, after which time metal hanks seized to the sail were used.

Spritsails

The sprit sail also has two special features: from the middle of the 17th century there were two holes on the extreme right and left of the bottom part, and from the first half of the 18th century there was often a third hole in the middle. These holes were sewn all round or enclosed with narrow bolt ropes. Their purpose was to allow any water which collected in the sail to run off as easily as possible – as this sail was set very low down, this could happen easily. The reef bands arranged diagonally served the same purpose, and they were found as standard on the sprit sail after 1680. With their help the sail could be tied up at an angle, i.e. shortened on the lee side so that it did not drag in the water.

Furled sails

If you wish to show your ship with sails furled on the yards, then the sails are made up in exactly the same way as described, but the following additional points should be noted.
The cloth dressing, as already stated, must be washed out very thoroughly. The cloth seams should not be folded and sewn up (and certainly not glued), but just indicated by two parallel seams on the sewing machine. The same goes for the linings; reef bands and reef points can be omitted. The sail, and in particular the foot, must be made up in exactly the same way as usual, but it is advisable to shorten the length of the sail by at least one third. The point of all these measures is to reduce the amount of material, and keep the sail as supple as possible, to avoid the finished furled sail looking like a fat, unruly ball of fabric. At the other extreme there should not be such a small amount of cloth that the furled sail looks like a skinny little sausage.
The sail is bent to the yard, but is allowed to hang down temporarily – do not roll it up straightaway. It is rigged in the normal way with clew lines, leech lines, sheets, etc. Only when all the running rigging is in place would it be furled (see the chapter RUNNING RIGGING).
If you want to show the sails furled very tightly to the yards, you can in certain circumstances use paper handkerchiefs, provided the plies are separated very neatly. Details of this method are given in the chapter RUNNING RIGGING.
The sails were furled with gaskets, 6 to 8 ropes of about ⅓ of the sail's depth in length, which were spaced out at regular intervals along the yard. They were always carried on the fore side of the sail. Before 1815 they were usually spliced round the yard. After 1815 the gaskets were attached to the jackstay, and hung in coils on the fore side of the sail.

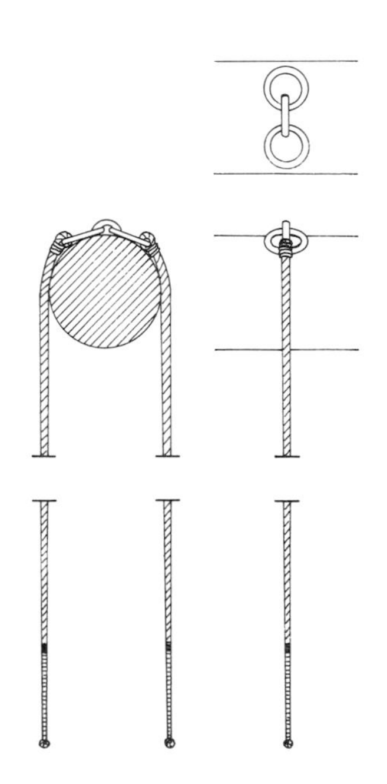

In the 16th and 17th centuries gaskets on Continental ships were secured to the spars with double ring bolts

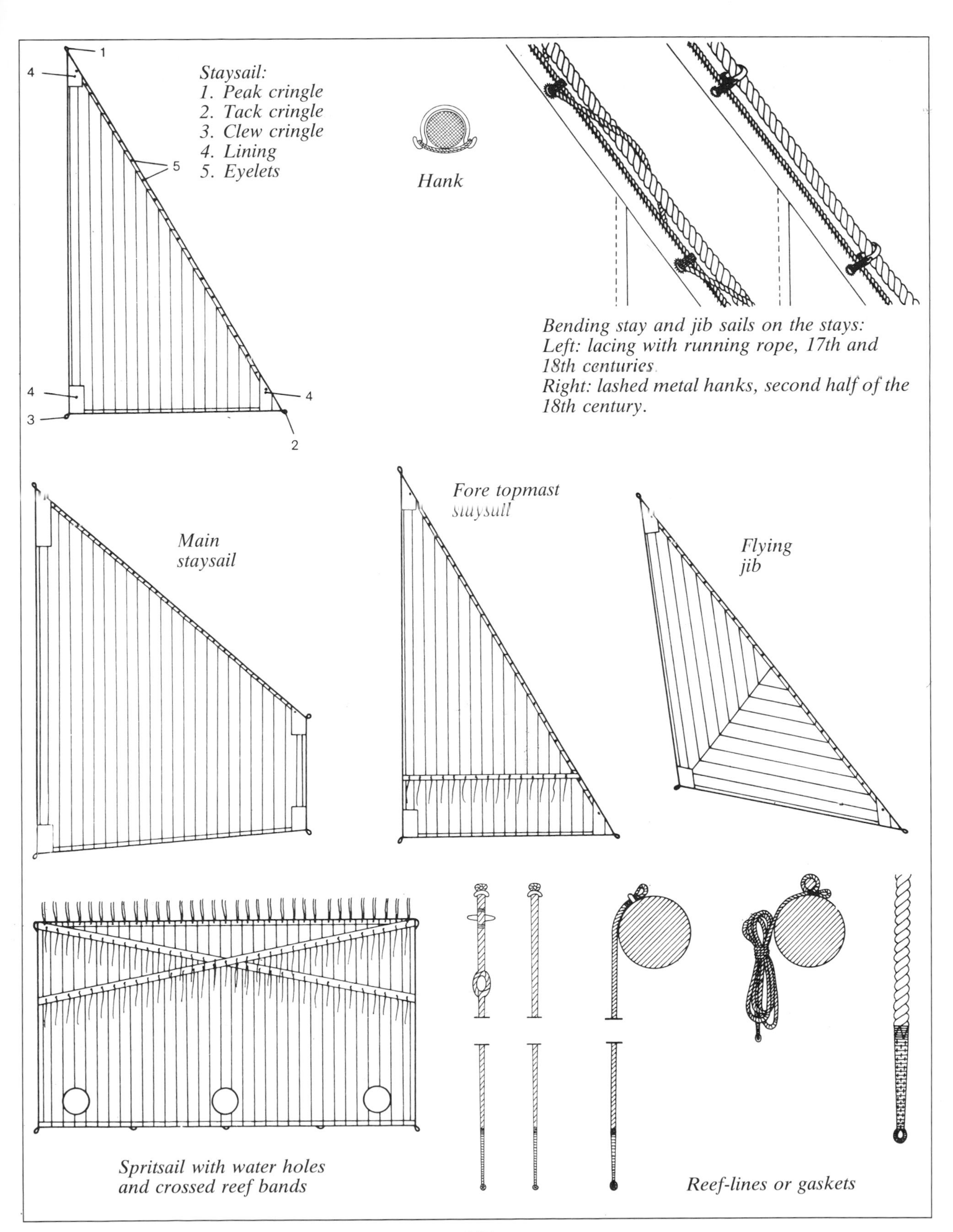

Bending stay and jib sails on the stays:
Left: lacing with running rope, 17th and 18th centuries.
Right: lashed metal hanks, second half of the 18th century.

Spritsail with water holes and crossed reef bands

Reef-lines or gaskets

Set of sails for a warship around 1750:

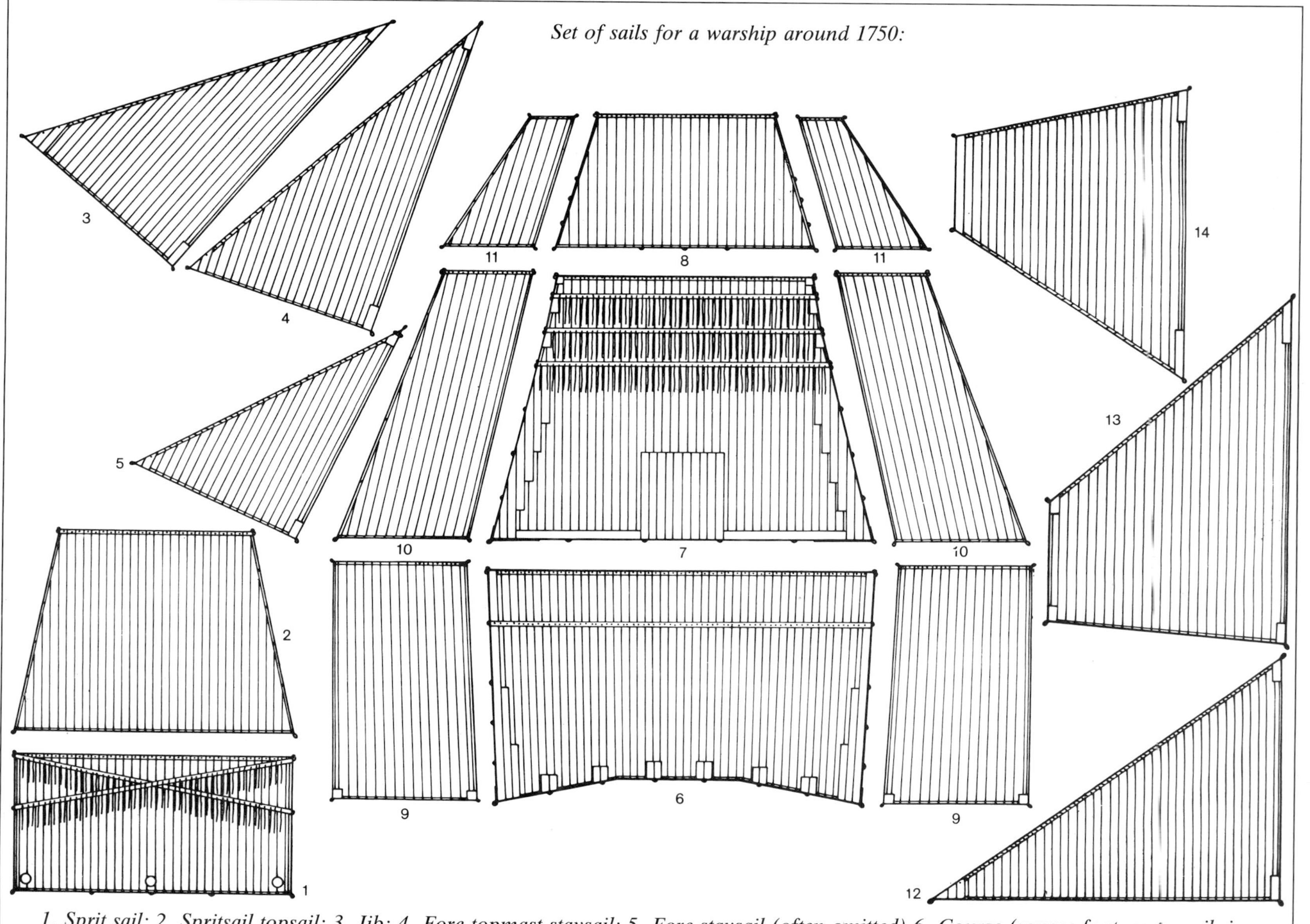

1. Sprit sail; 2. Spritsail topsail; 3. Jib; 4. Fore topmast staysail; 5. Fore staysail (often omitted) 6. Course (square foot, as topsail, in British ships); 7. Fore topsail; 8. Fore topgallant sail; 9. Fore studding sail; 10. Fore topmast studding sail; 11. Fore topgallant studding sail; 12. Main staysail; 13. Main topmast staysail; 14. Middle staysail

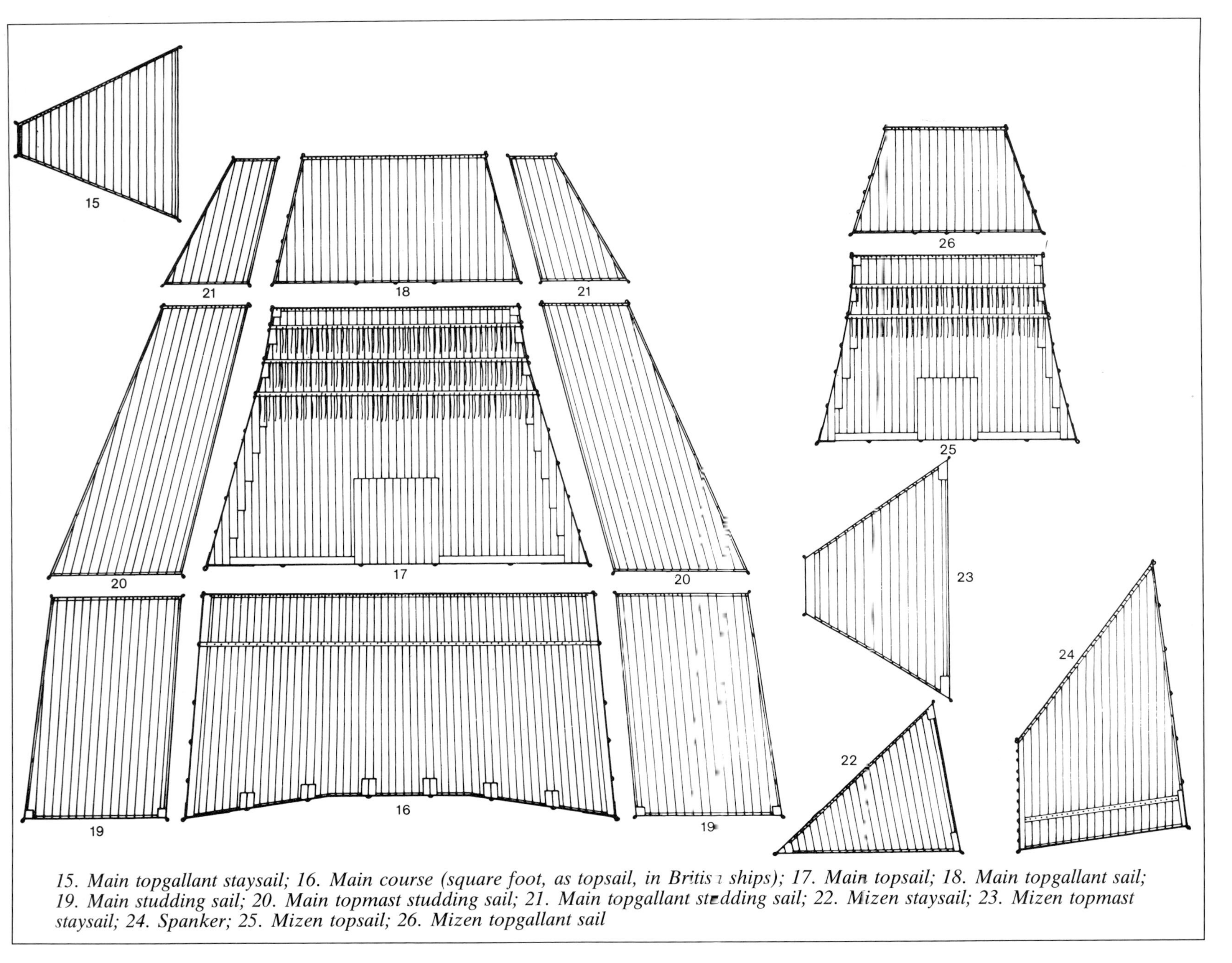

15. Main topgallant staysail; 16. Main course (square foot, as topsail, in British ships); 17. Main topsail; 18. Main topgallant sail; 19. Main studding sail; 20. Main topmast studding sail; 21. Main topgallant studding sail; 22. Mizen staysail; 23. Mizen topmast staysail; 24. Spanker; 25. Mizen topsail; 26. Mizen topgallant sail

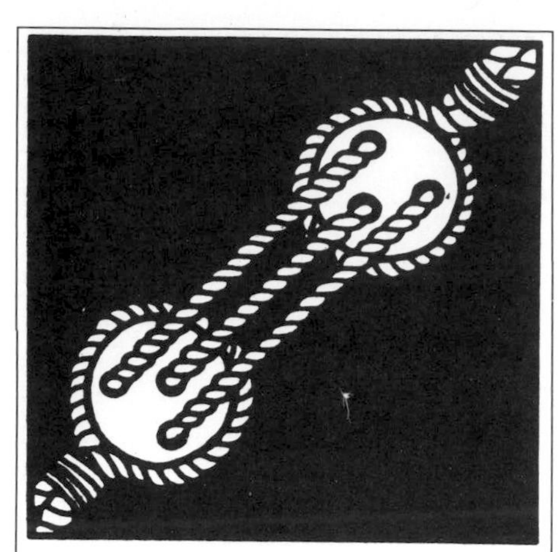

Standing rigging

Introduction
Standing rigging rope sizes
Gammoning · Bumkin shrouds · Outrigger guys
Bobstay · Bowsprit shrouds
Head stay · Loading gear
Burtons · Shrouds · Backstays
Stays · Sprit topmast backstay
Jibboom rigging

The term "standing rigging" covers all the ropes of a ship which serve to support the masts forward, aft and laterally. There are certain fundamental lines of development which can be observed in the design of the standing rigging through the centuries.

Until the middle of the 15th century the standing rigging was fairly simple; the ship carried just what it really needed. In the second half of the 15th century and in particular the whole of the 16th and the early part of the 17th century the standing rigging grew enormously complicated, and this complexity far outstripped the ships' requirements. We have to remember that the renaissance was not only a return to the consciousness of ancient times, but was also the first stage of an era of technology. New technical possibilities were deliberately indulged, with up to 16 pairs of shrouds per mast, double and triple crows feet on the mizen stay, fore topmast stay and backstay, lateen top and topgallant sails plus mizen and jigger masts, even when the ships were so over-rigged that their efficiency suffered markedly. In the 17th century this confused jungle of ropework was cleared up again under the leadership of Holland, Britain and France, and the standing rigging was again reduced to what was really necessary and useful.

In spite of the constant growth in mast heights and sail areas, the number of ropes did not increase in the 18th century, except for the stays. Instead the individual ropes of the standing rigging grew thicker and thicker. In the latter part of the 19th century, the hemp ropes used until that time finally became inadequate for the extremely tall-rigged ships, and it became standard practice to use steel wire rope for all or part of the standing rigging.

When fitting the standing rigging, work proceeds from the bow towards the stern, and from the bottom towards the top; in the case of shrouds and backstays individual ropes are fitted alternately to starboard then to port. This means: bowsprit gammoning – bobstay – bowsprit shrouds – fore tackle pendants – fore shrouds (starboard – port etc.) – forestay tackle pendants – main shrouds – mainstay – mizen burton pendants – mizen shrouds – mizen stay – fore topmast shrouds – fore topmast stay – main topmast shrouds – etc. etc.

As in full-size practice, the fitting of the standing rigging is a rather complicated matter on a period model – not so much because of the fiddly nature of the ropes, but because in every section a whole series of ropes have to be fitted at exactly the right tension to balance each other out.

The whole standing rigging system is based on the principle of tension and counter-tension, i.e. not only must each rope be pulled tight (that is, they must be under a certain amount of tension), but you have also to consider every other rope which exerts a pull in the opposite direction. An example might illustrate this principle: the shrouds pull the mast back towards the stern. If the shrouds are set up and tensioned, the mast assumes a slight curve towards the stern. If we now try to compensate for this by setting a corresponding amount of tension in the stay, the first pairs of shrouds will inevitably fall slack. For this reason it is of the utmost importance to leave all the lines and tackles of the standing rigging temporarily fixed until all the standing rigging has been fitted; then the tension of each component can be matched to the others, and the whole system balanced out.

Do allow yourself plenty of time for this. Masts that are curved or even bent by incorrect or asymmetrical tension look just as awful as loose shrouds, backstays or stays.

When the whole of the standing rigging has been fitted and balanced, the lines and tackles can be permanently fixed, the excess ends cut off, the crowsfeet attached to the main and fore stays, and the shrouds rattled down.

Admiralty model of the English three-decker St. Michael *of 1669*

Standing rigging sizes

Bowsprit and jib boom	16th/17th century	18th century	19th century hemp	19th century steel
Bowsprit				
Bowsprit gammoning	40%	40%		chain
Bobstay (single)	80%	80%	80%	chain
Lanyard	30%	30%	30%	
Bobstay (multiple)		46%	70%	chain
Lanyard		20%	30%	
Bowsprit shroud	25%	46%	50%	chain
Lanyard	10%	20%	25%	
Head stay	16%			
Lanyard	8%			
Sprit topmast				
Shrouds	16%	16%		
Lanyard	8%	8%		
Backstay	20%	20%		
Lanyard	10%	10%		
Jib				
Martingale stay		30%	60%	chain
Outer martingale stay		20%	55%	chain
Martingale backstay		20%	55%	20%
Outer jib boom guy		8%	53%	20%

The figures given refer to the thickness of the main stay, 0.166% of the diameter of the mainmast at the deck (100%).
These values are a guideline only, and national variations have not been taken into account.

In the case of a mainstay made of steel rope, the figures in the table are still based on the use of hemp rope but could be reduced for steel by about 33%.

Foremast	16th/17th century	18th century	19th century hemp	19th century steel
Lower mast				
Fore tackle pendants	40%	58%		
Tackles	20%	28%		
Shrouds	40%	58%	100%	44%
Lanyards	20%	30%	50%	
Stay	80%	90%	100%	44%
Lanyard	25%	30%	50%	
Preventer stay		60%	80%	35%
Lanyard		20%	40%	
Topmast				
Burton pendants	20%	30%		
Tackles	10%	15%		
Futtock staves	40%	58%		
Futtock shrouds	18%	20%		stave
Topmast shrouds	20%	30%	62%	31%
Lanyards	10%	15%	31%	
Backstays	20%	38%	88%	38%
Lanyards	10%	20%	44%	
Topmast stay	40%	48%	88%	38%
Lanyard	18%	20%	44%	
Topmast preventer stay		37%	62%	31%
Lanyard		18%	31%	
Topgallant mast				
Futtock staves	20%	30%		
Futtock shrouds	15%	15%		stave
Topgallant shrouds	16%	16%	50%	25%
Lanyards	8%	8%	25%	
Backstays	16%	21%	66%	33%
Lanyards	8%	10%	33%	
Topgallant stay	20%	21%	53%	26%
Royal backstays	8%	10%	40%	20%
Lanyards	4%	5%	20%	
Royal stay	10%	12%	34%	17%

Mainmast	16th/17th century	18th century	19th century hemp	19th century steel
Lower mast				
Main tackle pendants	50%	60%		
Tackles	25%	30%		
Shrouds	50%	62%	100%	44%
Lanyards	25%	30%	50%	
Stay	100%	100%	100%	44%
Stay collar	75%	92%		
Lanyard	30%	30%	50%	
Preventer stay		60%	100%	44%
Preventer stay collar		60%		
Lanyard		23%	50%	
Topmast				
Burton pendants	25%	34%		
Tackles	13%	17%		
Futtock staves	50%	62%		
Futtock shrouds	20%	20%		stave
Topmast shrouds	25%	33%	62%	31%
Lanyards	13%	17%	31%	
Backstays	25%	42%	88%	38%
Lanyards	12%	20%	44%	
Topmast stay	50%	51%	88%	38%
Lanyard	20%	21%	44%	
Topmast preventer stay		37%	62%	31%
Lanyard		18%	31%	
Topgallant mast				
Futtock staves	25%	33%		
Futtock shrouds	15%	17%		stave
Topgallant shrouds	16%	17%	50%	25%
Lanyard	8%	8%	25%	
Backstays	16%	22%	66%	33%
Lanyards	8%	10%	25%	
Topgallant stay	20%	25%	56%	28%
Royal backstays	8%	10%	40%	16%
Lanyards	4%	5%	20%	
Royal stay	10%	13%	37%	14%

Mizen mast	16th/17th century	18th century	19th century hemp	19th century steel
Lower mast				
Burton pendants	25%	40%		
Tackles	13%	20%		
Shrouds	25%	40%	75%	35%
Lanyards	13%	20%	37%	
Stay	40%	52%	88%	38%
Lanyard	20%	23%	44%	
Topmast				
Futtock staves	25%	40%		
Futtock shrouds	15%	17%		stave
Topmast shrouds	16%	22%	56%	28%
Lanyards	8%	11%	28%	
Backstays	16%	30%	56%	28%
Lanyards	8%	15%	28%	
Topmast stay	20%	28%	60%	30%
Lanyard	10%	14%	30%	
Topgallant backstays	8%	15%	52%	26%
Lanyards	4%	7%	26%	
Topgallant stay	10%	14%	47%	23%
Other ropes				
Stay tackle pendants	58%	58%	60%	
Guys	40%	40%	50%	
Tackles	20%	20%	25%	
Bumkin shrouds		16%	20%	
Lanyards		8%	10%	
Outrigger guys	16%			
Lanyard	8%			

Bowsprit gammoning

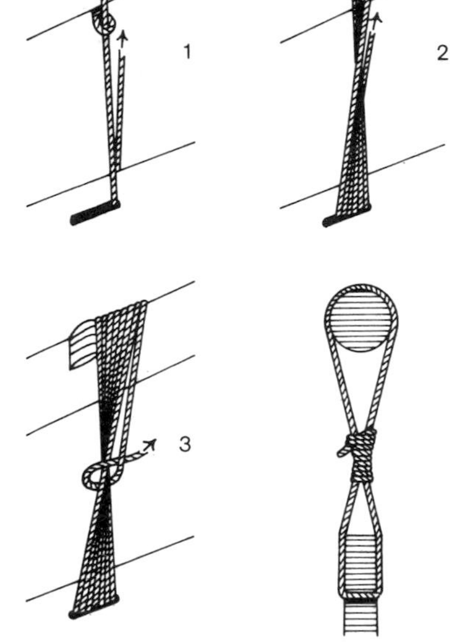

Sequence of the bowsprit gammoning

Until into the late 17th century the gammoning was the only standing rigging on the bowsprit, and in all cases it is the first rope to be attached when fitting the rigging.
Smaller ships mostly carried only one gammoning, and larger ships two. Until the beginning of the 17th century it was passed round the still very flat knee of the head, while on larger ships it ran through a heavy cleat on the beakhead platform. (see HEAD). After this time it ran through one or two slots in the knee of the head (sometimes also the gammoning knee); the arrangement should be shown on your plans.
The bowsprit gammoning was looped over the bowsprit, passed down to the knee of the head, through the gammoning hole, up again to the bowsprit and over it, back to the gammoning hole again etc., the whole repeated eight to eleven times. Note here that the rope always crossed over in the middle, that is, each new turn on the bowsprit was *in front of* the previous turn, and at the gammoning hole, was *behind* the previous turn (towards the stern).
The last turn was passed over the bowsprit to the middle of the gammoning, taken round the gammoning eight to ten times, and made fast. To prevent the bowsprit gammoning sliding, three to five thumb cleats were fitted to the bowsprit. They were slightly thicker than the rope, and as long as the gammoning itself on the bowsprit until the 18th century, slightly shorter in the 18th and 19th centuries.
In the 19th century (roughly from 1830) the bowsprit gammoning consisted of chains rather than ropes in many cases. In the late 19th century the gammoning largely disappeared, and completely disappeared on larger ships; smaller vessels continued to use it, especially in the Mediterranean.
In the 17th and 18th centuries a special block, the gammon lashing or rack block, was seized to the gammoning; this was a special block through which a part of the running rigging reeved; more detail on this in the chapter RUNNING RIGGING.

Bumkin shrouds

From the 18th century onward, the fore tacks were no longer taken through the knee of the head, but through blocks at the head of the bumkin. The bumkin itself was stayed by two bumkin shrouds, which prevented it bending upwards when under tension.
The forward shroud was led through a hole in the knee of the head and fixed to the bumkins to starboard and port. More often the shroud was fixed to a ring bolt on the knee of the head. The after shroud was made fast to a ring bolt in the hull. The bumkin shrouds were set up with a combination of blocks or deadeyes, and less often with hearts, and the tackle made fast to the bumkin shroud.

Outrigger guys

If the mizen or jigger was situated so far aft that the leech of the mizen or jigger sail projected out over the stern of the ship, as was often the case from the 15th to the early 17th century, an outrigger had to be fitted to take the sail's sheet. This outrigger in turn was supported by two guys, leading downwards at an angle on both sides.
A spliced eye in the outrigger guys was fitted over the end of the outrigger, and the other end fixed to ring bolts to starboard and port. Tensioning arrangements with blocks and deadeyes were extremely rare in the case of these guys.

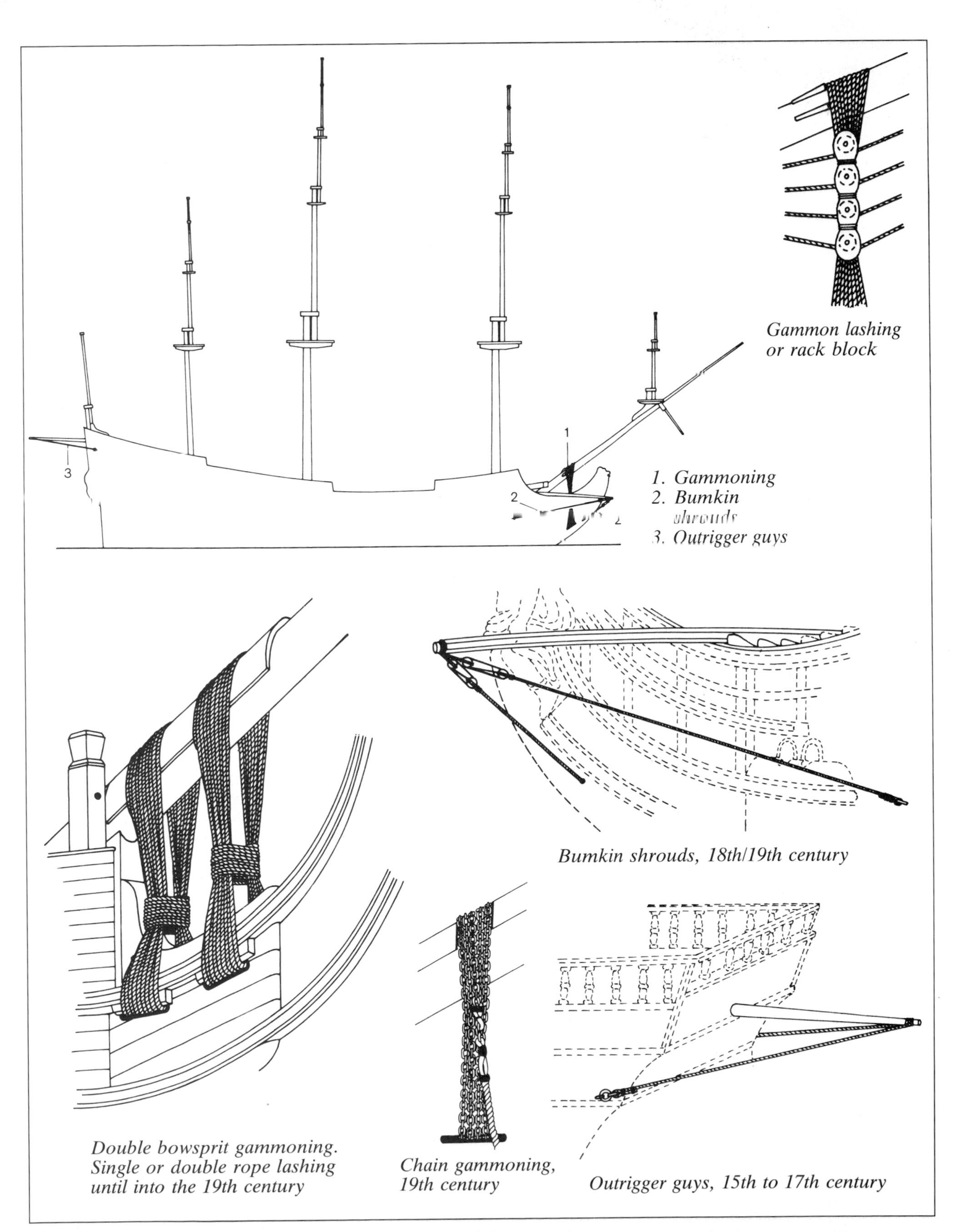

Gammon lashing or rack block

Bumkin shrouds, 18th/19th century

Double bowsprit gammoning. Single or double rope lashing until into the 19th century

Chain gammoning, 19th century

Outrigger guys, 15th to 17th century

The Bobstay

Around 1690 the bobstay began to appear, the purpose of which was to absorb the tension of the fore stay and the fore topmast stay. The bobstay was a French invention. A block was stropped to the knee of the head and a second one to the bowsprit, which was prevented from sliding by several thumb cleats. The blocks were linked by a tackle, which belayed to a cleat on the bowsprit, on the stem, or on the forecastle.

As early as 1695 the British followed the French example. In this case the bobstay was doubled over its full length, reeved at its lower end through the hole in the knee of the head, was spliced together at its upper end, and a deadeye was seized into it. The two parts were seized together in several places. A second deadeye was stropped to the bowsprit, and the bobstay was set up with a deadeye lanyard exactly as described for setting up the shrouds. This form was adopted by the French and the rest of the Continental shipbuilders by the beginning of the 18th century.

Until about 1850 the bobstay remained very largely unchanged, only the number of them being increased: around 1700 there were two, around 1740 three, and around 1770 a cap bobstay was fitted to the bowsprit cap.

The bobstays were tensioned with deadeyes, although from 1750 on hearts were used more and more on the Continent. After 1850 the bobstays – now usually fitted singly again – were made from chains, and set up with hearts or rigging screws (see also JIB RIGGING).

The Bowsprit shroud

From 1710 on the bowsprit was given lateral support with one or two pairs of shrouds. The bowsprit shrouds were fixed to the hull sides to starboard and port on eye bolts, and were initially set up with blocks, but soon after with deadeyes (Continental) or hearts (British, and from about 1770 also Continental). As with the bobstays chains were used for the bowsprit shrouds from about 1850, which were set up with hearts or rigging screws.

Head Stay. Fixed to an eye or ring bolt on the head, and set up to port and starboard on the forecastle bulkhead with deadeyes. Appeared around 1680, and disappeared again in 1720

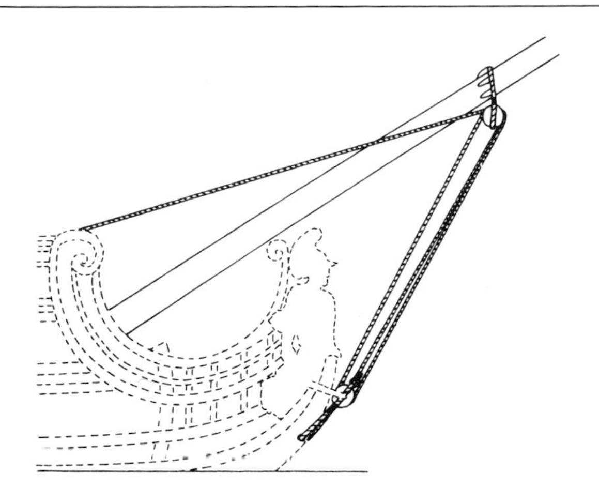

1. Bobstay, French 1690

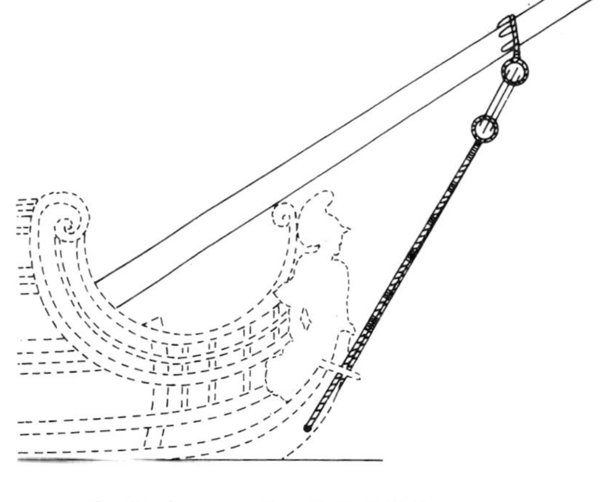

2. Bobstay, English 1695

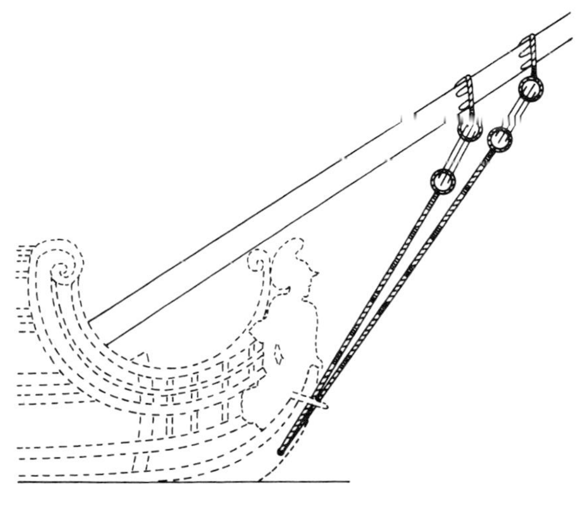

3. Bobstays, 1700

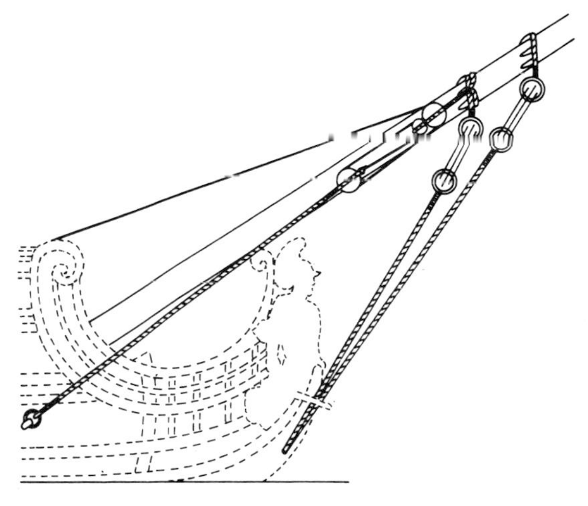

4. Bobstays and bowsprit shrouds, 1720

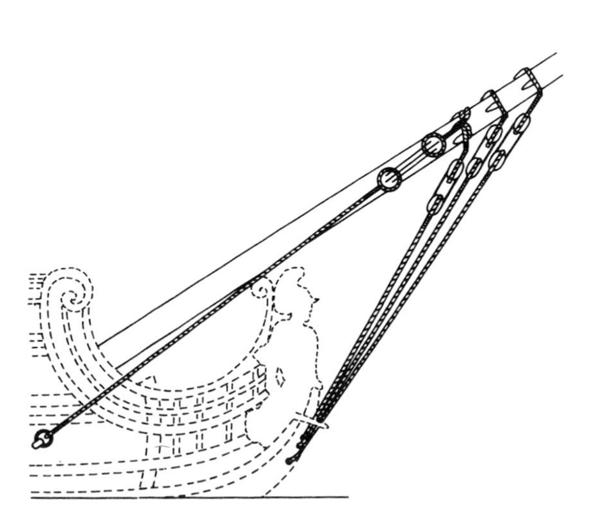

5. Bobstays and bowsprit shrouds, 1740

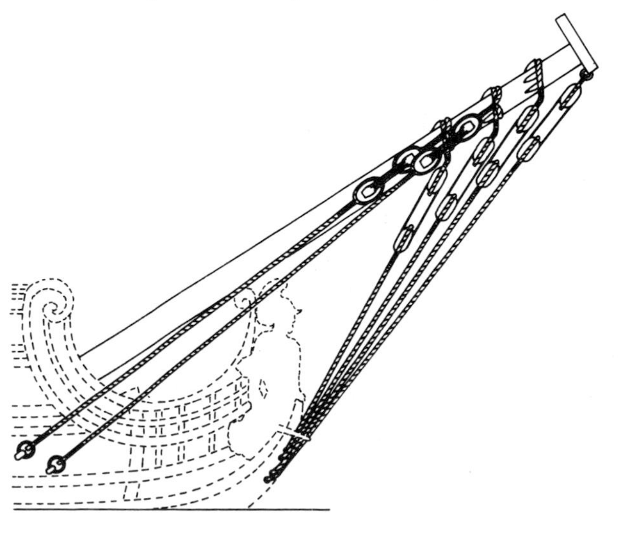

6. Bobstays and bowsprit shrouds, 1770

Loading tackles

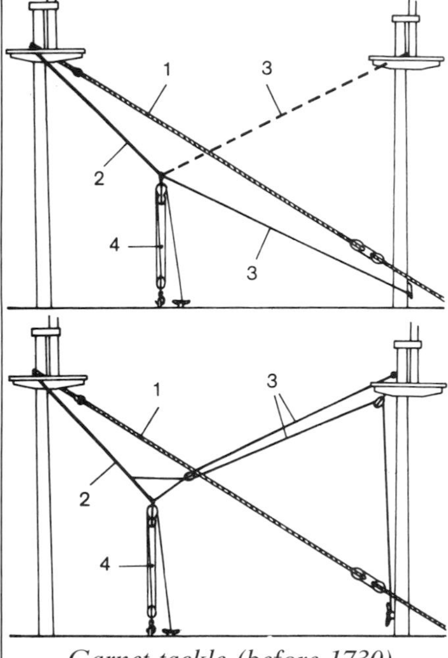

Garnet tackle (before 1730)
1. Mainstay; 2. Pendant;
3. Guy; 4. Tackle

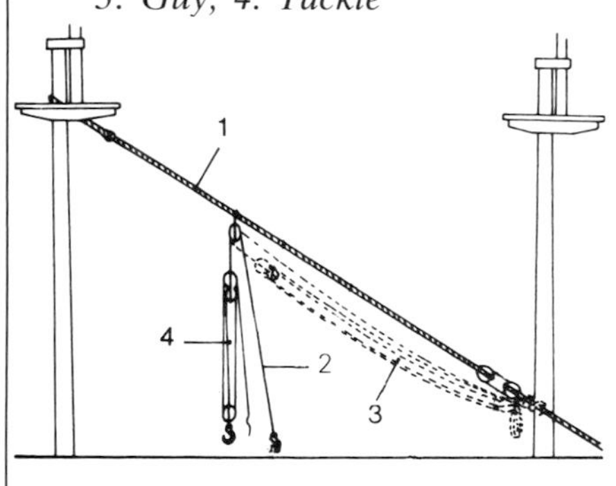

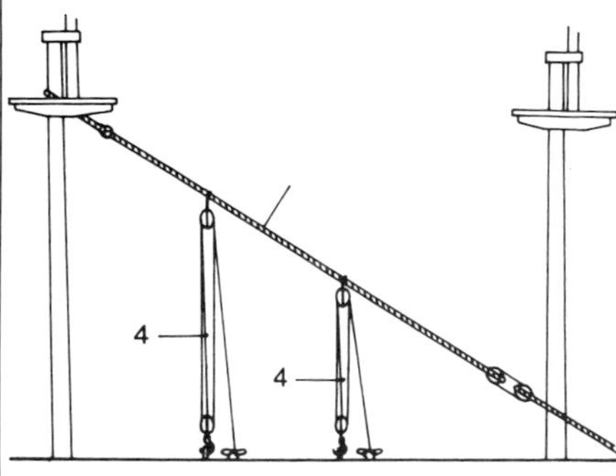

Stay tackle (after 1730)
1. Mainstay; 2. Runner;
3. Secured position; 4. Tackles

Various forms of tackles were used for moving loads, for tightening deadeye lanyards when setting up the shrouds, and for moving the ships' boats.

Lower mast tackles (Foretackle, maintackle and mizen burton tackle)
The lower mast tackles appeared in the course of the 16th century, initially on the mainmast and the foremast. A seized eye in the bight of a rope was fitted over the masthead of the main and fore lower masts below the shrouds, first to starboard then to port (more details on this in the chapter THE SHROUDS), so that on both sides two pendants hung down. A fiddle or double block was then spliced into the aftermost pendant at half to two thirds mast height, the mast tackle reeving through it. The foremost pendant was one foot shorter and was fitted with a single block for a runner.
In the single block form the runner reeved through the block, and was spliced into the upper block of the mast tackle. The standing end was fastened to an eyebolt in the deck. In the double block form a further double block completed the tackle. Hooks were stropped to the lower blocks, which were engaged in rings on the channel when the tackles were not in use. These rings were very frequently fitted with a small chain plate. The running part of the tackle belayed inboard on a belaying pin. By 1720 at the latest the pendants were served, as were the strops round the blocks and hooks.
Except on small ships the main and foremasts always carried double mast tackles. The mizen mast usually carried only one tackle called a burton on each side, which was fitted round the masthead with a spliced eye. Burton tackles were also carried on the main and fore topmasts in British ships as early as the very early 17th century, although only one on each side, and of correspondingly smaller dimensions, but on the Continent these only appeared from the last quarter of the 17th century. Burton tackles on the mizen topmasts were only carried by a few large ships prior to 1650 after which date they became extinct.

Garnet and stay tackles
The garnet tackle also appeared in the 16th century, and was still in use in the 19th century. Garnet tackles were usually double, and only smaller ships carried a single garnet tackle with a spliced eye.
The pendant of the garnet tackle was fitted with a cut splice, a lashed eye or a horseshoe splice, which was shipped over the shrouds on the main masthead in British ships, and in ships rigged after the British pattern. On Continental ships the pendant was in the form of a stay, but had no mouse; instead it had a seized eye as on the double shrouds, which was laid round the main masthead (see also SHROUDS AND STAYS).
Take care here. Although already discussed, the garnet tackle is the last part of the standing rigging to be fitted. The guy was fixed to the foremast or to the fore top with a seized eye.
A fiddle block was suspended between these two ropes, and formed a tackle with a lower hook block. The stay where the tackle was secured directly to the mainstay (drawing bottom left) came into use around the middle of the 18th century. When not in use the hook of the stay tackle was engaged in a ring on deck.

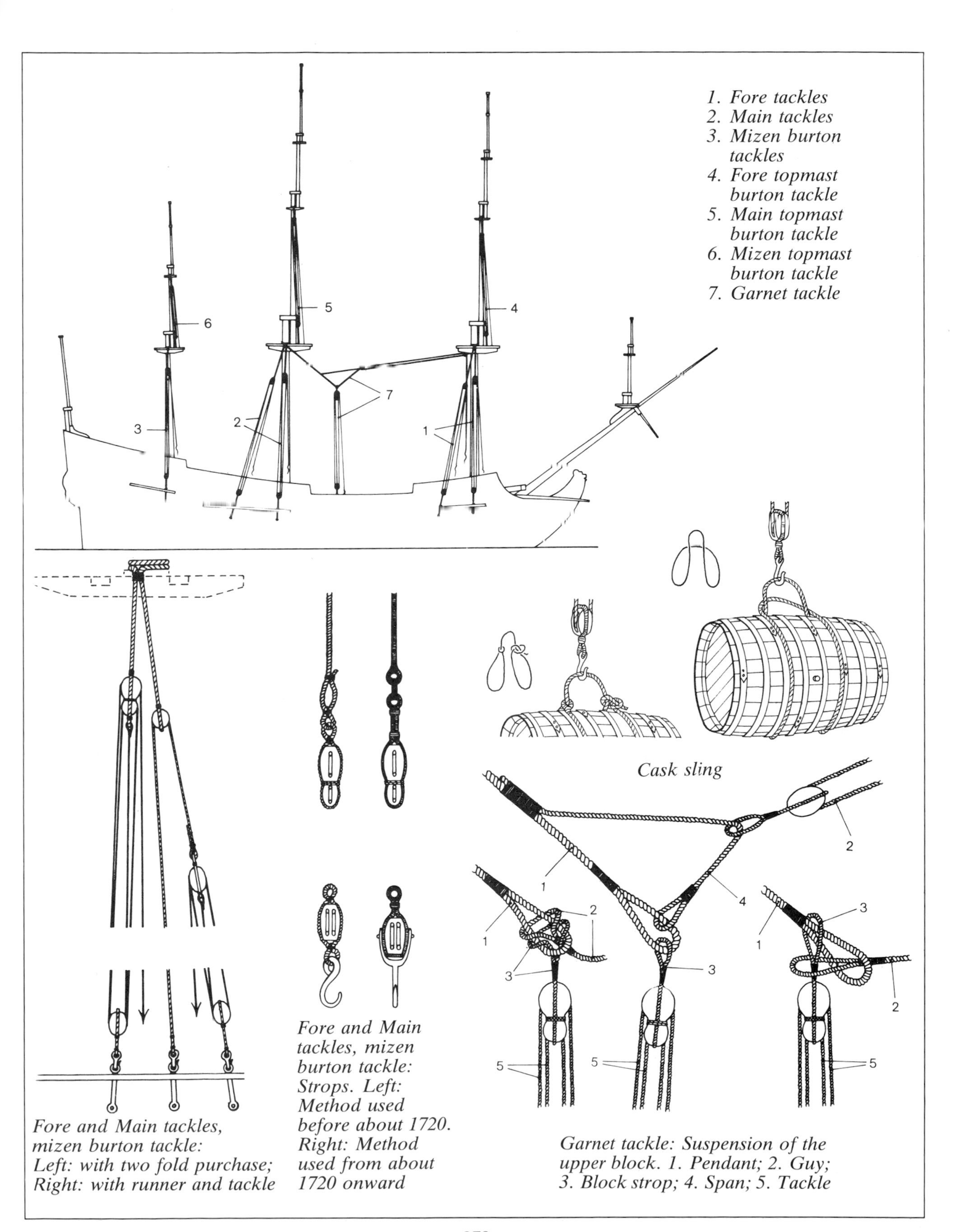

Fore and Main tackles, mizen burton tackle: Left: with two fold purchase; Right: with runner and tackle

Fore and Main tackles, mizen burton tackle: Strops. Left: Method used before about 1720. Right: Method used from about 1720 onward

Garnet tackle: Suspension of the upper block. 1. Pendant; 2. Guy; 3. Block strop; 4. Span; 5. Tackle

Shrouds

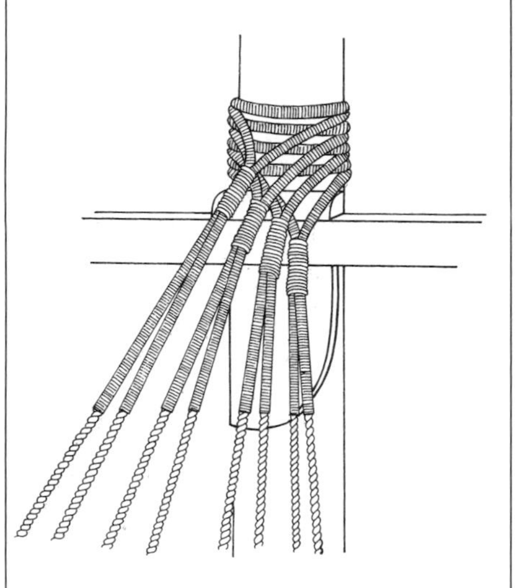

Sequence of shrouds

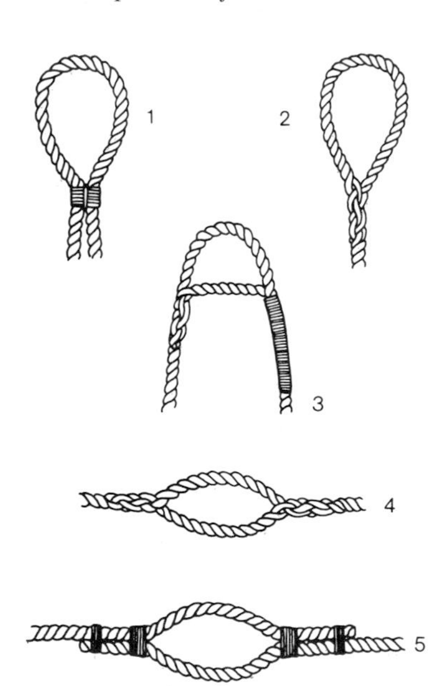

Eyes for shrouds and backstays: 1. Seized eye for double shrouds and backstays; 2. Spliced eye for single shrouds and backstays; 3. Horseshoe splice for double backstays; 4. Cut splice, and 5. Seized eye for single shrouds and backstays

The purpose of the shrouds was to provide the mast with lateral and after support. Until part way into the 14th century an average of one to three pairs of shrouds had proved adequate, but in the 15th and 16th centuries the number of pairs of shrouds increased by leaps and bounds. A dozen pairs of shrouds (one pair always counted as starboard – port) on the main mast was almost the rule, and 16 pairs was not exceptional, many ships carrying as many as 18 to 20 pairs. At the beginning of the 17th century this great mass of rope began to be reduced again to a more sensible amount. On large ships the number of pairs of shrouds on the mainmast varied from 9 to 11, on the foremast 8 to 10, on the mizen mast 4 to 6. On small ships the main mast had 6 or 7, the fore mast 5 or 6, the mizen mast 2 to 4 pairs. These figures remained the same until the 20th century.

Shrouds gang

In each case two shrouds formed a gang. This means that an eye was seized in to the middle of a rope of well over double the distance from channel to masthead. The eye was very slightly larger than the girth of the masthead, over which it was fitted and crossed over in such a way that the two ropes of the gang came down together on the same side – alternately starboard and port. The foremost gang was always on the starboard side. If there was an odd number of pairs of shrouds the last pair was either fitted singly with eye splices, or was doubled over the masthead with a horseshoe splice, cut splice or seized eye, in which case the one rope led downwards to starboard, the other to port.

Shrouds

In the second half of the 16th century the use of opposite laid ropes for the starboard and larboard shrouds was introduced although this practice never became universal. Right-handed shrouds were used for the larboard side, and left-handed shrouds on the starboard side.
The shrouds themselves were also wormed at the latest by the second half of the 16th century. The foremost shroud of each mast was wormed, parcelled and served from the first half of the 16th century on. From the middle of the 16th century in England, and from around 1680 on the Continent, the eye round the masthead was also served, initially as far as the seizing, but soon right down to just below the futtock stave. Serving at the lower end of the shroud, where it enclosed the deadeyes or the thimble of the rigging screw, first appeared during the 19th century.
The best sequence for the model maker is to make the shrouds first, that is to worm and serve them, and then fix them all over the masthead. The loose ends dangling down can be left hanging freely for the time being.

Turning in the deadeyes

Deadeyes were turned into the lower end of the shrouds, by means of which the shrouds were set up. The upper deadeyes should all be in a straight line parallel to the channels – this is easier advised than accomplished! For this reason all the seizings and deadeye lanyards are fixed temporarily at first; don't cut the rope ends short at this stage. Bear in mind what I said at the beginning of this chapter: the ropes should not be permanently fixed until the tension of all the shrouds, stays and backstays has been matched; the ropes can then be cut to the correct length.
Here is a little "wrinkle" which will undoubtedly make this job easier for you: set up only the first and last pairs of shrouds of the mast initially, and be sure that they are exactly an equal distance from

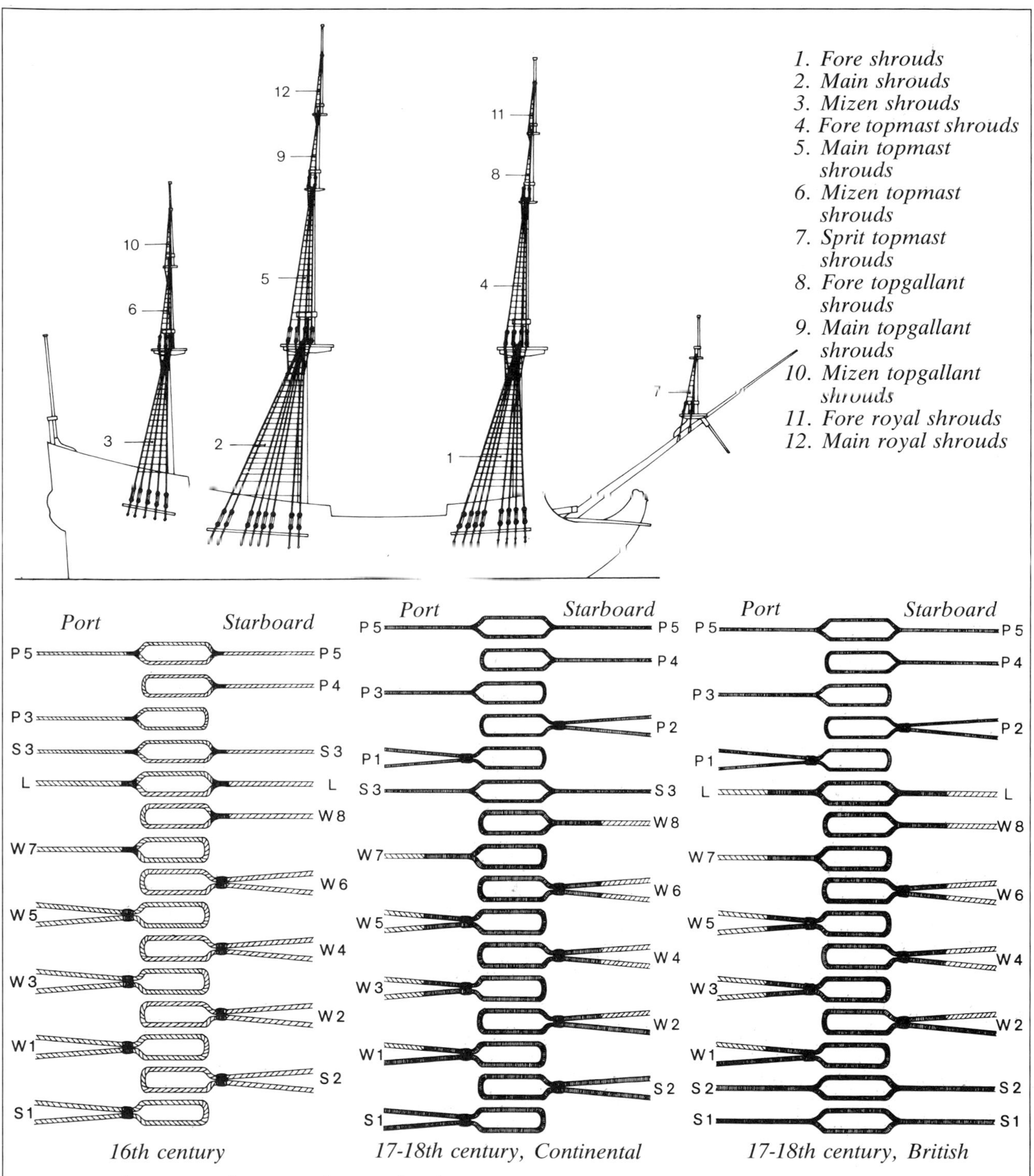

Sequence of ropes at the masthead:
Lower masthead: S1,2: Foretackle, Main tackle or Mizen burton tackle pendants, W1-6; pairs of shrouds, W7, 8: single shrouds or swifters (when number of shrouds was odd), L: Garnet pendant – Main mast only before 1730.
Topmast head: S1: Burton pendants – Fore and Main masts only, shrouds – as for lower shrouds, P1, 2: pairs of standing backstays, P3, 4: shifting backstays, single, P5: shifting backstays, cut splice

Shrouds

the channels. Now attach the mast stay and balance the tensions – this will not be the final setting, but any final alteration will be minimal. Now tie a thin guide batten above the first and last deadeyes – on ships after the middle of the 19th century the sheer pole assumes this task – and you will be able to align the remaining deadeyes with this batten without too much trouble. The deadeyes are turned in as follows: the shroud is passed round the deadeye, the short end crossing inboard of the standing part and the two parts seized together at the cross with a throat seizing. A further two round seizings secure the two parts together, the end being whipped and capped with canvas to keep the wet out.
If the shrouds are right-handed the short end is to the right of the standing part when viewed from inboard and vice versa. Consequently, with all shrouds right-handed the short end will be forward on the larboard side and aft on the starboard side; if all the shrouds are left-handed then the short end will be aft on the larboard side and forward on the starboard side. When the larboard shrouds are laid right-handed and the starboard shrouds left-handed, as previously mentioned, then all the short ends are forward.

The lanyards
The shrouds were set up by means of lanyards reeved through the deadeyes. The lanyard began with a stopper knot, on the inboard side of the outer hole of the upper deadeye, which was opposite the short end of the shroud.
N.B. When setting up the lanyard, never finish first the one side and then the other side, but always work alternately from starboard to port. For safety's sake, also check regularly with a small plumb bob that the mast has not moved from the vertical position on the centreline. The lanyard reeves through the deadeyes, as shown in the illustration, that is, always from inboard to outboard between the upper deadeye and the shroud, half hitching it round the two parts of the shrouds and expending the rest of the lanyard with turns round both parts and stopping the end; it is a good idea to secure the end of the lanyard in its place with a drop of glue.

The futtock stave
The futtock stave is a served piece of rope (sometimes, in the 16th and 17th centuries, a wooden spar or metal rod) which was seized to the shrouds the same distance below the upperside of the trestle trees as the underside of the cap was above the trestletrees. Generally the futtock stave was seized to the outside of the shrouds, but sometimes it was fitted inside or even double (inside and outside).

The futtock shrouds
The futtock plates of the topmast deadeyes were secured by the futtock shrouds. These were connected to the futtock plates by hooks, turned round the futtock stave, and seized to the shroud in three places. On Dutch ships of the 17th century double futtock shrouds also appeared.
From about the middle of the 18th century the futtock shrouds were occasionally seized to the futtock stave. From about 1830 on iron bars began to be used for the futtock shrouds. They were shackled to an iron band on the mast directly below the mast cheeks, and made the futtock stave obsolete. On large ships the topgallant futtock shrouds were made in the same way; on smaller ships they consisted of a served strop, with thimbles seized into the ends, through which the shackles passed.

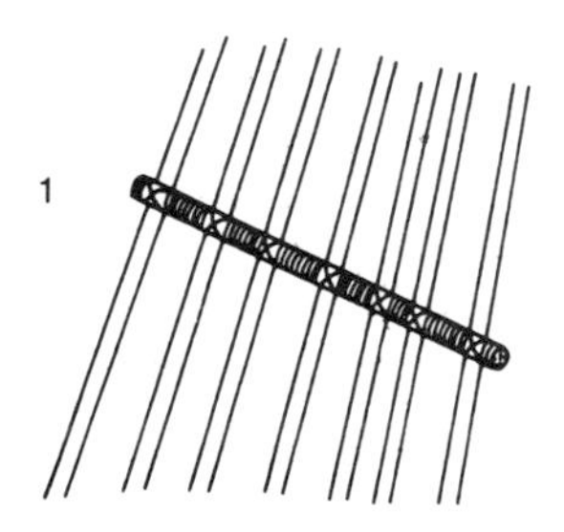

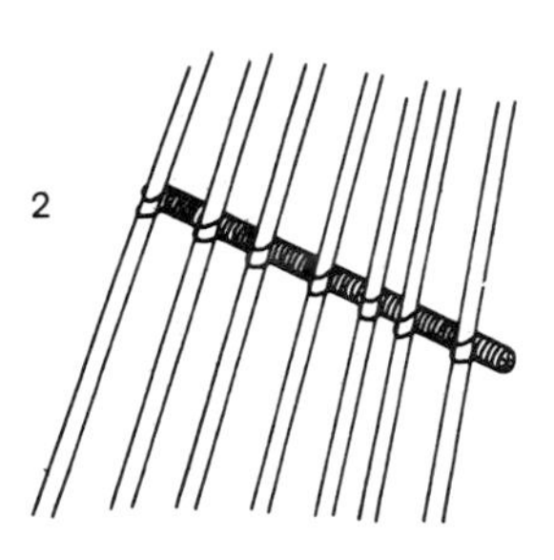

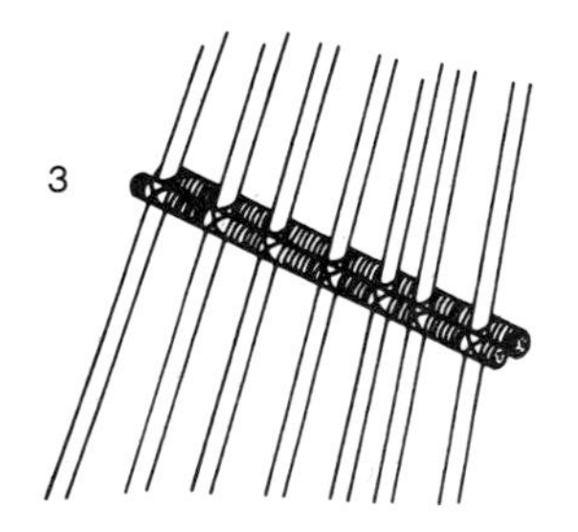

Futtock stave:
1. Single, outside the shrouds
2. Single, inside the shrouds
3. Double, both sides of the shrouds

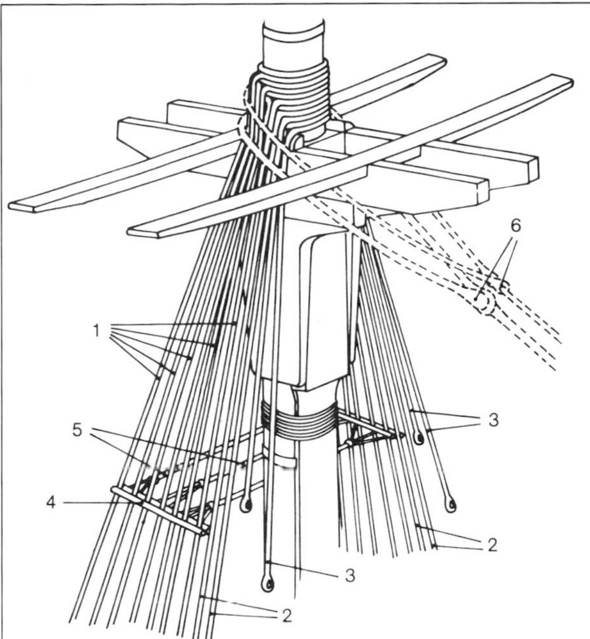

Sequence of the lower shrouds at the masthead: 1. Shrouds; 2. Single shrouds or swifters; 3. Fore tackle, Main tackle or Mizen burton tackle pendants; 4. Futtock stave; 5. Catharpins; 6. Stays

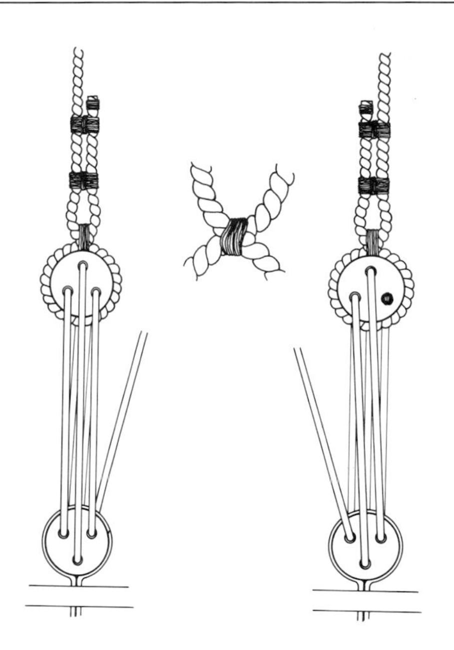

Lanyard: left from outboard, right from inboard. Enlarged sketch in the middle: the seizing above the upper deadeye. Note that it is vertical, and not horizontal like the two upper seizings, as shown on poor plans and models.

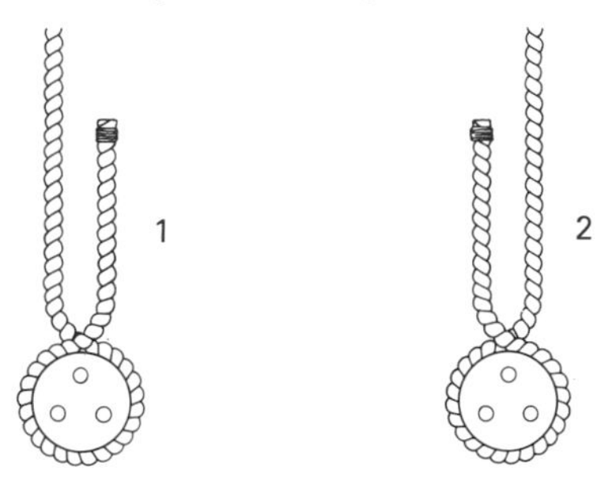

Shrouds laid in opposite directions: 1. Laid right; 2. Laid left

Shroud seizing and lead of the lanyard, seen from inboard

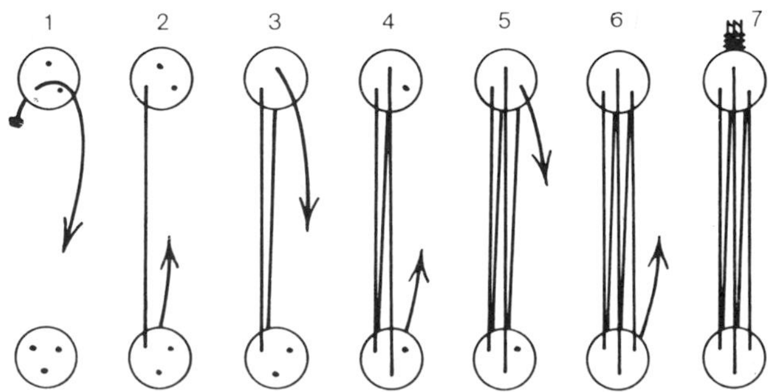

Run of the lanyard through the deadeyes – cable laid shrouds seen from outboard

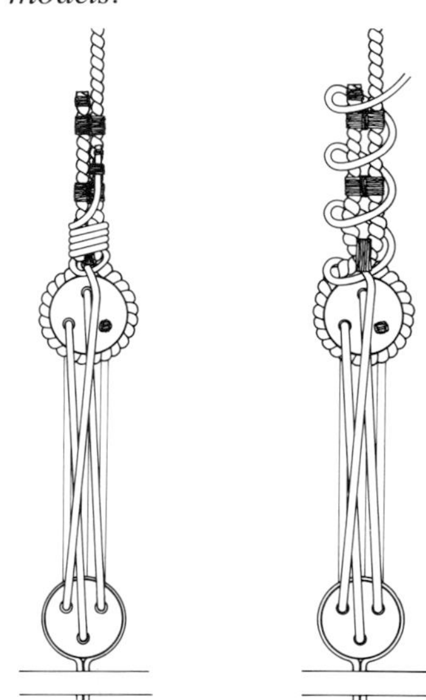

Run of the lanyard, seen from inboard. The lanyard is pulled through between deadeye and shroud, back under itself with a half hitch, then expended with round turns around the shroud and stopped to it.

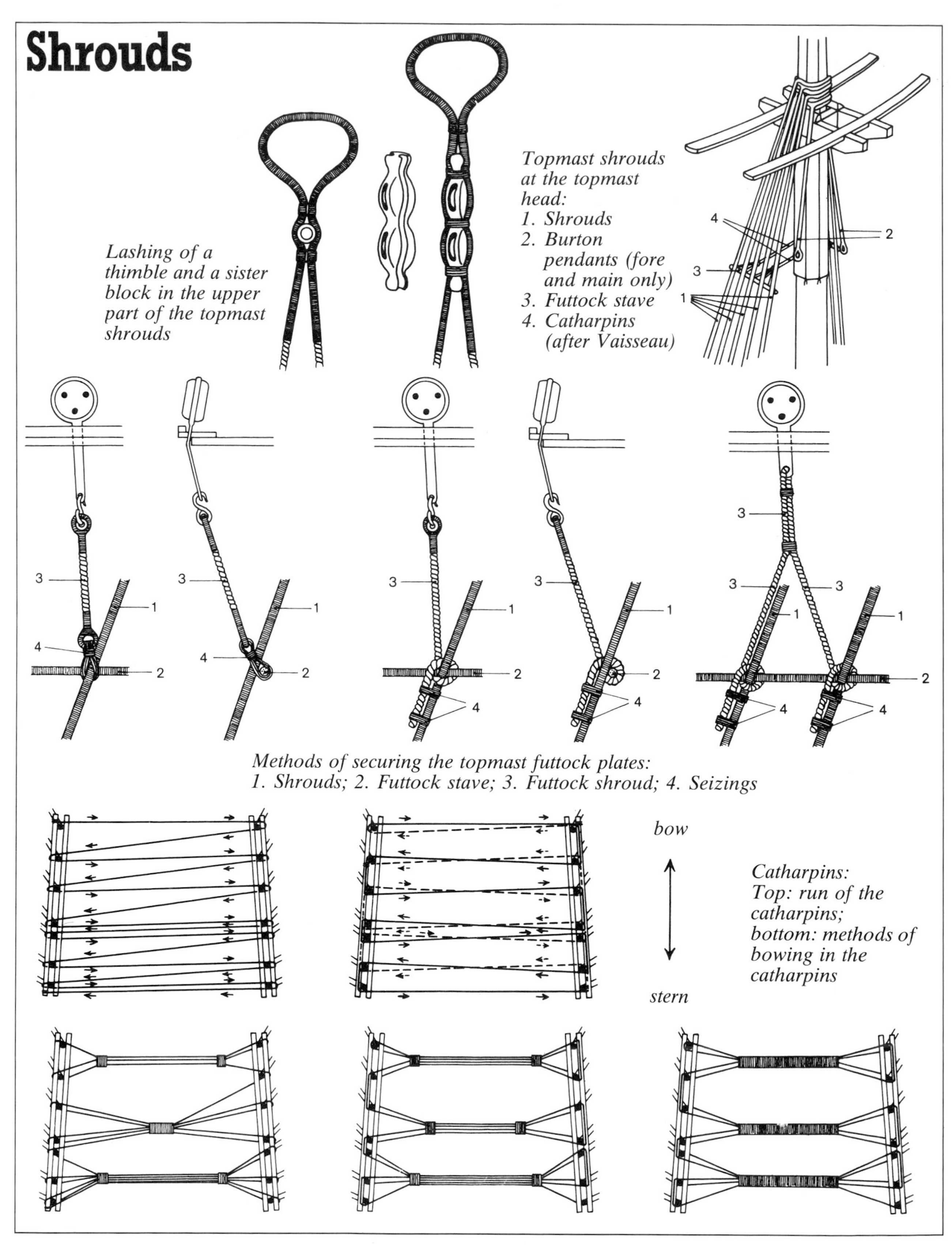
Shrouds
Lashing of a thimble and a sister block in the upper part of the topmast shrouds
Topmast shrouds at the topmast head:
1. Shrouds
2. Burton pendants (fore and main only)
3. Futtock stave
4. Catharpins
(after Vaisseau)
1
2
3
4
Methods of securing the topmast futtock plates:
1. Shrouds; 2. Futtock stave; 3. Futtock shroud; 4. Seizings
bow
stern
Catharpins:
Top: run of the catharpins;
bottom: methods of bowing in the catharpins

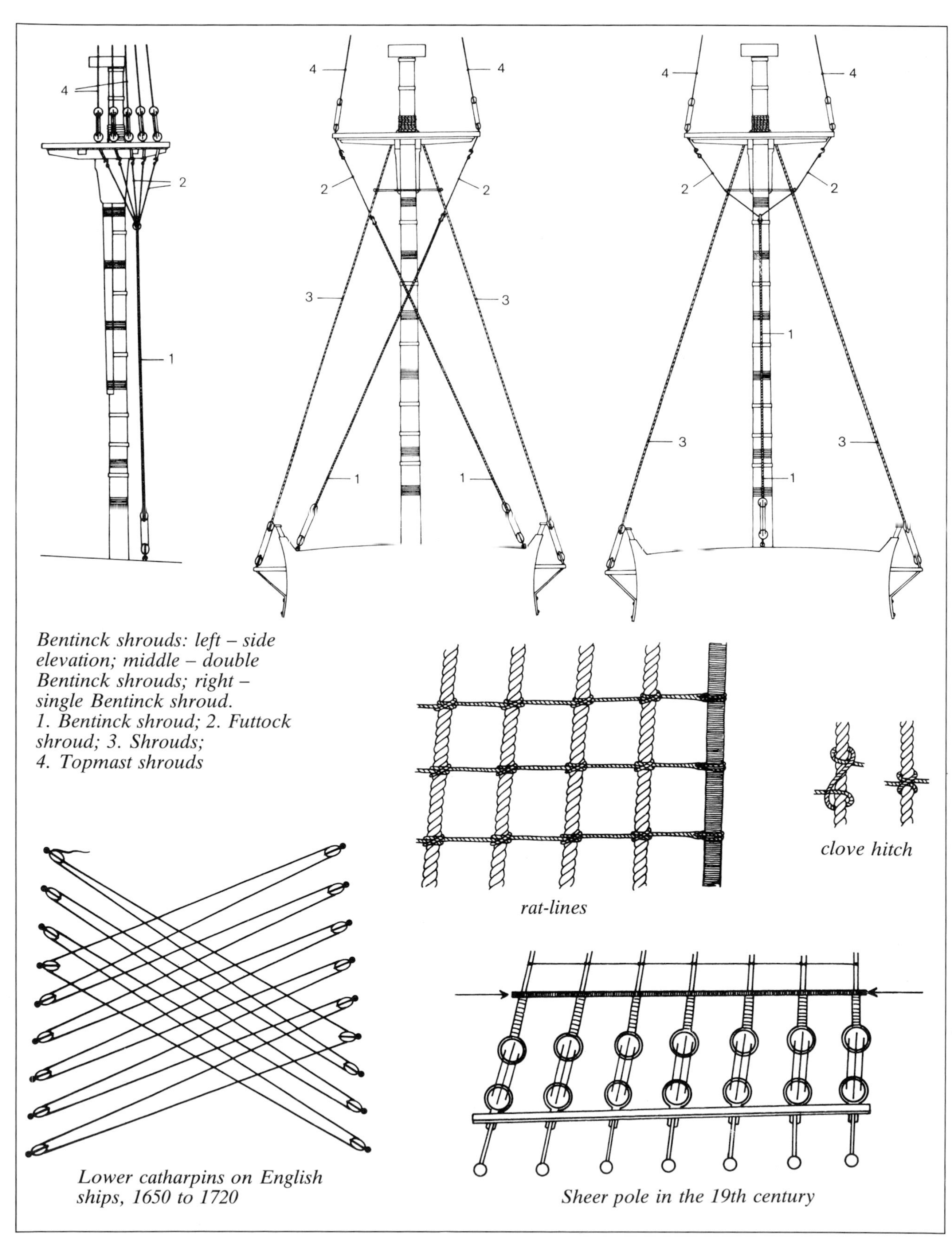

Bentinck shrouds: left – side elevation; middle – double Bentinck shrouds; right – single Bentinck shroud.
1. Bentinck shroud; 2. Futtock shroud; 3. Shrouds;
4. Topmast shrouds

rat-lines

clove hitch

Lower catharpins on English ships, 1650 to 1720

Sheer pole in the 19th century

Shrouds

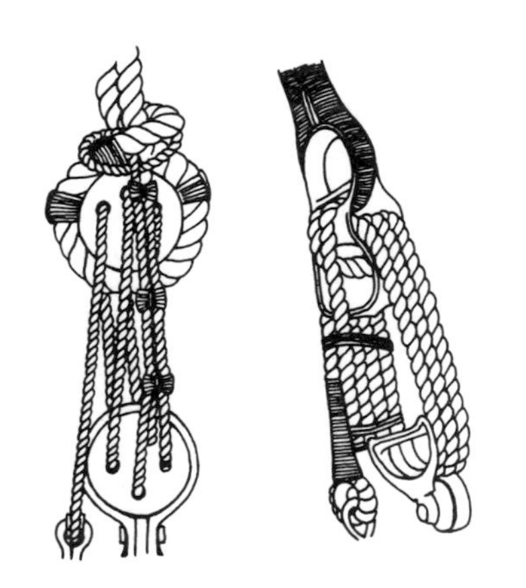

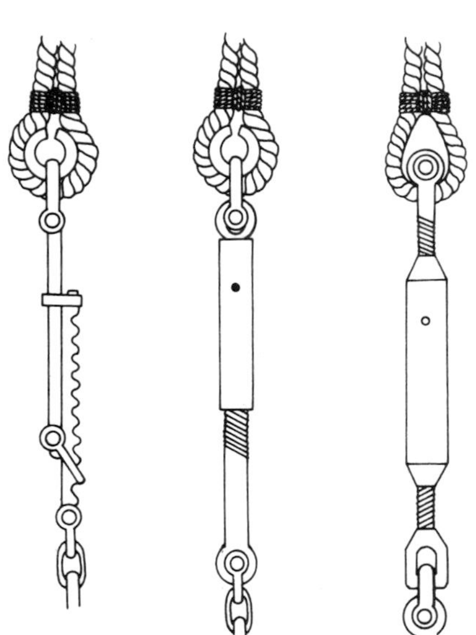

Methods of setting up the shrouds in the 19th century. Top: left, cutter stay fashion, right, iron heart. Bottom: left, rack; middle, rigging screw with single thread; right, rigging screw with left and right handed threads.

The bentinck shrouds
Additional shrouds for the lower masts, known as bentinck shrouds after their inventor Captain Wm. Bentinck, Royal Navy, were introduced into the British navy in the latter part of the 18th century. They were normally only rigged in very heavy weather.
Four or six short ropes with eyes spliced in one end were seized round the futtock stave and shrouds close up to the catharpins and led down through the shrouds where they were spliced into a common ring or seized to a thimble. In large ships the bentinck shroud was also spliced into this ring and led to a ringbolt in the opposite waterway where it was set up with a tackle. Small ships occasionally had the rings from both sides joined by a short span from which a single bentinck shroud led down to the foot of the mast and was set up in the same way.

The catharpins
From the middle of the 17th century on, it was usual to link the shrouds by catharpins. A line was looped round the futtock stave and the shrouds, and then lashed together with seizings – the various methods used are shown on the drawing. British warships occasionally had lower catharpins about one-third of the mast height above deck at the main and foremast, more rarely also on the mizen mast, which was rove through blocks seized to the shrouds. They were not used after 1730.

The topmast shrouds
The topmast shrouds were fitted and secured in the same way as the lower mast shrouds. The methods used for shipping the topmast shrouds on the masthead, the shrouds themselves, the deadeyes and lanyards were all identical to those used on the lower shrouds, except that the dimensions were correspondingly smaller and thinner. Around the middle of the 19th century it became standard practice in some areas to set up the topmast shrouds with small hearts or thimbles instead of deadeyes, especially in smaller ships.

The topgallant shrouds
In the 16th and 17th centuries the topgallant shrouds were attached by means of deadeyes, like the topmast shrouds.

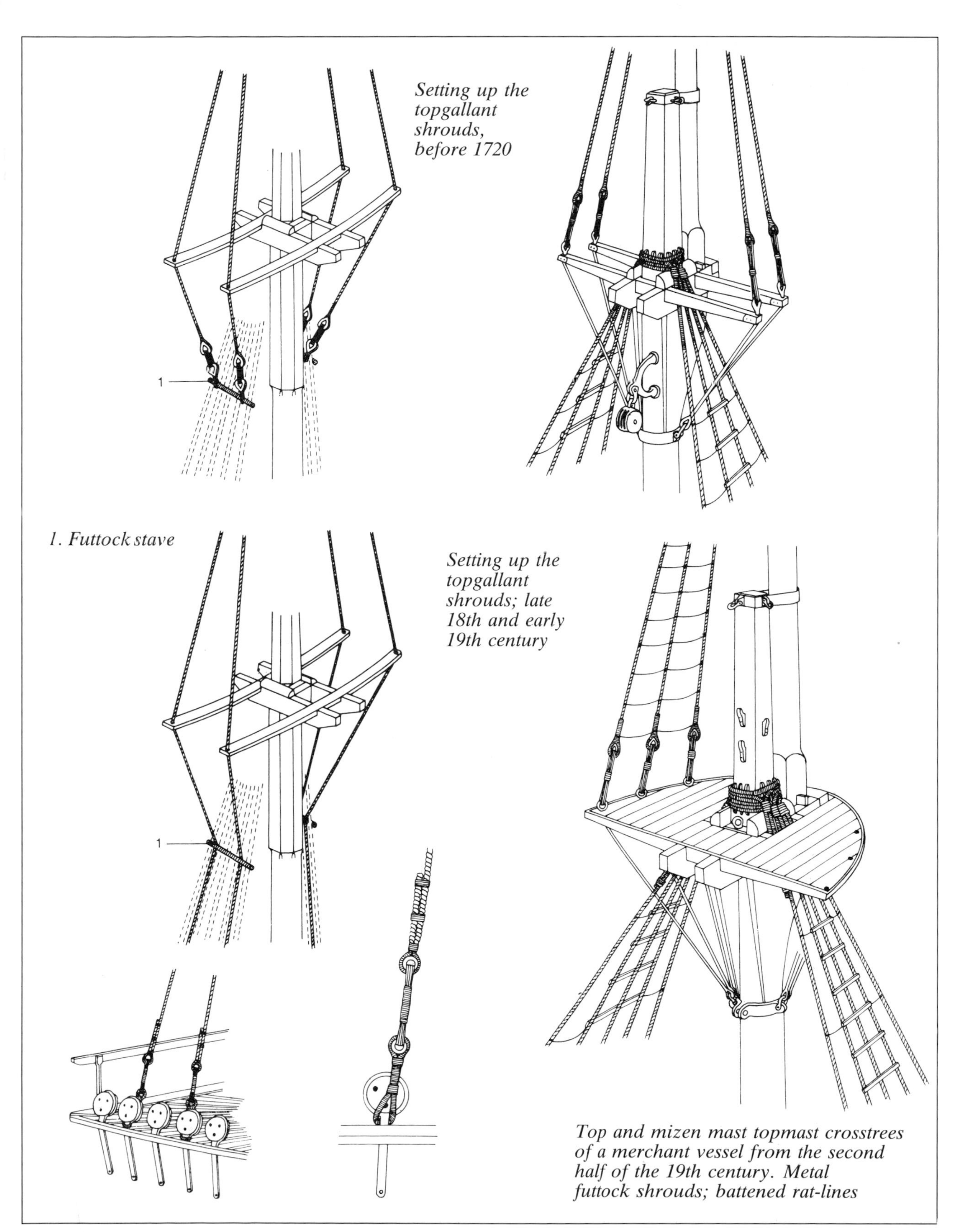

Setting up the topgallant shrouds, before 1720

1. Futtock stave

Setting up the topgallant shrouds; late 18th and early 19th century

Top and mizen mast topmast crosstrees of a merchant vessel from the second half of the 19th century. Metal futtock shrouds; battened rat-lines

Shrouds

Position of the shroud deadeyes (top) with reference to the channel deadeyes (bottom) and the channels

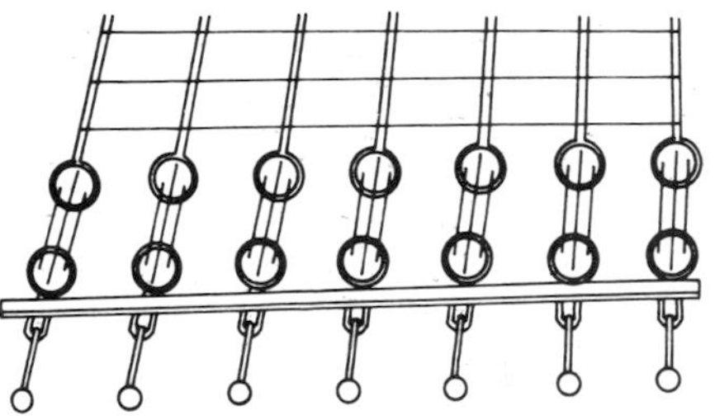

Correct!
Shroud deadeyes in one line, parallel to the channels

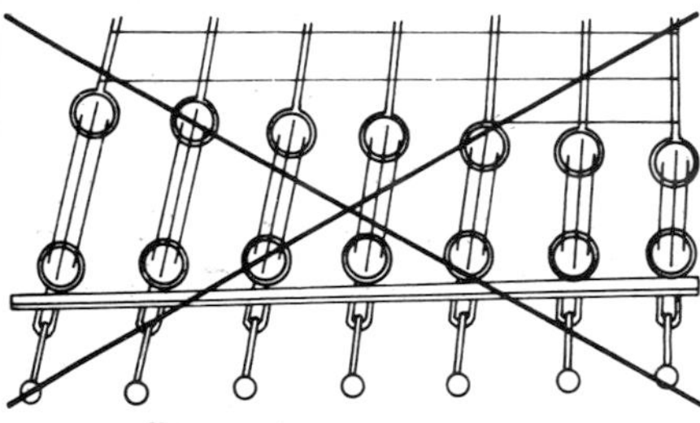

Wrong!
Shroud deadeyes rising towards the left

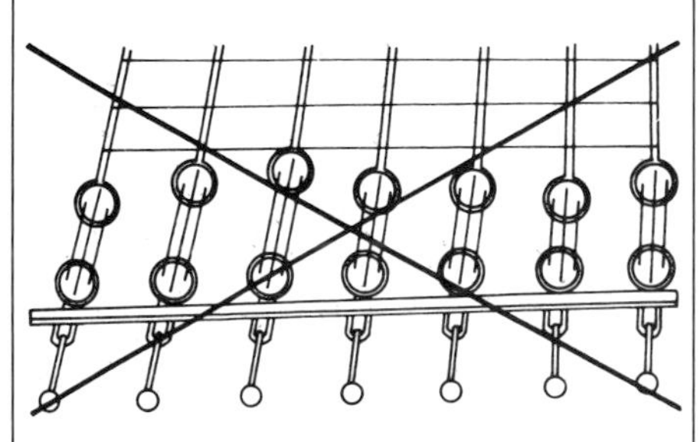

Wrong!
Shroud deadeyes at differing heights

After the early 18th century deadeyes were no longer used, and the topgallant shrouds were tensioned over the ends of the topmast crosstrees; on Continental ships they were attached to the futtock stave under the topmast crosstrees with small hearts or thimbles. In small ships they were simply lashed to the futtock stave and the topmast shrouds like the futtock shrouds. In British and American ships the topgallant shrouds were pulled through behind the futtock stave and taken down to the top, where they were set up with thimbles and lanyards with the lower thimble fixed to the chain plate of the lower top deadeye.

The royal shrouds
The royal shrouds were carried like the topgallant shrouds, and were fixed to the futtock stave of the topgallant shrouds.

The ratlines
The fitting of ratlines to the shrouds – known as rattling down – is rather a tedious task, but one which should be carried out with great accuracy. However, there is one way of making this job much easier: draw the first and last shroud on a piece of card, then draw in the ratlines as cross lines, and clamp the template behind the shrouds; the ratlines are then filled in following the template. The lower limit of the ratline is the rail, the upper limit is the futtock stave; the ratlines themselves should run parallel to the waterline. This job needs to be done on the lower shrouds, the futtock shrouds and the topmast shrouds, almost always the sprit topmast shrouds and the mizen topmast shrouds, but only rarely the topgallant shrouds, and never the royal shrouds.
The ratline spacing was about 15 or 16ins, and they were 1½ins in circumference. The ratlines must not be pulled tight; they should only form a loose connection between the shrouds. The drawing shows how they are attached. In the middle of the 19th century wooden battens were occasionally fitted between the middle shrouds instead of the ratlines. The drawing also shows how these were attached. They were originally about 1½ins high and ⅝in thick.

The sheer pole
Sheer poles were introduced in the middle of the 19th century to prevent the shrouds twisting. They were round iron bars which were seized to the shrouds above the deadeyes or rigging screws.

Rigging screws
After about 1830 rigging screws were frequently used in place of deadeyes for setting up shrouds, backstays and stays. Making rigging screws yourself is extremely difficult, indeed, almost impossible if you need metal ones. If you cast them in resin, you must be sure that they are strong enough to take the tension – and the occasional knock. Rigging screws, with opposite threads at either end, are just about impossible to make, although there are one or two commercial sources of rigging screws of this type of a very high quality.
Rigging screws were generally tarred black.

Model of a Flemish carrack of around 1480, from an engraving. A remarkable feature of the model is the number of shroud pairs: 8 on the foremast, 18 on the mainmast, 6 on the mizen mast. Main and fore shrouds are set up with the triangular deadeyes usual at the time, while the mizen shrouds are fitted with blocks, following the Mediterranean pattern. Rat-lines are not yet featured, in their place is a rope ladder. The small grapnel at the bowsprit is not an anchor, but a grappling hook.

Backstays

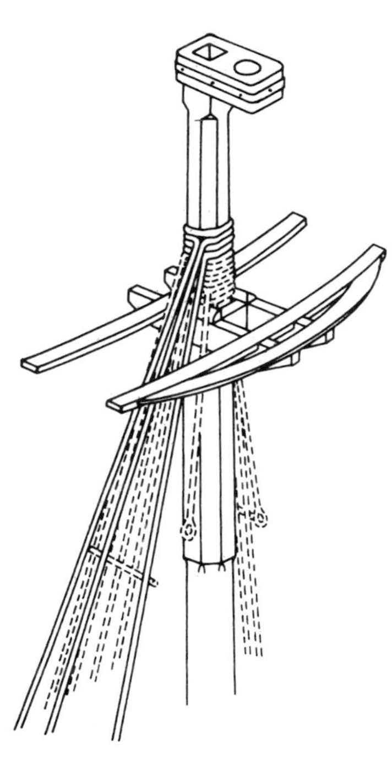

Backstays at the topmast head

During the course of the 17th century the topmasts grew longer, the topsails grew ever larger, and the topgallant masts and topgallant sails were added; by then the topmast and topgallant shrouds were no longer capable of providing adequate support. Initiall shifting backstays were fitted but by the middle of the 17th century standing backstays were added in Britain, initially one pair, but ultimately up to three pairs leading from the topmast crosstrees to th channels, and set up with deadeyes and lanyards.

The backstays were shipped round the topmast head above the topmas shrouds in exactly the same way as the topmast shrouds, and from th first half of the 18th century it became usual to serve many of them ove their full length. After 1840 backstays were often made of steel wire ropes, like the shrouds and stays.

We now to have to differentiate between shifting and standing backstays. Shifting backstays were set up with tackles, the running par of which belayed inboard on a belaying pin or cleat. Standing backstay were attached with deadeyes (they were the same size as the topmast shroud deadeyes), blocks (the running part of which was made fast above the upper block, as with the deadeyes), thimbles or rigging screws. The lower blocks of shifting backstays were fitted with a hook which was engaged in a ring bolt on the channel or on the ship's side abaft the channel. If this ring bolt was located on the channel, it usually had its own small chain plate.

The lower deadeyes, blocks and thimbles of standing backstays were fixed in place to the channels with small chain plates, although in some cases they had their own small backstay stools – or to ring bolts on the ship's side abaft the channels. Rigging screws were fixed to the channels or the ship's side with chain plates.

Backstays were fitted to topmasts, topgallant masts and royal masts. It was quite common to use a wide variety of methods to attach the backstays in one and the same ship. For example, including topgallan and royal masts HMS *Victory*, Lord Nelson's flagship at Trafalgar, carries three pairs of shifting backstays with blocks on the foremast, three pairs of standing backstays with deadeyes and one pai of standing backstays with thimbles, all on the fore channel; two pairs c shifting backstays with blocks and two pairs of standing backstays wit deadeyes on the main channel, plus one pair of shifting backstays with blocks, two pairs of standing backstays with deadeyes and one pair of standing backstays with thimbles on a stool abaft the main channel; on the mizen mast one pair of shifting backstays with blocks on the mizen channel, two pairs of standing backstays with deadeyes and one pair of standing backstays with thimbles on a stool abaft the mizen mast channel.

Before about the middle of the 19th century the backstays had a completely free run, but after that time they were led over spreaders on the crosstrees.

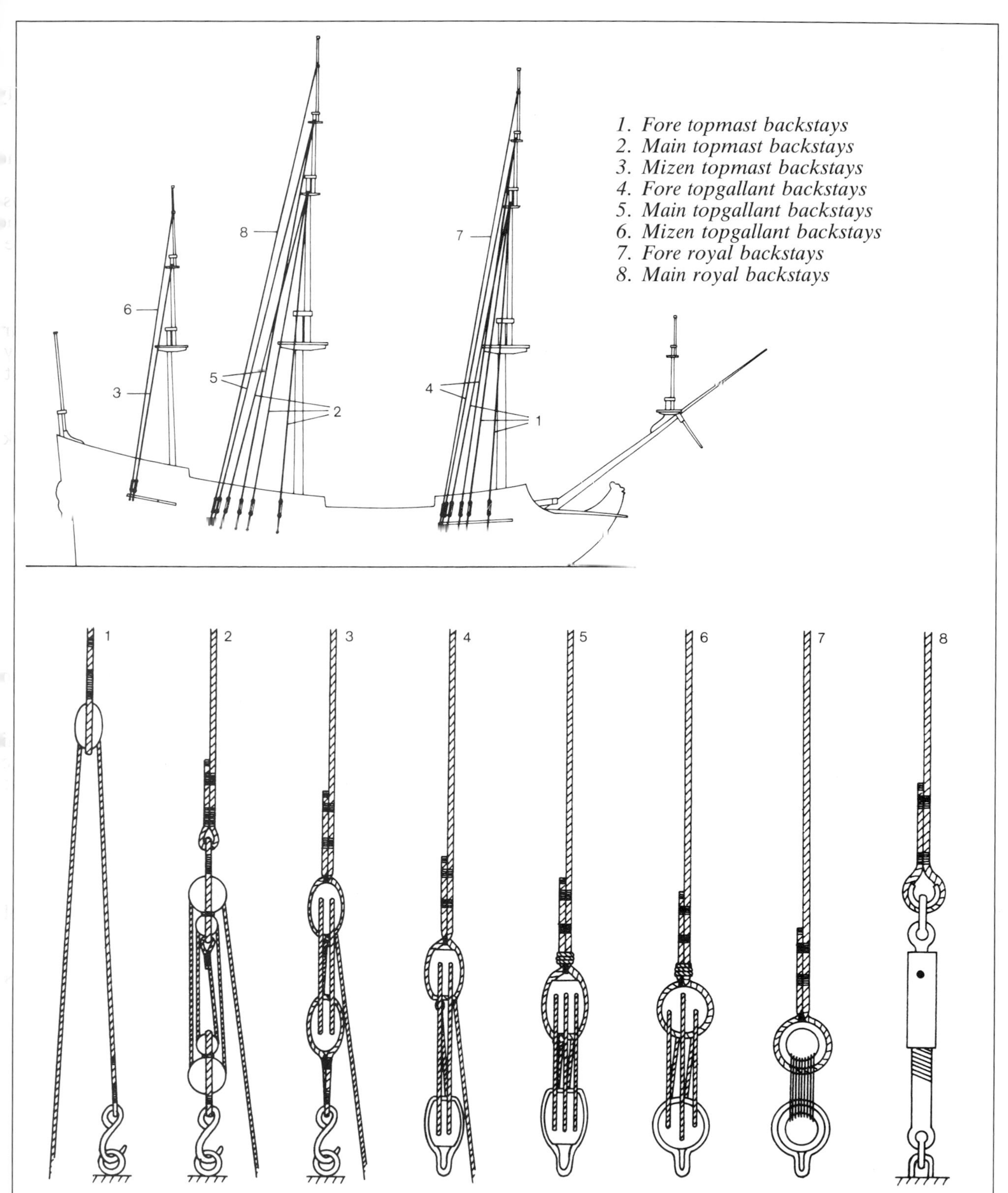

Methods of securing the backstays: 1. Shifting backstay, before 18th century; 2., 3. Shifting backstays, mid 18th century; 4. Shifting backstay, 18th/19th century; 5., 6. Standing backstays, 19th century; 7. Standing backstay, 18th/19th century; 8. Standing backstay, 19th century

The Stays

Lead of the stays:

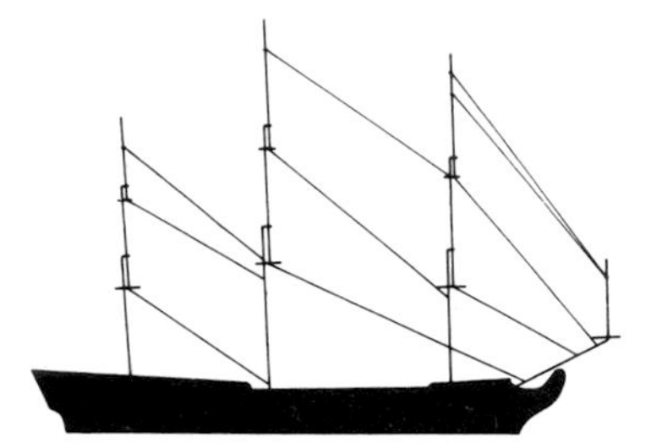

French warship, 1700

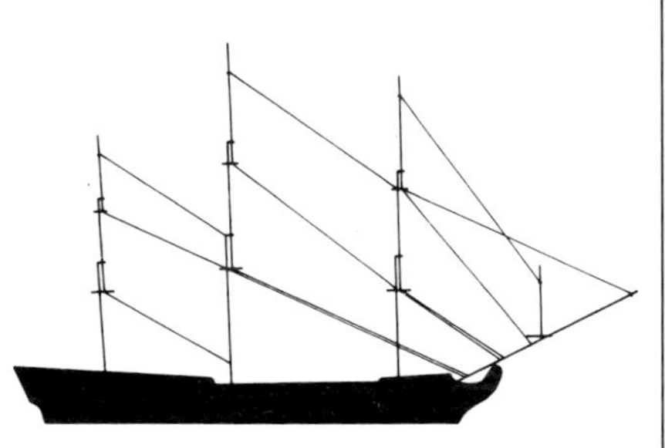

British warship, 1720

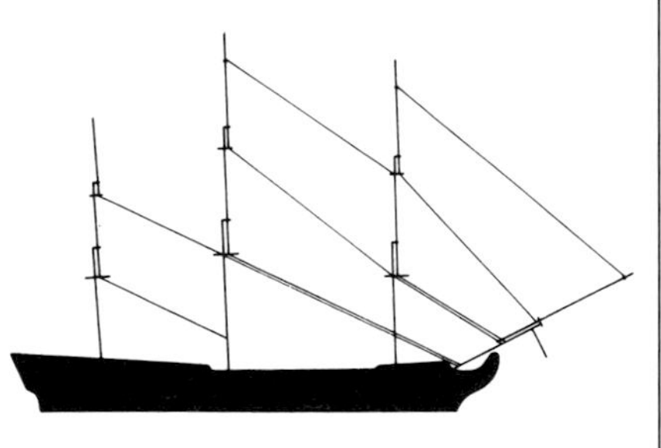

Swedish merchant ship, 1760

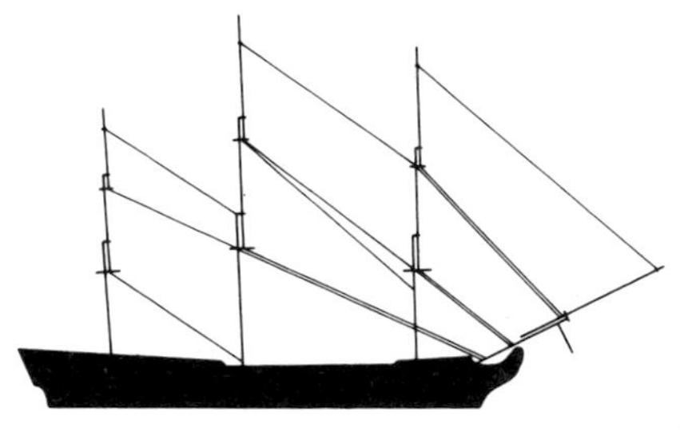

French warship, 1770

Next to the shrouds the stays are the most important part of the standing rigging, and in the history of the development of shipbuilding they are also the oldest part. They support the masts towards the bow, but they also serve to bring the shrouds and backstays to full supporting effect by exerting a balancing counter-tension. What I have already said twice in this chapter about equalising the tensions between shrouds, stays and backstays does not need to be repeated again here in detail, does it?

The stay eye

An eye was formed in the end of the stay which was rigged round the masthead over the shrouds and the trestletrees. Until the beginning of the 16th century a seized or spliced eye was used for this connection (although the latter was less durable), and in the case of double stays a seized eye was used, like those of the shrouds. The stay eye ended approximately below the front edge of the trestletrees.

In the first half of the 16th century a new method of forming the stay eye was introduced: the mouse. A small eye was spliced in at the upper end of the stay, which was just large enough for the rope itself to pass through, thus forming a loop. However, to prevent this eye tightening up on itself, the stay was locally thickened, this thicker part being termed the mouse.

The model mouse is made as follows: woollen thread is wrapped tightly round the stay to form the shape of the mouse, which in the 17th century was rounded, and in the 18th century more pear-shaped. It is a good idea not only to wrap the woollen threads round, but to glue them to the stay, so that the mouse cannot slip later. Then a loose ring of strong thread is fitted round the stay at both ends of the mouse. Using a needle and thread these two rings are then linked with a continuous series of vertical stitches. When this is complete, the thread is woven in and out as when darning, alternating above and below the thread all round. Take care always to take the thread alternately over and under the same thread, i.e. – for example – first round under, second round over, third round under, fourth round over etc., so forming a strong, evenly woven surface. Weaving a mouse evenly and neatly demands a degree of patience, but this is just the sort of small detail which makes a good model into an excellent one.

After the second half of the 16th century the stay eye itself was fully served, although the mouse was never served, thus leaving the elegant weaving exposed. Where the spliced eye of the stay end was located on the mouse, the rope was sheathed in a short leather sleeve for protection against chafing. The stay itself was wormed, like the shrouds, and was fully served from about the middle of the 19th century, when steel wire ropes were introduced. Around 1830 the mouse began to disappear; the upper end of the stay had a leg spliced into it with an eye spliced into the ends of both legs. They were seized together abaft the masthead with a rose lashing. A little later the system changed back again; the stay went over the masthead with the spliced eye, or – in the case of double stays – with a seized eye as used for the shrouds.

The mainstay

The mainstay was the strongest rope on the whole ship (with the exception of the anchor cables) and its blocks were the same length as the diameter of the main mast.

Until the middle of the 17th century the mainstay was set up with blocks or deadeyes.

After this time triple blocks were used exclusively on the Continent until

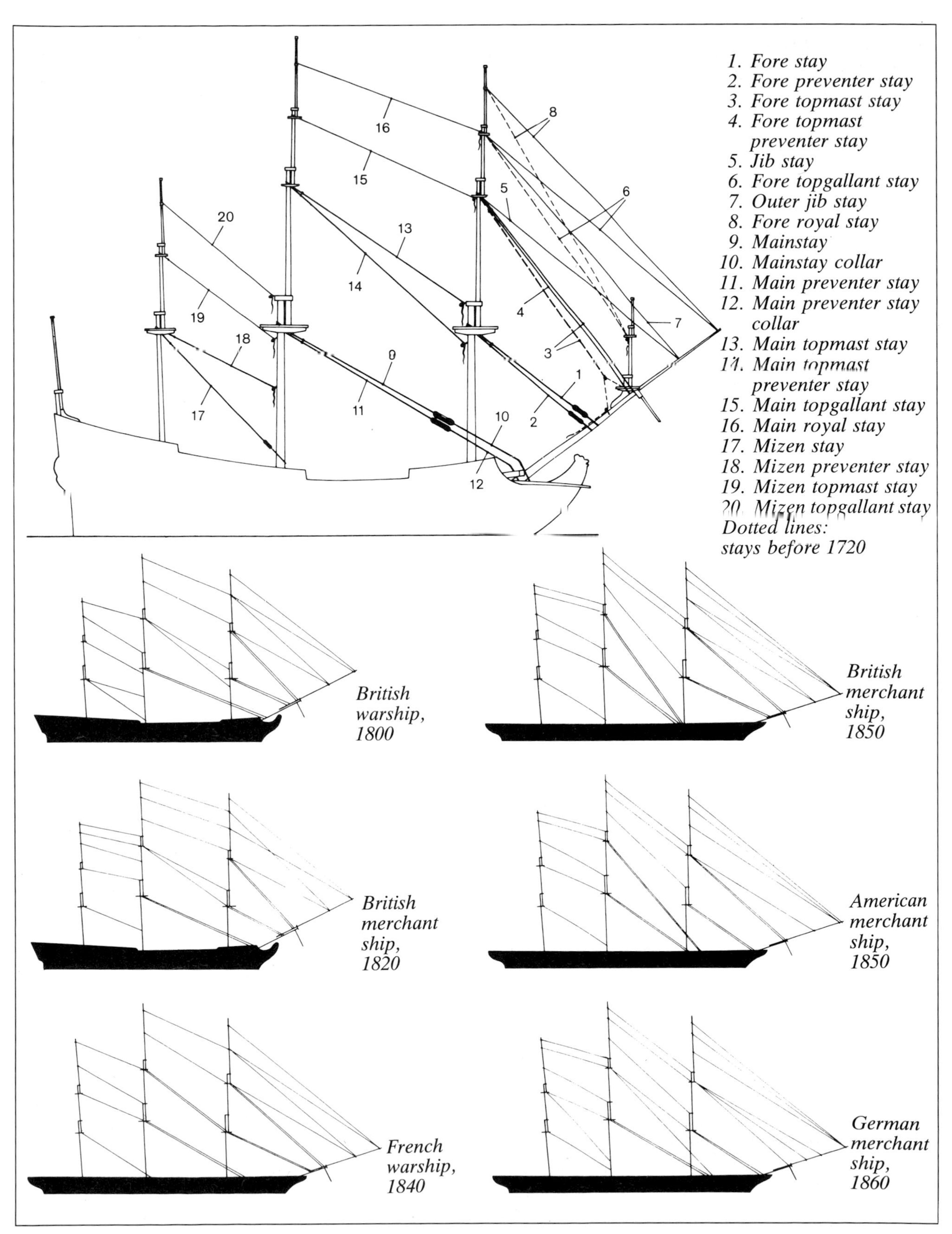
1. Fore stay
2. Fore preventer stay
3. Fore topmast stay
4. Fore topmast preventer stay
5. Jib stay
6. Fore topgallant stay
7. Outer jib stay
8. Fore royal stay
9. Mainstay
10. Mainstay collar
11. Main preventer stay
12. Main preventer stay collar
13. Main topmast stay
14. Main topmast preventer stay
15. Main topgallant stay
16. Main royal stay
17. Mizen stay
18. Mizen preventer stay
19. Mizen topmast stay
20. Mizen topgallant stay
Dotted lines: stays before 1720
British warship, 1800
British merchant ship, 1850
British merchant ship, 1820
American merchant ship, 1850
French warship, 1840
German merchant ship, 1860

The Stays

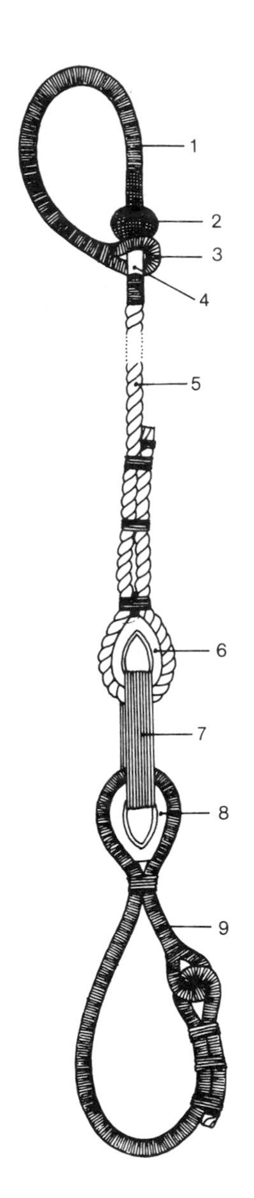

Mainstay with stay collar: 1. Stay eye at main masthead; 2. Mouse; 3. Spliced eye; 4. Leather parcelling; 5. Stay; 6. Upper heart; 7. Lanyard; 8. Lower heart; 9. Stay collar from 18th century, fully served

the first half of the 18th century. In Britain deadeyes were used up to 1690, and thereafter hearts, which also came more and more into use on the Continent after the middle of the 18th century. After 1830 the mainstay was set with rigging screws or thimbles. Continental ships also used deadeyes with 5 holes.
The lower stay block, deadeye or heart was seized into the stay collar, a rope, slightly thinner than the stay itself, which reeved through a hole in the gammoning knee, or engaged on the hook of the gammoning knee. The combination of blocks, deadeyes or hearts for setting up the stay could be located ahead of or abaft the foremast. If abaft the foremast, the stay collar was led either side of the foremast (at this point on the mast a rubbing sleeve was often fitted) and if ahead of the foremast, the mainstay usually passed to starboard of the mast.
The lanyard of the stay deadeyes was reeved and made fast in the same way as the shrouds. The fall of the stay tackle was attached to the lower block, and the free end was made fast by wrapping it round the middle of the lanyard several times; a similar arrangement was adopted if hearts were used.
A special feature of the mainstay of steam/sail driven ships of the 19th century should be noted. As the funnel was situated between the main and fore masts, the main stay was divided and made fast on the forecastle deck to starboard and port.

The forestay
The forestay was rigged in the same way as the mainstay, and made fast to the bowsprit. Various combinations of blocks were used up to the first half of the 16th century, whereafter the same method of setting up the forestay was adopted as for the mainstay, i.e. using blocks on the Continent and deadeyes in Britain, the lower of which was stropped to the bowsprit, where it was prevented from moving by thumb cleats.
Triangular hearts were used in British ships from 1690 until 1733 when an open lower heart was introduced through which the jib boom passed.

Main preventer stay and fore preventer stay
The preventer stays were slightly thinner than the stays proper, and their blocks, deadeyes, and hearts were correspondingly smaller; otherwise, however, they were attached in exactly the same way as the stays. From the middle of the 19th century, when double stays were fitted, the stay and preventer stay were one and the same rope.

The mizen stay
The mizen stay was attached to the masthead like the main and fore stays, and made fast with blocks, deadeyes or hearts at the foot of the mainmast.

The main topmast stay
Like the stays of the lower masts, the topmast stays were rigged over the topmast head by means of an eye secured with a mouse, or – in the 19th century – with a seized eye. The main topmast stay then passed through a leading block, which was stropped to the fore topmast just above the top, or to the foremast cap, and down to the deck, where it was set up with a tackle hooked to a ring bolt at the foot of the mast. In rare cases (mainly in the 16th century) the main topmast stay was attached to the fore top with deadeyes or blocks. The main topmast preventer stay followed the topmast stay, set up on the larboard side of the foremast with the main topmast stay set up to starboard.

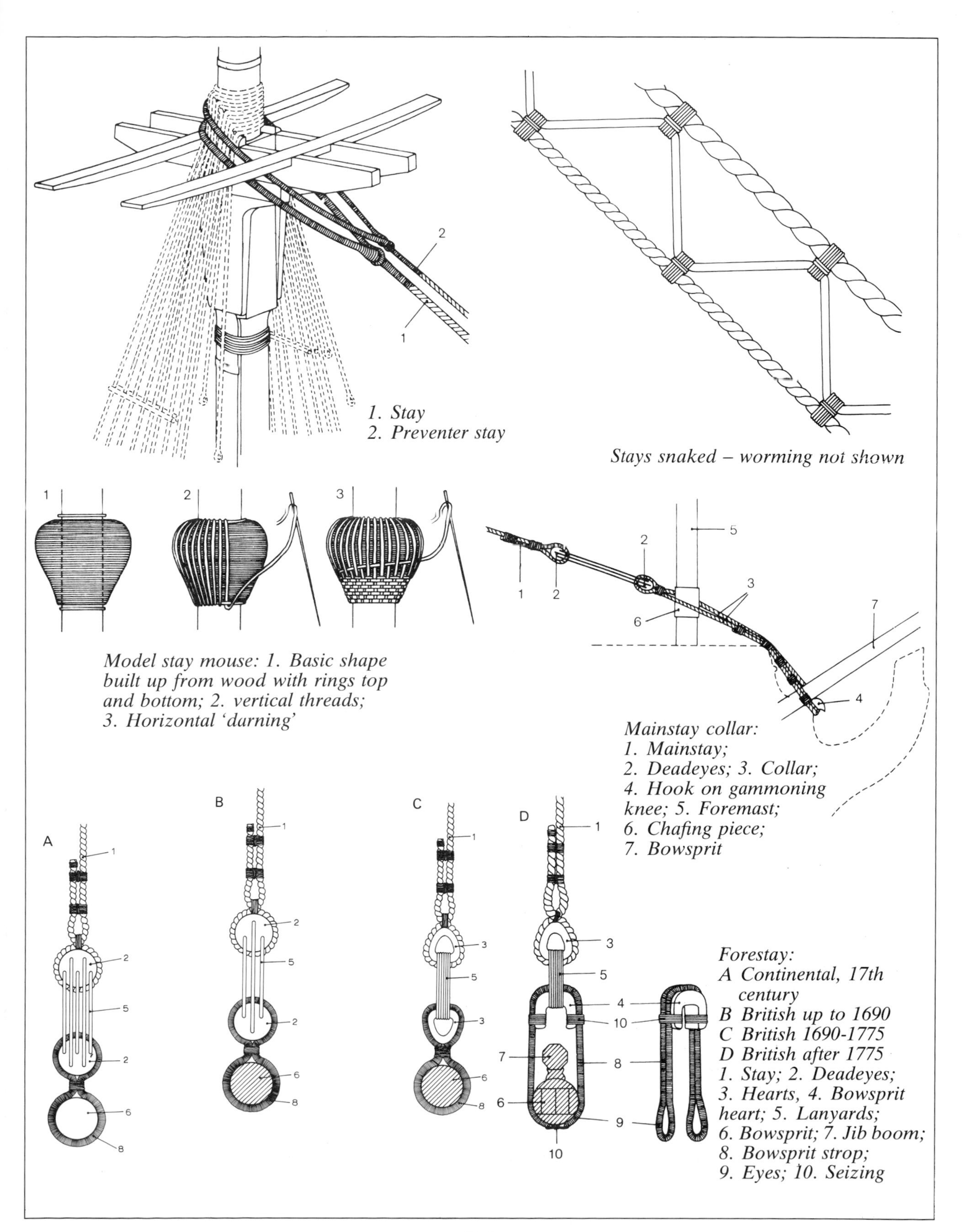

1. Stay
2. Preventer stay

Stays snaked – worming not shown

Model stay mouse: 1. Basic shape built up from wood with rings top and bottom; 2. vertical threads; 3. Horizontal 'darning'

Mainstay collar:
1. Mainstay;
2. Deadeyes; 3. Collar;
4. Hook on gammoning knee; 5. Foremast;
6. Chafing piece;
7. Bowsprit

Forestay:
A Continental, 17th century
B British up to 1690
C British 1690-1775
D British after 1775
1. Stay; 2. Deadeyes;
3. Hearts, 4. Bowsprit heart; 5. Lanyards;
6. Bowsprit; 7. Jib boom;
8. Bowsprit strop;
9. Eyes; 10. Seizing

The Stays

Methods of attaching the fore topmast stay in the 16th and 17th centuries

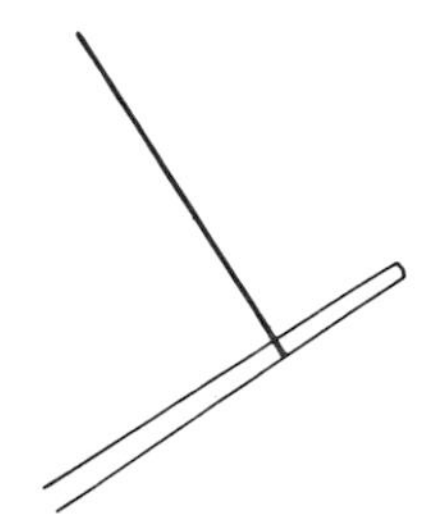

Portuguese 1490-1510; Spanish 1500-20

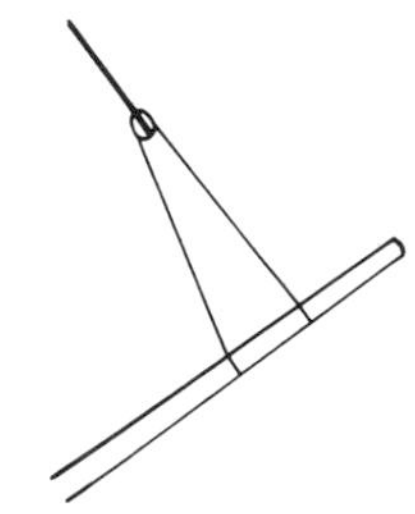

Portuguese 1510-1520; Spanish 1520-40, Dutch 1600

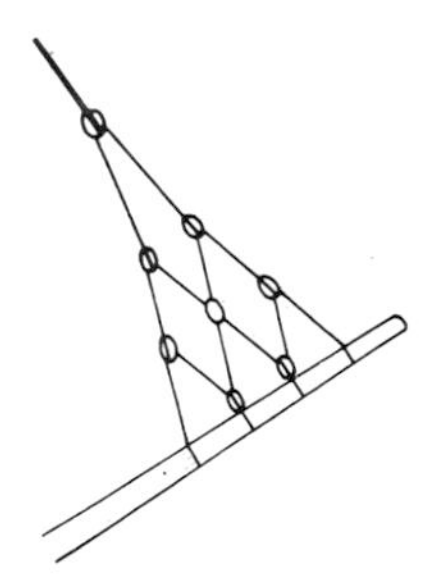

Spanish 1510-30; British 1520-40

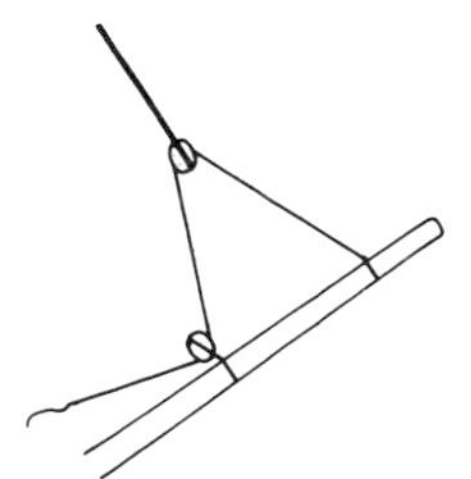

Portuguese 1520, British 1580, Genoan 1590-1600

The fore topmast stay

Until the introduction of the jib boom, that is, in the period between 1500 and 1720, the fore topmast stay was attached to the bowsprit with multiple block systems up to 1670, then deadeyes and lanyards in small ships.

There are no rules regarding the fitting of the topmast stay in respect of time, nor of nation, nor of ship type, as even on two ships of the same size, the same nationality and the same year of building, a wide variety of arrangements was used. The running part of the tackle usually belayed to a cleat on the bowsprit, and more rarely to a belaying pin on the beakhead bulwark. The collection of arrangements for attaching the fore topmast stay drawn on the facing page is not comprehensive. They are intended to show distinct trends only, and give you the chance to judge whether what your plan shows is likely to be right or not. In fact, the very wide variety of possibilities seduces many draughtsmen into drawing their own variant. However, when I see, for example, a fiddle block on the fore topmast stay of a ship built in 1630, then I have justifiable doubts. Fiddle blocks were used from 1660 on; they might be acceptable for 1650, but if they turn up on a plan for an older ship, then that cannot be right. If you have any doubts about the correctness of your plan on this point, and if a good museum model is not available to put you right, you would do better to stick to the types shown in this book.

With the introduction of the jib boom the run of the fore topmast stay was much simplified. Initially the fore topmast stay was made fast to the bowsprit bees with a simple combination of blocks. From the second half of the 18th century the two stays – fore topmast to starboard, fore topmast preventer stay to larboard – reeved through holes in the bees, and were set up at the foot of the bowsprit with a tackle. The running part belayed to a cleat on the bowsprit.

In the middle of the 19th century the fore topmast and fore topmast preventer stays were made fast to the bow on either side of the stem.

The mizen topmast stay

Until the middle of the 17th century the mizen topmast stay was divided and attached to the last pair of mainmast shrouds with a more or less complex arrangement of ropes and blocks to starboard and larboard . . .

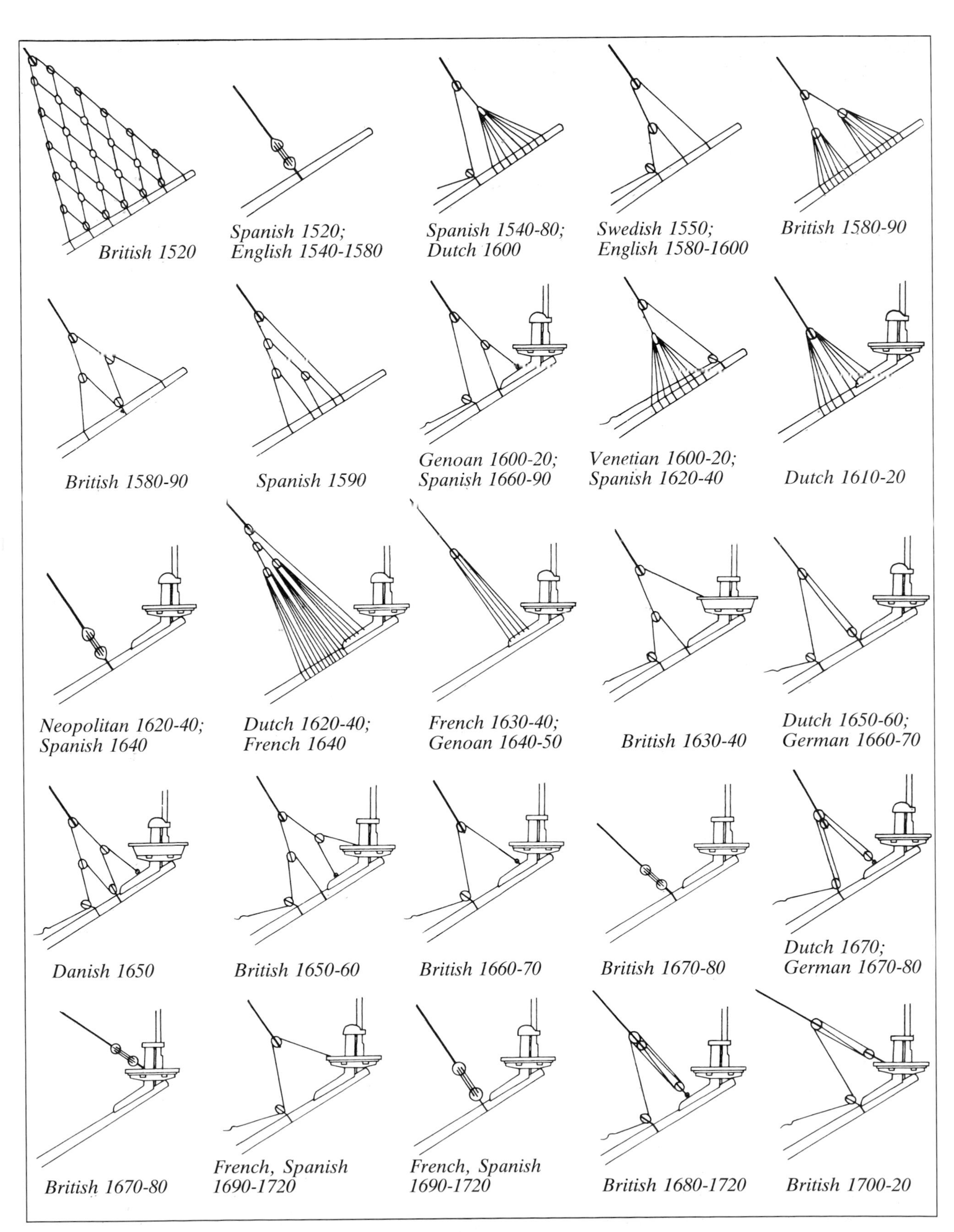
British 1520
Spanish 1520;
English 1540-1580
Spanish 1540-80;
Dutch 1600
Swedish 1550;
English 1580-1600
British 1580-90
British 1580-90
Spanish 1590
Genoan 1600-20;
Spanish 1660-90
Venetian 1600-20;
Spanish 1620-40
Dutch 1610-20
Neopolitan 1620-40;
Spanish 1640
Dutch 1620-40;
French 1640
French 1630-40;
Genoan 1640-50
British 1630-40
Dutch 1650-60;
German 1660-70
Danish 1650
British 1650-60
British 1660-70
British 1670-80
Dutch 1670;
German 1670-80
British 1670-80
French, Spanish
1690-1720
French, Spanish
1690-1720
British 1680-1720
British 1700-20

The Stays

Main and fore stay, second half of the 19th century

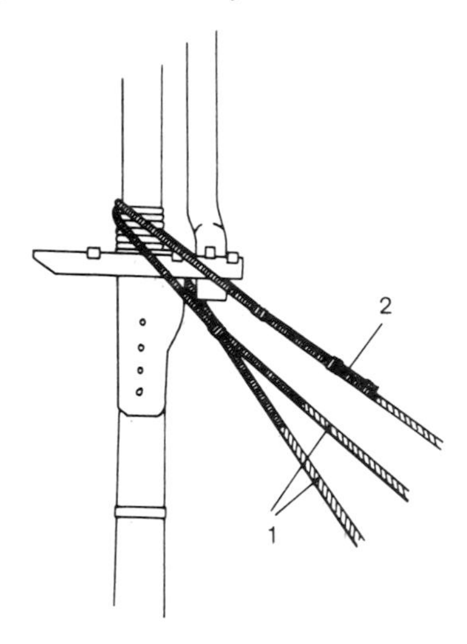

Mast head: 1. Double stay; 2. Single stay

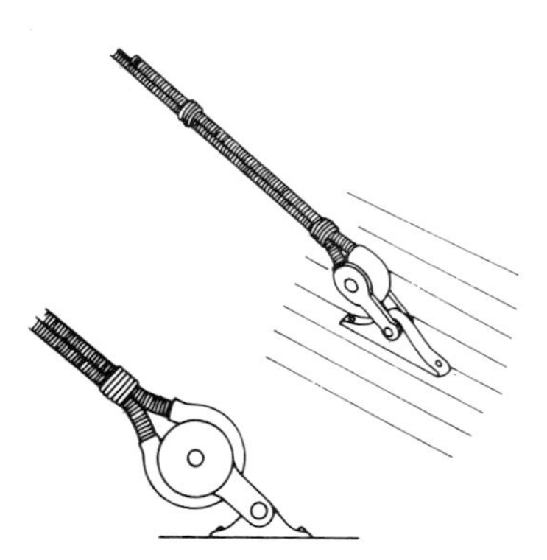

Setting up with a thimble

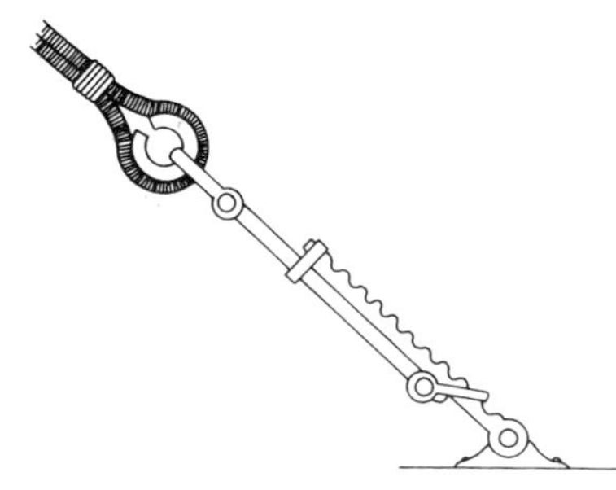

Setting up with a rack (late 19th century)

. . . After this time it was set up with blocks or deadeyes at the mainmast head or – rarely at first, then more commonly in the 18th century – reeved through a leading block, and set up with a tackle on the deck abaft the main mast, in a similar fashion to the main topmast stay.

The topgallant stays
The topgallant stays had no mouse, but were shipped over the masthead with a spliced or seized eye. Until 1720 the fore topgallant stay passed through a leading block in the sprit topmast crosstree and ended in a tackle in the sprit top. Thereafter, until the introduction of the dolphin striker it reeved through a block on the jib boom, and belayed on the forecastle.
After the introduction of the dolphin striker the stay led through a sheave on the jib boom and through a hole in the striker and into the head on the starboard side. The main topgallant stay passed through a leading block on the fore topgallant crosstrees and was set up in the foretop with blocks or thimbles. The mizen topgallant stay also reeved through a leading block, and set up with thimbles in the main top.

The royal stays
Generally speaking the information on the topgallant stays also applies to the royal stays. Please refer to the drawings in the section JIB RIGGING for the arrangement of the fore topgallant, fore topgallant preventer and fore royal stays to the jib boom and the outer jib boom.

Crowsfeet
To prevent the topsails blowing underneath the tops, crowsfeet were fitted between the fore edge of the tops and the stay. These consisted of a number of ropes which were laced from holes in the edge of the top and the euphroe. The euphroe was fixed to the stay with a simple tackle. Crowsfeet were always carried on the main and fore tops, and frequently also on the mizen top. Towards the end of the 18th century the crowsfeet disappeared.

Staysail
When staysails began to be introduced on large ships around 1660, they were set on staysail stays – with the exception of the mizen staysail and the mizen topmast staysail. These staysail stays ran below the stay proper, and were fitted to fore topmast stay, mainmast stay, and main topmast stay. The staysail stay was fitted to the stay below the mouse with a spliced eye, and made fast at its lower end with blocks or deadeyes to the mainstay collar, and foretopmast stay strop or the foretop.
The staysail stays only have to be fitted if you wish to set the staysails, as if the staysails were not set, the staysail stays were also taken down. In the first half of the 18th century most of the staysail stays disappeared, the staysails being set on the stays themselves or on the preventer stays.

Snaking the stays
In warships of the 18th and 19th centuries the stays and preventer stays were "snaked" together by a thin rope in wartime.
It is important that the distance between stay and preventer stay is not altered by the snaking. It is advisable to fit temporary spacers when fitting the snaking, which can be removed later.

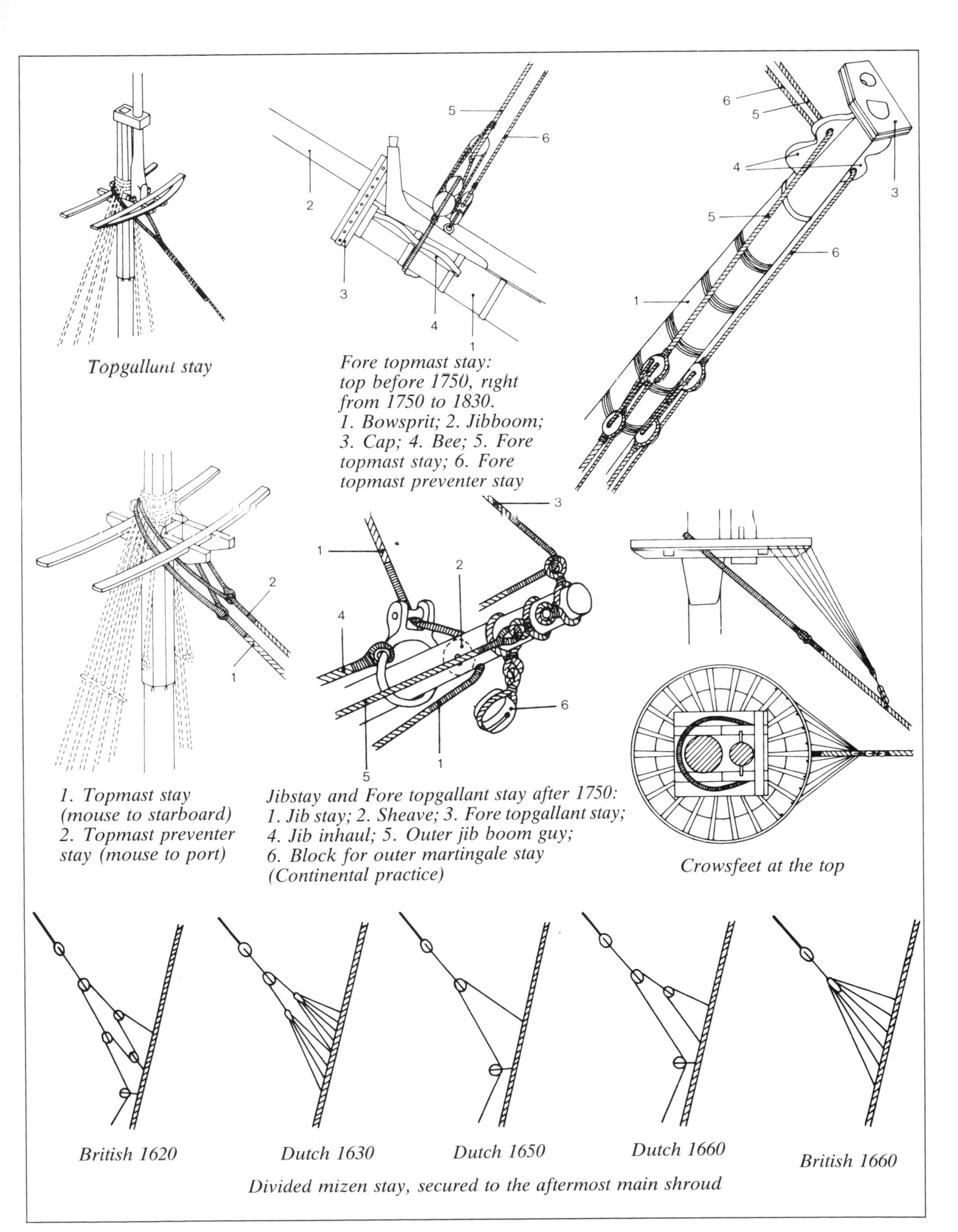

Topgallant stay

Fore topmast stay: top before 1750, right from 1750 to 1830. 1. Bowsprit; 2. Jibboom; 3. Cap; 4. Bee; 5. Fore topmast stay; 6. Fore topmast preventer stay

1. Topmast stay (mouse to starboard) 2. Topmast preventer stay (mouse to port)

Jibstay and Fore topgallant stay after 1750: 1. Jib stay; 2. Sheave; 3. Fore topgallant stay; 4. Jib inhaul; 5. Outer jib boom guy; 6. Block for outer martingale stay (Continental practice)

Crowsfeet at the top

British 1620 — *Dutch 1630* — *Dutch 1650* — *Dutch 1660* — *British 1660*

Divided mizen stay, secured to the aftermost main shroud

The Sprit topmast backstay

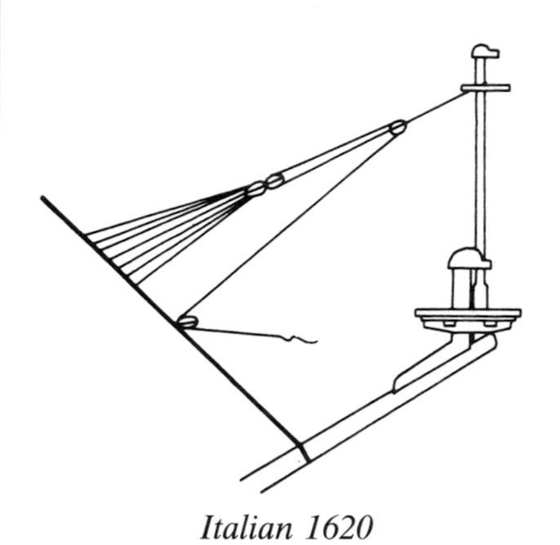

Italian 1620

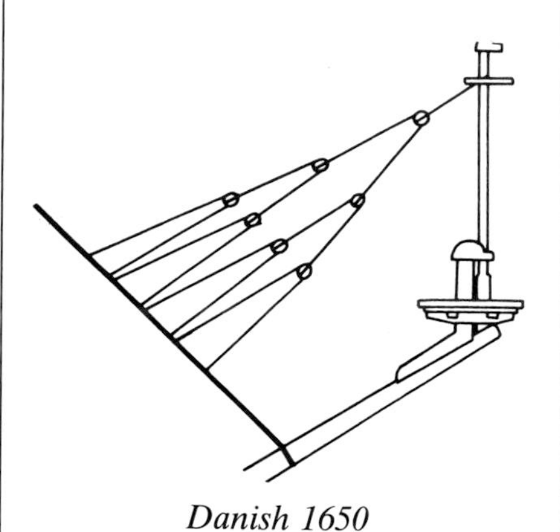

Danish 1650

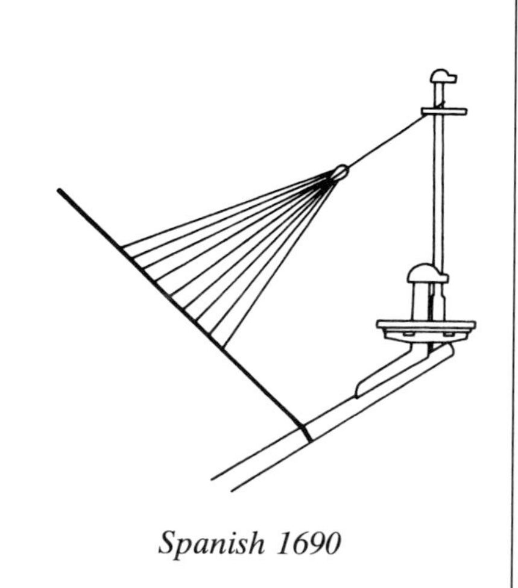

Spanish 1690

The sprit topmast backstay can be considered as the final member of the stay family. As long as a sprit topmast was carried, it was necessary to support this aft, and the sprit topmast backstay served this purpose. As with the fore topmast stay there were very many variations on this theme, which changed from time to time and from country to country, and sometimes even from ship to ship.

The system was based on a combination of crowsfeet and blocks, which were attached to the fore topmast stay and/or the foremast stay, sometimes standing, sometimes running – i.e. fitted with a tackle. The sprit topmast backstay was attached to the sprit topmast crosstress with a short seized or spliced eye, and ran from there aft between the trestletrees. The running part reeved through the last block of the combination (sometimes over a leading block on the bowsprit) and generally ran to a cleat in the sprit top, although sometimes to a cleat at the foot of the bowsprit, where it belayed.

As with the fore topmast stay drawings, the illustrations on the facing page are intended primarily to give you the chance to check your plans for accuracy, and if necessary to correct them, as this is another case where some plan makers draw in the first arrangement they come across without thinking twice.

With the disappearance of the sprit topmast around 1720 the sprit topmast backstay also vanished, as its function was assumed by the dolphin striker and the martingale stays – although in a quite different way. The sprit topmast backstay can present a few difficulties to the modeller. The most common problem is that the stay (fore topmast stay, foremast stay), to which the sprit topmast backstay is attached, is pulled towards the bow by it, and is then no longer straight. This can be countered by retensioning the fore topmast or foremast stay (take care – balance out the tensions), and in any case it can be allowed to deflect by a small amount; roughly 3%, or 1⁄10in in every 3ins of stay length. No more than that!

You are in a spot of trouble if the tension of the sprit topmast backstay causes the sprit mast to bend back towards the stern. This is why I emphasized so strongly when discussing the fixing of the sprit topmast that it must be really securely fixed. If the sprit topmast bends further aft than the vertical when you set up the sprit topmast backstay, there is only one redress: dismantle the standing rigging on the sprit topmast and fix it more strongly.

Many model makers try to get round the problem by leaving the backstay loose. Now, it does not need to be as taut as the shrouds, backstays and stays, but on the otherhand it must on no account look slack!

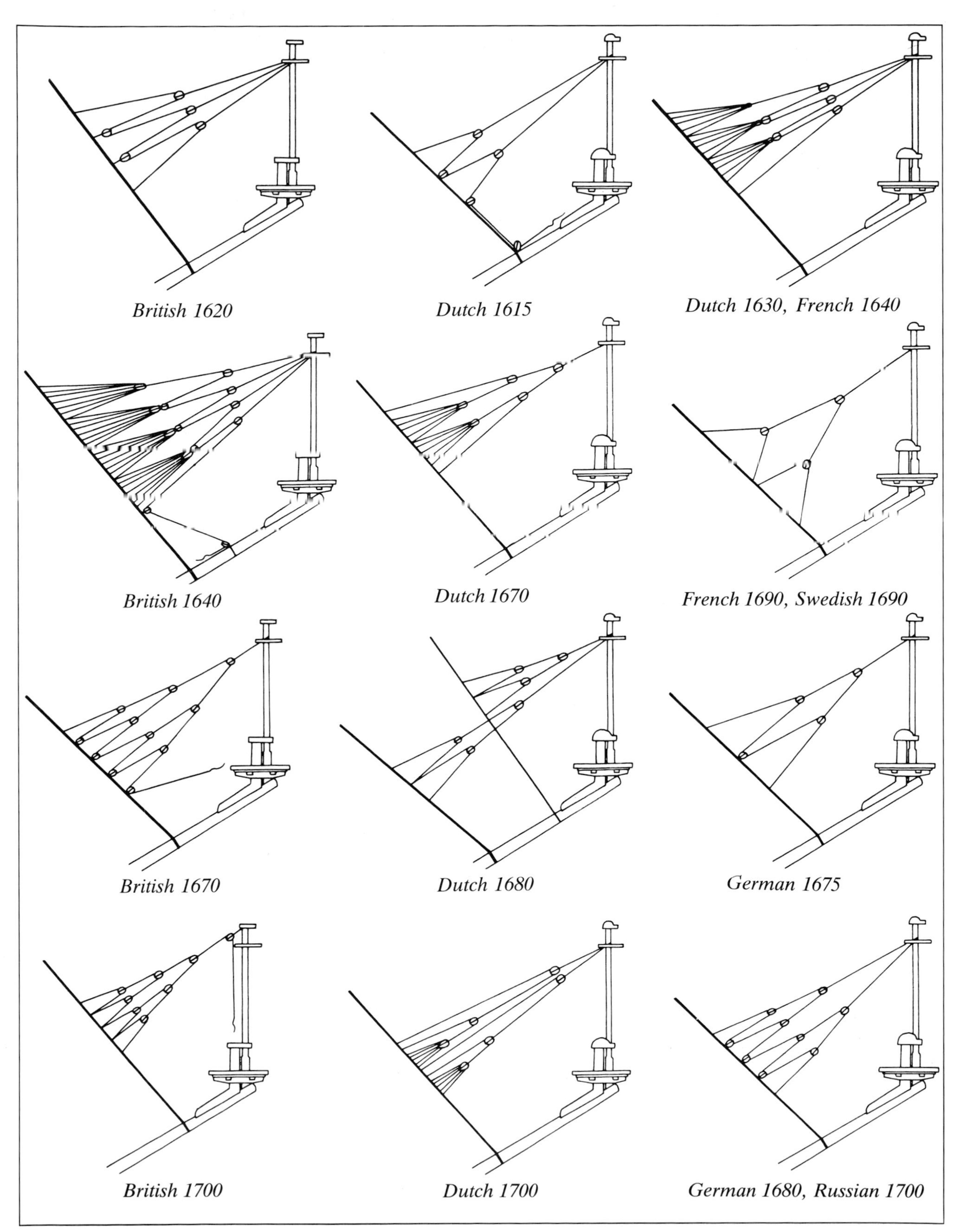
British 1620
Dutch 1615
Dutch 1630, French 1640
British 1640
Dutch 1670
French 1690, Swedish 1690
British 1670
Dutch 1680
German 1675
British 1700
Dutch 1700
German 1680, Russian 1700

The Jib boom rigging

Around 1715 an extension of the bowsprit was added below the sprit topmast. For a short period the jib boom, as it was called, and the sprit topmast existed together, then the sprit mast disappeared.

The crupper
Until the middle of the 18th century the crupper was the only standing rigging fitted to the jib boom. This was a lashing which connected the bowsprit and jib boom. It consisted of about seven turns around both the bowsprit and jib boom with cross turns between them. Around 1850 the crupper was in many cases replaced by a chain crupper and a heel lashing.

The martingale stay
In the second half of the 18th century the jib boom became so long that downwards support became an urgent necessity; this was the martingale stay. The martingale stay was secured at the head of the jib boom, then reeved through a hole in the dolphin striker, and was usually set up at the foot of the bowsprit with hearts.

The martingale back stays
This method was soon seen to be too complicated, and not strong enough. For this reason a change was made to two ropes supporting the dolphin striker from the bow – the martingale back stays, which were set up with hearts. The martingale stay, for which a chain was used after 1840, was just taken to the dolphin striker and fixed to an iron ring there.

The outer martingale stay
Eventually this method superseded all others, when at the end of the 18th century the jib boom was extended by the flying jib boom. The outer martingale stay was led from the flying jib boom to the dolphin striker in the same manner as the martingale stay, now known as the inner martingale stay. Occasionally the inner and the outer martingale stays were a single rope, which was rigged from the jib boom, through an eyebolt on the dolphin striker, and passed forward again to the flying jib boom. The martingale stays were tensioned by setting up the martingale back stays.

The jib and outer jib guys
The jib and outer jib guys were designed to give the jib and outer jib boom lateral support. They were attached in pairs to the jib boom band and the outer jib boom band. Until about 1830 they reeved through eyes on the spritsail yard, and were attached to the hull with hearts. When the spritsail disappeared, the guys ran directly to the hull, although in many cases the outer jib guys ran over whisker booms on the catheads, in order to spread them more widely.

The jib boom footropes
The jib boom footropes, usually fitted in pairs, fulfilled the same function as the foot ropes on the yards. They were secured to the bowsprit cap, and were often knotted at regular intervals, in order to provide the sailors with a better foothold. Nets were often stretched under this area to provide additional security for the crew.

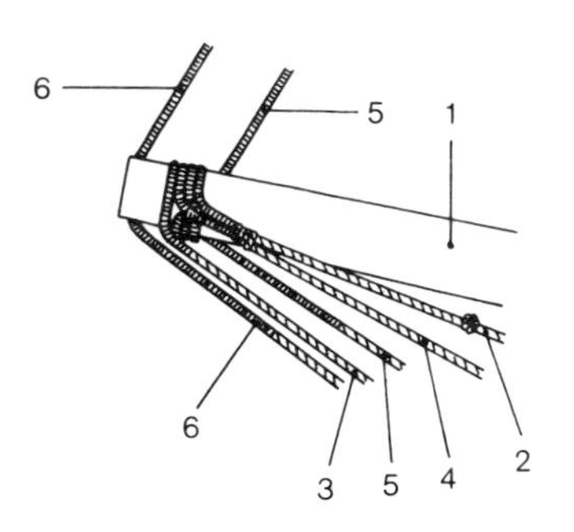

Flying jib boom around 1850:
1. Flying jib boom; 2. Horse;
3. Outer martingale stay;
4. Flying jib boom guys;
5. Topgallant stay;
6. Royal stay

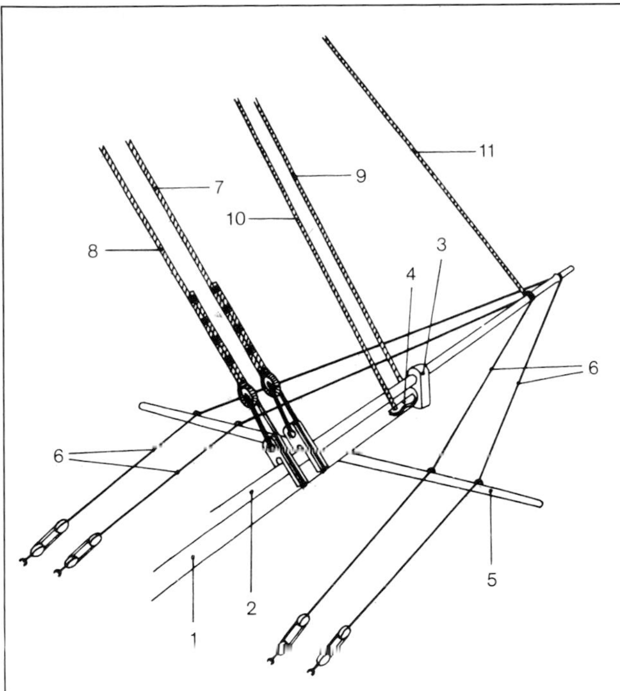

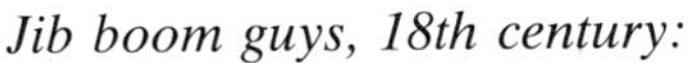

Jib boom guys, 18th century:
1. Bowsprit; 2. Jib boom; 3. Cap; 4. Bee; 5. Spritsail yard; 6. Jib boom guys; 7. Fore stay; 8. Fore preventer stay; 9. Fore topmast stay; 10. Fore topmast preventer stay; 11. Fore topgallant stay

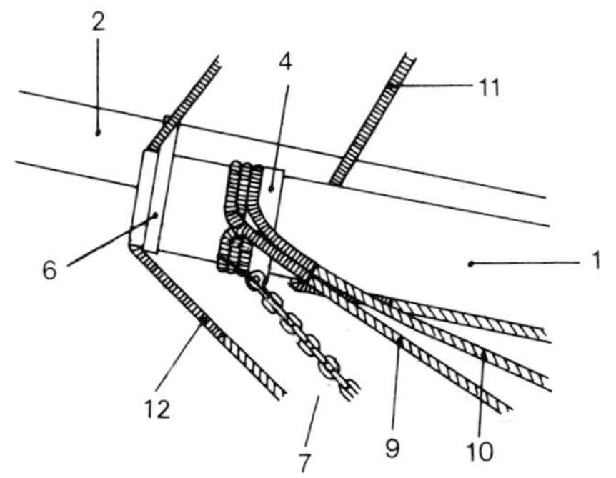

Jib boom, Fore end, with outer boom, around 1850

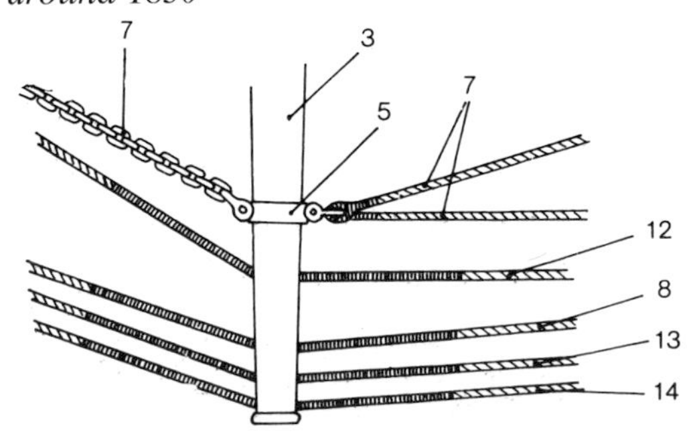

Dolphin striker, lower part, around 1850

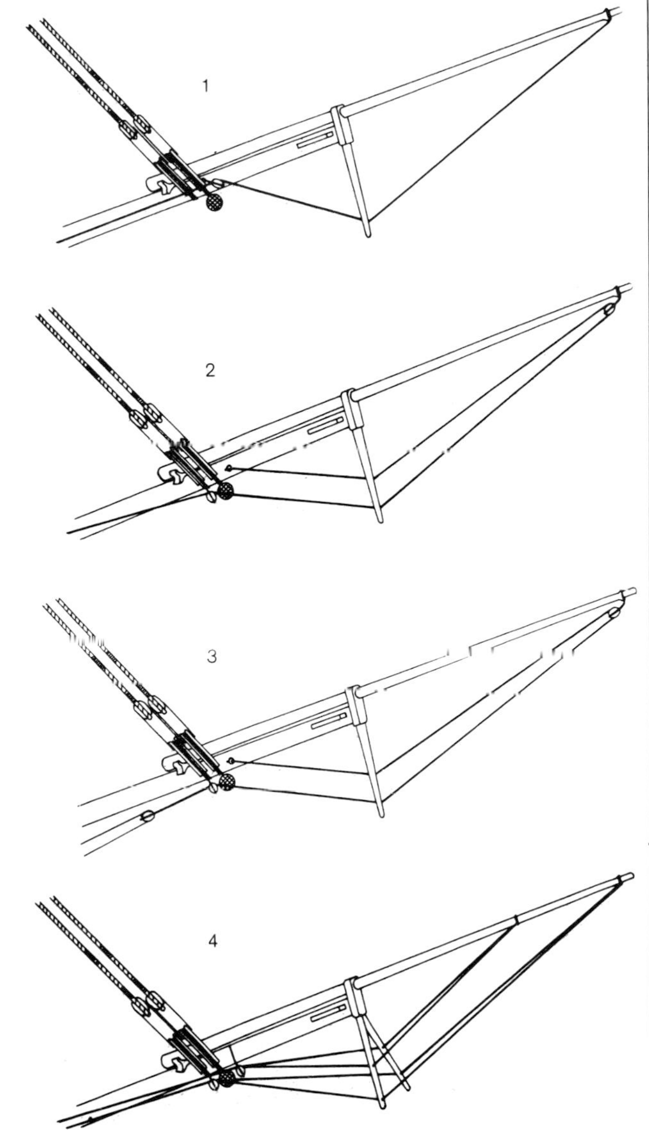

Development of martingale stay: (Continental practice)
1. Single martingale stay 1750
2. Double martingale stay 1780
3. Double martingale stay with tackle, 1790
4. Double martingale stays with double dolphin striker, 18/19th century

Jib boom and dolphin striker, 19th century:
1. Jib boom; 2. Flying jib boom; 3. Dolphin striker; 4. Martingale stay band; 5. Dolphin striker band; 6. Jib boom band; 7. Outer martingale stay; 8. Flying jib stay; 9. Jib boom guys; 10. Footrope; 11. Jib stay; 12. Fore topgallant stay; 13. Fore royal stay; 14. Flying martingale stay

The Jib boom rigging

The English opium clipper Falcon *in 1824.*
Note the spritsail yard. It is situated on top of the bowsprit abaft the jib boom. It could not carry sail at this stage, and its only purpose was to spread the jib boom and flying jib boom guys. Soon after this period the spritsail was replaced by a spreader.

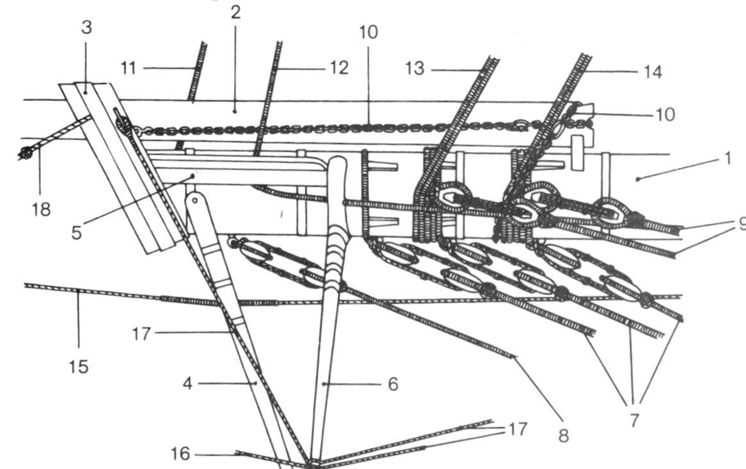

Fore end of bowsprit around 1850: 1. Bowsprit; 2. Jib boom; 3. Cap; 4. Fixed dolphin striker; 5. Bee; 6. Spreader; 7. Bobstays; 8. Cap bobstay; 9. Bowsprit shrouds; 10. Chain heel lashing; 11. Fore topmast stay; 12. Fore topmast preventer stay; 13. Fore stay; 14. Fore preventer stay; 15. Fore topgallant stay; 16. Jib boom guy; 17. Spreader guy; 18. Horse

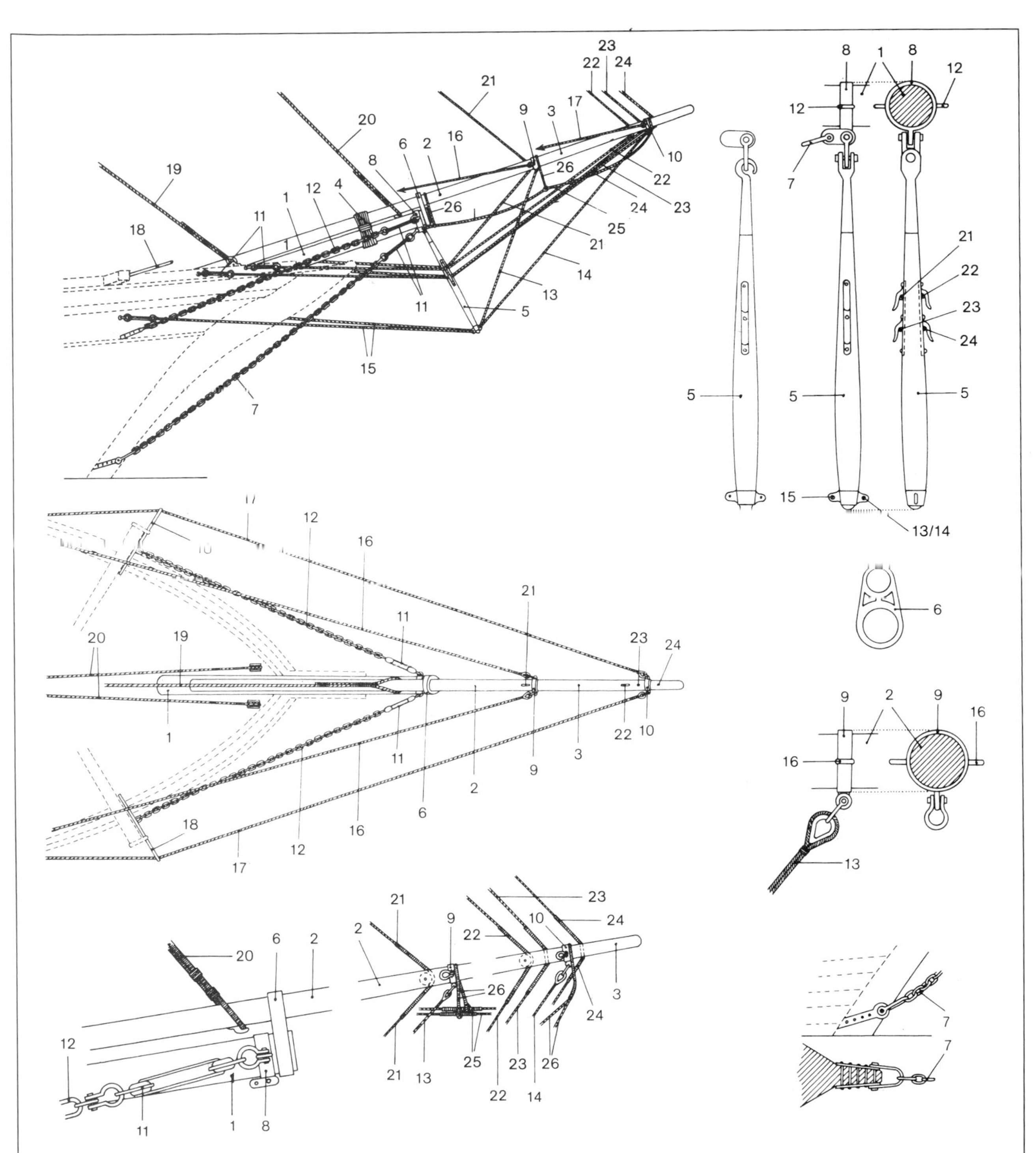

Jib boom rigging with a pivoted dolphin striker, second half of the 19th century: 1. Bowsprit; 2. Jib boom; 3. Jib boom head; 4. Crupper; 5. Dolphin striker or martingale (variant shown) 6. Iron bowsprit cap; 7. Bobstay; 8. Martingale band; 9. Jib stay band; 10. Outer jib stay band; 11. Lanyards; 12. Bowsprit guy; 13. Martingale stay; 14. Outer martingale stay; 15. Martingale backstays; 16. Inner jib boom guy; 17. Outer jib boom guy; 18. Whisker boom; 19. Fore stay; 20. Fore topmast stay; 21. Jib stay; 22. Outer jib stay; 23. Fore topgallant stay; 24. Fore royal stay; 25. Footrope; 26. Stirrup

Running rigging

Running rigging · Running rigging, rope sizes · Halyard Slings · Outhauler Parrals Lifts · Spritsail yard lifts Height of the yards · Braces Position of the yards · Sheets Tacks · Clew lines · Leech lines and bunt lines · Reef tackle · Bowlines · Bearing out spar · Topmast tye · Gaff sails Staysails · Staysail rope sizes Studding sails · Studding sail rope sizes · Furled sails Yards without sails · Lateen sails

The running rigging of a ship covers all the ropes which are used to manipulate yards and sails:
Halyards, tyes and jeers – for hoisting the yards on the mast.
Trusses and parrals – for holding the yards tight against the mast.
Lifts – for holding the yard horizontal, or topping up the yard (at an angle).
Braces – for swinging the yard to one side.
Sheets – for holding down the clews (lower sail corners).
Tacks – for hauling the clews forward.
Clew lines – for hauling up the clews when furling the sails.
Leech lines and bunt lines – for hauling the mass of the sailcloth on to the yard.
Reef tackles – for hauling up the reef bands onto the yard, when the sail is to be shortened.
Bowlines – for keeping the leech well out when sailing close-hauled.

In contrast to the standing rigging the running rigging underwent few major changes in the course of the centuries. There was good reason for this: the standing rigging was rigged up in port, where the time and leisure were available for fitting the most complex arrangements of rope, especially in the 16th century. The running rigging, on the other hand, had to be quick and straightforward to operate at sea, even in the worst weather, otherwise the safety of the whole ship was at risk. Hence while the standing rigging was subject to the latest aesthetic and technical fashions, the first consideration in the design of the running rigging was that it should work perfectly.

The ropework of the running rigging was generally in its natural state and therefore lighter in colour than most of the standing rigging. Steel wire ropes and chains gradually came into use after the middle of the 19th century, and here you should note that the chains of the running rigging – as with the standing rigging – were always of plain link rather than the stud link type.

Take care! Check the rope thicknesses and block size shown on your rigging plans very thoroughly, as advised for the standing rigging. On many plans, and especially if you are working from a kit, there is a tendency to make the lower yard rigging too heavy, and the upper yard rigging too light. You must also establish which ropes were taut, and which were carried loose.

Basically the halyards, trusses and parrals, lifts and braces, and all the upper sail sheets were set up taut. When the sails are set, the weather bowline is hauled taut, as also are the lee sheets and weather tacks.

Brails, clew lines and reef tackles are carried loosely when the sails are set. If the sail is hauled up to the yard, furled on the yard, or the model is shown without sails, then the clew lines, leech lines, bunt lines and reef tackles must also be hauled taut.

The running rigging is belayed to kevel blocks, staghorns, cleats and belaying pins. Until the beginning of the 17th century individual ropes were also simply wound round the rail; the thinner ropes of the topgallant and royal sails were also belayed in the tops in some instances.

Take care! The ropes of the running rigging must not be cut short after belaying. A certain amount of rope was generally coiled up by the belaying point, hung over the belaying pins (see BELAYING PINS), coiled up by the cleats, hung over the head of the kevel blocks, or hung over one of the horns of the staghorn.

The French corvette L'Astrolabe *of 1811*

Running rigging sizes

Bowsprit and jib boom	16th/17th century	18th century	19th century hemp	19th century steel
Spritsail				
Spritsail yard sling	40%	26%	88%	
Halliard	18%	20%	24%	
Lifts	20%	23%	23%	
Pendant	13%	15%		
Purchase	10%			
Braces	20%	23%		
Pendant	13%	15%	24%	
Sheets	20%	20%		
Clew lines	13%	13%		
Spritsail topsail (Spritsail topmast)				
Halyard	25%	25%		
Pendant	13%	13%		
Lifts	8%	8%		
Braces	12%	12%		
Sheets	20%	20%		
Clew lines	10%	10%		
Spritsail topsail (jib boom)				
Sprit topsail yard sling		20%		
Halliard		15%		
Lifts		11%		
Braces		11%		
Sheets		20%		
Clew lines		12%		
Leech and bunt lines		11%		

The figures given refer to the thickness of the main stay, 0.166% of the diameter of the mainmast at the deck (100%).
These values are a guideline only, and national variations have not been taken into account.

In the case of a mainstay made of steel rope, the figures in the table are still based on the use of hemp rope.

Foremast	16th/17th century	18th century	19th century hemp	19th century steel
Fore course				
Tye	50%	32%	50%	
Purchase	35%	20%	35%	
Slings		51%	60%	chain
Lifts	20%	22%	36%	12%
Braces	35%	32%		
Pendant	25%	23%	28%	
Sheets	37%	34%	45%	
Tacks	50%	30%	36%	
Clew lines	19%	22%	20%	
Leech and bunt lines	16%	15%	20%	
Bowlines	20%	26%	15%	
Fore topsail				
Top rope	50%	32%	48%	
Tye	50%	32%	48%	chain
Halyard	25%	20%	30%	
Lifts	13%	20%	28%	10%
Braces	20%	31%		
Pendants	13%	20%	24%	
Sheets	36%	46%	50%	chain
Clew lines	22%	20%	30%	
Leech and bunt lines	19%	15%	30%	
Bowlines	20%	22%	20%	
Reef tackle	14%	15%	20%	
Fore topgallant sail				
Tye	25%	23%	40%	chain
Halyard	13%	20%	28%	
Lifts	8%	12%	17%	
Braces	19%	19%		
Pendant	12%	12%	24%	
Sheets	20%	20%	24%	chain
Clew lines	10%	11%	15%	
Bowlines	10%	10%	17%	
Fore royal sail				
Tye	15%	15%	15%	chain
Halyard	10%	11%	11%	
Lifts	7%	10%	12%	
Braces	12%	12%	15%	
Sheets	12%	12%	15%	
Clew lines	7%	8%	11%	

Mainmast	16th/17th century	18th century	19th century hemp	19th century steel
Main Course				
Tye	50%	33%	50%	
Purchase	35%	22%	35%	
Sling		56%	60%	chain
Lifts	20%	22%	38%	13%
Braces	35%	32%		
Pendant	25%	23%	30%	
Sheets	37%	40%	45%	
Tacks	5[illegible]%	32%	40%	
Clew lines	19%	23%	28%	
Leech and bunt lines	16%	17%	28%	
Bowlines	20%	28%	23%	
Main topsail				
Top rope	30%	33%	10%	
Tye	50%	33%	48%	chain
Halyard	25%	22%	30%	
Lifts	13%	22%	30%	10%
Braces	20%	34%		
Pendants	13%	22%	26%	
Sheets	44%	50%	53%	chain
Clew lines	22%	22%	24%	
Leech and bunt lines	19%	17%	21%	
Bowlines	20%	25%	20%	
Reef tackle	12%	15%	34%	
Main topgallant sail				
Tye	25%	23%	44%	chain
Halyard	13%	20%	36%	
Lifts	8%	12%	20%	
Braces	19%	19%		
Pendants	12%	12%	26%	
Sheets	20%	22%	26%	chain
Clew lines	10%	12%	14%	
Bowlines	10%	10%	15%	
Main royal sail				
Tye	18%	20%	17%	chain
Halyard	12%	14%	14%	
Lifts	8%	10%	12%	
Braces	12%	13%	19%	
Sheets	12%	15%	17%	
Clew lines	8%	10%	12%	

Mizen mast	16th/17th century	18th century	19th century hemp	19th century steel
Crossjack yard				
Sling	25%	26%	30%	
Lifts	10%	15%	38%	13%
Braces	13%	18%		
Pendants	11%	15%	26%	
Mizen Course				
Tye	25%	23%	30%	chain
Halyard	13%	13%	24%	
Lifts	8%	13%	26%	10%
Braces	12%	19%		
Pendants	8%	13%	19%	
Sheets	20%	25%	30%	chain
Clew lines	10%	13%	19%	
Leech and bunt lines		12%	14%	
Bowlines	10%	12%	14%	
Reef tackle		10%	15%	
Mizen topgallant sail				
Tye		20%	36%	chain
Halyard		12%	21%	
Lifts		10%	14%	
Braces		13%	14%	
Sheets		13%	19%	
Clew lines		10%	11%	
Bowlines		10%	9%	
Mizen sail (lateen)				
Halyard	40%	30%		
Pendant	20%	15%		
Lift	20%	20%		
Bridles	8%			
Tack tackle	13%	20%		
Sheet	25%	18%		
Clew line	15%	13%		
Leech and bunt lines	15%	12%		
Mizen sail (gaff)				
Peak halyard		30%	30%	
Throat halyard		30%	28%	
Topping lift		40%	40%	
Sheet		30%	30%	
Vangs		19%	19%	
Tack		28%	28%	
Out haul		30%	30%	
Brails		19%	19%	
Signal halyard		6%	6%	

Halyards and slings

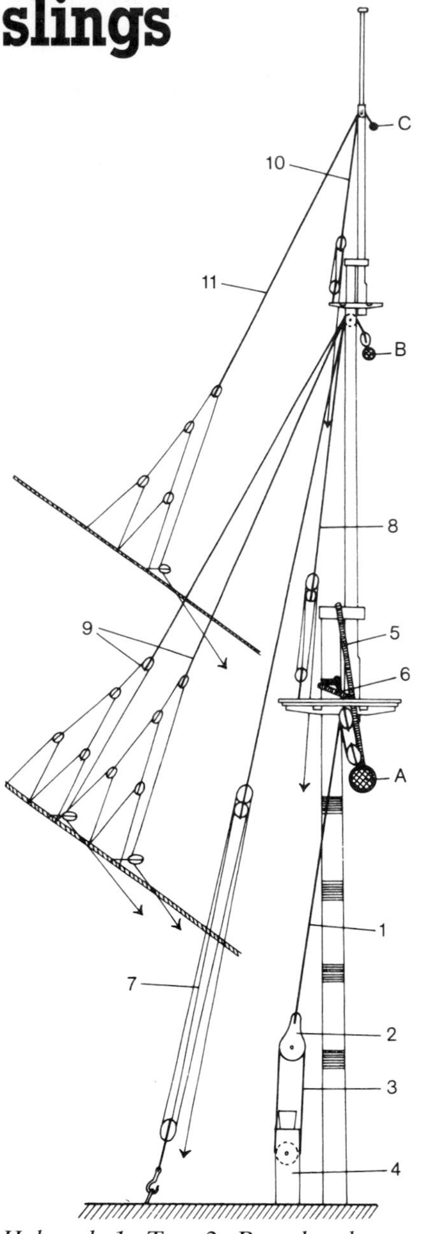

Halyard: *1. Tye; 2. Ramshead block; 3. Halyard tackle; 4. Knighthead; 5. British sling; 6. Continental sling; 7. Halyard, British before 1720; then generally; 8. Topsail halyard before 1720, Continental; 9. Fore topsail halyard before 1660; 10. Topgallant halyard; 11. Topgallant halyard before 1660. A. Lower yard; B. Topsail yard; C. Topgallant yard*

The lower yard tye and halyard
In the Middle Ages the tyes of the lower yards (fore yard, main yard) either reeved through sheave holes on the masthead or through blocks like the topsail halyards. A purchase was fitted abaft the mast to set them up taut. In the mid-16th century the tyes ran to a common ramshead block – they had previously been fitted individually – which with the knighthead formed the halliard purchase.
Towards the middle of the 16th century the tyes were taken through two sheaves in the mast, a system which was retained in Britain until the second half of the 17th century.
On the Continent the halyards were fitted over the round caps (see CAPS) after the late 16th century, where they passed through two holes on the forward, flat part, then ran back into the grooves and ended in the ramshead block. In Britain after 1650 two double blocks were fixed to the yard, and two triple blocks to the crosstrees. The jeers, which replaced the tyes and halyards, were secured to the yard, reeved through the blocks, and finally ran to the deck, where they belayed to the jeer bitts.
This form of lower yard jeers was also adopted on the Continent at the beginning of the 18th century. After the introduction of iron parrals in the second half of the 19th century the lower yard jeers fell out of use.

The slings
Slings were used from the early 18th century onward as an improved means of securing lower yards, which were very heavy. They were strong, served rope strops, which were slid round the masthead over the shrouds in Continental ships, and over the cap in British vessels, and were connected to a second rope sling seized to the yard. After the middle of the 19th century chains were used as slings in many cases.

The topsail halyard
The topsail tyes were attached with a strop round the yard on small ships, and with a block on large ships. They passed through a sheave in the topmast on smaller ships, and on larger ships through a block (on very large ships through two blocks) and on Continental ships in the 16th/17th centuries they led to the halyard purchase in the top. In Britain the topsail halyard purchase was taken down to the deck, and the running part belayed abaft the aftermost shroud. This system also became standard on the Continent in the 18th century.

The topgallant and royal halyards
The topgallant and royal tyes were always fixed with a strop, sometimes also with a hook on the yard, and then led through a sheave in the topmast to the topmast crosstrees and the halyard which belayed in the top.

The spritsail halyard
The spritsail halyard was attached to a block in the middle of the yard, reeved through a double or fiddle block on the bowsprit, and belayed to a cleat at the base of the bowsprit.

The crossjack yard sling
The crossjack yard had no halyard, but was held with a sling laid over the crosstrees.

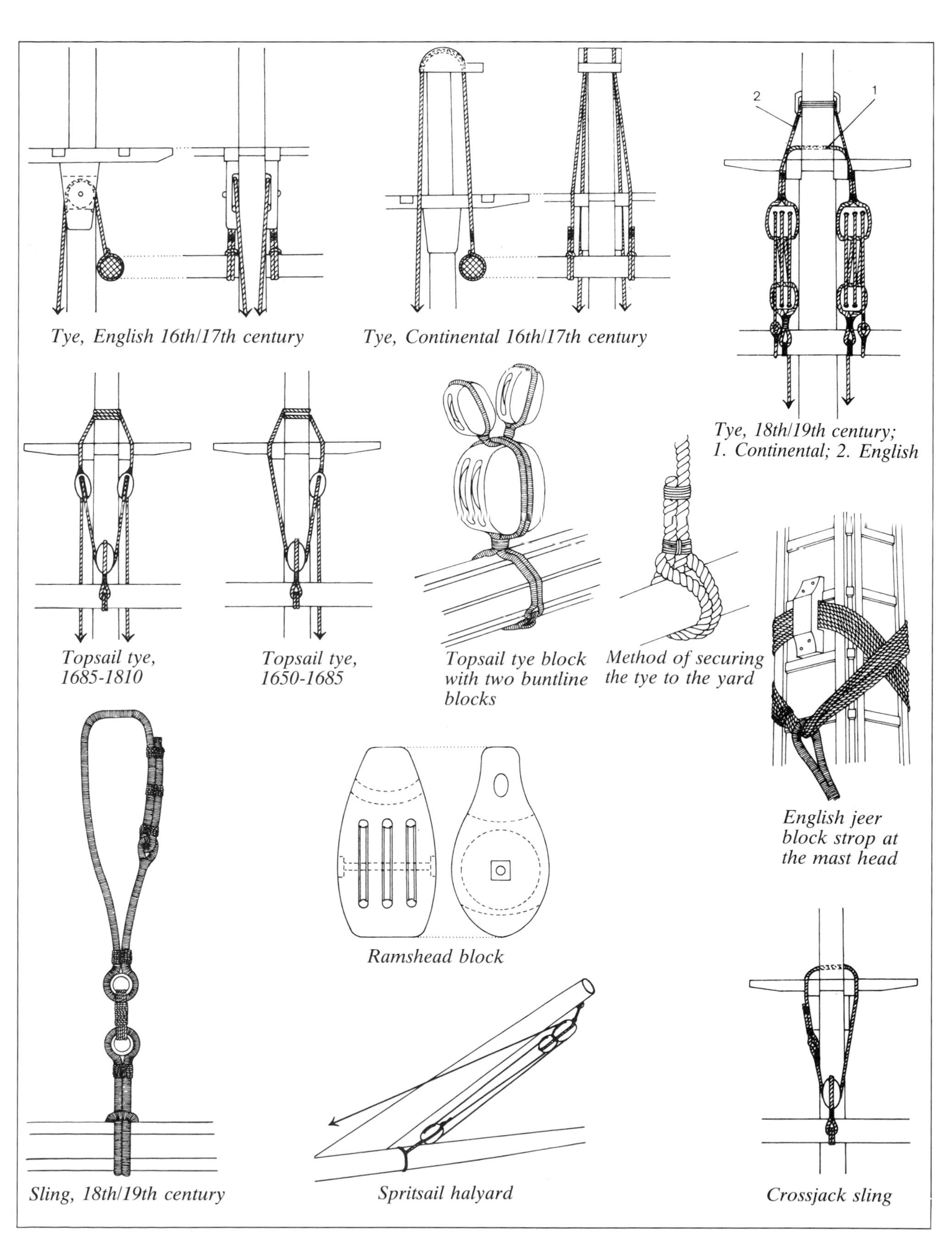

Tye, English 16th/17th century

Tye, Continental 16th/17th century

Tye, 18th/19th century; 1. Continental; 2. English

Topsail tye, 1685-1810

Topsail tye, 1650-1685

Topsail tye block with two buntline blocks

Method of securing the tye to the yard

English jeer block strop at the mast head

Ramshead block

Sling, 18th/19th century

Spritsail halyard

Crossjack sling

The Parral

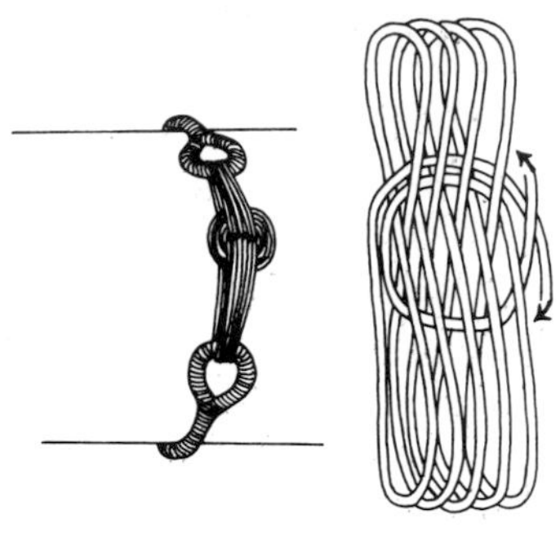

Rose lashing on the yard

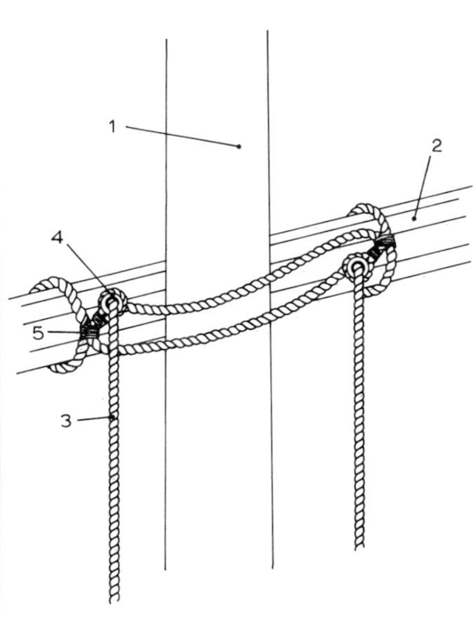

Truss pendants on the lower yards, 18th century; 1. Mast; 2. Yard; 3. Truss pendant; 4. Thimble; 5. Seizing

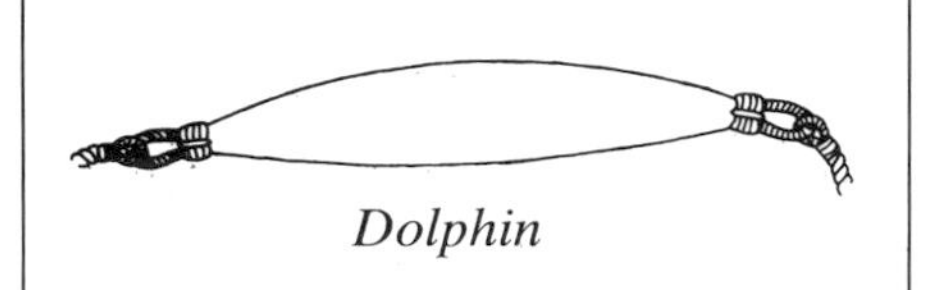

Dolphin

In ancient times and in the early Middle Ages the parral consisted of a strong rope strop which held the yard to the mast. Wooden balls known as trucks were threaded on to the parral from the 13th century on, to permit the parral to slide up and down the mast as easily as possible when the yard was hoisted or lowered. They were soon fitted with a tackle which ran down to the deck, so that the parral could be loosened when the yard was hoisted.

The lower yard parral

From the beginning of the 13th to the middle 18th century parrals with up to four rows of trucks were fitted for the lower yards, and ribs were used as spacers where there were two or more rows of trucks. The ribs of three-row parrals were about as long as the yard diameter, and sometimes slightly longer. A rope seizing was usually laid round the yard on the larboard side.

The parral ropes were fixed to this seizing, then passed round the mast and reeved through a thimble, which was seized to the yard on the starboard side. They were then spliced together just below the thimble, and led down to the deck, ending in a purchase.

In the 18th century parrals were no longer used on the lower yards. Two truss pendants were now used, which, as the drawing on the left shows, led to the top in Continental ships and to the deck in British ships up to 1810, after which they led to the top and could be set up with purchases. As this form of parral did not slide easily on the mast, it was fitted with a downhaul when the pendants led to the top. In the second half of the 19th century fixed iron trusses came into use, which no longer permitted the yards to be moved up and down.

The topsail yard parral

The topsail yards nearly always carried parrals with ribs and trucks until the first half of the 19th century, but in this case a purchase was not fitted, instead they were seized to the yard on either side.

In the first half of the 19th century rope parrals alone were used in some areas, in which case the part which passed round the topmast was protected from chafing with a leather sleeve. After this time the upper topsail yard and topgallant yard parrals were also made of iron, and fixed to a batten, as the drawing on the right shows.

The topgallant and royal parrals

Topgallant and royal parrals were sometimes fitted with trucks (but not ribs) until the end of the 17th century, after which time rope parrals were used exclusively without trucks until the middle of the 19th century.

The spritsail and crossjack parrals

Until the beginning of the 17th century various types of parral with two rows of trucks appeared, and after this time (and very often before this time) the spritsail yard was suspended from the bowsprit with just a double rope sling. A similar sling was used for the crossjack yard, which could also not be moved up and down.

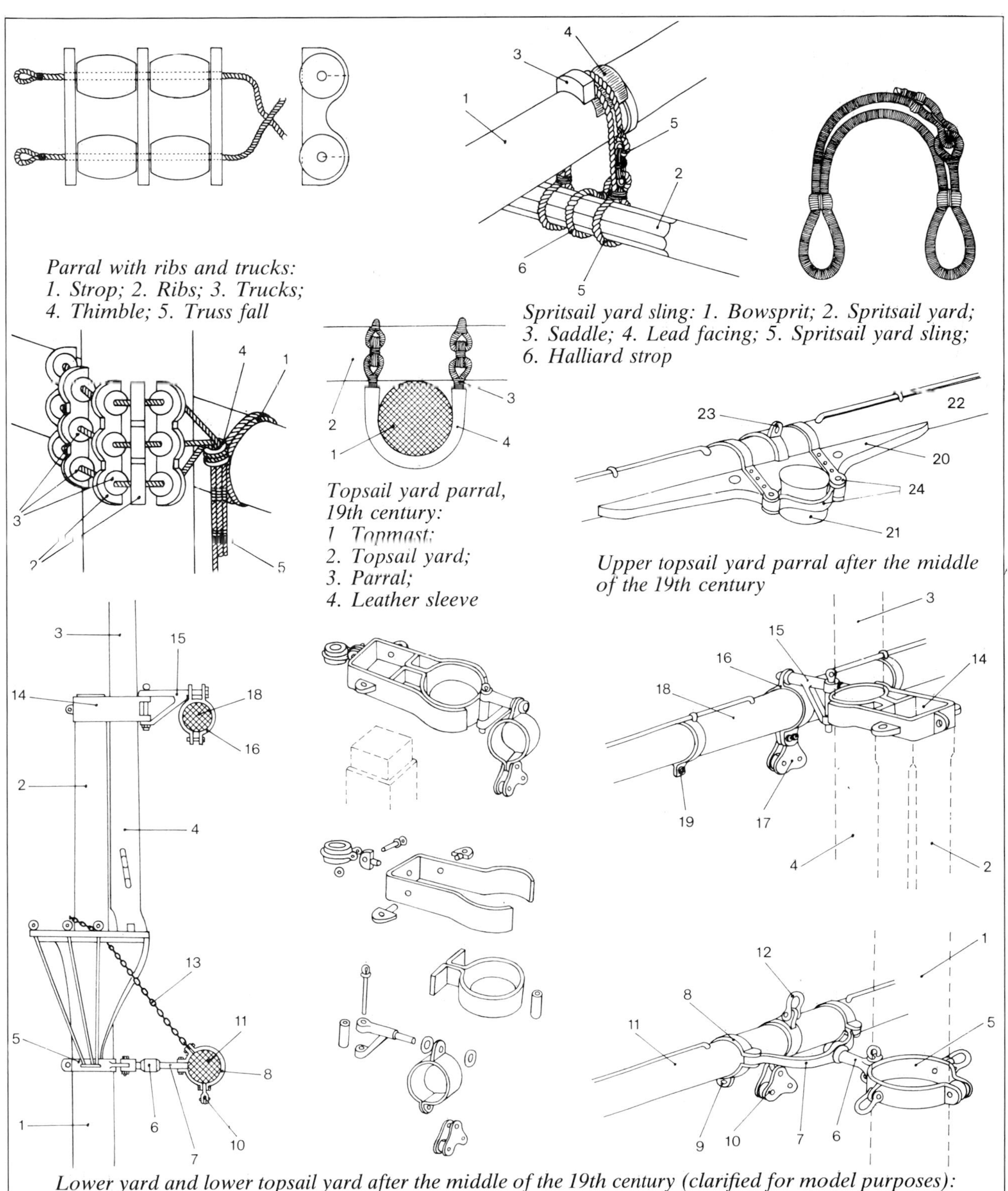

Parral with ribs and trucks: 1. Strop; 2. Ribs; 3. Trucks; 4. Thimble; 5. Truss fall

Spritsail yard sling: 1. Bowsprit; 2. Spritsail yard; 3. Saddle; 4. Lead facing; 5. Spritsail yard sling; 6. Halliard strop

Topsail yard parral, 19th century: 1. Topmast; 2. Topsail yard; 3. Parral; 4. Leather sleeve

Upper topsail yard parral after the middle of the 19th century

Lower yard and lower topsail yard after the middle of the 19th century (clarified for model purposes): 1. Lower mast; 2. Lower masthead; 3. Topmast; 4. Topmast heel; 5. Futtock band; 6. Truss link; 7. Truss span; 8. Yard bands; 9. Eye for clew lines block; 10. Clover leaf block; 11. Lower yard; 12. Sling shackle; 13. Chain sling; 14. Cap; 15. Truss crane; 16. Crane band; 17. Clover leaf block; 18. Lower topsail yard; 19. Eye for clew line block; 20. Parral batten; 21. Leather liner; 22. Upper topsail yard; 23. Eye for tye block; 24. Hinged parral

The Lifts

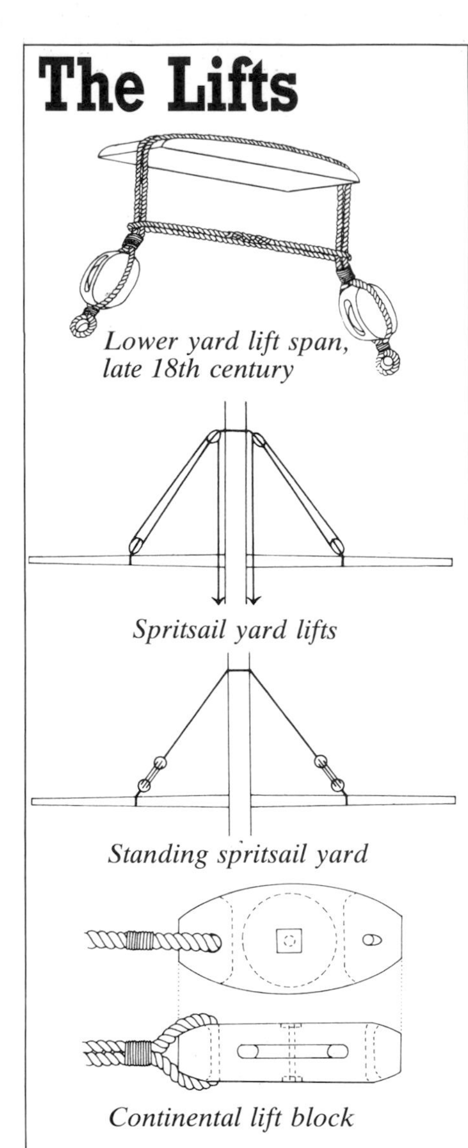

Lower yard lift span, late 18th century

Spritsail yard lifts

Standing spritsail yard

Continental lift block

The lifts' purpose was to hold the yards horizontal. They consisted of a pair of ropes, which ran from the yard arms to the mast and from there downwards to the deck. In ancient times and in the early Middle Ages the lift blocks were situated at the masthead; until the beginning of the 17th century they were on the crosstrees, and since then have been on the cap.
British ships employed either common or fiddle blocks for this purpose, while Continental practice varied: in the 17th century they had special extended lift blocks (see drawing on the left), from the early 18th century fiddle blocks were used for the lower yard lifts, and sometimes for the topsail yards, while common blocks were used for the upper yards.
From the middle of the 16th century in Britain the yard arm blocks were stropped to the sheet blocks, while on the Continent the lifts reeved through the upper part of the specially shaped sheet blocks (see SHEETS).
The lower yard lifts were almost always doubled, and sometimes even trebled, while those of the topsail yards were usually double, and those of the topgallant and royal yards were single. In smaller British ships the topgallant sail sheets sometimes doubled as topsail yard lifts.
The lower yard lifts belayed on pins in the bulwark, while the topsail lifts often belayed in the top until the first half of the 16th century. Later they also belayed to pins on the bulwark, while the topgallant lifts almost always belayed in the top. In the second half of the 19th century the lifts were sometimes made from steel wire rope, and in the case of non-lowering yards standing lifts were used i.e. the lifts were fixed to the yard arm with a shackle, without any blocks, taken to an eyebolt on the mast, and shackled in place there too.

The spritsail yard lifts
The spritsail yard lifts could be either fixed or movable. Standing lifts were connected to deadeyes stropped to the yard, and further deadeyes attached to the bowsprit on a long strop, the pairs of deadeyes being linked by a lanyard, like the shroud deadeyes. Running lifts consisted of two blocks on the yard and two blocks on the bowsprit, which were linked with falls and belayed at the foot of the bowsprit. The blocks or deadeyes of the spritsail yard lifts were not fitted at the yard arms, but half-way between the yard arms and the slings.

Height of the yards

One of the commonest mistakes on model ships is incorrect positioning of the yards. Basically it is safe to assume with earlier, smaller ships that the fore, main, mizen and crossjack yards were rigged just below the mast cheeks and were not normally lowered from this location; the spritsail yard and sprit topsail yard were also likely to remain in a "fixed" position. However, as ships grew larger the topsail, upper topsail, topgallant and royal yards, carried immediately below the hounds when the sails were set, were lowered to just above the cap below when the sails were furled or removed. A typical example is *La Jeanne d'Arc* on page 331. Inspection of museum models or reliable illustrations of ships of similar size and date to that under construction should resolve any doubt.

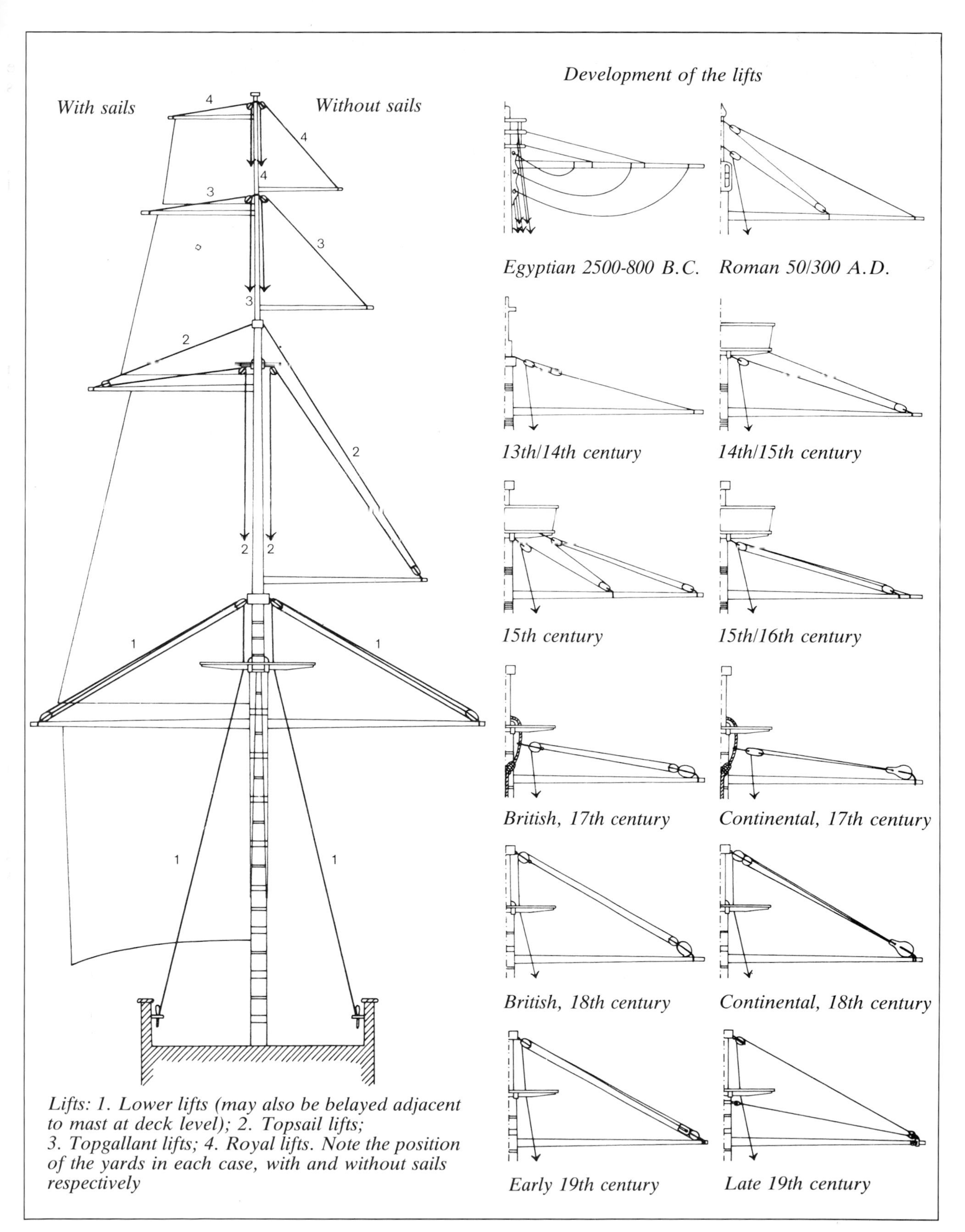

Lifts: 1. Lower lifts (may also be belayed adjacent to mast at deck level); 2. Topsail lifts; 3. Topgallant lifts; 4. Royal lifts. Note the position of the yards in each case, with and without sails respectively

The Braces

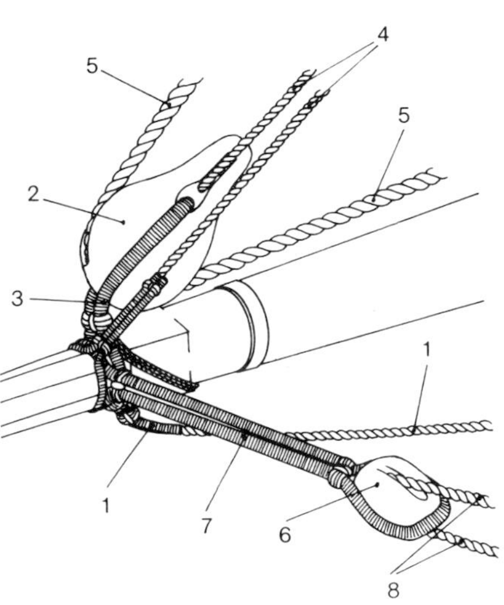

The lower yard arm:
1. Footrope; 2. Sheet block (Continental form); 3. Sheet block strop; 4. Lift; 5. Topsail sheet; 6. Brace block; 7. Brace block strop (before 1730 single brace); 8. Brace (after Vaisseau)

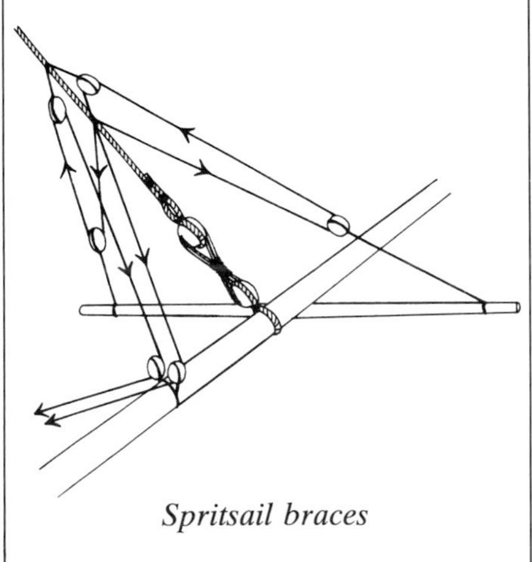

Spritsail braces

The braces were used to swing the yards laterally, and there is hardly any part of the rigging which has altered so little over a period of thousands of years. For smaller yards the braces were a rope with a seized or spliced eye secured to the yard arm, which was usually led down and aft to the deck.

On the larger yards a single block was stropped to the yard. This strop – the brace pendant – was very short in ancient times and in the early Middle Ages. From the 13th century the brace pendant grew longer and longer, until the 16th/17th centuries a length of about 4/10 of the yard length was reached. In the course of the 18th century it was shortened again, until around 1800 the block was situated immediately on the yard arm where it was shackled to a ring bolt in the 19th century.

The braces of the lower yards ran from a ring bolt on the ship's side, then reeved through the brace block, and usually belayed to a range cleat; on the Continent after 1500 it almost always belayed to a staghorn. This applied to all yards until the first half of the 16th century, then later to the main yard. The fore braces were attached to the mainstay after 1525, then reeved through the brace blocks and leading blocks on the main stay, and often belayed to small kevel blocks on the bulwarks until the early 18th century when they belayed to the main bitts.

The top, topgallant and royal braces followed a similar route to the lower braces, except that the topgallant braces were often single, and the royal braces almost always single, as the drawings on the right show. The crossjack braces were frequently attached to the last pair of main shrouds. The mizen and mizen topgallant braces were either taken to the main shrouds, or to the peak of the mizen lateen yard or the gaff, and from there again to the deck.

The spritsail braces followed a similar route to the foremast braces. They ran from the fore stay and were taken via leading blocks on the fore stay to a belaying pin on the bow rail of the forecastle, either directly, or via a further pair of leading blocks in the head.

The position of the yards

In some modelling books it is recommended to furl the lower sails and the spritsails to their yards, or at least to brail them up, and also to leave the staysails and studding sails out altogether, so that the deck superstructure and the rigging can be seen clearly; otherwise the sails would conceal too much detail. For the same reason many modellers prefer to leave off the sails altogether. There is good sense in this advice, but on the other hand much of the fine effect of a ship under full sail is lost if some of the sails are brailed up.

Now, there is a very simple and effective trick, by means of which all the sails – including the stay and studding sails – can be set, whilst still leaving the decks and rigging fully exposed; the trick is simply to swing the yards round to one side.

On a model with sails furled on the yard, or without sail altogether, the yards should always be at an angle of 90° to the ships' centreline. If you have set sails, this setting of the yards looks rather stolid and boring, and does not look very natural, since the wind would nearly always blow from one side or other to some extent. If you set the yards – and hence the sails – at 15° to a maximum of 35° from the ship's centreline, the effect is not only better visually, but you will also obtain a full and unobstructed view of the decks and rigging, at least from one side.

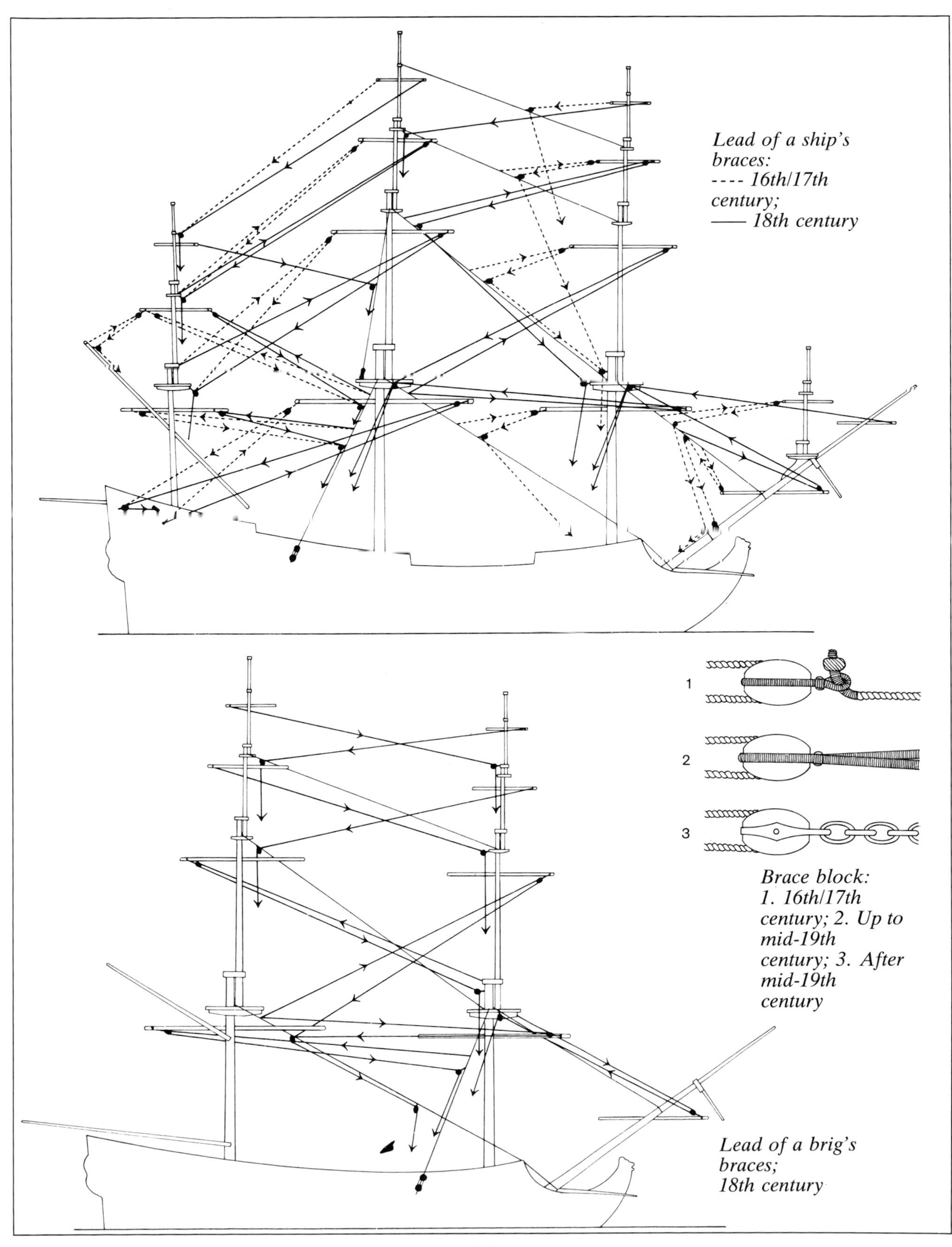

Lead of a ship's braces:
---- 16th/17th century;
—— 18th century

Brace block: 1. 16th/17th century; 2. Up to mid-19th century; 3. After mid-19th century

Lead of a brig's braces; 18th century

Sheets and tacks

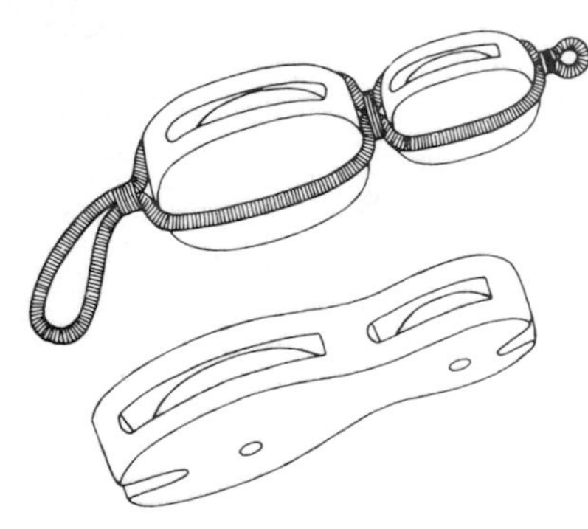

Top: Topsail sheet and tack block in single strop
Bottom: Fiddle block

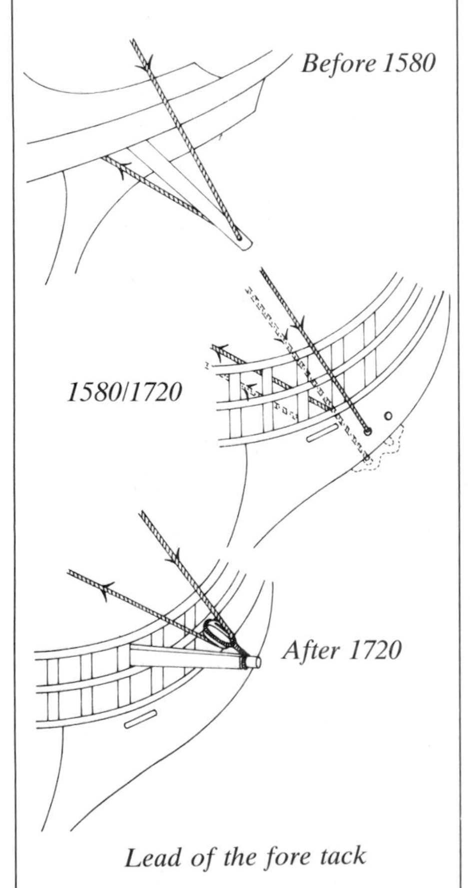

Lead of the fore tack

The course sheets
The sheets' task was to hold the leeward lower corners of the sails – the clews – against the wind pressure. From ancient times until the 19th century the method of guiding the course sheets remained the same. A single block was fixed to the clew. The sheet itself was fixed to a ring bolt on the outer side of the bulwarks, reeved through the sheet block, and ran directly inboard – or after the 15th century through a sheave in the bulwarks – where it belayed to a range cleat, or on the Continent from the early 16th century, to a staghorn.

Multiple sheets
Until the late 10th century multiple sheets were used in Viking ships; they were spliced into the foot rope of the sail, and 8 to 12 rope ends hung down to the deck for the men to hold. The Stenkyrka figurestone, illustrated on the right, shows a clear example of this type of multiple sheet.

The middle sheets
After the middle of the 14th century a further sheet was fitted to the middle of the foot rope, and after the middle of the 15th century there were two of them, one on the foot rope of the mainsail, and one on the foot rope of the bonnet. The sharp vertical centrefold, which can be seen on the mainsails and sometimes on the foresails of ships between the middle of the 14th and the middle of the 16th century, was a result of these middle sheets, which disappeared again in the mid-16th century.

The topsail sheets
In the second half of the 15th and the early 16th century, when the topsails were still very small, the sheets as well as the braces were taken to the top and belayed there. Shortly after 1500 the topsail sheets were led to the lower yard arm via small blocks, and thence to the deck parallel to the braces.

The topgallant and royal sheets
In the middle of the 16th century the topsail sheet was fixed to the clew with a stopper knot (pictured opposite), reeved through a block at the yard arm situated below it, then ran to a leading block on the inner third of the yard, and finally down to the deck, where it reeved through a sheave in a kevel block, and belayed to its head. The topgallant and royal sail sheets followed a similar course to the topsail sheets, and belayed to the bitts.

The tacks
Tacks were only used on the courses. Until the first half of the 18th century they were single ropes, which were attached to the clew with a stopper knot. The main tack reeved through the hole in the chesstree into the waist, and belayed on a range cleat. The fore tack ran through a square timber with two holes, fixed to the knee of the head until the beginning of the 17th century, around 1630 through a guide below the knee of the head, around 1650 through two holes in the knee of the head, and since the first half of the 18th century through a block on the outboard end of the bumkin. In the first half of the 18th century doubled tacks were fitted, reeved through a block fixed to the clew with a stopper knot. This was a Continental development, later adopted by the British.

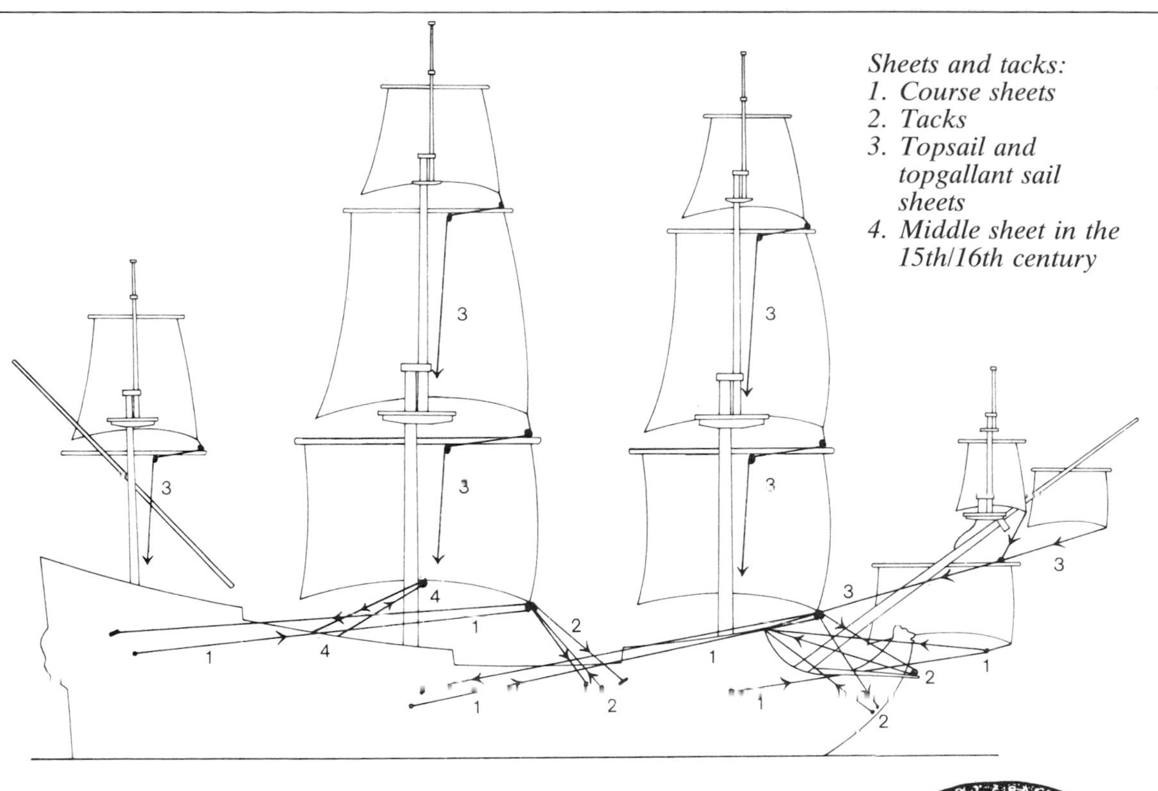

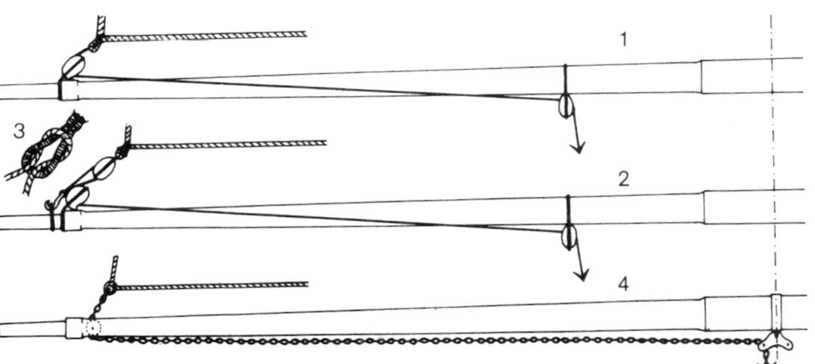

Topsail and topgallant sail sheet: 1. Single sheet; 2. Single sheet with tackle; 3. Clew; 4. Chain used after 1850

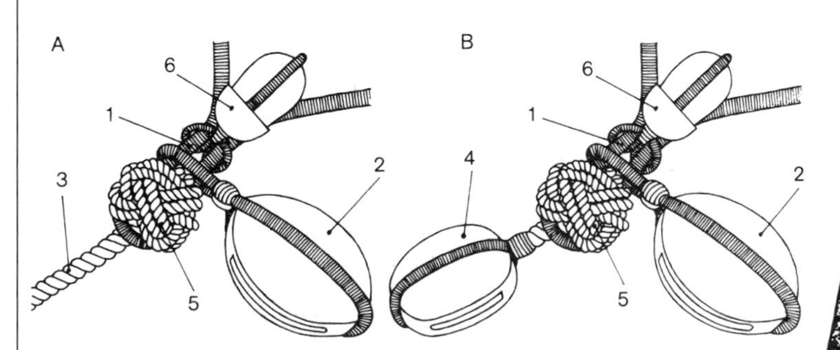

Clew of courses A. 14th/17th century; B. 18th/19th century; 1. Clew; 2. Sheet block; 3. Tack; 4. Tack block; 5. Stopper knot; 6. Clew line block

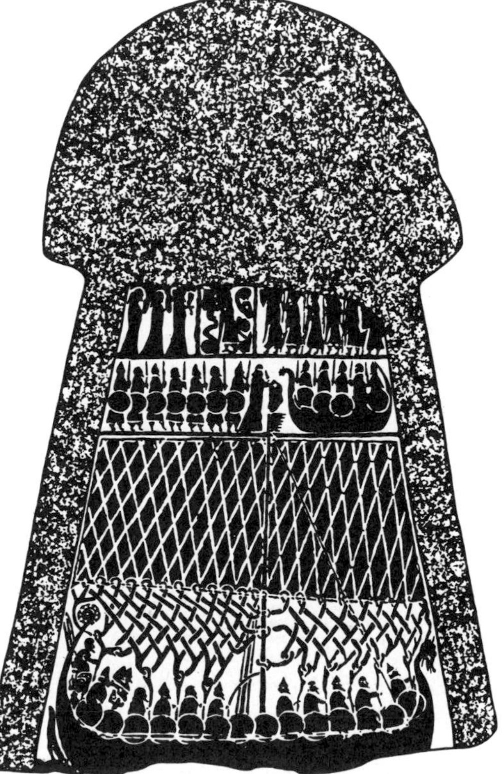

Multiple sheets of a Viking ship (Stenkyrka figurestone)

Clew lines

The clew lines (clew garnets on courses)
Clew lines have been used since the 14th century. The clew garnet and topsail clewlines were attached to the yards – ⅔ of the half-yard length plus 2ft from the middle of the yard – reeved through a block on the clew (see SHEETS), returned to a block on the yard – 2ft inside the attachment point – then reeved through a leading block at the top and through a shroud truck half-way up the shrouds, and belayed to a belaying pin. Topgallant clew lines – they were single ropes on smaller ships – were sometimes belayed in the top. Spritsail clew lines belayed to a cleat in the head before 1720, and later reeved through the gammon lashing or rack block and belayed to a timber head on the forecastle. The sprit topsail clew lines belayed in the sprit top before 1720, and after 1720 followed the same route as the spritsail clew lines. Clew-line blocks were almost always used for clew lines after 1670.

Leech lines and bunt lines

Leech line made off to cringle

First we have to differentiate between leech lines and bunt lines. Leech lines have been in use since the middle of the 15th century. They were attached to the leeches of the sail with martnets, and were always carried on both sides of the sail. After 1650 the leech lines were simplified, the various versions being shown in the drawings on the right. After 1720 simple leech lines of the British type were in general use.
Bunt lines were carried on the fore side of the sail only, and were attached to cringles in the foot rope. From the middle of the 16th century they were fitted to the courses, from the first half of the 17th century to the top sails, from the end of the 17th century to the topgallant sails. Before 1720 one pair was carried on the courses, and after 1720 two pairs on large ships; one pair was fitted on top sails, and often only a bunt line on the topgallant sails, attached with a thimble to a span between two foot cringles. The bunt lines ran below the top or to the stay collar via blocks, then down the shrouds through shroud trucks, and belayed to belaying pins. The spritsail possessed only bunt lines, often the same type as the topgallant bunt lines; the sprit topsail carried neither leech lines nor bunt lines.

Reef tackles

After the introduction of the reef on the topsails in the 17th century, reef tackles became necessary. They hooked into cringles in the leeches of the sail, reeved through a sheave in the yard arm, and ended in a tackle, which was stropped to the topmast head in Dutch ships, and in others to the parral ropes. The Dutch method became standard after 1710. The reef tackle belayed to the chain plate deadeyes in the top. Clew lines, leech lines, bunt lines and reef tackles are slack when the sails are set, that is, they just hang freely.

Yard tackles

From about 1685 the lower yards were fitted with yard tackles to augment the stay tackles.
A yard tackle consisted of a pendant, which was fixed to the yard arm, and which carried a long tackle block. The running part carried a hooked double block. When the ship was under sail, the yard tackle was hooked to the futtock shrouds and made up along the yard, as shown in the drawing on the right. Yard tackles were principally a feature of English ships; they were very seldom seen on Continental ships.

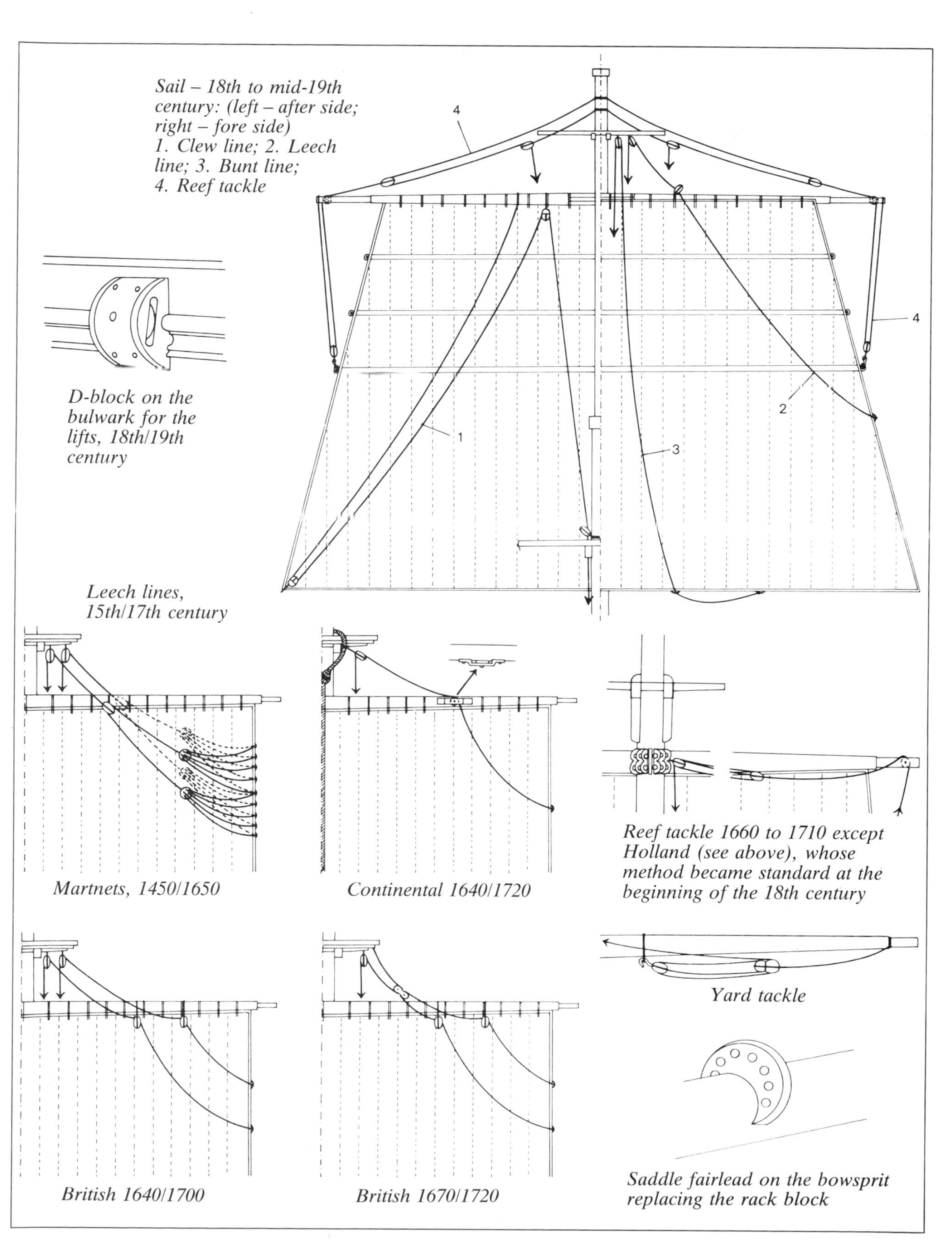

Sail – 18th to mid-19th century: (left – after side; right – fore side)
1. Clew line; 2. Leech line; 3. Bunt line; 4. Reef tackle
4
4
1
2
3
D-block on the bulwark for the lifts, 18th/19th century
Leech lines, 15th/17th century
Martnets, 1450/1650
Continental 1640/1720
Reef tackle 1660 to 1710 except Holland (see above), whose method became standard at the beginning of the 18th century
British 1640/1700
British 1670/1720
Yard tackle
Saddle fairlead on the bowsprit replacing the rack block

Bowlines

The purpose of the bowlines was to keep the weather leech well out when sailing close-hauled. Many ship historians have supposed that the ships of the ancient Greeks and Romans had bowlines, although they cannot prove it. Reliable evidence of their existence dates from the early 13th century.

The bearing out spar
Before bowlines were introduced the Viking ships and ships of the early Middle Ages carried bearing out spars in their ships. This was a wooden spar with a shoulder at its outboard end, which was plugged into a cringle in the leech rope. There were two wooden blocks with round depressions fixed inside the bulwarks, and level with the mast; the lower end of the spar was stepped in these, and by this means the sail was spread forward.

Bowlines
The run of the bowlines is usually shown clearly on the rigging plans. The bowline bridles were hitched to the cringles of the leech ropes – toggled after 1819. Until the late 15th century the bowlines were attached to the leech of the sail with two or at most three bridles.In the 16th century the number of bowline bridles increased dramatically in some areas, while in the early 17th century the number was reduced again as follows: courses three bridles, or if a bonnet was fitted, four bridles, the lowest of which was attached to the bonnet; fore topsail three or four bridles, main topsail four bridles, mizen topsail two or three bridles, topgallant sails two bridles. The bridles were joined together by means of spliced eyes, thimbles, or – more rarely – small blocks.
In the second half of the 19th century the bowlines disappeared.

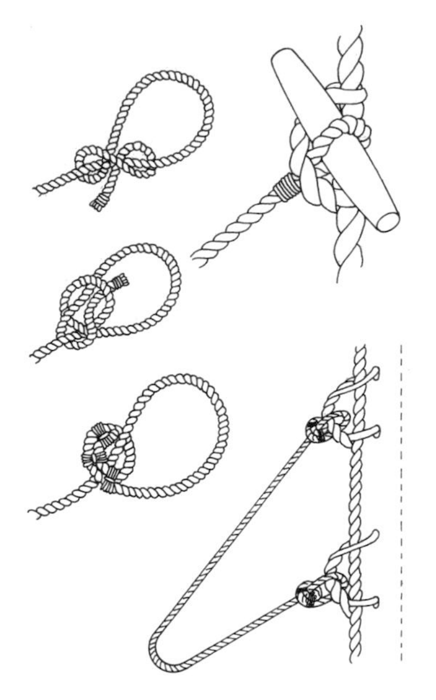

Hitches for bowline bridles

Top rope

The top rope was used to hoist and lower the topmasts. It was hooked under the underside of the cap, reeved through the sheave at the foot of the topmast, up through a block, which was hooked to the cap, and down to the deck. On a model the top rope can be omitted, as it was only used when sending up or striking the topmast, and was only rigged at those times. The only traces to be seen are two or four ringbolts on the underside of the cap.

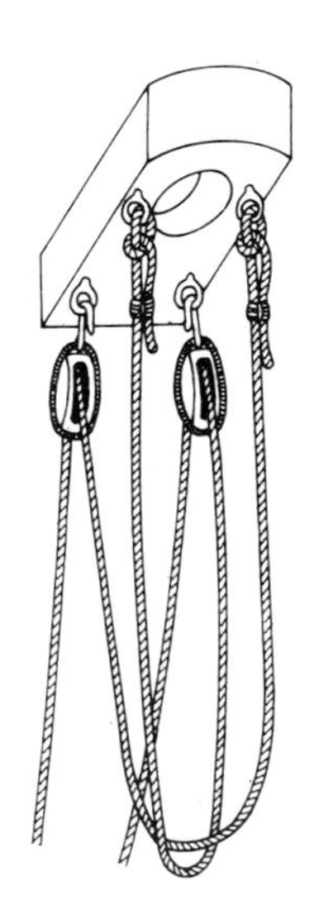

Top rope

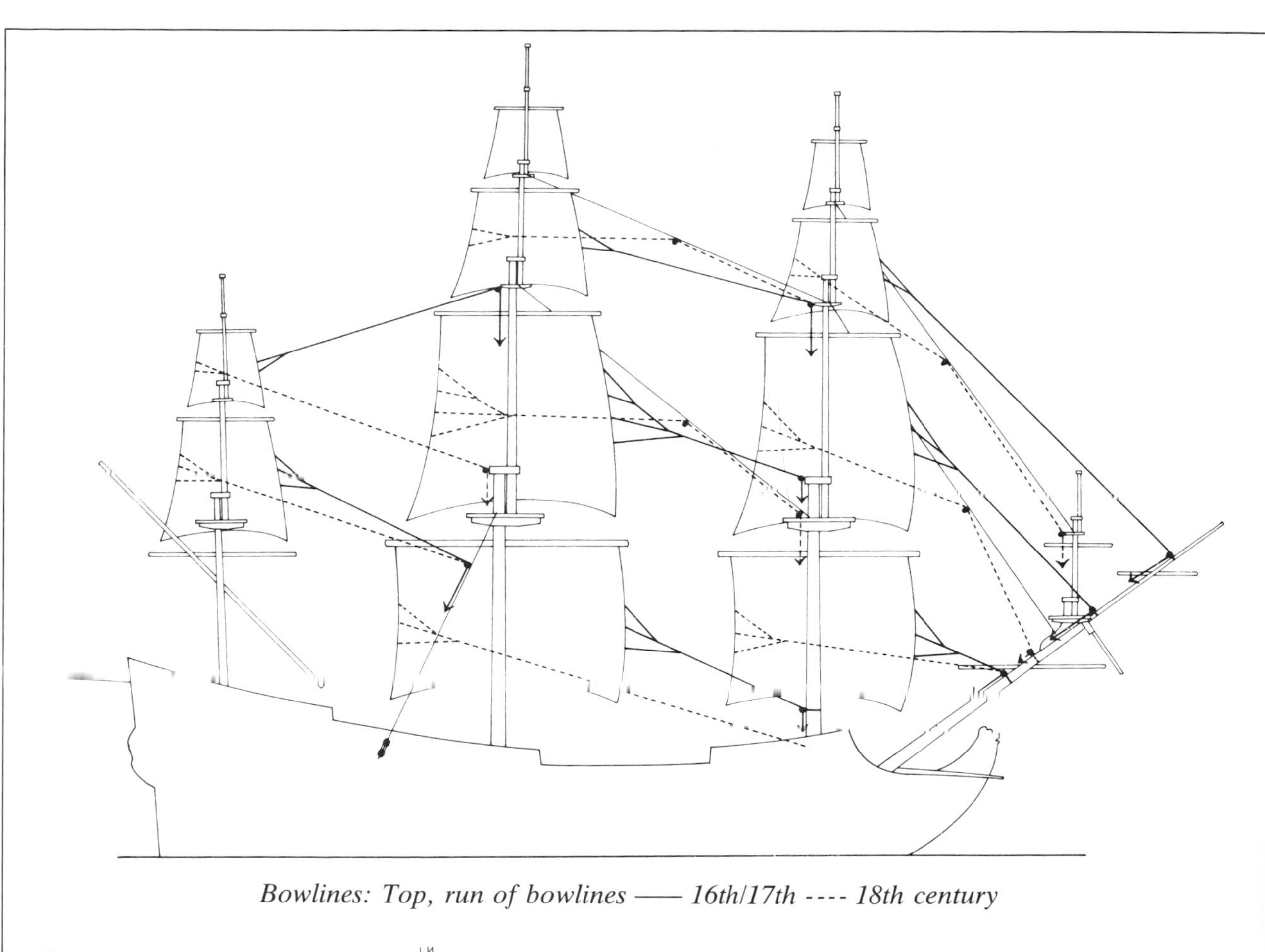

Bowlines: Top, run of bowlines —— 16th/17th ---- 18th century

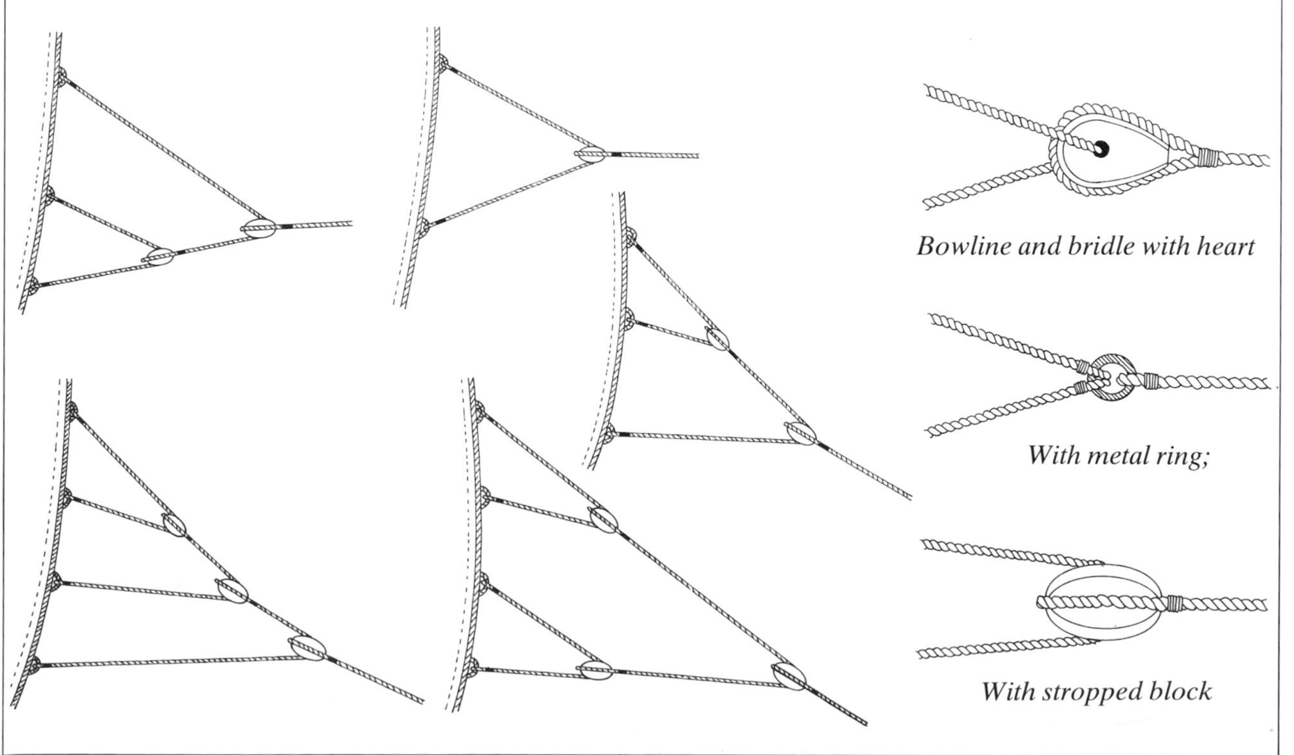

Bowline and bridle with heart

With metal ring;

With stropped block

Gaff sails

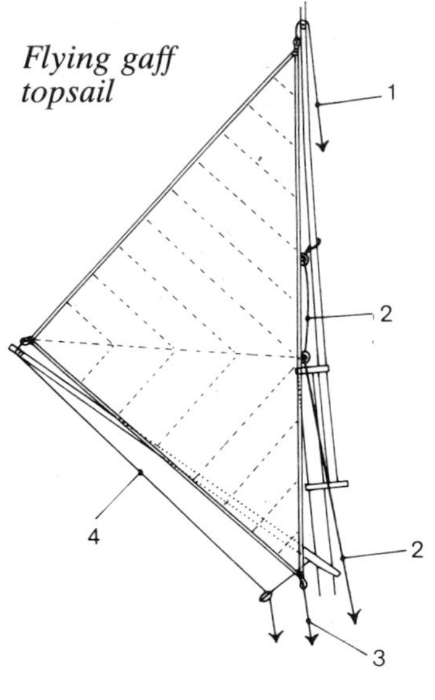

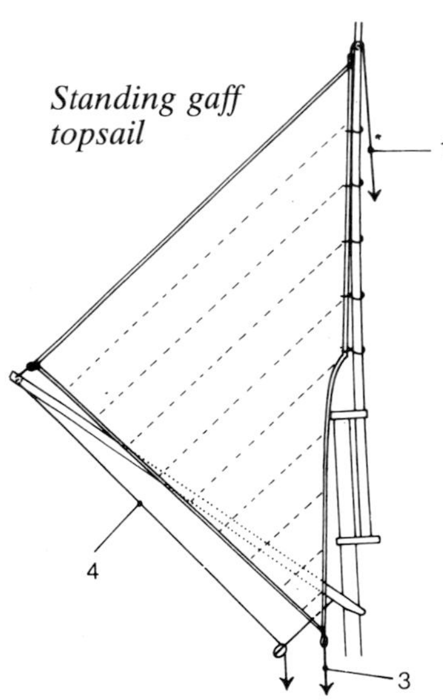

Gaff topsail: 1. Halyard; 2. Down haul; 3. Tack; 4. Sheet;

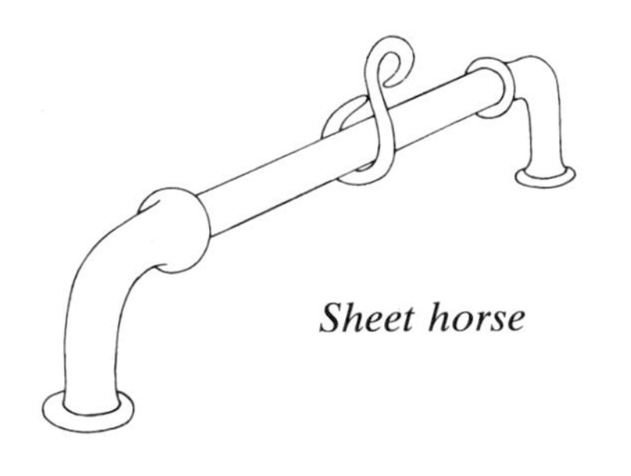

Sheet horse

In the first half of the 18th century gaff sails superseded mizen lateen sails. Initially they were still carried on lateen yards, then after the middle of the 18th century on the gaff proper in conjunction with a boom (driver), or without the boom (spanker). In the merchant service the name spanker was used for a mizen gaff sail with or without a boom. In the 19th century boomless gaff sails replaced staysails between the masts in the Royal Navy and were known as trysails. When fitted to merchant ships they were called spencers. After the late 18th century gaff topsails were also carried in many merchant ships on the mizen only.

The parral
The parrals for the gaff and driver boom were fitted with a series of trucks early on, but after the middle of the 19th century an iron goose neck was used (see GAFF and DRIVER BOOM).

The throat halyard
The throat halyard served to hoist the gaff. An upper block was suspended from the crosstrees, a lower one on a ring bolt in the gaff jaws. The two were joined by the throat halyard.

The peak halyard
The peak halyard assumed the job of lifts and set the correct angle of the gaff. There was a very wide variety of methods of attaching the peak halyard, as the drawings on the right show.

Vangs
The vangs served as braces to the gaff, and were rigged in a similar way.

The topping lift
The topping lift held the driver boom horizontal. It was attached to the cap, and there were various methods of rigging it.

The sheet
The sheet was used to control the driver boom. The strop of its upper block was prevented from slipping by a thumb cleat. The lower block was often hooked to a transverse iron rod, known as the horse. In the case of spencers the sheet was also hooked or shackled to a horse.

The peak outhaul
A rope ran via a sheave on the peak of the gaff to the peak of the sail and back to the mast; the sail was hoisted by this means.

The downhaul
A further rope was fixed to the peak, which passed to the jaws and on to the base of the mast; by this means the sail could be hauled down when it was to be furled.

The foot outhaul
The outhaul ran via a block or a sheave on the end of the boom and ran directly inboard on small ships, or by means of a purchase on large ships, then belayed to a cleat.

Brails
There were up to 5 brails, which were used to haul the sail to the mast when the sail was to be furled.

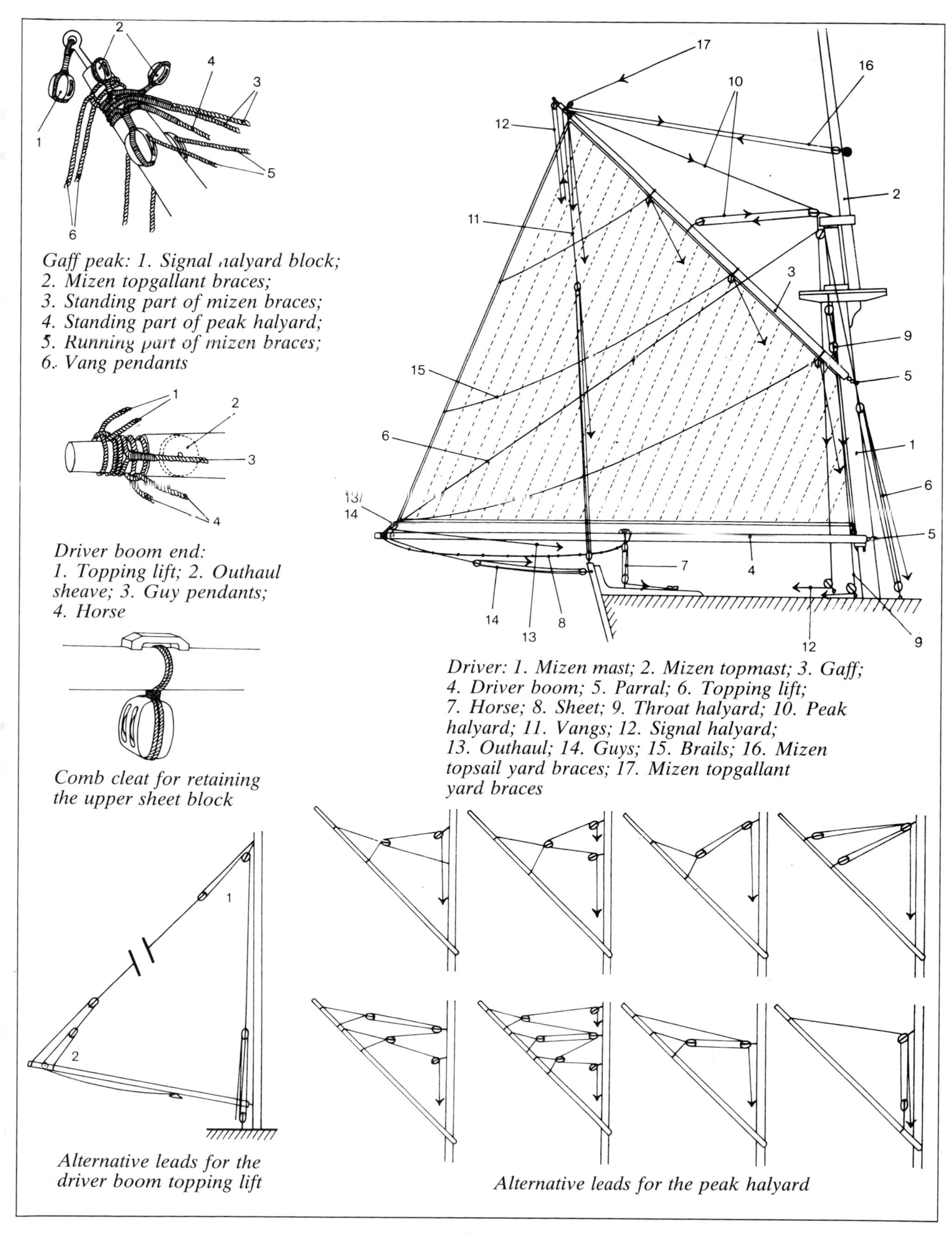

Gaff peak: 1. Signal halyard block; 2. Mizen topgallant braces; 3. Standing part of mizen braces; 4. Standing part of peak halyard; 5. Running part of mizen braces; 6. Vang pendants

Driver boom end: 1. Topping lift; 2. Outhaul sheave; 3. Guy pendants; 4. Horse

Comb cleat for retaining the upper sheet block

Driver: 1. Mizen mast; 2. Mizen topmast; 3. Gaff; 4. Driver boom; 5. Parral; 6. Topping lift; 7. Horse; 8. Sheet; 9. Throat halyard; 10. Peak halyard; 11. Vangs; 12. Signal halyard; 13. Outhaul; 14. Guys; 15. Brails; 16. Mizen topsail yard braces; 17. Mizen topgallant yard braces

Alternative leads for the driver boom topping lift

Alternative leads for the peak halyard

Staysails

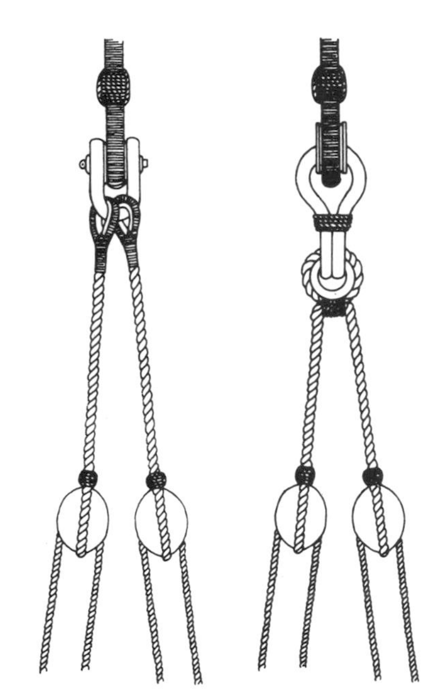

Methods of attaching the sheets to the clew, second half of the 19th century, using iron shackles or hook and thimble

Since their introduction on large ships in the second half of the 17th century the rigging of the staysails changed little. We have to differentiate between fixed staysails, which were bent to a stay, and jibs set flying, which were not.

The Staysail stay
As already described under STAYS, the staysails in the 17th and early 18th centuries were bent to false stays, which were removed when the staysails were furled.

The halyard
The halyard reeved through two single blocks, the upper of which was fixed to the mast or the crosstrees, the lower seized or hooked to the head of the sail. The halyard ran down to the deck, and was set up with a tackle in the case of large staysails.

The tack
The tack was a rope spliced into the tack cringle to secure the bottom of the staysail.

The sheet
Staysails featured double sheets with a block spliced in each end. The lee sheet was hauled taut, and the weather sheet hung loosely over the next stay.

The downhaul
On fixed staysails the downhaul was attached to the head – on large sails it sometimes ran on to the clew – and was used for hauling the sails down, when they were being furled Sails set flying had no downhaul.

The brails
Four-sided staysails carried a brail on both sides of the sail, which were used to haul the canvas to the mast when the sails were being furled.

Staysail rope sizes

Sail	False Stay	Halyard	Tack	Sheet	Down-haul	Brail
Outer jib	30%	15%	16%	28%	10%	
Inner jib	26%	15%	16%	26%	10%	
Fore topmast staysail	22%	21%	18%	23%	10%	
Main staysail	25%	20%	18%	22%	10%	10%
Main topmast staysail	25%	20%	18%	20%	10%	10%
Middle staysail	24%	16%	18%	16%	10%	10%
Main topgallant staysail	20%	12%	16%	12%	10%	10%
Mizen staysail	25%	15%	18%	15%	10%	10%
Mizen topmast staysail	20%	12%	16%	12%	10%	10%

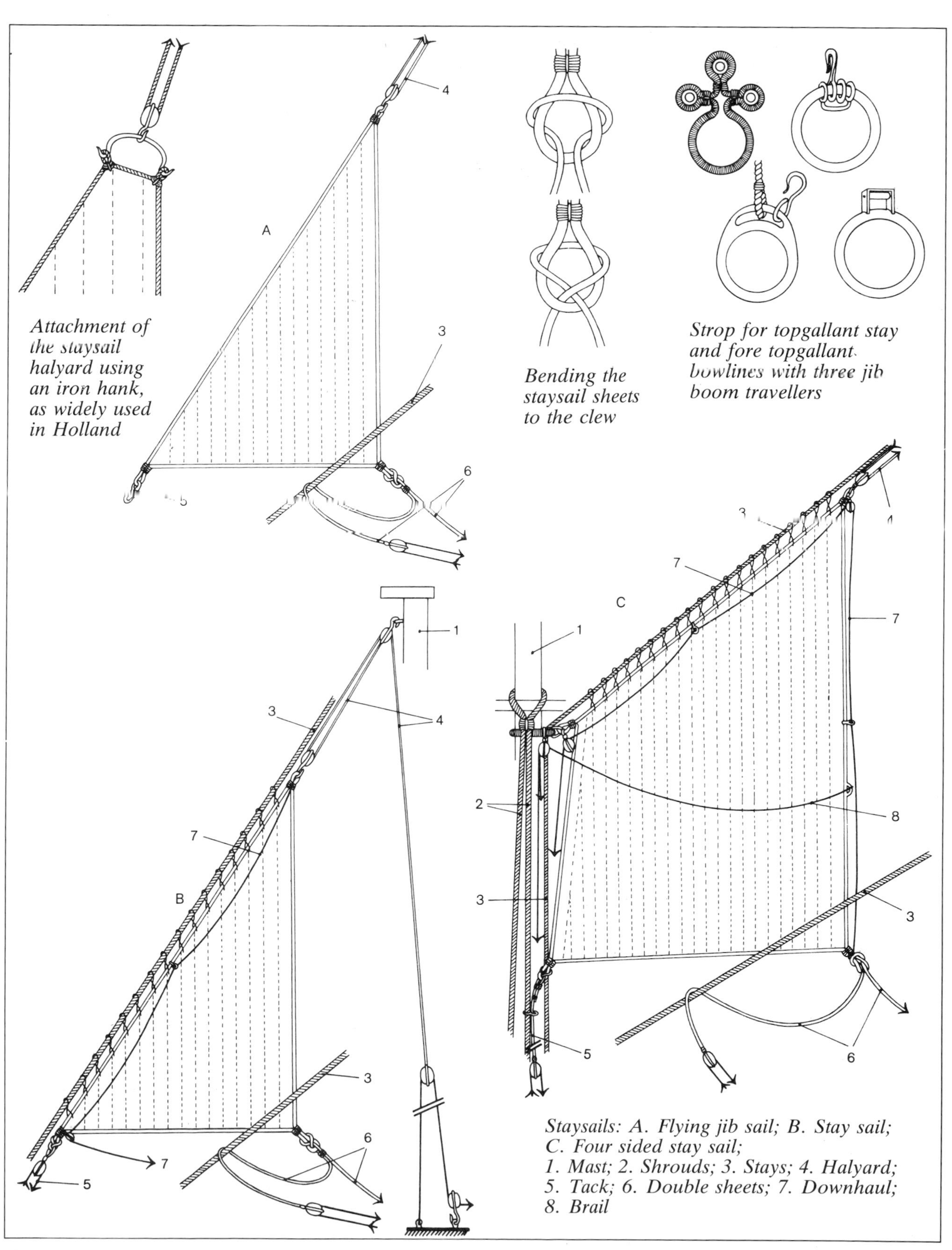

Attachment of the staysail halyard using an iron hank, as widely used in Holland

Staysails: A. Flying jib sail; B. Stay sail; C. Four sided stay sail; 1. Mast; 2. Shrouds; 3. Stays; 4. Halyard; 5. Tack; 6. Double sheets; 7. Downhaul; 8. Brail

Studding sails

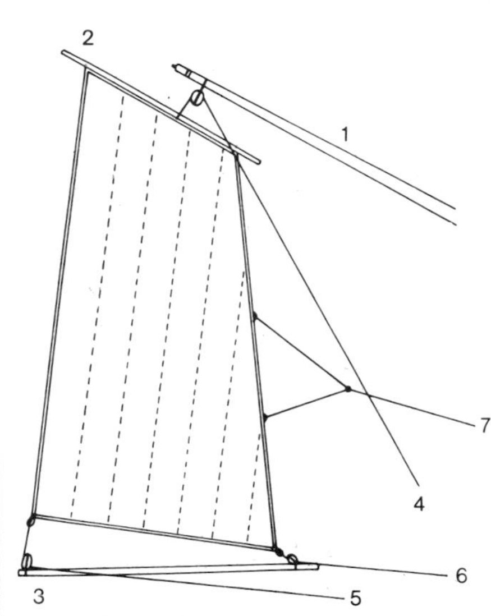

Ring tail or driver:
1. Gaff; 2. Ringtail or driver yard;
3. Ringtail or driver boom;
4. Halyard; 5. Outhaul; 6. Tack;
7. Bowline

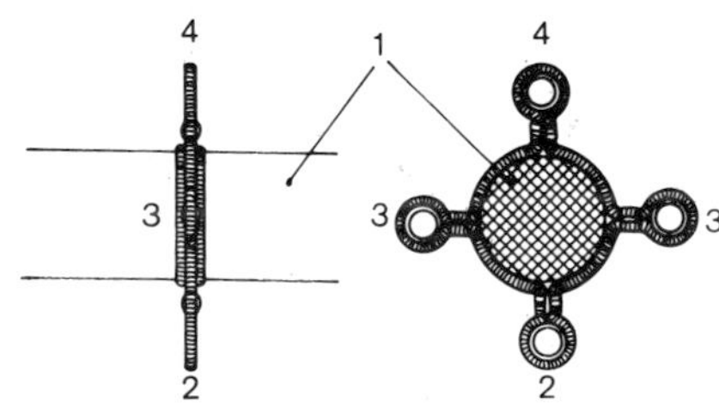

Studding sail boom strop:
1. Studding sail boom; 2. Thimble for martingale; 3. Thimble for guys; 4. Thimble for topping lift

The studding sails were used to increase the sail area when the wind was light and following. With the exception of the yard lashing, all of the studding sail gear was rigged when the studding sails were set; when they were unbent, the entire gear was sent down.

The spar and boom rigging
The studding sail booms were normally fixed to the yard with a lashing at their inboard end. The topmast studding sail boom was often fitted with a small additional brace on the Continent and the topmast studding sail tack was sometimes arranged that it also served as lift to the topmast studding sail boom on the Continent. The studding sail boom was held upwards by a lift, downwards with the martingale, and supported laterally by guys.

Studding sail yards and halyards
The studding sails were always bent on their own small yards. The lower studding sails up to about 1750 carried yards the full width of the sail, and after that time the yards were half the sail width, and the inner earing was hoisted with an inner halyard.
If no studding sail boom was carried, the lower studding sail was fitted with a lower yard of half sail width, and was set flying, with a tack which was attached to the lower yard with three bridles. The halyards of the studding sail yards were single, and reeved through blocks on the yard arms or the booms to leading blocks on the mast and down to the deck.

The tacks
Blocks were stropped at the outer ends of the booms, through which the tacks reeved; they were usually set up with a single whip, the fall of which ran down to the deck.

The sheets
On the mast side the studding sails were tensioned with double sheets which were belayed to the rail or the yard. They were usually bent to the clew of the sail without a block, and ran down to the deck via leading blocks.

The early 18th century driver
The original driver was a form of spanker studding sail and was similarly rigged. As well as the halyard, sheet and tack, it also carried a bowline on the leech. It was displaced in the late 18th century by the boom driver. Merchant ships in the late 19th century sometimes carried a similar sail outboard of the spanker, usually called a ringtail.

Studding sails, rope sizes

Rope	Studding sail boom	Topmast studding sail boom	Lower studding sail	Topmast studding sail	Topgallant studding sail
Martingale	22%				
Forward guy	20%				
After guy	20%				
Lift	20%				
Brace		10%			
Outer halyard			20%	18%	12%
Inner halyard			18%		
Tack			18%	15%	10%
Sheet			18%	15%	10%

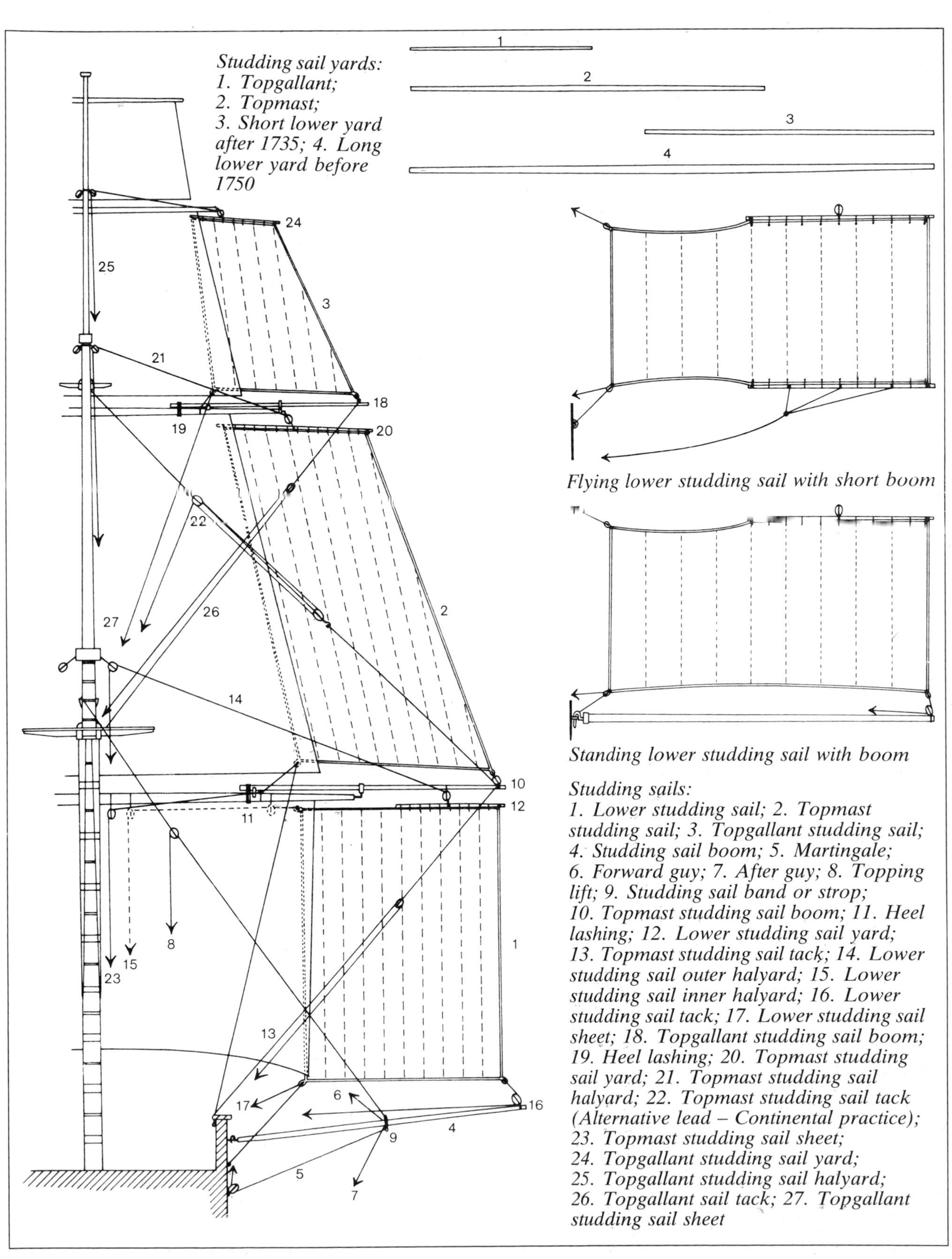
Studding sail yards:
1. Topgallant;
2. Topmast;
3. Short lower yard after 1735; 4. Long lower yard before 1750
1
2
3
4
24
25
3
21
18
19
20
22
2
26
27
14
10
12
11
15
8
23
1
13
17
6
16
9
4
5
7
Flying lower studding sail with short boom
Standing lower studding sail with boom
Studding sails:
1. Lower studding sail; 2. Topmast studding sail; 3. Topgallant studding sail; 4. Studding sail boom; 5. Martingale; 6. Forward guy; 7. After guy; 8. Topping lift; 9. Studding sail band or strop; 10. Topmast studding sail boom; 11. Heel lashing; 12. Lower studding sail yard; 13. Topmast studding sail tack; 14. Lower studding sail outer halyard; 15. Lower studding sail inner halyard; 16. Lower studding sail tack; 17. Lower studding sail sheet; 18. Topgallant studding sail boom; 19. Heel lashing; 20. Topmast studding sail yard; 21. Topmast studding sail halyard; 22. Topmast studding sail tack (Alternative lead – Continental practice); 23. Topmast studding sail sheet; 24. Topgallant studding sail yard; 25. Topgallant studding sail halyard; 26. Topgallant sail tack; 27. Topgallant studding sail sheet

Furled sails

If you wish to show your sails furled loosely on the yard, by this stage you should have prepared them as described under Furled Sails in the chapter Sails, and fitted them with all the appropriate ropework. The sheets and tacks are now left loose, and the sail is pulled up to the yard using clew lines, the leech lines and the bunt lines, so that they hang like a floppy bolster below the yard. A good example of this type is the model of the English galleon on page 23, and the French armoured frigate *La Gloire* on page 211.

If you do intend showing the sails completely furled on the yards, it is often advisable to fix the ropes (clew lines, leech lines, bunt lines and reef tackles) to the front of the yard, and to make the sails from de-laminated paper handkerchiefs or Japanese tissue.

Please note that up to the middle of the 19th century the sail was never furled in an even thickness along the yard; it was fairly thin towards the yard arms and was gathered up to a thick bundle in the bunt. In the latter part of the 19th century sails were clewed up to the yard arms instead of the bunt and the furled canvas was more evenly spread along the yard.

In many cases a bunt gasket was used for this, which was attached to larboard and starboard of the yard with two lines, and with a centre line reeved through a block on the top or the cap; the bunt of the sail was gathered up in the middle and held fast.

The furled sails are held in place on the yard with the gaskets, which are wound several times round the sail and the yard, and then knotted. Take care that the furled sail is the right thickness: neither too fat and bulging, nor too thin and mean-looking. The French armoured corvette *La Jeanne d'Arc* represents a particularly fine and successful example of sails furled on the yards – that is just how they should look!

Yards without sails

If the modeller decides to omit the sails from his model, he often does not quite know what to do with the various ropes which otherwise would be attached to the sails; you will sometimes see quite outlandish solutions to this problem.

Here are the general rules:

The stopper knot of the tack is passed through the stropped eye of the clew-line block, which would otherwise be fixed to the clew of the lower sail; the strop of the sheet block is then fitted over it. The whole combination is pulled up to the yard, with the lower and upper clew-line block retaining about one block's length between them.

The clew-lines and sheets of the topsails, topgallants and royals are arranged in a similar way.

The leech and bunt lines are fitted with stopper knots and pulled up on their yards as far as their leading blocks, so that the stropper knots are always located outboard of the block.

The bowlines are made fast to the yard, distributed along it at the same spacing as they would have with sails set. Take care here. When sails were furled or unbent, the yards were always set at right-angles to the centre line, i.e. parallel to the midships frame. Be sure to locate the yards correctly (see Lifts).

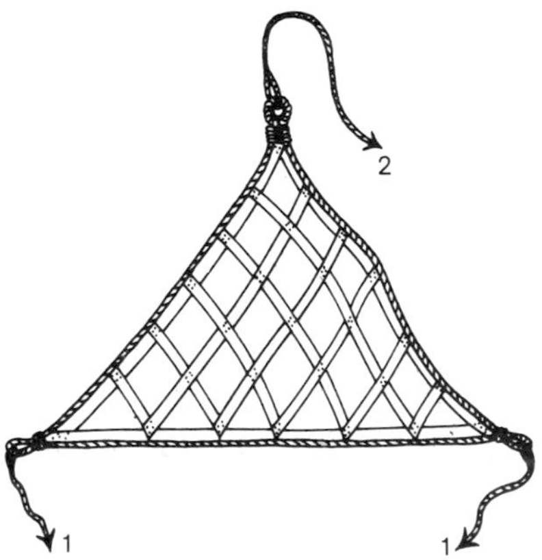

Bunt gasket for furling the sails: 1. Sennet for securing gasket to the yard (behind the sail); 2. Sennet for securing gasket to mast

French armoured corvette La Jeanne d'Arc *of 1867*
The sails furled on the yards are very finely modelled here.

Lateen sails

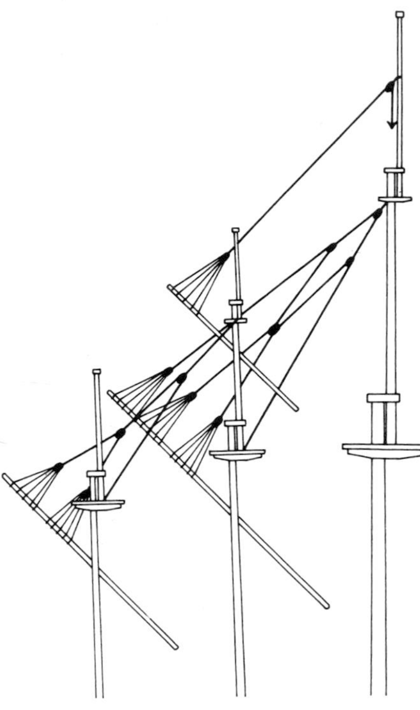

Mizen lifts, 16th century

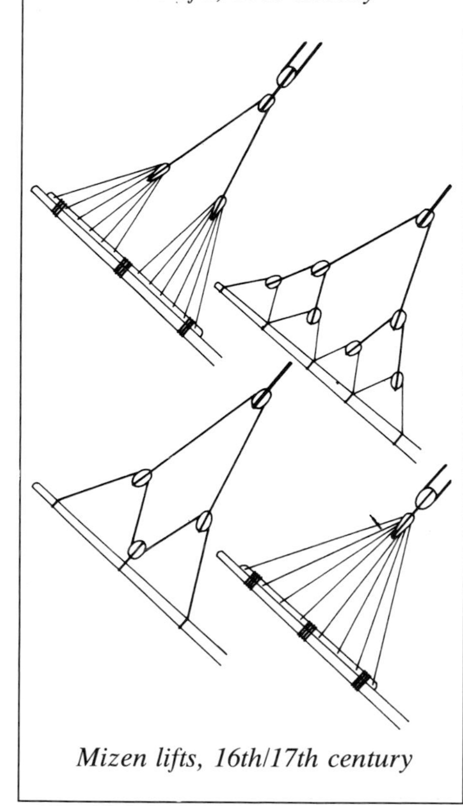

Mizen lifts, 16th/17th century

First we have to differentiate between the lateen sails of the Mediterranean which were often the only sails rigged, and the mizen lateen sails of ships which were otherwise square-rigged.

The Parral
The parral was fitted with two rows of trucks, and on square-rigged ships with ribs also; ribs were not used in the Mediterranean. It was not attached directly to the yard, but instead enclosed the halyard. If it reeved through a block, then it ended in a purchase at the foot of the mast; if it reeved through a two-hole deadeye, the purchase was in many cases belayed to the yard.

The jeers
In the Mediterranean the jeers generally reeved through a sheave at the masthead. On square-rigged ships the jeers frequently reeved through blocks, which were attached to the crosstrees. The jeers were attached to a halyard, which reeved through blocks or through a kevel block.

The lift
The lift was only carried on square-rigged ships. It was attached to the peak of the yard with a more or less complex arrangement of crowsfeet, ran to the mizen topmast and/or the mainmast, and ended at the deck with a purchase.

The toggles
Almost all ropes, including the shrouds, were fitted with toggles in the Mediterranean, which facilitated rapid connection and disconnection of the ropes.

The tack tackles
The two tack tackles braced round the foot. On square-rigged ships they were attached to the aftermost main shrouds, and in the Mediterranean to the bulwarks. They reeved through blocks at the foot of the yard and belayed to belaying pins or cleats. In the Mediterranean a third tack tackle was often fitted in the centre.

The vangs
In the Mediterranean a pair of vangs was fixed to the upper third of the gaff, which were intended to prevent it bending, as they were often very long. In this case the weather vang was set up taut, and the lee vang left slack.

The sheet
Lateen sails were only fitted with one sheet. Its lower block was fixed to the ensign staff knee, to a ring bolt on deck, or to the outrigger while the sheet itself was belayed to a cleat.

The leech lines
The widest imaginable variety of leech lines was carried, sometimes in addition to brails, as shown in the drawings on the right.

The tack
If a bonnet was carried (never in the Mediterranean!) its forward end was held by a tack, similar in form to the sheet.

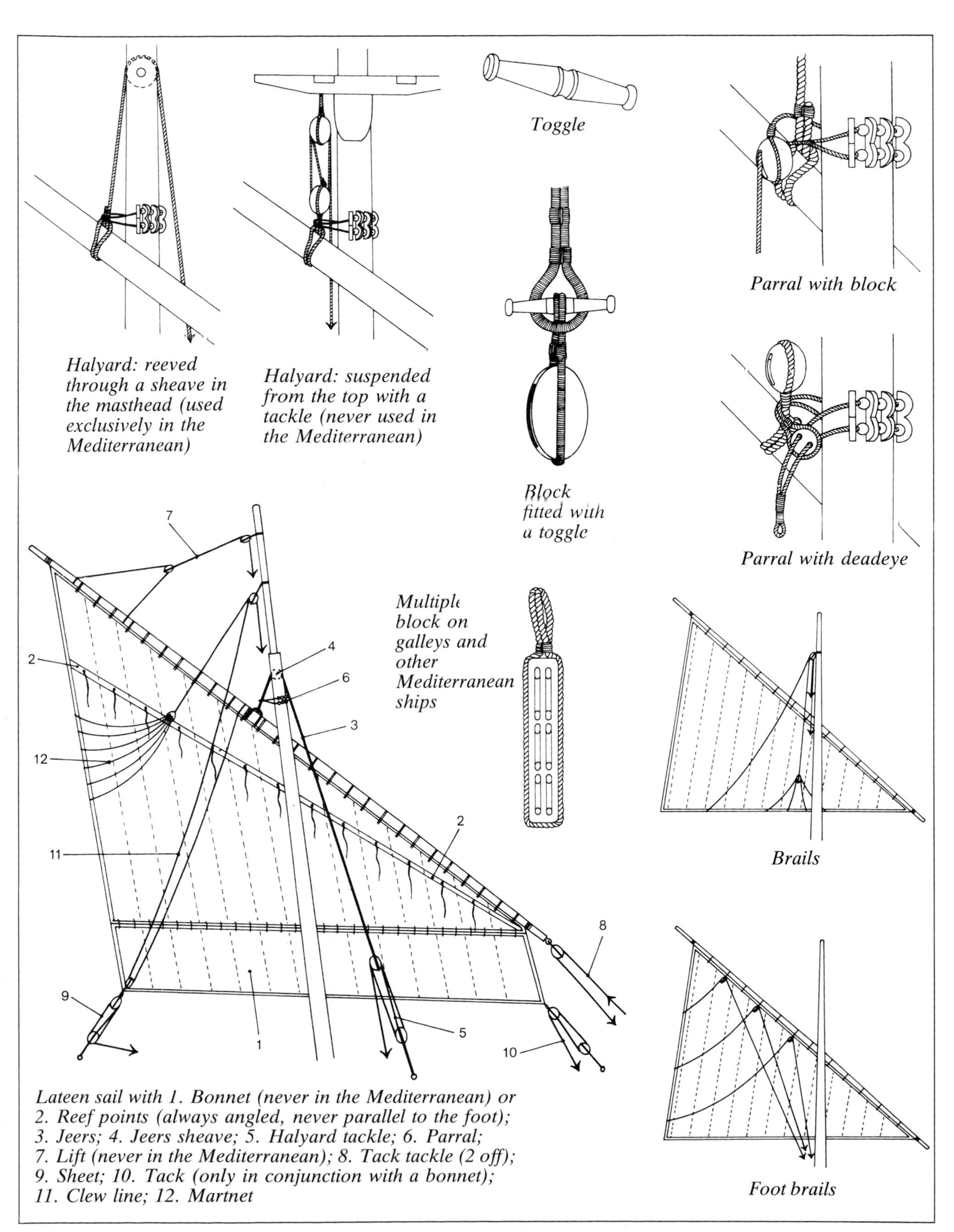

Lateen sail with 1. Bonnet (never in the Mediterranean) or 2. Reef points (always angled, never parallel to the foot); 3. Jeers; 4. Jeers sheave; 5. Halyard tackle; 6. Parral; 7. Lift (never in the Mediterranean); 8. Tack tackle (2 off); 9. Sheet; 10. Tack (only in conjunction with a bonnet); 11. Clew line; 12. Martnet

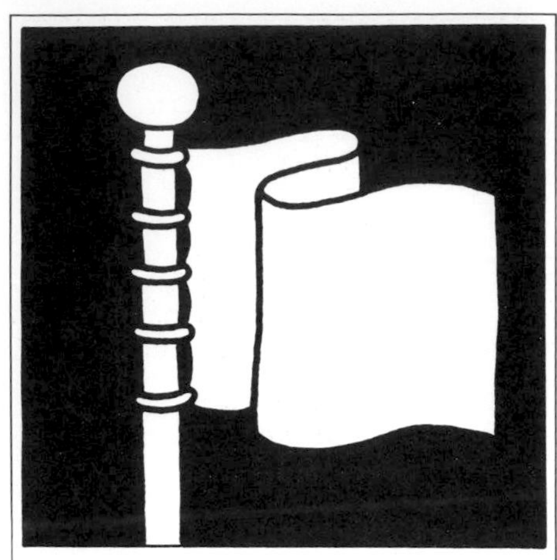

Flags

Flags, banners, ensigns, pennants, standards – all seafaring nations made a minor religion of these things. The model builder should also take the trouble to fit the appropriate flags and pennants to his model to finish the job off and add the splashes of colour which set the whole model off. We have to differentiate between the following:

Flags: Rectangular in shape, they were flown at the masthead. The main mast usually carried a command flag, while the fore and mizen masts flew command, regional, squadron or shipping company flags. These flags were attached with rope or metal hanks, although in some cases they were nailed up. In the 17th century signal halyards came into use, which enabled the flags to be hoisted and lowered. The sprit topmast, or later the jack staff, usually carried a state flag.

Ensigns: Also rectangular and generally worn at the stern. They were usually the state flags. Until the middle of the 18th century they were carried on large ensign staffs on the taffarel at all times, and then after the introduction of the driver boom were flown from the peak of the gaff when at sea.

Standards: This was the term for the personal or corporate flag which was often used until the 16th century, and even later on galleys. (Royal, Presidential and other standards are still in use today).

Burgees: These were long pennants, usually with a bifurcated fly. They were attached to a batten which in turn was hung on the mast head or on the yards by a thin line. Burgees were extremely popular on sailing ships from the late 15th to the beginning of the 18th century.

Pennants: There were three versions:

1. Short, narrow, rectangular strips of cloth. They were sometimes carried on the mizen mast instead of a flag.
2. Long, narrow and tapering, with a batten sewn into the hoist (the side nearest the mast); bent to the halyard with a 2 or 3 legged span. Warships of all the major seafaring nations, not wearing a command flag, had a commissioning pennant of this form at the mast head.
3. Long, narrow and tapering, but without a batten. They were then fitted to the flag pole or halyard. Frequently used after the mid 18th century as signal flags, in conjunction with rectangular flags.

Burgees and pennants could reach considerable lengths, in some cases as long as the whole mast.

Standards and banners: Strictly speaking, these are not part of a ship's flag equipment. In the 16th century they were extremely popular. They were fitted on their own banner staffs, and then lashed to the rail to provide additional decoration.

The modeller should heed the following points in respect of flags:

1. Choice of flags. They must, of course, be strictly correct in historical terms, in respect of their appearance and also their size and location. This is sometimes by no means easy. The appearance of the flags, e.g. in Great Britain, often altered several times over a short period; there are few reliable reference books available on this subject, and plans are also not always accurate. The safest source for the appearance of the flags is contemporary paintings and engravings.
2. Materials and fabrication. The flags are best made, like the sails, from cotton cambric (very thin silk or Japanese tissue are also possibilities). Tempera or water colour paints are used to colour in the coats of arms etc. Flags should never stand stiff and straight, but always have a slight natural wavy shape. As the material is too stiff to fold up in the right way by itself, the flags have to be moulded before fitting. Creases are avoided by rolling the flags over a pencil.
3. Arrangement. On sailing ships all the flags stream down wind, and in practice this means the direction in which the sails are swelling. If your model has no sails, the flags should be arranged aligned towards the bow along the keel line.

Papal

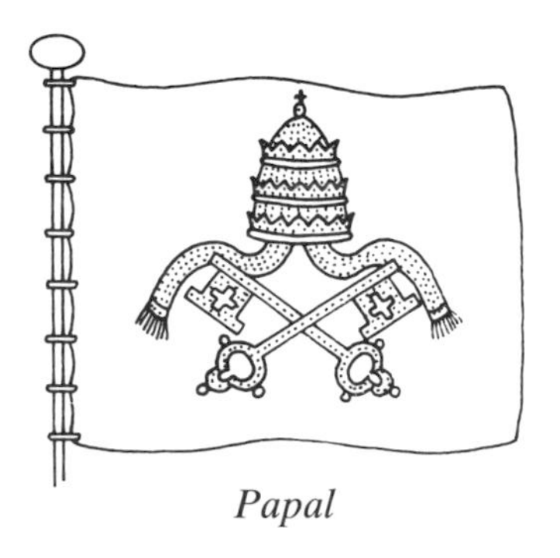

Papal

Jerusalem

Portuguese Admiralty flag

Portuguese pennant

Portuguese state flag

Portugal

Portuguese pennant

Burgundian war flag

Spain, Royal flag

Spanish Royal flag

Burgundian trade flag

Spain, state flag

Spanish pennant

white

yellow

red

blue

green

black

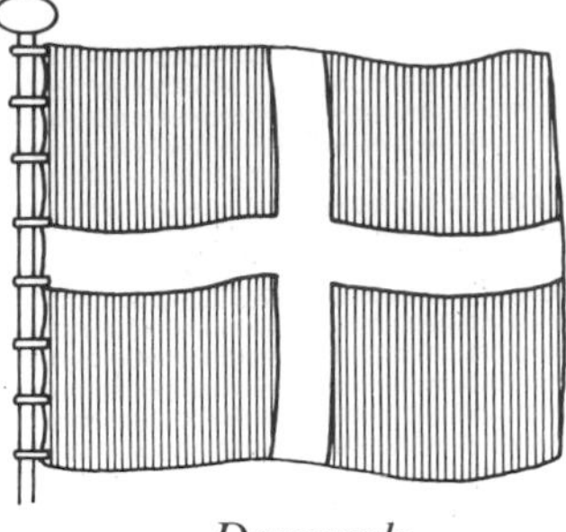
Denmark state flag

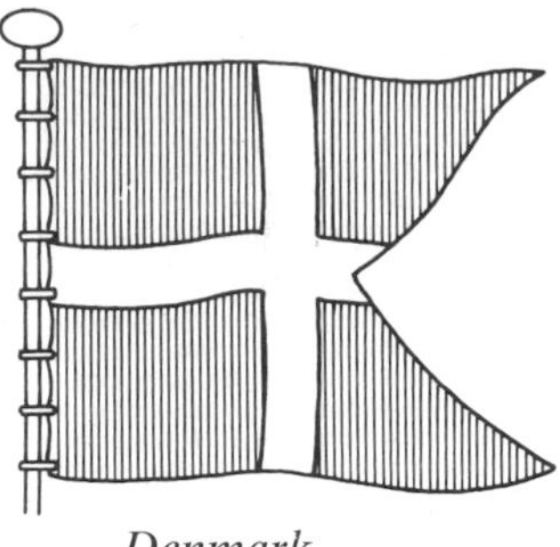
Denmark, Royal flag

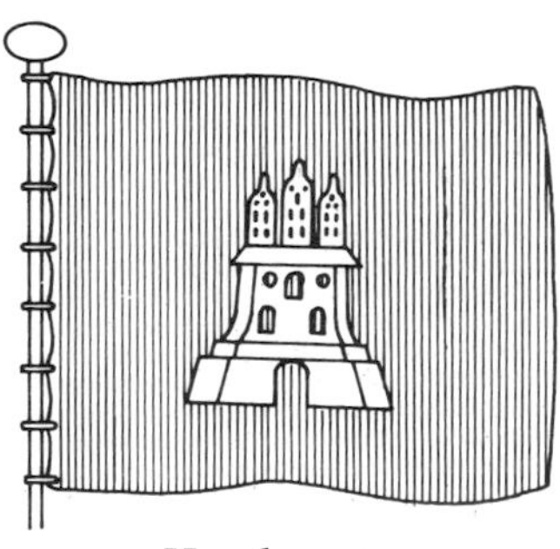
Hamburg

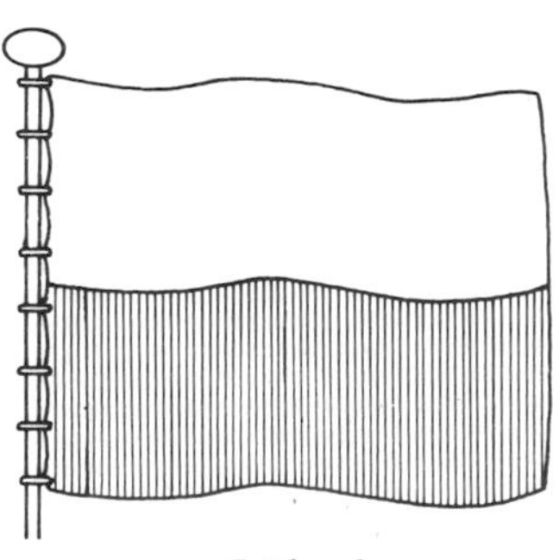
Lübeck

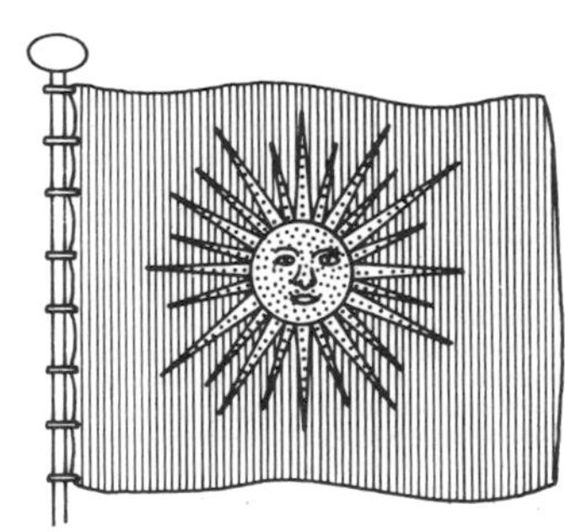
Stralsund

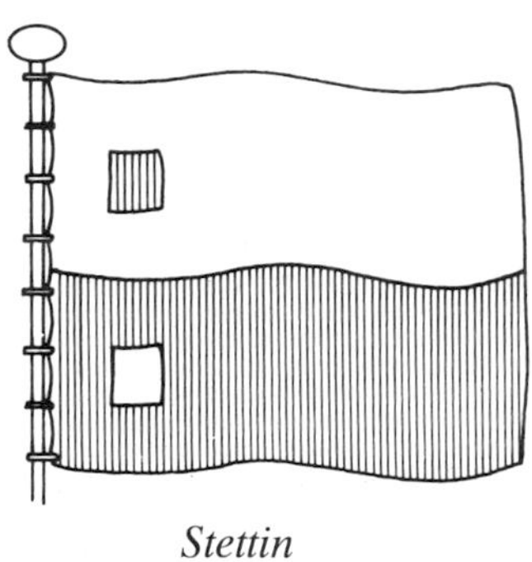
Stettin

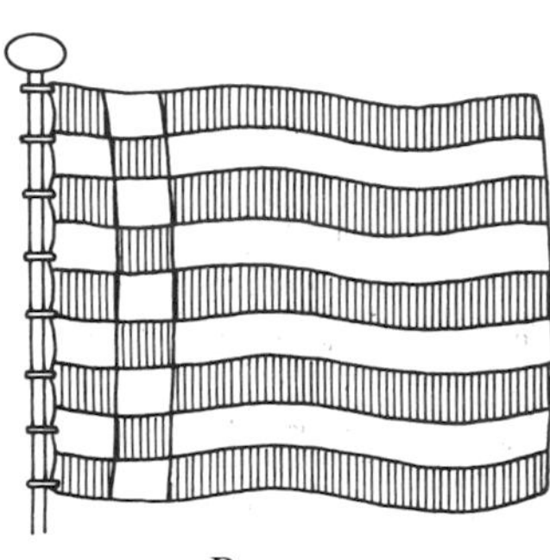
Bremen

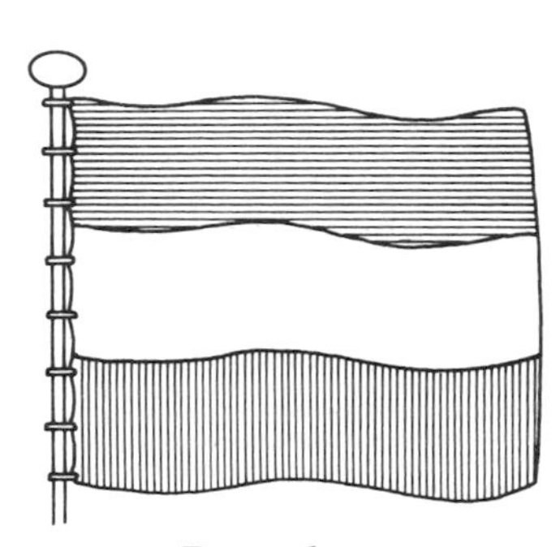
Rostock

Brandenburg principality flag

Brandenburg

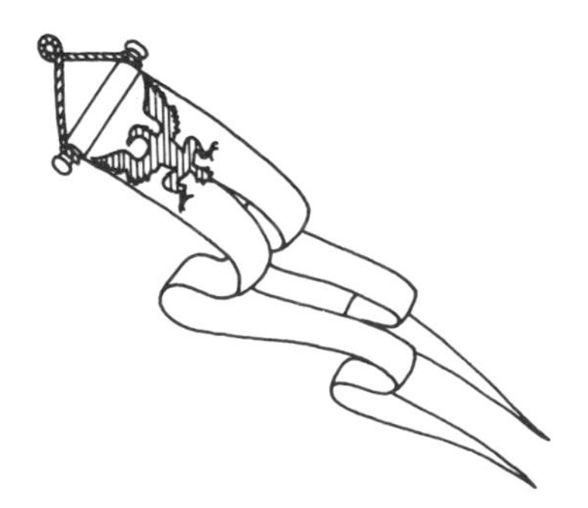
Brandenburg pennant

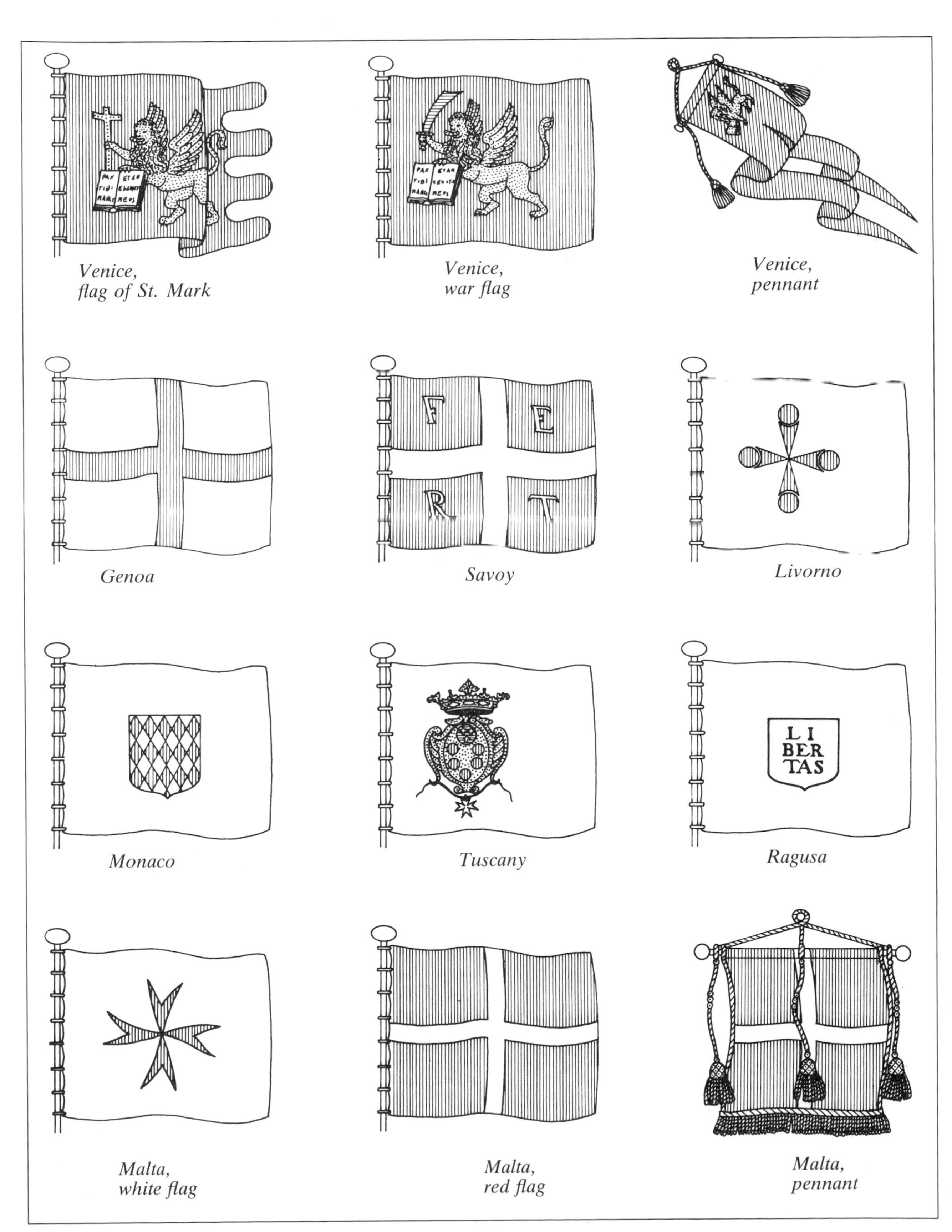

Venice, flag of St. Mark

Venice, war flag

Venice, pennant

Genoa

Savoy

Livorno

Monaco

Tuscany

Ragusa

Malta, white flag

Malta, red flag

Malta, pennant

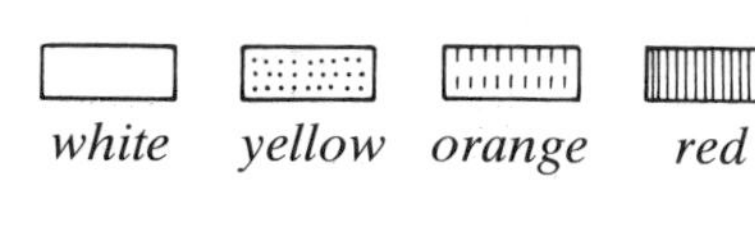

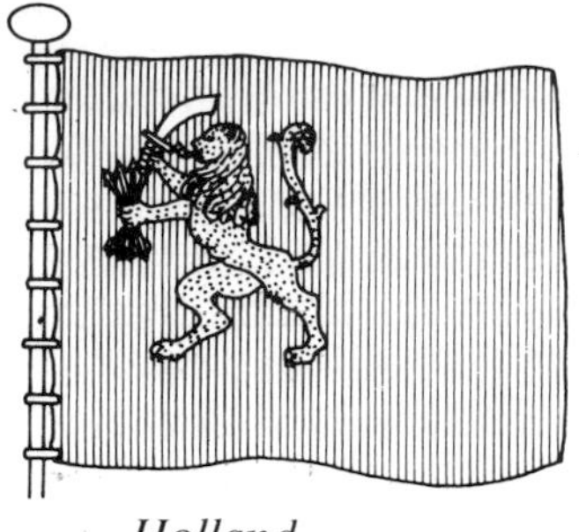

Holland,
state flag

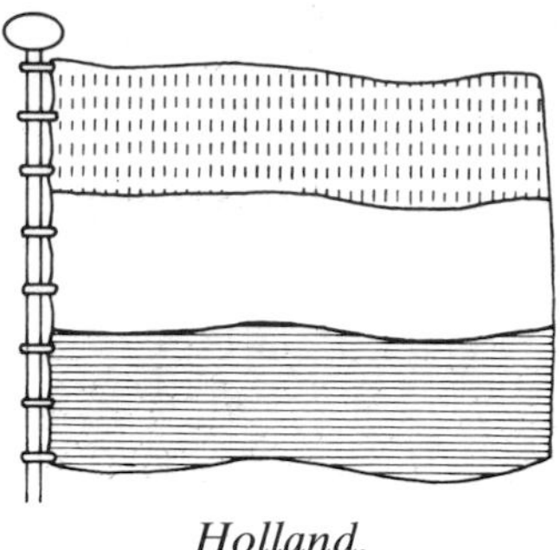

Holland,
state flag

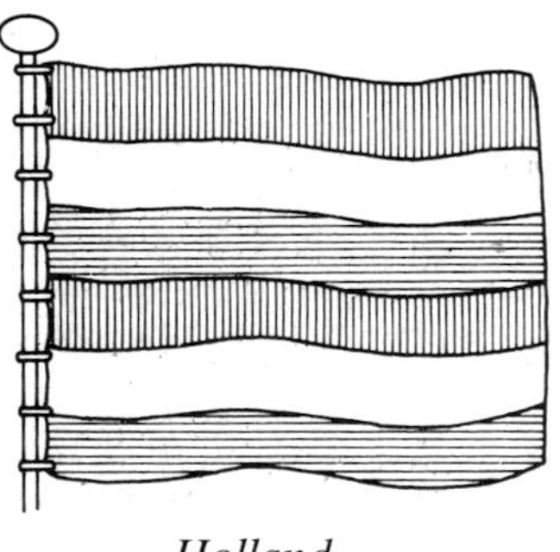

Holland,
state flag

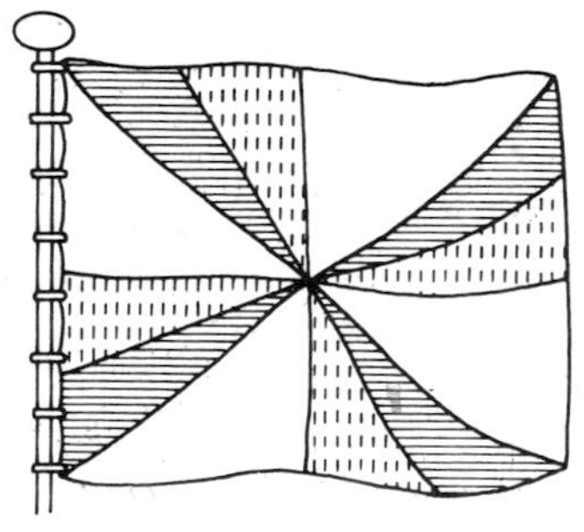

Holland,
Prince's flag

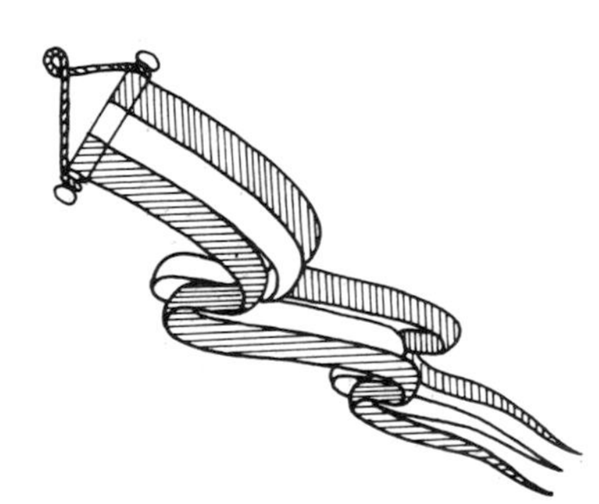

Holland,
pennant

Amsterdam

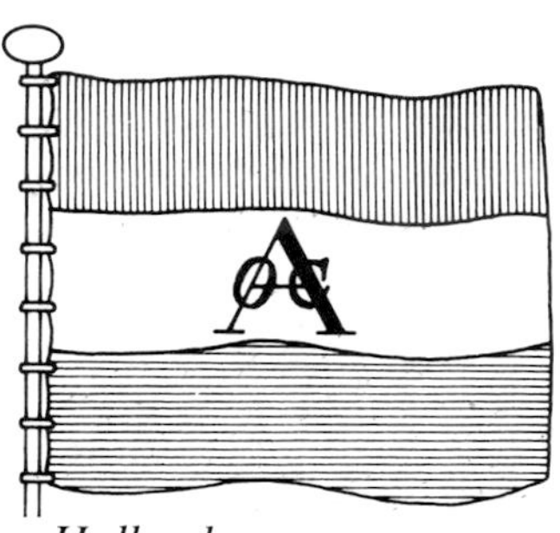

Holland,
East India Company

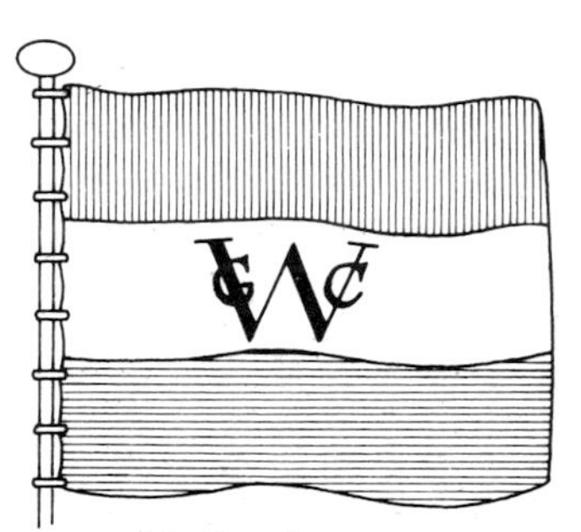

Holland,
West India Company

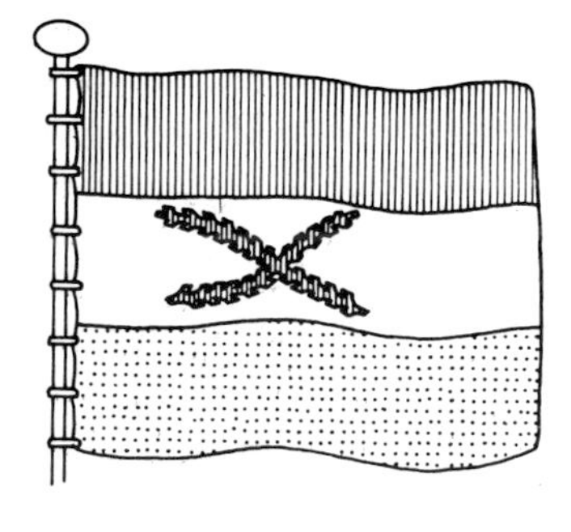

Flanders

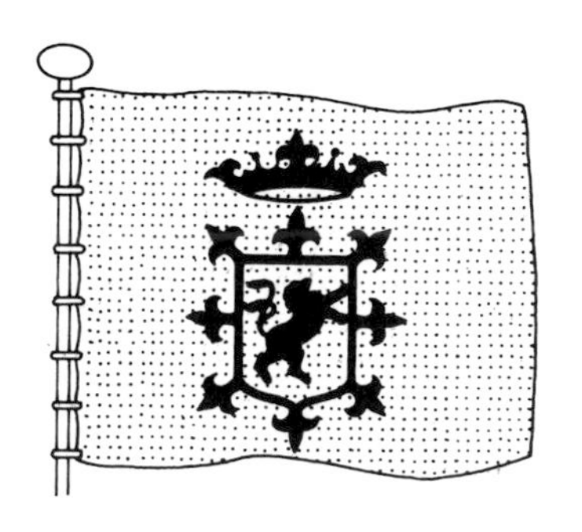

Flanders

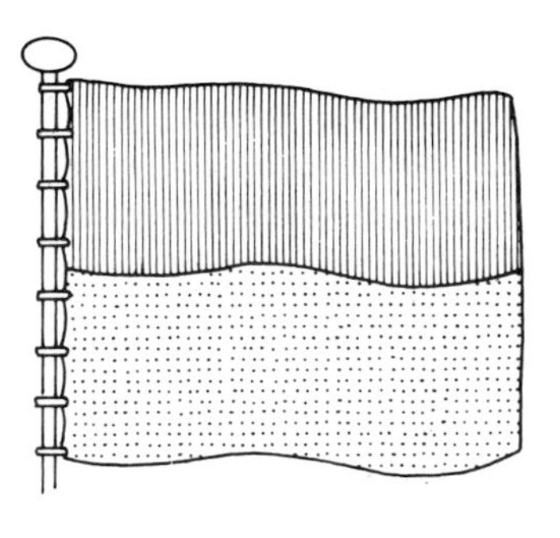

Ostend

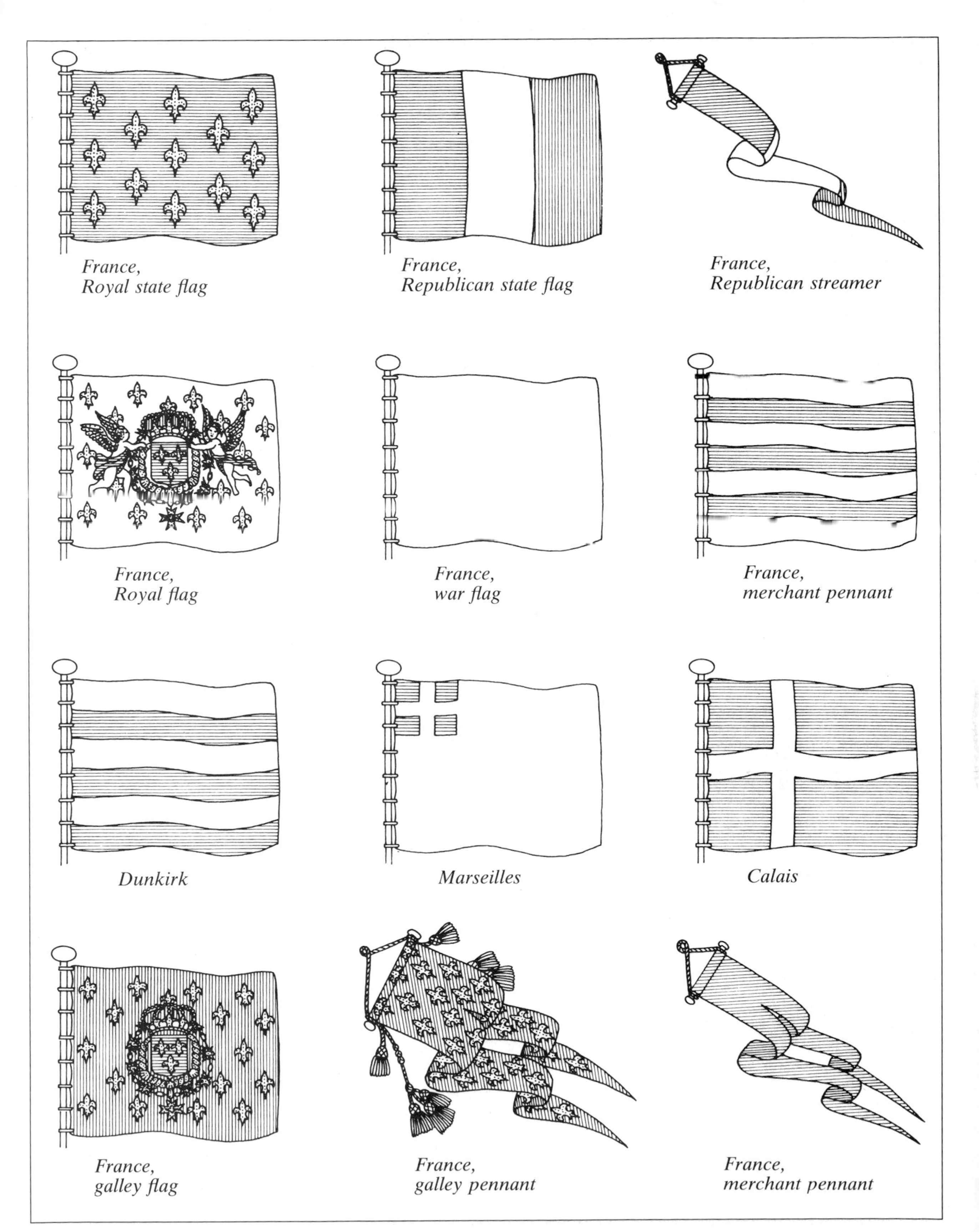

France, Royal state flag

France, Republican state flag

France, Republican streamer

France, Royal flag

France, war flag

France, merchant pennant

Dunkirk

Marseilles

Calais

France, galley flag

France, galley pennant

France, merchant pennant

Flags

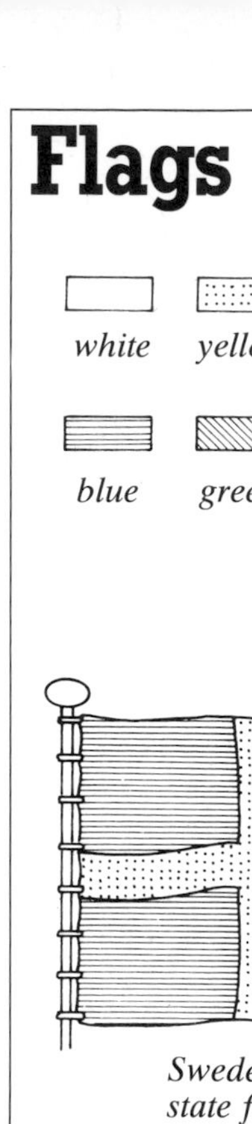

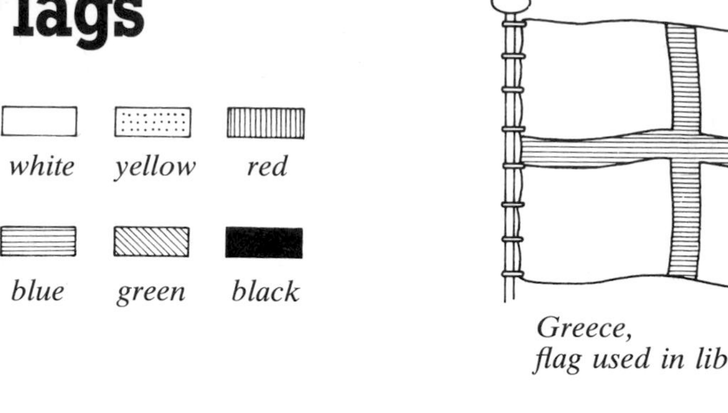

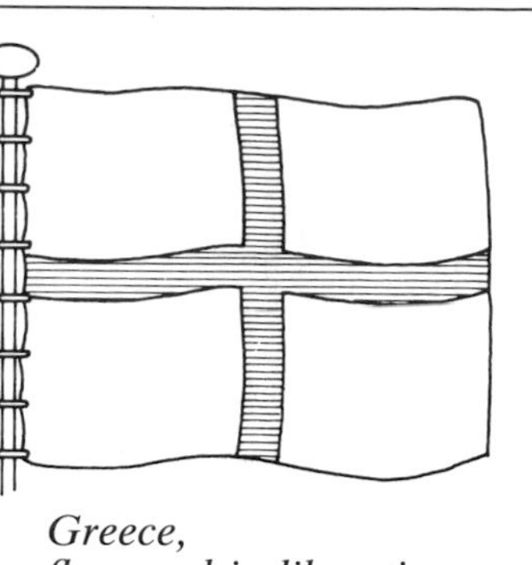

Greece,
flag used in liberation war

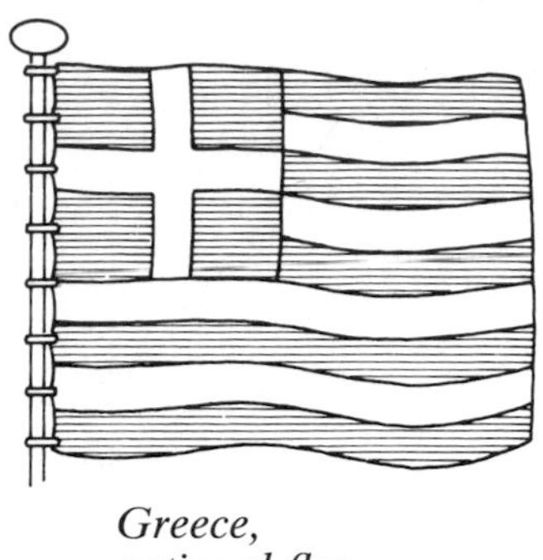

Greece,
national flag

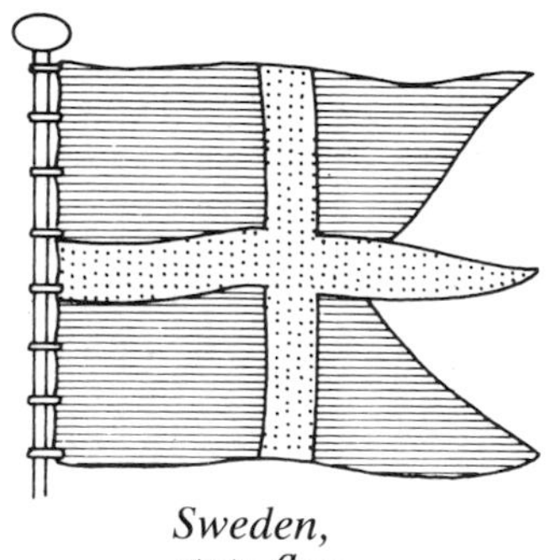

Sweden,
state flag

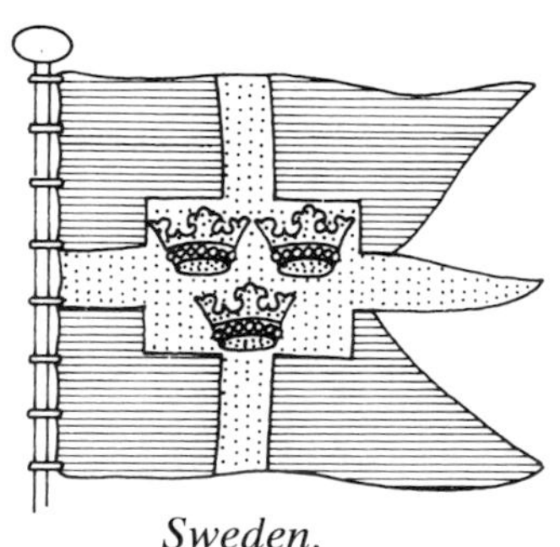

Sweden,
royal flag

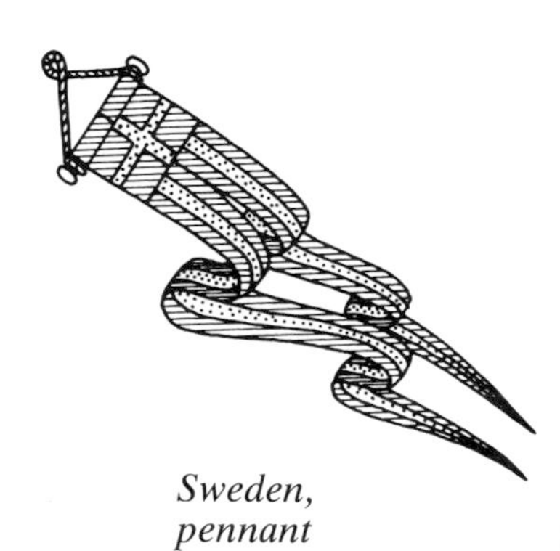

Sweden,
pennant

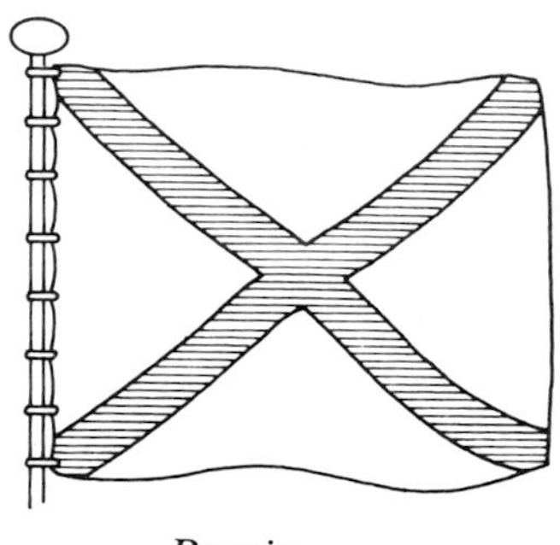

Russia,
state flag

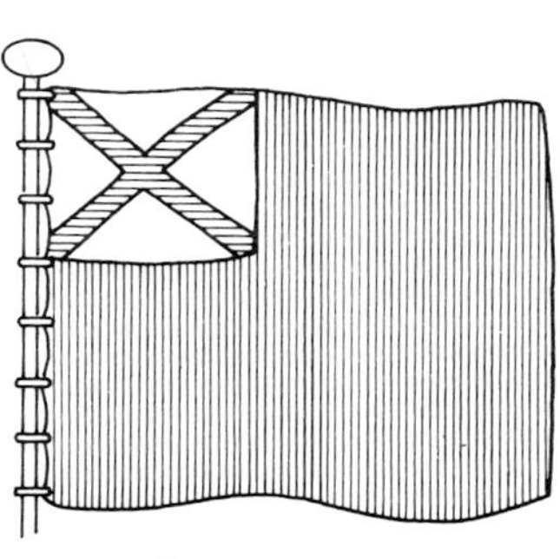

Russia,
war flag

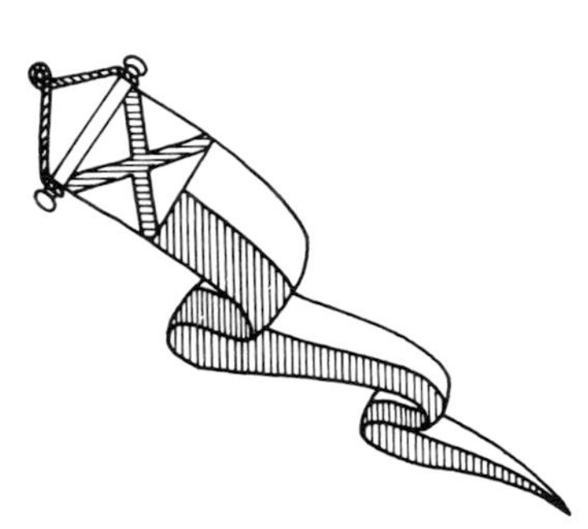

Russia,
pennant

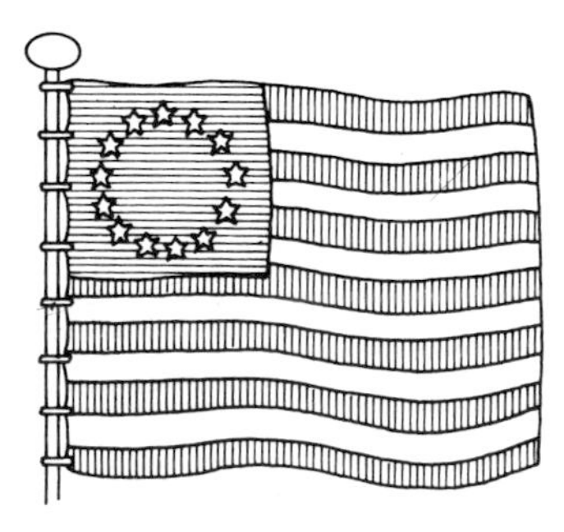

America,
state flag, 1776

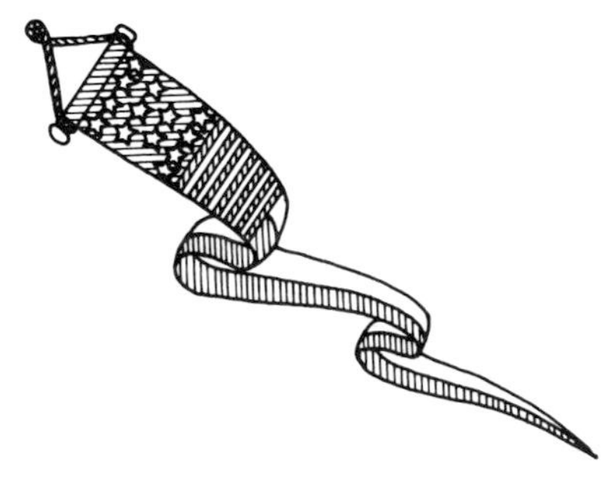

America,
pennant, 1776

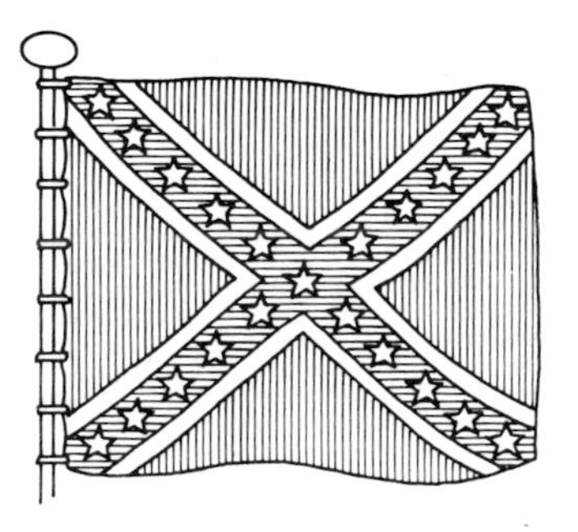

America,
Confederate flag, 1861

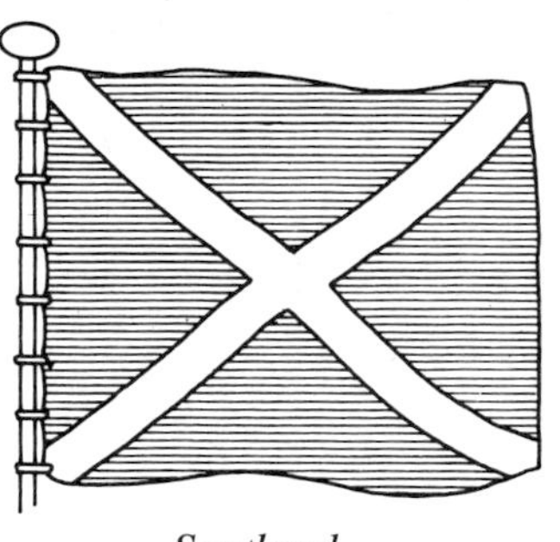

Scotland, National flag

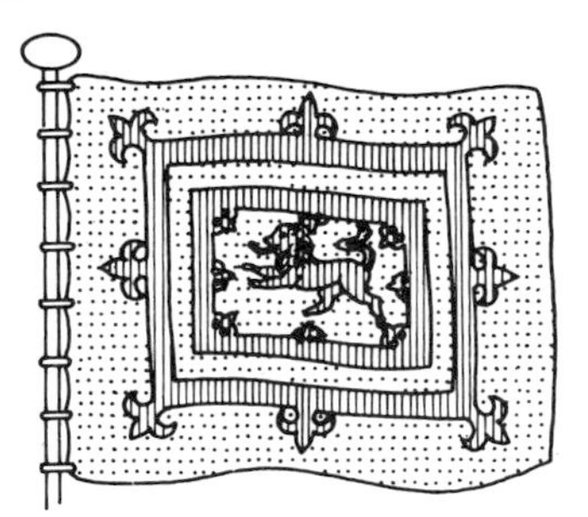

Scotland, Royal flag

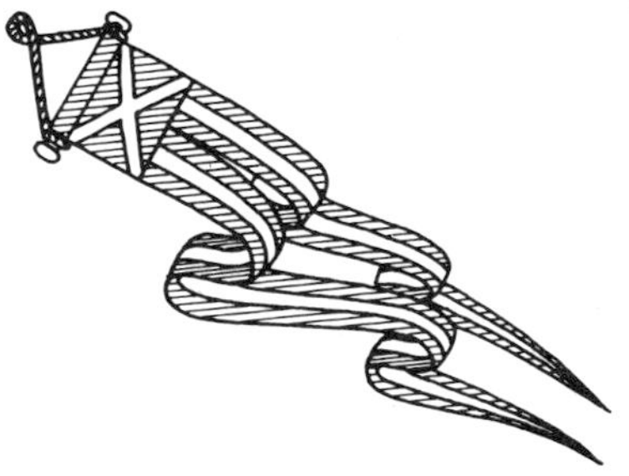

Scotland, pennant

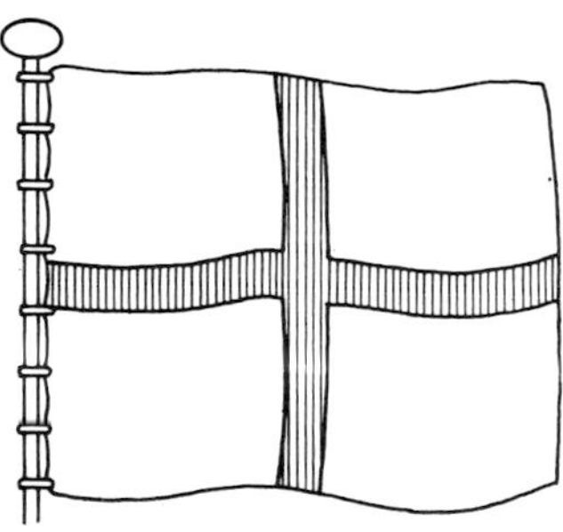

England, National flag

England, Tudor flag

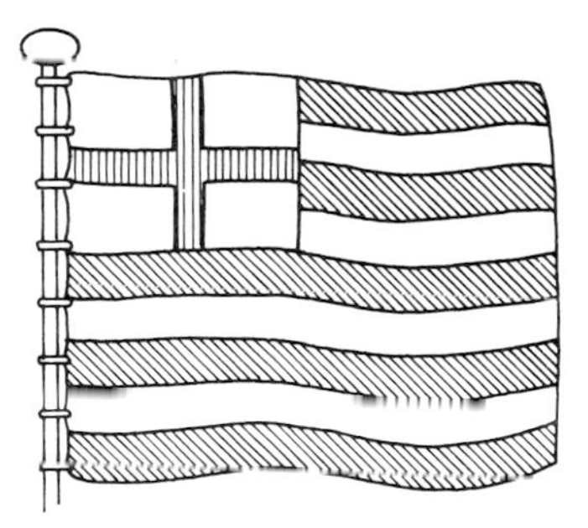

England, Tudor flag

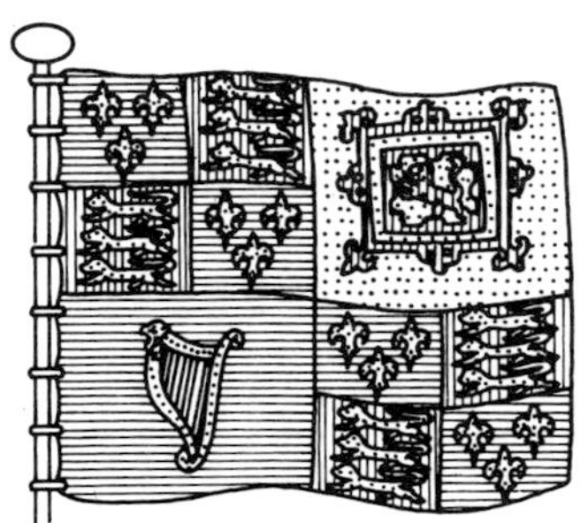

Great Britain, Royal Standard

Great Britain, Royal flag

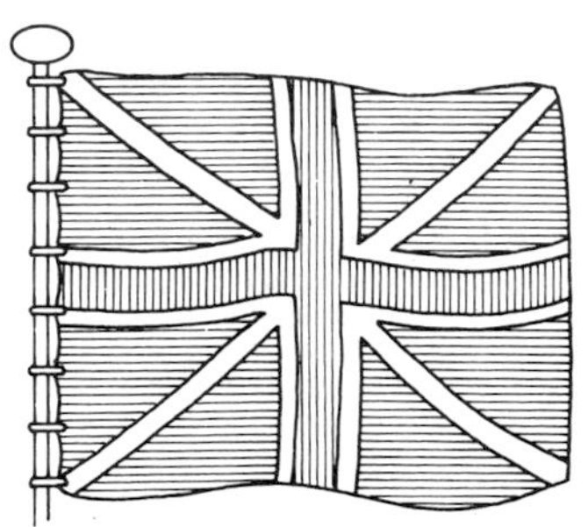

Great Britain, Union Flag before 1803

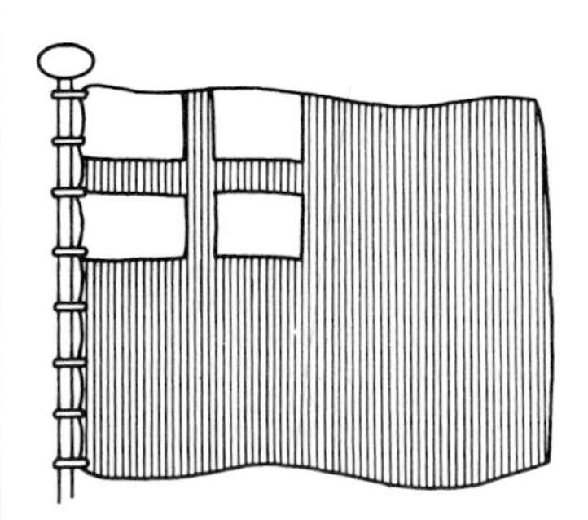

England – Red Ensign

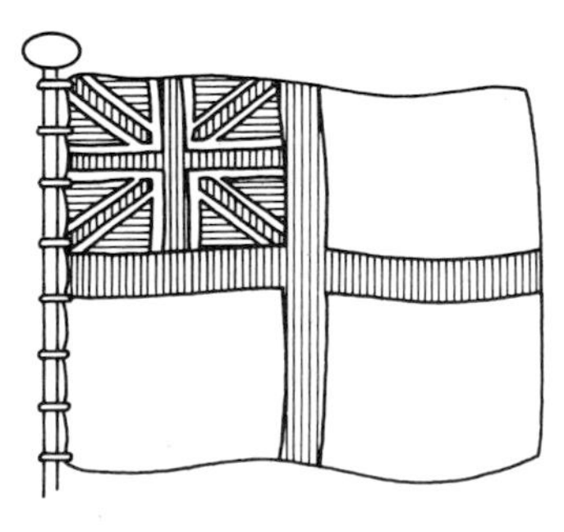

Royal Navy, White Ensign after 1803

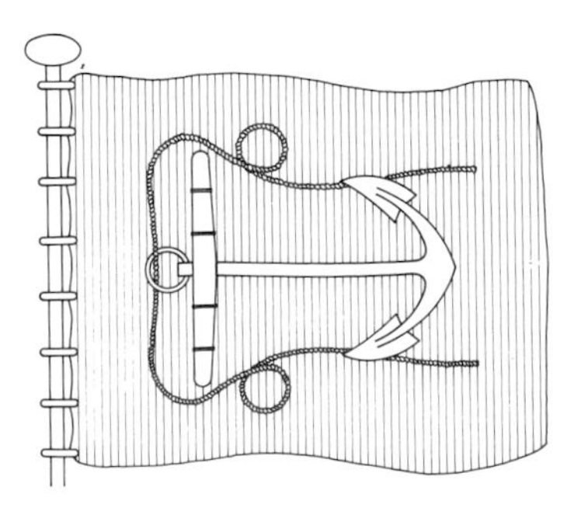

Great Britain, Admiralty flag

Museums

Figurehead of the Dutch corvette Heldin, *19th century*

Belgium:	Antwerpen, Nationaal Scheepvaart Museum
Denmark:	Helsingör, Handels-og Söfartsmuseum paa Kronborg, Kopenhaven, Orlogmuseet
	Roskilde, Vikingeskibshallen
Germany:	Brake, Schiffahrtsmuseum der Oldenburgischen Weserhäfen
	Bremen, Fokke-Museum
	Bremen, Heimatmuseum Vegesack
	Bremen, Übersee-Museum
	Bremerhaven, Deutsches Schiffahrtsmuseum
	Hamburg, Altonaer Museum
	Hamburg, Museum für Hamburgische Geschichte
	München, Deutsches Museum
Finland:	Abo, Sjöfartsmuseum vid Abo Akademi
France:	Marseille, Musée de Marine et d'Outre-Mer
	Paris, Musée de la Marine
	Dunkirk, Musée des Beaux Arts
	Rochefort, Musée de la Marine
	Saint Martin de Ré (Ile de Ré)
Greece:	Athen-Piräus, Naval Museum of Greece
Great Britain:	Edinburgh, Royal Scottish Museum
	London, National Maritime Museum Greenwich
	London, Science Museum South Kensington
Italy:	Genoa, Museo Civico Navale
	La Spezia, Museo Navale
	Venedig, Museo Storico Navale
Israel:	Haifa, National Maritime Museum
Lebanon:	Beirut, Musée de Beyrouth
Holland:	Amsterdam, Nederlandsch Historisch Scheepvaart Museum
	Amsterdam, Rijksmuseum
	Dronten, Zuiderzeemuseum
	Groningen, Noordelijk Scheepvaartmuseum
	Rotterdam, Maritiem Museum "Prins Hendrik"
Norway:	Bergen, Bergens Sjöfartsmuseum
	Oslo, Norsk Sjöfartsmuseum
	Oslo, Universitetets Oldsaksamling
Portugal:	Lisbon, Museu de Marinha
Sweden:	Göteborg, Sjöfartsmuseum
	Karlskrona, Marinemuseet och Modellkammaren
	Stockholm, Statens Sjöhistoriska Museum
	Stockholm, Wasa Museum (Wasavarvet)
	Visby, Gotlands Fornsal
Spain:	Barcelona, Museo Maritimo
	Madrid, Museo Naval
Turkey:	Istanbul/Beşiktaş, Deniz Müzesi Müdürlügü
Soviet Union:	Leningrad, Marinemuseum
USA:	Annapolis/Maryland, United States Naval Academy
	Mystic/Connecticut, Marine Historical Association
	Nantucket/Massachusetts, Whaling Museum
	New Bedford/Massachusetts, Whaling Museum
	New York/New York, Marine Museum of the Seaman's
	Salem/Massachusetts, Peabody Museum

ENGLISH	German	French	Spanish	Italian
anchor	Anker	ancre	ancla	ancora
backstay	Pardune	galhauban	burda	paterazzo
belaying pin	Belegnagel	cabillot	cabilla	caviglia
bitt	Beting	bitte	bita	bitta
block	Block	poulie	motón	bozzolo
bobstay	Wassertag	sous-barbe de beaupré	barbiquejo del bauprés	briglia di bompresso
bolt-rope	Liektau	ralingue	relinga	gratile
bow	Bug	avant	proa	prua
bowline	Bulin	bouline	bolina	bolina
bowsprit	Bugspriet	beaupré	bauprés	bompresso
brace	Brasse	bras	brazo	braccio
breeching	Brooktau	étrangloir	candaliza de boca de cangrejo	imbroglio de gola di sotto
cap	Eslshaupt	chouquet	tamborete	testa de moro
capstan	Spill	cabestan	cabrestante	argano
cathead	Kranbalken	bossoir de capon	serviola	gru di capone
chainplate	Pütting	cadène chaîne	cadena de obenque cadenote	landa
channel	Rüste	porte-hauban	mesa de guarnición	parasartie
cleat	Klampe	taquet	cornamusa	galloccia
clew line	Geitau	aurigue	cargadera	imbroglio
companion hatch	Niedergang	descende	descendo	boccaporto
cringle	Legel	putto	garrucho de cabo	brancarella
crossjack	Kreuzsegel	voile barrée	mesana	vela di contromezzana
crossjack yard	Bagienrah	vergue de fortune	verga de un trinquete volante	peronne per trevo di tortuna
davit	Davit	bossoir	pescante	gru
deadeye	Jungfer	cap de mouton	vigota	bigota
deck	Deck	ponte	coverta	ponte
dolphin boom	Stampfstock	arc-boutant de martingale	moco del bauprés	buffafuori di briglia
dolphin striker				pennaccion
driver boom	Gaffelbaum	gui	botavara	boma
eyelet holes	Gat	oillets	ollaos	occhiello
fender	Fender	défense	defensa	parabordo
foot rope	Ruule	marchepied	marchapié	marchapiede
fore -	Fock-	- de misaine	- de trinquete	- di trinchetto
foremast	Fockmast	mât de misaine	palo de trinquete	albero di trinchetto
fore sail	Focksegel	misaine	trinquete	vela di trinchetto
foreyard	Fockrah	vergue de misaine	verga de trinquete	peronne di trinchetto
frame	Spant	couple	cuoderna	ordinata
gaff-	Gaffel-	- à corne	- de cangrejo	- picco
gaff sail	Gaffelsegel	voile à corne	vela cangreja	randa
gratings	Gräting	caillebotis grillage	enjaretado rejilla	carabottino grata
hammock netting	Finknetz	bastingage	batayola	bastingaggio
hatch	Ladeluke	écoutille	escotilla	boccaporto
hawse	Ankerklüse	écubier d'ancre	escobén del ancla	cubia d'ancora
head (of which the knee is part)	Galion	guibre	beque tajamar	serpe
hull	Rumpf	coque	casco	scafo
jackstay	Jackstag	filière d'envergure	nervio de envergadura	infertitura
jib boom	Klüverbaum	bâton de foc	botalón de foque	asta di fiocco
jigger	Kreuzsegel	voile barrée	mesana	vela di contromezzana
jigger-	Bonaventur-	- d'artimon derrière	- de contromesana	- di contromezzana
jigger-mast	Bonaventurmast	mât d'artimon derrière	palo de contromesana	
jigger sail	Bonaventursegel	petit artimon	cangreja de popa	vanda di contromezzana
keel	Kiel	quille	quilla	chiglia
lashing	Zurring	aiguillette	trinca	rizza
leech line and bunt line (collectively)	Gording			
lift	Toppnanten	balancine	amantillo	mantiglio
lug sail	Luggersegel	voile à bourcet	bela al tercio	vela al terzo
main-	Groß-	grand -	- mayor	- di maestra
main mast	Großmast	grand mât	palo mayor	albero di maestro
main sail	Großsegel	grand voile	vela mayor	vela maestra
main yard	Großrah	grand vergue	verga mayor	peronne di maestra
mast	Mast	mât	palo	albero
mast head	Top	tête de mât	tope del mastil	testa d'albero
mizen-	Besan-	- d'artimon	- de mesana	- di mezzana
mizen-mast	Besanmast Kreuzmast	grand mât arriere	palo de mesana	albero di mezzana
oar	Riemen	aviron	remo	remo
outrigger	Ausleger	arc boutant	arbotante	buttafuori di crocetta
parral	Rack	racage	racamiento	trozza
peak	Nock	pic	peñol	varea
pin rail	Nagelbank	râtelier à cabillots	cabillero	cavigliera
planking	Beplankung	bordé	forro de planchas	fasciame di legno
preventer stay	Borgstag	faux étai	contraestay	controstaglio
pump	Pumpe	pompe	bomba	pompa
rail	Reling	lisse de pavois	regala	filaretto
rat-lines	Webeleine	enflechûres	flecharduras	griselle
recuperator	Vorholer	récupérateur	recuperador	ricuperatore
reef	Reff	ris	rizo	terzaruolo
rigging screw	Spannschraube	ridoir à vis	tensor de tornillo	arridatoio a vite
rope	Tau	câbe	cabo	cavo
rudder	Ruder	gouvernail	timón	timone
rudder pendants	Sorgleine	sauvegardes	varones del timón	bracotti del timone
rudder pintles	Fingerlinge	aiguillots	manchos del timón	agugliotti del timone
running rigging	laufendes Gut	manoeuvres courantes	jarcias de labor	manovri correnti
sail	Segel	voile	vela	vela
scupper	Speigat	dalot	imbornal	ombriale
servant	Knecht	valet	escotra	servo

English	German	French	Spanish	Italian
sheavehole	Scheibgat	mortaise	cajera	cavatoia
sheet	Schot	écoute	escota	scotta
shroud	Want	hauban	obenque	sartia
sling	Hanger	cercle de suspente	aro de boza de una verga mayor	collare di sospensione
spanker	Besansegel	artimon (grand a.)	vela de mesana	vanda di mezzana
spreader	Saling	barre de hune	cruceta	crocetta
sprit-	Blinde-	- à livarde	- tarquia	- tarchia
sprit sail	Blindesegel	tente à livarde	vela tarquia	vela tarchia
spritsail halyard	Vorholer	récupérateur	recuperador	ricuperatore
spritsail yard	Blinderah	porte lof	servioleta	peronne di bompresso
staghorn	Kreuzholz	oreille d'âne	manigueta	cazzasotte
standing rigging	stehendes Gut	manoeuvres dormantes	jarcias muertas	manovre dormienti
stay	Stag	étai	estay	straglio
staysail	Stagsegel	voile d'étai	vela de estay	vela di straglio
stem	Vordersteven	étrave	roda	dritto di prua
sternpost	Achtersteven	étambot	codaste	dritto di poppa
	Heck	arrière	popa	poppa
strand	Kardeel	toron	cordón	legnuolo
strop	Stropp	estrope	gaza	stroppo
studding sail	Leesegel	bonnette	ala	vela di caccia
studding sail boom	Leesegelspiere	bout - dehors de bonnette	botalón de ala	buffafuori di vela
tack	Hals	amure	amura	amura
tackle	Talje	palan	aparejo	palanca
thimble	Kausch	cosse	guardacabo	radancia
top	Mars	hune	cofa	coffa
topping lift	Dirk	balancine de gui	amantillo	mantiglio
top sail	Marssegel	hunier	gravia	vela di gabbia
topgallant-	Bram-	- de perroquet	- de juanete	- de velaccio
topgallant sail	Bramsegel	perroquet	juanete	velaccio
topmast	Stenge	mât de hune	mastelero de gavia	albero di gabbia
		mât de flèche	mastelero de galope	albero di freccia
tye	Fall	drisse	driza	drizza
vang	Geere	palan de garde	osta	ostino
wale	Barkholz	préceinte	cinta	incintone
waterline	Wasserlinie	ligne de flottaison	linea de flotación	linea di galleggiamento
woolding	Wuling	rousture	reata	trincatura
yard	Rah	vergue	verga	peronne

GERMAN	English	French	Spanish	Italian
Achtersteven	sternpost	étambot	codaste	dritto di poppa
Anker	anchor	ancre	ancla	ancora
Ankerklüse	hawse	écubier d'ancre	escobén del ancla	cubia d'ancora
Ausleger	outrigger	arc boutant	arbotante	buttafuori di crocetta
Bagienrah	crossjack yard	vergue de fortune	verga de un trinquete volante	peronne per trevo di fortuna
Barkholz	wale	préceinte	cinta	incintone
Belegnagel	belaying pin	cabillot	cabilla	caviglia
Beplankung	planking	bordé	forro de planchas	fasciame di legno
Besan-	mizen-	- d'artimon	- de mesana	- di mezzana
Besanmast	mizen-mast	grand mât arriere	palo de mesana	albero di mezzana
Besansegel	spanker	artimon (grand a.)	vela de mesana	vanda di mezzana
Beting	bitt	bitte	bita	bitta
Blinde-	sprit-	- à livarde	- tarquia	- tarchia
Blinderah	spritsail yard	porte of	servioleta	peronne di bompresso
Blindesegel	sprit sail	tente à livarde	vewla tarquia	vela tarchia
Block	block	poulie	motón	bozzolo
Bonaventur-	jigger-	- d'artimon derrière	- de contromesana	- di contromezzana
Bonaventurmast	jigger-mast	mât d'artimon derrière	palo de contromesana	albero di contromezzana
Bonaventursegel	jigger sail	petit artimon	cangreja de popa	vanda di contromezzana
Borstag	preventer stay	faux étai	contraestay	controstaglio
Bram-	topgallant-	- de perroquet	- de juanete	- de velaccio
Bramsegel	topgallant sail	perroquet	juanete	velaccio
Brasse	brace	bras	brazo	braccio
Brooktau	breeching	étrangloir	candaliza de boca de cangrejo	imbroglio de gola di sotto
Bug	bow	avant	proa	prua
Bugspriet	bowsprit	beaupré	baupres	bompresso
Bulin	bowline	bouline	bolina	bolina
Davit	davit	bossoir	pescante	gru
Deck	deck	ponte	coverta	ponte
Dirk	topping lift	balancine de gui	amantillo	mantiglio
Eselshaupt	cap	chouquet	tamborete	testa di moro
Fall	tye	drisse	driza	drizza
Fender	fender	défense	defensa	parabordo
Fingerlinge	rudder pintles	aiguillots	manchos del timón	agugliotti del timone
Finknetz	hammock netting	bastingage	batayola	bastingaggio
Fock-	fore-	- de misaine	- de trinquete	- di trinchetto
Fockmast	foremast	mât de misaine	palo de trinquete	albero di trinchetto
Fockrah	foreyard	vergue de misaine	verga de trinquete	peronne di trinchetto

German	English	French	Spanish	Italian
Focksegel	fore sail	misaine	trinquete	vela di trinchetto
Gaffel-	gaff-	- à corne	- de cangrejo	- picco
Gaffelbaum	driver boom	gui	botavara	boma
Gaffelsegel	gaff sail	voile à corne	vela cangreja	randa
Galion	head (of which the knee	gibre	beque	serpe
	of the head is part)		tajamar	
Gat	eyelet holes	oillets	ollaos	occhiello
Geere	vang	palan de garde	osta	ostino
Geitau	clew line	aurigue	cargadera	imbroglio
Gording	leech line and bunt line			
	(collectively)			
Gräting	gratings	caillebotis	enjaretado	carabottino
		grillage	rejilla	grata
Groß-	main-	grand -	- mayor	- di maestra
Großmast	main mast	grand mât	palo mayor	albero di maestro
Großrah	main yard	grand vergue	verga mayor	peronne di maestra
Großsegel	main sail	grand voile	vela mayor	vela maestra
Hals	tack	amure	amura	amura
Hanger	sling	cercle de suspente	aro de boza de una verga	collare di sospensione
			mayor	
Heck	stern	arrière	popa	poppa
Jackstag	jackstay	filière d'envergure	nervio de envergadura	infertitura
Jungfer	deadeye	cap de mouton	vigota	bigota
Kardeel	strand	toron	cordón	legnuolo
Kausch	thimble	cosse	guardacabo	radancia
Kiel	keel	quille	quilla	chiglia
Klampe	cleat	taquet	cornamusa	galloccia
Llüverbaum	jib boom	bâton de foc	botalón de foque	asta di fiocco
Knecht	servant	valet	escotera	servo
Krankbalken	cathead	bossoir de capon	serviola	gru di capone
Kreuzholz	staghorn	oreille de'âne	manigueta	cazzasotte
Kreuzmast	mizen mast	mât d'artimon	palo mesana	albero di mezzana
Kreuzsegel	jigger	voile barrée	mesana	vela di contromezzana
	crossjack			
Ladeluke	hatch	écoutille	escotilla	boccaporto
laufendes Gut	running rigging	manoeuvres courantes	jarcias de labor	manovri correnti
Leesegel	studding sail	bonnette	ala	vela di caccia
Leesegelspiere	studding sail boom	bout-dehors de bonnette	botalón de ala	buffafuori di vela
Legel	cringle	patte	garrucho de cabo	brancarella
Liektau	bolt-rope	ralingue	relinga	gratile
Luggersegel	lug sail	voile à bourcet	vela al tercio	vela al terzo
Mars	top	hune	cofa	coffa
Marssegel	top sail	hunier	gravia	vela di gabbia
Mast	mast	mât	palo	albero
Nagelbank	pin rail	râtelier à cabillots	cabillero	cavigliera
Niedergang	companion hatch	descende	descendo	boccaporto
Nock	peak	pic	peñol	varea
Pardune	back stay	galhauben	burda	paterazzo
Perde	foot rope	marchepied	marchapié	marciapiede
Pumpe	pump	pompe	bomba	pompa
Pütting	chain plate	cadène	cadena de obenque	landa
		chaîne	cadenote	
Rack	parral	racage	racamiento	trozza
Rah	yard	vergue	verga	peronne
Reff	reef	ris	rizo	terzaruolo
Reling	rail	lisse de pavois	regala	filaretto
Riemen	oar	aviron	remo	remo
Ruder	rudder	gouvernail	timón	timone
Rumpf	hull	coque	casco	scafo
Rüste	channel	porte-hauban	mesa de guarnición	parasartie
Saling	spreader	barre de hune	cruceta	crocetta
Sceibgat	sheavehole	mortaise	cajera	cavatoia
Schot	sheet	écoute	escota	scotta
Schott	bulkhead	cloison	mamparo	paratia
Segel	sail	voile	vela	vela
Sorgleine	rudder pendants	sauvegardes	varones del timón	bracotti del timone
Spannschraube	rigging screw	ridoir à vis	tensor de tornillo	arridatoio a vite
Spant	frame	couple	cuoderna	ordinata
Speigat	scupper	dalot	imbornal	ombriale
Spill	capstan	cabestan	cabrestante	argano
Stag	stay	étai	estay	straglio
Stagsegel	staysail	voile d'étai	vela de estay	vela di straglio
Stampfstock	dolphin boom	arc-boutant de	moco del bauprés	buffafuori di briglia
	dolphin striker	martingale		pennaccino
stehendes Gut	standing rigging	manoeuvres dormantes	jarcias muertas	manovre dormienti
Stenge	topmast	mât de hune	mastelero de gavia	albero di gabbia
		mât de flèche	mastelero de galope	albero di freccia
Stropp	strop	estrope	gaza	stroppo
Talje	tackle	palan	aparejo	palanca
Tau	rope	câble	cabo	cavo
Top	mast head	tête de mât	tope del mastil	testa d'albero
Toppnanten	lift	balancine	amantillo	mantiglio
Vordersteven	stem	étrave	roda	dritto di prua
Vorholer	spritsail halyard	récupérateur	recuperador	ricuperatore
Want	shroud	hauban	obenque	sartia
Wasserlinie	waterline	ligne de flottaison	linea de flotación	linea di galleggiamento
Wassertag	bobstay	sous-barbe de beaupré	barbiquejo del bauprés	briglia di bompresso
Webeleine	rat-lines	enflechûres	flecharduras	griselle
Wuling	woolding	rousture	reata	trincatura
Zurring	lashing	aiguillette	trinca	rizza

FRENCH	English	German	Spanish	Italian
aiguillette	lashing	Zurring	trinca	rizza
aiguillots	rudder pintles	Fingerlinge	manchos del timón	agugliotti del timone
amure	tack	Hals	amura	amura
ancre	anchor	Anker	ancla	ancora
arc boutant	outrigger	Ausleger	arbotante	buttafuori di crocetta
arc-boutant de martingale	dolphin boom dolphin striker	Stampfstock	moco del bauprés	buffafuori di briglia pennaccino
arrière	stern	Heck	popa	poppa
artimon (grand a.)	spanker	Besansegel	vela de mesana	vanda di mezzana
- d'artimon	mizen-	Besan-	- de mesana	- di mezzana
- d'artimon derrière	jigger-	Bonaventur-	- de contromesana	- di contromezzana
aurigue	clew line	Geitau	cargadera	imbroglio
	leech line and bunt line (collectively)	Gording		
avant	bow	Bug	proa	prua
aviron	oar	Riemen	remo	remo
balancine	lift	Toppnanten	amantillo	mantiglio
balancine de gui	topping lift	Dirk		
barre de hune	spreader	Saling	cruceta	crocetta
bastingage	hammock netting	Finknetz	batayola	bastingaggio
bâton de foc	jib boom	Klüverbaum	botalón de foque	asta di fiocco
beaupré	bowsprit	Bugspriet	bauprés	bompresso
bitte	bitt	Beting	bita	bitta
bonnette	studding sail	Leesegel	ala	vela di caccia
bordé	planking	Beplankung	forro de planchas	fasciame di legno
bossoir	davit	Davit	oescante	gru
bossoir de capon	cat head	Kranbalken	serviola	gru di capone
bouline	bowline	Bulin	bolina	bolina
bout-dehors de bonnette	studding sail boom	Leesegelspiere	botalón de ala	buffafuori di vela
bras	brace	Brasse	brazo	braccio
cabestan	capstan	Spill	cabrestante	argano
câble	rope	Tau	cabo	cavo
cabillot	belaying pin	Belegnagel	cabilla	caviglia
cadène	chain plate	Pütting	cadena de obenque	landa
caillebotis	grating	Gräting	enjaretado	carabottino
cap de mouton	deadeye	Jungfer	vigota	bigota
cercle de suspente	sling	Hanger	aro de boza de una verga mayor	collare di sospensione
chaîne	chain plate	Pütting	cadenote	landa
chouquet	cap	Eselshaupt	tamborete	testa di moro
cloison	bulkhead	Schott	mamparo	paratia
coque	hull	Rumpf	casco	scafo
- à corne	gaff-	Gaffel-	- de cangrejo	- picco
cosse	thimble	Kausch	guardacabo	radancia
couple	frame	Spant	couderna	ordinata
dalot	scupper	Speigat	imbornal	ombriale
défense	fender	Fender	defensa	parabordo
descende	companion hatch	Niedergang	descendo	boccaporto
drisse	tye	Fall	driza	drizza
écoute	sheet	Schot	escota	scotta
écoutille	hatch	Ladeluke	escotilla	boccaporto
écubier d'ancre	hawse	Ankerklüse	escobén del ancla	cubia d'ancora
enfelchûres	rat-lines	Webeleine	flechardura	griselle
estrope	strop	Stropp	gaza	stroppa
étai	stay	Stag	estay	straglio
étambot	sternpost	Achtersteven	codaste	dritto di poppa
étrangloir	breeching	Brooktau	candaliza de boca de cangrejo	imbroglio de gola di sotto
étrave	stem	Vordersteven	roda	dritto di prua
faux étai	preventer stay	Borgstag	contraestay	controstaglio
filière d'envergure	jackstay	Jackstag	nervio de envergadura	infertitura
galhauban	back stay	Pardune	burda	paterazzo
gouvernail	rudder	Ruder	timón	timone
grand -	main-	Groß-	- mayor	- di maestra
grand mât	main mast	Großmast	palo mayor	albero di maestro
grand mât arriere	mizen-mast	Besanmast	palo de mesana	albero di mezzana
grand voile	main sail	Großsegel	vela mayor	vela maestra
grand vergue	main yard	Großrah	verga mayor	peronne di maestra
grillage	gratings	Gräting	rejilla	grata
gui	driver boom	Gaffelbaum	botavara	boma
guibre	head (of which the knee of the head is part)	Galion	beque tajamar	serpe
hauban	shroud	Want	obenque	sartia
hune	top	Mars	cofa	coffa
hunier	top sail	Marssegel	gravia	vela di gabbia
ligne de flottaison	waterline	Wasserlinie	linea de flotación	linea di galleggiamento
lisse de pavois	rail	Reling	regala	filaretto
- à livarde	sprit-	Blinde-	- tarquia	- tarchia
manoeuvres courantes	running rigging	laufendes Gut	jarcias de labor	manovri correnti
manoeuvres dormantes	standing rigging	stehendes Gut	jarcias muertas	manovri dormienti
marchepied	foot rope	Perde	marchapié	marciapiede
mât	mast	Mast	palo	albero
mât d'artimon	mizen mast	Kreuzmast	palo mesana	albero di mezzana
mât d'artimon derrière	jigger-mast	Bonaventurmast	palo di contromesana	albero di contromezzana
mât de flèche	topmast	Stenge	mastelero de galope	albero di freccia
mât de hune			mastelero de gavia	albero di gabbia
mât de misaine	foremast	Fockmast	palo de trinquete	albero di trinchetto
misaine	fore sail	Focksegel	trinquete	vela di trinchetto
- de misaine	fore-	Fock-	- de trinquete	- di trinchetto
mortaise	sheavehole	Scheibgat	cajera	cavatoia
oillets	eyelet holes	Gat	ollaos	occhiello
oreille d'âne	staghorn	Kreuzholz	manigueta	cazzasotte

French	English	German	Spanish	Italian
palan	tackle	Talje	aparejo	palanca
palan de garde	vang	Geere	osta	ostino
patte	cringle	Legel	garrucho de cabo	brancarella
perroquet	topgallant sail	Bramsegel	juanete	velaccio
- de perroquet	topgallant-	Bram-	- de juanete	- di velaccio
petit artimon	jigger sail	Bonaventursegel	cangrejo de popa	vanda di contromezzana
pic	peak	Nock	peñol	varea
pope	pump	Pumpe	bomba	pompa
ponte	deck	Deck	coverta	ponte
porte-hauban	channel	Rüste	mesa de guarnición	parasartie
porte lof	spritsail yard	Blinderah	servioleta	peronne di bompresso
poulie	block	Block	motón	bozzolo
préceinte	wale	Barkholz	cinta	incintone
quille	keel	Kiel	quilla	chiglia
racage	parral	Rack	racamiento	trozza
ralingue	bolt-rope	Liektau	relinga	gratile
râtelier à cabillots	pin rail	Nagelbank	cabillero	cavigliera
récupérateur	spritsail halyard	Vorholer	recuperador	ricuperatore
ridoir à vis	rigging screw	Spannschraube	tensor de tornillo	arridatoio a vite
ris	reef	Reff	rizo	terzaruolo
rousture	woolding	Wuling	reata	trincatura
sauvegardes	rudder pendants	Sorgleine	varones del timón	bracotti del timone
sous-barbe de beaupré	bobstay	Wassertag	barbiquejo del bauprés	briglia di bompresso
taquet	cleat	Klampe	cornamusa	galloccia
tente à livarde	sprit sail	Blindesegel	vela tarquia	vela tarchia
tête de mât	mast head	Top	tope del mastil	testa d'albero
toron	strand	Kardeel	cordón	legnuolo
valet	servant	Knecht	escotera	servo
vergue	yard	Rah	verga	peronne
vergue de fortune	crossjack yard	Bagienrah	verga de un trinquete volante	peronne per trevo di fortuna
vergue de misaine	foreyard	Fockrah	verga de trinquete	peronne di trinchetto
voile	sail	Segel	vela	vela
voile barrée	jigger crossjack	Kreuzsegel	mesana	vela di contromezzana
voile à bourcet	lug sail	Luggersegel	vela al tercio	vela al terzo
voile à corne	gaff sail	Gaffelsegel	vela cangreja	randa
voile d'étai	staysail	Stagsegel	vela de estay	vela di straglio

SPANISH	English	German	French	Italian
ala	studding sail	Leesegel	bonnette	vela di caccia
amantillo	topping lift	Dirk	balancine de gui	mantiglio
	lift	Toppnanten	balancine	
amura	tack	Hals	amure	amura
ancla	anchor	Anker	ancre	ancora
aparejo	tackle	Talje	palan	palanca
arbotante	outrigger	Ausleger	arc boutant	buttafuori di crocetta
aro de boza de una verga mayor	sling	Hanger	cercle de suspente	collare di sospensione
barbiquejo del bauprés	bobstay	Wassertag	sous-barbe de beaupré	
batayola	hammock netting	Finknetz	bastingage	bastingaggio
bauprés	bowsprit	Bugspriet	beaupré	bompresso
beque	head (of which the knee of the head is part)	Galion	guibre	serpe
bita	bitt	Beting	bitte	bitta
bolina	bowline	Bulin	bouline	bolina
bomba	pump	Pumpe	pompe	pompa
botalón de ala	studding sail boom	Leesegelspiere	bout-dehors de bonnette	buttafuori di vela
botalón de foque	jib boom	Klüverbaum	bâton de foc	
botavara	driver boom	Gaffelbaum	gui	boma
brazo	brace	Brasse	bras	braccio
burda	backstay	Pardune	galhauban	paterazzo
cabilla	belaying pin	Belegnagel	cabillot	caviglia
cabillero	pin rail	Nagelbank	râtelier à cabillots	cavigliera
cabo	rope	Tau	câble	cavo
cabrestante	capstan	Spill	cabestan	argano
cadena de obenque	chainplate	Pütting	cadène	landa
cadenote			chaîne	
cajera	sheavehole	Scheibgat	mortaise	cavatoia
candeliza de boca de cangrejo	breeching	Brooktau	étrangloir	imbroglio de gola di sotto
cangrejo de popa	jigger sail	Bonaventursegel	petit artimon	vanda di contromezzana
- de cangrejo	gaff-	Gaffel-	- à corne	- picco
cargadera	clew line	Geitau	aurigue	imbroglio
	leech line and bunt line (collectively)	Gording		
casco	hull	Rumpf	coque	scafo
cinta	wale	Barkholz	préceinte	incintone
codaste	sternpost	Achtrsteven	étambot	dritto di poppa
cofa	top	Mars	hune	coffa
contraestay	preventer stay	Borgstag	faux etai	controstaglio

Spanish	English	German	French	Italian
- de contromesana	jigger-	Bonaventur-	- d'artimon derrière	- di contromezzana
cordón	strand	Kardeel	toron	legnuolo
cornamusa	cleat	Klampe	taquet	galloccia
coverta	deck	Deck	ponte	ponte
cruceta	spreader	Saling	barre de hune	crocetta
cuoderna	frame	Spant	couple	ordinata
defensa	fender	Fender	défense	parabordo
descendo	companion hatch	Niedergang	descende	boccaporto
driza	tye	Fall	drisse	drizza
enjaretado	gratings	Gräting	caillebotis	carabottino
escobén del ancla	hawse	Ankerklüse	écubier d'ancre	cubia d'ancora
escota	sheet	Schot	écoute	scotta
escotera	servant	Knecht	valet	servo
escotilla	hatch	Ladeluke	écoutille	boccaporto
estay	stay	Stag	étai	straglio
flechaduras	rat-lines	Webeleine	enflechûres	griselle
forro de planchas	planking	Beplankug	bordé	fasciame di legno
garrucho de cabo	cringle	Legel	patte	brancarella
gazza	strop	Stropp	estrope	stroppo
gravia	top sail	Marssegel	hunier	vela di gabbia
guardacabo	thimble	Kausch	cosse	radancia
imbornal	scupper	Speigat	dalot	ombriale
jarcias de labor	running rigging	laufendes Gut	manoeuvres courantes	manovri correnti
jarcias muertas	standing rigging	stehendes Gut	manoeuvres dormantes	manovri dormienti
juanete	topgallant sail	Bramsegel	perroquet	velaccio
- de juanete	topgallant-	Bram-	- de perroquet	- de velaccio
linea de flotación	waterline	Wasserlinie	ligne de flottaison	linea di galleggiamento
mamparo	bulkhead	Schott	cloison	paratia
manchos de timón	rudder pintles	Fingerlinge	aiguillots	agugliotti del timone
manigueta	staghorn	Kreuzholz	oreille d'âne	cazzasotte
marchapié	foot rope	Perde	marchepied	marciapiede
mastelero de galope	topmast	Stenge	mât de flèche	albero di freccia
mastelero de gavia			mât de hune	albero di gabbia
- mayor	main-	Groß-	grand -	- di maestra
mesa de guarnición	channel	Rüste	porte-hauban	parasartie
mesana	jigger	Kreuzsegel	voile barrée	vela di contromezzana
	crossjack			
- de mesana	mizen-	Besan-	- d'artimon	- di mezzana
moco del bauprés	dolphin boom	Stampfstock	arc-boutant de martingale	buffafuori di briglia
	dolphin striker			pennaccino
motón	block	Block	poulie	bozzolo
nervio de envergadura	jackstay	Jackstag	filière d'envergure	infertitura
obenque	shroud	Want	hauban	sartia
ollaos	eyelet holes	Gat	oillets	occhiello
osta	vang	Geere	palan de garde	ostino
palo	mast	Mast	mât	albero
palo de contromesana	jigger-mast	Bonaventurmast	mât d'artimon derrière	albero di contomezzana
palo mayor	main mast	Großmst	grand mât	albero di maestro
palo mesana	mizen-mast	Kreuzmast	mât d'artimon	albero di mezzana
		Besanmast	grand mât arriere	
palo de trinquete	foremast	Fockmast	mât de misaine	albero di trinchetto
peñol	peak	Nock	pic	varea
pescante	davit	Davit	bossoir	gru
popa	stern	Heck	arrière	poppa
proa	bow	Bug	avant	prua
quilla	keel	Kiel	quille	chiglia
racamiento	parral	Rack	racage	trozza
reata	woolding	Wuling	rousture	trincatura
recuperador	spritsail halyard	Vorholer	récupérateur	ricuperatore
regala	rail	Reling	lisse de pavois	filaretto
rejilla	gratings	Gräting	grillage	grata
relinga	bolt-rope	Liektau	ralingue	gratile
remo	oar	Riemen	aviron	remo
rizo	reef	Reff	ris	terzaruolo
roda	stem	Vordersteven	étrave	dritto di prua
serviola	cat head	Krankbalken	bossoir de capon	gru di capone
servioleta	spritsail yard	Blinderah	porte lof	peronne di bompresso
tajamar	Head (of which the knee of the head is part)	Galion	guibre	serpe
tamborete	cap	Eselshaupt	chouquet	testa di moro
-tarquia	sprit-	Blinde-	- à livarde	- tarchia
tensor de tornillo	rigging screw	Spannschraube	ridoir à vis	arridatoio a vite
timón	rudder	Ruder	gouvernail	timone
tope del mastil	mast head	Top	tête de mât	testa d'albero
trinca	lashing	Zurring	aiguillette	rizza
trinquete	fore sail	Focksegel	misaine	vela di trinchetto
- de trinquete	fore-	Fock-	- de misaine	- di trinchetto
varones del timón	rudder pendants	Sorgleine	sauvegardes	bracotti del timone
vela	sail	Segel	voile	vela
vela cangreja	gaff sail	Gaffelsegel	voile à corne	randa
vela de estay	staysail	Stagsegel	voile d'étai	vela di straglio
vela mayor	main sail	Großsegel	grand voile	vela maestra
vela de mesana	spanker	Besansegel	artimon (grand a.)	vanda di mezzana
vela tarquia	sprit sail	Blindesegel	tente à livarde	vela tarchia
vela al tercio	lug sail	Luggersegel	voile à bourcet	vela al terzo
verga	yard	Rah	vergue	peronne
verga mayor	main yard	Großrah	grand vergue	peronne di maestra
verga de trinquete	foreyard	Fockrah	vergue de misaine	peronne di trinchetto
verga de un trinquete volante	crossjack yard	Bagienrah	vergue de fortune	peronne per trevo di fortuna
vigota	deadeye	Jungfer	cap de mouton	bigota

ITALIAN	English	German	French	Spanish
agugliotti del timone	rudder pintles	Fingerlinge	aiguillots	manchos del timón
albero	mast	Mast	mât	palo
albero di contromezzana	jigger-mast	Bonaventurmast	mât d'artimon derrière	palo de contromesana
albero di freccia	topmast	Stenge	mât de flèche	mastelero de galope
albero di gabbia			mât de hune	mastelero de gavia
albero di maestro	mainmast	Großmast	grand mât	palo mayor
albero di mezzana	mizen mast	Besanmast	grand mât arriere	palo de mesana
		Kreuzmast	mât d'artimon	
albero di trinchetto	foremast	Fockmast	mât de misaine	palo de trinquete
amura	tack	Hals	amure	amura
ancora	anchor	Anker	ancre	ancla
argano	capstan	Spill	cabestan	cabrestante
arridatoio a vite	rigging screw	Spannschraube	ridoir à vis	tensor de tornillo
asta di fiocco	jib boom	Klüverbaum	bâton de foc	botalón de foque
bastingaggio	hammock netting	Finknetz	bastingage	batayola
bigota	deadeye	Jungfer	cap de mouton	vigota
bitta	bitt	Beting	bitte	bita
boccaporto	hatch	Ladeluke	écoutille	escotilla
	companion hatch	Niedergang	descende	descendo
bolina	bowline	Bulin	bouline	bolina
boma	Driver boom	Gaffelbaum	gui	botavara
bompresso	bowsprit	Bugspriet	beaupré	bauprés
bozzolo	block	Block	poulie	motón
braccio	brace	Brasse	bras	brazo
bracotti del timone	rudder pendants	Sorgleine	sauvegardes	varones del timón
brancarella	cringle	Legel	patte	garrucho de cabo
briglia di bompresso	bobstay	Wasserstag	sous-barbe de beaupré	barbiquejo del bauprés
buffafuori di briglia	dolphin boom	Stampfstock	arc-boutant de	moco del bauprés
	dolphin striker		martingale	
buffafuori di crocetta	outrigger	Ausleger	arc boutant	arbotante
buffafuori di vela	studding sail boom	Leesegelspiere	bout-dehors de bonnette	botalón de ala
carabottino	gratings	Gräting	caillebotis	enjaretado
cavatoia	sheavehole	Scheibgat	mortaise	cajera
caviglia	belaying pin	Belegnagel	cabillot	cabilla
cavigliera	pin rail	Nagelbank	râtelier à cabillots	cabillero
cavo	rope	Tau	cable	[illegible]
cazzasotte	staghorn	Kreuzholz	oreille d'âne	manigueta
chiglia	keel	Kiel	quille	quilla
coffa	top	Mars	hune	cofa
collare di sospensione	slig	Hanger	cercle de suspente	aro de boza de una verga mayor
- di contromezzana	jigger-	Bonaventur-	- d'artimon derrière	- de contromesana
controstaglio	preventer stay	Borgstag	faux étai	contraestay
corcetta	spreader	Saling	barre de hune	cruceta
cubia d'ancora	hawse	Ankerlüse	écubier d'ancre	escobén del ancla
dritto di poppa	sternpost	Achtersteven	étambot	codaste
dritto di prua	stem	Vordersteven	étrave	roda
drizza	tye	Fall	drisse	driza
fasciame di legno	planking	Beplankung	bordé	forro de planchas
filaretto	rail	Reling	lisse de pavois	regala
galloccia	cleat	Klampe	taquet	cornamusa
grata	gratings	Gräting	grillage	rejilla
gratile	bolt-rope	Liektau	ralingue	relinga
griselle	rat-lines	Webeleine	enflechûres	flecharduras
gru	davit	Davit	bossoir	pescante
gru di capone	cat head	Kranbalken	bossoir de capon	serviola
imbroglio	clew line	Geitau	aurigue	cargedera
	Leech line and bunt line (collectively)	Gording		
imbroglio de gola di sotto	breeching	Brooktau	étrangloir	candaliza de boca de cangrejo
incintone	wale	Barkholz	préceinte	cinta
infertitura	jackstay	Jackstag	filière d'envergure	nervio de envergadura
landa	chain plate	Pütting	cadène	cadena de obenque
			chaîne	cadenote
legnuolo	strand	Kardeel	toron	cordón
linea di galleggiamento	waterline	Wasserlinie	ligne de flottaison	linea de flotación
- di maestra	main-	Groß-	grand -	- mayor
manovri correnti	running rigging	laufendes Gut	manoeuvres courantes	jarcias de labor
manovri dormienti	standing rigging	stehendes Gut	manoeuvres dormantes	jarcias muertas
mantiglio	topping lift	Dirk	balancine de gui	amantillo
	lift	Toppnanten	balancine	
marciapiede	foot rope	Perde	marchepied	marchapié
- di mezzana	mizen-	Besan-	- d'artimon	- de mesana
occhiello	eyelet holes	Gat	oillets	ollaos
ombriale	scupper	Speigat	dalot	imbornal
ordinata	frame	Spant	couple	cuoderna
ostino	vang	Geere	palan de garde	osta
palanca	tackle	Talje	palan	aparejo
parabordo	fender	Fender	défense	defensa
parasartie	channel	Rüste	porte-hauban	mesa de guarnición
paratia	bulkhead	Schott	cloison	mamparo
paterazzo	back stay	Pardune	galhauban	burda
peronne	yard	Rah	vergue	verga
peronne di bompresso	spritsail yard	Blinderah	porte lof	servioleta
peronne di maestra	main yard	Großrah	grand vergue	verga mayor
peronne per treve di fortuna	crossjack yard	Bagienrah	vergue de fortune	verga de un trinquete volante
peronne di trinchetto	foreyard	Fockrah	vergue de misaine	verga de trinquete
pompa	pump	Pumpe	pompe	bomba
- picco	gaff-	Gaffel-	- à corne	- de cangrejo
ponte	deck	Deck	ponte	coverta
poppa	stern	Heck	arrière	popa

Italian	English	German	French	Spanish
prua	bow	Bug	avant	proa
radancia	thimble	Kausch	cosse	guardacabo
randa	gaff sail	Gaffelsegel	voile à corne	vela cangreja
remo	oar	Riemen	aviron	remo
ricuperatore	spritsail halyard	Vorholer	récupérateur	recuperdor
rizza	lashing	Zurring	aiguillette	trica
sartia	shroud	Want	hauban	obenque
scafo	hull	Rumpf	coque	casco
scotta	sheet	Schot	écoute	escota
serpe	head (of which the knee of the head is part)	Galion	guibre	beque tajamar
servo	servant	Knecht	valet	escotera
straglio	stay	Stag	étai	estay
stroppo	strop	Stropp	estrope	gaza
- tarchia	sprit-	Blinde-	- àlivarde	- tarquia
terzaruolo	reef	Reff	ris	rizo
testa d'albero	mast head	Top	tête de mât	tope del mastil
testa di moro	cap	Eselhaupt	chouquet	tamborete
timone	rudder	Ruder	gouvernail	timón
trincatura	woolding	Wuling	rousture	reata
- di trinchetto	fore-	Fock-	- de misaine	- de trinquete
trozza	parral	Rack	racage	racamiento
vanda di contromezzana	jigger sail	Bonaventursegel	petit artimon	cangreja de popa
vanda di mezzana	spanker	Besansegel	artimon (grand a.)	vela de mesana
varea	peak	Nock	pic	peñol
vela	sail	Segel	voile	vela
vela di caccia	studding sail	Leesegel	bonnette	ala
vela di contromezzana	jigger crossjack	Kreuzsegel	voile barrée	mesana
vela di gabbia	top sail	Marssegel	hunier	gravia
vela maestra	main sail	Großsegel	grand voile	vela mayor
vela di straglio	staysail	Stagsegel	voile d'étai	vela de estay
vela tarchia	sprit sail	Blindesegel	tente à livarde	vela tarquia
vela al terzo	lug sail	Luggersegel	voile à bourcet	vela al tercio
vela di trinchetto	fore sail	Focksegel	misaine	trinquete
velaccio	topgallant sail	Bramsegel	perroquet	juanete
- de velaccio	topgallant -	Bram-	- de perroquet	- de juanete

Index